Walter Richard Cassels

Supernatural religion:

An inquiry into the reality of divine revelation - Vol. 2

Walter Richard Cassels

Supernatural religion:
An inquiry into the reality of divine revelation - Vol. 2

ISBN/EAN: 9783337717636

Printed in Europe, USA, Canada, Australia, Japan

Cover: Foto ©Lupo / pixelio.de

More available books at **www.hansebooks.com**

SUPERNATURAL RELIGION:

AN INQUIRY

INTO

THE REALITY OF DIVINE REVELATION.

IN THREE VOLUMES.

VOL. II.

COMPLETE EDITION.

CAREFULLY REVISED.

LONDON:
LONGMANS, GREEN, AND CO.,
1879.

[*The Right of Translation is Reserved.*]

LONDON
BRADBURY, AGNEW, & CO., PRINTERS, WHITEFRIARS.

THE SECOND VOLUME.

PART II.

(Continued.)

CHAPTER V.

	PAGE
THE CLEMENTINES	1
THE EPISTLE TO DIOGNETUS	38

CHAPTER VI.

BASILIDES	41
VALENTINUS	55

CHAPTER VII.

MARCION	79

CHAPTER VIII.

TATIAN	144
DIONYSIUS OF CORINTH	159

CHAPTER IX.

MELITO OF SARDIS	169
CLAUDIUS APOLLINARIS	182
ATHENAGORAS	190
EPISTLE OF VIENNE AND LYONS	198

CHAPTER X.

PTOLEMÆUS AND HERACLEON	203
CELSUS	225
THE CANON OF MURATORI	235
RESULTS	246

CONTENTS.

PART III.
THE FOURTH GOSPEL.

CHAPTER I.
THE EXTERNAL EVIDENCE 249

CHAPTER II.
THE AUTHORSHIP AND CHARACTER OF THE FOURTH GOSPEL . . 385

AN INQUIRY

INTO THE

REALITY OF DIVINE REVELATION.

PART II.

CHAPTER V.

THE CLEMENTINES—THE EPISTLE TO DIOGNETUS.

WE must now as briefly as possible examine the evidence furnished by the apocryphal religious romance generally known by the name of "The Clementines," and assuming, falsely of course,[1] to be the composition of the Roman Clement. The Clementines are composed of three principal works, the Homilies, Recognitions, and a so-called Epitome. The Homilies, again, are prefaced by a pretended epistle addressed by the Apostle Peter to James, and another from Clement. These Homilies were only known in an imperfect form till 1853, when Dressel[2] published a complete Greek text. Of the Recognitions we only possess a Latin translation by Rufinus (A.D. 402).

---

[1] *Baur*, Dogmengesch., 1865, I. i. p. 155; *Bunsen*, Hippolytus, i. p. 431; *Cotelerius*, Patr. Apost. Opp., i. p. 490, 607; *Ewald*, Gesch. d. V. Isr., vii. p. 183; *Gallandi*, Patr. Bibl., ii. Proleg., p. lv.; *Guericke*, H'Luch K. G., i. p. 117, anm. 2; *Hilgenfeld*, Der Kanon, p. 30, p. 204, anm. 1; Die apost. Väter, p. 287; *Kirchhofer*, Quellensamml., p. 461, anm. 47; *Lechler*, Das apost. u. nachap. Zeit., p. 454, 500; *Nicolas*, Et. sur les Ev. Apocr., 1866, p. 87 ff.; *Ritschl*, Entst. altk. Kirche, p. 204 f.

[2] Clementis R. quæ feruntur Homiliæ xx. nunc primum integræ. Ed. A. R. M. Dressel.

Although there is much difference of opinion regarding the claims to priority of the Homilies and Recognitions, many critics assigning that place to the Homilies,[1] whilst others assert the earlier origin of the Recognitions,[2] all are agreed that the one is merely a version of the other, the former being embodied almost word for word in the latter, whilst the Epitome is a blending of the other two, probably intended to purge them from heretical doctrine. These works, however, which are generally admitted to have emanated from the Ebionitic party of the early Church,[3] are supposed to be based upon older Petrine writings, such as the "Preaching of Peter" (Κήρυγμα Πέτρου), and the "Travels of Peter" (Περίοδοι Πέτρου).[4]

---

[1] *Credner*, Beiträge, i. p. 280 f.; *Dorner*, Lehre von d. Person Christi, 1845, i. p. 348, anm. 192; *Ewald*, Gesch. d. V. Isr., vii. p. 183, anm. 2; *Engelhardt*, Zeitschr. f. hist. Theol., 1852, i. p. 104 f.; *Guericke*, H'buch K. G., i. p. 117, anm. 2; *Lücke*, Comment. Ev. Joh., i. p. 225; *Mansel*, The Gnostic Heresies, 1875, p. 222; *Reuss*, Gesch. N. T., p. 254; *Schwegler*, Das nachap. Zeit., i. p. 481; *Schliemann*, Die Clement. Recog., 1843, p. 265 ff.; *Tischendorf*, Wann wurden u. s. w., p. vii., anm. 1; *Uhlhorn*, Die Homil. u. Recogn., p. 343 ff., &c., &c., &c.

[2] *Hilgenfeld*, Die ap. Väter, p. 288 f.; Zeitschr. f. wiss. Theol., 1869, p. 353 ff.; *Köstlin*, Hallische Allg. Lit. Zeitung, 1849, No. 73—77; *Nicolas*, Etudes Crit. sur les Ev. Apocr., p. 77, note 2; *Ritschl*, Entst. altk. Kirche, p. 264, anm. 1; cf. p. 451, anm. 1; *Thiersch*, Die Kirche im ap. Zeit., p. 341 f.; *Volkmar*, Der Ursprung, p. 62, p. 137, &c., &c., &c.

[3] *Baur*, Paulus, i. p. 381 f.; Unters. kan. Evv., p. 562; *Credner*, Beiträge, i. p. 279 ff.; *Hilgenfeld*, Die ap. Väter, p. 288 ff.; *Kirchhofer*, Quellensamml., p. 461, anm. 47; *Lechler*, D. ap. u. nachap. Zeit., p. 500; *Nicolas*, Etudes sur les Ev. Ap., p. 87; *Reuss*, Hist. du Canon, 1863, p. 63, note 1; Gesch. N. T., p. 253; *Ritschl*, Entst. altk. K., p. 204 f.; *Schwegler*, Das nachap. Zeit., i. p. 363 ff.; *Westcott*, On the Canon, p. 251; *Zeller*, Die Apostelgeschichte, 1854, p. 53.

[4] *Baur*, Unters. kan. Evv., p. 536 ff.; *Credner*, Beiträge, i. p. 331 f.; *Gfrörer*, Allg. K. G., i. p. 256 ff.; *Hilgenfeld*, Das Markus Ev., p. 113 f.; Die ap. Väter, p. 289 ff.; Zeitschr. wiss. Theol., 1869, p. 361 ff.; *Holtzmann* in Bunsen's Bibelwerk, viii. p. 500 ff.; *Köstlin*, Der Ursprung synopt. Evv., p. 395; *Kayser*, Rev. de Théol., 1851, iii. p. 131; *Mayerhoff*, Einl. petr. Schr. p. 314 ff.; *Reuss*, Gesch. N. T., p. 251 f.; *Ritschl*, Entst. altk. Kirche, p. 264 ff.; *Thiersch*, Die Kirche im ap. Zeit., p. 340 f.; *Volkmar*, Der Ursprung, p. 62.

It is not necessary for our purpose to go into any analysis of the character of the Clementines. It will suffice to say that they almost entirely consist of discussions between the Apostle Peter and Simon the Magician regarding the identity of the true Mosaic and Christian religions. Peter follows the Magician from city to city for the purpose of exposing and refuting him, the one, in fact, representing Apostolic doctrine and the other heresy, and in the course of these discussions occur the very numerous quotations of sayings of Jesus and of Christian history which we have to examine.

The Clementine Recognitions, as we have already remarked, are only known to us through the Latin translation of Rufinus; and from a comparison of the evangelical quotations occurring in that work with the same in the Homilies, it is evident that Rufinus has assimilated them in the course of translation to the parallel passages of our Gospels. It is admitted, therefore, that no argument regarding the source of the quotations can rightly be based upon the Recognitions, and that work may, consequently, be entirely set aside,[1] and the Clementine Homilies alone need occupy our attention.

We need scarcely remark that, unless the date at which these Homilies were composed can be ascertained, their value as testimony for the existence of our Synoptic Gospels is seriously affected. The difficulty of arriving at a correct conclusion regarding this point, great under almost any circumstances, is of course increased by the fact that the work is altogether apocryphal, and most certainly not held by any one to have

[1] *Credner*, Beiträge, i. p. 280 ff.; *Schwegler*, Das nachap. Zeit., i. p. 481 ff.; *Hilgenfeld*, Die Evv. Justin's, p. 370 f.; *Nicolas*, Et. sur les Ev. Apocr., p. 60, note 2; *Scholten*, Die ält. Zeugnisse, p. 55 f., anm. 10; *Westcott*, On the Canon, p. 251, n. 2; *Zeller*, Die Apostelgesch., p. 60.

been written by the person whose name it bears. There is in fact nothing but internal evidence by which to fix the date, and that internal evidence is of a character which admits of very wide extension down the course of time, although a sharp limit is set beyond which it cannot mount upwards. Of external evidence there is almost none, and what little exists does not warrant an early date. Origen, it is true, mentions Περίοδοι Κλήμεντος,[1] which, it is conjectured, may either be the same work as the Ἀναγνωρισμός, or Recognitions, translated by Rufinus, or related to it, and Epiphanius and others refer to Περίοδοι Πέτρου;[2] but our Clementine Homilies are not mentioned by any writer before pseudo-Athanasius.[3] The work, therefore, can at the best afford no substantial testimony to the antiquity and apostolic origin of our Gospels. Hilgenfeld, following in the steps of Baur, arrives at the conclusion that the Homilies are directed against the Gnosticism of Marcion (and also, as we shall hereafter see, against the Apostle Paul), and he, therefore, necessarily assigns to them a date subsequent to A.D. 160. As Reuss, however, inquires: upon this ground, why should a still later date not be named, since even Tertullian wrote vehemently against the same Gnosis.[4] There can be little doubt that the author was a representative of Ebionitic Gnosticism, which had once been the purest form of primitive Christianity, but later, through its own development, though still more through the rapid growth around it of Paulinian doctrine, had

[1] Comment. in Genesin Philoc., 22.
[2] *Hilgenfeld* considers Recog. iv.—vi., Hom. vii.—xi. a version of the περίοδοι Πέτρου· Die ap. Väter, p. 291 ff.; *Ritschl* does not consider that this can be decidedly proved, Entst. Altk. Kirche, p. 204 f.; so also *Uhlhorn*, Die Hom. u. Recog., p. 71 ff.
[3] Synops. Sacr. Script., sub finem.   [4] Gesch. N. T., p. 254.

assumed a position closely verging upon heresy. It is not necessary for us, however, to enter upon any exhaustive discussion of the date at which the Clementines were written; it is sufficient to show that there is no certain ground upon which a decision can be based, and that even an approximate conjecture can scarcely be reasonably advanced. Critics variously date the composition of the original Recognitions from about the middle of the second century to the end of the third, though the majority are agreed in placing them at least in the latter century.[1] They assign to the Homilies an origin at different dates within a period commencing about the middle of the second century, and extending to a century later.[2]

In the Homilies there are very numerous quotations

[1] A.D. 150, *Volkmar*, Der Ursprung, p. 163, cf. 93 f.; Circa A.D. 140—150, *Hilgenfeld*, Die ap. Väter, p. 297, anm. 11; Der Paschastreit, p. 194. After A.D. 170, *Maran.*, Divinit. D. N. J. C., lib. ii., cap. 7, § 4, p. 250 ff. Beginning 3rd century, *Dorner*, Lehre von d. Person Christi, 1845, i. p. 348, anm. 192; *Reuss*, Gesch. N. T., p. 254; *Zeller*, Die Apostelgesch., p. 64. Between A.D. 212—230, *Schwegler*, Das nachap. Zeit., i. p. 481; *Schliemann*, Die Clementinen, 1844, p. 326, f. Not before A.D. 216, *Gallandi*, Vet. Patr. Bibl., ii, Proleg., p. lv. Between A.D. 218—231, *Dodwell*, Dissert. vi. in Iren., § xi. p. 443. C.A.D. 220, *Keim*, Aus d. Urchristenthum, 1878, p. 225, anm. 1. End 3rd century, *Credner*, Beiträge, i. p. 281.

[2] Before middle 2nd century, *Credner*, Gesch. N. T. Kan., p. 45; cf. Beiträge, i. p. 281. Middle 2nd century, *Ritschl*, Entst. altk. K., p. 264, 451; *Kern*, Tüb. Zeitschr. 1835, H. 2, p. 112; *Gfrörer*, Allg. K. G., i. p. 256; *Tischendorf*, Wann wurden u. s. w., p. 90; *Réville*, Essais de Crit. Religieuse, 1860, p. 35. Soon after middle 2nd century, *Schliemann*, Die Clementinen, p. 548 f. C.A.D. 150—160, *Renan*, St. Paul, 1869, p. 303, note 8. A.D. 160, *Lechler*, Das ap. u. nachap. Zeit., p. 461; *Mansel*, The Gnostic Heresies, 1875, p. 222 f. A.D. 150—170, *Scholten*, Die ält. Zeugnisse, p. 55. Before A.D. 180, *Kayser*, Rev. de Théol., 1851, p. 155. A.D. 161—180, *Hilgenfeld*, Zeitschr. wiss. Theol., 1869, p. 353, anm. 1; cf. Die ap. Väter, p. 301; Der Paschastreit, p. 194; Einl. N. T., 1875, p. 43. A.D. 175—180, *Volkmar*, Der Ursprung, p. 164; cf. 137, 63; *Keim*, Aus d. Urchristenthum, 1878, p. 224 f. Second half 2nd century, *Dorner*, Lehre Person Christi, i. p. 341, anm. 190. End of 2nd century, *Baur*,

of sayings of Jesus and of Gospel history, which are generally placed in the mouth of Peter, or introduced with such formulæ as: "The teacher said," "Jesus said," "He said," "The prophet said," but in no case does the author name the source from which these sayings and quotations are derived. That he does, however, quote from a written source, and not from tradition, is clear from the use of such expressions as "in another place (ἄλλῃ που)[1] he has said," which refer not to other localities or circumstances, but another part of a written history.[2] There are in the Clementine Homilies upwards of a hundred quotations of sayings of Jesus or references to his history, too many by far for us to examine in detail here; but, notwithstanding the number of these passages, so systematically do they vary, more or less, from the parallels in our canonical Gospels, that, as in the case of Justin, Apologists are obliged to have recourse to the elastic explanation, already worn so threadbare, of "free quotation from memory" and "blending of passages" to account for the remarkable phenomena presented. It must, however, be evident that the necessity for such an apology at all shows the insufficiency of the evidence furnished by these quotations. De Wette says: "The quotations of evangelical works and histories in the pseudo-Clementine writings, from their nature free and inaccurate, permit only an uncertain conclusion to be

---

Dogmengesch., 1865, I. i. p. 155; *Ewald*, Gesch. d. V. Israel, vii. p. 183; cf. 386, anm. 1; *Gieseler*, Kirchengeschichte, 1844, I. i. p. 1337; *Lücke*, Comment. Ev. Joh. 1840, i. p. 225; *Neander*, Genet. Entw. Gnost. Systeme, p. 370; *Reuss*, Gesch. N. T., p. 254; *Schwegler*, Das nachap. Zeit. p. 405 f. *Zimmermann*, Lebensgesch. d. Kirche J. C. 2 Ausg., ii. p. 118. Second or third century, *Kirchhofer*, Quellensamml. p. 461, anm. 47. A.D. 250, *Gallandi*, Vet. Patr. Bibl. Proleg., p. lv.; *Mill*, Proleg. N. T. Gr., 1707, p. lxiv. Fourth century, *Lentz*, Dogmengeschichte, i. p. 58. Their groundwork 2nd or 3rd century, *Guericke*, H'buch K. G., p. 146.

[1] See several instances, Hom. xix. 2. [2] *Credner*, Beiträge, i. p. 283.

drawn as to their written source."[1] Critics have maintained very different and conflicting views regarding that source. Apologists, of course, assert that the quotations in the Homilies are taken from our Gospels only.[2] Others ascribe them to our Gospels, with a supplementary apocryphal work: the Gospel according to the Hebrews, or the Gospel according to Peter.[3] Some, whilst admitting a subsidiary use of some of our Gospels, assert that the author of the Homilies employs, in preference, the Gospel according to Peter;[4] whilst others, recognizing also the similarity of the phenomena presented by these quotations with those of Justin's, conclude that the author does not quote our Gospels at all, but makes use of the Gospel according to Peter, or the Gospel according to the Hebrews.[5] Evidence permitting of such divergent conclusions manifestly cannot be of a decided character. We may affirm, however, that few of those who are

[1] Die Anführungen evangelischer Werke und Geschichten in den pseudo-clementinischen Schriften, ihrer Natur nach frei und ungenau, lassen nur unsichere auf ihre schriftliche Quelle zurückschliessen. Einl. N. T. p. 115.

[2] *Lechler*, Das ap. u. nachap. Zeit., p. 458, anm.; *Orelli*, Selecta Patr. Eccles., cap. 1821, p. 22; *Semisch*, Denkw. d. M. Just., p. 356 ff.; *Tischendorf*, Wann wurden u. s. w., p. 90; *Westcott*, On the Canon, p. 251.

[3] *Franck*, Die evang. Citate in d. Clem. Hom., Stud. w. Geistlichkeit, 1847, 2, p. 144 ff.; *Holtzmann* in Bunsen's Bibelwerk, viii. p. 553; *Kirchhofer*, Quellensamml., p. 461, anm. 47, 48; *Köstlin*, Der Ursprung synopt. Evv., p. 372 f.; *Scholten*, Die ält. Zeugnisse, p. 58; *Uhlhorn*, Die Homilien u. Recog. d. Clem. Rom., 1854, p. 119—137; Herzog's Realencyclop., Art. Clementinen; *De Wette*, Einl. N. T., p. 115 f.; *Weisse*, Der evang. Gesch., i. p. 27, anm. * * *; Cf. *Westcott*, Canon, 4th ed. p. 287.

[4] *Baur*, Unters. kan. Evv., p. 575 ff.; *Hilgenfeld*, Die Evv. Justin's, p. 388; *Volkmar*, Der Ursprung, p. 62; *Zeller*, Die Apostelgesch., p. 59.

[5] *Credner*, Beiträge, i. p. 330 ff.; *Neander*, Genetische Entw. der vorn. Gnost. Syst., p. 418 f.; *Nicolas*, Et. sur les Evang. Apocr., p. 69 ff.; *Reuss*, Gesch. N. T., p. 193; *Schwegler*, Das nachap. Zeit., i. p. 207.

Credner, Schwegler, Hilgenfeld, Volkmar, Zeller, and others consider that the author uses the same Gospel as Justin. See references in note 3.

willing to admit the use of our Synoptics by the author of the Homilies along with other sources, make that concession on the strength of the absolute isolated evidence of the Homilies themselves, but they are generally moved by antecedent views on the point. In an inquiry like that which we have undertaken, however, such easy and indifferent judgment would obviously be out of place, and the point we have to determine is not whether an author may have been acquainted with our Gospels, but whether he furnishes testimony that he actually was in possession of our present Gospels and regarded them as authoritative.

We have already mentioned that the author of the Clementine Homilies never names the source from which his quotations are derived. Of these very numerous quotations we must again distinctly state that only two or three, of a very brief and fragmentary character, literally agree with our Synoptics, whilst all the rest differ more or less widely from the parallel passages in those Gospels. Some of these quotations are repeated more than once with the same persistent and characteristic variations, and in several cases, as we have already seen, they agree more or less closely with quotations of Justin from the Memoirs of the Apostles. Others, again, have no parallels at all in our Gospels, and even Apologists are consequently compelled to admit the collateral use of an apocryphal Gospel. As in the case of Justin, therefore, the singular phenomenon is presented of a vast number of quotations of which only one or two brief phrases, too fragmentary to avail as evidence, perfectly agree with our Gospels; whilst of the rest, which all vary more or less, some merely resemble combined passages of two Gospels, others merely contain the sense, some present variations likewise found in other writers or in various parts of the Homilies are repeatedly quoted with the same variations, and others are not found in our Gospels at all. Such phenomena cannot be fairly accounted for by any mere theory of imperfect memory or negligence. The systematic variation from our Synoptics, variation proved by repetition not to be accidental, coupled with quotations which have no parallels at all in our Gospels, more naturally point to the use of a different Gospel. In no case can the Homilies be accepted as furnishing evidence even of the existence of our Gospels.

As it is impossible here to examine in detail all of the quotations in the Clementine Homilies, we must content ourselves with this distinct statement of their character, and merely illustrate briefly the different classes of quotations, exhausting, however, those which literally agree with passages in the Gospels. The most determined of recent Apologists do not afford us an opportunity of testing the passages upon which they base their assertion of the use of our Synoptics, for they simply assume that the author used them without producing instances.[1]

The first quotation agreeing with a passage in our Synoptics occurs in Hom. iii. 52: "And he cried, saying: Come unto me all ye that are weary," which agrees with the opening words of Matt. xi. 28, but the phrase does

[1] *Tischendorf* only devotes a dozen lines, with a note, to the Clementines, and only in connection with our fourth Gospel, which shall hereafter have our attention. Wann wurden u. s. w., p. 90. In the same way Canon Westcott passes them over in a short paragraph, merely asserting the allusions to our Gospels to be "generally admitted," and only directly referring to one supposed quotation from Mark which we shall presently examine, and one which he affirms to be from the fourth Gospel. On the Canon, p. 251 f. [In the 4th edition he has enlarged his remarks, p. 282 ff.]

not continue, and is followed by the explanation: "that is, who are seeking the truth and not finding it."[1] It is evident, that so short and fragmentary a phrase cannot prove anything.[2]

The next passage occurs in Hom. xviii. 15: "For Isaiah said: I will open my mouth in parables, and I will utter things that have been kept secret from the foundation of the world."[3] Now this passage, with a slightly different order of words, is found in Matt. xiii. 35. After giving a series of parables, the author of the Gospel says (v. 34), "All these things spake Jesus unto the multitudes in parables; and without a parable spake he not unto them; (v. 35) That it might be fulfilled which was spoken by the prophet (Isaiah), saying: I will open my mouth in parables, &c." There are two peculiarities which must be pointed out in this passage. It is not found in Isaiah, but in Psalm lxxviii. 2,[4] and it presents a variation from the version of the lxx. Both the variation and the erroneous reference to Isaiah, therefore, occur also in the Homily. The first part of the sentence agrees with, but the latter part is quite different from, the Greek of the lxx., which reads: "I will utter problems from the beginning," φθέγξομαι προβλήματα ἀπ' ἀρχῆς.[5]

The Psalm from which the quotation is really taken is, by its superscription, ascribed to Asaph, who, in the Septuagint version of II. Chronicles xxix. 30, is called a

---

[1] Διὸ καὶ ἐβόα λέγων· 'Δεῦτε πρὸς μὲ πάντες οἱ κοπιῶντες.' τουτέστιν, οἱ τὴν ἀλήθειαν ζητοῦντες καὶ μὴ εὑρίσκοντες αὐτήν. Hom. iii. 52.

[2] *Hilgenfeld*, Die Evv. Justin's, u. s. w., p. 351.

[3] Καὶ τὸν Ἡσαΐαν εἰπεῖν· 'Ἀνοίξω τὸ στόμα μου ἐν παραβολαῖς καὶ ἐξερεύξομαι κεκρυμμένα ἀπὸ καταβολῆς κόσμου. Hom. xviii. 15.

[4] The Vulgate reads: aperiam in parabolis os meum: loquar propositiones ab initio. Ps. lxxviii. 2.

[5] Ps. lxxvii. 2.

prophet.[1] It was, therefore, early asserted that the original reading of Matthew was "Asaph," instead of "Isaiah." Porphyry, in the third century, twitted Christians with this erroneous ascription by their inspired evangelist to Isaiah of a passage from a Psalm, and reduced the Fathers to great straits. Eusebius, in his commentary on this verse of the Psalm, attributes the insertion of the words, "by the prophet Isaiah," to unintelligent copyists, and asserts that in accurate MSS. the name is not added to the word prophet. Jerome likewise ascribes the insertion of the name Isaiah for that of Asaph, which was originally written, to an ignorant scribe,[2] and in the commentary on the Psalms, generally, though probably falsely, ascribed to him, the remark is made that many copies of the Gospel to that day had the name "Isaiah," for which Porphyry had reproached Christians,[3] and the writer of the same commentary actually allows himself to make the assertion that Asaph was found in all the old codices, but ignorant men had removed it.[4] The fact is, that the reading "Asaph" for "Isaiah" is not found in any extant MS., and, although "Isaiah" has disappeared from all but a few obscure codices, it cannot be denied that the name anciently stood in the text.[5] In the Sinaitic Codex, which is probably the earliest MS. extant, and which is assigned to the fourth century, "the prophet *Isaiah*" stands in the text by the first hand, but is erased by the second (B).

[1] ἐν λόγοις Δαυὶδ καὶ Ἀσὰφ τοῦ προφήτου. [2] Comment. Matt., xiii. 35.
[3] Multa evangelia usque hodie ita habent: Ut impleretur, quod scriptum est per *Isaiam* prophetam, &c., &c. *Hieron.*, Opp., vii. p. 270 f.
[4] Asaph invenitur in omnibus veteribus codicibus, sed homines ignorantes tulerunt illud. To this *Credner* pertinently remarks: "Die Noth, in welche die guten Kirchenväter durch Porphyrius gekommen waren, erlaubte auch eine Lüge. Sie geschah ja: *in majorem Dei gloriam.* Beiträge, i. p. 304. [5] Cf. *Credner*, Beiträge, i. p. 303 f.

The quotation in the Homily, however, is clearly not from our Gospel. It is introduced by the words "For Isaiah says:" and the context is so different from that in Matthew, that it seems most improbable that the author of the Homily could have had the passage suggested to him by the Gospel. It occurs in a discussion between Simon the Magician and Peter. The former undertakes to prove that the Maker of the world is not the highest God, and amongst other arguments he advances the passage: "No man knew the Father, &c.," to show that the Father had remained concealed from the Patriarchs, &c., until revealed by the Son, and in reply to Peter he retorts, that if the supposition that the Patriarchs were not deemed worthy to know the Father was unjust, the Christian teacher was himself to blame, who said: "I thank thee, Lord of heaven and earth, that what was concealed from the wise thou hast revealed to suckling babes." Peter argues that in the statement of Jesus: "No man knew the Father, &c.," he cannot be considered to indicate another God and Father from him who made the world, and he continues: "For the concealed things of which he spoke may be those of the Creator himself; for Isaiah says: 'I will open my mouth, &c.' Do you admit, therefore, that the prophet was not ignorant of the things concealed,"[1] and so on. There is absolutely nothing in this argument to indicate that the passage was suggested by the Gospel, but, on the contrary, it is used in a totally different way, and is quoted not as an evangelical text, but as a saying from the Old Testament, and treated in connection with the prophet himself, and not with its supposed fulfilment in Jesus. It may be remarked, that in the corresponding part of

[1] Hom., xviii. 1—15.

the Recognitions, whether that work be of older or more recent date, the passage does not occur at all. Now, although it is impossible to say how and where this erroneous reference to a passage of the Old Testament first occurred, there is no reason for affirming that it originated in our first Synoptic, and as little for asserting that its occurrence in the Clementine Homilies, with so different a context and object, involves the conclusion that their author derived it from the Gospel, and not from the Old Testament or some other source. On the contrary, the peculiar argument based upon it in the Homilies suggests a different origin, and it is very probable that the passage, with its erroneous reference, was derived by both from another and common source.

Another passage is a phrase from the "Lord's Prayer," which occurs in Hom. xix. 2: "But also in the prayer which he commended to us, we have it said: Deliver us from the evil one" ('Ρῦσαι ἡμᾶς ἀπὸ τοῦ πονηροῦ). It need scarcely be said, however, that few Gospels can have been composed without including this prayer, and the occurrence of this short phrase demonstrates nothing more than the mere fact, that the author of the Homilies was acquainted with one of the most universally known lessons of Jesus, or made use of a Gospel which contained it. There would have been cause for wonder had he been ignorant of it.

The only other passage which agrees literally with our Gospels is also a mere fragment from the parable of the Talents, and when the other references to the same parable are added, it is evident that the quotation is not from our Gospels. In Hom. iii. 65, the address to the good servant is introduced: "Well done, good and faithful servant" (Εὖ, δοῦλε ἀγαθὲ καὶ πιστέ), which agrees with the words in Matt. xxv. 21. The allusion to the parable of the talents in the context is perfectly clear, and the passage occurs in an address of the Apostle Peter to overcome the modest scruples of Zaccheus, the former publican, who has been selected by Peter as his successor in the Church of Cæsarea when he is about to leave in pursuit of Simon the Magician. Anticipating the possibility of his hesitating to accept the office, Peter, in an earlier part of his address, however, makes fuller allusions to the same parable of the talents, which we must contrast with the parallel in the first Synoptic. "But if any of those present, having the ability to instruct the ignorance of men, shrink back from it, considering only his own ease, then let him expect to hear:"

Hom. III. 61.	Matt. xxv. 26—30.
Thou wicked and slothful servant;	v. 26. Thou wicked and slothful servant, thou knowest that I reap where I sowed not, and gather from where I strawed not.
thou oughtest to have put out my money with the exchangers, and at my coming I should have exacted mine own.	v. 27. Thou oughtest therefore to have put my money to the exchangers, and at my coming I should have received mine own with usury.
	v. 28, 29. Take therefore, &c. &c.
Cast ye the unprofitable servant into the darkness without.	v. 30. And cast ye the unprofitable servant into the darkness without; there shall be weeping and gnashing of teeth.
Δοῦλε πονηρὲ καὶ ὀκνηρέ,	v. 26. Πονηρὲ δοῦλε καὶ ὀκνηρέ, ᾔδεις ὅτι θερίζω, κ.τ.λ.
ἔδει σε τὸ ἀργύριόν μου προβαλεῖν ἐπὶ τῶν τραπεζιτῶν, καὶ ἐγὼ ἂν ἐλθὼν ἔπραξα τὸ ἐμόν·	v. 27. ἔδει σε οὖν βαλεῖν τὸ ἀργύριόν μου τοῖς τραπεζίταις, καὶ ἐλθὼν ἐγὼ ἐκομισάμην[1] ἂν τὸ ἐμὸν σὺν τόκῳ.
	v. 28, 29. ἄρατε οὖν, κ.τ.λ.
ἐκβάλετε τὸν ἀχρεῖον δοῦλον εἰς τὸ σκότος τὸ ἐξώτερον.	v. 30. καὶ τὸν ἀχρεῖον δοῦλον ἐκβάλετε εἰς τὸ σκότος τὸ ἐξώτερον· ἐκεῖ ἔσται ὁ κλαυθμὸς, κ.τ.λ.

[1] Luke xix. 23, substitutes ἔπραξα for ἐκομισάμην.

The Homily does not end here, however, but continues in words not found in our Gospels at all: "And reasonably: 'For,' he says, 'it is thine, O man, to put my words as silver with exchangers, and to prove them as money.'"[1] This passage is very analogous to another saying of Jesus, frequently quoted from an apocryphal Gospel, by the author of the Homilies, to which we shall hereafter more particularly refer, but here merely point out: "Be ye approved money-changers" (γίνεσθε τραπεζῖται δόκιμοι).[2] The variations from the parallel passages in the first and third Gospels, the peculiar application of the parable to the *words* of Jesus, and the addition of a saying not found in our Gospels, warrant us in denying that the quotations we are considering can be appropriated by our canonical Gospels, and, on the contrary, give good reason for the conclusion, that the author derived his knowledge of the parable from another source.

There is no other quotation in the Clementine Homilies which literally agrees with our Gospels, and it is difficult, without incurring the charge of partial selection, to illustrate the systematic variation in such very numerous passages as occur in these writings. It would be tedious and unnecessary to repeat the test applied to the quotations of Justin, and give in detail the passages from the Sermon on the Mount which are found in the Homilies. Some of these will come before us presently, but with regard to the whole, which are not less than fifty, we may broadly and positively state that they all more or less differ from our Gospels. To take the

---

[1] Καὶ εὐλόγως. Σοῦ γὰρ, φησὶν, ἄνθρωπε, τοὺς λόγους μου ὡς ἀργύριον ἐπὶ τραπεζιτῶν βαλεῖν, καὶ ὡς χρήματα δοκιμάσαι. Hom. iii. 61.
[2] Hom. iii. 50, ii. 51, &c., &c.

severest test, however, we shall compare those further passages which are specially adduced as most closely following our Gospels, and neglect the vast majority which most widely differ from them. In addition to the passages which we have already examined, Credner[1] points out the following. The first is from Hom. xix. 2.[2] "If Satan cast out Satan he is divided against himself: how then can his kingdom stand?" In the first part of this sentence, the Homily reads, ἐκβάλλῃ for the ἐκβάλλει of the first Gospel, and the last phrase in each is as follows :—

Hom. πῶς οὖν αὐτοῦ στήκῃ ἡ βασιλεία;
Matt. πῶς οὖν σταθήσεται ἡ βασιλεία αὐτοῦ;

The third Gospel differs from the first as the Homily does from both. The next passage is from Hom. xix. 7.[3] "For thus, said our Father, who was without deceit: out of abundance of heart mouth speaketh." The Greek compared with that of Matt. xii. 34.

Hom. Ἐκ   περισσεύματος καρδίας στόμα λαλεῖ
Matt. Ἐκ γὰρ τοῦ περισσεύματος τῆς καρδίας τὸ στόμα λαλεῖ.

The form of the homily is much more proverbial. The next passage occurs in Hom. iii. 52: "Every plant which the heavenly Father did not plant shall be rooted up." This agrees with the parallel in Matt. xv. 13, with the important exception, that although in the mouth of Jesus, "*the* heavenly Father" is substituted for the "*my* heavenly Father" of the Gospel. The last passage pointed out by Credner, is from Hom. viii. 4: "But also 'many,' he said, 'called, but few chosen;'" which may be compared with Matt. xx. 16, &c.

Hom. Ἀλλὰ καὶ, πολλοί, φησὶν, κλητοί, ὀλίγοι δὲ ἐκλεκτοί.
Matt.   πολλοὶ γάρ εἰσιν κλητοί, ὀλίγοι δὲ ἐκλεκτοί.

[1] *Credner*, Beiträge, i. p. 285; cf. p. 302.
[2] Cf. Matt. xii. 26.
[3] Cf. Matt. xii. 34.

We have already fully discussed this passage of the Gospel in connection with the "Epistle of Barnabas,"[1] and need not say more here.

The variations in these passages, it may be argued, are not very important. Certainly, if they were the exceptional variations amongst a mass of quotations perfectly agreeing with parallels in our Gospels, it might be exaggeration to base upon such divergences a conclusion that they were derived from a different source. When it is considered, however, that the very reverse is the case, and that these are passages selected for their closer agreement out of a multitude of others either more decidedly differing from our Gospels or not found in them at all, the case entirely changes, and variations being the rule instead of the exception, these, however slight, become evidence of the use of a Gospel different from ours. As an illustration of the importance of slight variations in connection with the question as to the source from which quotations are derived, the following may at random be pointed out. The passage "See thou say nothing to any man, but go thy way, show thyself to the priest" ("Ορα μηδενὶ μηδὲν εἴπῃς, ἀλλὰ ὕπαγε σεαυτὸν δεῖξον τῷ ἱερεῖ) occurring in a work like the Homilies would, supposing our second Gospel no longer extant, be referred to Matt. viii. 4, with which it entirely agrees with the exception of its containing the one extra word μηδέν. It is however actually taken from Mark i. 44, and not from the first Gospel. Then again, supposing that our first Gospel had shared the fate of so many others of the πολλοί of Luke, and in some early work the following passage were found: "A prophet is not without honour except in his own country

[1] Vol. i. p. 236 ff.

and in his own house" (Οὐκ ἔστιν προφήτης ἄτιμος εἰ μὴ ἐν τῇ ἰδίᾳ[1] πατρίδι αὐτοῦ καὶ ἐν τῇ οἰκίᾳ αὐτοῦ), this passage would undoubtedly be claimed by apologists as a quotation from Mark vi. 4, and as proving the existence and use of that Gospel. The omission of the words "and among his own kin" (καὶ ἐν τοῖς συγγενέσιν αὐτοῦ) would at first be explained as mere abbreviation, or defect of memory, but on the discovery that part or all of these words are omitted from some MSS., that for instance the phrase is erased from the oldest manuscript known, the Cod. Sinaiticus, the derivation from the second Gospel would be considered as established. The author notwithstanding might never have seen that Gospel, for the quotation is taken from Matt. xiii. 57.[2]

We have already quoted the opinion of De Wette as to the inconclusive nature of the deductions to be drawn from the quotations in the pseudo-Clementine writings regarding their source, but in pursuance of the plan we have adopted we shall now examine the passages which he cites as most nearly agreeing with our Gospels.[3] The first of these occurs in Hom. iii. 18 : "The Scribes and the Pharisees sit upon Moses' seat ; all things therefore, whatsoever they speak to you, hear them," which is compared with Matt. xxiii. 2, 3 : "The Scribes and the Pharisees sit upon Moses' seat ; all things therefore, whatsoever they say to you, do and observe." We subjoin the Greek of the latter half of these passages.

Hom. πάντα οὖν ὅσα λέγωσιν ὑμῖν, ἀκούετε αὐτῶν.
Matt. πάντα οὖν ὅσα ἐὰν εἴπωσιν ὑμῖν ποιήσατε καὶ τηρεῖτε.[4]

[1] ἰδίᾳ, though not found in all MSS., has the authority of the Cod. Sinaiticus and other ancient texts.
[2] Cf. Matt. viii. 19—22; Luke ix. 57—60, &c., &c.
[3] Einl. N. T., p. 115.
[4] It is unnecessary to point out the various readings of the three last

That the variation in the Homily is deliberate and derived from the Gospel used by the author is clear from the continuation: "Hear *them* (αὐτῶν), he said, as entrusted with the key of the kingdom, which is knowledge, which alone is able to open the gate of life, through which alone is the entrance to eternal life. But verily, he says: They possess the key indeed, but to those who wish to enter in they do not grant it."[1] The αὐτῶν is here emphatically repeated, and the further quotation and reference to the denunciation of the Scribes and Pharisees continues to differ distinctly from the account both in our first and third Gospels. The passage in Matt. xxiii. 13, reads: "But woe unto you, Scribes and Pharisees, hypocrites! for ye shut the kingdom of heaven against men; for ye go not in yourselves neither suffer ye them that are entering to go in."[2] The parallel in Luke xi. 52 is not closer. There the passage regarding Moses' seat is altogether wanting, and in ver. 52, where the greatest similarity exists, the "lawyers" instead of the "Scribes and Pharisees" are addressed. The verse reads: "Woe unto you, Lawyers! for ye have taken away the key of knowledge: ye entered not in yourselves, and them that were entering in ye hindered."[3] The first Gospel has not the direct image of the key at all: the Scribes and Pharisees "shut the kingdom of

words in various MSS. Whether shortened or inverted, the difference from the Homily remains the same.

[1] Αὐτῶν δὲ, εἶπεν, ὡς τὴν κλεῖδα τῆς βασιλείας πεπιστευμένων, ἥτις ἐστὶ γνῶσις, ἡ μόνη τὴν πύλην τῆς ζωῆς ἀνοῖξαι δύναται, δι' ἧς μόνης εἰς τὴν αἰωνίαν ζωὴν εἰσελθεῖν ἔστιν. . 'Ἀλλὰ ναί, φησὶν, κρατοῦσι μὲν τὴν κλεῖν, τοῖς δὲ βουλομένοις εἰσελθεῖν οὐ παρέχουσιν. Hom. iii. 18 ; cf. Hom. iii. 70, xviii. 15, 16.

[2] Οὐαὶ, κ.τ.λ. . . . . ὅτι κλείετε τὴν βασιλείαν τῶν οὐρανῶν ἔμπροσθεν τῶν ἀνθρώπων· ὑμεῖς γὰρ οὐκ εἰσέρχεσθε, οὐδὲ τοὺς εἰσερχομένους ἀφίετε εἰσελθεῖν. Matt. xxiii. 13.

[3] Οὐαὶ ὑμῖν τοῖς νομικοῖς, ὅτι ἤρατε τὴν κλεῖδα τῆς γνώσεως· αὐτοὶ οὐκ εἰσήλθατε καὶ τοὺς εἰσερχομένους ἐκωλύσατε. Luke xi. 52.

heaven;" the third has "the key of knowledge" (κλεῖδα τῆς γνώσεως) taken away by the lawyers, and not by the Scribes and Pharisees, whilst the Gospel of the Homilies has the key of the kingdom (κλεῖδα τῆς βασιλείας), and explains that this key is knowledge (ἥτις ἐστὶ γνῶσις). It is apparent that the first Gospel uses an expression more direct than the others, whilst the third Gospel explains it, but the Gospel of the Homilies has in all probability the simpler original words: the "key of the kingdom," which both of the others have altered for the purpose of more immediate clearness. In any case it is certain that the passage does not agree with our Gospel.[1]

The next quotation referred to by De Wette is in Hom. iii. 51: "And also that he said: 'I am not come to destroy the law . . . . the heaven and the earth will pass away, but one jot or one tittle shall in nowise pass from the law.'" This is compared with Matt. v. 17, 18:[2] "Think not that I am come to destroy the law or the prophets: I am not come to destroy but to fulfil. (v. 18) For verily I say unto you: Till heaven and earth pass away one jot or one tittle shall in nowise pass from the law, till all be fulfilled." The Greek of both passages reads as follows:—

Hom. iii. 51.	Matt. v. 17, 18.
Τὸ δὲ καὶ εἰπεῖν αὐτόν·	Μὴ νομίσητε ὅτι ἦλθον καταλῦσαι τὸν νόμον ἢ τοὺς προφήτας· οὐκ ἦλθον καταλῦσαι ἀλλὰ πληρῶσαι.
Οὐκ ἦλθον καταλῦσαι τὸν νόμον.	
* * * *	v. 18. ἀμὴν γὰρ λέγω ὑμῖν, ἕως ἂν παρέλθῃ ὁ οὐρανὸς καὶ ἡ γῆ, ἰῶτα ἐν ἢ μία κεραία οὐ μὴ παρέλθῃ ἀπὸ τοῦ νόμου, ἕως ἂν πάντα γένηται.
Ὁ οὐρανὸς καὶ ἡ γῆ παρελεύσονται ἰῶτα δὲ ἐν ᾗ μία κεραία οὐ μὴ παρέλθῃ ἀπὸ τοῦ νόμου.	

[1] *Credner*, Beiträge, i. p. 317 f.; *Hilgenfeld*, Die Evv. Justin's, p. 366 f. *Zeller*, Die Apostelgesch., p. 57 f.
Cf. Luke xvi. 17.

That the omissions and variations in this passage are not accidental is proved by the fact that the same quotation occurs again literally in the Epistle from Peter[1] which is prefixed to the Homilies in which the παρελεύσονται is repeated, and the sentence closes at the same point. The author in that place adds: "This he said that all might be fulfilled" (τοῦτο δὲ εἴρηκεν, ἵνα τὰ πάντα γίνηται). Hilgenfeld considers this Epistle of much more early date than the Homilies, and that this agreement bespeaks a particular text.[2] The quotation does not agree with our Gospels, and must be assigned to another source.

The next passage pointed out by De Wette is the erroneous quotation from Isaiah which we have already examined.[3] That which follows is found in Hom. viii. 7: "For on this account our Jesus himself said to one who frequently called him Lord, yet did nothing which he commanded: Why dost thou say to me Lord, Lord, and doest not the things which I say?" This is compared with Luke vi. 46 :[4] "But why call ye me Lord, Lord, and do not the things which I say?"

Hom. viii. 7.	Luke vi. 46.
Τί με λέγεις, Κύριε, κύριε, καὶ οὐ ποιεῖς ἃ λέγω ;	Τί δέ με καλεῖτε Κύριε, κύριε, καὶ οὐ ποιεῖτε ἃ λέγω ;

This passage differs from our Gospels in having the second person singular instead of the plural, and in substituting λέγεις for καλεῖτε in the first phrase. The Homily, moreover, in accordance with the use of the second person singular, distinctly states that the saying was addressed to a person who frequently called Jesus "Lord," whereas in the Gospels it forms part of the Sermon on the Mount with a totally impersonal application to the multitude.

[1] § ii.   [2] Die Evv. Justin's, p. 340.
[3] P. 10. Cf. Hom. xviii. 15; Matt. xiii. 35.   [4] Cf. Matt. vii. 21.

The next passage referred to by De Wette is in Hom. xix. 2: "And he declared that he saw the evil one as lightning fall from heaven." This is compared with Luke x. 18, which has no parallel in the other Gospels: "And he said to them, I beheld Satan as lightning fall from heaven."

Hom. xix. 2.	Luke x. 18.
Καὶ ὅτι ἑώρακε τὸν πονηρὸν ὡς ἀστραπὴν πεσόντα ἐκ τοῦ οὐρανοῦ ἐδήλωσεν.	Εἶπεν δὲ αὐτοῖς Ἐθεώρουν τὸν σατανᾶν ὡς ἀστραπὴν ἐκ τοῦ οὐρανοῦ πεσόντα.

The substitution of τὸν πονηρὸν for τὸν σατανᾶν, had he found the latter in his Gospel, would be all the more remarkable from the fact that the author of the Homilies has just before quoted the saying "If Satan cast out Satan,"[1] &c. and he continues in the above words to show that Satan had been cast out, so that the evidence would have been strengthened by the retention of the word in Luke had he quoted that Gospel. The variations, however, indicate that he quoted from another source.[2]

The next passage pointed out by De Wette likewise finds a parallel only in the third Gospel. It occurs in Hom. ix. 22: "Nevertheless, though all demons with all the diseases flee before you, in this only is not to be your rejoicing, but in that, through grace, your names, as of the ever-living, are recorded in heaven." This is compared with Luke x. 20: "Notwithstanding, in this rejoice not that the spirits are subject unto you, but rejoice that your names are written in the heavens."

Hom. ix. 22.	Luke x. 20.
Ἀλλ' ὅμως κἂν πάντες δαίμονες μετὰ πάντων τῶν παθῶν ὑμᾶς φεύγωσιν, οὐκ ἔστιν ἐν τούτῳ μόνῳ χαίρειν, ἀλλ' ἐν τῷ δι' εὐαρεστίαν τὰ ὀνόματα ὑμῶν ἐν οὐρανῷ ὡς ἀεὶ ζώντων ἀναγραφῆναι.	Πλὴν ἐν τούτῳ μὴ χαίρετε, ὅτι τὰ πνεύματα ὑμῖν ὑποτάσσεται, χαίρετε δὲ ὅτι τὰ ὀνόματα ὑμῶν ἐγγέγραπται ἐν τοῖς οὐρανοῖς.

[1] See p. 16. [2] Cf. *Hilgenfeld*, Die Evv. Justin's, p. 346 f.

The differences between these two passages are too great and the peculiarities of the Homily too marked to require any argument to demonstrate that the quotation cannot be successfully claimed by our third Gospel. On the contrary, as one of so many other passages systematically varying from the canonical Gospels, it must rather be assigned to another source.

De Wette says: "A few others (quotations) presuppose (voraussetzen) the Gospel of Mark,"[1] and he gives them. The first occurs in Hom. ii. 19: "There is a certain Justa[2] amongst us, a Syrophœnician, a Canaanite by race, whose daughter was affected by a sore disease, and who came to our Lord crying out and supplicating that he would heal her daughter. But he being also asked by us, said: 'It is not meet to heal the Gentiles who are like dogs from their using different meats and practices, whilst the table in the kingdom has been granted to the sons of Israel.' But she, hearing this and exchanging her former manner of life for that of the sons of the kingdom, in order that she might, like a dog, partake of the crumbs falling from that same table, obtained, as she desired, healing for her daughter."[3] This is compared with Mark vii. 24—30,[4] as it is the only Gospel which calls the woman a Syrophœnician. The Homily, however, not only calls her so, a very unimportant point, but gives her name as "Justa."

---

[1] Einl. N. T., p. 115.   [2] Cf. Hom. iii. 73; xiii. 7.

[3] Ἰουστά τις ἐν ἡμῖν ἐστι Συροφοινίκισσα, τὸ γένος Χαναανῖτις, ἧς τὸ θυγάτριον ὑπὸ χαλεπῆς νόσου συνείχετο, ἣ καὶ τῷ Κυρίῳ ἡμῶν προσῆλθε βοῶσα καὶ ἱκετεύουσα, ὅπως αὐτῆς τὸ θυγάτριον θεραπεύσῃ. Ὁ δὲ, καὶ ὑφ' ἡμῶν ἀξιωθείς, εἶπεν· Οὐκ ἔξεστιν ἰᾶσθαι τὰ ἔθνη, ἐοικότα κυσὶν, διὰ τὸ διαφόροις χρῆσθαι τροφαῖς καὶ πράξεσιν, ἀποδεδομένης τῆς κατὰ τὴν βασιλείαν τραπέζης τοῖς υἱοῖς Ἰσραήλ. Ἡ δὲ τοῦτο ἀκούσασα, καὶ τῆς αὐτῆς τραπέζης, ὡς κύων, ψιχίων ἀποπιπτόντων συμμεταλαμβάνειν μετατεθεμένη ὅπερ ἦν, τῷ ὁμοίως διαιτᾶσθαι τοῖς τῆς βασιλεία υἱοῖς, τῆς εἰς τὴν θυγατέρα, ὡς ἠξίωσεν ἔτυχεν ἰάσεως. Hom. ii. 19.

[4] Cf. Matt. xv. 21—28.

If, therefore, it be argued that the mention of her nationality supposes that the author found the fact in his Gospel, and that as we know no other but Mark[1] which gives that information, that he therefore derived it from our second Gospel, the additional mention of the name of "Justa" on the same grounds necessarily points to the use of a Gospel which likewise contained it, which our Gospel does not. Nothing can be more decided than the variation in language throughout this whole passage from the account in Mark, and the reply of Jesus is quite foreign to our Gospels. In Mark (vii. 25) the daughter has "an unclean spirit" (πνεῦμα ἀκάθαρτον); in Matthew (xv. 22) she is "grievously possessed by a devil" (κακῶς δαιμονίζεται), but in the Homily she is "affected by a sore disease" (ὑπὸ χαλεπῆς νόσου συνείχετο). The second Gospel knows nothing of any intercession on the part of the disciples, but Matthew has: "And the disciples came and besought him (ἠρώτων αὐτὸν) saying: 'Send her away, for she crieth after us,'"[2] whilst the Homily has merely "being also asked by us," (ἀξιωθεὶς) in the sense of intercession in her favour. The second Gospel gives the reply of Jesus as follows: "Let the children first be filled: for it is not meet to take the bread of the children, and to cast it to the dogs. And she answered and said unto him: 'Yea, Lord, for the dogs also eat under the table of the crumbs of the children. And he said unto her: For this saying go thy way; the devil is gone out of thy daughter."[3] The nature of the reply of the woman is,

---

[1] "The woman was a Greek, a Syrophenician by nation." (ἡ δὲ γυνὴ ἦν Ἑλληνίς, Σύρα Φοινίκισσα τῷ γένει). Mark vii. 26. "A woman of Canaan" (γυνὴ Χαναναία). Matt. xv. 22.   [2] Matt. xv. 23.

[3] Mark vii. 27—29. Ἄφες πρῶτον χορτασθῆναι τὰ τέκνα· οὐ γάρ ἐστιν καλὸν λαβεῖν τὸν ἄρτον τῶν τέκνων καὶ τοῖς κυναρίοις βαλεῖν. ἡ δὲ ἀπεκρίθη καὶ λέγει αὐτῷ, Ναί, κύριε· καὶ γὰρ τὰ κυνάρια ὑποκάτω τῆς τραπέζης ἐσθίουσιν ἀπὸ τῶν ψιχίων τῶν παιδίων. κ.τ.λ.

in the Gospels, the reason given for granting her request; but in the Homily the woman's conversion to Judaism,[1] that is to say Judeo-Christianity, is prominently advanced as the cause of her successful pleading. It is certain from the whole character of this passage, the variation of the language, and the reply of Jesus which is not in our Gospels at all, that the narrative cannot rightly be assigned to them, but the more reasonable inference is that it was derived from another source.[2]

The last of De Wette's[3] passages is from Hom. iii. 57: "Hear, O Israel; the Lord thy[4] God is one Lord." This is a quotation from Deuteronomy vi. 4, which is likewise quoted in the second Gospel, xii. 29, in reply to the question, "Which is the first Commandment of all? Jesus answered: The first is, Hear, O Israel; the Lord our God is one Lord, and thou shalt love the Lord thy God," &c. &c. In the Homily, however, the quotation is made in a totally different connection, for there is no question of commandments at all, but a clear statement of the circumstances under which the passage was used, which excludes the idea that this quotation was derived from Mark xii. 29. The context in the Homily is as follows: "But to those who were beguiled to imagine many gods as the Scriptures say, he said: Hear, O Israel," &c., &c.[5] There is no hint of the assertion of many gods in the Gospels; but, on the contrary, the question is put by one of the scribes in Mark to whom Jesus says: "Thou art not far from the Kingdom of God."[6] The quotation,

[1] Cf. Hom. xiii. 7.
[2] Cf. *Hilgenfeld*, Die Evv. Justin's, p. 353 f.
[3] Einl. N. T., p. 115.
[4] Although most MSS. have σου in this place, some, as for instance that edited by Cotelerius, read ὑμῶν.
[5] Τοῖς δὲ ἠπατημένοις πολλοὺς θεοὺς ὑπονοεῖν, ὡς αἱ Γραφαὶ λέγουσιν, ἔφη Ἄκουε, Ἰσραήλ, κ.τ.λ. Hom. iii. 57.
[6] Mark xii. 34.

therefore, beyond doubt, cannot be legitimately appropriated by the second Synoptic, but may with much greater probability be assigned to a different Gospel.

We may here refer to the passage, the only one pointed out by him in connection with the Synoptics, the discovery of which Canon Westcott affirms, "has removed the doubts which had long been raised about those (allusions) to St. Mark."[1] The discovery referred to is that of the Codex Ottobonianus by Dressel, which contains the concluding part of the Homilies, and which was first published by him in 1853. Canon Westcott says: "Though St. Mark has few peculiar phrases, one of these is repeated verbally in the concluding part of the 19th Homily."[2] The passage is as follows: Hom. xix. 20: "Wherefore also he explained to his disciples privately the mysteries of the kingdom of the heavens." This is compared with Mark iv. 34. . . . "and privately to his own disciples, he explained all things."

Hom. xix. 20.	Mark iv. 34.
Διὸ καὶ τοῖς αὐτοῦ μαθηταῖς κατ' ἰδίαν ἐπέλυε τῆς τῶν οὐρανῶν βασιλείας τὰ μυστήρια.	. . . . κατ' ἰδίαν δὲ τοῖς ἰδίοις μαθηταῖς ἐπέλυεν πάντα.[3]

We have only a few words to add to complete the whole of Dr. Westcott's remarks upon the subject. He adds after the quotation: "This is the only place where ἐπιλύω occurs in the Gospels."[4] We may, however, point out that it occurs also in Acts xix. 39 and 2 Peter i. 20. It is upon the coincidence of this word that

---

[1] On the Canon, p. 251.   [2] Cf. *Ib.*, p. 252.

[3] Dr. Westcott quotes this reading, which is supported by the Codices B, C, Sinaiticus and others. The Codex Alexandrinus and a majority of other MSS. read for τοῖς ἰδίοις μαθηταῖς,—"τοῖς μαθηταῖς αὐτοῦ," which is closer to the passage in the Homily. It is fair that this should be pointed out.

[4] On the Canon, p. 252, note 1.

Canon Westcott rests his argument that this passage is a reference to Mark. Nothing, however, could be more untenable than such a conclusion from such an indication. The phrase in the Homily presents a very marked variation from the passage in Mark. The "all things" ($\pi\acute{a}\nu\tau a$) of the Gospel, reads: "The mysteries of the kingdom of the heavens" ($\tau\hat{\eta}s$ $\tau\hat{\omega}\nu$ $o\mathring{\nu}\rho a\nu\hat{\omega}\nu$ $\beta a\sigma\iota\lambda\epsilon\acute{\iota}as$ $\tau\grave{a}$ $\mu\nu\sigma\tau\acute{\eta}\rho\iota a$) in the Homily. The passage in Mark iv. 11, to which Dr. Westcott does not refer, reads $\tau\grave{o}$ $\mu\nu\sigma\tau\acute{\eta}\rho\iota o\nu$ $\tau\hat{\eta}s$ $\beta a\sigma\iota\lambda\epsilon\acute{\iota}as$ $\tau o\hat{\nu}$ $\theta\epsilon o\hat{\nu}$. There is one very important matter, however, which our Apologist has omitted to point out, and which, it seems to us, decides the case—the context in the Homily. The chapter commences thus: "And Peter said: We remember that our Lord and Teacher, as commanding, said to us: 'Guard the mysteries for me, and the sons of my house.' Wherefore also he explained to his disciples privately," &c.:[1] and then comes our passage. Now, here is a command of Jesus, in immediate connection with which the phrase before us is quoted, which does not appear in our Gospels at all, and which clearly establishes the use of a different source. The phrase itself which differs from Mark, as we have seen, may with all right be referred to the same unknown Gospel.

It must be borne in mind that all the quotations which we have hitherto examined are those which have been selected as most closely approximating to passages in our Gospels. Space forbids our giving illustrations of the vast number which so much more widely differ from parallel texts in the Synoptics. We shall confine our-

[1] Καὶ ὁ Πέτρος· Μεμνήμεθα τοῦ Κυρίου ἡμῶν καὶ Διδασκάλου, ὡς ἐντελλόμενος, εἶπεν ἡμῖν· Τὰ μυστήρια ἐμοὶ καὶ τοῖς υἱοῖς τοῦ οἴκου μου φυλάξατε. κ.τ.λ. Hom. xix. 20.

selves to pointing out in the briefest possible manner some of the passages which are persistent in their variations or recall similar passages in the Memoirs of Justin. The first of these is the injunction in Hom. iii. 55 : "Let your yea be yea, your nay nay, for whatsoever is more than these cometh of the evil one." The same saying is repeated in Hom. xix. with the sole addition of "and." We subjoin the Greek of these, together with that of the Gospel and Justin with which the Homilies agree.

    Hom. iii. 55. Ἔστω   ὑμῶν τὸ ναὶ ναί   τὸ οὒ οὔ.
    Hom. xix. 2. Ἔστω   ὑμῶν τὸ ναὶ ναί καὶ τὸ οὒ οὔ.
    Apol. i. 16.   Ἔστω δὲ   ὑμῶν τὸ ναὶ ναί καὶ τὸ οὒ οὔ.
    Matt. v. 37.   Ἔστω δὲ ὁ λόγος ὑμῶν   ναὶ ναί   οὒ οὔ.

As we have already discussed this passage [1] we need not repeat our remarks here. That this passage comes from a source different from our Gospels is rendered still more probable by the quotation in Hom. xix. 2 being preceded by another which has no parallel at all in our Gospels. "And elsewhere he said, 'He who sowed the bad seed is the devil' (Ὁ δὲ τὸ κακὸν σπέρμα σπείρας ἐστὶν ὁ διάβολος [2]): and again : ' Give no pretext to the evil one.' [2] (Μὴ δότε πρόφασιν τῷ πονηρῷ.) But in exhorting he prescribes : 'Let your yea be yea,'" &c. The first of these phrases differs markedly from our Gospels ; the second is not in them at all ; the third, which we are considering, differs likewise in an important degree in common with Justin's quotation, and there is every reason for supposing that the whole were derived from the same unknown source. [3]

In the same Homily, xix. 2, there occurs also the passage which exhibits variations likewise found in Justin, which we have already examined, [4] and now

---

[1] Vol. i. p. 354, p. 375 f.   [2] Cf. Matt. xiii. 39.
[3] Cf. Credner, Beiträge, i. p. 306 ; Hilgenfeld, Die Evv. Justin's, p. 360.   [4] Vol. i. p. 353 n. 1, p. 375 f.

merely point out: "Begone into the darkness without, which the Father hath prepared for the devil and his angels."[1] The quotation in Justin (Dial. 76) agrees exactly with this, with the exception that Justin has Σατανᾷ instead of διαβόλῳ, which is not important, whilst the agreement in the marked variation from the parallel in the first Gospel establishes the probability of a common source different from ours.[2]

We have also already[3] referred to the passage in Hom. xvii. 4. "No one knew (ἔγνω) the Father but the Son, even as no one knoweth the Son but the Father and those to whom the Son is minded to reveal him." This quotation differs from Matt. xi. 27 in form, in language, and in meaning, but agrees with Justin's reading of the same text, and as we have shown the use of the aorist here, and the transposition of the order, were characteristics of Gospels used by Gnostics and other parties in the early Church, and the passage with these variations was regarded by them as the basis of some of their leading doctrines.[4] That the variation is not accidental, but a deliberate quotation from a written source, is proved by this, and by the circumstance that the author of the Homilies repeatedly quotes it elsewhere in the same form.[5] It is unreasonable to suppose that the quotations in these Homilies are so systematically and consistently erroneous, and not only can they not, from their actual variations, be legitimately referred to the Synoptics exclusively, but, considering all the circumstances, the

---

[1] 'Ὑπάγετε εἰς τὸ σκότος τὸ ἐξώτερον, ὃ ἡτοίμασεν ὁ Πατὴρ τῷ διαβόλῳ καὶ τοῖς ἀγγέλοις αὐτοῦ. Hom. xix. 2; cf. Matt. xxv. 41.

[2] *Hilgenfeld*, Die Evv. Justin's, pp. 369, 233 f.; *Credner*, Beiträge, i. p. 211, p. 330; *Mayerhoff*, Einl. petr. Schr., p. 245 f.

[3] Vol. i. p. 402 ff.

[4] *Irenæus*, Adv. Hær., iv. 6, §§ 1, 3, 7; cf. vol. i. p. 406 f.

[5] Hom. xviii. 4, 6, 7, 8, 13, 20.

only natural conclusion is that they are derived from a source different from our Gospels.¹

Another passage occurs in Hom. iii. 50 : "Wherefore ye do err, not knowing the true things of the Scriptures ; and on this account ye are ignorant of the power of God." This is compared with Mark xii. 24 :² "Do ye not therefore err, not knowing the Scriptures nor the power of God ? "

Hom. iii. 50.	Mark xii. 24.
Διὰ τοῦτο πλανᾶσθε, μὴ εἰδότες τὰ ἀληθῆ τῶν γραφῶν, οὗ εἵνεκεν ἀγνοεῖτε τὴν δύναμιν τοῦ Θεοῦ.	Οὐ διὰ τοῦτο πλανᾶσθε μὴ εἰδότες τὰς γραφὰς μηδὲ τὴν δύναμιν τοῦ Θεοῦ ;

The very same quotation is made both in Hom. ii. 51 and xviii. 20, and in each case in which the passage is introduced it is in connection with the assertion that there are true and false Scriptures, and that as there are in the Scriptures some true sayings and some false, Jesus by this saying showed to those who erred by reason of the false the cause of their error. There can scarcely be a doubt that the author of the Homilies quotes this passage from a Gospel different from ours, and this is demonstrated both by the important variation from our text and also by its consistent repetition, and by the context in which it stands.³

Upon each occasion, also, that the author of the Homilies quotes the foregoing passage he likewise quotes another saying of Jesus which is foreign to our Gospels.: "Be ye approved money-changers," γίνεσθε τραπεζῖται δόκιμοι.⁴ The saying is thrice quoted without

---

[1] *Baur*, Unters. kan. Evv., p. 576 ; *Credner*, Beiträge, i. p. 210 f., 248 f., 314, 330 ; *Hilgenfeld*, Die Evv. Justin's, p. 201 ff., 351 ; *Mayerhoff*, Einl. petr. Schr., p. 245 ; *Zeller*, Die Apostelgesch., p. 48.

[2] Cf. Matt. xxii. 29, which is still more remote.

[3] *Hilgenfeld*, Die Evv. Justin's, p. 365.

[4] Hom. ii. 51, iii. 50, xviii. 20.

variation, and each time, together with the preceding passage, it refers to the necessity of discrimination between true and false sayings in the Scriptures, as for instance: "And Peter said: If, therefore, of the Scriptures some are true and some are false, our Teacher rightly said: 'Be ye approved money-changers,' as in the Scriptures there are some approved sayings and some spurious."[1] This is one of the best known of the apocryphal sayings of Jesus, and it is quoted by nearly all the Fathers,[2] by many as from Holy Scripture, and by some ascribed to the Gospel of the Nazarenes, or the Gospel according to the Hebrews. There can be no question here that the author quotes an apocryphal Gospel.[3]

There is, in immediate connection with both the preceding passages, another saying of Jesus quoted which is not found in our Gospels: "Why do ye not discern the good reason of the Scriptures?" "Διὰ τί οὐ νοεῖτε τὸ εὔλογον τῶν γραφῶν;"[4] This passage also comes from a Gospel different from ours,[5] and the connection and sequence of these quotations is very significant.

One further illustration, and we have done. We find the following in Hom. iii. 55: "And to those who

---

[1] Hom. ii. 51.
[2] Apost. Constit., ii. 36; cf. 37; *Clem. Al.*, Strom., i. 28, § 177; cf. ii. 4, § 15, vi. 10, § 81, vii. 15, § 90; *Origen*, in Joan. T. xix., vol. iv. p. 289; *Epiphanius*, Hær., xliv. 2, p. 382; *Hieron.*, Ep. ad Minerv. et Alex., 119 (al. 152); Comm. in Ep. ad Ephes., iv.; *Grabe*, Spicil. Patr., i. p. 13 f., 326; *Cotelerius*, Patr. Ap., i. p. 249 f.; *Fabricius*, Cod. Apocr. N. T., ii. p. 524.
[3] *Credner*, Beiträge, i. p. 326 f.; *Hilgenfeld*, Die Evv. Justin's, p. 369; *De Wette*, Einl. N. T., p. 115, anm. f.
[4] Hom. iii. 50.
[5] *Cotelerius*, Not. ad Clem. Hom., iii. 50; *Credner*, Beiträge, i. p. 326; *Hilgenfeld*, Die Evv. Justin's, p. 365; *De Wette*, Einl. N. T., p. 115, anm. f.

think that God tempts, as the Scriptures say, he said: 'The evil one is the tempter,' who also tempted himself."[1] This short saying is not found in our Gospels. It probably occurred in the Gospel of the Homilies in connection with the temptation of Jesus. It is not improbable that the writer of the Epistle of James, who shows acquaintance with a Gospel different from ours,[2] also knew this saying.[3] We are here again directed to the Ebionite Gospel. Certainly the quotation is derived from a source different from our Gospels.[4]

These illustrations of the evangelical quotations in the Clementine Homilies give but an imperfect impression of the character of the extremely numerous passages which occur in the work. We have selected for our examination the quotations which have been specially cited by critics as closest to parallels in our Gospels, and have thus submitted the question to the test which is most favourable to the claims of our Synoptics. Space forbids our adequately showing the much wider divergence which exists in the great majority of cases between them and the quotations in the Homilies. To sum up the case: Out of more than a hundred of these quotations only four brief and fragmentary phrases really agree with parallels in our Synoptics, and these, we have shown, are either not used in the same context as in our Gospels or are of a nature far from special to them. Of the rest, all without exception systematically vary more or less from our Gospels, and many in their variations agree with similar quotations in other writers,

---

[1] Τοῖς δὲ οἰομένοις ὅτι ὁ θεὸς πειράζει, ὡς αἱ Γραφαὶ λέγουσιν ἔφη· Ὁ πονηρός ἐστιν ὁ πειράζων, ὁ καὶ αὐτὸν πειράσας. Hom. iii. 55.

[2] Cf. ch. v. 12.   [3] Cf. ch. i. 13.

[4] *Credner*, Beiträge, i. p. 306; *Hilgenfeld*, Die Evv. Justin's, p. 339.

or on repeated quotation always present the same peculiarities, whilst others, professed to be direct quotations of sayings of Jesus, have no parallels in our Gospels at all. Upon the hypothesis that the author made use of our Gospels, such systematic divergence would be perfectly unintelligible and astounding. On the other hand, it must be remembered that the agreement of a few passages with parallels in our Gospels cannot prove anything. The only extraordinary circumstance is that, even using a totally different source, there should not have been a greater agreement with our Synoptics. But for the universal inaccuracy of the human mind, every important historical saying, having obviously only one distinct original form, would in all truthful histories have been reported in that one unvarying form. The nature of the quotations in the Clementine Homilies leads to the inevitable conclusion that their author derived them from a Gospel different from ours; at least, since the source of these quotations is never named throughout the work, and there is not the faintest direct indication of our Gospels, the Clementine Homilies cannot be considered witnesses of any value as to the origin and authenticity of the canonical Gospels. That this can be said of a work written a century and a half after the establishment of Christianity, and abounding with quotations of the discourses of Jesus, is in itself singularly suggestive.

It is scarcely necessary to add that the author of the Homilies has no idea whatever of any canonical writings but those of the Old Testament, though even with regard to these some of our quotations have shown that he held peculiar views, and believed that they contained spurious elements. There is no reference in the

Homilies to any of the Epistles of the New Testament.[1]

One of the most striking points in this work, on the other hand, is its determined animosity against the Apostle Paul. We have seen that a strong anti-Pauline tendency was exhibited by many of the Fathers, who, like the author of the Homilies, made use of Judeo-Christian Gospels different from ours. In this work, however, the antagonism against the "Apostle of the Gentiles" assumes a tone of peculiar virulence. There cannot be a doubt that the Apostle Paul is attacked in it, as the great enemy of the true faith, under the hated name of Simon the Magician,[2] whom Peter follows everywhere for the purpose of unmasking and confuting him. He is robbed of his title of "Apostle of the Gentiles," which, together with the honour of founding the Church of Antioch, of Laodicæa, and of Rome, is ascribed to Peter. All that opposition to Paul which is implied in the Epistle to the Galatians and elsewhere[3] is here realized and exaggerated, and

---

[1] *Westcott*, On the Canon, p. 252, note 2; *Scholten*, Die ält. Zeugnisse, p. 57.

[2] *Baur*, Paulus, i. p. 97 ff., 148, anm. 1, p. 250; K. G. d. 3 erst. Jahrh., p. 87 ff., 93, anm. 1; Tübinger Zeitschr. f. Th., 1831, h. 4, p. 136 f.; Dogmengesch. I., i. p. 155; *Davidson*, Introd. N. T., ii. p. 286 f.; *Gfrörer*, Allg. K. G., i. p. 257 ff.; *Hilgenfeld*, Die Clem. Recogn. u. Hom., p. 319; Zeitschr. f. wiss. Theol., 1869, p. 353 ff.; Der Kanon, p. 11 f.; *A. Kayser*, Rev. de Théol., 1851, p. 142 f.; *Lechler*, Das apost. u. nachap. Zeit., p. 457 f., p. 500; *Lightfoot*, The Eps. of St. Paul, Galatians, 5th ed. p. 61, p. 327 ff; *Lipsius*, Die Quell. d. röm. Petrussage, 1872, p. 80 f.; *Mansel*, The Gnostic Heresies, 1875, p. 231; *Réville*, Essais de Crit. Relig., 1860, p. 35 f.; *Renan*, St. Paul, 1869, p. 303, note 8; *Reuss*, Hist. du Canon, p. 63, note 1; *Ritschl*, Entst. altk. Kirche, p. 277 ff.; *Scholten*, Die ält. Zeugn., p. 57; *Schwegler*, Das nachap. Zeit., i. p. 372 ff.; *Uhlhorn*, Die Homilien, u. s. w., 1854, p. 297; *Volkmar*, Theol. Jahrb., 1856, p. 279 ff.; *Westcott*, On the Canon, p. 252, note 2; *Zeller*, Apostelgeschichte, p. 158 f.

[3] 1 Cor. i. 11, 12; 2 Cor. xi. 13, 20 f.; Philip. i. 15, 16.

the personal difference with Peter to which Paul refers[1] is widened into the most bitter animosity. In the Epistle of Peter to James which is prefixed to the Homilies, Peter says, in allusion to Paul: "For some among the Gentiles have rejected my lawful preaching and accepted certain lawless and foolish teaching of the hostile man."[2] First expounding a doctrine of duality, as heaven and earth, day and night, life and death,[3] Peter asserts that in nature the greater things come first, but amongst men the opposite is the case, and the first is worse and the second better.[4] He then says to Clement that it is easy according to this order to discern to what class Simon (Paul) belongs, "who came before me to the Gentiles, and to which I belong who have come after him, and have followed him as light upon darkness, as knowledge upon ignorance, as health upon disease."[5] He continues: "If he had been known he would not have been believed, but now, not being known, he is wrongly believed; and though by his acts he is a hater, he has been loved; and although an enemy, he has been welcomed as a friend; and though he is death, he has been desired as a saviour; and though fire, esteemed as light; and though a deceiver, he is listened to as speaking the truth."[6] There is much more of this acrimonious abuse put into the mouth of Peter.[7] The indications that it is Paul who is really attacked under the name of Simon are much too clear to admit of doubt. In Hom. xi. 35, Peter, warning the Church against false

---

[1] Gal. ii. 11; cf. 1 Cor. i. 11, 12.
[2] Epist. Petri ad Jacobum, § 2. Canon Westcott quotes this passage with the observation, "There can be no doubt that St. Paul is referred to as 'the enemy.'" On the Canon, p. 252, note 2.
[3] Hom. ii. 15.   [4] Ib., ii. 16.   [5] Ib., ii. 17.
[6] Ib., ii. 18.   [7] Cf. Hom. iii. 59; vii. 2, 4, 10, 11.

teachers, says: "He who hath sent us, our Lord and Prophet, declared to us that the evil one . . . . announced that he would send from amongst his followers apostles[1] to deceive. Therefore, above all remember to avoid every apostle, or teacher, or prophet, who first does not accurately compare his teaching with that of James called the brother of my Lord, and to whom was confided the ordering of the Church of the Hebrews in Jerusalem," &c., lest this evil one should send a false preacher to them, "as he has sent to us Simon preaching a counterfeit of truth in the name of our Lord and disseminating error."[2] Further on he speaks more plainly still. Simon maintains that he has a truer appreciation of the doctrines and teaching of Jesus because he has received his inspiration by supernatural vision, and not merely by the common experience of the senses,[3] and Peter replies: "If, therefore, our Jesus indeed was seen in a vision, was known by thee, and conversed with thee, it was only as one angry with an adversary. . . . But can any one through a vision be made wise to teach? And if thou sayest: 'It is possible,' then wherefore did the Teacher remain and discourse for a whole year to us who were awake? And how can we believe thy story that he was seen by thee? And how could he have been seen by thee when thy thoughts are contrary to his teaching? But if seen and taught by him for a single hour thou becamest an apostle:[4] preach his words, interpret his sayings, love his

---

[1] We have already pointed out that this declaration is not in our Gospels.
[2] Hom. xi. 35; cf. Galat. i. 7 ff. [3] Ib., xvii. 13 ff.
[4] Cf. 1 Cor. ix. 1 ff. "Am I not an Apostle? have I not seen Jesus our Lord?" Cf. Galat. i. 1; i. 12, "For neither did I myself receive it by man, nor was I taught it, but by revelation of Jesus Christ."

apostles, oppose not me who consorted with him. For thou hast directly withstood me who am a firm rock, the foundation of the Church. If thou hadst not been an adversary thou wouldst not have calumniated me, thou wouldst not have reviled my teaching in order that, when declaring what I have myself heard from the Lord, I might not be believed, as though I were condemned. . . . But if thou callest me condemned, thou speakest against God who revealed Christ to me,'"[1] &c. This last phrase: "If thou callest me condemned" (*Η εἰ κατεγνωσμένον με λέγεις) is an evident allusion to Galat. ii. 11: "I withstood him to the face, because he was condemned" (ὅτι κατεγνωσμένος ἦν).

We have digressed to a greater extent than we intended, but it is not unimportant to show the general character and tendency of the work we have been examining. The Clementine Homilies,—written perhaps about the end of the second century, which never name nor indicate any Gospel as the source of the author's knowledge of evangelical history, whose quotations of sayings of Jesus, numerous as they are, systematically differ from the parallel passages of our Synoptics, or are altogether foreign to them, which denounce the Apostle Paul as an impostor, enemy of the faith, and disseminator of false doctrine, and therefore repudiate his Epistles, at the same time equally ignoring all the other writings of the New Testament,—can scarcely be considered as giving much support to any theory of the early formation of the New Testament Canon, or as affording evidence even of the existence of its separate books.

[1] Hom. xvii. 19.

2.

Among the writings which used formerly to be ascribed to Justin Martyr, and to be published along with his genuine works, is the short composition commonly known as the "Epistle to Diognetus." The ascription of this composition to Justin arose solely from the fact that in the only known MS. of the letter there is an inscription Τοῦ αὐτοῦ πρὸς Διόγνητον which, from its connection, was referred to Justin.[1] The style and contents of the work, however, soon convinced critics that it could not possibly be written by Justin,[2] and although it has been ascribed by various isolated writers to Apollos, Clement, Marcion, Quadratus, and others, none of these guesses have been seriously supported, and critics are almost universally agreed in confessing that the author of the Epistle is entirely unknown.

Such being the case, it need scarcely be said that the difficulty of assigning a date to the work with any degree of certainty is extreme, if it be not absolutely impossible to do so. This difficulty, however, is increased by several circumstances. The first and most important of these is the fact that the Epistle to Diognetus is neither quoted nor mentioned by any ancient

---

[1] *Otto*, Ep. ad Diognetum, &c., 1852, p. 11 f.

[2] *Baur*, Dogmengesch. I., i. p. 255; Gesch. chr. Kirche, i. p. 373; *Bunsen*, Analecta Ante-Nic., i. p. 103 ff.; Christianity and Mankind, i. p. 170 f.; *Credner*, Beiträge, i. p. 50; *Davidson*, Introd. N. T., ii. p. 399; *Donaldson*, Hist. Chr. Lit. and Doctr., ii. p. 168 ff.; *Ewald*, Gesch. Volkes Isr., vii. p. 251; *Guericke*, H'buch K. G., p. 152; *C. D. a. Grossheim*, De ep. ad Diogn. Comm., 1828; *Hollenberg*, Der Br. ad Diogn., 1853; *Hilgenfeld*, Die ap. Väter, p. 1, cf. 9 f.; *Kayser*, Rev. de Théol., xiii. 1856, p. 258 ff.; *Kirchhofer*, Quellensamml., p. 36, anm. 1; *Möhler*, Ueb. d. Br. an Diogn. Werke, 1839, i. p. 19 ff.; *Reuss*, Gesch. N. T., p. 289; *Scholten*, Die ält. Zeugnisse, p. 101; *Tischendorf*, Wann wurden, u. s. w., p. 40; *Tillemont*, Mém. eccl., tom. ii. pt. 1, p. 366, 493, note 1; *Westcott*, On the Canon, p. 74 f.; *Zeller*, Die Apostelgesch., p. 50.

writer, and consequently there is no external evidence whatever to indicate the period of its composition.[1] Moreover, it is not only anonymous but incomplete, or, at least, as we have it, not the work of a single writer. At the end of Chapter x. a break is indicated, and the two concluding chapters are unmistakably by a different and later hand.[2] It is not singular, therefore, that there exists a wide difference of opinion as to the date of the first ten chapters, although all agree regarding the later composition of the concluding portion. It is assigned by critics to various periods ranging from about the end of the first quarter of the second century to the end of the third century or later,[3] whilst some denounce it as a mere modern forgery.[4] Nothing can be more insecure in one

[1] *Donaldson*, Hist. Chr. Lit. and Doctr., ii. p. 126; *Kirchhofer*, Quellensamml. p. 36, anm. 1.

[2] *Credner*, Der Kanon, p. 59 ff., 67, 76; *Davidson*, Introd. N. T., ii. p. 339; *Donaldson*, Hist. Chr. Lit. and Doctr., ii. p. 142; *Ewald*, Gesch. V. Isr., vii. p. 251, anm. 1; *Hilgenfeld*, Die ap. Väter, p. 1; *Otto*, Just. Mart., ii. p. 201 n.; *Reuss*, Gesch. N. T., p. 290; *Westcott*, On the Canon, p. 75.

[3] c. A.D. 117. *Westcott*, On the Canon, p. 76. A.D. 120—130, *Ewald*, Gesch. V. Isr., vii. p. 252. *Between Trajan and Marc. Aurel. Kayser*, Rev. de Théol., xiii. 1856, p. 258. *An elder contemporary of Justin. Tischendorf*, Wann wurden, u. s. w., p. 40. A.D. 133—135, *Otto*, De Ep. ad Diogn., 1845; *Bunsen*, Chr. and Mankind, i. p. 170. A.D. 135, *Reuss*, Gesch. N. T., p. 289. A.D. 140, *Credner*, Der Kanon, p. 59; cf. Beiträge, i. p. 50. After A.D. 170, *Scholten*, Die ält. Zeugnisse, p. 101. Hardly before A.D. 180, *Davidson*, Introd. N. T., ii. p. 399. End of 2nd cent., *Lipsius*, Lit. Central-Blatt, n. 40, 1873. *Hilgenfeld* excludes it from the second century. Die ap. Väter, p. 9 f. *Zeller* considers it of no value, even if it contained quotations, on account of its late date. Die Apostelgesch., p. 51; Theol. Jahrb., iv. p. 619 f. *Zahn* dates it between A.D. 250—310, Gött. Gel. Anz. 1873, 3, 5, 10 f.; *De Gebhardt* and *Harnack*, between A.D. 170—310, Patr. ap. Opp. Fasc. i. 1875, p. 214; Fasc. i. 2, 1878, p. 152.

[4] *Donaldson* is inclined to consider it either a forgery by H. Stephanus the first editor, or, more likely, a composition by Greeks who came over to Italy when Constantinople was threatened by the Turks. Hist. Chr. Lit. and Doctr., ii. p. 141 f. *Overbeck* decides it to be a fictitious production written after the time of Constantine; Ueb. d. pseudojust. Br. an Dioguet. Programm. 1872, p. 73; Stud. zur. Gesch. d. Kirche, 1875, p. 10 ff. So also apparently *Harnack*, Zeitschr. f. Kirchengesch., 1876,

direction than the date of a work derived alone from internal evidence. Allusions to actual occurrences may with certainty prove that a work could only have been written after they had taken place. The mere absence of later indications in an anonymous Epistle only found in a single MS. of the thirteenth or fourteenth century, however, and which may have been, and probably was, written expressly in imitation of early Christian feeling, cannot furnish any solid basis for an early date. It must be evident that the determination of the date of this Epistle cannot therefore be regarded as otherwise than doubtful and arbitrary. It is certain that the purity of its Greek and the elegance of its style distinguish it from all other Christian works of the period to which so many assign it.[1]

The Epistle to Diognetus, however, does not furnish any evidence even of the existence of our Synoptics, for it is admitted that it does not contain a single direct quotation from any evangelical work.[2] We shall hereafter have to refer to this Epistle in connection with the fourth Gospel, but in the meantime it may be well to add that in Chapter xii., one of those, it will be remembered, which are admitted to be of later date, a brief quotation is made from 1 Cor. viii. 1, introduced merely by the words, ὁ ἀπόστολος λέγει.

p. 122 f. A remarkable paper on the Epistle in the Church Quart. Rev., April, 1877, p. 42 ff., a continuation of which is promised, seems likely finally to dispose of the question of date, and to assign the composition to a very late period.

[1] *Davidson*, Introd. N. T., ii. p. 399; *Donaldson*, Hist. Chr. Lit. and Doctr., ii. p. 134 ff.; *Ewald*, Gesch. V. Isr., vii. p. 253; *Kayser*, Rev. de Théol., xiii. 1856, p. 257; *Scholten*, Die ält. Zeugnisse, p. 102; *Westcott*, On the Canon, p. 74 f.

[2] *Credner*, Beiträge, i. p. 50; *Kayser*, Rev. de Théol., 1856, p. 257; *Reuss*, Hist. du Canon, p. 40 f.; *Scholten*, Die ält. Zeugnisse, p. 102; *Tischendorf*, Wann wurden, u. s. w., p. 40; *Westcott*, On the Canon, p. 78.

CHAPTER VI.

BASILIDES—VALENTINUS.

WE must now turn back to an earlier period, and consider any evidence regarding the Synoptic Gospels which may be furnished by the so-called heretical writers of the second century. The first of these who claims our attention is Basilides, the founder of a system of Gnosticism, who lived in Alexandria about the year 125 of our era.[1] With the exception of a very few brief fragments,[2] none of the writings of this Gnostic have been preserved, and all our information regarding them is, therefore, derived at second-hand from ecclesiastical writers opposed to him and his doctrines; and their statements, especially where acquaintance with, and the use of, the New Testament Scriptures are assumed, must be received with very great caution. The uncritical and inaccurate character of the Fathers rendered them peculiarly liable to be misled by foregone devout conclusions.

Eusebius states that Agrippa Castor, who had written a refutation of the doctrines of Basilides: "says that he had composed twenty-four books upon the Gospel."[3]

---

[1] *Eusebius*, H. E., iv. 7, 8, 9. *Baur*, Gesch. chr. K., i. p. 196; *Davidson*, Introd. N. T., ii. p. 388; *Guericke*, H'buch K. G., i. p. 182; *Lechler*, Das ap. und nachap. Zeit., p. 498; *Scholten*, Die ält. Zeugnisse, p. 64. From A.D. 117 to 138, *Mansel*, The Gnostic Heresies, p. 145; *Tischendorf*, Wann wurden, u. s. w., p. 50.

[2] *Grabe*, Spicil. Patr., ii. p. 39 ff., 65 ff.

[3] Φησὶν αὐτὸν εἰς μὲν τὸ εὐαγγέλιον τέσσαρα πρὸς τοῖς εἴκοσι συντάξαι βιβλία. H. E., iv. 7.

This is interpreted by Tischendorf, without argument, and in a most arbitrary and erroneous manner, to imply that the work was a commentary upon our four canonical Gospels;[1] a conclusion the audacity of which can scarcely be exceeded. This is, however, almost surpassed by the treatment of Canon Westcott, who writes regarding Basilides: "It appears, moreover, that he himself published a Gospel—a 'Life of Christ' as it would perhaps be called in our days, or 'The Philosophy of Christianity'[2]—but he admitted the historic truth of all the facts contained in the canonical Gospels, and used them as Scripture. For, in spite of his peculiar opinions, the testimony of Basilides to our 'acknowledged' books is comprehensive and clear. In the few pages of his writings which remain there are certain references to the Gospels of St. Matthew, St. Luke, and St. John,"[3] &c. Now in making, in such a manner, these assertions: in totally ignoring the whole of the discussion with regard to the supposed quotations of Basilides in the work commonly ascribed to Hippolytus and the adverse results of learned criticism: in the unqualified assertions thus made and the absence either of explanation of the facts or the reasons for the conclusion: this statement must be condemned as only calculated to mislead readers who must generally be ignorant of the actual facts of the case.

We know from the evidence of antiquity that Basilides made use of a Gospel, written by himself it is said, but certainly called after his own name.[4] An attempt has

---

[1] Wann wurden, u. s. w., p. 51 f.

[2] These names are pure inventions of Dr. Westcott's fancy, of course.

[3] On the Canon, p. 255 f. [Since these remarks were first made, Dr. Westcott has somewhat enlarged his account of Basilides, but we still consider that his treatment of the subject is deceptive and incomplete.]

[4] Ausus fuit et Basilides scribere Evangelium et suo illud nomine titu-

been made to explain this by suggesting that perhaps the work mentioned by Agrippa Castor may have been mistaken for a Gospel;[1] but the fragments of that work which are still extant[2] are of a character which precludes the possibility that any writing of which they formed a part could have been considered a Gospel.[3] Various opinions have been expressed as to the exact nature of the Gospel of Basilides. Neander affirmed it to be the Gospel according to the Hebrews which he brought from Syria to Egypt;[4] whilst Schneckenburger held it to be the Gospel according to the Egyptians.[5] Others believe it to have at least been based upon one or other of these Gospels.[6] There seems most reason for the hypothesis that it was a form of the Gospel according to the Hebrews, which was so generally in use.

Returning to the passage already quoted, in which Eusebius states, on the authority of Agrippa Castor, whose works are no longer extant, that Basilides had composed a work in twenty-four books on the Gospel

---

lare. *Origen*, Hom. i. in Lucam. Ausus est etiam Basilides Evangelium scribere quod dicitur secundum Basilidem. *Ambros.*, Comment in Luc. Proem. *Hieron.*, Præf. in Matt. Cf. *Credner*, Beiträge, i. p. 37; Gesch. N. T. Kanon, p. 11; *Davidson*, Introd. N. T., ii. p. 389; *Holtzmann*, in Bunsen's Bibelwerk, viii. p. 568; *Kirchhofer*, Quellensamml., p. 414, anm. 3, p. 475; *Neudecker*, Einl. N. T., 1840, p. 85 f.; *Schott*, Isagogo, p. 23; *Scholten*, Die ält. Zeugnisse, p. 64.

[1] *Gfrörer*, Allg. K. G., i., p. 340, anm.***; *Kirchhofer*, Quellensamml., p. 414, anm. 3; *Nicolas*, Et. sur les Ev. Apocr., p. 134; *Tischendorf*, Wann wurden, u. s. w., p. 52, anm. 1; *Westcott*, On the Canon, p. 255 f., note 4.

[2] *Grabe*, Spicil. Patr., ii. p. 39 ff., 65 ff.; *Clemens Al.*, Strom., iv. 12.

[3] Dr. Westcott admits this. On the Canon, p. 255, note 4.

[4] Gnost. Syst., p. 84; cf. K. G., 1843, ii. p. 709, anm. 2; *Nicolas*, Et. sur les Ev. Apocr., p. 134.

[5] Ueb. d. Ev. d. Ægypt., 1834; cf. *Gieseler*, Entst. schr. Evv., p. 19.

[6] *Gieseler*, Entst. schr. Evv., p. 19; *Holtzmann*, in Bunsen's Bibelwerk, viii. p. 568. Cf. *Fabricius*, Cod. Ap. N. T., i. p. 343, note m.

(τὸ εὐαγγέλιον), and to the unwarrantable inference that this must have been a work on our four Gospels, we must add that, so far from deriving his doctrines from our Gospels or other New Testament writings, or acknowledging their authority, Basilides professed that he received his knowledge of the truth from Glaucias, "the interpreter of Peter," whose disciple he claimed to be,[1] and thus practically sets Gospels aside and prefers tradition.[2] Basilides also claimed to have received from a certain Matthias the report of private discourses which he had heard from the Saviour for his special instruction.[3] Agrippa Castor further stated, according to Eusebius, that in his ἐξηγητικά Basilides named for himself, as prophets, Barcabbas and Barcoph (Parchor[4]), as well as invented others who never existed, and claimed their authority for his doctrines.[5] With regard to all this Canon Westcott writes: "Since Basilides lived on the verge of the apostolic times, it is not surprising that he made use of other sources of Christian doctrine besides the canonical books. The belief in Divine Inspiration was still fresh and real,"[6] &c. It is apparent, however, that Basilides, in basing his doctrines upon tradition and

---

[1] . . . . . καθάπερ ὁ Βασιλείδης κἂν Γλαυκίαν ἐπιγράφηται διδάσκαλον, ὡς αὐχοῦσιν αὐτοὶ, τὸν Πέτρου ἑρμηνέα. *Clemens Al.*, Strom., vii. 17, § 106.

[2] *Credner*, Beiträge, i. p. 37; *Gfrörer*, Allg. K. G., i. p. 310; *Scholten*, Die ält. Zeugnisse, p. 64. Cf. *Holtzmann* in Bunsen's Bibelwerk, viii. p. 508.

[3] Βασιλείδης τοίνυν καὶ Ἰσίδωρος, ὁ Βασιλείδου παῖς γνήσιος καὶ μαθητής, φασὶν εἰρηκέναι Ματθίαν αὐτοῖς λόγους ἀποκρύφους, οὓς ἤκουσε παρὰ τοῦ σωτῆρος κατ' ἰδίαν διδαχθείς. *Hippolytus*, Refut. Omn. Haer., vii. 20; ed. Duncker et Schneidewin, 1859.

[4] Isidorus, his son and disciple, wrote a commentary on the prophecy of Parchor (*Clem. Al.*, Strom., vi. 6, § 53), in which he further refers to the "prophecy of Cham." Cf. *Neander*, Allg. K. G., 1843, ii. p. 703 ff.

[5] . . . . . προφήτας δὲ ἑαυτῷ ὀνομάσαι Βαρκαββᾶν καὶ Βαρκὼφ καὶ ἄλλους ἀνυπάρκτους τινὰς ἑαυτῷ συστησάμενον, κ.τ.λ. *Euseb.*, H. E., iv. 7.

[6] On the Canon, p. 255.

upon these Apocryphal books as inspired, and in having a special Gospel called after his own name, which, therefore, he clearly adopts as the exponent of his ideas of Christian truth, completely ignores the canonical Gospels, and not only does not offer any evidence for their existence, but proves, on the contrary, that he did not recognize any such works as of authority. There is no ground, therefore, for Tischendorf's assumption that the commentary of Basilides "on the Gospel" was written upon our Gospels, but that idea is negatived in the strongest way by all the facts of the case.[1] The perfectly simple interpretation of the statement is that long ago suggested by Valesius,[2] that the Commentary of Basilides was composed upon his own Gospel,[3] whether it was the Gospel according to the Hebrews or the Egyptians.

Moreover, it must be borne in mind that Basilides used the word "Gospel" in a peculiar sense. Hippolytus, in the work usually ascribed to him, writing of the Basilidians and describing their doctrines, says: "When therefore it was necessary, he (?) says, that we, the children of God, should be revealed, in expectation of whose revelation, he says, the creation groaned and travailed, the Gospel came into the world, and passed through every principality and power and dominion, and every name that is named."[4] "The Gospel, therefore,

[1] *Credner*, Der Kanon, p. 24; *Davidson*, Introd. N. T., ii. p. 389; *Scholten*, Die ält. Zeugnisse, p. 64.
[2] Cf. *Fabricius*, Cod. Apocr. N. T., i. p. 343, not. m.
[3] *Neudecker*, Einl. N. T., p. 85 f.; *Nicolas*, Et. sur les Ev. Apocr., p. 134.
[4] ’Επεὶ οὖν ἔδει ἀποκαλυφθῆναι, φησίν, ἡμᾶς τὰ τέκνα τοῦ θεοῦ, περὶ ὧν ἐστέναξε, φησίν, ἡ κτίσις καὶ ὤδινεν, ἀπεκδεχομένη τὴν ἀποκάλυψιν, ἦλθε τὸ εὐαγγέλιον εἰς τὸν κόσμον, καὶ διῆλθε διὰ πάσης ἀρχῆς καὶ ἐξουσίας καὶ κυριότητος καὶ παντὸς ὀνόματος ὀνομαζομένου, κ.τ.λ. *Hippolytus*, Refut. Omn. Hær., vii. 25.

came first from the Sonship, he says, through the Son, sitting by the Archon, to the Archon, and the Archon learnt that he was not the God of all things but begotten,"[1] &c. "The Gospel, according to them, is the knowledge of supramundane matters,"[2] &c. This may not be very intelligible, but it is sufficient to show that "the Gospel" in a technical sense[3] formed a very important part of the system of Basilides. Now there is nothing whatever to show that the twenty-four books which he composed "on the Gospel" were not in elucidation of the Gospel as technically understood by him, illustrated by extracts from his own special Gospel and from the tradition handed down to him by Glaucias and Matthias.

The emphatic assertion of Canon Westcott that Basilides "admitted the historic truth of all the facts contained in the canonical Gospels," is based solely upon the following sentence of the work attributed to Hippolytus; "Jesus, however, was generated according to these (followers of Basilides) as we have already said.[4] But when the generation which has already been declared had taken place, all things regarding the Saviour, according to them, occurred in like manner as they have been written in the Gospel."[5] There are, however, several important points to be borne in mind in reference to this passage. The statement in question is not made in con-

---

[1] Ἦλθεν οὖν τὸ εὐαγγέλιον πρῶτον ἀπὸ τῆς υἱότητος, φησί, διὰ τοῦ παρακαθημένου τῷ ἄρχοντι υἱοῦ πρὸς τὸν ἄρχοντα, καὶ ἔμαθεν ὁ ἄρχων, ὅτι οὐκ ἦν θεὸς τῶν ὅλων, ἀλλ' ἦν γεννητὸς, κ.τ.λ. *Ib.*, vii. 26; cf. 27, &c.

[2] Εὐαγγέλιον ἐστί κατ' αὐτοὺς ἡ τῶν ὑπερκοσμίων γνῶσις, κ.τ.λ. *Ib.*, vii. 27.

[3] Canon Westcott admits this technical use of the word, of course. On the Canon, p. 255 f., note 4.

[4] He refers to a mystical account of the incarnation.

[5] Ὁ δὲ Ἰησοῦς γεγένηται κατ' αὐτοὺς ὡς προείρηκαμεν. Γεγενημένης δὲ τῆς γενέσεως τῆς προδεδηλωμένης, γέγονε πάντα ὁμοίως κατ' αὐτοὺς τὰ περὶ τοῦ σωτῆρος ὡς ἐν τοῖς εὐαγγελίοις γέγραπται. *Hippolytus*, Ref. Omn. Hær., vii. 27.

nection with Basilides himself, but distinctly in reference to his followers, of whom there were many in the time of Hippolytus and long after him. It is, moreover, a general observation the accuracy of which we have no means of testing, and upon the correctness of which there is no special reason to rely. The remark, made at the beginning of the third century, however, that the followers of Basilides believed that the actual events of the life of Jesus occurred in the way in which they have been written in the Gospels, is no proof whatever that either they or Basilides used or admitted the authority of our Gospels. The exclusive use by any one of the Gospel according to the Hebrews, for instance, would be perfectly consistent with the statement. No one who considers what is known of that Gospel, or who thinks of the use made of it in the first half of the second century by perfectly orthodox Fathers, can doubt this. The passage is, therefore, of no weight as evidence for the use of our Gospels. Canon Westcott himself admits that in the extant fragments of Isidorus, the son and disciple of Basilides, who "maintained the doctrines of his father," he has "noticed nothing bearing on the books of the New Testament."[1] On the supposition that Basilides actually wrote a Commentary on our Gospels, and used them as Scripture, it is indeed passing strange that we have so little evidence on the point.

We must now, however, examine in detail all of the quotations, and they are few, alleged to show the use of our Gospels, and we shall commence with those of Tischendorf. The first passage which he points out is found in the Stromata of Clement of Alexandria. Tischendorf guards himself, in reference to these quotations,

[1] On the Canon, p. 257.

by merely speaking of them as "Basilidian" (Basilidianisch),[1] but it might have been more frank to have stated clearly that Clement distinctly assigns the quotation to the followers of Basilides (οἱ δὲ ἀπὸ Βασιλείδου),[2] and not to Basilides himself.[3] The supposed quotation, therefore, however surely traced to our Gospels, could really not prove anything in regard to Basilides. The passage itself compared with the parallel in Matt. xix. 11, 12, is as follows:—

STROM. III. 1, § 1.	MATT. XIX. 11, 12.
They say the Lord answered: All men cannot receive this saying.	v. 11. But he said unto them: All men cannot receive this saying, but only they to whom it is given.
For there are some who are eunuchs from birth, others by constraint.	v. 12. For there are eunuchs which were so born from their mother's womb: and there are eunuchs which were made eunuchs by men, &c. &c.
Οὐ πάντες χωροῦσι τὸν λόγον τοῦτον, εἰσὶ γὰρ εὐνοῦχοι, οἱ μὲν ἐκ γενετῆς, οἱ δὲ ἐξ ἀνάγκης.	Οὐ πάντες χωροῦσιν τὸν λόγον τοῦτον, ἀλλ' οἷς δέδοται· εἰσὶν γὰρ εὐνοῦχοι οἵτινες ἐκ κοιλίας μητρὸς ἐγεννήθησαν οὕτως, καὶ εἰσὶν εὐνοῦχοι οἵτινες εὐνουχίσθησαν ὑπὸ τῶν ἀνθρώπων, κ.τ.λ.

Now this passage in its affinity to, and material variation from, our first Gospel might be quoted as evidence for the use of another Gospel, but it cannot reasonably be cited as evidence for the use of Matthew. Apologists in their anxiety to grasp at the faintest analogies as testimony seem altogether to ignore the history of the creation of written Gospels, and to forget the very existence of the πολλοί of Luke.[4]

The next passage referred to by Tischendorf[5] is one

---

[1] Wann wurden, u. s. w., p. 51.
[2] Οἱ δὲ ἀπὸ Βασιλείδου πυθομένων φασὶ τῶν ἀποστόλων μή ποτε ἄμεινόν ἐστι τὸ μὴ γαμεῖν ἀποκρίνασθαι λέγουσι τὸν κύριον, κ.τ.λ. Strom., iii. 1, § 1.
[3] Canon Westcott does not refer to this quotation at all.
[4] Cf. Ewald, Jahrb. bibl. Wiss., 1849, p. 208.
[5] Wann wurden, u. s. w., p. 51.

quoted by Epiphanius[1] which we subjoin in contrast with the parallel in Matt. vii. 6 :—

Hær. xxiv. 5.	Matt. vii. 6.
And therefore he said : Cast not ye pearls before swine, neither give that which is holy unto dogs.	Give not that which is holy unto dogs, neither cast ye your pearls before swine, lest they trample them under their feet, and turn again and rend you.
Μὴ βάλητε τοὺς μαργαρίτας ἔμπροσ- θεν τῶν χοίρων, μηδὲ δότε τὸ ἅγιον τοῖς κυσί.	Μὴ δῶτε τὸ ἅγιον τοῖς κυσίν, μηδὲ βάλητε τοὺς μαργαρίτας ὑμῶν ἔμπροσ- θεν τῶν χοίρων, κ.τ.λ.

Here, again, the variation in order is just what one might have expected from the use of the Gospel according to the Hebrews or a similar work, and there is no indication whatever that the passage did not end here, without the continuation of our first Synoptic. What is still more important, although Tischendorf does not mention the fact, nor otherwise hint a doubt than by the use, again, of an unexplained description of this quotation as " Basilidianisch " instead of a more direct ascription of it to Basilides himself, this passage is by no means attributed by Epiphanius to that heretic. It is introduced into the section of his work directed against the Basilidians, but he uses, like Clement, the indefinite φησί, and as in dealing with all these heresies there is continual interchange of reference to the head and the later followers, there is no certainty who is referred to in these quotations and, in this instance, nothing to indicate that this passage is ascribed to Basilides himself. His name is mentioned in the first line of the first chapter of this " heresy," but not again before this φησί occurs in chapter v. Tischendorf does not claim any other quotations.

[1] Hær., xxiv. 5, p. 72

Canon Westcott states: "In the few pages of his (Basilides') writings which remain there are certain references to the Gospels of St. Matthew, St. Luke,"[1] &c. One might suppose from this that the "certain" references occurred in actual extracts made from his works, and that the quotations, therefore, appeared set in a context of his own words. This impression is strengthened when we read as an introduction to the instances: "The following examples will be sufficient to show his method of quotation."[2] The fact is, however, that these examples are found in the work of Hippolytus, in an epitome of the views of the school by that writer himself, with nothing more definite than a subjectless φησί to indicate who is referred to. The only examples Canon Westcott can give of these "certain references" to our first and third Synoptics, do not show his "method of quotation" to much advantage. The first is not a quotation at all, but a mere reference to the Magi and the Star. "But that every thing, he says (φησί), has its own seasons, the Saviour sufficiently teaches when he says: . . . and the Magi having seen the star,"[3] &c. This of course Canon Westcott considers a reference to Matt. ii. 1, 2, but we need scarcely point out that this falls to the ground instantly, if it be admitted, as it must be, that the Star and the Magi may have been mentioned in other Gospels than the first Synoptic. We have already seen, when examining the evidence of Justin, that this is the case. The only quotation asserted to be taken from Luke is the phrase: "The Holy Spirit shall come upon thee, and the power of the Highest shall overshadow

---

[1] On the Canon, p. 256.   [2] *Ib.*, p. 256, note 3.
[3] Ὅτι δὲ, φησίν, ἕκαστον ἰδίους ἔχει καιρούς, ἱκανὸς ὁ σωτὴρ λέγων· . . . . καὶ οἱ μάγοι τὸν ἀστέρα τεθεαμένοι. *Hippolytus*, Ref. Omn. Haer., vii. 27.

thee,"[1] which agrees with Luke i. 35. This again is introduced by Hippolytus with another subjectless "he says," and apart from the uncertainty as to who "he" is, this is very unsatisfactory evidence as to the form of the quotation in the original text, for it may easily have been corrected by Hippolytus, consciously or unconsciously, in the course of transfer to his pages. We have already met with this passage as quoted by Justin from a Gospel different from ours.

As we have already stated, however, none of the quotations which we have considered are directly referred to Basilides himself, but they are all introduced by the utterly vague expression, "he says," (φησί) without any subject accompanying the verb. Now it is admitted that writers of the time of Hippolytus, and notably Hippolytus himself, made use of the name of the founder of a sect to represent the whole of his school, and applied to him, apparently, quotations taken from unknown and later followers.[2] The passages which he cites, therefore, and which appear to indicate the use of Gospels, instead of being extracted from the works of the founder himself, in all probability were taken from writings of Gnostics of his own time. Canon Westcott himself admits the possibility of this, in writing of other early heretics. He says: "The evidence that has been collected from

---

[1] Πνεῦμα ἅγιον ἐπελεύσεται ἐπὶ σέ, καὶ δύναμις ὑψίστου ἐπισκιάσει σοι. *Hippolytus*, Ref. Omn. Hær., vii. 26.

[2] *Zeller*, Theol. Jahrb., 1853, p. 148 ff.; Die Apostelgesch., p. 63 f.; *Volkmar*, Theol. Jahrb., 1854, p. 108 ff.; Hippolytus, u. d. röm. Zeitgenossen, 1855, p. 167; Der Ursprung, p. 70 f.; *Hilgenfeld*, Die Evangelien, p. 345 f., anm. 5; *Reuss*, Gesch. N. T., p. 287; *Scholten*, Die ält. Zeugnisse, p. 65 f.; Das Ev. n. Johan., p. 427; *Rumpf*, Rev. de Théol., 1867, p. 17 ff.; *Davidson*, Introd. N. T., ii. p. 388 ff.; *J. J. Tayler*, The Fourth Gospel, 1867, p. 57; *Luthardt*, Der johann. Ursprung d. viert. Ev., 1874, p. 85 f. See further references p. 53, n. 3.

the documents of these primitive sects is necessarily somewhat vague. It would be more satisfactory to know the exact position of their authors, and the precise date of their being composed. It is just possible that Hippolytus made use of writings which were current in his own time without further examination, and transferred to the apostolic age forms of thought and expression which had been the growth of two, or even of three generations."[1] So much as to the reliance to be placed on the work ascribed to Hippolytus. It is certain, for instance, that in writing of the sect of Naaseni and Ophites, Hippolytus perpetually quotes passages from the writings of the school, with the indefinite φησί,[2] as he likewise does in dealing with the Peratici,[3] and Docetæ,[4] no individual author being named; yet he evidently quotes various writers, passing from one to another without explanation, and making use of the same unvarying φησί. In one place,[5] where he has "the Greeks say," (φασὶν οἱ Ἕλληνες) he gives, without further indication, a quotation from Pindar.[6] A still more apt instance of his method is that pointed out by Volkmar,[7] where Hippolytus, writing of "Marcion, or some one of his hounds," uses, without further explanation, the subjectless φησί to introduce matter from the later followers of Marcion.[8] Now, with regard to

---

[1] On the Canon, p. 252.
[2] *Hippolytus*, Ref. Omn. Hær., v. 6 ff.
[3] *Ib.*, v. 16, 17.   [4] *Ib.*, viii. 9, 10.
[5] *Ib.*, v. 7.
[6] *Hippol.*, Ref. Omn. Hær. ed. Duncker et Schneidewin not. in loc., p. 134. *Zeller*, Theol. Jahrb., 1853, p. 149 f.; *Scholten*, Die ält. Zeugnisse, p. 65 f.; *Davidson*, Introd. N. T., ii. p. 389.
[7] Theol. Jahrb., 1854, p. 108 ff.; Der Ursprung, p. 70.
[8] *Hippolytus*, Ref. Omn. Hær., vii. 30. *Scholten*, Die ält. Zeugnisse, p. 66.

Basilides, Hippolytus directly refers not only to the heretic chief, but also to his disciple Isidorus and all their followers,[1] (καὶ Ἰσίδωρος καὶ πᾶς ὁ τούτων χορός) and then proceeds to use the indefinite "he says," interspersed with references in the plural to these heretics, exhibiting the same careless method of quotation, and leaving the same complete uncertainty as to the speaker's identity as in the other cases mentioned.[2] On the other hand, it has been demonstrated by Hilgenfeld, that the gnosticism ascribed to Basilides by Hippolytus, in connection with these quotations, is of a much later and more developed type than that which Basilides himself held,[3] as shown in the actual fragments of his own writings which are still extant, and as reported by Irenæus,[4] Clement of Alexandria,[5] and the work "Adversus omnes Hæreses," annexed to the "Præscriptio hæreticorum" of Tertullian, which is

---

[1] *Hippolytus, ib.*, vii. 20; cf. 22.

[2] *Zeller*, Theol. Jahrb., 1853, p. 148 ff.; *Volkmar*, Theol. Jahrb., 1854, p. 108 f.; Der Ursprung, p. 71 f., anm.; *Scholten*, Die ält. Zeugnisse, p. 65; *Davidson*, Introd. N. T., ii. p. 388; *Rumpf*, Rev. de Théol., 1867, p. 18 f.

[3] *Hilgenfeld*, Theol. Jahrb., 1856, p. 86 ff., 786 ff.; Die jüd. Apok., 1857, p. 287 ff.; Zeitschr. wiss. Theol., 1862, p. 452 ff.; 1878, p. 228 ff.; *Volkmar*, Hippolytus u. d. röm. Zeitgenossen, p. 167; Zeitschr. wiss. Theol., 1860, p. 295 ff.; Der Ursprung, p. 70; *Lipsius*, Der Gnosticismus. Ersch. u. Gruber's Allg. Encyclop., 1, sect. 71, 1860, p. 90, 152; Zur Quellenkr. d. Epiphanius, 1866, p. 100 ff.; *Guericke*, II'buch K. G., i. p. 184; *Scholten*, Die ält. Zeugnisse, p. 66; *Luthardt*, Der johann. Urspr. d. viert. Ev., 1874, p. 85 f.; *Mangold*, Zu Bleek's Einl. N. T., 1875, p. 265; *Zundert*, Zeitschr. luth. Theol., 1855, h. 2, 1856, h. 1, 3. The following differ from the view taken by Hilgenfeld: *Baur*, Die chr. Kirche 3 erst. Jahrh., p. 187 f.; Theol. Jahrb., 1856, p. 121 ff.; *Bunsen*, Hippolytus u. s. Zeit., 1852, i. p. 65 ff.; *Jacobi*, Basilides Phil. Gnost. ex. Hyppolyti lib. nuper reperto illustr., 1852; Zeitschr. f. Kirchengesch., 1877, p. 481 ff.; *Möller*, Gesch. d. Kosmologied. griech. Kirsho, 1860, p. 344 f.; *Uhlhorn*, Das Basilidianische System, u. s. w., 1855.

[4] Adv. Hær., i. 24.

[5] Stromata, vi. 3.

considered to be the epitome of an earlier work of Hippolytus. The fact probably is that Hippolytus derived his views of the doctrines of Basilides from the writings of his later followers, and from them made the quotations which are attributed to the founder of the school.[1] In any case there is no ground for referring these quotations with an indefinite φησί to Basilides himself.

Of all this there is not a word from Canon Westcott,[2] but he ventures to speak of "the testimony of Basilides to our 'acknowledged' books," as "comprehensive and clear."[3] We have seen, however, that the passages referred to have no weight whatever as evidence for the use of our Synoptics. The formulæ (as τὸ εἰρημένον to that compared with Luke i. 35, and ὡς γέγραπται, ἡ γραφή with references compared with some of the Epistles) which accompany these quotations, and to which Canon Westcott points as an indication that the New Testament writings were already recognized as Holy Scripture,[4] need no special attention, because, as it cannot be shown that the expressions were used by Basilides himself at all, they do not come into question. If anything, however, were required to complete the evidence that these quotations are not from the works of Basilides himself, but from later writings by his followers, it would be the use of such formulæ, for as the writings of pseudo-Ignatius, Polycarp, Justin Martyr, Papias, Hegesippus,

---

[1] *Davidson*, Introd. N. T., ii. p. 388 ff.; *Rumpf*, Rev. de Théol., 1867, p. 18 ff.; *Scholten*, Die ält. Zeugnisse, p. 66; *Volkmar*, Der Ursprung, p. 69 ff.; *Zeller*, Apostelgesch., p. 65 f.; Theol. Jahrb., 1853, p. 148 ff.

[2] And very little from Tischendorf. [In the 4th ed. of his work, Dr. Westcott has added some observations regarding these subjectless quotations, but still most inadequately states the case.]

[3] On the Canon, p. 256.

[4] On the Canon, p. 256.

and others of the Fathers in several ways positively demonstrate, the New Testament writings were not admitted, even amongst orthodox Fathers, to the rank of Holy Scripture, until a very much later period.[1]

2.

Much of what has been said with regard to the claim which is laid to Basilides, by some apologists, as a witness for the Gospels and the existence of a New Testament Canon, and the manner in which that claim is advanced, likewise applies to Valentinus, another Gnostic leader, who, about the year 140, came from Alexandria to Rome and flourished till about A.D. 160.[2] Very little remains of the writings of this Gnostic, and we gain our only knowledge of them from a few short quotations in the works of Clement of Alexandria, and some doubtful fragments preserved by others. We shall presently have occasion to refer more directly to these, and need not here more particularly mention them.

Tischendorf, the self-constituted modern Defensor fidei,[3] asserts, with an assurance which can scarcely be characterized otherwise than as an unpardonable calculation upon the ignorance of his readers, that Valentinus used

---

[1] *Scholten*, Die ält. Zeugnisse, p. 69 ; *Zeller*, Die Apostelgesch., p. 65, anm. 3; Theol. Jahrb., 1853, p. 148.

[2] *Irenæus*, Adv. Hær., iii. 4, § 3; *Eusebius*, H. E., iv. 11. *Anger*, Synops. Ev. Proleg., p. xxxv.; *Baur*, Gesch. chr. Kirche, i. p. 196; *Bleek*, Einl. N. T., p. 227 ; *Credner*, Beiträge, i. p. 38 ; *Davidson*, Introd. N. T., ii. p. 390 ; *Guericke*, H'buch K. G., i. p. 184; *Mansel*, The Gnostic Heresies, 1875, p. 163; *Reuss*, Gesch. N. T., p. 243; *Scholten*, Die ält. Zeugnisse, p. 67 ; *Tischendorf*, Wann wurden, u. s. w., p. 43; *Westcott*, On the Canon, p. 258 f.

[3] *Hilgenfeld*, Zeitschr. wiss. Theol., 1865, p. 329.

the whole of our four Canonical Gospels. To do him full justice, we shall as much as possible give his own words; and, although we set aside systematically all discussion regarding the fourth Gospel for separate treatment hereafter, we must, in order to convey the full sense of Dr. Tischendorf's proceeding, commence with a sentence regarding that Gospel. Referring to a statement of Irenæus, that the followers of Valentinus made use of the fourth Gospel, Tischendorf continues: "Hippolytus confirms and completes the statement of Irenæus, for he quotes several expressions of John, which Valentinus employed. This most clearly occurs in the case of John x. 8; for Hippolytus writes: 'Because the prophets and the law, according to the doctrine of Valentinus, were only filled with a subordinate and foolish spirit, Valentinus says: On account of this, the Saviour says: All who came before me were thieves and robbers.'"[1] Now this, to begin with, is a practical falsification of the text of the Philosophumena, which reads: "Therefore all the Prophets and the Law spoke under the influence of the Demiurge, a foolish God, he says, (they themselves being) foolish, knowing nothing. On this account, he says, the Saviour saith: All who came before me," &c. &c.[2] There is no mention whatever of the name of Valentinus in the passage, and, as we shall presently

---

[1] Die Angabe des Irenäus bestärkt und vervollständigt Hippolytus, denn er führt einzelne Johanneische Aussprüche an, welche Valentin benutzt hat. Am deutlichsten geschicht dies mit Joh. x. 8; denn Hippolytus schreibt: Weil die Propheten und das Gesetz, nach Valentins Lehre, nur von einem untergeordneten und thörichten Geiste erfüllt waren, so sagt Valentin: Eben deshalb spricht der Erlöser: Alle die vor mir gekommen sind, sind Diebe und Mörder gewesen." Wann wurden, u. s. w., p. 44.

[2] Πάντες οὖν οἱ προφῆται καὶ ὁ νόμος ἐλάλησαν ἀπὸ τοῦ δημιουργοῦ, μωροῦ λέγει θεοῦ, μωροὶ οὐδὲν εἰδότες. Διὰ τοῦτο, φησί, λέγει ὁ σωτήρ· Πάντες, κ.τ.λ. *Hippolytus*, Ref. Omn. Hær., vi. 35.

show, there is no direct reference in the whole chapter to Valentinus himself. The introduction of his name in this manner into the text, without a word of explanation, is highly reprehensible. It is true that in a note Tischendorf gives a closer translation of the passage, without, however, any explanation; and here again he adds, in parenthesis to the "says he," "namely, Valentinus." Such a note, however, which would probably be unread by a majority of readers, does not rectify the impression conveyed by so positive and emphatic an assertion as is conveyed by the alteration in the text.

Tischendorf continues: "And as the Gospel of John, so also were the other Gospels used by Valentinus. According to the statement of Irenæus (I. 7, § 4), he found the said subordinate spirit, which he calls Demiurge, Masterworker, emblematically represented by the Centurion of Capernaum (Matt. viii. 9, Luke vii. 8); in the dead and resuscitated daughter of Jairus, when twelve years old, (Luke viii. 41), he recognized a symbol of his 'Wisdom' (Achamoth), the mother of the Masterworker (I. 8, § 2); in like manner, he saw represented in the history of the woman who had suffered twelve years from the bloody issue, and was cured by the Lord (Matt. ix. 20), the sufferings and salvation of his twelfth primitive spirit (Aeon) (I. 3, § 3); the expression of the Lord (Matt. v. 18) on the numerical value of the iota ('the smallest letter') he applied to his ten æons in repose."[1] Now, in every instance where Tischendorf here speaks of Valentinus by the singular "he," Irenæus uses the plural "they," referring not to the original founder of the sect, but to his followers in his own day, and the

[1] Wann wurden, u. s. w., p. 44 f.

text is thus again in every instance falsified by the pious zeal of the apologist. In the case of the Centurion: "they say" (λέγουσι) that he is the Demiurge;[1] "they declare" (διηγοῦνται) that the daughter of Jairus is the type of Achamoth;[2] "they say" (λέγουσι) that the apostasy of Judas points to the passion in connection with the twelfth æon, and also the fact that Jesus suffered in the twelfth month after his baptism; for they will have it (βούλονται) that he only preached for one year. The case of the woman with the bloody issue for twelve years, and the power which went forth from the Son to heal her, "they will have to be Horos" (εἶναι δὲ ταύτην τὸν Ὅρον θέλουσιν).[3] In like manner they assert that the ten æons are indicated (σημαίνεσθαι λέγουσι) by the letter "Iota," mentioned in the Saviour's expression, Matt. v. 18.[4] At the end of these and numerous other similar references in this chapter to New Testament expressions and passages, Irenæus says: "Thus they interpret," &c. (ἑρμηνεύουσιν εἰρῆσθαι).[5] The plural "they" is employed throughout.

Tischendorf proceeds to give the answer to his statement which is supposed to be made by objectors. "They say: all that has reference to the Gospel of John was not advanced by Valentinus himself, but by his disciples. And in fact, in Irenæus, 'they—the Valentinians—say,' occurs much oftener than 'he—Valentinus —says.' But who is there so sapient as to draw the line between what the master alone says, and that which the disciples state without in the least repeating the

---

[1] *Irenæus*, Adv. Hær., i. 7, § 4.
[2] *Ib.*, Adv. Hær., i. 8, § 2.
[3] *Ib.*, i. 3, § 3.
[4] *Ib.*, i. 3, § 2.
[5] *Ib.*, i. 3, § 4.

master?"[1] Tischendorf solves the difficulty by referring everything indiscriminately to the master. Now, in reply to these observations, we must remark in the first place that the admission here made by Tischendorf, that Irenæus much more often uses "they say" than "he says" is still quite disingenuous, inasmuch as invariably, and without exception, Irenæus uses the plural in connection with the texts in question. Secondly, it is quite obvious that a Gnostic, writing about A.D. 185—195, was likely to use arguments which were never thought of by a Gnostic, writing at the middle of the second century. At the end of the century, the writings of the New Testament had acquired consideration and authority, and Gnostic writers had therefore a reason to refer to them, and to endeavour to show that they supported their peculiar views, which did not exist at all at the time when Valentinus propounded his system. Tischendorf, however, cannot be allowed the benefit even of such a doubt as he insinuates, as to what belongs to the master, and what to the followers. Such doubtful testimony could not establish anything, but it is in point of fact also totally excluded by the statement of Irenæus himself.

In the preface to the first book of his great work, Irenæus clearly states the motives and objects for which he writes. He says: "I considered it necessary, having read the commentaries ($\dot{\upsilon}\pi o\mu\nu\acute{\eta}\mu a\sigma\iota$) *of the disciples of Valentinus*, as they call themselves, and having had personal intercourse with some of them and acquired full knowledge of their opinions, to unfold to thee," &c., and he goes on to say that he intends to set forth "the opinions of those who are *now* teaching heresy; I speak

[1] Wann wurden, u. s. w., p. 45.

particularly of the followers of Ptolemæus, whose system is an offshoot of the school of Valentinus."[1] Nothing could be more explicit than this statement that Irenæus neither intended nor pretended to write upon the works of Valentinus himself, but upon the commentaries of his followers of his own time, with some of whom he had had personal intercourse, and that the system which he intended to attack was that actually being taught in his day by Ptolemæus and his school, the offshoot from Valentinus. All the quotations to which Tischendorf refers are made within a few pages of this explicit declaration. Immediately after the passage about the Centurion, he says: "such is their system" (τοιαύτης δὲ τῆς ὑποθέσεως αὐτῶν οὔσης), and three lines below he states that they derive their views from unwritten sources (ἐξ ἀγράφων ἀναγινώσκοντες).[2] The first direct reference to Valentinus does not occur until after these quotations, and is for the purpose of showing the variation of opinion of his followers. He says: "Let us now see the uncertain opinions of these heretics, for there are two or three of them, how they do not speak alike of the same things, but contradicted one another in facts and names." Then he continues: "For the first of them, Valentinus, having derived his principles from the so-called Gnostic heresy, and adapted them to the peculiar character of his school declared this:" &c., &c.[3] And

---

[1] ... ἀναγκαῖον ἡγησάμην, ἐντυχὼν τοῖς ὑπομνήμασι τῶν, ὡς αὐτοὶ λέγουσιν, Οὐαλεντίνου μαθητῶν, ἐνίοις δὲ αὐτῶν καὶ συμβαλών, καὶ καταλαβόμενος τὴν γνώμην αὐτῶν, μηνῦσαί σοι, κ.τ.λ. ... τήν τε γνώμην αὐτῶν τῶν νῦν παραδιδασκόντων, λέγω δὴ τῶν περὶ Πτολεμαῖον, ἀπάνθισμα οὖσαν τῆς Οὐαλεντίνου σχολῆς, κ.τ.λ. Irenæus, Adv. Hær. Præf., i. § 2.

[2] Irenæus, Adv. Hær., i. 8, § 1.

[3] Ἴδωμεν νῦν καὶ τὴν τούτων ἄστατον γνώμην, δύο που καὶ τριῶν ὄντων, πῶς περὶ τῶν αὐτῶν οὐ τὰ αὐτὰ λέγουσιν, ἀλλὰ τοῖς πράγμασι καὶ τοῖς ὀνόμασιν ἐναντία ἀποφαίνονται. Ὁ μὲν γὰρ πρῶτος ἀπὸ τῆς λεγομένης Γνωστικῆς αἱρέσεως

after a brief description of his system, in which no Scriptural allusion occurs, he goes on to compare the views of the rest, and in chap. xii. he returns to Ptolemæus and his followers (Ὁ Πτολεμαῖος, καὶ οἱ σὺν αὐτῷ, κ.τ.λ.).

In the preface to Book ii., he again says that he has been exposing the falsity of the followers of Valentinus (qui sunt a Valentino) and will proceed to establish what he has advanced; and everywhere he uses the plural "they," with occasional direct references to the followers of Valentinus (qui sunt a Valentino).[1] The same course is adopted in Book iii., the plural being systematically used, and the same distinct definition introduced at intervals.[2] And again, in the preface to Book iv. he recapitulates that the preceding books had been written against these, "qui sunt a Valentino" (§ 2). In fact, it would almost be impossible for any writer more frequently and emphatically to show that he is not, as he began by declaring, dealing with the founder of the school himself, but with his followers living and teaching at the time at which he wrote.

Canon Westcott, with whose system of positively enunciating unsupported and controverted statements we are already acquainted, is only slightly outstripped by the German apologist in his misrepresentation of the evidence of Valentinus. It must be stated, however, that, acknowledging, as no doubt he does, that Irenæus never refers to Valentinus himself, Canon Westcott passes over in complete silence the supposed references upon

---

τὰς ἀρχὰς εἰς ἴδιον χαρακτῆρα διδασκαλείου μεθαρμόσας Οὐαλεντῖνος, οὕτως ἐξηροφόρησεν, κ.τ.λ. *Irenæus*, Adv. Hær., i. 11, § 1.

[1] As, for instance, ii. 16, § 4.

[2] For instance, "Secundum autem eos qui sunt a Valentino," iii. 11, § 2. "Secundum autem illos," § 3; "ab omnibus illos," § 3. " Iii autem qui sunt a Valentino," &c., § 7, *ib.* § 9, &c. &c.

which Tischendorf relies as his only evidence for the use of the Synoptics by that Gnostic. He, however, makes the following extraordinary statement regarding Valentinus: "The fragments of his writings which remain show the same natural and trustful use of Scripture as other Christian works of the same period; and there is no diversity of character in this respect between the quotations given in Hippolytus and those found in Clement of Alexandria. He cites the Epistle to the Ephesians as 'Scripture,' and refers clearly to the Gospels of St. Matthew, St. Luke, and St. John, to the Epistles to the Romans,"[1] &c.

We shall now give the passages which he points out in support of these assertions.[2] The first two are said to occur in the Stromata of the Alexandrian Clement, who professes to quote the very words of a letter of Valentinus to certain people regarding the passions, which are called by the followers of Basilides "the appendages of the soul." The passage is as follows: "But one only is good, whose presence is the manifestation through the Son, and

---

[1] On the Canon, p. 259 f. [In the 4th ed. of his work, published since the above remarks were made, Dr. Westcott has modified or withdrawn his assertions regarding Valentinus. As we cannot well omit the above passage, it is right to state that the lines quoted now read: "The few unquestionable fragments of Valentinus contain but little which points to passages of Scripture. If it were clear that the anonymous quotations in Hippolytus were derived from Valentinus himself, the list would be much enlarged, and include a citation of the Epistle to the Ephesians as 'Scripture,' and clear references to the Gospels of St. Luke and St. John, to 1 Corinthians, perhaps also to the Epistle to the Hebrews, and the first Epistle of St. John," (p. 295 f.). In a note he adds: "But a fresh and careful examination of the whole section of Hippolytus makes me feel that the evidence is so uncertain, that I cannot be sure in this case, as in the case of Basilides, that Hippolytus is quoting the words of the Founder" (p. 295, n. 5). Under these circumstances the statements even in the amended edition present many curious features.]

[2] Ib., p. 260, note 2.

through Him alone will the heart be enabled to become pure, by the expulsion of every evil spirit from the heart. For many spirits dwelling in it do not allow it to be pure, but each of them, while in divers parts they riot there in unseemly lusts, performs its own works. And, it seems to me, the heart is somewhat like an inn. For that, also, is both bored and dug into, and often filled with the ordure of men, who abide there in revelry, and bestow not one single thought upon the place, seeing it is the property of another. And in such wise is it with the heart, so long as no thought is given to it, being impure, and the dwelling-place of many demons, but as soon as the alone good Father has visited it, it is sanctified and shines through with light, and the possessor of such a heart becomes so blessed, that he shall see God." [1] According to Canon Westcott this passage contains two of the "clear references" to our Gospels upon which he bases his statement, namely to Matt. v. 8, and to Matt. xix. 17.

Now it is clear that there is no actual quotation from any evangelical work in this passage from the Epistle of Valentinus, and the utmost for which the most zealous apologist could contend is, that there is a slight similarity with some words in the Gospel, and Canon

---

[1] Εἷς δέ ἐστιν ἀγαθός, οὗ παρρησίᾳ (Grabe—Spicil. Patr. ii. p. 52—suggests παρουσία, which we adopt.) ἡ διὰ τοῦ υἱοῦ φανέρωσις, καὶ δι' αὐτοῦ μόνου δύναιτο ἂν ἡ καρδία καθαρὰ γενέσθαι παντὸς πονηροῦ πνεύματος ἐξωθουμένου τῆς καρδίας. πολλὰ γὰρ ἐνοικοῦντα αὐτῇ πνεύματα οὐκ ἐᾷ καθαρεύειν, ἕκαστον δὲ αὐτῶν τὰ ἴδια ἐκτελεῖ ἔργα πολλαχῶς ἐνυβριζόντων ἐπιθυμίαις οὐ προσηκούσαις. καί μοι δοκεῖ ὅμοιόν τι πάσχειν τῷ πανδοχείῳ ἡ καρδία· καὶ γὰρ ἐκεῖνο κατατιτρᾶταί τε καὶ ὀρύττεται καὶ πολλάκις κόπρου πίμπλαται ἀνθρώπων ἀσελγῶς ἐμμενόντων καὶ μηδὲ μίαν πρόνοιαν ποιουμένων τοῦ χωρίου, καθάπερ ἀλλοτρίου καθεστῶτος· τὸν τρόπον τοῦτον καὶ ἡ καρδία μέχρι μὴ προνοίας τυγχάνει, ἀκάθαρτος οὖσα, πολλῶν οὖσα δαιμόνων οἰκητήριον, ἐπειδὰν δὲ ἐπισκέψηται αὐτὴν ὁ μόνος ἀγαθὸς πατήρ, ἡγίασται καὶ φωτὶ διαλάμπει, καὶ οὕτω μακαρίζεται ὁ ἔχων τὴν τοιαύτην καρδίαν, ὅτι ὄψεται τὸν θεόν. Clem. Al., Strom., ii. 20, § 114.

Westcott himself does not venture to call them more than "references." That such distant coincidences should be quoted as evidence for the use of the first Gospel shows how weak is his case. At best such vague allusions could not prove anything, but when the passages to which reference is supposed to be made are examined, it will be apparent that nothing could be more unfounded or arbitrary than the claim of reference specially to our Gospel, to the exclusion of the other Gospels then existing, which to our knowledge contained both passages. We may, indeed, go still further, and affirm that if these coincidences are references to any Gospel at all, that Gospel is not the canonical, but one different from it.

The first reference alluded to consists of the following two phrases: "But one only is good (εἷς δέ ἐστιν ἀγαθός). .... the alone good Father" (ὁ μόνος ἀγαθὸς πατήρ). This is compared with Matt. xix. 17 :[1] "Why askest thou me concerning good? there is one that is good" (εἷς ἐστιν ὁ ἀγαθός).[2] Now the passage in the epistle, if a reference to any parallel episode, such as Matt. xix. 17, indicates with certainty the reading: "One is good the Father" εἷς ἐστιν ἀγαθὸς ὁ πατήρ. There is no such reading in any of our Gospels. But although this reading does not exist in any of the Canonical Gospels, it is well known that it did exist in uncanonical Gospels no longer extant, and that the passage was one upon which various sects of so-called heretics laid great stress. Irenæus quotes it as one of

---

[1] *Westcott*, On the Canon, p. 260, note 2.
[2] Mark x. 18, and Luke xviii. 18, are linguistically more distant. "Why callest thou me good? There is none good but God only." οὐδεὶς ἀγαθὸς εἰ μὴ εἷς ὁ θεός.

the texts to which the Marcosians, who made use of apocryphal Gospels,[1] and notably of the Gospel according to the Hebrews, gave a different colouring: εἷς ἐστιν ἀγαθὸς, ὁ πατήρ.[2] Epiphanius also quotes this reading as one of the variations of the Marcionites: εἷς ἐστιν ἀγαθὸς, ὁ θεὸς, ὁ πατήρ.[3] Origen, likewise, remarks that this passage is misused by some Heretics: "Velut proprie sibi datum scutum putant (hæretici) quod dixit Dominus in Evangelio: Nemo bonus nisi unus Deus pater."[4] Justin Martyr quotes the same reading from a source different from our Gospels,[5] εἷς ἐστιν ἀγαθὸς ὁ πατήρ μου, κ.τ.λ.,[6] and in agreement with the repeated similar readings of the Clementine Homilies, which likewise derived it from an extra canonical source,[7] ὁ γὰρ ἀγαθὸς εἷς ἐστιν, ὁ πατήρ.[8] The use of a similar expression by Clement of Alexandria,[9] as well as by Origen, only serves to prove the existence of the reading in extinct Gospels, although it is not found in any MS. of any of our Gospels.

The second of the supposed references is more diffuse: "One is good and through him alone will the heart be enabled to become pure (ἡ καρδία καθαρὰ γενέσθαι) . . . but when the alone good Father has visited it, it is sanctified and shines through with light, and the possessor of such a heart becomes so blessed, that he shall see God" (καὶ οὕτω μακαρίζεται ὁ ἔχων τὴν τοιαύτην

---

[1] Adv. Hær., i. 20, § 1. [2] Ib., i. 20, § 2.
[3] Epiphanius, Hær., xlii.; Schol. L. ed. Pet., p. 339.
[4] De Principiis, i. 2, § 13; cf. de Orat., 15; Exhort. ad Mart., 7; Contra Cels., v. 11; cf. Griesbach, Symb. Crit., ii. p. 305, 349, 388.
[5] Hilgenfeld, Die Evv. Justin's, p. 220 ff.; Credner, Beiträge, i. p. 243 ff. [6] Apol., i. 16.
[7] Hilgenfeld, Die Evv. Justin's, p. 362 f.; Credner, Beiträge, i. p. 321.
[8] Hom., xviii. 1; 3.
[9] οὐδεὶς ἀγαθὸς, εἰ μὴ ὁ πατήρ μου, κ.τ.λ. Pædag., i. 8, § 72, cf. § 74; εἷς ἀγαθὸς ὁ πατήρ. Strom., v. 10, § 64.

καρδίαν, ὅτι ὄψεται τὸν θεόν). This is compared[1] with Matthew v. 8: "Blessed are the pure in heart, for they shall see God" (μακάριοι οἱ καθαροὶ τῇ καρδίᾳ, ὅτι αὐτοὶ τὸν θεὸν ὄψονται). It might be argued that this is quite as much a reference to Psalm xxiv. 3-6 as to Matt. v. 8, but even if treated as a reference to the Sermon on the Mount, nothing is more certain than the fact that this discourse had its place in much older forms of the Gospel than our present Canonical Gospels,[2] and that it formed part of the Gospel according to the Hebrews and other evangelical writings in circulation in the early Church. Such a reference as this is absolutely worthless as evidence of special acquaintance with our first Synoptic.[3]

Tischendorf does not appeal at all to these supposed references contained in the passages preserved by Clement, but both the German and the English apologist join in relying upon the testimony of Hippolytus,[4] with regard to the use of the Gospels by Valentinus, although it must be admitted that the former does so with greater fairness of treatment than Canon Westcott. Tischendorf does refer to, and admit, some of the difficulties of the case, as we shall presently see, whilst Canon Westcott, as in the case of Basilides, boldly makes his assertion, and totally ignores all adverse facts. The only Gospel

---

[1] *Westcott*, On the Canon, p. 260, note 2.
[2] Ewald assigns it to the Spruchsammlung. Die drei erst. Evv., p. 7.
[3] The supposed reference to the Ep. to the Romans i. 20; cf. *Clem. Al.*, Strom., iv. 13, § 91, 92, is much more distant than either of the preceding. It is not necessary for us to discuss it, but as Canon Westcott merely gives references to all of the passages without quoting any of the words, a good strong assertion becomes a powerful argument, since few readers have the means of verifying its correctness.
[4] By a misprint Canon Westcott ascribes all his references of Valentinus to the N. T., except three, to the extracts from his writings in the Stromata of Clement, although he should have indicated the work of Hippolytus. Cf. On the Canon, 1866, p. 260, note 2.

reference which can be adduced even in the Philosophumena, exclusive of one asserted to be to the fourth Gospel, which will be separately considered hereafter, is advanced by Canon Westcott, for Tischendorf does not refer to it, but confines himself solely to the supposed reference to the fourth Gospel. The passage is the same as one also imputed to Basilides: "The Holy Spirit shall come upon thee and the power of the Highest shall overshadow thee;" which happens to agree with the words in Luke i. 35; but, as we have seen in connection with Justin, there is good reason for concluding that the narrative to which it belongs was contained in other Gospels.[1] In this instance, however, the quotation is carried further and presents an important variation from the text of Luke. "The Holy Spirit shall come upon thee, and the power of the Highest shall overshadow thee; therefore the thing begotten of thee shall be called holy"[2] (διὸ τὸ γεννώμενον ἐκ σοῦ ἅγιον κληθήσεται). The reading of Luke is: "Therefore also the holy thing begotten shall be called the Son of God" (διὸ καὶ τὸ γεννώμενον ἅγιον κληθήσεται υἱὸς θεοῦ). It is probable that the passage referred to in connection with the followers of Basilides may have ended in the same way as this, and been derived from the same source. Nothing, however, can be clearer than the fact that this quotation, by whoever made, is not taken from our third Synoptic, inasmuch as there does not exist a single MS. which contains such a passage.

We again, however, come to the question: Who really made the quotations which Hippolytus introduces so indefinitely? We have already, in speaking of Basilides,

---

[1] Cf. *Hilgenfeld*, Die Evv. Justin's, p. 141 ff.
[2] *Hippolytus*, Adv. Hær., vi. 35.

pointed out the loose manner in which Hippolytus and other early writers, in dealing with different schools of heretics, indifferently quote the founder or his followers without indicating the precise person quoted. This practice is particularly apparent in the work of Hippolytus when the followers of Valentinus are in question. Tischendorf himself is obliged to admit this. He asks: "Even though it be also incontestable that the author (Hippolytus) does not always sharply distinguish between the sect and the founder of the sect, does this apply to the present case?"[1] He denies that it does in the instance to which he refers, but he admits the general fact. In the same way another apologist of the fourth Gospel (and as the use of that Gospel is maintained in consequence of a quotation in the very same chapter as we are now considering, only a few lines higher up, both the third and fourth are in the same position) is forced to admit: "The use of the Gospel of John by Valentinus cannot so certainly be proved from our refutation-writing (the work of Hippolytus). Certainly in the statement of these doctrines it gives abstracts, which contain an expression of John (x. 8), and there cannot be any doubt that this is taken from some writing of the sect. But the apologist, in his expressions regarding the Valentinian doctrines, does not seem to confine himself to one and the same work, but to have alternately made use of different writings of the school, for which reason we cannot say anything as to the age of this quotation, and from this testimony, therefore, we merely have further confirmation that the Gospel was early[2] (?) used in the

---

[1] Wenn nun auch unbestreitbar ist, dass der Verfasser nicht immer streng zwischen der Sekte sondert und dem Urheber der Sekte, findet dies auf den vorliegenden Fall Anwendung? Wann wurden, u. s. w., p. 46.

[2] Why "early"? since Hippolytus writes about A.D. 225.

School of the Valentinians,"[1] &c. Of all this not a word from Canon Westcott, who adheres to his system of bare assertion.

Now we have already quoted [2] the opening sentence of Book vi. 35, of the work ascribed to Hippolytus, in which the quotation from John x. 8, referred to above occurs, and ten lines further on, with another intermediate and equally indefinite "he says" (φησί), occurs the supposed quotation from Luke i. 35, which, equally with that from the fourth Gospel, must, according to Weizsäcker, be abandoned as a quotation which can fairly be ascribed to Valentinus himself, whose name is not once mentioned in the whole chapter. A few lines below the quotation, however, a passage occurs which throws much light upon the question. After explaining the views of the Valentinians regarding the verse: "The Holy Ghost shall come upon thee," &c., the writer thus proceeds: "Regarding this there is among them (αὐτοῖς) a great question, a cause both of schism and dissension. And hence their (αὐτῶν) teaching has become divided, and the one teaching according to them (κατ' αὐτούς) is called Eastern (ἀνατολική) and the other Italian. They from Italy, of whom is Heracleon and Ptolemæus, say (φασί) that the body of Jesus was animal, and on account of this, on the occasion of the baptism, the Holy Spirit like a dove came down—that is, the Logos from the Mother above, Sophia—and became joined to the animal, and raised him from the dead. This, *he says* (φησί) is the declaration (τὸ εἰρημένον),"—and here be it observed we come to another of the "clear refer-

---

[1] *Weizsäcker*, Unters. üb. d. evang. Gesch., 1864, p. 234. Cf. *Luthardt*, Der johann. Urspr. viert. Ev. 1874, p. 88 f.

[2] Vol. ii. p. 57, "Therefore all the Prophets," &c.

ences" which Canon Westcott ventures, deliberately and without a word of doubt, to attribute to Valentinus himself,[1]—"This, he says, is the declaration: 'He who raised Christ from the dead shall also quicken your mortal bodies,'[2] that is animal. For the earth has come under a curse: 'For dust, he says (φησί) thou art and unto dust shalt thou return.'[3] On the other hand, those from the East (οἱ δ' αὖ ἀπὸ τῆς ἀνατολῆς), of whom is Axionicus and Bardesanes, say (λέγουσιν) that the body of the Saviour was spiritual, for the Holy Spirit came upon Mary, that is the Sophia and the power of the Highest,"[4] &c.

In this passage we have a good illustration of the mode in which the writer introduces his quotations with the subjectless "he says." Here he is conveying the divergent opinions of the two parties of Valentinians, and explaining the peculiar doctrines of the Italian school "of whom is Heracleon and Ptolemæus," and he suddenly departs from the plural "they" to quote the passage from Romans viii. 11, in support of their views with the singular "he says." Nothing can be more obvious than that "he" cannot possibly be Valentinus himself, for the schism is represented as taking place

[1] On the Canon, p. 260. [He no longer does so. *See* back p. 62, n. [1].]
[2] Cf. Rom. viii. 11. [3] Cf. Gen. iii. 19.
[4] Περὶ τούτου ζήτησις μεγάλη ἐστὶν αὐτοῖς καὶ σχισμάτων καὶ διαφορᾶς ἀφορμή. Καὶ γέγονεν ἐντεῦθεν ἡ διδασκαλία αὐτῶν διῃρημένη, καὶ καλεῖται ἡ μὲν ἀνατολικὴ τις διδασκαλία κατ' αὐτούς, ἡ δὲ Ἰταλιωτική. Οἱ μὲν ἀπὸ τῆς Ἰταλίας, ὧν ἐστιν Ἡρακλέων καὶ Πτολεμαῖος, ψυχικόν φασι τὸ σῶμα τοῦ Ἰησοῦ γεγονέναι, καὶ διὰ τοῦτο ἐπὶ τοῦ βαπτίσματος τὸ πνεῦμα ὡς περιστερὰ κατελήλυθε, τουτέστιν ὁ λόγος ὁ τῆς μητρὸς ἄνωθεν τῆς σοφίας, καὶ γέγονε τῷ ψυχικῷ, καὶ ἐγήγερκεν αὐτὸν ἐκ νεκρῶν. Τοῦτο ἐστί, φησί, τὸ εἰρημένον· Ὁ ἐγείρας Χριστὸν ἐκ νεκρῶν, ζωοποιήσει καὶ τὰ θνητὰ σώματα ὑμῶν, ἤτοι ψυχικά. Ὁ χοῦς γὰρ ὑπὸ κατάραν ἐλήλυθε. Γῆ γὰρ, φησίν, εἶ, καὶ εἰς γῆν ἀπελεύσῃ. Οἱ δ' αὖ ἀπὸ τῆς ἀνατολῆς λέγουσιν, ὧν ἐστὶν Ἀξιόνικος καὶ Ἀρδησιάνης, ὅτι πνευματικὸν ἦν τὸ σῶμα τοῦ σωτῆρος. πνεῦμα γὰρ ἅγιον ἦλθεν ἐπὶ τὴν Μαρίαν, τουτέστιν ἡ σοφία, καὶ ἡ δύναμις τοῦ ὑψίστου, κ.τ.λ. *Hippolytus*, Ref. Omn. Hær., vi. 35.

amongst his followers, and the quotation is evidently made by one of them to support the views of his party in the schism, but whether Hippolytus is quoting from Heracleon or Ptolemæus or some other of the Italian[1] school, there is no means of knowing. Of all this, again, nothing is said by Canon Westcott, who quietly asserts without hesitation or argument, that Valentinus himself is the person who here makes the quotation.

We have already said that the name of Valentinus does not occur once in the whole chapter (vi. 35) which we have been examining, and if we turn back we find that the preceding context confirms the result at which we have arrived, that the $\phi\eta\sigma\iota$ has no reference to the Founder himself, but is applicable only to some later member of his school, most probably contemporary with Hippolytus. In vi. 21, Hippolytus discusses the heresy of Valentinus, which he traces to Pythagoras and Plato, but in Ch. 29 he passes from direct reference to the Founder to deal entirely with his school. This is so manifest, that the learned editors of the work of Hippolytus, Professors Duncker and Schneidewin, alter the preceding heading at that part from "Valentinus" to "Valentiniani." At the beginning of Ch. 29 Hippolytus writes: "Valentinus, therefore, and Heracleon and Ptolemæus and the whole school of these (heretics) . . . have laid down as the fundamental principle of their teaching the arithmetical system. For according to these," &c. And a few lines lower down: "There is discernible amongst them, however, considerable difference of opinion. For many of them, in order that

---

[1] The quotation from an Epistle to the Romans by the Italian school is appropriate.

the Pythagorean doctrine of Valentinus may be wholly pure, suppose, &c., but others," &c. He shortly after says that he will proceed to state their doctrines as they themselves teach them (μνημονεύσαντες ὡς ἐκεῖνοι διδάσκουσιν ἐροῦμεν). He then continues : "There is, he says (φησί)," &c. &c., quoting evidently one of these followers who want to keep the doctrine of Valentinus pure, or of the "others," although without naming him, and three lines further on again, without any preparation, returning to the plural "they say" (λέγουσι) and so on through the following chapters, "he says" alternating with the plural, as the author apparently has in view something said by individuals or merely expresses general views. In the Chapter (34) preceding that which we have principally been examining, Hippolytus begins by referring to "the Quaternion according to Valentinus," but after five lines on it, he continues : "This is what they say : ταῦτά ἐστιν ἃ λέγουσιν,"[1] and then goes on to speak of "their whole teaching" (τὴν πᾶσαν αὐτῶν διδασκαλίαν), and lower down he distinctly sets himself to discuss the opinions of the school in the plural : "Thus these (Valentinians) subdivide the contents of the Pleroma," &c. (οὕτως οὗτοι, κ.τ.λ.), and continues with an occasional "according to them" (κατ' αὐτοὺς) until, without any name being mentioned, he makes use of the indefinite "he says" to introduce the quotation referred to by Canon Westcott as a citation by Valentinus himself of "the Epistle to the Ephesians as Scripture."[2] "This is, he says, what is written in Scripture," and there follows a quotation which, it may merely be mentioned as Canon Westcott says nothing of it, differs considerably from the passage in the Epistle

---

[1] vi. 34. [2] On the Canon, p. 260.

iii. 14—18. Immediately after, another of Canon Westcott's quotations from 1 Cor. ii. 14, is given, with the same indefinite " he says," and in the same way, without further mention of names, the quotations in Ch. 35 compared with John x. 8, and Luke i. 35. There is, therefore, absolutely no ground whatever for referring these φησί to Valentinus himself; but, on the contrary, Hippolytus shows in the clearest way that he is discussing the views of the later writers of the sect, and it is one of these, and not the Founder himself, whom in his usual indefinite way he thus quotes.

We have been forced by these bald and unsupported assertions of apologists to go at such length into these questions at the risk of being very wearisome to our readers, but it has been our aim as much as possible to make no statements without placing before those who are interested the materials for forming an intelligent opinion. Any other course would be to meet mere assertion by simple denial, and it is only by bold and unsubstantiated statements which have been simply and in good faith accepted by ordinary readers who have not the opportunity, if they have even the will, to test their veracity, that apologists have so long held their ground. Our results regarding Valentinus so far may be stated as follows: the quotations which without any explanation are so positively imputed to Valentinus are not made by him, but by later writers of his school;[1] and, moreover, the passages which are indicated by the English apologist as references to our two Synoptic Gospels not only do

---

[1] *Bretschneider*, Probabilia de Evang. et Ep.Joannis, 1820, p. 212 ff.; *Davidson*, Introd. N. T., ii. p. 390, p. 516; *Hilgenfeld*, Die Evangelien, p. 345, anm. 5; *Rumpf*, Rev. de Théol., 1867, p. 17 ff.; *Scholten*, Die ält. Zeugnisse, p. 68 ff.; *J. J. Tayler*, The Fourth Gospel, 1867, p. 57; *Volkmar*, Der Ursprung, p. 70 f.; Theol. Jahrb., 1854, p. 108 ff., 125 f.;

not emanate from Valentinus, but do not agree with our Gospels, and are apparently derived from other sources.[1]

The remarks of Canon Westcott with regard to the connection of Valentinus with our New Testament are on a par with the rest of his assertions. He says: "There is no reason to suppose that Valentinus differed from Catholic writers on the Canon of the New Testament."[2] We might ironically adopt this sentence, for as no writer whatever of the time of Valentinus, as we have seen, recognized any New Testament Canon at all, he certainly did not in this respect differ from the other writers of that period. Canon Westcott relies upon the statement of Tertullian, but even here, although he quotes the Latin passage in a note, he does not fully give its real sense in his text. He writes in immediate continuation of the quotation given above: "Tertullian says that in this he differed from Marcion, that he at least professed to accept 'the whole instrument,' perverting the interpretation, where Marcion mutilated the text." Now the assertion of Tertullian has a very important modification, which, to any one acquainted with the very unscrupulous boldness of the "Great African" in dealing with religious controversy, is extremely significant. He does not make the assertion positively and of his own knowledge, but modifies it by saying: "Nor, indeed, if Valentinus seems to use the

Weizsäcker, Unters. evang. Gesch., p. 234; *Zeller*, Die Apostelgesch., p. 65 ff.; Theol. Jahrb., 1853, p. 151 ff. Cf. *Kirchhofer*, Quellensamml., p. 387, anm. 1.

[1] Cf. *Zeller*, Die Apostelgesch., p. 67 f.; *Kirchhofer*, Quellensamml., p. 387, anm. 1.

[2] On the Canon, p. 259. [Dr. Westcott omits these words from his 4th ed., but he uses others here and elsewhere which imply very nearly the same assertion.]

whole instrument, (neque enim si Valentinus integro instrumento uti videtur),"[1] &c. Tertullian evidently knew very little of Valentinus himself, and had probably not read his writings at all.[2] His treatise against the Valentinians is avowedly not original, but, as he himself admits, is compiled from the writings of Justin, Miltiades, Irenæus, and Proclus.[3] Tertullian would not have hesitated to affirm anything of this kind positively, had there been any ground for it, but his assertion is at once too uncertain, and the value of his statements of this nature much too small, for such a remark to have any weight as evidence.[4] Besides, by his own showing Valentinus altered Scripture (sine dubio emendans),[5] which he could not have done had he recognized it as of canonical authority.[6] We cannot, however, place any reliance upon criticism emanating from Tertullian.

All that Origen seems to know on this subject is that the followers of Valentinus (τοὺς ἀπὸ Οὐαλεντίνου) have altered the form of the Gospel (μεταχαράξαντες τὸ εὐαγγέλιον).[7] Clement of Alexandria, however, informs us that Valentinus, like Basilides, professed to have direct traditions from the Apostles, his teacher being Theodas, a disciple of the Apostle Paul.[8] If he had known any Gospels which he believed to have apostolic authority, there would clearly not have been any need of such tradition. Hippolytus distinctly affirms that Valentinus derived his system from Pythagoras and Plato,

---

[1] De Præscrip. Hær., 38.
[2] *Scholten*, Die ält. Zeugnisse, p. 67; *Davidson*, Introd. N. T., ii. p. 390.   [3] Adv. Valent., 5.
[4] *Baur*, Unters. kan. Evv., p. 357; *Davidson*, Introd. N. T., ii. p. 390.
[5] De Præscrip. Hær., 30.   [6] *Credner*, Beiträge, i. p. 38.
[7] Contra Cels., ii. 27.   [8] Strom., vii. 17, § 106.

and "not from the Gospels" (οὐκ ἀπὸ τῶν εὐαγγελίων), and that consequently he might more properly be considered a Pythagorean and Platonist than a Christian.[1] Irenæus, in like manner, asserts that the Valentinians derive their views from unwritten sources (ἐξ ἀγράφων ἀναγινώσκοντες),[2] and he accuses them of rejecting the Gospels, for after enumerating them,[3] he continues: "When, indeed, they are refuted out of the Scriptures, they turn round in accusation of these same Scriptures, as though they were not correct, nor of authority . . . For (they say) that it (the truth) was not conveyed by written records but by the living voice."[4] In the same chapter he goes on to show that the Valentinians not only reject the authority of Scripture, but also reject ecclesiastical tradition. He says: "But, again, when we refer them to that tradition which is from the Apostles, which has been preserved through a succession of Presbyters in the Churches, they are opposed to tradition, affirming themselves wiser not only than Presbyters, but even than the Apostles, in that they have discovered the uncorrupted truth. For (they say) the Apostles mixed up matters which are of the law with the words of the Saviour, &c. . . . It comes to this, they neither consent to Scripture nor to tradition. (Evenit itaque, neque Scripturis jam, neque Traditioni consentire eos.)"[5] We find, therefore, that even in the time of Irenæus the Valentinians rejected the writings

---

[1] Ref. Omn. Hær., vi. 29; cf. vi. 21.
[2] Adv. Hær., i. 8, § 1.   [3] Ib., iii. 1, § 1.
[4] Cum enim ex Scripturis arguuntur, in accusationem convertuntur ipsarum Scripturarum, quasi non recte habeant, neque sint ex auctoritate. . . . . Non enim per litteras traditam illam, sed per vivam vocem, &c. Irenæus, Adv. Hær., iii. 2, § 1.
[5] Ib., iii. 2, § 2.

of the New Testament as authoritative documents, which they certainly would not have done had the Founder of their sect himself acknowledged them. So far from this being the case, there was absolutely no New Testament Canon for Valentinus himself to deal with,[1] and his perfectly orthodox contemporaries recognized no other Holy Scriptures than those of the Old Testament.

Irenæus, however, goes still further, and states that the Valentinians of his time not only had many Gospels, but that they possessed one peculiar to themselves. "Those indeed who are followers of Valentinus," he says, "again passing beyond all fear, and putting forth their own compositions, boast that they have more Gospels than there actually are. Indeed they have proceeded so far in audacity that they entitle their not long written work, agreeing in nothing with the Gospels of the Apostles, the Gospel of Truth, so that there cannot be any Gospel among them without blasphemy."[2] It follows clearly, from the very name of the Valentinian Gospel, that they did not consider that others contained the truth,[3] and indeed Irenæus himself perceived this, for he continues: "For if what is published by them be the Gospel of Truth, yet is dissimilar from those which have been delivered to us by the Apostles, any may perceive who please, as is demonstrated by these very Scriptures, that that which has been handed down from the Apostles is not the Gospel of Truth."[4] These passages speak for

---

[1] *Credner*, Gesch. N. T. Kan., p. 24; *Reuss*, Hist. du Canon, p. 69 f.

[2] Hi vero, qui sunt a Valentino, iterum exsistentes extra omnem timorem, suas conscriptiones proferentes, plura habere gloriantur, quam sint ipsa Evangelia. Siquidem in tantum processerunt audaciæ, uti quod ab his non olim conscriptum est, veritatis Evangelium titulent, in nihilo conveniens apostolorum Evangeliis, ut nec Evangelium quidem sit apud eos sine blasphemia. *Irenæus*, Adv. Hær., iii. 11, § 9.

[3] *Credner*, Beiträge, i. p. 38, f.   [4] *Irenæus*, Adv. Hær., iii. 11, § 9.

themselves. It has been suggested that the "Gospel of Truth" was a harmony of the four Gospels.[1] This, however, cannot by any possibility have been the case, inasmuch as Irenæus distinctly says that it did not agree in anything with the Gospels of the Apostles. We have been compelled to devote too much space to Valentinus, and we now leave him with the certainty that in nothing does he afford any evidence even of the existence of our Synoptic Gospels.

[1] *Bleek*, Einl. N. T., p. 638.

CHAPTER VII.

MARCION.

We must now turn to the great Heresiarch of the second century, Marcion, and consider the evidence regarding our Gospels which may be derived from what we know of him. The importance, and at the same time the difficulty, of arriving at a just conclusion from the materials within our reach have rendered Marcion's Gospel the object of very elaborate criticism, and the discussion of its actual character has continued with fluctuating results for nearly a century.

Marcion was born at Sinope, in Pontus, of which place his father was Bishop,[1] and although it is said that he aspired to the first place in the Church of Rome,[2] the Presbyters refused him communion on account of his peculiar views of Christianity. We shall presently more fully refer to his opinions, but here it will be sufficient to say that he objected to what he considered the debasement of true Christianity by Jewish elements, and he upheld the teaching of Paul alone, in opposition to that of all the other Apostles, whom he accused of mixing

---

[1] *Epiphanius*, Hær., xlii. 1 ed. Petav., p. 302; *Bleek*, Einl. N. T., p. 125; *Credner*, Beiträge, i. p. 40 f.; *Tischendorf*, Wann wurden, u. s. w., p. 57; *Westcott*, On the Canon, p. 272.

[2] *Epiph.*, Hær., xlii. 1.

up matters of the law with the Gospel of Christ, and falsifying Christianity,[1] as Paul himself had protested.[2] He came to Rome about A.D. 139—142,[3] and continued teaching for some twenty years.[4] His high personal character and elevated views produced a powerful effect upon his time,[5] and, although during his own lifetime and long afterwards vehemently and with every opprobrious epithet denounced by ecclesiastical writers, his opinions were so widely adopted that in the time of Epiphanius his followers were to be found throughout the whole world.[6]

Marcion is said to have recognized as his sources of Christian doctrine, besides tradition, a single Gospel and ten Epistles of Paul, which in his collection stood in the following order;—Epistle to Galatians, Corinthians (2), Romans, Thessalonians (2), Ephesians (which he had with

---

[1] *Irenæus*, Adv. Hær., iii. 2, § 2; cf. 12, § 12; *Tertullian*, Adv. Marc., iv. 2, 3; cf. i. 20; *Origen*, in Joann. T. v., § 4. *Neander*, Allg. K. G., 1843, ii. p. 815 f.; cf. p. 795; *Schleiermacher*, Lit. nachlass iii. Sämmtl. Werke, viii.; Einl. N. T., 1845, p. 214 f.; *Westcott*, On the Canon, p. 273 f.

[2] Gal. i. 6 ff.; cf. ii. 4 ff., 11 ff.; cf. 2 Cor. xi. 1 ff.

[3] *Anger*, Synops. Ev., p. xxiv.; *Baur*, Gesch. chr. Kirche, i. p. 196; *Bleek*, Einl. N. T., p. 126; *Burton*, Lectures on Eccl. History of first Three Centuries, ii. p. 105 ff.; *Credner*, Beiträge, i. p. 40 f.; *Hilgenfeld*, Der Kanon, p. 21 f.; *Holtzmann*, in Bunsen's Bibelwerk, viii. p. 562; *Lipsius*, Zeitschr. wiss. Theol., 1867, p. 75 ff.; *Reuss*, Gesch. N. T., p. 244; *Scholten*, Die ält. Zeugnisse, p. 73; *Schleiermacher*, Gesch. chr. Kirche, Sämmtl. Werke, 1840, xi. 1 abth., p. 107; *Tischendorf*, Wann wurden, u. s. w., p. 57; *Volkmar*, Theol. Jahrb., 1850, p. 120, ib., 1855, p. 270 ff.; *Westcott*, On the Canon, p. 273. The accounts of the Fathers are careless and conflicting. Cf. *Tertullian*, Adv. Marc., i. 19; *Epiph.*, Hær., xlii. 1; *Irenæus*, Adv. Hær., iii. 4, § 3; *Clem. Al.*, Strom., vii. 17, A.D. 140—150; *Bertholdt*, Einl. A. und N. T., i. p. 103.

[4] *Reuss*, Gesch. N. T., p. 244; *Lipsius*, Zeitschr. wiss. Theol., 1867, p. 75 ff.; *Volkmar*, Theol. Jahrb., 1855, p. 270 ff.

[5] *Credner*, Beiträge, i. p. 40; *Schleiermacher*, Sämmtl. Werke, viii.; Einl. N. T., 1845, p. 64; *Westcott*, On the Canon, p. 272 f.

[6] *Epiph.*, Hær., xlii. 1.

the superscription "to the Laodiceans"),[1] Colossians, Philippians, and Philemon.[2] None of the other books which now form part of the canonical New Testament were either mentioned or recognized by Marcion.[3] This is the oldest collection of Apostolic writings of which there is any trace,[4] but there was at that time no other "Holy Scripture" than the Old Testament, and no New Testament Canon had yet been imagined. Marcion neither claimed canonical authority for these writings,[5] nor did he associate with them any idea of divine inspiration.[6] We have already seen the animosity expressed by contemporaries of Marcion against the Apostle Paul.

The principal interest in connection with the collection of Marcion, however, centres in his single Gospel, the nature, origin, and identity of which have long been actively and minutely discussed by learned men of all shades of opinion with very varying results. The work itself is unfortunately no longer extant, and our only knowledge of it is derived from the bitter and very inaccurate opponents of Marcion. It seems to have borne much the same analogy to our third Canonical Gospel which existed between the Gospel according to

[1] *Tertullian*, Adv. Marc., v. 11, 17; *Epiph.*, Hær., xlii. 9; cf. 10, Schol. xl.
[2] *Tertullian*, Adv. Marc., v.; *Epiph.*, Hær., xlii. 9. (Epiphanius transposes the order of the last two Epistles.)
[3] *Credner*, Beiträge, i. p. 42 f.; *Hug*, Einl. N. T., i. p. 68 ff.; *Westcott*, On the Canon, p. 275.
[4] *Baur*, Paulus, i. p. 277 f.; *Reuss*, Hist. du Canon, p. 76 f.; *Tischendorf*, Wann wurden, u. s. w., p. 57; *Westcott*, On the Canon, p. 272.
[5] *Credner*, Beiträge, i. p. 42 f., 44 f.; Gesch. N. T. Kan., p. 23; *Bleek*, Einl. N. T., p. 126; *Hilgenfeld*, Der Kanon, p. 22 f.; *Holtzmann* in Bunsen's Bibelwerk, viii. p. 563; *Reuss*, Gesch. N. T., p. 244, p. 286; Hist. du Canon, p. 72; *Ritschl*, Theol. Jahrb., 1851, p. 529; *Scholten*, Die ält. Zeugnisse, p. 74; Het Paulinisch Evangelie, p. 6. Cf. *Köstlin*, Theol. Jahrb., 1851, p. 151.
[6] *Credner*, Beiträge, i. p. 45 f.

the Hebrews and our first Synoptic.¹ The Fathers, whose uncritical and, in such matters, prejudiced character led them to denounce every variation from their actual texts as a mere falsification, and without argument to assume the exclusive authenticity and originality of our Gospels, which towards the beginning of the third century had acquired wide circulation in the Church, vehemently stigmatized Marcion as an audacious adulterator of the Gospel, and affirmed his evangelical work to be merely a mutilated and falsified version of the "Gospel according to Luke."²

This view continued to prevail, almost without question or examination, till towards the end of the eighteenth century, when Biblical criticism began to exhibit the earnestness and activity which have ever since more or less characterized it. Semler first abandoned the prevalent tradition, and, after analyzing the evidence, he concluded that Marcion's Gospel and Luke's were different versions of an earlier work,³ and that the so-called heretical Gospel was one of the numerous Gospels from amongst which the Canonical had been selected by the Church.⁴ Griesbach about the same time also rejected the ruling opinion, and denied the close relationship usually asserted to exist between the two Gospels.⁵ Löffler⁶ and Corrodi⁷ strongly supported Semler's con-

[1] *Schwegler*, Das nachap. Zeitalter, i. p. 260.

[2] *Irenæus*, Adv. Hær., i. 27, § 2; iii. 12, § 12; *Tertullian*, Adv. Marc., iv. 2—6; *Epiphanius*, Hær., xlii. 9, 11; *Origen*, Contra Cels., ii. 27; *Theodoret*, Hær. fab., i. 24.

[3] Vorrede zu Townson's Abhandl. üb. d. vier Evv., 1783.

[4] Neuer Versuch, die Gemeinnützige Auslegung u. anwend. der N. T. zu befördern, 1786, p. 162 f.; cf. Prolegg. in Ep. ad Galatas.

[5] Curæ in hist. textus epist. Pauli, 1799, sect. iii., Opuscula Academica, ii. p. 124 ff.

[6] Marcionem Pauli epist. et Lucæ evang. adulterasse dubitatur, 1788, in Velthusen Kuinœl et Ruperti Comment. Theologicæ, 1794, i. pp. 180—218.

[7] Versuch einer Beleuchtung d. Gesch. des jüd. u. Christl. Bibelkanons, 1792, ii. p. 158 ff. 169.

clusion, that Marcion was no mere falsifier of Luke's Gospel, and J. E. C. Schmidt[1] went still further, and asserted that Marcion's Gospel was the genuine Luke, and our actual Gospel a later version of it with alterations and additions. Eichhorn,[2] after a fuller and more exhaustive examination, adopted similar views; he repudiated the statements of Tertullian regarding Marcion's Gospel as utterly untrustworthy, asserting that he had not that work itself before him at all, and he maintained that Marcion's Gospel was the more original text and one of the sources of Luke. Bolten,[3] Bertholdt,[4] Schleiermacher,[5] and D. Schulz[6] likewise maintained that Marcion's Gospel was by no means a mutilated version of Luke, but, on the contrary, an independent original Gospel. A similar conclusion was arrived at by Gieseler,[7] but later, after Hahn's criticism, he abandoned it, and adopted the opinion that Marcion's Gospel was constructed out of Luke.[8]

On the other hand, the traditional view was maintained by Storr,[9] Arneth,[10] Hug,[11] Neander,[12] and Gratz,[13] although with little originality of investigation or argument; and

[1] Ueber das ächte Evang. des Lucas, in Henke's Mag. für Religionsphilos., u. s. w., iii. 1796, p. 468 ff., 482 f., 507 f.
[2] Einl. N. T., 1820, i. pp. 43—84.
[3] Bericht des Lucas von Jesu dem Messia. Vorbericht, 1796, p. 29 f.
[4] Einl. A. u. N. T., 1813, iii. p. 1293 ff.
[5] Sämmtl. Werke, viii.; Einl. N. T., 1845, p. 64 f., 197 f., 214 f.
[6] Theol. Stud. u. Krit., 1829, 3, pp. 586—595.
[7] Entst. schr. Evv., 1818, p. 24 ff.
[8] Recens. d. Hahn's Das Ev. Marcion's in Hall. Allg. Litt. Z., 1823, p. 225 ff.; K. G., i. § 45.
[9] Zweck d. Evang. Gesch. u. Br. Johan., 1786, pp. 254—265.
[10] Ueber d. Bekanntsch. Marcion's mit. n. Kanon, u. s. w., 1809.
[11] Einl. N. T., 1847, i. p. 64 ff.
[12] Genet. Entwickl. d. vorn. Gnost. Syst., 1818, p. 311 ff.; cf. Allg. K. G., 1843, ii. pp. 792—816.
[13] Krit. Unters. üb. Marcion's Evang., 1818.

Paulus[1] sought to reconcile both views by admitting that Marcion had before him the Gospel of Luke, but denying that he mutilated it, arguing that Tertullian did not base his arguments on the actual Gospel of Marcion, but upon his work, the "Antitheses." Hahn,[2] however, undertook a more exhaustive examination of the problem, attempting to reconstruct the text of Marcion's Gospel[3] from the statements of Tertullian and Epiphanius, and he came to the conclusion that the work was a mere version, with omissions and alterations made by the Heresiarch in the interest of his system, of the third Canonical Gospel. Olshausen[4] arrived at the same result, and with more or less of modification but no detailed argument, similar opinions were expressed by Credner,[5] De Wette,[6] and others.[7]

Not satisfied, however, with the method and results of

---

[1] Theol. exeg. Conserv., 1822, Lief. i. p. 115 ff.

[2] Das Evang. Marcion's in seiner ursprüngl. Gestalt, 1823.

[3] The reconstructed text also in Thilo's Cod. Apocr. N. T., 1832, pp. 403—486.

[4] Die Echtheit der vier kan. Evv., 1823, pp. 107—215.

[5] Beiträge, i. p. 43.

[6] Einl. N. T., 6th ausg., 1860, p. 119 ff.

[7] The following writers, either before Hahn's work was written or subsequently, have maintained the dependence, in one shape or another, of Marcion's Gospel on Luke. *Anger*, Synopsis Ev. Proleg., xxiv. ff.; *Becker*, Exam. Crit. de l'Ev. de Marcion, 1837; *Bleek*, Einl. N. T., p. 135; *Cellérier*, Introd. Crit. N. T., 1823, p. 25 f.; *Davidson*, Introd. N. T., ii. p. 51 f.; *Ebrard*, Wiss. krit. evang. Gesch., p. 810; *Ewald*, Jahrb. bibl. Wiss., 1853—54, p. 48; *Guericke*, Gesammtgesch. N. T., p. 231; H'buch K. G., i. p. 190; *Gfrörer*, Allg. K. G., i. p. 363 ff.; *Harting*, Quæst. de Marcione Lucani Evangelii, &c., 1849; *Holtzmann* in Bunsen's Bibelwerk, viii. p. 505 f.; *Kirchhofer*, Quellensamml., p. 48, p. 361, anm. 10; *Meyer*, Krit.-exeg. Kommentar N. T., 1867, 1 abth. 2 hälfte, p. 228; *Michaelis*, Einl. N. T., 1788, i. p. 40; *Neudecker*, Einl. N. T., 1840, p. 68 ff.; *Nicolas*, Et. sur les Ev. Apocr., 1866, p. 157 f.; *Rhode*, Prolegg. ad Quæst. de evang. Marcionis denuo instit. 1834; *Reuss*, Gesch. N. T., p. 244 f.; Rev. de Théol., 1857, p. 4 f.; *Rumpf*, Rev. de Théol., 1867, p. 20 f.; *Schott*, Isagoge, 1830, p. 13 ff., note 7; *Scholten*, Die ält. Zeugnisse, p. 73 f.; *Tischendorf*, Wann wurden, u. s. w., pp. 56—65; *Westcott*,

Hahn and Olshausen, whose examination, although more minute than any previously undertaken, still left much to be desired, Ritschl[1] made a further thorough investigation of the character of Marcion's Gospel, and decided that it was in no case a mutilated version of Luke, but, on the contrary, an original and independent work, from which the Canonical Gospel was produced by the introduction of anti-Marcionitish passages and readings. Baur[2] strongly enunciated similar views, and maintained that the whole error lay in the mistake of the Fathers, who had, with characteristic assumption, asserted the earlier and shorter Gospel of Marcion to be an abbreviation of the later Canonical Gospel, instead of recognizing the latter as a mere extension of the former. Schwegler[3] had already, in a remarkable criticism of Marcion's Gospel declared it to be an independent and original work, and in no sense a mutilated Luke, but, on the contrary, probably the source of that Gospel. Köstlin,[4] while stating that the theory that Marcion's Gospel was an earlier work and the basis of that ascribed to Luke was not very probable, affirmed that much of the Marcionitish text was more original than the Canonical, and that both Gospels must be considered versions of the same original, although Luke's was the later and more corrupt.

These results, however, did not satisfy Volkmar,[5] who entered afresh upon a searching examination of the whole subject, and concluded that whilst, on the one hand, the

On the Canon, p. 272 ff.; *Wilcke*, Tradition u. Mythe, 1837, p. 28; *Zeller*, Die Apostelgesch., p. 12 ff.

[1] Das Evangelium Marcion's, 1846.
[2] Krit. Unters. kan. Evv., 1847, p. 397 ff.
[3] Das nachap. Zeit., 1846, i. p. 260 ff.
[4] Der Ursprung d. synopt. Evv., 1853, p. 303 ff.
[5] Theol. Jahrb., 1850, pp. 110—138, pp. 185—235.

Gospel of Marcion was not a mere falsified and mutilated form of the Canonical Gospel, neither was it, on the other, an earlier work, and still less the original Gospel of Luke, but merely a Gnostic compilation from what, so far as we are concerned, may be called the oldest codex of Luke's Gospel, which itself is nothing more than a similar Pauline edition of the original Gospel. Volkmar's analysis, together with the arguments of Hilgenfeld, succeeded in convincing Ritschl,[1] who withdrew from his previous opinions, and, with those critics, merely maintained some of Marcion's readings to be more original than those of Luke,[2] and generally defended Marcion from the aspersions of the Fathers, on the ground that his procedure with regard to Luke's Gospel was precisely that of the Canonical Evangelists to each other;[3] Luke himself being clearly dependent both on Mark and Matthew.[4] Baur was likewise induced by Volkmar's and Hilgenfeld's arguments to modify his views;[5] but although for the first time he admitted that Marcion had altered the original of his Gospel frequently for dogmatic reasons, he still maintained that there was an older form of the Gospel without the earlier chapters, from which both Marcion and Luke directly constructed their Gospels;—both of them stood in the same line in regard to the original; both altered it; the one abbreviated, the other extended it.[6] Encouraged by this success, but not yet satisfied, Volkmar immediately undertook a further and more exhaustive examination of the text of Marcion, in the hope of finally settling the

---

[1] Theol. Jahrb., 1851, p. 528 ff. [2] *Ib.*, p. 530 ff.
[3] *Ib.*, p. 529. [4] *Ib.*, p. 534 ff.
[5] Das Markusevang. Anhang üb. das Ev. Marcion's, 1851, p. 191 ff.
[6] *Ib.*, p. 225 f.

discussion, and he again, but with greater emphasis, confirmed his previous results.[1] In the meantime Hilgenfeld[2] had seriously attacked the problem, and, like Hahn and Volkmar, had sought to reconstruct the text of Marcion, and, whilst admitting many more original and genuine readings in the text of Marcion, he had also decided that his Gospel was dependent on Luke, although he further concluded that the text of Luke had subsequently gone through another, though slight, manipulation before it assumed its present form. These conclusions he again fully confirmed after a renewed investigation of the subject.[3]

This brief sketch of the controversy which has so long occupied the attention of critics will at least show the uncertainty of the data upon which any decision is to be based. We have not attempted to give more than the barest outlines, but it will appear as we go on that most of those who decide against the general independence of Marcion's Gospel, at the same time admit his partial originality and the superiority of some of his readings over those of the third Synoptic, and justify his treatment of Luke as a procedure common to the Evangelists, and warranted not only by their example but by the fact that no Gospels had in his time emerged from the position of private documents in limited circulation.

Marcion's Gospel not being any longer extant, it is important to establish clearly the nature of our knowledge regarding it, and the exact value of the data from which various attempts have been made to reconstruct the text. It is manifest that the evidential force of any deductions from a reconstructed text is almost wholly

[1] Das Evang. Marcion's, 1852.
[2] Ueb. die Evv. Justin's der Clem. Hom. und Marcion's, 1850, p. 389 ff.
[3] Theol. Jahrb., 1853. pp. 192—244.

dependent on the accuracy and sufficiency of the materials from which that text is derived.

The principal sources of our information regarding Marcion's Gospel are the works of his most bitter denouncers Tertullian and Epiphanius, who, however, it must be borne in mind, wrote long after his time,—the work of Tertullian against Marcion having been composed about A.D. 208,[1] and that of Epiphanius a century later. We may likewise merely mention here the "*Dialogus de recta in deum fide*," commonly attributed to Origen, although it cannot have been composed earlier than the middle of the fourth century.[2] The first three sections are directed against the Marcionites, but only deal with a late form of their doctrines.[3] As Volkmar admits that the author clearly had only a general acquaintance with the "Antitheses," and principal proof passages of the Marcionites, but, although he certainly possessed the Epistles, had not the Gospel of Marcion itself,[4] we need not now more particularly consider it.

We are, therefore, dependent upon the "dogmatic and partly blind and unjust adversaries"[5] of Marcion for our only knowledge of the text they stigmatize; and when the character of polemical discussion in the early centuries of our era is considered, it is certain that great caution must be exercised, and not too much weight attached to the statements of opponents who regarded a heretic with abhorrence, and attacked him with an acrimony which carried them far beyond the limits of fairness and truth. Their religious controversy bristles with

---

[1] Cf. *Tertullian*, Adv. Marc., i. 15. *Neander*, Antignosticus, 1849, p. 398; *Scholten*, Die ält. Zeugnisse, p. 75.
[2] *Volkmar*, Das Ev. Marcion's, p. 52.
[3] *Ib.*, p. 52 f.   [4] *Ib.*, p. 53.
[5] *Volkmar*, Theol. Jahrb., 1850, p. 120.

misstatements, and is turbid with pious abuse. Tertullian was a master of this style, and the vehement vituperation with which he opens[1] and often interlards his work against " the impious and sacrilegious Marcion" offers anything but a guarantee of fair and legitimate criticism. Epiphanius was, if possible, still more passionate and exaggerated in his representations against him.[2] Undue importance must not, therefore, be attributed to their statements.[3]

Not only should there be caution exercised in receiving the representations of one side in a religious discussion, but more particularly is such caution necessary in the case of Tertullian, whose trustworthiness is very far from being above suspicion, and whose inaccuracy is often apparent.[4] " Son christianisme," says Reuss, " est ardent, sincère, profondément ancré dans son âme. L'on voit qu'il en vit. Mais ce christianisme est âpre, insolent, brutal, ferrailleur. Il est sans onction et sans charité, quelquefois même sans loyauté, dès qu'il se trouve en face d'une opposition quelconque. C'est un soldat qui ne sait que se battre et qui oublie, tout en se battant, qu'il faut aussi respecter son ennemi. Dialecticien subtil et rusé, il excelle à ridiculiser ses adversaires. L'injure, le sarcasme, un langage qui rappelle parfois en vérité le genre de Rabelais, une effronterie d'affirmation dans les moments de faiblesse qui frise et atteint même la mauvaise foi, voilà ses armes. Je sais ce qu'il faut en cela mettre sur le compte de l'époque. . . . Si, au second siècle,

---

[1] Adv. Marc., i. 1.   [2] Cf. *De Wette*, Einl. N. T., p. 122.
[3] *Reuss*, Hist. du Canon, p. 71 ff.; *Gieseler*, Entst. schr. Evv., p. 25; *Scholten*, Die ält. Zeugnisse, p. 75; *Volkmar*, Theol. Jahrb., 1850, p. 120; *Westcott*, On the Canon, p. 276; *De Wette*, Einl. N. T., p. 122.
[4] *Baur*, Unters. kan. Evv., 1847, p. 357; *Reuss*, Rev. de Théol., 1857, p. 67 f.; *Schwegler*, Das nachap. Zeitalter, i. p. 278 f.

tous les partis, sauf quelques gnostiques, sont intolérants, Tertullien l'est plus que tout le monde." [1]

The charge of mutilating and interpolating the Gospel of Luke is first brought against Marcion by Irenæus,[2] and it is repeated with still greater vehemence and fulness by Tertullian,[3] and Epiphanius;[4] but the mere assertion by Fathers at the end of the second and in the third centuries, that a Gospel different from their own was one of the Canonical Gospels falsified and mutilated, can have no weight whatever in itself in the inquiry as to the real nature of that work.[5] Their arbitrary assumption of exclusive originality and priority for the four Gospels of the Church led them, without any attempt at argument, to treat every other evangelical work as an offshoot or falsification of these. The arguments by which Tertullian endeavours to establish that the Gospels of Luke and the other Canonical Evangelists were more ancient than that of Marcion[6] show that he had no idea of historical or critical evidence.[7] We are, however, driven back upon such actual data regarding the text and contents of Marcion's Gospel as are given by the Fathers, as the only basis, in the absence of the Gospel itself, upon which any hypothesis as to its real character can be built. The question therefore is: Are these data sufficiently ample and trustworthy for a decisive judgment

---

[1] *Reuss*, Rev. de Théol., xv. 1857, p. 67 f. Cf. *Mansel*, The Gnostic Heresies, 1875, p. 250, p. 259 f.

[2] Et super hæc, id quod est secundum Lucam Evangelium circumcidens..... *Irenæus*, Adv. Hær., i. 27, § 2; cf. iii. 11, § 7; 12, § 12; 14, § 4.

[3] Adv. Marc., iv. 1, 2, 4 et passim.   [4] Hær., xlii. 9, 10 et passim.

[5] *Hilgenfeld*, Die Evv. Justin's, p. 446 f., 448; *Reuss*, Hist. du Canon, p. 72 f.; *Volkmar*, Theol. Jahrb., 1850, p. 120; *Ritschl*, Das Evang. Marcion's, p. 23 ff.

[6] Adv. Marc., iv. 5.

[7] *Eichhorn*, Einl. N. T., i. p. 73 f.; *Schwegler*, Das nachap. Zeit., i. p. 276 f.

from internal evidence? if indeed internal evidence in such a case can be decisive at all.

All that we know, then, of Marcion's Gospel is simply what Tertullian and Epiphanius have stated with regard to it. It is, however, undeniable, and indeed is universally admitted, that their object in dealing with it at all was entirely dogmatic, and not in the least degree critical[1]. The spirit of that age was indeed so essentially uncritical[2] that not even the canonical text could waken it into activity. Tertullian very clearly states what his object was in attacking Marcion's Gospel. After asserting that the whole aim of the Heresiarch was to prove a disagreement between the Old Testament and the New, and that for this purpose he had erased from the Gospel all that was contrary to his opinion, and retained all that he had considered favourable, Tertullian proceeds to examine the passages retained,[3] with the view of proving that the Heretic has shown the same "blindness of heresy" both in that which he has erased and in that which he has retained, inasmuch as the passages which Marcion has allowed to remain are as opposed to his system, as those which he has omitted. He conducts the controversy in a free and discursive manner, and whilst he appears to go through Marcion's Gospel with some regularity, it will be apparent, as we proceed, that

---

[1] *Hilgenfeld*, Die Evv. Justin's, p. 447 f.; *Kirchhofer*, Quellensamml., p. 361, anm. 10, p. 362 f., anm. 12, 15, 16, 17; *Reuss*, Rev. de Théol., xv. 1857. p. 4; *Tischendorf*, Wann wurden, u. s. w., p. 62; *Volkmar*, Theol. Jahrb., 1850, p. 120; Das Evang. Marcion's, 1852, pp. 29 f., 31 f.; *De Wette*, Einl. N. T., p. 123.

[2] *Westcott*, On the Canon, p. 8.

[3] Hæc conveniemus, hæc amplectemur, si nobiscum magis fuerint, si Marcionis præsumptionem percusserint. Tunc et illa constabit eodem vitio hæreticæ cæcitatis erasa quo et hæc reservata. Sic habebit intentio et forma opusculi nostri, &c., &c. *Tertullian*, Adv. Marc. iv. 6.

mere conjecture has to play a large part in any attempt to reconstruct, from his data, the actual text of Marcion. Epiphanius explains his aim with equal clearness. He had made a number of extracts from the so-called Gospel of Marcion which seemed to him to refute the heretic, and after giving a detailed and numbered list of these passages, which he calls σχόλια, he takes them consecutively and to each adds his "Refutation." His intention is to show how wickedly and disgracefully Marcion has mutilated and falsified the Gospel, and how fruitlessly he has done so, inasmuch as he has stupidly, or by oversight, allowed much to remain in his Gospel by which he may be completely refuted.[1]

As it is impossible within our limits fully to illustrate the procedure of the Fathers with regard to Marcion's Gospel, and the nature and value of the materials they supply, we shall as far as possible quote the declarations of critics, and more especially of Volkmar and Hilgenfeld, who, in the true and enlightened spirit of criticism, impartially state the character of the data available for the understanding of the text. As these two critics have, by their able and learned investigations, done more than any others to educe and render possible a decision of the problem, their own estimate of the materials upon which a judgment has to be formed is of double value.

With regard to Tertullian, Volkmar explains that his desire is totally to annihilate the most dangerous heretic of his time,—first (Books i.—iii.), to overthrow Marcion's system in general as expounded in his "Antitheses,"—and then (Book iv.) to show that even the Gospel of Marcion

---

[1] *Epiphanius*, Hær., xlii. 9 f.

only contains Catholic doctrine (he concludes, "*Christus Jesus in Evangelio tuo meus est,*" c. 43); and therefore he examines the Gospel only so far as may serve to establish his own view and refute that of Marcion. "To show," Volkmar continues, "wherein this Gospel was falsified or mutilated, *i.e.*, varied from his own, on the contrary, is in no way his design, for he perceives that Marcion could retort the reproach of interpolation, and in his time proof from internal grounds was hardly possible, so that only exceptionally, where a variation seems to him remarkable, does he specially mention it."[1] On the other hand Volkmar remarks that Tertullian's Latin rendering of the text of Marcion which lay before him,—which, although certainly free and having chiefly the substance in view, is still in weightier passages verbally accurate,—directly indicates important variations in that text. He goes on to argue that the silence of Tertullian may be weighty testimony for the fact that passages which exist in Luke, but which he does not mention, were missing in Marcion's Gospel, but he does so with considerable reservation. "But his silence *alone*," he says, "can only under certain conditions represent with diplomatic certainty an omission in Marcion. It is indeed probable that he would not lightly have passed over a passage in the Gospel of Marcion which might in any way be contradictory to its system, if one altogether similar had not preceded it, all the more as he frequently drags in by force such proof passages from Marcion's text, and often plainly with but a certain sophistry tries to refute his adversary out of the words of his own Gospel. But it remains always possible that in his eagerness he has

[1] *Volkmar*, Das Evang. Marcion's, p. 29.

overlooked much; and besides, he believes that by his replies to particular passages he has already sufficiently dealt with many others of a similar kind; indeed, avowedly, he will not willingly repeat himself. A certain conclusion, therefore, can only be deduced from the silence of Tertullian when special circumstances enter." [1] Volkmar, however, deduces with certainty from the statements of Tertullian that, whilst he wrote, he had not before him the Gospel of Luke, but intentionally laid it aside, and merely referred to the Marcionitish text, and further that, like all the Fathers of the third Century, he preferred the Gospel according to Matthew to the other Synoptics, and was well acquainted with it alone, so that in speaking of the Gospel generally he only has in his memory the sense, and the sense alone of Luke except in so far as it agrees or seems to agree with Matthew.[2]

With regard to the manner in which Tertullian performed the work he had undertaken, Hilgenfeld remarks: " As Tertullian, in going through the Marcionitish Gospel, has only the object of refutation in view, he very rarely states explicitly what is missing in it; and as, on the one hand, we can only venture to conclude from the silence of Tertullian that a passage is wanting, when it is altogether inexplicable that he should not have made use of it for the purpose of refutation; so, on the other, we must also know how Marcion used and interpreted the Gospel, and should never lose sight of Tertullian's refutation and defence." [3]

Hahn substantially expresses the same opinions. He

---

[1] *Volkmar*, Das Evang. Marcion's, p. 29 f.; cf. Theol. Jahrb., 1855, p. 237.
[2] Das Ev. Marcion's, p. 30 f.   [3] Die Evv. Justin's, p. 397.

says: "Inasmuch as Tertullian goes through the Marcionitish text with the view of refuting the heretic out of that which he accepts, and not of critically pointing out all variations, falsifications, and passages rejected, he frequently quotes the falsified or altered Marcionitish text without expressly mentioning the variations.'... Yet he cannot refrain—although this was not his object—occasionally, from noticing amongst other things any falsifications and omissions which, when he perhaps examined the text of Luke or had a lively recollection of it, struck and too grievously offended him."[2]

Volkmar's opinion of the procedure of Epiphanius is still more unfavourable. Contrasting it with that of Tertullian, he characterizes it as "more superficial," and he considers that its only merit is its presenting an independent view of Marcion's Gospel. Further than this, however, he says: "How far we can build upon his statements, whether as regards their completeness or their trustworthiness is not yet made altogether clear."[3] Volkmar goes on to show how thoroughly Epiphanius intended to do his work, and yet that, although from what he himself leads us to expect, we might hope to find a complete statement of Marcion's sins, the Father himself disappoints such an expectation by his own admission of incompleteness. He complains generally of his free and misleading method of quotation, such, for instance, as his alteration of the text without explanation; alteration of the same passage on different occasions in more than one way; abbreviations, and omissions of parts of quotations; the sudden breaking off of passages just commenced with

---

[1] Das Ev. Marcion's, p. 96.   [2] *Ib.* p. 98.
[3] *Volkmar*, Das Ev. Marcion's, p. 32, cf. p. 43.

the indefinite καὶ τὰ ἑξῆς or καὶ τὸ λοιπόν, without any indication how much this may include.¹

Volkmar, indeed, explains that Epiphanius is only thoroughly trustworthy where, and *so far as*, he wishes to state in his Scholia an omission or variation in Marcion's text from his own Canonical Gospel, in which case he minutely registers the smallest point, but this is to be clearly distinguished from any charge of falsification brought against Marcion in his Refutations; for only while earlier drawing up his Scholia had he the Marcionitish Gospel before him and compared it with Luke; but in the case of the Refutations, on the contrary, which he wrote later, he did not at least again compare the Gospel of Luke. "It is, however, altogether different," continues Volkmar, "as regards the statements of Epiphanius concerning the part of the Gospel of Luke which is preserved in Marcion. Whilst he desires to be *strictly literal* in the account of the *variations*, and also with two exceptions *is* so, he so generally adheres *only to the purport* of the passages retained by Marcion, that altogether literal quotations are quite exceptional; *throughout*, however, where passages of greater extent are referred to, these are not merely abbreviated, but also are quoted in *very free* fashion, and nowhere can we reckon that the passage in Marcion ran verbally as Epiphanius quotes it."² And to this we may add a remark made further on: "We cannot in general rely upon the accuracy of his statements in regard to that which Marcion had in common with Luke."³ On the other hand Volkmar had previously

---

¹ *Volkmar*, Das Ev. Marcion's, p. 33 ff.; cf. *Hahn*, Das Ev. Marcion's, p. 123 ff.

² *Volkmar*, Das Ev. Marcion's, p. 43 f.; cf. p. 31.

³ *Volkmar*, Das Ev. Marcion's, p. 45.

said: "Absolute completeness in regard to that which Marcion's Gospel did not contain is not to be reckoned upon in his Scholia. He has certainly not intended to pass over anything, but in the eagerness which so easily renders men superficial and blind much has escaped him."[1]

Hahn bears similar testimony to the incompleteness of Epiphanius. "It was not his purpose," he says, "fully to notice all falsifications, variations, and omissions, although he does mark most of them, but merely to extract from the Gospel of Marcion, as well as from his collection of Epistles, what seemed to him well suited for refutation."[2] But he immediately adds: "When he quotes a passage from Marcion's text, however, in which such falsifications occur, he generally,—but not always, —notes them more or less precisely, and he had himself laid it down as a subsidiary object of his work to pay attention to such falsifications."[3] A little further on he says: "In the quotations of the remaining passages which Epiphanius did not find different from the Gospel of Luke, and where he therefore says nothing of falsification or omission, he is often very free, neither adhering strictly to the particular words, nor to their arrangement, but his favourite practice is to give their substance and sense for the purpose of refuting his opponent. He presupposes the words known from the Gospel of Luke."[4]

It must be stated, however, that both Volkmar[5] and Hilgenfeld[6] consider that the representations of

---

[1] *Volkmar*, Das Ev. Marcion's, p. 33; cf. *Neudecker*, Einl. N. T., p. 75 ff.; *Hahn*, Das Ev. Marcion's, p. 111 f.; *De Wette*, Einl. N. T., p. 123; *Kirchhofer*, Quellensamml., p. 361, anm. 10, p. 362 f., anm. 15, 16, 17.

[2] *Hahn*, Das Ev. Marcion's, p. 121.

[3] *Ib.*, p. 122. [4] *Ib.*, p. 123 f.

[5] *Volkmar*, Das Ev. M., p. 45 ff. [6] Die Evv. Justin's, p. 397 f.

Tertullian and Epiphanius supplement each other and enable the contents of Marcion's Gospel to be ascertained with tolerable certainty. Yet a few pages earlier Volkmar had pointed out that: "The ground for a certain fixture of the text of the Marcionitish Gospel, however, seems completely taken away by the fact that Tertullian and Epiphanius, in their statements regarding its state, not merely repeatedly seem to, but in part actually do, directly contradict each other."[1] Hahn endeavours to explain some of these contradictions by imagining that later Marcionites had altered the text of their Gospel, and that Epiphanius had the one form and Tertullian another;[2] but such a doubt only renders the whole of the statements regarding the work more uncertain and insecure. That it is not without some reason, however, appears from the charge which Tertullian brings against the disciples of Marcion: "for they daily alter it (their Gospel) as they are daily refuted by us."[3] In fact, we have no assurance whatever that the work upon which Tertullian and Epiphanius base their charge against Marcion of falsification and mutilation of Luke was Marcion's original Gospel at all, and we certainly have no historical evidence on the point.[4]

The question even arises, whether Tertullian, and indeed Epiphanius, had Marcion's Gospel in any shape before them when they wrote, or merely his work the

---

[1] *Volkmar*, Das Ev. Marcion's, p. 22 f., p. 46 ff.; Theol. Jahrb., 1854, p. 106.

[2] *Hahn*, Das Ev. Marcion's, p. 130 f., p. 169, p. 224 ff.; cf. *Neudecker*, Einl. N. T., p. 82.

[3] Nam et quotidie reformant illud, prout a nobis quotidie revincuntur Adv. Marc., iv. 5; cf. Dial. de recta in deum fide, § 5; *Orig.*, Opp., i. p. 867.

[4] *Schwegler*, Das nachap. Zeit., i. p. 262 f.; cf. *Volkmar*, Theol. Jahrb., 1854, p. 106 f.

"Antitheses."[1] In commencing his onslaught on Marcion's Gospel, Tertullian says: "Marcion seems (videtur) to have selected Luke, to mutilate it."[2] This is the first serious introduction of his "mutilation hypothesis," which he thenceforward presses with so much assurance, but the expression is very uncertain for so decided a controversialist, if he had been able to speak more positively.[3] We have seen that it is admitted that Epiphanius wrote without again comparing the Gospel of Marcion with Luke, and it is also conceded that Tertullian at least had not the Canonical Gospel, but in professing to quote Luke evidently does so from memory, and approximates his text to Matthew, with which Gospel, like most of the Fathers, he was better acquainted. This may be illustrated by the fact that both Tertullian and Epiphanius reproach Marcion with erasing passages from the Gospel of Luke, which never were in Luke at all.[4] In one place Tertullian says: "Marcion, you must also remove this from the Gospel: 'I am not sent but unto the lost sheep of the house of Israel,'[5] and: 'It is not meet to take the children's bread, and give it to dogs,'[6] in order, be it known, that Christ may not seem to be an Israelite."[7] The "Great African"

---

[1] *Eichhorn*, Einl. N. T., i. p. 45, anm. i.; cf. p. 77 f., p. 83; *Schwegler*, Das nachap. Zeit., i. p. 279 f.

[2] Nam ex iis commentatoribus, quos habemus, Lucam videtur Marcion elegisse, quem crederet. Adv. Marc., iv. 2.

[3] *Eichhorn*, Einl. N. T., i. p. 78, anm. g. p. 83; cf. *Hilgenfeld*, Die Evv. Justin's, p. 447, anm. 1.

[4] *Schwegler*, Das nachap. Zeit., i. p. 278 f.; *Eichhorn*, Einl. N. T., i. p. 45 f., anm. i. cf. p. 77; *Volkmar*, Das Ev. Marcion's, p. 43; cf. *Hahn*, Das Ev. Marcion's, p. 264.

[5] Matt. xv. 24.   [6] *Ib.*, xv. 26.

[7] Marcion, aufer etiam illud de evangelio: non sum missus, nisi ad oves perditas domus Israel; et: non est auferre panem filiis et dare cum canibus, ne scilicet Christus Israelis videretur. Adv. Marc., iv. 7.

thus taunts his opponent, evidently under the impression that the two passages were in Luke, immediately after he had accused Marcion of having actually expunged from that Gospel, "as an interpolation,"[1] the saying that Christ had not come to destroy the law and the prophets, but to fulfil them,[2] which likewise never formed part of it. He repeats a similar charge on several other occasions.[3] Epiphanius commits the same mistake of reproaching Marcion with omitting from Luke what is only found in Matthew.[4] We have, in fact, no certain guarantee of the accuracy or trustworthiness of their statements.

We have said enough, we trust, to show that the sources for the reconstruction of a text of Marcion's Gospel are most unsatisfactory, and no one who attentively studies the analysis of Hahn, Ritschl, Volkmar, Hilgenfeld, and others, who have examined and systematized the data of the Fathers, can fail to be struck by the uncertainty which prevails throughout, the almost continuous vagueness and consequent opening, nay, necessity, for conjecture, and the absence of really sure indications. The Fathers had no intention of showing what Marcion's text actually was, and their object being solely dogmatic and not critical, their statements are very insufficient for the purpose.[5] The materials have had to be ingeniously collected and sifted from polemical writings whose authors, so far from professing to furnish them, were only bent upon seeking in Marcion's Gospel such points as could legitimately, or by sophistical skill, be used against him. Passing observations, general

---

[1] Hoc enim Marcion ut additum erasit. Adv. Mar., iv. 7.
[2] Matt. v. 17.   [3] Adv. Marc., iv. 9, 12; ii. 17, iv. 17, 36.
[4] Hær., xlii. p. 322 f., Ref. 1 ; cf. Luke v. 14 ; Matt. viii. 4.
[5] *Kirchhofer*, Quellensamml., p. 361, anm. 10, p. 362 f. ; anm. 15, 16, 17.

remarks, as well as direct statements, have too often been the only indications guiding the patient explorers and, in the absence of certain information, the silence of the angry Fathers has been made the basis for important conclusions. It is evident that not only is such a procedure necessarily uncertain and insecure, but that it rests upon assumptions with regard to the intelligence, care and accuracy of Tertullian and Epiphanius, which are not sufficiently justified by that part of their treatment of Marcion's text which we can examine and appreciate. And when all these doubtful landmarks have failed, too many passages have been left to the mere judgment of critics, as to whether they were too opposed to Marcion's system to have been retained by him, or too favourable to have been omitted. The reconstructed texts, as might be expected, differ from each other, and one Editor finds the results of his predecessors incomplete or unsatisfactory,[1] although naturally at each successive attempt, the materials previously collected and adopted have contributed to an apparently more complete result. After complaining of the incompleteness and uncertainty of the statements of Tertullian and Epiphanius, Ritschl affirms that they furnish so little solid material on which to base a hypothesis, that rather by means of a hypothesis must we determine the remains of the Gospel from Tertullian.[2] Hilgenfeld quotes this with approval, and adds, that at least Ritschl's opinion is so far right, that all the facts of the case can no longer be settled from external data, and that the general view regarding the

---

[1] *Ritschl*, Das Ev. Marcion's, p. 55 f. ; *Volkmar*, Das Ev. Marc., p. 5 f., p. 19 ff. ; *Hilgenfeld*, Die Evv. Justin's, p. 444 f., p. 394 f.; Theol. Jahrb., 1853, p. 194 f., p. 211 f.

[2] *Ritschl*, Das Evv. Marcion's, p. 55.

Gospel only can decide many points.¹ This means of course that hypothesis is to supply that which is wanting in the Fathers. Volkmar, in the introduction to his last comprehensive work on Marcion's Gospel, says: "And, in fact, it is no wonder that critics have for so long, and substantially to so little effect, fought over the protean question, for there has been so much uncertainty as to the very basis (Fundament) itself,—the precise text of the remarkable document,—that Baur has found full ground for rejecting, as unfounded, the supposition on which that finally-attained decision (his previous one) rested."² Critics of all shades of opinion are forced to admit the incompleteness of the materials for any certain reconstruction of Marcion's text and, consequently, for an absolute settlement of the question from internal evidence,³ although the labours of Volkmar and Hilgenfeld have materially increased our knowledge of the contents of his Gospel. We must contend, however, that, desirable and important as it is to ascertain as perfectly as possible the precise nature of Marcion's text, the question of its origin and relation to Luke would not by any means be settled even by its final reconstruction. There would, as we shall presently show, remain unsolved the problem of its place in that successive manipulation of materials by which a few Gospels gradually absorbed and displaced the rest. Our own synoptics

---

[1] *Hilgenfeld*, Die Evv. Justin's, p. 445.
[2] *Volkmar*, Das Ev. Marcion's, 1852, p. 19 f.
[3] *Bleek*, Einl. N. T., p. 126; *Hilgenfeld*, Theol. Jahrb., 1853, p. 194 ff., 211 ff.; *Holtzmann* in Bunsen's Bibelwerk, viii. p. 565; *Hug*, Einl. N. T., i. p. 58 ff., cf. *Hahn*, Das Ev. Marcion's, p. 114 f.; *Kirchhofer*, Quellensamml., p. 361, anm. 10; *Neudecker*, Einl. N. T., p. 75 ff.; *Reuss*, Rev. de Théol., 1857, p. 3; *Schwegler*, Das nachap. Zeitalter, i. p. 262 f.; *Tischendorf*, Wann wurden, u. s. w., p. 60 f.; *Volkmar*, Das Ev. Marcion's, 19 ff., 22 ff.

exhibit unmistakable traces of the process, and clearly forbid our lightly setting aside the claim of Marcion's Gospel to be considered a genuine work, and no mere falsification and abbreviation of Luke.

Before proceeding to a closer examination of Marcion's Gospel and the general evidence bearing upon it, it may be well here briefly to refer to the system of the Heresiarch whose high personal character exerted so powerful an influence upon his own time,[1] and whose views continued to prevail widely for a couple of centuries after his death. It was the misfortune of Marcion to live in an age when Christianity had passed out of the pure morality of its infancy, when, untroubled by complicated questions of dogma, simple faith and pious enthusiasm had been the one great bond of Christian brotherhood, into a phase of ecclesiastical development in which religion was fast degenerating into theology, and complicated doctrines were rapidly assuming that rampant attitude which led to so much bitterness, persecution, and schism. In later times Marcion might have been honoured as a reformer, in his own he was denounced as a heretic.[2] Austere and ascetic in his opinions, he aimed at superhuman purity, and although his clerical adversaries might scoff at his impracticable doctrines regarding marriage and the subjugation of the flesh, they have had their parallels amongst those whom the Church has since most delighted to honour; and at least the whole tendency of his system was markedly towards the side of virtue.[3] It would of course be foreign to our

---

[1] *Credner*, Beiträge, i. p. 40; *Schleiermacher*, Sämmtl. Werke, viii.; Einl. N. T., 1845, p. 64; *Westcott*, On the Canon, p. 272 f.

[2] Cf. *Neander*, Allg. K. G., 1843, ii. p. 792, 815 f.; *Schleiermacher*, Einl. N. T., 1845, p. 64.

[3] *Gfrörer*, Allg. K. G., i. p. 356 ff.; *Hagenbach*, K. G., 1869, i. p. 134 f.;

purpose to enter upon any detailed statement of its principles, and we must confine ourselves to such particulars only as are necessary to an understanding of the question before us.

As we have already frequently had occasion to mention, there were two broad parties in the primitive Church, and the very existence of Christianity was in one sense endangered by the national exclusiveness of the people amongst whom it originated. The one party considered Christianity a mere continuation of the Law, and dwarfed it into an Israelitish institution, a narrow sect of Judaism; the other represented the glad tidings as the introduction of a new system applicable to all and supplanting the Mosaic dispensation of the Law by a universal dispensation of grace. These two parties were popularly represented in the early Church by the Apostles Peter and Paul, and their antagonism is faintly revealed in the Epistle to the Galatians. Marcion, a gentile Christian, appreciating the true character of the new religion and its elevated spirituality, and profoundly impressed by the comparatively degraded and anthropomorphic features of Judaism, drew a very sharp line of demarcation between them, and represented Christianity as an entirely new and separate system abrogating the old and having absolutely no connection with it. Jesus was not to him the Messiah of the Jews, the son of David come permanently to establish the Law and the Prophets, but a divine being sent to reveal to man a wholly new spiritual religion, and a hitherto unknown God of goodness and grace. The Creator ($\Delta\eta\mu\iota\text{o}\nu\rho\gamma\text{ό}\varsigma$),

---

Hug, Einl. N. T., i. p. 56 ff.; *Milman*, Hist. of Chr., 1867, ii. p. 77 ff.; *Neander*, Allg. K. G., ii. p. 791 ff.; *Volkmar*, Das Ev. Marc., p. 25 ff.

the God of the Old Testament, was different from the God of grace who had sent Jesus to reveal the Truth, to bring reconciliation and salvation to all, and to abrogate the Jewish God of the World and of the Law, who was opposed to the God and Father of Jesus Christ as Matter is to Spirit, impurity to purity. Christianity was in distinct antagonism to Judaism, the Spiritual God of heaven, whose goodness and love were for the Universe, to the God of the World, whose chosen and peculiar people were the Jews, the Gospel of Grace to the dispensation of the Old Testament. Christianity, therefore, must be kept pure from the Judaistic elements humanly thrust into it, which were so essentially opposed to its whole spirit.

Marcion wrote a work called "Antitheses" ('Αντιθέσεις), in which he contrasted the old system with the new, the God of the one with the God of the other, the Law with the Gospel, and in this he maintained opinions which anticipated many held in our own time. Tertullian attacks this work in the first three books of his treatise against Marcion, and he enters upon the discussion of its details with true theological vigour: "Now, then, ye hounds, yelping at the God of truth, whom the Apostle casts out,[1] to all your questions! These are the bones of contention which ye gnaw!"[2] The poverty of the "Great African's" arguments keeps pace with his abuse. Marcion objected: If the God of the Old Testament be good, prescient of the future, and able to avert evil, why did he allow man, made in his own image, to be deceived

---

[1] Rev. xxii. 15.

[2] Jam hinc ad quæstiones omnes, canes, quos foras apostolus expellit, latrantes in deum veritatis. Hæc sunt argumentationum ossa, quæ obroditis. Adv. Marc., ii. 5.

by the devil, and to fall from obedience of the Law into sin and death?[1] How came the devil, the origin of lying and deceit, to be made at all?[2] After the fall, God became a judge both severe and cruel; woman is at once condemned to bring forth in sorrow and to serve her husband, changed from a help into a slave; the earth is cursed which before was blessed, and man is doomed to labour and to death.[3] The law was one of retaliation and not of justice,—lex talionis—eye for eye, tooth for tooth, stripe for stripe.[4] And it was not consistent, for in contravention of the Decalogue, God is made to instigate the Israelites to spoil the Egyptians, and fraudulently rob them of their gold and silver;[5] to incite them to work on the Sabbath by ordering them to carry the ark for eight days round Jericho;[6] to break the second commandment by making and setting up the brazen serpent and the golden cherubim.[7] Then God is inconstant, electing men, as Saul and Solomon, whom he subsequently rejects;[8] repenting that he had set up Saul, and that he had doomed the Ninevites,[9] and so on. God calls out: Adam, where art thou? inquires whether he had eaten the forbidden fruit; asks of Cain where his brother was, as if he had not yet heard the blood of Abel crying from the ground, and did not already know all these things.[10] Anticipating the results of modern criticism, Marcion denies the applicability to Jesus of the so-called Messianic prophecies. The Emmanuel of

---

[1] *Tertullian*, Adv. Marc., ii. 5; cf. 9. [2] *Ib.*, ii. 10.
[3] *Ib.*, ii. 11. [4] *Ib.*, ii. 18.
[5] *Ib.*, ii. 20. Tertullian introduces this by likening the Marcionites to the cuttle-fish, like which "they vomit the blackness of blasphemy" (tenebras blasphemiæ intervomunt), l. c.
[6] *Ib.*, ii. 21. [7] *Ib.*, ii. 22. [8] *Ib.*, ii. 23.
[9] *Ib.*, ii. 24. [10] *Ib.*, ii. 25.

Isaiah (vii. 14, cf. viii. 4) is not Christ;[1] the "Virgin" his mother is simply a "young woman" according to Jewish phraseology;[2] and the sufferings of the Servant of God (Isaiah lii. 13—liii. 9) are not predictions of the death of Jesus.[3] There is a complete severance between the Law and the Gospel, and the God of the latter is the Antithesis of that of the former.[4] "The one was perfect, pure, beneficent, passionless; the other, though not unjust by nature, infected by matter,—subject to all the passions of man,— cruel, changeable; the New Testament, especially as remodelled by Marcion,[5] was holy, wise, amiable; the Old Testament, the Law, barbarous, inhuman, contradictory, and detestable."[6]

Marcion ardently maintained the doctrine of the impurity of matter, and he carried it to its logical conclusion, both in speculation and practice. He, therefore, asserting the incredibility of an incarnate God, denied the corporeal reality of the flesh of Christ. His body was a mere semblance and not of human substance, was not born of a human mother, and the divine nature was not degraded by contact with the flesh.[7] Marcion finds in Paul the purest promulgator of the truth as he understands it, and emboldened by the Epistle to the Galatians, in which that Apostle rebukes even Apostles for "not walking uprightly according to the truth of the Gospel," he accuses the other Apostles of having depraved the pure form of the Gospel doctrines delivered to them by

---

[1] Adv. Marc., iii. 12. [2] Ib., iii. 13.
[3] Ib., iii. 17, 18. [4] Ib., iv. 1.
[5] We give this quotation as a *résumé* by an English historian and divine, but the idea of the "New Testament remodelled by Marcion," is a mere ecclesiastical imagination.
[6] *Milman*, Hist. of Christianity, 1867, ii. p. 77 f.
[7] *Tertullian*, Adv. Marc., iii. 8 ff.

Jesus,[1] "mixing up matters of the Law with the words of the Saviour."[2]

Tertullian reproaches Marcion with having written the work in which he details the contrasts between Judaism and Christianity, of which we have given the briefest sketch, as an introduction and encouragement to belief in his Gospel, which he ironically calls "the Gospel according to the Antitheses;"[3] and the charge which the Fathers bring against Marcion is that he laid violent hands on the Canonical Gospel of Luke, and manipulated it to suit his own views. "For certainly the whole object at which he laboured in drawing up the 'Antitheses,'" says Tertullian, "amounts to this: that he may prove a disagreement between the Old and New Testament, so that his own Christ may be separated from the Creator, as of another God, as alien from the Law and the Prophets. For this purpose it is certain that he has erased whatever was contrary to his own opinion and in harmony with the Creator, as if interpolated by his partisans, but has retained everything consistent with his own opinion."[4] The whole hypothesis that Marcion's Gospel is a mutilated version of our third Synoptic in fact rested upon this accusation. It is obvious that if it cannot be shown that Marcion's Gospel was our Canonical Gospel merely garbled by the Heresiarch for dogmatic reasons in the interest of his system,—for there could not be any other conceivable

---

[1] Adv. Marc., iv. 3.
[2] Apostolos enim admiscuisse ea quae sunt legalia salvatoris verbis. *Irenæus*, Adv. Hær., iii. 2, § 2; cf. iii. 12, § 12.   [3] Adv. Marc., iv. 1.
[4] Certe enim totum, quod elaboravit, etiam Antitheses præstruendo, in hoc cogit, ut veteris et novi testamenti diversitatem constituat, proinde Christum suum a creatore separaturus ut dei alterius, ut alienum legis et prophetarum. Certe propterea contraria quæque sententiæ suæ erasit, conspirantia cum creatore, quasi ab adsertoribus eius intexta; competentia autem sententiæ suæ reservavit. Adv. Marc., iv. 6.

reason for tampering with it,—the claim of Marcion's Gospel to the rank of a more original and authentic work than Luke's acquires double force. We must, therefore, inquire into the character of the variations between the so-called heretical, and the Canonical Gospels, and see how far the hypothesis of the Fathers accords with the contents of Marcion's Gospel so far as we are acquainted with it.

At the very outset we are met by the singular phenomenon, that both Tertullian and Epiphanius, who accuse Marcion of omitting everything which was unfavourable, and retaining only what was favourable to his views, undertake to refute him out of what remains in his Gospel. Tertullian says: "It will then be proved that he has shown the same defect of blindness of heresy both in that which he has erased and that which he has retained."[1] Epiphanius also confidently states that, out of that which Marcion has allowed to remain of the Gospel, he can prove his fraud and imposture, and thoroughly refute him.[2] Now if Marcion mutilated Luke to so little purpose as this, what was the use of his touching it at all? He is known as an able man, the most influential and distinguished of all the heretical leaders of the second century, and it seems unreasonable to suppose that, on the theory of his erasing or altering all that contradicted his system, he should have done his work so imperfectly.[3] The Fathers say that he endeavours to get rid of the contradictory passages which remain by a system of false interpretation; but surely he would not have allowed himself to be driven

---

[1] Tunc et illa constabit eodem vitio hæreticæ cæcitatis erasa, quo et hæc reservata. Adv. Marc., iv. 6.   [2] Hær., xlii. 9 f., p. 310 f.
Eichhorn, Einl. N. T., i. p. 75.

to this extremity, leaving weapons in the hands of his opponents, when he might so easily have excised the obnoxious texts along with the rest? It is admitted by critics, moreover, that passages said to have been omitted by Marcion are often not opposed to his system at all, and sometimes, indeed, even in favour of it;[1] and on the other hand, that passages which were retained are contradictory to his views.[2] This is not intelligible upon any theory of arbitrary garbling of a Gospel in the interest of a system.

It may be well to give a few instances of the anomalies presented, upon this hypothesis, by Marcion's text. Some critics believe that the verses Luke vii. 29—35, were wanting in Marcion's Gospel.[3] Hahn accounts for the omission of verses 29, 30, regarding the baptism of John, because they represented the relation of the Baptist to Jesus in a way which Marcion did not admit.[4] But as he allowed the preceding verses to remain, such a proceeding was absurd. In verse 26 he calls John a prophet, and much more than a prophet, and in the next verse (27) quotes respecting him the words of

---

[1] *Baur*, Unters. kan. Evv., p. 423 ff.; *Hilgenfeld*, Die Evv. Just., p. 444 ff.; *Nicolas*, Et. sur les Ev. Apocr., p. 151; *Ritschl*, Theol. Jahrb., 1851, p. 529 f.; *Schwegler*, Das nachap. Zeit., i. p. 263 ff., 273 ff.; *De Wette*, Einl. N. T., p. 132; *Volkmar*, Das Ev. Marcion's, p. 74 ff., p. 107 ff., p. 175 f.; cf. Theol. Jahrb., 1850, p. 214 f.

[2] *Baur*, Unters. kan. Evv., p. 423 ff.; *Eichhorn*, Einl. N. T., i. p. 75 ff.; *Guericke*, Gesammtgesch. N. T., p. 231, anm. 1; *Hilgenfeld*, Die Evv. J., p. 444 ff.; *Kirchhofer*, Quellensamml., p. 362, anm. 13; *Neander*, Allg. K. G., ii. p. 816; *Nicolas*, Et. sur les Ev. Apocr., p. 151 ff.; *Ritschl*, Theol. Jahrb., 1851, p. 529 f.; *Schwegler*, Das nachap. Zeit., i. p. 263 ff., 273 ff.; *Volkmar*, Das Ev. Marcion's, p. 107 ff.

[3] Tertullian and Epiphanius pass them over in silence. Cf. *Hahn*, Ev. Marc. in *Thilo*, Cod. Apocr. N. T., p. 418, anm. 24; *Ritschl*, Das Ev. Marc., p. 78 f.; *De Wette*, Einl. N. T., p. 125. *Volkmar* (Das Ev. Marc., p. 156 f.) and *Hilgenfeld* (Die Evv. Justin's, p. 407; cf. 441) retain them.   [4] Das Ev. Marc., p. 147.

Malachi iii. 1: "This is he of whom it is written: Behold I send my messenger before thy face, which shall prepare thy way before thee." It is impossible on any reasonable ground to account for the retention of such honourable mention of the Baptist, if verses 29, 30 were erased for such dogmatic reasons.[1] Still more incomprehensible on such a hypothesis is the omission of Luke vii. 31—35, where that generation is likened unto children playing in the market-place and calling to each other: "We piped unto you and ye danced not," and Jesus continues: "For John is come neither eating bread nor drinking wine; and ye say, He hath a devil (34). The Son of Man is come, eating and drinking; and ye say: Behold a gluttonous man and a winebibber, a friend of publicans and sinners." Hahn attributes the omission of these verses to the sensuous representation they give of Jesus as eating and drinking.[2] What was the use of eliminating these verses when he allowed to remain unaltered verse 36 of the same chapter,[3] in which Jesus is invited to eat with the Pharisee, and goes into his house and sits down to meat? or v. 29—35,[4] in which Jesus accepts the feast of Levi, and defends his disciples for eating and drinking against the murmurs of the Scribes and Pharisees? or xv. 2,[5]

---

[1] *Ritschl*, Das Ev. Marc., p. 78 f.; *Schwegler*, Das nachap. Zeitalter, i. p. 263; *De Wette*, Einl. N. T., p. 132. Cf. *Volkmar*, Das Ev. Marcion's, p. 156; *Hilgenfeld*, Die Evv. Justin's, p. 406 f.; *Tertullian*, Adv. Marc., iv. 18; *Epiphanius*, Hær., xlii., Sch. viii. f.; Ref. viii. f.

[2] Das Ev. M., p. 147 f.; Evang. Marc. in *Thilo*, Cod. ap. N. T., p. 418, anm. 24; *Ritschl*, Das Ev. Marc, p. 78 f. Cf. *Volkmar*, Das Ev. Marc., p. 156; *Hilgenfeld*, Die Evv. Justin's, p. 407.

[3] *Hahn*, Evang. Marc. *Thilo*, p. 418, 419, anm. 25; *Volkmar*, Das Ev. Marc., p. 157.

[4] *Hahn*, Ev. Marc. in *Thilo*, p. 408; *Volkmar*, Das Ev. Marc., p. 155; *Tertullian*, Adv. Marc., iv. 11.

[5] *Hahn*, Ev. M. in *Thilo*, p. 451; *Volkmar*, Das Ev. Marc., p. 162; cf. *Tertullian*, Adv. M., iv. 32.

where the Pharisees say of him: "This man receiveth sinners and eateth with them?" How absurdly futile the omission of the one passage for dogmatic reasons, while so many others were allowed to remain unaltered.[1]

The next passage to which we must refer is one of the most important in connection with Marcion's Docetic doctrine of the person of Jesus. It is said that he omitted viii. 19: "And his mother and his brethren came to him and could not come at him for the crowd," and that he inserted in verse 21, τίς μου μήτηρ καὶ οἱ ἀδελφοί; making the whole episode in his Gospel read (20): "And it was told him by certain which said: Thy mother and thy brethren stand without desiring to see thee: 21. But he answered and said unto them: Who are my mother and brethren? My mother and my brethren are these," &c.[2] The omission of verse 19 is said to have been made because, according to Marcion, Christ was not born like an ordinary man, and consequently had neither mother nor brethren.[3] The mere fact, however, that Marcion retains verse 20, in which the crowd simply state as a matter fully recognized, the relationship of those who were seeking Jesus, renders the omission of the preceding verse useless,[4] except on the ground of mere redundancy.

Marcion is reported not to have had the word αἰώνιον in x. 25,[5] so that the question of the lawyer simply ran:

[1] *Schwegler*, Das nachap. Zeit., i. p. 263; *De Wette*, Einl. N. T., p. 132.

[2] *Epiph.*, Hær., xlii., Sch. 12; *Tertullian*, Adv. Marc., iv. 19, de carne Christi, § 7. *Hahn*, Ev. M. in *Thilo*, p. 421, anm. 26; *Volkmar*, Das Ev. Marc., p. 150; *De Wette*, Einl. N. T., p. 125; *Hilgenfeld*, Die Evv. Justin's, p. 408 f., 441; *Baur*, Das Markusev., p. 192 f.

[3] *Hahn*, Das Ev. M., p. 148 f.; Ev. M. in *Thilo*, p. 421, anm. 26; cf. *Volkmar*, Das Ev. M., p. 56 f. [4] *Schwegler*, Das nachap. Zeit., i. p. 264.

[5] *Hahn*, Ev. M. in *Thilo*, p. 434; *Volkmar*, Das Ev. M., p. 57 f.; *Hilgenfeld*, Die Evv. J., p. 441; *De Wette*, Einl. N. T., p. 126.

"Master, what shall I do to inherit life?" The omission of this word is supposed to have been made in order to make the passage refer back to the God of the Old Testament, who promises merely long life on earth for keeping the commandments, whilst it is only in the Gospel that *eternal* life is promised.[1] But in the corresponding passage, xviii. 18,[2] the αἰώνιον is retained, and the question of the ruler is: "Good master, what shall I do to inherit eternal life?" It has been argued that the introduction of the one thing still lacking (verse 22) after the keeping of the law and the injunction to sell all and give to the poor, changes the context, and justifies the use there of *eternal* life as the reward for fulfilment of the higher commandment.[3] This reasoning, however, seems to us without grounds, and merely an ingenious attempt to account for an embarrassing fact. In reality the very same context occurs in the other passage, for, explaining the meaning of the word "neighbour," love to whom is enjoined as part of the way to obtain "life," Jesus inculcates the very same duty as in xviii. 22, of distributing to the poor (cf. x. 28—37). There seems, therefore, no reasonable motive for omitting the word from the one passage whilst retaining it in the other.[4]

The passage in Luke xi. 29—32, from the concluding words of verse 29, "but the sign of the prophet Jonah"

---

[1] *Hahn*, Das Ev. M., p. 161; Ev. M. in *Thilo*, p. 435, an. 42; *Volkmar*, Das Ev. M., p. 58, p. 159; *Tertullian*, Adv. M. iv. 25; *Baur*, Das Markusev., p. 193.

[2] *Hahn*, Ev. M. in *Thilo*, p. 461; *Epiph.*, Hær., xlii. Sch. 50; *Tertullian*, Adv. M. iv. 36.

[3] *Volkmar*, Das Ev. M., p. 58; *Hilgenfeld*, Die Evv. Just., p. 426; *Baur*, Das Markusev., p. 193.

[4] *Schwegler*, Das nachap. Zeit., i. p. 264.

was not found in Marcion's Gospel.[1] This omission is accounted for on the ground that such a respectful reference to the Old Testament was quite contrary to the system of Marcion.[2] Verses 49—51 of the same chapter, containing the saying of the "Wisdom of God," regarding the sending of the prophets that the Jews might slay them, and their blood be required of that generation, were also omitted.[3] The reason given for this omission is, that the words of the God of the Old Testament are too respectfully quoted and adopted to suit the views of the Heretic.[4] The words in verses 31—32, "And a greater than Solomon—than Jonah is here," might well have been allowed to remain in the text, for the superiority of Christ over the kings and prophets of the Old Testament which is asserted directly suits and supports the system of Marcion. How much less, however, is the omission of these passages to be explained upon any intelligent dogmatic principle, when we find in Marcion's text the passage in which Jesus justifies his conduct on the Sabbath by the example of David (vi. 3—4),[5] and that in which he assures the disciples of the greatness of their reward in heaven for the persecutions they were to endure:

---

[1] *Hahn*, Ev. M. in *Thilo*, 438, anm. 46; *Volkmar*, Das Ev. M., p. 151; *De Wette*, Einl. N. T., p. 126; *Hilgenfeld*, Die Evv. J., p. 441; *Epiph.*, Hær., xlii. Sch. 25; cf. Ref. It is conjectured that the words πονηρά ἐστι were also wanting. Epiphanius does not use them, but he is thought to be quoting "freely." The words, however, equally fail in Codex 235.

[2] *Hahn*, Das Ev. M., p. 163 f.; *Volkmar*, Das Ev. M., p. 58; *Baur*, Das Markusev., p. 194.

[3] *Hahn*, Das Ev. M. in *Thilo*, 439, anm. 47; *Volkmar*, Das Ev. M., p. 151.

[4] *Hahn*, Das Ev. M., p. 165; Ev. M. in *Thilo*, 440, anm. 47; *Volkmar*, Das Ev. M., p. 58 f.

[5] *Hahn*, Ev. M. in *Thilo*, 410; *Volkmar*, Das Ev. M., 155.

"For behold your reward is great in heaven: for after the same manner did their fathers unto the prophets" (vi. 23).[1] As we have seen, Jesus is also allowed to quote an Old Testament prophecy (vii. 27) as fulfilled in the coming of John to prepare the way for himself. The questions which Jesus puts to the Scribes (xx. 41—44) regarding the Christ being David's son, with the quotation from Ps. cx. 1, which Marcion is stated to have retained,[2] equally refute the supposition as to his motive for "omitting" xi. 29 ff. It has been argued with regard to the last passage that Jesus merely uses the words of the Old Testament to meet his own theory,[3] but the dilemma in which Jesus places the Scribes is clearly not the real object of his question: its aim is a suggestion of the true character of the Christ. But amongst his other sins with regard to Luke's Gospel, Marcion is also accused of interpolating it. And in what way? Why the Heresiarch, who is so averse to all references to the Old Testament that he is supposed to erase them, actually, amongst his few interpolations, adds a reference to the Old Testament. Between xvii. 14 and 15 (some critics say in verse 18) Marcion introduced the verse which is found in Luke iv. 27: "And many lepers were in Israel in the time of Elisha the prophet; and none of them was cleansed saving Naaman, the Syrian."[4] Now is it conceivable that a man who inserts, as it is said, references to the

---

[1] *Hahn*, Ev. M. in *Thilo*, 412; *Volkmar*, Das Ev. M. 156.
[2] *Hahn*, in *Thilo*, 468; *Volkmar*, ib., p. 165.
[3] *Volkmar*, ib., p. 59 f.; *Hilgenfeld*, Die Ev. J., p. 453.
[4] *Epiph.*, Hær., xlii. Sch. 48; *Tertullian*, Adv. M., iv. 35. *Baur*, Das Markusev., p. 213; *Eichhorn*, Einl. N. T., p. 77; *Hahn*, Ev. M. in *Thilo*, p. 457, anm. 67; *Hilgenfeld*, Die Evv. J., p. 424 f.; *Volkmar*, Theol. Jahrb., 1850, p. 131; Das Ev. M., p. 163, p. 82 ff.; *De Wette*, Einl. N. T., p. 128 f.

Old Testament into his text so gratuitously, can have been so inconsistent as to have omitted these passages because they contain similar references? We must say that the whole of the reasoning regarding these passages omitted and retained, and the fine distinctions which are drawn between them, are anything but convincing. A general theory being adopted, nothing is more easy than to harmonise everything with it in this way; nothing is more easy than to assign some reason, good or bad, apparently in accordance with the foregone conclusion, why one passage was retained, and why another was omitted, but in almost every case the reasoning might with equal propriety be reversed if the passages were so, and the retention of the omitted passage as well as the omission of that retained be quite as reasonably justified. The critics who have examined Marcion's Gospel do not trouble themselves to inquire if the general connection of the text be improved by the absence of passages supposed to be omitted, but simply try whether the supposed omissions are explainable on the ground of a dogmatic tendency in Marcion. In fact, the argument throughout is based upon foregone conclusions, and rarely upon any solid grounds whatever. The retention of such passages as we have quoted above renders the omission of the other for dogmatic reasons quite purposeless.[1]

The passage, xii. 6, 7, which argues that as the sparrows are not forgotten before God, and the hairs of our head are numbered, the disciples need not fear, was not found in Marcion's Gospel.[2] The supposed omission

---

[1] *Schwegler*, Das nachap. Zeit., p. 264; *Ritschl*, Das. Ev. M., p. 87 f.
[2] *Hahn*, Ev. M. in *Thilo*, p. 441; *Volkmar*, Das Ev. M., p. 151, cf. 94; *Hilgenfeld*, Die Evv. J., p. 441; Theol. Jahrb., 1853, p. 204.

is explained on the ground that, according to Marcion's system, God does not interest himself about such trifles as sparrows and the hairs of our head, but merely about souls.[1] That such reasoning is arbitrary, however, is apparent from the fact, that Marcion's text had verse 24 of the same chapter:[2] "Consider the ravens," &c., &c., and "God feedeth them:" &c., and also v. 28,[3] "But if God so clothe the grass," &c., &c., "how much more will he clothe you, O! ye of little faith?" As no one ventures to argue that Marcion limited the providence of God to the ravens, and to the grass, but excluded the sparrows and the hair, no dogmatic reason can be assigned for the omission of the one, whilst the other is retained.[4]

The first nine verses of ch. xiii. were likewise absent from Marcion's text,[5] wherein Jesus declares that like the Galilæans, whose blood Pilate had mixed with their sacrifices (v. 1, 2), and the eighteen upon whom the tower in Siloam fell (v. 4), "except ye repent, ye shall all likewise perish," (v. 3 and 5), and then recites the parable of the unfruitful fig-tree (v. 6—9), which the master of the vineyard orders to be cut down (v. 7), but then spares for a season (v. 8, 9). The theory advanced to account for the asserted "omission" of these

---

[1] *Hahn*, Das Ev. M., p. 167; Ev. M. in *Thilo*, p. 441, anm. 49.
[2] *Hahn*, Ev. M. in *Thilo*, p. 442.
[3] *Hahn*, Ev. M. in *Thilo*, p. 443, anm. 51; *Volkmar*, Das Ev. M., p. 160; *De Wette*, Einl. N. T., p. 127. This verse was wanting according to *Epiph.*, Sch., 31, but was in the text by the decided statement of *Tertullian*, Adv. M., iv. 29; *Volkmar* (Das Ev. M., 46 ff.), and *Hilgenfeld* (Theol. Jahrb., 1853, p. 204), agree that this arose solely from an accidental absence of the verse in the copy of Epiphanius.
[4] *Schwegler*, Das nachap. Zeit., i. p. 265; *Ritschl*, Das Ev. M., p. 91; cf. *De Wette*, Einl. N. T., p. 132.
[5] *Hahn*, Ev. M. in *Thilo*, p. 446; *Volkmar*, Das Ev. M., p. 151. (He omits xiii. 1—10); *Hilgenfeld*, Theol. Jahrb., 1853, p. 204. (He had previously,—Die Ev. J., p. 441,—only admitted the absence of xiii. 1—5.) *De Wette*, Einl. N. T., i. p. 127 f.

verses is that they could not be reconciled with Marcion's system, according to which the good God never positively punishes the wicked, but merely leaves them to punish themselves in that, by not accepting the proffered grace, they have no part in the blessedness of Christians.[1] In his earlier work, Volkmar distinctly admitted that the whole of this passage might be omitted without prejudice to the text of Luke, and that he could not state any ground, in connection with Marcion's system, which rendered its omission either necessary or even conceivable. He then decided that the passage was not contained at all in the version of Luke, which Marcion possessed, but was inserted at a later period in our Codices.[2] It was only on his second attempt to account for all omissions on dogmatic grounds that he argued as above. In like manner Hilgenfeld also, with Rettig, considered that the passage did not form part of the original Luke, so that here again Marcion's text was free from a very abrupt passage, not belonging to the more pure and primitive Gospel.[3] Baur recognizes not only that there is no dogmatic ground to explain the omission, but on the contrary, that the passage fully agrees with the system of Marcion.[4] The total insufficiency of the argument to explain the omission, however, is apparent from the numerous passages, which were allowed to remain in the text, which still more clearly outraged this part of Marcion's system. In the parable of the great supper, xiv. 15—24, the Lord is angry (v. 21), and declares that none of those who were

---

[1] *Hahn*, Das Ev. M., p. 175; Ev. M. in *Thilo*, p. 446, anm. 55; *Volkmar*, Das Ev. M., p. 64 f.

[2] Theol. Jahrb., 1850, p. 207 f.

[3] Die Ev. J., p. 470.

[4] Das Markusev., p. 195 f.

bidden should taste of his supper (v. 24). In xii. 5, Jesus warns his own disciples: "Fear him, which after he hath killed hath power to cast into hell; yea, I say unto you: fear him." It is not permissible to argue that Marcion here understands the God of the Old Testament, the Creator, for he would thus represent his Christ as forewarning his own disciples to fear the power of that very Demiurge, whose reign he had come to terminate. Then again, in the parable of the wise steward, and the foolish servants, xii. 41 ff, he declares (v. 46), that the lord of the foolish servant "will cut him in sunder, and will appoint him his portion with the unbelievers," and (vs. 47, 48) that the servants shall be beaten with stripes, in proportion to their fault. In the parable of the nobleman who goes to a far country and leaves the ten pounds with his servants, xix. 11 ff, the lord orders his enemies, who would not that he should reign over them, to be brought and slain before him (v. 27). Then, how very much there was in the Epistles of Paul, which he upheld, of a still more contradictory character. There is no dogmatic reason for such inconsistency.[1]

Marcion is accused of having falsified xiii. 28 in the following manner: "There shall be weeping and gnashing of teeth, when ye shall see *all the just* (πάντας τοὺς δικαίους) in the kingdom of God, but you yourselves being thrust, *and bound* (καὶ κρατουμένους) without." The substitution of "all the just" for "Abraham, Isaac, and Jacob, and all the prophets," is one of those variations which the supporter of the dogmatic theory greedily lays hold of, as bearing evident tokens of falsification in anti-judaistic interest.[2] But Marcion had in his Gospel

[1] *Schwegler*, Das nachap. Zeit., i. p. 265; *Baur*, Das Markusev. p. 195.
[2] *Hahn*, Das Ev. M., p. 177; Ev. M. in *Thilo*, p. 448, anm. 58; cf.

the parable of the rich man and Lazarus, xvi. 19—31, where the beggar is carried up into Abraham's bosom.[1] And again, there was the account of the Transfiguration, ix. 28—36, in which Moses and Elias are seen in converse with Jesus.[2] The alteration of the one passage for dogmatic reasons, whilst the parable of Lazarus is retained, would have been useless. Hilgenfeld, however, in agreement with Baur and Ritschl, has shown that Marcion's reading πάντας τοὺς δικαίους is evidently the contrast to the ἐργάται τῆς ἀδικίας of the preceding verse, and is superior to the canonical version, which was either altered after Matth. viii. 12, or with the anti-Marcionitish object of bringing the rejected Patriarchs into recognition.[3] The whole theory in this case again goes into thin air, and it is consequently weakened in every other.

Marcion's Gospel did not contain the parable of the Prodigal Son, xv. 11—23.[4] The omission of this passage,

---

Volkmar (Das Ev. M., p. 62 f.), and *Hilgenfeld* (Die Evv. J., p. 420), who explain the omission differently, and consider Hahn in error.

[1] *Tertullian* (Adv. M., iv. 34), gives an elaborate explanation of the interpretation by which Marcion does away with the offensive part of the parable, but in this and every case erasure was surely more simple than explanation if Marcion erased anything at all.

[2] *Hahn*, in verse 30 reads συνέστησαν for συνελάλουν, the two men "stood" with him instead of "talked" with him, as in Luke. This he derives from the obscure words of Tertullian, which, however, really refer to v. 32 (Adv. M. iv. 22), but *Epiphanius* (Sch. 17) has very distinctly the reading of Luke. Hahn omits v. 31 altogether, on the very undecided evidence of Tertullian and Epiphanius; *Hahn*, Ev. M. in *Thilo*, p. 427, anm. *; Das Ev. M., p. 154; *Volkmar* (Das Ev. Marc., p. 158, cf. 151), and *Hilgenfeld* (Die Evv. J., p. 411 f., 466 f.), prove that the reading was unaltered in v. 30, and that v. 31 stood in Marcion's text. The whole discussion, as showing the uncertainty of the text, is very instructive. Cf. *Ritschl*, Das Ev. M., p. 80 ff.

[3] *Hilgenfeld*, Die Evv. J., p. 470; *Baur*, Das Markusev., p. 206 f.; *Ritschl*, Das Ev. M., p. 94 f.

[4] *Hahn*, Ev. M. in *Thilo*, p. 452; *Volkmar*, Das Ev. M., p. 162; *Hilgenfeld*, Die Evv. J., p. 441; *De Wette*, Einl. N. T., p. 128: *Epiphanius*,

which is universally recognized as in the purest Paulinian spirit, is accounted for partly on the ground that a portion of it (v. 22—32) was repugnant to the ascetic discipline of Marcion, to whom the killing of the fatted calf, the feasting, dancing and merry-making, must have been obnoxious, and, partly because, understanding under the similitude of the elder son the Jews, and of the younger son the Gentiles, the identity of the God of the Jews and of the Christians would be recognized.[1] There is, however, the very greatest doubt admitted as to the interpretation which Marcion would be likely to put upon this parable, and certainly the representation which it gives of the Gentiles, not only as received completely on a par with the Jews, but as only having been lost for a time, and found again, is thoroughly in harmony with the teaching of Paul, who was held by Marcion to be the only true Apostle. It could not, therefore, have been repugnant to him. Any points of disagreement could very easily have been explained away, as his critics are so fond of asserting to be his practice in other passages.[2] As to the supposed dislike of Marcion for the festive character of the parable, what object could he have had for omitting this, when he retained the parable of the

Hær., xlii. Sch. 42. *Tertullian* (Adv. Marc., iv. 32) passes it over in silence.

[1] *Hahn*, Das. Ev. M., p. 182; Ev. M. in *Thilo*, p. 452, anm. 62; *Olshausen*, Echtheit d. vier Can. Evv., 1823, p. 208 f. Hahn and Olshausen did not hold the second part of this explanation, but applied the parable merely to Judaic and Gentile Christians, under which circumstances critics would not admit reason for the omission. *Volkmar*, Das Ev. M., p. 66; *Baur*, Das Markusev., p. 194 f.

[2] *Volkmar* talks of the intentional omission of the parable by Marcion as being "fully conceivable" (völlig begreiflich), but it is almost impossible to find anything for which a reason cannot be discovered if the question asked be: "Is the intentional omission on any ground conceivable?"

great supper, xiv. 15—24; the feast in the house of Levi, v. 27—32; the statements of Jesus eating with the Pharisees, vii. 36, xv. 2? If Marcion had any objection to such matters, he had still greater to marriage, and yet Jesus justifies his disciples for eating and drinking by the similitude of a marriage feast, himself being the bridegroom: v. 34, 35, "Can ye make the sons of the bridechamber fast, while the bridegroom is with them? But the days will come when the bridegroom shall be taken away from them: then will they fast in those days." And he bids his disciples to be ready "like men that wait for their lord, when he shall return from the wedding," (xii. 36), and makes another parable on a wedding feast (xiv. 7—10). Leaving these passages, it is impossible to see any dogmatic reason for excluding the others.[1]

The omission of a passage in every way so suitable to Marcion's system as the parable of the vineyard, xx. 9—16, is equally unintelligible upon the dogmatic theory.

Marcion is accused of falsifying xvi. 17, by altering τοῦ νόμου to τῶν λόγων μου,[2] making the passage read: "But it is easier for heaven and earth to pass, than for one tittle of my words to fail." The words in the canonical Gospel, it is argued, were too repugnant to him to be allowed to remain unaltered, representing as they do the permanency of "the Law" to which he was opposed.[3] Upon this hypothesis, why did he leave

---

[1] *Schwegler*, Das nachap. Zeitalter, i. p. 266 f.; *Nicolas*, Et. sur les Ev. apocr., p. 153; cf. *Hilgenfeld*, Die Evv. J., p. 454.

[2] *Volkmar*, Das Ev. M., p. 151; *Hilgenfeld*, Die Evv. J., p. 441; *Hahn*, reads τῶν λόγων τοῦ κυρίου. Ev. M. in *Thilo*, p. 454; Das Ev. M., p. 185.

[3] *Hahn*, Ev. M. in *Thilo*, p. 454, anm. 63; Das Ev. M., p. 185; *Volkmar*, Das Ev. M., p. 65 f.

x. 25 f. (especially v. 26) and xviii. 18 ff, in which the keeping of the law is made essential to life? or xvii. 14, where Jesus bids the lepers conform to the requirements of the law? or xvi. 29, where the answer is given to the rich man pleading for his relatives: "They have Moses and the prophets, let them hear them"?[1] Hilgenfeld, however, with others, points out that it has been fully proved that the reading in Marcion's text is not an arbitrary alteration at all, but the original expression, and that the version in Luke xvi. 17, on the contrary, is a variation of the original introduced to give the passage an anti-Marcionitish tendency.[2] Here, again, it is clear that the supposed falsification is rather a falsification on the part of the editor of the third canonical Gospel.[3]

One more illustration may be given. Marcion is accused of omitting from xix. 9 the words: "forasmuch as he also is a son of Abraham," ($\kappa\alpha\theta\acute{o}\tau\iota$ $\kappa\alpha\grave{\iota}$ $\alpha\grave{\upsilon}\tau\grave{o}\varsigma$ $\upsilon\acute{\iota}\grave{o}\varsigma$ $\vphantom{x}^{\prime}A\beta\rho\alpha\acute{\alpha}\mu$ $\dot{\epsilon}\sigma\tau\iota\nu$) leaving merely: "And Jesus said unto him: This day is salvation come to this house."[4] Marcion's system, it is said, could not tolerate the phrase which was erased.[5] It was one, however, eminently in the spirit of his Apostle Paul, and in his favourite Epistle to the Galatians he retained the very parallel

---

[1] *Schwegler*, Das nachap. Zeit., i. p. 267; *Eichhorn*, Einl. N. T., i. p. 75.

[2] *Hilgenfeld*, Die Ev. J., p. 470; *Ritschl*, Das Ev. M., p. 97 f.; *Baur*, Unters. kan. Evv., p. 402; Das Markusev., p. 196 ff. *Baur*, in the last-mentioned work, argues that even Tertullian himself (Adv. M., iv. 33), represents Marcion's reading as the original.

[3] *Ritschl*, Das Ev. M., p. 98.

[4] *Hahn*, Ev. M. in *Thilo*, p. 463; *Volkmar*, Das Ev. M., p. 152; *Hilgenfeld*, Die Evv. J., p. 442.

[5] *Hahn*, Das Ev. M., p. 195; Ev. M. in *Thilo*, p. 463, anm. 74. "Quæ non potuit ferre Marcion, cujus Christus potius servavit eum quem filii Abrahami damnabant."

passage iii. 7, "Ye know, therefore, that they which are of faith, these are the sons of Abraham."[1] How could he, therefore, find any difficulty in such words addressed to the repentant Zacchæus, who had just believed in the mission of Christ? Moreover, why should he have erased the words here, and left them standing in xiii. 16, in regard to the woman healed of the "spirit of infirmity:" "and ought not this woman, *being a daughter of Abraham*, whom Satan hath bound, lo! these eighteen years, to be loosed from this bond on the Sabbath day?" No reasoning can explain away the substantial identity of the two phrases. Upon what principle of dogmatic interest, then, can Marcion have erased the one while he retained the other?[2]

We have taken a very few passages for illustration, and treated them very briefly, but it may roundly be said that there is scarcely a single variation of Marcion's text regarding which similar reasons are not given, and which do not present similar anomalies in consequence of what has elsewhere been retained.[3] As we have already stated, much that is really contradictory to Marcion's system was found in his text, and much which either is not opposed or is favourable to it is omitted

---

[1] Cf. Rom. iv. 11, 12, 16. It has been argued from Tertullian's obscure reference that Marcion omitted the last phrase of Gal. iii. 7, but *Epiph.* does not say so, and the statement of Jerome (*Comm. in Ep. ad Gal.*) was evidently not from the direct source, but was probably derived from a hasty perusal of Tertullian, and there is no real ground whatever for affirming it. Even Tertullian himself does not positively do so. *Ritschl*, Das Ev. M., p. 154 ff.; *Baur*, Unters. kan. Evv., p. 412 ff.; *Westcott*, On the Canon, p. 274.

[2] *Schwegler*, Das nachap. Zeit., i. p. 268; *Ritschl*, Das Ev. M., p. 98 f.; cf. *Hilgenfeld*, Die Evv. J., p. 427.

[3] *Baur*, Unters. kan. Evv., p. 411 ff.; Das Markusev., p. 191 f.; *Nicolas*, Et. sur les Ev. apocr., p. 155; *Ritschl*, Theol. Jahrb., 1851, p. 530 ff.; cf. Das Ev. M., p. 46. Cf. *Westcott*, On the Canon, p. 274 f.

and cannot be set down to arbitrary alteration. Moreover, it has never been shown that the supposed alterations were made by Marcion himself,[1] and till this is done the pith of the whole theory is wanting. There is no principle of intelligent motive which can account for the anomalies presented by Marcion's Gospel, considered as a version of Luke mutilated and falsified in the interest of his system. The contrast of what is retained with that which is omitted reduces the hypothesis *ad absurdum*. Marcion was too able a man to do his work so imperfectly, if he had proposed to assimilate the Gospel of Luke to his own views. As it is avowedly necessary to explain away by false and forced interpretations requiring intricate definitions[2] very much of what was allowed to remain in his text, it is inconceivable that he should not have cut the Gordian knot with the same unscrupulous knife with which it is asserted he excised the rest. The ingenuity of most able and learned critics endeavouring to discover whether a motive in the interest of his system cannot be conceived for every alteration is, notwithstanding the evident scope afforded by the procedure, often foiled. Yet a more elastic hypothesis could not possibly have been advanced, and that the text obstinately refuses to fit into it, is even more than could have been expected. Marcion is like a prisoner at the bar without witnesses, who is treated from the first as guilty, attacked by able and passionate adversaries who warp every possible circumstance against him, and yet who cannot be convicted. The foregone conclusion by which every supposed omission from his Gospel is explained, is, as we have shown, almost in

---

[1] *Westcott*, On the Canon, p. 274.
[2] *Hilgenfeld*, Die Evv. J., p. 443 f.

every case contradicted by passages which have been allowed to remain, and this is rendered more significant by the fact, which is generally admitted, that Marcion's text contains many readings which are manifestly superior to, and more original than, the form in which the passages stand in our third Synoptic.[1] The only one of these to which we shall refer is the interesting variation from the passage in Luke xi. 2, in the substitution of a prayer for the Holy Spirit for the "hallowed be thy name,"—ἐλθέτω τὸ ἅγιον πνεῦμά σου ἐφ᾽ ἡμᾶς instead of ἁγιασθήτω τὸ ὄνομά σου. The former is recognized to be the true original reading. This phrase is evidently referred to in v. 13. We are, therefore, indebted to Marcion for the correct version of "the Lord's Prayer."[2]

There can be no doubt that Marcion's Gospel bore great analogy to our Luke, although it was very considerably shorter. It is, however, unnecessary to repeat that there were many Gospels in the second century which, although nearly related to those which have become canonical, were independent works, and the most favourable interpretation which can be given of the relationship between our three Synoptics leaves them very much in a line with Marcion's work. His Gospel was chiefly distinguished

---

[1] *Anger*, Synops. Ev. Proleg., p. xxv. ff.; *Baur*, Das Markusev., p. 195 ff., p. 223 ff.; *Bertholdt*, Einl., 1813, iii. p. 1294 ff.; *Eichhorn*, Einl. N. T., i. p. 72 ff.; *Hilgenfeld*, Die Evv. J., p. 473; Theol. Jahrb., 1853, p. 222 ff.; Die Evangelien, p. 30; *Köstlin*, Der Urspr. synopt. Evv., p. 303; *Michaelis*, Einl. N. T., 1788, i. p. 40, p. 342 f., p. 751; *Reuss*, Rev. de Théol., 1857, p. 4; *Ritschl*, Theol. Jahrb., 1851, p. 530 ff.; Das Ev. M., p. 46; *Volkmar*, Das Ev. M., p. 187—199, p. 256 f.; Der Ursprung, p. 75; *De Wette*, Einl. N. T., p. 132 ff.; *Zeller*, Die Apostelgesch., p. 13 ff., p. 23 ff. Cf. *Westcott*, On the Canon, p. 275.

[2] *Ritschl*, Das Ev. M., p. 71; *Baur*, Das Markusev., p. 207; *Volkmar*, Das Ev. M., p. 197 f., p. 256 f.; Der Ursprung, p. 75; *Hilgenfeld*, Die Evv. J., p. 441, p. 415 f. Cf. *Tertullian*, Adv. Marc., iv. 26.

by a shorter text,[1] but besides large and important omissions there are a few additions,[2] and very many variations of text. The whole of the first two chapters of Luke, as well as all the third, was wanting, with the exception of part of the first verse of the third chapter, which, joined to iv. 31, formed the commencement of the Gospel. Of chapter iv. verses 1—13, 17—20 and 24 were likewise probably absent. Some of the other more important omissions are xi. 29—32, 49—51, xiii. 1—9, 29—35, xv. 11—32, xvii. 5—10 (probably), xviii. 31—34, xix. 29—48, xx. 9—19, 37—38, xxi. 1—4, 18, 21—22, xxii. 16—18, 28—30, 35—38, 49—51, and there is great doubt about the concluding verses of xxiv. from 44 to the end, but it may have terminated with v. 49. It is not certain whether the order was the same as Luke,[3] but there are instances of decided variation, especially at the opening. As the peculiarities of the opening variations have had an important effect in inclining some critics towards the acceptance of the mutilation hypothesis,[4] it may be well for us briefly to examine the more important amongst them.

Marcion's Gospel is generally said to have commenced thus: "In the fifteenth year of the reign of Tiberius Cæsar, Jesus came down to Capernaum, a city of Galilee."[5]

---

[1] *Eichhorn*, Einl. N. T., i. p. 53 ff., p. 58 ff., 68 ff.; *Volkmar*, Das Ev. M., p. 2 ff.

[2] *Volkmar*, Das Ev. M., p. 80 f.; *Eichhorn*, Einl. N. T., i. p. 77; *Bleek*, Einl. N. T., p. 128.

[3] Cf. *Epiphanius*, Hær., xlii., ed. Pet., p. 312; *Eichhorn*, Einl. N. T., i. p. 46; *Volkmar*, Das Ev. M., p. 141; *Hilgenfeld*, Theol. Jahrb., 1853, p. 199.

[4] *Baur*, Das Markusev., p. 209; *Guericke*, Gesammtgesch, p. 232; *Reuss*, Rev. de Théol., xv. 1857, p. 54.

[5] Hahn incorrectly reads, "God came down" (ὁ θεὸς κατῆλθεν) Ev. M. in *Thilo*, p. 403. Cf. *Volkmar*, Das Ev. M., p. 150, anm. 3; *Baur*, Unters. kan. Evv., p. 406, anm. *; *Hilgenfeld*, Die Evv. J., p. 398, anm. 1.

There are various slightly differing readings of this. Epiphanius gives the opening words, Ἐν τῷ πεντεκαιδεκάτῳ ἔτει Τιβερίου Καίσαρος, καὶ τὰ ἑξῆς.[1] Tertullian has : Anno quintodecimo principatus Tiberiani. . . . descendisse in civitatem Galilææ Capharnaum."[2] The καὶ τὰ ἑξῆς of Epiphanius has permitted the conjecture that there might have been an additional indication of the time, such as "Pontius Pilate being governor of Judæa,"[3] but this has not been generally adopted.[4] It is not necessary for us to discuss the sense in which the "came down" (κατῆλθε) was interpreted, since it is the word used in Luke. Marcion's Gospel then proceeds with iv. 31 : "and taught them on the sabbath days, (v. 32), and they were exceedingly astonished at his teaching, for his word was power." Then follow vs. 33—39 containing the healing of the man with an unclean spirit,[5] and of Simon's wife's mother, with the important omission of the expression "of Nazareth" (Ναζαρηνέ)[6] after "Jesus" in the cry of the possessed (v. 34). The vs. 16—30[7] immediately *follow* iv. 39, with important

[1] Hær., xlii., ed. Pet., p. 312.
[2] Adv. M., iv. 7.
[3] Cf. Dial. de recta fide ; *Orig.*, Opp., i. p. 868 ; *Irenæus*, Adv. Hær., i. 27, § 2.
[4] *Volkmar* has it, Das Ev. M., p. 154, 224, p. 126 ; *Hahn* omits it, Ev. M. in *Thilo*, l. c., as do also *Baur* (Unters. kan. Ev., p. 406, who after the statement of Epiph. also rightly leaves open the τῆς ἡγεμονίας and καίσαρος), and *Hilgenfeld* (who conjectured the second date), Die Evv. J., p. 398 ; cf. Theol. Jahrb., 1853, p. 197.
[5] *Volkmar* omits v. 37 ; *Hahn*, *Hilgenfeld*, and others retain it. *Ritschl* rejects 38, 39, the healing of Simon's wife's mother, which are passed over in silence by *Tertullian* (Adv. M., iv. 8), Das Ev. M., p. 76 f., in which he is joined by Baur only. The whole of this examination illustrates the uncertainties of the text and of the data on which critics attempt to reconstruct it.
[6] *Hahn*, in *Thilo*, p. 404, anm. 4 ; *Volkmar*, Das Ev. M., p. 150 ; cf. 56, 131 ; *Hilgenfeld*, Die Evv. J., p. 441 ; Theol. Jahrb., 1853, p. 198.
[7] *Volkmar* also includes the latter part of v. 14, and all of 15, "And

omissions and variations. In iv. 16, where Jesus comes to Nazareth, the words "where he had been brought up" are omitted, as is also the concluding phrase "and stood up to read."[1] Verses 17—19, in which Jesus reads from Isaiah, are altogether wanting.[2] Volkmar omits the whole of v. 20, Hilgenfeld only the first half down to the sitting down, retaining the rest; Hahn retains from "and he sat down" to the end.[3] Of v. 21 only: "He began to speak to them" is retained.[4] From v. 22 the concluding phrase: "And said: Is not this Joseph's son" is omitted,[5] as are also the words "in thy country" from v. 23.[6] Verse 24, containing the proverb: "A prophet has no honour" is wholly omitted,[7] but the best critics differ regarding the two following verses 25—26; they are omitted according to Hahn, Ritschl and De Wette,[8] but retained by Volkmar and Hilgenfeld.[9] Verse 27,

---

there went out a fame of him," &c., &c. (Das Ev. M., p. 152, cf. 154), but in this he is unsupported by others. Cf. *Tertullian*, Adv. Marc., iv. 8.

[1] *Hahn*, in *Thilo*, p. 404, 405, anm. 7; *Ritschl*, Das Ev. M., p. 76; *Volkmar*, Das Ev. M., p. 150, cf. 154; *Hilgenfeld*, Die Evv. Justin's, p. 441, cf. 399; *De Wette*, Einl. N. T., p. 124.

[2] *Hahn*, in *Thilo*, 404; Das Ev. M., p. 136; *Ritschl*, Das Ev. M., 76, anm. 1; *Volkmar*, Das Ev. M., p. 150; *Hilgenfeld*, Theol. Jahrb., 1853, p. 199; In Die Evv. J., p. 399 (cf. 441), he considers it probable, but does not speak with certainty. *Tertullian* is silent, Adv. M., iv. 8.

[3] *Volkmar*, Das Ev. M., p. 150, 154; *Hilgenfeld*, Theol. Jahrb., 1853, p. 199; *Hahn*, in *Thilo*, p. 404.

[4] *Volkmar* reads καὶ ἤρξατο κηρύσσειν αὐτοῖς, Das. Ev. M., p. 154; *Hahn* has λέγειν πρὸς αὐτούς, in *Thilo*, p. 404; *Ritschl*, Das Ev. M., 76 anm. 1; *Hilgenfeld* suggests λαλεῖν for λέγειν, Theol. Jahrb., 1853, p. 199.

[5] *Hahn*, Ev. M. in *Thilo*, p. 405; *Ritschl*, Das Ev. M., p. 76, anm. 1; *Volkmar*, Das Ev. M., p. 150, 154, *Hilgenfeld*, Theol. Jahrb., 1853, p. 199; Die Evv. J., p. 441.

[6] *Hahn*, in *Thilo*, p. 405; *Volkmar*, Das Ev. M., p. 150, 154; *Hilgenfeld*, Theol. Jahrb. 1853, p. 199.

[7] *Ib.*

[8] *Hahn*, in *Thilo*, p. 405; *Ritschl*, Das Ev. M., 76 anm. 1; *De Wette*, Einl. N. T., p. 124.

[9] *Volkmar*, Das Ev. M., p. 154; *Hilgenfeld*, Th. Jahrb., 1853, p. 199.

referring to the leprosy of Naaman, which, it will be remembered, is interpolated at xvii. 14, is omitted here by most critics, but retained by Volkmar.[1] Verses 28—30 come next,[2] and the four verses iv. 40—44, which then immediately follow, complete the chapter. This brief analysis, with the accompanying notes, illustrates the uncertainty of the text, and, throughout the whole Gospel, conjecture similarly plays the larger part. We do not propose to criticise minutely the various conclusions arrived at as to the state of the text, but must emphatically remark that where there is so little certainty there cannot be any safe ground for delicate deductions regarding motives and sequences of matter. Nothing is more certain than that, if we criticise and compare the Synoptics on the same principle, we meet with the most startling results and the most irreconcileable difficulties.[3] The opening of Marcion's Gospel is more free from abruptness and crudity than that of Luke.

It is not necessary to show that the first three chapters of Luke present very many differences from the other Synoptics. Mark omits them altogether, and they do not even agree with the account in Matthew. Some of the oldest Gospels of which we have any knowledge, such as the Gospel according to the Hebrews, are said not to have had the narrative of the first two chapters at all,[4] and there is much more than doubt as to their originality. The mere omission of the history of

---

[1] *Volkmar*, Das Ev. M., p. 154. Cf. *Hahn*, in *Thilo*, 405; *Ritschl*, Das Ev. M., p. 76, anm. 1; *Hilgenfeld*, Theol. Jahrb., 1853, p. 199 f.; *De Wette*, Einl. N. T., p. 124.

[2] Volkmar adds to " went his way" the words " to Capernaum," Das Ev. M., p. 155.

[3] Cf. *Baur*, Das Markusev., p. 211 ff.; *Volkmar*, Theol. Jahrb., 1850, p. 126 ff.

[4] *Epiphanius*, Hær., xxix. 9; cf. xxx. 13 f.

the infancy, &c., from Mark, however, renders it unnecessary to show that the absence of these chapters from Marcion's Gospel has the strongest support and justification. Now Luke's account of the early events and geography of the Gospel history is briefly as follows: Nazareth is the permanent dwelling-place of Joseph and Mary,[1] but on account of the census they travel to Bethlehem, where Jesus is born;[2] and after visiting Jerusalem to present him at the Temple,[3] they return "to their own city Nazareth."[4] After the baptism and temptation Jesus comes to Nazareth "where he had been brought up,"[5] and in the course of his address to the people he says: "Ye will surely say unto me this proverb: Physician heal thyself: whatsoever we have heard done in Capernaum do also here in thy country."[6] No mention, however, has before this been made of Capernaum, and no account has been given of any works done there; but, on the contrary, after escaping from the angry mob at Nazareth, Jesus goes for the first time to Capernaum, which, on being thus first mentioned, is particularized as "a city of Galilee,"[7] where he heals a man who had an unclean spirit, in the synagogue, who addresses him as "Jesus of Nazareth;"[8] and the fame of him goes throughout the country.[9] He cures Simon's wife's mother of a fever[10] and when the sun is set they bring the sick and he heals them.[11]

The account in Matthew contradicts this in many points, some of which had better be indicated here. Jesus is born in Bethlehem, which is the ordinary

---

[1] Luke i. 26, ii. 4. [2] ii. 4.
[3] ii. 22. [4] ii. 39; cf. 42, 51. [5] iv. 16.
[6] iv. 23. [7] iv. 31. [8] iv. 33 ff.
[9] iv. 37. [10] iv. 38 f. [11] iv. 40—44.

dwelling-place of the family;[1] his parents fly thence with him into Egypt,[2] and on their return, they dwell "in a city called Nazareth; that it might be fulfilled which was spoken by the prophets: He shall be called a Nazarene."[3] After John's imprisonment, Jesus leaves Nazareth, and goes to dwell in Capernaum.[4] From that time he begins to preach.[5] Here then, he commences his public career in Capernaum.

In Mark, Jesus comes from Nazareth to be baptized,[6] and after the imprisonment of John, he comes into Galilee preaching.[7] In Capernaum, he heals the man of the unclean spirit, and Simon's wife's mother,[8] and then retires to a solitary place,[9] returns after some days to Capernaum[10] without going to Nazareth at all, and it is only at a later period that he comes to his own country, and quotes the proverb regarding a prophet.[11]

It is evident from this comparison, that there is very considerable difference between the three Synoptics, regarding the outset of the career of Jesus, and that there must have been decided elasticity in the tradition, and variety in the early written accounts of this part of the Gospel narrative. Luke alone commits the error of making Jesus appear in the synagogue at Nazareth, and refer to works wrought at Capernaum, before any mention had been made of his having preached or worked wonders there to justify the allusions

---

[1] Matt. ii. 1, 5 ff.   [2] ii. 13 ff.
[3] ii. 23. We need not pause here to point out that there is no such prophecy known in the Old Testament. The reference may very probably be a singularly mistaken application of the word in Isaiah xi. 1, the Hebrew word for branch being נֵצֶר, Nazer.
[4] iv. 12—13, for the fulfilment of another supposed prophecy, v. 14 ff.
[5] iv. 17.   [6] Mark i. 9.   [7] i. 14 f.
[8] i. 21 ff.   [9] i. 35.   [10] ii. 1.
[11] vi. 1—6; cf. Matt. xiii. 54.

and the consequent agitation. It is obvious that there has been confusion in the arrangement of the third Synoptic and a transposition of the episodes, clearly pointing to a combination of passages from other sources.[1] Now Marcion's Gospel did not contain these anomalies. It represented Jesus as first appearing in Capernaum, teaching in the synagogue, and performing mighty works there, and *then* going to Nazareth, and addressing the people with the natural reference to the previous events at Capernaum, and in this it is not only more consecutive, but also adheres more closely to the other two Synoptics.

That Luke happens to be the only one of our canonical Gospels, which has the words with which Marcion's Gospel commences, is no proof that these words were original in that work, and not found in several of the writings which existed before the third Synoptic was compiled. Indeed, the close relationship between the first three Gospels is standing testimony to the fact that one Gospel was built upon the basis of others previously existing. This which has been called "the chief prop of the mutilation hypothesis,"[2] has really no solid ground to stand on beyond the accident that only one of three Gospels survives out of many which may have had the phrase. The fact that Marcion's Gospel really had the words of Luke, moreover, is mere conjecture, inasmuch as Epiphanius, who alone gives the Greek, shows a distinct variation of reading. He has: Ἐν τῷ πεντε-

---

[1] Cf. Luke iv. 23; Matt. viii. 54; Mark vi. 1—6. We do not go into the question as to the sufficiency of the motives ascribed for the agitation at Nazareth, or the contradiction between the facts narrated as to the attempt to kill Jesus, and the statement of their wonder at his gracious words, v. 22, &c. There is no evidence where the various discrepancies arose, and no certain conclusions can be based upon such arguments.

[2] "Die Haupstütze der Verstümmelungshypothese." Baur, Das Markusev., p. 209.

καιδεκάτῳ ἔτει Τιβερίου Καίσαρος, καὶ τὰ ἑξῆς.[1] Luke reads : Ἐν ἔτει δὲ πεντεκαιδεκάτῳ τῆς ἡγεμονίας Τιβερίου Καίσαρος. We do not of course lay much stress upon this, but the fact that there is a variation should be noticed. Critics quietly assume, because there is a difference, that Epiphanius has abbreviated, but that is by no means sure. In any case, instances could be multiplied to show that if one of our Synoptic Gospels were lost, one of the survivors would in this manner have credit for passages which it had in reality either derived from the lost Gospel, or with it drawn from a common original source.

Now starting from the undeniable fact that the Synoptic Gospels are in no case purely original independent works, but are based upon older writings, or upon each other, each Gospel remodelling and adding to already existing materials, as the author of the third Gospel, indeed, very frankly and distinctly indicates,[2] it seems a bold thing to affirm that Marcion's Gospel must necessarily have been derived from the latter. Ewald has made a minute analysis of the Synoptics assigning the materials of each to what he considers their original source. We do not of course attach any very specific importance to such results, for it is clear that they must to a great extent be arbitrary and incapable of proof, but being effected without any reference to the question before us, it may be interesting to compare Ewald's conclusions regarding the parallel part of Luke, with the first chapter of Marcion's Gospel. Ewald details the materials from which our Synoptic Gospels

---

[1] Haer., xlii. ed. Pet., p. 312.
[2] Luke i. 1—4. He professes to write in order the things in which Theophilus had already been instructed, not to tell something new, but merely that he might know the certainty thereof.

were derived, and the order of their composition as follows, each Synoptic of course making use of the earlier materials: I. the oldest Gospel. II. the collection of Discourses (Spruchsammlung). III. Mark. IV. the Book of earlier History. V. our present Matthew. VI. the sixth recognizable book. VII. the seventh book. VIII. the eighth book; and IX. Luke.[1] Now the only part of our third canonical Gospel corresponding with any part of the first chapter of Marcion's Gospel which Ewald ascribes to the author of our actual Luke is the opening date.[2] The passage to which the few opening words are joined, and which constitute the commencement of Marcion's Gospel, Luke iv. 31—39, is a section commencing with verse 31, and extending to the end of the chapter, thereby including verses 40—44, which Ewald assigns to Mark.[3] Verses 16—24, which immediately follow, also form a complete and isolated passage assigned by Ewald, to the "sixth recognizable book."[4] Verses 25—27, also are the whole

---

[1] *Ewald*, Die drei ersten Evangelien, 1850, p. 1; cf. Jahrb. bibl. Wiss., 1848—49.

[2] The verses iv. 14—15, which Volkmar wished to include, but which all other critics reject (see p. 128, note 7), from Marcion's text, Ewald likewise identifies as an isolated couple of verses by the author of our Luke inserted between episodes derived from other written sources. Cf. *Ewald*, l. c.

[3] *Ewald*, Die drei erst. Evv., p. 104 f.; cf. p. 1. We hold that Marcion's Gospel read continuously, v. 31—44, and that v. 16 ff. then immediately followed. This would make the reference at Nazareth to the works done at Capernaum much more complete, and would remove the incongruity of attributing v. 40—44, to the evening of the day of escape from Nazareth and return to Capernaum or to Nazareth itself. The only reason for not joining 40—44 to the preceding section 31—39, is the broken order of reference by *Tertullian* (Adv. Marc. iv. 8), but there is no statement that he follows the actual order of Marcion in this, and his argument would fully account for the order of his references without dividing this passage. Cf. *Volkmar*, Das Ev. M., p. 146 ff.; *Hilgenfeld*, Die Evv. J., p. 462 ff.; Theol. Jahrb., 1853, p. 198 f.

[4] *Ewald*, Die drei erst. Evv., p. 104, cf. p. 1; v. 24 is omitted.

of another isolated section attributed by Ewald, to the "Book of earlier history," whilst 28—30, in like manner form another complete and isolated episode, assigned by him to the "eighth recognizable book."[1] According to Ewald, therefore, Luke's Gospel at this place is a mere patchwork of older writings, and if this be in any degree accepted, as in the abstract, indeed, it is by the great mass of critics, then the Gospel of Marcion might be an arrangement different from Luke of materials not his, but previously existing, and of which, therefore, there is no warrant to limit the use and reproduction to the canonical Gospel.

The course pursued by critics, with regard to Marcion's Gospel, is necessarily very unsatisfactory. They commence with a definite hypothesis, and try whether all the peculiarities of the text may not be more or less well explained by it. On the other hand, the attempt to settle the question by a comparison of the reconstructed text with Luke's is equally inconclusive. The determination of priority of composition from internal evidence, where there are no chronological references, must as a general rule be arbitrary, and can rarely be accepted as final. Internal evidence would, indeed, decidedly favour the priority of Marcion's Gospel. The great uncertainty of the whole system, even when applied under the most favourable circumstances, is well illustrated by the contradictory results at which critics have arrived as to the order of production and dependence on each other of our three Synoptics. Without going into details, we may say that critics who are all agreed upon the mutual dependence of those Gospels have variously arranged them in the following order: I. Matthew—

[1] *Ewald, ib., p. 104, cf. p. 1.*

Mark—Luke.[1] II. Matthew—Luke—Mark.[2] III. Mark—Matthew—Luke.[3] IV. Mark—Luke—Matthew.[4] V. Luke—Matthew—Mark.[5] VI. All three out of common written sources.[6] Were we to state the various theories still more in detail, we might largely increase the variety of conclusions. These, however, suffice to show the uncertainty of results derived from internal evidence.

It is always assumed that Marcion altered a Gospel to suit his own particular system, but as one of his most orthodox critics, while asserting that Luke's narrative lay at the basis of his Gospel, admits: "it is not equally clear that all the changes were due to Marcion himself;"[7] and, although he considers that "some of the omissions can be explained by his peculiar doctrines," he continues: "others are unlike arbitrary corrections, and must be considered as various readings of the greatest interest, dating as they do from a time anterior to all

---

[1] Of course we only pretend to indicate a few of the critics who adopt each order. So Bengel, Bolton, Ebrard, Grotius, Hengstenberg, Hug, Hilgenfeld, Holtzmann, Mill, Seiler, Townson, Wetstein.

[2] So Ammon, Baur, Bleek, Delitzsch, Fritzsche, Gfrörer, Griesbach, Kern, Köstlin, Neudecker, Saunier, Schwarz, Schwegler, Sieffert, Stroth, Theile, Owen, Paulus, De Wette.

[3] So Credner, Ewald, Hitzig, Lachmann, (?) Reuss, Ritschl, Meyer, Storr, Thiersch.

[4] B. Bauer, Hitzig (?) Schneckenburger, Volkmar, Weisse, Wilke.

[5] Büsching, Evanson.

[6] Bertholdt, Le Clerc, Corrodi, Eichhorn, Gratz, Hänlein, Koppe, Kuinoel, Lessing, Marsh, Michaelis, Niemeyer, Semler, Schleiermacher, Schmidt, Weber. This view was partly shared by many of those mentioned under other orders.

[7] *Westcott*, On the Canon, p. 275. We do not pause to discuss *Tertullian's* insinuations (Adv. Marc., iv. 4), that Marcion himself admitted that he had amended St. Luke's Gospel, for the statement was repudiated by the Marcionites, abandoned practically by Tertullian himself, and has been rejected by the mass of critics. Cf. *Ritschl*, Das Ev. M., p. 23 ff.; *Schwegler*, Das nachap. Zeit., i. 283, anm. 2; *Volkmar*, Theol. Jahrb., 1850, p. 120; Das Ev. M., p. 4, anm. 2; *Hilgenfeld*, Die Evv. J., p. 446 f.

other authorities in our possession."[1] Now, undoubtedly, the more developed forms of the Gospel narrative were the result of additions, materially influenced by dogmatic and other reasons, made to earlier and more fragmentary works, but it is an argument contrary to general critical experience to affirm that a Gospel, the distinguishing characteristic of which is greater brevity, was produced by omissions in the interest of a system from a longer work.

In the earlier editions of this work, we contended that the theory that Marcion's Gospel was a mutilated form of our third Synoptic had not been established, and that more probably it was an earlier work, from which our Gospel might have been elaborated. We leave the statement of the case, so far, nearly in its former shape, in order that the true nature of the problem and the varying results and gradual development of critical opinion may be better understood. Since the sixth edition of this work was completed, however, a very able examination of Marcion's Gospel has been made by Dr. Sanday,[2] which has convinced us that our earlier hypothesis is untenable, that the portions of our third Synoptic excluded from Marcion's Gospel were really written by the same pen which composed the mass of the work and, consequently, that our third Synoptic existed in his time, and was substantially in the hands of Marcion. This conviction is mainly the result of the linguistic analysis, sufficiently indicated by Dr. Sanday and, since, exhaustively carried out for ourselves. We still consider the argument based upon the mere dogmatic views of Marcion, which has hitherto been almost

[1] *Westcott*, On the Canon, p. 275.
[2] Fortnightly Review, 1875, p. 855, ff.; The Gospels in Second Century, 1876, p. 204 ff.

exclusively relied on, quite inconclusive by itself, but the linguistic test, applied practically for the first time in this controversy by Dr. Sanday, must, we think, prove irresistible to all who are familiar with the comparatively limited vocabulary of New Testament writers. Throughout the omitted sections, peculiarities of language and expression abound which clearly distinguish the general composer of the third Gospel, and it is, consequently, not possible reasonably to maintain that these sections are additions subsequently made by a different hand, which seems to be the only legitimate course open to those who would deny that Marcion's Gospel originally contained them.

Here, then, we find evidence of the existence of our third Synoptic about the year 140, and it may of course be inferred that it must have been composed at least some time before that date. It is important, however, to estimate aright the facts actually before us and the deductions which may be drawn from them. The testimony of Marcion does not throw any light upon the authorship or origin of the Gospel of which he made use. Its superscription was simply: "The Gospel," or, "The Gospel of the Lord" (τὸ εὐαγγελιον, or εὐαγγέλιον τοῦ Κυρίου),[1] and no author's name was attached to it. The Heresiarch did not pretend to have written it himself, nor did he ascribe it to any other person. Tertullian, in fact, reproaches him with its anonymity. "And here

---

[1] Marcion Evangelio suo nullum adscribit auctorem. *Tertullian*, Adv. Marc., iv. 2; Dial. de recta fide, § 1. Cf. *Bertholdt*, Einl., iii. p. 1293 ff.; *Bleek*, Einl. N. T., p. 126; *Credner*, Beiträge, i. p. 43; *Eichhorn*, Einl. N. T., i. p. 79 f.; *Hahn*, Ev. M. in *Thilo*, p. 403; Das Ev. M., p. 132; *Holtzmann*, in Bunsen's Bibelwerk, viii. p. 563; *Neudecker*, Einl. N. T., p. 74, anm.; *Schwegler*, Das nachap. Zeit. i. p. 280 f., p. 261; *Scholten*, Het Paulin. Evangelie, p. 8; *Tischendorf*, Wann wurden, u. s. w., p. 61; *De Wette*, Einl. N. T., p. 119 f.

already I might make a stand," he says at the very opening of his attack on Marcion's Gospel, "contending that a work should not be recognized which does not hold its front erect . . . which does not give a pledge of its trustworthiness by the fulness of its title, and the due declaration of its author."[1] Not only did Marcion himself not in any way connect the name of Luke with his Gospel, but his followers repudiated the idea that Luke was its author.[2] In establishing the substantial identity of Marcion's Gospel and our third Synoptic, therefore, no advance is made towards establishing the authorship of Luke. The Gospel remains anonymous still. On the other hand we ascertain the important fact that, so far from its having any authoritative or infallible character at that time, Marcion regarded our Synoptic as a work perverted by Jewish influences, and requiring to be freely expurgated in the interests of truth.[3] Amended by very considerable omissions and alterations, Marcion certainly held it in high respect as a record of the teaching of Jesus, but beyond this circumstance, and the mere fact of its existence in his day, we learn nothing from the evidence of Marcion. It can scarcely be maintained that this does much to authenticate the third Synoptic as a record of miracles and a witness for the reality of Divine Revelation.

---

[1] Et possem hic jam gradum figere, non agnoscendum contendens opus, quod non erigat frontem, quod nullam constantiam præferat, nullam fidem repromittat de plenitudine tituli et professione debita auctoris. *Tertullian*, Adv. Marc., iv. 2.

[2] Dial. de recta fide, § 1. Cf. *Bertholdt*, Einl. iii. p. 1295, 1218 ff.; *Eichhorn*, Einl. N. T., i. p. 79 f.; *Gieseler*, Entst. schr. Evv., p. 25; *Holtzmann*, in Bunsen's Bibelwerk, viii. p. 563. The later Marcionites affirmed their Gospel to have been written by Christ himself, and the particulars of the Crucifixion, &c., to have been added by Paul.

[3] Cf. *Credner*, Beiträge, i. p. 44 f.

There is no evidence whatever that Marcion had any knowledge of the other canonical Gospels in any form.[1] None of his writings are extant, and no direct assertion is made even by the Fathers that he knew them, although from their dogmatic point of view they assume that these Gospels existed from the very first, and therefore insinuate that as he only recognized one Gospel, he rejected the rest.[2] When Irenæus says: "He persuaded his disciples that he himself was more veracious than were the apostles who handed down the Gospel, though he delivered to them not the Gospel, but part of the Gospel,"[3] it is quite clear that he speaks of the Gospel—the good tidings—Christianity—and not of specific written Gospels. In another passage which is referred to by Apologists, Irenæus says of the Marcionites that they have asserted: "That even the apostles proclaimed the Gospel still under the influence of Jewish sentiments; but that they themselves are more sound and more judicious than the apostles. Wherefore also Marcion and his followers have had recourse to mutilating the Scriptures, not recognizing some books at all, but curtailing the Gospel according to Luke and the Epistles of Paul; these they say are alone authentic which they themselves have abbreviated."[4]

---

[1] *Eichhorn*, Einl. N. T., i. p. 84; *Gieseler*, Entst. schr. Evv. p. 25; *Rumpf*, Rev. de Théol., 1867, p. 21; *Schleiermacher*, Einl. N. T., p. 214 f.

[2] *Irenæus*, Adv. Hær., i. 27, § 2; cf. iii. 2; 12, § 12; *Tertullian*, Adv. Marc., iv. 3; cf. De Carne Christi, 2, 3.

[3] Semetipsum esse veraciorem, quam sunt hi, qui Evangelium tradiderunt, apostoli, suasit discipulis suis; non Evangelium, sed particulam Evangelii tradens eis. Adv. Hær., i. 27, § 2.

[4] Et apostolos quidem adhuc quæ sunt Judæorum sentientes, annuntiasse Evangelium; se autem sinceriores, et prudentiores apostolis esse. Unde et Marcion, et qui ab eo sunt, ad intercidendas conversi sunt Scripturas, quasdam quidem in totum non cognoscentes, secundum Lucam autem Evangelium, et Epistolas Pauli decurtantes, hæc sola legitima esse dicunt, quæ ipsi minoraverunt. Adv. Hær., iii. 12, § 12.

These remarks chiefly refer to the followers of Marcion, and as we have shown, when treating of Valentinus, Irenæus is expressly writing against members of heretical sects living in his own day and not of the founders of those sects.[1] The Marcionites of the time of Irenæus no doubt deliberately rejected the Gospels, but it does not by any means follow that Marcion himself knew anything of them. As yet we have not met with any evidence even of their existence.

The evidence of Tertullian is not a whit more valuable. In the passage usually cited, he says: "But Marcion, lighting upon the Epistle of Paul to the Galatians, in which he reproaches even Apostles for not walking uprightly according to the truth of the Gospel, as well as accuses certain false Apostles of perverting the Gospel of Christ, tries with all his might to destroy the status of those Gospels which are put forth as genuine and under the name of Apostles or at least of contemporaries of the Apostles, in order, be it known, to confer upon his own the credit which he takes from them."[2] Now here again it is clear that Tertullian is simply applying, by inference, Marcion's views with regard to the preaching of the Gospel by the two parties in the Church, represented by the Apostle Paul and the "pillar" Apostles whose leaning to Jewish doctrines he condemned, to the written Gospels recognized in his day though not in Marcion's. "It is uncertain," says even Canon Westcott,

---

[1] Cf. Adv. Hær., i. Præf. § 2; iii. Præf., &c.
[2] Sed enim Marcion nactus epistolam Pauli ad Galatas, etiam ipsos apostolos suggillantis ut non recto pede incedentes ad veritatem evangelii, simul et accusantis pseudapostolos quosdam pervertentes evangelium Christi, connititur ad destruendum statum eorum evangeliorum, quæ propria et sub apostolorum nomine eduntur, vel etiam apostolicorum, ut scilicet fidem, quam illis adimit, suo conferat. Adv. Marc., iv. 3; cf. de Carne Christi, 2, 3.

"whether Tertullian in the passage quoted speaks from a knowledge of what Marcion may have written on the subject, or simply from his own point of sight."[1] Any doubt is, however, removed on examining the context, for Tertullian proceeds to argue that if Paul censured Peter, John and James, it was for changing their company from respect of persons, and similarly, "if false apostles crept in," they betrayed their character by insisting on Jewish observances. "So that it was *not on account of their preaching*, but of their conversation that they were pointed out by Paul,"[2] and he goes on to argue that if Marcion thus accuses Apostles of having depraved the Gospel by their dissimulation, he accuses Christ in accusing those whom Christ selected.[3] It is palpable, therefore, that Marcion, in whatever he may have written, referred to the preaching of the Gospel, or Christianity, by Apostles who retained their Jewish prejudices in favour of circumcision and legal observances, and not to written Gospels. Tertullian merely assumes, with his usual audacity, that the Church had the four Gospels from the very first, and therefore that Marcion, who had only one Gospel, knew the others and deliberately rejected them.

[1] On the Canon, p. 276, note 1.
[2] Adeo non de prædicatione, sed de conversatione a Paulo denotabantur. Adv. Marc., iv. 3.
[3] Adv. Marc., iv. 3.

CHAPTER VIII.

TATIAN—DIONYSIUS OF CORINTH.

From Marcion we now turn to Tatian, another so-called heretic leader. Tatian, an Assyrian by birth,[1] embraced Christianity and became a disciple of Justin Martyr[2] in Rome, sharing with him, as it seems, the persecution excited by Crescens the Cynic[3] to which Justin fell a victim. After the death of Justin, Tatian, who till then had continued thoroughly orthodox, left Rome, and joined the sect of the Encratites, of which, however, he was not the founder,[4] and became the leading exponent of their austere and ascetic doctrines.[5]

The only one of his writings which is still extant is his "Oration to the Greeks" (λόγος πρὸς Ἕλληνας). This work was written after the death of Justin, for in it he refers to that event,[6] and it is generally dated between

---

[1] Oratio ad Græcos, ed Otto, § 42.
[2] Ib., § 18.   [3] Ib., § 19.
[4] *Anger*, Synops. Ev. Proleg., p. xxviii.; *Credner*, Beiträge, i. p. 437; *Volkmar*, Der Ursprung, p. 34; *Westcott*, On the Canon, p. 277.
[5] *Eusebius*, H. E., iv. 29; *Irenæus*, Adv. Hær., i. 28; *Epiphanius*, Hær., xlvi. 1; *Hieron*., De Vir. Illustr., 29; *Theodoret*, Hær. fab., i. 20. *Beausobre*, Hist. du Manichéisme, i. p. 303 f.; *Credner*, Beiträge, i. p. 437 f.; *Donaldson*, Hist. Chr. Lit. and Doctr., iii. p. 3 ff.; *Holtzmann*, in Bunsen's Bibelwerk, viii. p. 562; *Lardner*, Credibility, &c., Works, ii. p. 136 ff; *Matter*, Hist. du Christianisme, 2 éd., i. p. 172 f.; *Volkmar*, Der Ursprung, p. 34.
[6] Orat. ad Gr., § 19. *Credner*, Beiträge, i. 438; *Keim*, Jesu v. Nazara, i. p. 145; *Scholten*, Die ält. Zeugnisse, p. 93; *Tischendorf*, Wann wurden, u. s. w., p. 16, anm. 1.

A.D. 170—175.¹ Tischendorf does not assert that there is any quotation in this address taken from the Synoptic Gospels;² and Canon Westcott only affirms that it contains a "clear reference" to "a parable recorded by St. Matthew," and he excuses the slightness of this evidence by adding: "The absence of more explicit testimony to the books of the New Testament is to be accounted for by the style of his writing, and not by his unworthy estimate of their importance."³ This remark is without foundation, as we know nothing whatever with regard to Tatian's estimate of any such books.

The supposed "clear reference" is as follows: "For by means of a certain hidden treasure (ἀποκρύφου θησαυροῦ) he made himself lord of all that we possess, in digging for which though we were covered with dust, yet we give it the occasion of falling into our hands and abiding with us."⁴ This is claimed as a reference to Matt. xiii. 44: "The kingdom of heaven is like unto treasure hidden (θησαυρῷ κεκρυμμένῳ) in the field, which a man found and hid, and for his joy he goeth and selleth all that he hath and buyeth that field." So faint a similarity could not prove anything, but it is evident that there are decided differences here. Were the probability fifty times greater

---

[1] *Credner* (after Justin's death), Beiträge, i. p. 438; *Donaldson*, Hist. Chr. Lit. and Doctr., iii. p. 10; *Keim*, Jesu v. Nazara, i. p. 145; *Lardner* (between 165—172), Credibility, &c., Works, ii. p. 139; *Scholten*, Die ält. Zeugnisse, p. 93; *Tischendorf* (between 166—170), Wann wurden, u. s. w., p. 16, anm. 1, p. 17; *Volkmar* (between 165—175), Der Ursprung, p. 163, cf. p. 34 ff.; *De Wette* († 176), Einl. A. T., 1852, p. 24.

[2] Cf. Wann wurden, u. s. w., p. 16 f.

[3] On the Canon, p. 278.

[4] Διὰ τινὸς γὰρ ἀποκρύφου θησαυροῦ τῶν ἡμετέρων ἐπεκράτησεν, ὃν ὀρύττοντες κονιορτῷ μὲν ἡμεῖς ἐνεπλήσθημεν, τούτῳ δὲ τοῦ συνεστάναι τὴν ἀφορμὴν παρέχομεν. Orat. ad Gr., § 30.

than it is that Tatian had in his mind the parable, which is reported in our first Gospel, nothing could be more unwarrantable than the deduction that he must have derived it from our Matthew, and not from any other of the numerous Gospels which we know to have early been in circulation. Ewald ascribes the parable in Matthew originally to the "Spruchsammlung" or collection of Discourses, the second of the four works out of which he considers our first Synoptic to have been compiled.[1] As evidence even for the existence of our first canonical Gospel, no such anonymous allusion could have the slightest value.

Although neither Tischendorf nor Canon Westcott think it worth while to refer to it, some apologists claim another passage in the Oration as a reference to our third Synoptic. "Laugh ye: nevertheless you shall weep."[2] This is compared with Luke vi. 25: "Woe unto you that laugh now: for ye shall mourn and weep."[3] Here again, it is impossible to trace a reference in the words of Tatian specially to our third Gospel, and manifestly nothing could be more foolish than to build upon such vague similarity any hypothesis of Tatian's acquaintance with Luke. If there be one part of the Gospel which was more known than another in the first ages of Christianity, it was the Sermon on the Mount, and there can be no doubt that many evangelical works now lost contained versions of it. Ewald likewise assigns this passage of Luke originally to the Spruchsammlung,[4] and no one can doubt that the saying was recorded long before the writer of the third Gospel

---

[1] Die drei ersten Evv., l. c.
[2] Γελᾶτε δὲ ὑμεῖς, ὡς καὶ κλαύσοντες. Orat. ad Gr., § 32.
[3] οὐαὶ ὑμῖν οἱ γελῶντες νῦν· ὅτι πενθήσετε καὶ κλαύσετε. Luke vi. 25.
[4] Die drei ersten Evv., l. c.

undertook to compile evangelical history, as so many had done before him.

Further on, however, Canon Westcott says: "it can be gathered from Clement of Alexandria . . . that he (Tatian) endeavoured to derive authority for his peculiar opinions from the Epistles to the Corinthians and Galatians, and probably from the Epistle to the Ephesians, and the Gospel of St. Matthew."[1] The allusion here is to a passage in the Stromata of Clement, in which reference is supposed by the apologist to be made to Tatian. No writer, however, is named, and Clement merely introduces his remark by the words: "a certain person," (τις) and then proceeds to give his application of the Saviour's words "not to treasure upon earth where moth and rust corrupt" (ἐπὶ γῆς μὴ θησαυρίζειν ὅπου σὴς καὶ βρῶσις ἀφανίζει).[2] The parallel passage in Matthew vi. 19, reads: "Lay not up for yourselves treasures upon earth, where moth and rust doth corrupt," &c. (μὴ θησαυρίζετε ὑμῖν θησαυροὺς ἐπὶ τῆς γῆς, κ.τ.λ.). Canon Westcott, it is true, merely suggests that "probably" this may be ascribed to Tatian, but it is almost absolutely certain that it was not attributed to him by Clement. Tatian is several times referred to in the course of the same chapter, and his words are continued by the use of φησί or γράφει, and it is in the highest degree improbable that Clement should introduce another quotation from him in such immediate context by the vague and distant reference "a certain person" (τις). On the other hand reference is made in the chapter to

---

[1] On the Canon, p. 279. [In the 4th edition Dr. Westcott has altered the "probably" of the above sentence to "perhaps," and in a note has added: "These two last references are from an anonymous citation (τις) which has been commonly assigned to Tatian." P. 318, n. 1.]

[2] Strom. iii. 12, § 86.

other writers and sects, to one of whom with infinitely greater propriety this expression applies. No weight, therefore, could be attached to any such passage in connection with Tatian. Moreover the quotation not only does not agree with our Synoptic, but may much more probably have been derived from the Gospel according to the Hebrews.[1] It will be remembered that Justin Martyr quotes the same passage, with the same omission of "θησαυρούς," from a Gospel different from our Synoptics.[2]

Tatian, however, is claimed by apologists as a witness for the existence of our Gospels—more than this he could not possibly be—principally on the ground that his Gospel was called by some Diatessaron (διὰ τεσσάρων) or "by four," and it is assumed to have been a harmony of four Gospels. The work is no longer extant and, as we shall see, our information regarding it is of the scantiest and most unsatisfactory description. Critics have arrived at very various conclusions with regard to the composition of the work. Some of course affirm, with more or less of hesitation nevertheless, that it was nothing else than a harmony of our four canonical Gospels;[3] many of these, however, are constrained to admit that it was also partly based upon the Gospel according to the Hebrews.[4] Some maintain that it was

---

[1] Cf. *Credner*, Beiträge, i. p. 445.
[2] *Justin*, Apol., i. 15, see Vol. i. p. 348 f., p. 370 f.
[3] *Anger*, Synops. Ev. Proleg., p. xxviii.; *Bleek*, Einl. N. T., p. 231; *Bindemann*, Th. Stud. u. Krit., 1842, p. 471 ff.; *Celérier*, Essai d'une Introd. N. T., p. 21; *Delitzsch*, Urspr. Mt. Ev., p. 30; *Feilmoser*, Einl. N. B., p. 276; *Guericke*, Gesammtgesch. N. T., p. 227; *Hug*, Einl. N. T., i. p. 40 ff.; *Kirchhofer*, Quellensamml., p. 43, anm. 1; *Neudecker*, Lehrb. Einl. N. T., p. 45 f.; *Olshausen*, Echth. vier can. Evv. p. 336 ff.; *Tischendorf*, Wann wurden, u. s. w., p. 16 f.; *Westcott*, On the Canon, p. 279 ff.
[4] *Guericke*, Gesammtgesch., p. 227; *Kirchhofer*, Quellensamml.,

a harmony of our three Synoptics together with the Gospel according to the Hebrews;[1] whilst many deny that it was composed of our Gospels at all,[2] and either declare it to have been a harmony of the Gospel according to the Hebrews with three other Gospels whose identity cannot be determined, or that it was simply the Gospel according to the Hebrews itself,[3] by which name, as Epiphanius states, it was called by some in his day.[4]

Tatian's Gospel, however, was not only called Diatessaron, but, according to Victor of Capua, it was also called Diapente (διὰ πέντε) "by five,"[5] a complication which shows the incorrectness of the ecclesiastical theory of its composition.

Tischendorf, anxious to date Tatian's Gospel as early as possible, says that in all probability it was composed earlier than the address to the Greeks.[6] Of this, however, he does not offer any evidence, and upon examina-

---

p. 44, anm. 1; *Neudecker*, Einl. N. T., p. 45 f.; *Simon*, Hist. Crit. N. T., p. 74; *De Wette*, Einl. N. T., p. 116 f. Cf. *Michaelis*, Einl. N. T., ii. p. 1007 f., 1042.

[1] *Holtzmann* in Bunson's Bibelwerk, viii. p. 562; *Scholten*, Die ält. Zeugnisse, p. 94; cf. 98.

[2] *Credner*, Beiträge, i. p. 48, p. 443 f.; *Eichhorn*, Einl. N. T., i. p. 120 ff.; *Reuss*, Gesch. N. T., p. 193; *Schmidt*, Einl. N. T., i. p. 125 ff.; *Wilcke*, Tradition u. Mytho, p. 15.

[3] *Baur*, Unters. kan Evv., p. 573; *Credner*, Beiträge, i. p. 444; Gesch. N. T. Kanons, p. 17 ff.; *Eichhorn*, Einl. N. T., i. p. 123; *Nicolas*, Et. sur les Ev. apocr., p. 137; *Reuss*, Gesch. N. T., p. 193; *Schwegler*, Das nachap. Zeit., i. p. 235.

[4] *Epiphanius*, Haer., xlvi. 1.

[5] Præf. ad anon. Harm. Evang. Cf. *Fabricius*, Cod. N. T., i. p. 378; *Beausobre*, Hist. du Manichéisme, i. p. 303 f.; *Davidson*, Introd. N. T., ii. p. 397; *Kirchhofer*, Quellensamml., p. 44; *Lardner*, Credibility, &c., Works, ii. p. 138 f.; *Michaelis*, Einl. N. T., ii. p. 1008; *Neudecker*, Einl. N. T., p. 44 f., anm. p. 45 f., p. 47, anm. 2; *Nicolas*, Et. Evang. apocr., p. 137; *Reuss*, Gesch. N. T., p. 193; *Schott*, Isagoge, p. 22, anm. 3; *Simon*, Hist. Crit. N. T., ch. vii.; *Westcott*, On the Canon, p. 282, note 1.

[6] Wann wurden, u. s. w., p. 16, anm. 1.

tion it is very evident that the work was, on the contrary, composed or adopted after the Oration and his avowal of heretical opinions. Theodoret states that Tatian had in it omitted the genealogies and all other passages showing that Christ was born of David according to the flesh, and he condemned the work, and caused it to be abandoned, on account of its evil design.[1] If the assumption be correct, therefore, as Tischendorf maintains, that Tatian altered our Gospels, and did not merely from the first, like his master Justin, make use of Gospels different from those which afterwards became canonical, he must have composed the work after the death of Justin, up to which time he is stated to have remained quite orthodox.[2] The date may with much greater probability be set between A.D. 170—180.[3]

The earliest writer who mentions Tatian's Gospel is Eusebius,[4] who wrote some century and a half after its supposed composition, without, however, having himself seen the work at all, or being really acquainted with its nature and contents.[5] Eusebius says: "Tatian, however, their former chief, having put together a certain amalgamation and collection, I know not how, of the Gospels, named this the Diatessaron, which even now is current with some."[6]

[1] Hæret. fab., i. 20.
[2] *Irenæus*, Adv. Hær., i. 28; *Eusebius*, H. E., iv. 29.
[3] *Volkmar*, Der Ursprung, p. 164, p. 35.
[4] *Credner*, Beiträge, i. p. 441; *Feilmoser*, Einl. N. B., p. 275; *Hilgenfeld*, Der Kanon, p. 83, anm. 6; *Westcott*, On the Canon, p. 279.
[5] *Célérier*, Introd. N. T., p. 22; *Credner*, Beiträge, i. p. 441 f.; *Davidson*, Introd. N. T., ii. p. 396; *Donaldson*, Hist. Chr. Lit. and Doctr., iii. p. 24; *Feilmoser*, Einl. N. B., p. 275; *Holtzmann* in Bunsen's Bibelwerk, viii. p. 562; *Hug*, Einl. N. T., i. p. 42; *Lardner*, Credibility, &c., Works, ii. p. 138; *Reuss*, Gesch. N. T., p. 193; *Scholten*, Die ält. Zeugnisse, p. 94; *Westcott*, On the Canon, p. 279 f., note 4.
[6] Ὁ μέντοι γε πρότερος αὐτῶν ἀρχηγὸς ὁ Τατιανὸς συνάφειάν τινα καὶ συναγωγὴν οὐκ οἶδ᾽ ὅπως τῶν εὐαγγελίων συνθείς, τὸ διὰ τεσσάρων τοῦτο προσωνόμασεν· Ὃ καὶ παρά τισιν εἰσέτι νῦν φέρεται. H. E., iv. 29.

It is clear that such hearsay information is not to be relied on.

Neither Irenæus, Clement of Alexandria, nor Jerome, who refer to other works of Tatian, make any mention of this one. Epiphanius, however, does so, but, like Eusebius, evidently without having himself seen it.[1] This second reference to Tatian's Gospel is made upwards of two centuries after its supposed composition. Epiphanius says: "It is said that he (Tatian) composed the Diatessaron, which is called by some the Gospel according to the Hebrews."[2] It must be observed that it is not said that Tatian himself gave this Gospel the name of Diatessaron,[3] but on the contrary the expression of Epiphanius implies that he did not do so,[4] and the fact that it was also called by some the Gospel according to the Hebrews, and Diapente, shows that the work had no superscription from Tatian of a contradictory character. Theodoret, Bishop of Cyrus (†457), is the next writer who mentions Tatian's Gospel, and he is the only one who had personally seen it. He says: " He (Tatian) also composed the Gospel which is called *Diatessaron*, excising the genealogies and all the other parts which declare that the Lord was born of the seed of David according to the flesh. This was used not only by those of his own sect, but also by those who held the apostolic doctrines, who did not perceive the evil of the composition, but made use of the book in simplicity on account of its conciseness. I myself found upwards of two hundred such

---

[1] *Credner*, Beiträge, i. p. 442; *Davidson*, Introd. N. T., ii. p. 396; *Donaldson*, Hist. Chr. Lit. and Doctr., iii. p. 24.
[2] Λέγεται δὲ τὸ διὰ τεσσάρων εὐαγγέλιον ἐπ' αὐτοῦ γεγενῆσθαι ὅπερ, Κατὰ Ἑβραίους τινὲς καλοῦσι. *Epiph.*, Hær., xlvi. 1.
[3] *Credner*, Gesch. N. T. Kanon, p. 18; *Neudecker*, Einl. N. T., p. 47, anm. 2; *Scholten*, Die ält. Zeugnisse, p. 95; *Volkmar*, Der Ursprung, p. 34.
[4] *Davidson*, Introd. N. T., ii. p. 397.

books held in honour among our churches, and collecting them all together, I had them put aside and, instead, introduced the Gospels of the four Evangelists." Again it must be observed that Theodoret does not say that the Gospel of Tatian *was* a Diatessaron, but merely that it was called so (διὰ τεσσάρων καλούμενον).[1]

After quoting this passage, and that from Epiphanius, Canon Westcott says with an assurance which, considering the nature of the evidence, is singular:—" Not only then was the Diatessaron grounded on the four canonical Gospels, but in its general form it was so orthodox as to enjoy a wide ecclesiastical popularity. The heretical character of the book was not evident upon the surface of it, and consisted rather in faults of defect than in erroneous teaching. Theodoret had certainly examined it, and he, like earlier writers, regarded it as a compilation from the four Gospels. He speaks of omissions which were at least in part natural in a Harmony, but notices no such apocryphal additions as would have found place in any Gospel not derived from canonical sources."[2] Now it must be remembered that the evidence regarding Tatian's Gospel is of the very vaguest description. It is not mentioned by any writer until a century and a half after the date of its supposed

---

[1] Οὗτος καὶ τὸ διὰ τεσσάρων καλούμενον συντέθεικεν εὐαγγέλιον, τάς τε γενεαλογίας περικόψας, καὶ τὰ ἄλλα ὅσα ἐκ σπέρματος Δαβὶδ κατὰ σάρκα γεγενημένον τὸν κύριον δείκνυσιν. Ἐχρήσαντο δὲ τούτῳ οὐ μόνον οἱ τῆς ἐκείνου συμμορίας, ἀλλὰ καὶ οἱ τοῖς ἀποστολικοῖς ἐπόμενοι δόγμασι, τὴν τῆς συνθήκης κακουργίαν οὐκ ἐγνωκότες, ἀλλ' ἁπλούστερον ὡς συντόμῳ τῷ βιβλίῳ χρησάμενοι. Εὗρον δὲ κἀγὼ πλείους ἢ διακοσίας βίβλους τοιαύτας ἐν ταῖς παρ' ἡμῖν ἐκκλησίαις τετιμημένας, καὶ πάσας συναγαγὼν ἀπεθέμην, καὶ τὰ τῶν τεττάρων εὐαγγελιστῶν ἀντεισήγαγον εὐαγγέλια. Hær. fab., i. 20.

[2] On the Canon, p. 281. [In the 4th edition, the first sentence in the above passage is altered to: "From this statement it is clear that the *Diatessaron* was so orthodox as to enjoy a wide ecclesiastical popularity." P. 320.]

composition, and then only referred to by Eusebius, who had not seen the work, and candidly confesses his ignorance with regard to it, so that a critic who is almost as orthodox as Canon Westcott himself acknowledges: "For the truth is that we know no more about Tatian's work than what Eusebius, who never saw it, knew."[1] The only other writer who refers to it, Epiphanius, had not seen it either, and while showing that the title of Diatessaron had not been given to it by Tatian himself, he states the important fact that some called it the Gospel according to the Hebrews. Theodoret, the last writer who mentions it, and of whom Dr. Donaldson also says: "Theodoret's information cannot be depended upon,"[2] not only does not say that it is based upon our four Gospels, but, on the contrary, points out that Tatian's Gospel did not contain the genealogies and passages tracing the descent of Jesus through the race of David, which our Synoptics possess, and he so much condemned the mischievous design of the work that he confiscated the copies in circulation in his diocese as heretical. Canon Westcott's assertion that Theodoret regarded it as a compilation of our four Gospels is most arbitrary. Omissions, as he himself points out, are natural to a Harmony, and conciseness certainly would be the last quality for which it could have been so highly prized, if every part of the four Gospels had been retained. The omission of the parts referred to, which are equally omitted from the canonical fourth Gospel, could not have been sufficient to merit the condemnation of the work as heretical, and had Tatian's Gospel not been different in various respects from our four Gospels, such summary treatment would have been totally

---

[1] Donaldson, Hist. Chr. Lit. and Doctr., iii. p. 26.   [2] Ib., iii. p. 25.

unwarrantable. The statement, moreover, that in place of Tatian's Gospel, Theodoret " introduced the Gospels of the four Evangelists," seems to indicate that the displaced Gospel was not a compilation from them, but a substantially different work. Had this not been the case, Theodoret would naturally have qualified such an expression.

Speaking of the difficulty of distinguishing Tatian's Harmony from others which must, the writer supposes, have been composed in his time, Dr. Donaldson points out : " And then we must remember that the Harmony of Tatian was confounded with the Gospel according to the Hebrews ; and it is not beyond the reach of possibility that Theodoret should have made some such mistake."[1] That is to say, that the only writer who refers to Tatian's Gospel who professes to have seen the work is not only "not to be depended on," but may actually have mistaken for it the Gospel according to the Hebrews. There is, therefore, no authority for saying that Tatian's Gospel was a harmony of four Gospels at all, and the name Diatessaron was not only not given by Tatian himself to the work, but was probably the usual foregone conclusion of the Christians of the third and fourth centuries, that everything in the shape of evangelical literature must be dependent on the Gospels adopted by the Church. Those, however, who called the Gospel used by Tatian the Gospel according to the Hebrews must apparently have read the work, and all that we know confirms their conclusion. The Gospel was, in point of fact, found in wide circulation precisely in the places in which, earlier, the Gospel according to the Hebrews was more particularly current.[2] The singular

---

[1] *Donaldson*, Hist. of Chr. Lit. and Doctr., iii. p. 25.

[2] *Credner*, Beiträge, i. p. 445; cf. *Westcott*, On the Canon, p. 280, note 2.

fact that the earliest reference to Tatian's "Harmony," is made a century and a half after its supposed composition, and that no writer before the fifth century had seen the work itself, indeed that only two writers before that period mention it at all, receives its natural explanation in the conclusion that Tatian did not compose any Harmony at all, but simply made use of the same Gospel as his master Justin Martyr, namely, the Gospel according to the Hebrews,[1] by which name his Gospel had been actually called by those best informed.

Although Theodoret, writing in the fifth century, says in the usual arbitrary manner of early Christian writers, that Tatian "excised" from his Gospel the genealogies and certain passages found in the Synoptics, he offers no explanation or proof of his assertion, and the utmost that can be received is that Tatian's Gospel did not contain them.[2] Did he omit them or merely use a Gospel which never included them? The latter is the more probable conclusion. Neither Justin's Gospel nor the Gospel according to the Hebrews contained the genealogies or references to the Son of David, and why, as Credner suggests, should Tatian have taken the trouble to prepare a Harmony with these omissions when he already found one such as he desired in Justin's Gospel? Tatian's Gospel, like that of his master Justin, or the Gospel according to the Hebrews, was different from, yet nearly related to, our canonical Gospels, and as we have already seen, Justin's Gospel, like Tatian's, was considered by many to be a harmony of our Gospels.[3] No

---

[1] Cf. *Credner*, Beiträge, i. p. 443 ff.; *Schmidt*, Einl. N. T., i. p. 124 ff.; *Scholten*, Die ält. Zeugnisse, p. 96 f.

[2] Cf. *Eichhorn*, Einl. N. T., p. 121 f.; *Hug*, Einl. N. T., i. p. 42; *Volkmar*, Der Ursprung, p. 35 f.

[3] *Credner*, Beiträge, i. p. 443 ff.

one seems to have seen Tatian's "Harmony," probably for the very simple reason that there was no such work, and the real Gospel used by him was that according to the Hebrews, as some distinctly and correctly called it. The name Diatessaron is first heard of in a work of the fourth century, when it is naturally given by people accustomed to trace every such work to our four Gospels, but as we have clearly seen, there is not up to the time of Tatian any evidence even of the existence of three of our Gospels, and much less of the four in a collected form. Here is an attempt to identify a supposed, but not demonstrated, harmony of Gospels whose separate existence has not been heard of. Even Dr. Westcott states that Tatian's Diatessaron " is apparently the first recognition of a fourfold Gospel,"[1] but, as we have seen, that recognition emanates only from a writer of the fourth century who had not seen the work of which he speaks. No such modern ideas, based upon mere foregone conclusions, can be allowed to enter into a discussion regarding a work dating from the time of Tatian.[2]

The fact that the work found by Theodoret in his diocese was used by orthodox Christians without con-

[1] On the Canon, p. 279.
[2] Dr. Lightfoot (Contemp. Rev., 1876-77, p. 1137) refers to an apocryphal work, "The Doctrine of Addai," recently edited and published by Dr. Phillips, in which it is stated that a large multitude assembled daily at Edessa for prayer and the reading of the Old Testament, "and the new of the Diatessaron." Dr. Lightfoot assumes that this is Tatian's Gospel. Even if it were so, however, we cannot discover in this any addition to our information regarding the composition of the work. We have already the fuller statement of Theodoret respecting the use of Tatian's work in the churches of his diocese, so that beyond an interesting reference, no fresh light is thrown upon the question by the phrase quoted. But we cannot see any ground for asserting that the Diatessaron here spoken of was Tatian's Gospel. On the contrary, it seems perfectly clear that the writer speaks only of the four Gospels of the New Testament.

sciousness of its supposed heterodoxy, is quite consistent with the fact that it was the Gospel according to the Hebrews, which at one time was in very general use, but later gradually became an object of suspicion and jealousy in the Church as our canonical Gospels took its place. The manner in which Theodoret dealt with Tatian's Gospel, or that "according to the Hebrews," recalls the treatment by Serapion of another form of the same work: the Gospel according to Peter. He found that work in circulation and greatly valued amongst the Christians of Rhossus, and allowed them peaceably to retain it for a time, until, alarmed at the Docetic heresy, he more closely examined the Gospel, and discovered in it what he considered heretical matter.[1] The Gospel according to the Hebrews, which narrowly missed a permanent place in the Canon of the Church, might well seem orthodox to the simple Christians of Cyrus, yet as different from, though closely related to, the Canonical Gospels, it would seem heretical to their Bishop. As different from the Gospels of the four evangelists, it was doubtless suppressed by Theodoret with perfect indifference as to whether it were called Tatian's Gospel or the Gospel according to the Hebrews.

It is obvious that there is no evidence of any value connecting Tatian's Gospel with those in our Canon. We know so little about the work in question, indeed, that as Dr. Donaldson frankly admits, "we should not be able to identify it, even if it did come down to us, unless it told us something reliable about itself."[2] Its earlier history is enveloped in obscurity, and as Canon Westcott observes: "The later history of the Diatessaron is

---

[1] *Eusebius*, H. E., vi. 12.
[2] Hist. Chr. Lit. and Doctr., iii. p. 26.

involved in confusion."¹ We have seen that in the sixth century it was described by Victor of Capua as Diapente, "by five," instead of "by four." It was also confounded with another Harmony written, not long after Tatian's day, by Ammonius of Alexandria (†243). Dionysius Bar-Salibi,² a writer of the latter half of the twelfth century, mentions that the Syrian Ephrem, about the middle of the fourth century, wrote a commentary on the Diatessaron of Tatian, which Diatessaron commenced with the opening words of the fourth Gospel: "In the beginning was the word." The statement of Bar-Salibi, however, is contradicted by Gregory Bar-Hebræus, Bishop of Tagrit, who says that Ephrem Syrus wrote his Commentary on the Diatessaron of Ammonius, and that this Diatessaron commenced with the words of the fourth Gospel: "In the beginning was the word."³ The Syrian Ebed-Jesu (†1308) held Tatian and Ammonius to be one and the same person; and it is probable that Dionysius mistook the Harmony of Ammonius for that of Tatian. It is not necessary further to follow this discussion, for it in no way affects our question, and no important deduction can be derived from it.⁴ We allude to the point for the mere sake of showing that, up to the last, we have no certain information throwing light on the composition of Tatian's Gospel. All that we do know of it,—what it did not contain—the places where it largely circulated, and the name by which it was

---

[1] On the Canon, p. 281.
[2] *Jos. Sim. Assemani*, Bibl. Orient., ii. p. 159 f.
[3] *Assemani*, Bibl. Orient., i. p. 57 f.
[4] *Credner*, Beiträge, i. p. 446 ff.; Gesch. N. T. Kan., p. 19 ff; *Donaldson*, Hist. Chr. Lit. and Doctr., iii. p. 25 f.; *Davidson*, Introd. N. T., ii. p. 397; *Eichhorn*, Einl. N. T., p. 120, anm.; *Gieseler*, Entst. schr. Evv., p. 17; *Hug*, Einl. N. T., i. p. 40 ff.; *Michaelis*, Einl. N. T., i. p. 898; *Scholten*, Die ält. Zeugnisse, p. 95 f.; *Westcott*, On the Canon, p. 281 f.

called, tends to identify it with the Gospel according to the Hebrews.

For the rest, Tatian had no idea of a New Testament Canon, and evidently did not recognize as inspired, any Scriptures except those of the Old Testament.[1] It is well known that the sect of the Encratites made use of apocryphal Gospels until a much later period, and rejected the authority of the Apostle Paul, and Tatian himself is accused of repudiating some of the Pauline Epistles, and of altering and mutilating others.[2]

2.

Dionysius of Corinth need not detain us long. Eusebius informs us that he was the author of seven Epistles addressed to various Christian communities, and also of a letter to Chrysophora, "a most faithful sister." Eusebius speaks of these writings as Catholic Epistles, and briefly characterizes each, but with the exception of a few short fragments preserved by him, none of these fruits of the "inspired industry" (ἐνθέου φιλοπονίας) of Dionysius are now extant.[3] These fragments are all from an Epistle said to have been addressed to Soter, Bishop of Rome, and give us a clue to the time at which they were written. The Bishopric of Soter is generally dated between A.D. 168—176,[4] during which years the Epistle must have been composed. It could not have

---

[1] *Credner*, Beiträge, i. p. 47 f., p. 441; Gesch. N. T. Kanons, p. 21; *Scholten*, Die ält. Zeugnisse, p. 98; *Volkmar*, Der Ursprung, p. 35.

[2] *Epiphanius*, Hær. xlvii. 1; *Eusebius*, H. E., iv. 29; *Hieron.*, Præf. in Tit. *Credner*, Beiträge, i. p. 47, p. 438; *Lardner*, Credibility, &c., Works, ii. p. 138; *Scholten*, Die ält. Zeugnisse, p. 97 f.; *Westcott*, On the Canon, p. 278, 280, note 1.

[3] *Eusebius*, H. E., iv. 23; *Hieron.*, De Vir. Ill., 27; *Grabe*, Spicil. Patr., ii. p. 217 f.; *Routh*, Reliq. Sacræ, i. p. 180 ff.

[4] *Eusebius*, H. E., iv. 19.

been written, however, until after Dionysius became Bishop of Corinth in A.D. 170,[1] and it was probably written some years after.[2]

No quotation from, or allusion to, any writing of the New Testament occurs in any of the fragments of the Epistles still extant; nor does Eusebius make mention of any such reference in the Epistles which have perished. As testimony for our Gospels, therefore, Dionysius is an absolute blank. Some expressions and statements, however, are put forward by apologists which we must examine. In the few lines which Tischendorf accords to Dionysius he refers to two of these. The first is an expression used, not by Dionysius himself, but by Eusebius, in speaking of the Epistles to the Churches at Amastris and at Pontus. Eusebius says that Dionysius adds some "expositions of Divine Scriptures" (γραφῶν θείων ἐξηγήσεις).[3] There can be no doubt, we think, that this refers to the Old Testament only, and Tischendorf himself does not deny it.[4]

The second passage which Tischendorf[5] points out, and which he claims with some other apologists as evidence of the actual existence of a New Testament Canon when Dionysius wrote, occurs in a fragment from the Epistle

[1] *Anger*, Synops. Ev. Proleg., p. xxxii.; *Hilgenfeld*, Der Kanon, p. 77; *Kirchhofer*, Quellensamml., p. 479; *Lardner*, Credibility, &c., Works, ii. p. 133; *Reuss*, Gesch. N. T., p. 290; *Scholten*, Die ält. Zeugnisse, p. 107; *Tischendorf*, Wann wurden, u. s. w., p. 18; *Volkmar*, Der Ursprung, p. 164; cf. p. 37. *Eusebius* in his Chronicon sets it in A.D. 171.

[2] *Anger* places it between 173–177, Synops. Ev. Proleg., xxxii.; cf. *Credner*, Gesch. N. T. Kan., p. 79. Jerome states that Dionysius flourished under M. Aurel. Verus and L. Aurel. Commodus. De Vir. Ill., 27.

[3] *Eusebius*, H. E., iv. 23.

[4] *Tischendorf*, Wann wurden, u. s. w., p. 18 f.; *Volkmar*, Der Ursprung, p. 38; *Donaldson*, Hist. Chr. Lit. and Doctr., iii. p. 217. Dr. Westcott's opinion is shown by his not even referring to the expression.

[5] Wann wurden, u. s. w., p. 18 f.

to Soter and the Romans which is preserved by Eusebius. It is as follows: "For the brethren having requested me to write Epistles, I wrote them. And the Apostles of the devil have filled these with tares, both taking away parts and adding others; for whom the woe is destined. It is not surprising then if some have recklessly ventured to adulterate the Scriptures of the Lord (τῶν κυριακῶν γραφῶν) when they have formed designs against these which are not of such importance."[1] Regarding this passage, Canon Westcott, with his usual boldness, says: "It is evident that the 'Scriptures of the Lord'—the writings of the New Testament—were at this time collected, that they were distinguished from other books, that they were jealously guarded, that they had been corrupted for heretical purposes."[2] We have seen, however, that there has not been a trace of any New Testament Canon in the writings of the Fathers before and during this age, and it is not permissible to put such an interpretation upon the remark of Dionysius. Dr. Donaldson, with greater critical justice and reserve, remarks regarding the expression "Scriptures of the

---

[1] Ἐπιστολὰς γὰρ ἀδελφῶν ἀξιωσάντων με γράψαι, ἔγραψα. Καὶ ταύτας οἱ τοῦ διαβόλου ἀπόστολοι ζιζανίων γεγέμικαν, ἃ μὲν ἐξαιροῦντες, ἃ δὲ προστιθέντες. Οἷς τὸ οὐαὶ κεῖται. Οὐ θαυμαστὸν ἄρα εἰ καὶ τῶν κυριακῶν ῥαδιουργῆσαί τινες ἐπιβέβληνται γραφῶν, ὁπότε καὶ ταῖς οὐ τοιαύταις ἐπιβεβουλεύκασι. Eusebius, H. E., iv. 23.

[2] On the Canon, p. 166. Dr. Wescottt, in the first instance, translates the expression: τῶν κυριακῶν γραφῶν: "the Scriptures of the New Testament." In a note to his fourth edition, however, he is kind enough to explain: "Of course it is not affirmed that the collection here called αἱ κυριακαὶ γραφαί was identical with our 'New Testament,' but simply that the phrase shows that a collection of writings belonging to the New Testament existed," p. 188, n. 2. Such a translation, in such a work, assuming as it does the whole question, and concealing what is doubtful, is most unwarrantable. The fact is that not only is there no mention of the New Testament at all, but the words as little necessarily imply a "collection" of writings as they do a "collection" of the Epistles of Dionysius.

Lord:" "It is not easy to settle what this term means," although he adds his own personal opinion, "but most probably it refers to the Gospels as containing the sayings and doings of the Lord. It is not likely, as Lardner supposes, that such a term would be applied to the whole of the New Testament."[1] The idea of our collected New Testament being referred to is of course quite untenable, and although it is open to argument that Dionysius may have referred to evangelical works, it is obvious that there are no means of proving the fact, and much less that he referred specially to our Gospels. In fact, the fragments of Dionysius present no evidence whatever of the existence of our Synoptics.

In order further to illustrate the inconclusiveness of the arguments based upon so vague an expression, we may add that it does not of necessity apply to any Gospels or works of Christian history at all, and may with perfect propriety have indicated the Scriptures of the Old Testament. We find Justin Martyr complaining in the same spirit as Dionysius, through several chapters, that the Old Testament Scriptures, and more especially those relating to the Lord, had been adulterated, that parts had been taken away, and others added, with the intention of destroying or weakening their application to Christ.[2] Justin's argument throughout is, that the whole of the Old Testament Scriptures refer to Christ, and Tryphon, his antagonist, the representative of Jewish opinion, is made to avow that the Jews not only wait for Christ, but, he adds: "We admit that all the Scriptures which you have cited refer to him."[3] Not only, therefore, were the Scriptures of the Old Testament

---

[1] Hist. Chr. Lit. and Doctr., iii. p. 217.
[2] Dial. c. Tryph., lxx.—lxxv. [3] Dial., lxxxix.

closely connected with their Lord by the Fathers and, at the date of which we are treating, were the only "Holy Scriptures" recognised, but they made the same complaints which we meet with in Dionysius that these Scriptures were adulterated by omissions and interpolations.[1] The expression of Eusebius regarding "expositions of Divine Scriptures" (γραφῶν θείων ἐξηγήσεις) added by Dionysius, which applied to the Old Testament, tends to connect the Old Testament also with this term "Scriptures of the Lord."

If the term "Scriptures of the Lord," however, be referred to Gospels, the difficulty of using it as evidence continues undiminished. We have no indication of the particular evangelical works which were in the Bishop's mind. We have seen that other Gospels were used by the Fathers, and in exclusive circulation amongst various communities, and even until much later times many works were regarded by them as divinely inspired which have no place in our Canon. The Gospel according to the Hebrews for instance was probably used by some at least of the Apostolic Fathers,[2] by pseudo-Ignatius,[3] Polycarp,[4] Papias,[5] Hegesippus,[6] Justin Martyr,[7] and at least employed along with our Gospels by Clement of Alexandria, Origen, and Jerome.[8] The fact that Serapion, in the third century allowed the Gospel of Peter to be used in the church of Rhossus[9] shows at the same time the consideration in which it was held, and the incompleteness of the Canonical position of the New Testament writings. So does the circumstance

---

[1] This charge is made with insistance throughout the Clementine Homilies.
[2] Cf. i. p. 223 ff., p. 230 ff.   [3] Cf. i. p. 272 f.   [4] Cf. i. p. 279.
[5] Cf. i. p. 484.   [6] Cf. i. p. 433 f.   [7] Cf. i. p. 288 ff.
[8] Cf. i. p. 422 f.   [9] *Eusebius, H. E.*, vi. 12.

that in the fifth century Theodoret found the Gospel according to the Hebrews, or Tatian's Gospel, widely circulated and held in honour amongst orthodox churches in his diocese.[1] The Pastor of Hermas, which was read in the Churches and nearly secured a permanent place in the Canon, was quoted as inspired by Irenæus.[2] The Epistle of Barnabas was held in similar honour, and quoted as inspired by Clement of Alexandria[3] and by Origen,[4] as was likewise the Epistle of the Roman Clement. The Apocalypse of Peter was included by Clement of Alexandria in his account of the Canonical Scriptures and those which are disputed, such as the Epistle of Jude and the other Catholic Epistles,[5] and it stands side by side with the Apocalypse of John in the Canon of Muratori, being long after publicly read in the Churches of Palestine.[6] Tischendorf indeed conjectures that a blank in the Codex Sinaiticus after the New Testament was formerly filled by it. Justin, Clement of Alexandria, and Lactantius quote the Sibylline books as the Word of God, and pay similar honour to the Book of Hystaspes.[7] So great indeed was the consideration and use of the Sibylline Books in the Church of the second and third centuries, that Christians from that fact were nicknamed Sibyllists.[8] It is unnecessary to multiply, as

[1] *Theodoret*, Hær. fab., i. 20; cf. *Epiph.*, Hær., xlvi. 1; cf. *Theodoret*, Hær. fab., ii. 2.

[2] Adv. Hær., iv. 20, § 2; *Eusebius*, H. E., v. 8; cf. iii. 3.

[3] Strom., ii. 8, iv. 17.   [4] Philocal., 18.

[5] *Eusebius*, H. E., vi. 14.   [6] *Sozom.*, H. E., vii. 19.

[7] *Justin*, Apol., i. 20, 44; *Clem. Al.*, Strom., vi. 5, §§ 42, 43; *Lactantius*, Instit. Div., i. 6, 7, vii. 15, 19. Clement of Alexandria quotes with perfect faith and seriousness some apocryphal book, in which, he says, the Apostle Paul recommends the Hellenic books, the Sibyl and the books of Hystaspes, as giving notably clear prophetic descriptions of the Son of God. Strom., vi. 5, § 42, 43.

[8] *Origen*, Contra Cels., v. 6; cf. vii. 53.

might so easily be done, these illustrations; it is too well known that a vast number of Gospels and similar works, which have been excluded from the Canon, were held in the deepest veneration by the Church in the second century, to which the words of Dionysius may apply. So vague and indefinite an expression at any rate is useless as evidence for the existence of our Canonical Gospels.

Canon Westcott's deduction from the words of Dionysius, that not only were the writings of the New Testament already collected, but that they were "jealously guarded," is imaginative indeed. It is much and devoutly to be wished that they had been as carefully guarded as he supposes, but it is well known that this was not the case, and that numerous interpolations have been introduced into the text. The whole history of the Canon and of Christian literature in the second and third centuries displays the most deplorable carelessness and want of critical judgment on the part of the Fathers. Whatever was considered as conducive to Christian edification was blindly adopted by them, and a vast number of works were launched into circulation and falsely ascribed to Apostles and others likely to secure for them greater consideration. Such pious fraud was rarely suspected, still more rarely detected in the early ages of Christianity, and several of such pseudographs have secured a place in our New Testament. The words of Dionysius need not receive any wider signification than a reference to well-known Epistles. It is clear from the words attributed to the Apostle Paul in 2 Thess. ii. 2, iii. 17, that his Epistles were falsified, and setting aside some of those which bear his name in our Canon, spurious Epistles were long ascribed to him, such as the Epistle to the Laodiceans and a third Epistle to the Corinthians. We need not do more than allude to the second Epistle falsely bearing the name of Clement of Rome, as well as the Clementine Homilies and Recognitions, the Apostolical Constitutions, and the spurious letters of Ignatius, the letters and legend of Abgarus quoted by Eusebius, and the Epistles of Paul and Seneca, in addition to others already pointed out, as instances of the wholesale falsification of that period, many of which gross forgeries were at once accepted as genuine by the Fathers, so slight was their critical faculty and so ready their credulity.[1] In one case the Church punished the author who, from mistaken zeal for the honour of the Apostle Paul, fabricated the *Acta Pauli et Theclæ* in his name,[2] but the forged production was not the less made use of in the Church. There was, therefore, no lack of falsification and adulteration of works of Apostles and others of greater note than himself to warrant the remark of Dionysius, without any forced application of it to our Gospels or to a New Testament Canon, the existence of which there is nothing to substantiate, but on the contrary every reason to discredit.

Before leaving this passage we may add that although even Tischendorf does not, Canon Westcott does find in it references to our first Synoptic, and to the Apocalypse. "The short fragment just quoted," he says, "contains two obvious allusions, one to the Gospel of St. Matthew, and one to the Apocalypse."[3] The words: "the Apostles of the devil have filled these with tares," are, he supposes,

---

[1] The Epistle of Jude quotes as genuine the Assumption of Moses, and also the Book of Enoch, and the defence of the authenticity of the latter by Tertullian (*de Cultu fem.*, i. 3) will not be forgotten.

[2] *Tertullian*, De Baptismo, 17.   [3] On the Canon, p. 167.

an allusion to Matt. xiii. 24 ff. But even if the expression were an echo of the Parable of the Wheat and Tares, it is not permissible to refer it in this arbitrary way to our first Gospel, to the exclusion of the numerous other works which existed, many of which doubtless contained it. Obviously the words have no evidential value.

Continuing his previous assertions, however, Canon Westcott affirms with equal boldness: "The allusion in the last clause"—to the "Scriptures of the Lord"—"will be clear when it is remembered that Dionysius 'warred against the heresy of Marcion and defended the rule of truth'" (παρίστασθαι κανόνι ἀλ.).[1] Tischendorf, who is ready enough to strain every expression into evidence, recognizes too well that this is not capable of such an interpretation. Dr. Westcott omits to mention that the words, moreover, are not used by Dionysius at all, but simply proceed from Eusebius.[2] Dr. Donaldson distinctly states the fact that, "there is no reference to the Bible in the words of Eusebius: he defends the rule of the truth"[3] (τῷ τῆς ἀληθείας παρίσταται κανόνι).

There is only one other point to mention. Canon Westcott refers to the passage in the Epistle of Dionysius, which has already been quoted in this work regarding the reading of Christian writings in churches. "To-day," he writes to Soter, "we have kept the Lord's holy day, in which we have read your Epistle, from the reading of which we shall ever derive admonition, as we do from the former one written to us by Clement."[4] It is evident that there was no idea, in selecting the works to be read at the weekly assembly of Christians, of any

---

[1] On the Canon, p. 166 f.   [2] H. E., iv. 23.
[3] Hist. Chr. Lit. and Doctr., iii. p. 217 f.
[4] Euseb., H. E., iv. 23.

Canon of a New Testament. We here learn that the Epistles of Clement and of Soter were habitually read, and while we hear of this, and of the similar reading of Justin's "Memoirs of the Apostles,"[1] of the Pastor of Hermas,[2] of the Apocalypse of Peter,[3] and other apocryphal works, we do not at the same time hear of the public reading of our Gospels.

[1] *Justin*, Apol., i. 67.
[2] *Euseb.*, H. E., iii. 3; *Hieron.*, De Vir. Ill., 10.
[3] *Sozom.*, H. E., vii. 9.

CHAPTER IX.

MELITO OF SARDIS—CLAUDIUS APOLLINARIS—ATHENA-GORAS—THE EPISTLE OF VIENNE AND LYONS.

We might here altogether have passed over Melito, Bishop of Sardis in Lydia, had it not been for the use of certain fragments of his writings made by Canon Westcott. Melito, naturally, is not cited by Tischendorf at all, but the English Apologist, with greater zeal, we think, than critical discretion, forces him into service as evidence for the Gospels and a New Testament Canon. The date of Melito, it is generally agreed, falls after A.D. 176, a phrase in his apology presented to Marcus Antoninus preserved in Eusebius [1] (μετὰ τοῦ παιδός) indicating that Commodus had already been admitted to a share of the Government.[2]

Canon Westcott affirms that, in a fragment preserved by Eusebius, Melito speaks of the books of the New Testament in a collected form. He says: "The words of Melito on the other hand are simple and casual, and yet their meaning can scarcely be mistaken. He writes to Onesimus, a fellow-Christian who had urged him ' to

---

[1] H. E., iv. 26.
[2] *Basnage*, Ann. Polit. Eccles., 177, § 3; *Dupin*, Biblioth. des Auteurs Eccl., i. p. 63; *Lardner*, Credibility, &c., Works, ii. p. 147; *Tillemont*, Mém. Hist. Eccl., ii. p. 707, note 1 f.; *Westcott*, On the Canon, p. 193, note 2; *Woog*, De Melitone, § 5; cf. *Donaldson*, Hist. Chr. Lit. and Doctr., iii. p. 229. Compare, however, *Waddington*, Fastes des Prov. Asiatiques, p. 731, as to the date of the work on the Passover.

make selections for him from the Law and the Prophets concerning the Saviour and the faith generally, and furthermore desired to learn the accurate account of the Old (παλαιῶν) Books;' 'having gone therefore to the East,' Melito says, 'and reached the spot where [each thing] was preached and done, and having learned accurately the Books of the Old Testament, I have sent a list of them.' The mention of 'the Old Books'—'the Books of the Old Testament,' naturally implies a definite New Testament, a written antitype to the Old; and the form of language implies a familiar recognition of its contents."[1] This is truly astonishing! The "form of language" can only refer to the words: "concerning the Saviour and the faith generally," which must have an amazing fulness of meaning to convey to Canon Westcott the implication of a "familiar recognition" of the contents of a supposed already collected New Testament, seeing that a simple Christian, not to say a Bishop, might at least know of a Saviour and the faith generally from the oral preaching of the Gospel, from a single Epistle of Paul, or from any of the πολλοί of Luke. This reasoning forms a worthy pendant to his argument that because Melito speaks of the books of the Old Testament he implies the existence of a definite collected New Testament. Such an assertion is calculated to mislead a large class of readers.[2]

The fragment of Melito is as follows: " Melito to his

[1] On the Canon, p. 193. [In the fourth edition Dr. Westcott omits the last phrase, making a full stop at " Old." p. 218.]

[2] It must be said, however, that Canon Westcott merely follows and exaggerates Lardner, here, who says: " From this passage I would conclude that there was then also a volume or collection of books called the New Testament, containing the writings of Apostles and Apostolical men, but we cannot from hence infer the names or the exact number of those books." Credibility, &c., Works, ii. p. 148.

brother Onesimus, greeting. As thou hast frequently desired in thy zeal for the word (λόγον) to have extracts made for thee, both from the law and the prophets concerning the Saviour and our whole faith; nay, more, hast wished to learn the exact statement of the old books (παλαιῶν βιβλίων), how many they are and what is their order, I have earnestly endeavoured to accomplish this, knowing thy zeal concerning the faith, and thy desire to be informed concerning the word (λόγον), and especially that thou preferrest these matters to all others from love towards God, striving to gain eternal salvation. Having, therefore, gone to the East, and reached the place where this was preached and done, and having accurately ascertained the books of the Old Testament (τὰ τῆς παλαιᾶς διαθήκης βιβλία), I have, subjoined, sent a list of them unto thee, of which these are the names"—then follows a list of the books of the Old Testament, omitting, however, Esther. He then concludes with the words: "Of these I have made the extracts dividing them into six books."[1]

Canon Westcott's assertion that the expression "Old Books," "Books of the Old Testament," involves here by antithesis a definite *written* New Testament, requires us to say a few words as to the name of "Testament" as applied to both divisions of the Bible. It is of course well known that this word came into use originally from the translation of the Hebrew word "covenant" (בְּרִית), or compact made between God and the Israelites,[2] in the Septuagint version, by the Greek word Διαθήκη, which in a legal sense also means a will or Testament,[3] and that word is adopted throughout the New Testa-

---

[1] *Eusebius*, H. E., iv. 26.   [2] Cf. Exod. xxiv. 7.
[3] The legal sense of διαθήκη as a Will or Testament is distinctly in-

ment.[1] The Vulgate translation, instead of retaining the original Hebrew signification, translated the word in the Gospels and Epistles, "*Testamentum*," and ἡ παλαιὰ διαθήκη became "*Vetus Testamentum*," instead of "*Vetus Fœdus*," and whenever the word occurs in the English version it is almost invariably rendered "Testament" instead of covenant. The expression "Book of the Covenant," or "Testament," βίβλος τῆς διαθήκης, frequently occurs in the LXX version of the Old Testament and its Apocrypha,[2] and in Jeremiah xxxi. 31–34,[3] the prophet speaks of making a "new covenant" (καινὴ διαθήκη) with the house of Israel, which is indeed quoted in Hebrews viii. 8. It is the doctrinal idea of the new covenant, through Christ confirming the former one made to the Israelites, which has led to the distinction of the Old and New Testaments. Generally the Old Testament was, in the first ages of Christianity, indicated by the simple expressions "The Books" (τὰ βιβλία), "Holy Scriptures" (ἱερὰ γράμματα,[4] or γραφαὶ ἅγιαι),[5] or "The Scriptures" (αἱ γραφαί),[6] but the preparation for the distinction of "Old Testament" began very early in the development of the doctrinal idea of the New Testament of Christ, before there was any part of the New Testament books written at all. The expression "New Testament," derived thus

---

tended in Heb. ix. 16. "For where a Testament (διαθήκη) is, there must also of necessity be the death of the testator" (διαθεμένου). The same word διαθήκη is employed throughout the whole passage. Heb. ix. 15—20.

[1] 2 Cor. iii. 14; Heb. viii. 6—13, xii. 24; Rom. ix. 4, xi. 26—28; Gal. iii. 14—17; Ephes. ii. 12, &c., &c.

[2] Cf. Exod. xxiv. 7; 2 Chron. xxxiv. 30; 2 Kings xxiii. 2; 1 Maccab. i. 57; Sirach, xxiv. 23, &c., &c.

[3] In the Septuagint version, xxxviii. 31—34.

[4] 2 Tim. iii. 15.   [5] Rom. i. 2.   [6] Matt. xxii. 29.

antithetically from the "Old Testament," occurs constantly throughout the second part of the Bible. In the Epistle to the Hebrews viii. 6–13, the Mosaic dispensation is contrasted with the Christian, and Jesus is called the Mediator of a better Testament ($\delta\iota\alpha\theta\acute{\eta}\kappa\eta$).[1] The first Testament not being faultless, is replaced by the second, and the writer quotes the passage from Jeremiah to which we have referred regarding a New Testament, winding up his argument with the words, v. 13 : "In that he saith a new (Testament) he hath made the first old." Again, in our first Gospel, during the Last Supper, Jesus is represented as saying : "This is my blood of the New Testament" ($\tau\hat{\eta}s$ $\kappa\alpha\iota\nu\hat{\eta}s$ $\delta\iota\alpha\theta\acute{\eta}\kappa\eta s$) ;[2] and in Luke he says : "This cup is the New Testament ($\dot{\eta}$ $\kappa\alpha\iota\nu\grave{\eta}$ $\delta\iota\alpha\theta\acute{\eta}\kappa\eta$) in my blood."[3] There is, therefore, a very distinct reference made to the two Testaments as "New" and "Old," and in speaking of the books of the Law and the Prophets as the "Old Books" and "Books of the old Testament," after the general acceptance of the Gospel of Jesus as the New Testament or Covenant, there was no antithetical implication whatever of a written New Testament, but a mere reference to the doctrinal idea. We might multiply illustrations showing how ever-present to the mind of the early Church was the contrast of the Mosaic and Christian Covenants as Old and New. Two more we may venture to point out. In Romans ix. 4, and Gal. iv. 24, the two Testaments or Covenants ($\alpha\acute{\iota}$ $\delta\acute{\upsilon}o$ $\delta\iota\alpha\theta\hat{\eta}\kappa\alpha\iota$), typified by Sinai and the heavenly Jerusalem, are discussed, and the superiority of the latter asserted. There is, however, a passage, still more clear and decisive. Paul says in 2 Corinthians iii. 6 : "Who also (God) made us sufficient to be ministers of the New

---

[1] Cf. ix. 15, xii. 24.   [2] Matt. xxvi. 28.   [3] Luke xxii. 20.

Testament (καινῆς διαθήκης) not of the letter, but of the spirit" (οὐ γράμματος ἀλλὰ πνεύματος). Why does not Canon Westcott boldly claim this as evidence of a definite written New Testament, when not only is there reference to the name, but a distinction drawn between the letter and the spirit of it, from which an apologist might make a telling argument? But proceeding to contrast the glory of the New with the Old dispensation, the Apostle, in reference to the veil with which Moses covered his face, says: "But their understandings were hardened: for until this very day remaineth the same veil in the reading of the Old Testament" (ἐπὶ τῇ ἀναγνώσει τῆς παλαιᾶς διαθήκης);[1] and as if to make the matter still clearer he repeats in the next verse: "But even unto this day when Moses is read, the veil lieth upon their heart." Now here the actual reading of the *Old* Testament (παλαιᾶς διαθήκης) is distinctly mentioned, and the expression quite as aptly as that of Melito, "implies a definite New Testament, a written antitype to the Old," but even Canon Westcott would not dare to suggest that, when the second Epistle to the Corinthians was composed, there was a "definite written New Testament" in existence. This conclusively shows that the whole argument from Melito's mention of the books of the Old Testament is absolutely groundless.

On the contrary, Canon Westcott should know very well that the first general designation for the New Testament collection was "The Gospel" (εὐαγγέλιον, εὐαγγελικόν, εὐαγγελικά) and "The Apostle" (ἀπόστολος, ἀποστολικόν, ἀποστολικά), for the two portions of the collection, in contrast with the divisions of the Old Testament, the Law and the Prophets (ὁ νόμος, οἱ

[1] Verse 14.

προφῆται),[1] and the name New Testament occurs for the very first time in the third century, when Tertullian called the collection of Christian Scriptures *Novum Instrumentum* and *Novum Testamentum*.[2] The term ἡ καινὴ διαθήκη is not, so far as we are aware, applied in the Greek to the "New Testament" collection in any earlier work than Origen's *De Principiis*, iv. 1. It was only in the second half of the third century that the double designation τὸ εὐαγγέλιον καὶ ὁ ἀπόστολος was generally abandoned.[3]

As to the evidence for a New Testament Canon, which Dr. Westcott supposes he gains by his unfounded inference from Melito's expression, we may judge of its value from the fact that he himself, like Lardner, admits: "But there is little evidence in the fragment of Melito to show what writings he would have included in the new collection."[4] Little evidence? There is none at all.

There is, however, one singular and instructive point in this fragment to which Canon Westcott does not in any way refer, but which well merits attention as illus-

---

[1] Cf. *Irenæus*, Adv. Hær., i. 3, § 6; *Clemens Al.*, Strom., v. 5, § 31; *Tertullian*, De Præscr., 36; Adv. Marc., iv. 2, Apolog., 18; *Origen*, Hom. xix. in Jerem. T. iii. p. 364. The Canon of Muratori says that the Pastor of Hermas can neither be classed "inter Prophetas neque inter Apostolos." In a translation of the *Clavis*, a spurious work attributed to Melito himself—and Dr. Westcott admits it to be spurious (p. 198, note 1) —the Gospels are referred to simply by the formula "*in evangelio*," and the Epistles generally "*in apostolo*."

[2] Adv. Prax., 15, 20; Adv. Marc., iv. 1. He says in the latter place "instrumenti," referring to Old and New Testaments, "vel, quod magis usui est dicere, testamenti."

[3] *Bertholdt*, Einl. a. u. N. Test., i. p. 22; *Credner*, Gesch. N. T. Kanon, p. 23 ff.; *Eichhorn*, Einl. N. T., iv. p. 25 ff., p. 38 ff.; *Guericke*, Gesammtgesch. N. T., p. 4 f.; *Reithmayr*, Einl. N. B., 1852, p. 22 ff.; *Scholz*, Einl. H. S. des A. u. N. T., 1845, i. p. 264; *De Wette*, Lehrb. Einl. A. T., 1852, p. 8 ff.

[4] On the Canon, p. 194.

trating the state of religious knowledge at that time, and, by analogy, giving a glimpse of the difficulties which beset early Christian literature. We are told by Melito that Onesimus had frequently urged him to give him exact information as to the number and order of the books of the Old Testament, and to have extracts made for him from them concerning the Saviour and the faith. Now it is apparent that Melito, though a Bishop, was not able to give the desired information regarding the number and order of the books of the Old Testament himself, but that he had to make a journey to collect it. If this was the extent of knowledge possessed by the Bishop of Sardis of what was to the Fathers the only Holy Scripture, how ignorant his flock must have been, and how unfitted, both, to form any critical judgment as to the connection of Christianity with the Mosaic dispensation. The formation of a Christian Canon at a period when such ignorance was not only possible but generally prevailed, and when the zeal of believers led to the composition of such a mass of pseudonymic and other literature, in which every consideration of correctness and truth was subordinated to a childish desire for edification, must have been slow indeed and uncertain; and in such an age fortuitous circumstances must have mainly led to the canonization or actual loss of many a work. So far from affording any evidence of the existence of a New Testament Canon, the fragment of Melito only shows the ignorance of the Bishop of Sardis as to the Canon even of the Old Testament.

We have not yet finished with Melito in connection with Canon Westcott, however, and it is necessary to follow him further in order fully to appreciate the nature of the evidence for the New Testament Canon, which, in default of better, he is obliged to offer. Eusebius gives a list of the works of Melito which have come to his knowledge, and in addition to the fragment already quoted, he extracts a brief passage from Melito's work on the Passover, and some much longer quotations from his Apology, to which we have in passing referred.[1] With these exceptions, none of Melito's writings are now extant. Dr. Cureton, however, has published a Syriac version, with translation, of a so-called "Oration of Meliton, the Philosopher, who was in the presence of Antoninus Cæsar," together with five other fragments attributed to Melito.[2] With regard to this Syriac Oration, Canon Westcott says : "Though if it be entire, it is not the Apology with which Eusebius was acquainted, the general character of the writing leads to the belief that it is a genuine book of Melito of Sardis ; "[3] and he proceeds to treat it as authentic. In the first place, we have so little of Melito's genuine compositions extant, that it is hazardous indeed to draw any positive deduction from the "character of the writing." Cureton, Bunsen, and others maintain that this Apology is not a fragment, and it cannot be the work mentioned by Eusebius, for it does not contain the quotations from the authentic Orations which he has preserved, and which are considerable. It is, however, clear from the substance of the composition that it cannot have been spoken before the Emperor,[4] and, moreover, it has in no way the character of an "Apology," for there is not a single word in it about either Christianity or Christians. There is

---

[1] *Euseb.*, H. E., iv. 26.
[2] Spicilegium Syriacum, 1855, pp. 41—56 ; *Pitra*, Spicil. Solesm., 1855, ii. Proleg. xxxviii. ff.
[3] On the Canon, p. 194.
[4] *Donaldson*, Hist. Chr. Lit. and Doctr., iii. p. 234 f.

every reason to believe that it is not a genuine work of Melito.[1] There is no ground whatever for supposing that he wrote two Apologies, nor is this ascribed to him upon any other ground than the inscription of an unknown Syriac writer. This, however, is not the only spurious work attributed to Melito. Of this work Canon Westcott says: "Like other Apologies, this oration contains only indirect references to the Christian Scriptures. The allusions in it to the Gospels are extremely rare, and except so far as they show the influence of St. John's writings, of no special interest."[2] It would have been more correct to have said that there are no allusions in it to the Gospels at all.

Canon Westcott is somewhat enthusiastic in speaking of Melito and his literary activity as evinced in the titles of his works recorded by Eusebius, and he quotes a fragment, said to be from a treatise "On Faith," amongst these Syriac remains, and which he considers to be "a very striking expansion of the early historic creed of the Church."[3] As usual, we shall give the entire fragment: "We have made collections from the Law and the Prophets relative to those things which have been declared respecting our Lord Jesus Christ, that we may prove to your love that he is perfect Reason, the Word of God; who was begotten before the light; who was Creator together with the Father; who was the Fashioner of man; who was all in all; who among the Patriarchs was Patriarch; who in the Law was the Law; among the Priests chief Priest; among Kings Governor; among the Prophets the Prophet;

---

[1] *Donaldson, ib.*, iii. p. 234; *Freppel, Les Apologistes*, 2 ser. p. 374 f.; *Davidson*, Introd. N. T., ii. p. 478.
[2] *On the Canon*, p. 194.
[3] *On the Canon*, p. 196.

among the Angels Archangel; in the voice the Word; among Spirits Spirit; in the Father the Son; in God God the King for ever and ever. For this was he who was Pilot to Noah; who conducted Abraham; who was bound with Isaac; who was in exile with Jacob; who was sold with Joseph; who was captain with Moses; who was the Divider of the inheritance with Jesus the son of Nun; who in David and the Prophets foretold his own sufferings; who was incarnate in the Virgin; who was born at Bethlehem; who was wrapped in swaddling clothes in the manger; who was seen of shepherds; who was glorified of angels; who was worshipped by the Magi; who was pointed out by John; who assembled the Apostles; who preached the kingdom; who healed the maimed; who gave light to the blind; who raised the dead; who appeared in the Temple; who was not believed by the people; who was betrayed by Judas; who was laid hold of by the Priests; who was condemned by Pilate; who was pierced in the flesh; who was hanged upon the tree; who was buried in the earth; who rose from the dead; who appeared to the Apostles; who ascended to heaven; who sitteth on the right hand of the Father; who is the Rest of those who are departed; the Recoverer of those who are lost; the Light of those who are in darkness; the Deliverer of those who are captives; the Finder of those who have gone astray; the Refuge of the afflicted; the Bridegroom of the Church; the Charioteer of the Cherubim; the Captain of the Angels; God who is of God; the Son who is of the Father; Jesus Christ, the King for ever and ever. Amen." [1]

[1] *Cureton*, Spicil. Syriacum, p. 53 f.; *Pitra*, Spicil. Solesm., ii. Prolog. lix. f.; *Westcott*, On the Canon, p. 196 f.

Canon Westcott commences his commentary upon this passage with the remark: "No writer could state the fundamental truths of Christianity more unhesitatingly, or quote the Scriptures of the Old and New Testaments with more perfect confidence."[1] We need not do more than remark that there is not a single quotation in the fragment, and that there is not a single one of the references to Gospel history or to ecclesiastical dogmas which might not have been derived from the Epistles of Paul, from any of the forms of the Gospel according to the Hebrews, the Protevangelium of James, or from many another apocryphal Gospel, or the oral teaching of the Church. It is singular, however, that the only hint which Canon Westcott gives of the more than doubtful authenticity of this fragment consists of the introductory remark, after alluding to the titles of his genuine and supposititious writings: "Of these multifarious writings very few fragments remain in the original Greek, but the general tone of them is so decided in its theological character as to go far to establish the genuineness of those which are preserved in the Syriac translation."[2]

Now, the fragment "On Faith" which has just been quoted is one of the five Syriac pieces of Dr. Cureton to which we have referred, and which even Apologists agree "cannot be regarded as genuine."[3] It is well known that there were other writers in the early Church bearing the names of Melito and Miletius or Meletius,[4]

---

[1] On the Canon, p. 197.
[2] On the Canon, p. 196.
[3] *Donaldson*, Hist. Chr. Lit. and Doctr., iii. p. 236. Cf. *Sanday*, Gospels in Sec. Cent., p. 245.
[4] *Woog*, Dissert., i. § 2; cf. *Donaldson*, ib., iii. p. 234, 236; *Cureton*, Spicil. Syriac., p. 96 f.

which were frequently confounded. Of these five Syriac fragments one bears the superscription: "Of Meliton, Bishop of the city of Attica," and another, "Of the holy Meliton, Bishop of Utica," and Cureton himself evidently leant to the opinion that they are not by our Melito, but by a Meletius or Melitius, Bishop of Sebastopolis in Pontus.[1] The third fragment is said to be taken from a discourse "On the Cross," which was unknown to Eusebius, and from its doctrinal peculiarities was probably written after his time.[2] Another fragment purports to be from a work on the "Soul and Body;" and the last one from the treatise "On Faith," which we are discussing. The last two works are mentioned by Eusebius, but these fragments, besides coming in such suspicious company, must for other reasons be pronounced spurious.[3] They have in fact no attestation whatever except that of the Syriac translator, who is unknown, and which therefore is worthless, and, on the other hand, the whole style and thought of the fragments are unlike anything else of Melito's time, and clearly indicate a later stage of theological development.[4] Moreover, in the Mechitarist Library at Venice there is a shorter version of the same passage in a Syriac MS., and an Armenian version of the extract as given above, with some variation of the opening lines, in both of which the passage is distinctly ascribed to Irenæus.[5] Besides the Oration and the five Syriac fragments, we have other two works extant falsely attributed to Melito, one, "De Transitu Virginis Mariæ," describing the miraculous presence of the Apostles at the

[1] Spicil. Syriac., p. 96 f.
[2] *Donaldson*, Hist. Chr. Lit. and Doctr., iii. p. 237.
[3] *Donaldson*, ib., iii. p. 227.   [4] *Ib.*, iii. p. 236.
[5] They are given by *Pitra*, Spicil. Solesm., i. p. 3 ff.

death of Mary;[1] and the other, "De Actibus Joannis Apostoli," relates the history of miracles performed by the Apostle John. Both are universally admitted to be spurious,[2] as are a few other fragments also bearing his name. Melito did not escape from the falsification to which many of his more distinguished predecessors and contemporaries were victims, through the literary activity and unscrupulous religious zeal of the first three or four centuries of our era.

2.

Very little is known regarding Claudius Apollinaris to whom we must now for a moment turn. Eusebius informs us that he was Bishop of Hierapolis,[3] and in this he is supported by the fragment of a letter of Serapion Bishop of Antioch preserved to us by him, which refers to Apollinaris as the "most blessed."[4] Tischendorf, without any precise date, sets him down as contemporary with Tatian and Theophilus (the latter of whom, he thinks, wrote his work addressed to Autolycus about A.D. 180—181).[5] Eusebius[6] mentions that, like his somewhat earlier contemporary Melito of Sardis, Apollinaris presented an "Apology" to the Emperor Marcus Antoninus, and he gives us further materials for a date[7] by stating that Claudius Apollinaris, probably in his Apology, refers to

---

[1] It is worthy of remark that the Virgin is introduced into all these fragments in a manner quite foreign to the period at which Melito lived.

[2] *Donaldson*, Hist. Chr. Lit. and Doctr., iii. p. 238; *Woog*, Dissert., ii. § 25; *Pitra*, Spicil. Solesm., ii. Proleg. xxxi. f.

[3] H. E., iv. 21, 26. [4] *Ib.*, v. 19.

[5] Wann wurden, u. s. w., p. 16, anm. 1.

[6] H. E., iv. 26, 27; cf. *Hieron.*, De Vir. Ill., 26.

[7] Eusebius himself sets him down in his Chronicle as flourishing in the eleventh year of Marcus, or A.D. 171, a year later than he dates Melito.

the miracle of the "Thundering Legion," which is said to have occurred during the war of Marcus Antoninus against the Marcomanni in A.D. 174.[1] The date of his writings may, therefore, with moderation be fixed between A.D. 177—180.[2]

Eusebius and others mention various works composed by him,[3] none of which, however, are extant; and we have only to deal with two brief fragments in connection with the Paschal controversy, which are ascribed to Apollinaris in the Paschal Chronicle of Alexandria. This controversy, as to the day upon which the Christian Passover should be celebrated, broke out about A.D. 170, and long continued to divide the Church.[4] In the preface to the Paschal Chronicle, a work of the seventh century, the unknown chronicler says: "Now even Apollinaris, the most holy Bishop of Hierapolis, in Asia, who lived near apostolic times, taught the like things in his work on the Passover, saying thus: 'There are some, however, who through ignorance raise contentions regarding these matters in a way which

---

[1] *Eusebius*, H. E., v. 5; *Mosheim*, Inst. Hist. Eccles., Book i. cent. ii. part. i. ch. i. § 9. Apollinaris states that in consequence of this miracle, the Emperor had bestowed upon the Legion the name of the "Thundering Legion." We cannot here discuss this subject, but the whole story illustrates the rapidity with which a fiction is magnified into truth by religious zeal, and is surrounded by false circumstantial evidence. Cf. *Tertullian*, Apol. 5, ad Scapulam, 4; *Dion Cassius*, lib. 55; *Scaliger*, Animadv. in Euseb., p. 223 f.; cf. *Donaldson*, Hist. Chr. Lit. and Doctr., iii. p. 241 f.

[2] *Baur*, Unters. kan. Evv. p. 356; *Donaldson*, Hist. Chr. Lit. and Doctr., iii. p. 240; *Lardner*, Credibility, &c., Works, ii. p. 291; *Newman*, Essays on Miracles, 1870, p. 241; *Scholten*, Das Evang. n. Johann., 1867, p. 14 ff.; Die ält. Zeugnisse, p. 106; *Volkmar*, Der Ursprung, p. 164, p. 31 f.

[3] *Eusebius*, H. E., iv. 27; cf. 26, v. 19; *Hieron.*, Vir. Ill., 26; *Theodoret*, Hær. Fab. ii. 21, iii. 2; *Photius*, Biblioth. Cod. 14.

[4] Cf. *Hilgenfeld*, Der Paschastreit, p. 250 ff.; Die Evangelien, p. 344 ff.; *Baur*, K. G. drei erst. Jahrh., p. 156 ff.; Unters. kan. Evv., p. 340 f., p. 356 f.; *Volkmar*, Der Ursprung, p. 31 f.; *Davidson*, Int. N. T. ii. p. 403 ff.

should be pardoned, for ignorance does not admit of accusation, but requires instruction. And they say that the Lord, together with his disciples, ate the sheep (τὸ πρόβατον) on the 14th Nisan, but himself suffered on the great day of unleavened bread. And they state (διηγοῦνται) that Matthew says precisely what they have understood; hence their understanding of it is at variance with the law, and according to them the Gospels seem to contradict each other.'"[1] The last sentence is interpreted as pointing out that the first synoptic Gospel is supposed to be at variance with our fourth Gospel. This fragment is claimed by Tischendorf[2] and others as evidence of the general acceptance at that time both of the Synoptics and the fourth Gospel. Canon Westcott, with obvious exaggeration, says: "The Gospels are evidently quoted as books certainly known and recognized; their authority is placed on the same footing as the Old Testament."[3] The Gospels are referred to merely for the settlement of the historical fact as to the day on which the last Passover had been eaten, a narrative of which they contained.

There are, however, very grave reasons for doubting the authenticity of the two fragments ascribed to Apolli-

---

[1] Καὶ Ἀπολινάριος δὲ ὁ ὁσιώτατος ἐπίσκοπος Ἱεραπόλεως τῆς Ἀσίας, ὁ ἐγγὺς τῶν ἀποστολικῶν χρόνων γεγονώς, ἐν τῷ περὶ τοῦ Πάσχα λόγῳ τὰ παραπλήσια ἐδίδαξε, λέγων οὕτως· Εἰσὶ τοίνυν οἱ δι' ἄγνοιαν φιλονεικοῦσι περὶ τούτων συγγνωστὸν πρᾶγμα πεπονθότες· ἄγνοια γὰρ οὐ κατηγορίαν ἀναδέχεται, ἀλλὰ διδαχῆς προσδεῖται. καὶ λέγουσιν ὅτι τῇ ιδ' τὸ πρόβατον μετὰ τῶν μαθητῶν ἔφαγεν ὁ Κύριος· τῇ δὲ μεγάλῃ ἡμέρᾳ τῶν ἀζύμων αὐτὸς ἔπαθεν· καὶ διηγοῦνται Ματθαῖον οὕτω λέγειν ὡς νενοήκασιν· ὅθεν ἀσύμφωνός τε νόμῳ ἡ νόησις αὐτῶν· καὶ στασιάζειν δοκεῖ κατ' αὐτοὺς τὰ εὐαγγέλια. Præfat. Chron. Pasch. sive Alex. ed. Ducange, p. 6; Routh, Reliq. Sacr., i. p. 160. We need not quote the second fragment here, as it has nothing to do with our Synoptics; but, indeed, neither of the passages being by Apollinaris, it is scarcely necessary to refer to the other at all.

[2] Wann wurden, u. s. w., p. 18. [3] On the Canon, p. 199.

naris, and we must mention that these doubts are much less those of German critics, who, on the whole, either do not raise the question at all, or hastily dispose of it, than doubts entertained by orthodox Apologists, who see little ground for accepting them as genuine.[1] Eusebius, who gives a catalogue of the works of Apollinaris which had reached him,[2] was evidently not acquainted with any writing of his on the Passover. It is argued, however, that "there is not any sufficient ground for doubting the genuineness of these fragments 'On Easter,' in the fact that Eusebius mentions no such book by Apollinaris."[3] It is quite true that Eusebius does not pretend to give a complete list of these works, but merely says that there are many preserved by many, and that he mentions those with which he had met.[4] At the same time, entering with great interest, as he does, into the Paschal Controversy, and acquainted with the principal writings on the subject,[5] it would indeed have been strange had he not met with the work itself, or at least with some notice of it in the works of others. Eusebius gives an account of the writings of Melito and Apollinaris together. He was acquainted with the work of Melito on the Passover, and quotes it,[6] and it is extremely improbable that he could have been ignorant of a treatise by his distinguished contemporary

---

[1] *Donaldson*, Hist. Chr. Lit. and Doctr., iii. p. 247 f.; *Lardner*, Credibility, &c., Works, 1788, ii. p. 296; *Tillemont*, Mém. Hist. Eccles., ii. pt. iii. p. 91; Cf. *Neander*, K. G. 1842, i. p. 513 anm. 1.

[2] H. E., iv. 27.

[3] *Westcott*, On the Canon, p. 198, note 3; cf. *Baur*, Unters. kan. Evv., p. 340 f. This is the only remark which Dr. Westcott makes as to any doubt of the authenticity of these fragments. Tischendorf does not mention a doubt at all.

[4] Τοῦ δὲ Ἀπολιναρίου πολλῶν παρὰ πολλοῖς σωζομένων, τὰ εἰς ἡμᾶς ἐλθόντα ἐστὶ τάδε· κ.τ.λ. H. E., iv. 27.

[5] *Eusebius*, H. E., v. 23, 24.   [6] *Ib.*, H. E., iv. 26.

on the same subject, had he actually written one. Not only, however, does Eusebius seem to know nothing of his having composed such a work, but neither do Theodoret,[1] Jerome,[2] nor Photius,[3] who refer to his writings, mention it; and we cannot suppose that it was referred to in the lost works of Irenæus or Clement of Alexandria on the Passover. Eusebius, who quotes from them,[4] would in that case have probably mentioned the fact, as he does the statement by Clement regarding Melito's work, or at least would have been aware of the existence of such a writing, and alluded to it when speaking of the works of Apollinaris.

This silence is equally significant whether we regard Apollinaris as a Quartodeciman or as a supporter of the views of Victor and the Church of Rome. On the one hand, Eusebius states that "all the churches of Asia"[5] kept the 14th Nisan, and it is difficult to believe that, had Apollinaris differed from this practice and, more especially, had he written against it, the name of so eminent an exception would not have been mentioned. The views of the Bishop of Hierapolis, as a prominent representative of the Asiatic Church, must have been quoted in many controversial works on the subject, and even if the writing itself had not come into their hands, Eusebius and others could scarcely fail to become indirectly acquainted with it. On the other hand, supposing Apollinaris to have been a Quartodeciman, whilst the ignorance of Eusebius and others regarding any contribution by him to the discussion is scarcely less remarkable, it is still more surprising that no allusion is made to

---

[1] Hæret. Fab., ii. 21, iii. 2.
[2] Vir. Ill. 26.
[3] Biblioth. Cod., 14.
[4] H. E., v. 24; iv. 26; cf. vi. 13.
[5] *Eusebius*, H. E., v. 23.

him by Polycrates[1] when he names so many less distinguished men of Asia, then passed away, who kept the 14th Nisan, such as Thaseas of Eumenia, Sagoris of Laodicea, Papirius of Sardis, and the seven Bishops of his kindred, not to mention Polycarp of Smyrna and the Apostles Philip and John. He also cites Melito of Sardis: why does he not refer to Apollinaris of Hierapolis? If it be argued that he was still living, then why does Eusebius not mention him amongst those who protested against the measures of Victor of Rome?[2]

There has been much discussion as to the view taken by the writer of these fragments, Hilgenfeld and others[3] maintaining that he is opposed to the Quartodeciman party. Into this it is not necessary for us to enter, as our contention simply is that in no case can the authenticity of the fragments be established. Supposing them, however, to be directed against those who kept the 14th Nisan, how can it be credited that this isolated convert to the views of Victor and the Roman Church, could write of so vast and distinguished a majority of the Churches of Asia, including Polycarp and Melito, as "some who through ignorance raised contentions" on the point, when they really raised no new contention at all, but, as Polycrates represented, followed the tradition handed down to them from their Fathers, and authorized by the practice of the Apostle John himself?

None of his contemporaries nor writers about his own time seem to have known that Apollinaris wrote any work from which these fragments can have been taken, and there is absolutely no independent evidence that he

---

[1] *Eusebius*, H. E., v. 24.   [2] *Ib.* H. E., v. 23, 24.
[3] *Hilgenfeld*, Der Paschastreit, 1860, p. 255 ff.; *Baur*, K. G., i. p. 157; *Davidson*, Int. N. T., ii. p. 406 ff.

ever took any part in the Paschal controversy at all. The only ground we have for attributing these fragments to him is the Preface to the Paschal Chronicle of Alexandria, written by an unknown author of the seventh century, some five hundred years after the time of Apollinaris, whose testimony has rightly been described as ' worth almost nothing."[1] Most certainly many passages preserved by him are inauthentic, and generally allowed to be so.[2] The two fragments have by some been conjecturally ascribed to Pierius of Alexandria,[3] a writer of the third century, who composed a work on Easter, but there is no evidence on the point. In any case, there is such exceedingly slight reason for attributing these fragments to Claudius Apollinaris, and so many strong grounds for believing that he cannot have written them, that they have no material value as evidence for the antiquity of the Gospels.

3.

We know little or nothing of Athenagoras. He is not mentioned by Eusebius, and our only information regarding him is derived from a fragment of Philip Sidetes, a writer of the fifth century, first published by

---

[1] *Donaldson*, Hist. Chr. Lit. and Doctr., iii. p. 247; *Lardner*, Credibility, &c., Works, ii. p. 296.

[2] Dr. Donaldson rightly calls a fragment in the Chronicle ascribed to Melito, "unquestionably spurious." Hist. Chr. Lit. and Doctr., iii. p. 231.

[3] Cf. *Lardner*, Credibility, &c., Works, ii. p. 296; *Donaldson*, Hist. Chr. Lit. and Doctr. iii. p. 218 f.

Dodwell.¹ Philip states that he was the first leader of the school of Alexandria during the time of Hadrian and Antoninus, to the latter of whom he addressed his Apology, and he further says that Clement of Alexandria was his disciple, and that Pantænus was the disciple of Clement. Part of this statement we know to be erroneous, and the Christian History of Philip, from which the fragment is taken, is very slightingly spoken of both by Socrates² and Photius.³ No reliance can be placed upon this information.⁴

The only works ascribed to Athenagoras are an Apology—called an Embassy, πρεσβεία—bearing the inscription: "The Embassy of Athenagoras the Athenian, a philosopher and a Christian, concerning Christians, to the Emperors Marcus Aurelius Antoninus and Lucius Aurelius Commodus, Armeniaci Sarmatici and, above all, philosophers"; and further, a Treatise: "On the Resurrection of the Dead." A quotation from the Apology by Methodius in his work on the Resurrection of the Body, is preserved by Epiphanius⁵ and Photius,⁶ and this, the mention by Philip Sidetes, and the inscription by an unknown hand, just quoted, are all the evidence we possess regarding the Apology. We have no evidence at all regarding the treatise on the Resurrection, beyond the inscription. The authenticity of neither, therefore, stands on very sure grounds.⁷ The address of the Apology and internal evidence furnished by it, into which we need not go, show that it could not

---

¹ Append. ad Diss. Iren., p. 488. The extract from Philip's History is made by an unknown author.
² H. E., vii. 27.   ³ Bibl. Cod., xxxv. p. 21.
⁴ *Basnage*, Ann. Polit. Eccl., 176, § 6; *Lardner*, Works, ii. p. 180; *Donaldson*, Hist. Chr. Lit. and Doctr., iii. p. 108 f.
⁵ Hær., lxiv. 21.   ⁶ Bibl. Cod., ccxxxiv. p. 908.
⁷ *Donaldson*, Hist. Chr. Lit. and Doctr., iii. p. 114 f.

have been written before A.D. 176—177, the date assigned to it by most critics,[1] although there are many reasons for dating it some years later.

In the six lines which Tischendorf devotes to Athenagoras, he says that the Apology contains "several quotations from Matthew and Luke,"[2] without, however, indicating them. In the very few sentences which Canon Westcott vouchsafes to him, he says: "Athenagoras quotes the words of our Lord as they stand in St. Matthew four times, and appears to allude to passages in St. Mark and St. John, but he nowhere mentions the name of an Evangelist."[3] Here the third Synoptic is not mentioned. In another place he says: "Athenagoras at Athens, and Theophilus at Antioch, make use of the same books generally, and treat them with the same respect;" and in a note: "Athenagoras quotes the Gospels of St. Matthew and St. John."[4] Here it will be observed that also the Gospel of Mark is quietly dropped out of sight, but still the positive manner in which it is asserted that Athenagoras quotes from "the Gospel of St. Matthew," without further explanation, is calculated to mislead. We shall refer to each of the supposed quotations.

Athenagoras not only does not mention any Gospel, but singularly enough he never once introduces the

---

[1] *Anger*, Synops. Ev. Proleg., xxxii.; *Basnage*, Annal. Polit. Eccles. 176, § 6; *Credner*, Beiträge, i. p. 53; *Fabricius*, (A.D. 177—180), Bibl. Græc., vi. p. 86; *Donaldson*, Hist. Chr. Lit. and Doctr., iii. p. 111 f.; *Kirchhofer*, Quellensamml., p. 473; *Lardner*, (A.D. 177—178), Works, ii. p. 181; *Mosheim*, Diss. de vera ætat. Apol. Athenag.; *Reuss*, Gesch. N. T., p. 290; *Scholten*, Die ält. Zeugnisse, p. 109; *Tillemont*, Mém. Hist. Eccles., t. ii. art. 8, note x.; *Tischendorf*, Wann wurden, u. s. w., p. 19; *Volkmar*, Der Ursprung, p. 34; *De Wette*, († 180), Einl. N. T., 1852, p. 25.

[2] Wann wurden, u. s. w., p. 19.

[3] On the Canon, p. 103.

[4] *Ib.*, p. 304, and note 2.

name of "Christ" into the works ascribed to him, and all the "words of the Lord" referred to are introduced simply by the indefinite "he says," φησί, and without any indication whatever of a written source.[1] The only exception to this is an occasion on which he puts into the mouth of "the Logos" a saying which is not found in any of our Gospels. The first passage to which Canon Westcott alludes is the following, which we contrast with the supposed parallel in the Gospel:—

ATHENAGORAS.	MATT. v. 39—40.
For we have learnt not only not to render a blow, nor to go to law (δικάζεσθαι) with those who spoil and plunder us, but even to those who should strike (us) on one side of the forehead (κατὰ κόρρης προσπηλακίζωσι) to offer for a blow the other side of the head also; and to those who should take away (ἀφαιροῖντο) the coat, to give also (ἐπιδιδόναι) the cloke besides.[2]	But I say unto you: that ye resist not evil: but whosoever shall smite thee on thy right cheek (σε ῥαπίσει ἐπὶ τὴν δεξιάν σου σιαγόνα) turn to him the other also. And if any man be minded to sue thee at the law (κριθῆναι) and take away (λαβεῖν) thy coat, let him have (ἄφες αὐτῷ) thy cloke also.[3]

It is scarcely possible to imagine a greater difference in language conveying a similar idea than that which exists between Athenagoras and the first Gospel, and the parallel passage in Luke is in many respects still more distant. No echo of the words in Matthew has lingered in the ear of the writer, for he employs utterly different phraseology throughout, and nothing can be more certain

---

[1] *Credner*, Beiträge, i. p. 54 f.; *Donaldson*, Hist. Chr. Lit. and Doctr., iii. p. 172.

[2] .... οὐ μόνον τὸ ἀντιπαίειν, οὐδὲ μὴν δικάζεσθαι τοῖς ἄγουσι καὶ ἁρπάζουσιν ἡμᾶς, μεμαθηκότες· ἀλλὰ τοῖς μὲν, κἂν κατὰ κόρρης προσπηλακίζωσι, καὶ τὸ ἕτερον παίειν παρέχειν τῆς κεφαλῆς μέρος· τοῖς δὲ, εἰ τὸν χιτῶνα ἀφαιροῖντο, ἐπιδιδόναι καὶ τὸ ἱμάτιον, κ.τ.λ. Legatio pro Christianis, § 1.

[3] Ἐγὼ δὲ λέγω ὑμῖν μὴ ἀντιστῆναι τῷ πονηρῷ· ἀλλ᾽ ὅστις σε ῥαπίσει ἐπὶ τὴν δεξιάν σου σιαγόνα, στρέψον αὐτῷ καὶ τὴν ἄλλην· καὶ τῷ θέλοντί σοι κριθῆναι καὶ τὸν χιτῶνά σου λαβεῖν, ἄφες αὐτῷ καὶ τὸ ἱμάτιον. Matt. v. 39, 40; cf. Luke vi. 29.

than the fact that there is not a linguistic trace in it of acquaintance with our Synoptics.

The next passage which is referred to is as follows:

ATHENAGORAS.	MATT. v. 44—45.
What, then, are those precepts in which we are instructed? I say unto you: love your enemies, bless them that curse, pray for them that persecute you: that ye may be sons of your Father which is in the heavens who (ὅς) maketh his sun, &c.[1]	But I say unto you, Love your enemies, bless them that curse you,[2] do good to them that hate you, and pray for them that[3] persecute you: That ye may be sons of your Father which is in heaven: for (ὅτι) he maketh his sun, &c.[4]

The same idea is continued in the next chapter, in which the following passage occurs:

ATHENAGORAS.	MATT. v. 46.
For if ye love (ἀγαπᾶτε), he says, (φησί) them which love, and lend to them which lend to you, what reward shall ye have?[5]	For if ye should love (ἀγαπήσητε) them which love you, what reward have ye?[6]

There is no parallel at all in the first Gospel to the phrase "and lend to them that lend to you," and in Luke vi. 34, the passage reads: "and if ye lend to them of whom ye hope to receive, what thank have ye?"

---

[1] Λέγω ὑμῖν· Ἀγαπᾶτε τοὺς ἐχθροὺς ὑμῶν, εὐλογεῖτε τοὺς καταρωμένους, προσεύχεσθε ὑπὲρ τῶν διωκόντων ὑμᾶς, ὅπως γένησθε υἱοὶ τοῦ Πατρὸς ὑμῶν τοῦ ἐν τοῖς οὐρανοῖς, ὃς τὸν ἥλιον αὐτοῦ ἀνατέλλει, κ.τ.λ. Leg. pro Christ., § 11.

[2] The expressions εὐλογεῖτε τοὺς καταρωμένους ὑμᾶς, καλῶς ποιεῖτε τοὺς μισοῦντας ὑμᾶς, "bless them that curse you, do good to them that hate you," are omitted from some of the oldest MSS., but we do not know any in which the first of these two doubtful phrases is retained, as in Athenagoras, and the "do good to them that hate you," is omitted.

[3] The phrase ἐπηρεαζόντων ὑμᾶς, "despitefully use you," is omitted from many ancient codices.

[4] Ἐγὼ δὲ λέγω ὑμῖν, ἀγαπᾶτε τοὺς ἐχθροὺς ὑμῶν καὶ προσεύχεσθε ὑπὲρ τῶν διωκόντων ὑμᾶς· ὅπως γένησθε υἱοὶ τοῦ Πατρὸς ὑμῶν τοῦ ἐν οὐρανοῖς, ὅτι τὸν ἥλιον αὐτοῦ ἀνατέλλει, κ.τ.λ. Matt. v. 44, 45.

[5] Ἐὰν γὰρ ἀγαπᾶτε, φησίν, τοὺς ἀγαπῶντας, καὶ δανείζετε τοῖς δανείζουσιν ὑμῖν, τίνα μισθὸν ἕξετε; Leg. pro Chr., § 12.

[6] Ἐὰν γὰρ ἀγαπήσητε τοὺς ἀγαπῶντας ὑμᾶς, τίνα μισθὸν ἔχετε; Matt. v. 46.

(καὶ ἐὰν δανίζετε παρ' ὧν ἐλπίζετε λαβεῖν, ποία ὑμῖν χάρις ἐστίν;) It is evident, therefore, that there are decided variations here, and that the passage of Athenagoras does not agree with either of the Synoptics. We have seen the persistent variation in the quotations from the "Sermon on the Mount" which occur in Justin,[1] and there is no part of the discourses of Jesus more certain to have been preserved by living Christian tradition, or to have been recorded in every form of Gospel. The differences in these passages from our Synoptic present the same features as mark the several versions of the same discourse in our first and third Gospels, and indicate a distinct source. The same remarks also apply to the next passage:

ATHENAGORAS.	MATT. v. 28.
For whosoever, he says (φησί), looketh on a woman to lust after her, hath committed adultery (μεμοιχευκεν) already in his heart.[2]	But I say unto you, That whosoever looketh on a woman to lust after her, hath committed adultery with her (ἐμοίχευσεν αὐτήν) already in his heart.[3]

The omission of αὐτήν, "with her," is not accidental, but is an important variation in the sense, which we have already met with in the Gospel used by Justin Martyr.[4] There is another passage, in the next chapter, the parallel to which follows closely on this in the great Sermon as reported in our first Gospel, to which Canon Westcott does not refer, but which we must point out:

ATHENAGORAS.	MATT. v. 32.
For whosoever, he says (φησί),	But I say unto you, That whoso-

---

[1] Justin likewise has ἀγαπᾶτε for ἀγαπήσητε in this passage.
[2] Ὁ γὰρ βλέπων, φησί, γυναῖκα πρὸς τὸ ἐπιθυμῆσαι αὐτῆς, ἤδη μεμοίχευκεν ἐν τῇ καρδίᾳ αὐτοῦ. Leg. pro Christ., § 32.
[3] Ἐγὼ δὲ λέγω ὑμῖν ὅτι πᾶς ὁ βλέπων γυναῖκα πρὸς τὸ ἐπιθυμῆσαι αὐτὴν ἤδη ἐμοίχευσεν αὐτὴν ἐν τῇ καρδίᾳ αὐτοῦ.
[4] Apol., i. 15.

shall put away his wife and marry another committeth adultery.[1]

ever shall put away his wife, saving for the cause of fornication, causeth her to commit adultery: and whosoever shall marry her when divorced committeth adultery.[2]

It is evident that the passage in the Apology is quite different from that in the "Sermon on the Mount" in the first Synoptic. If we compare it with Matt. xix. 9, there still remains the express limitation μὴ ἐπὶ πορνείᾳ, which Athenagoras does not admit, his own express doctrine being in accordance with the positive declaration in his text. In the immediate context, indeed, he insists that even to marry another wife after the death of the first is cloaked adultery. We find in Luke xvi. 18, the reading of Athenagoras,[3] but with important linguistic variations:

ATHENAGORAS.	LUKE XVI. 18.
Ὃς γὰρ ἂν ἀπολύσῃ τὴν γυναῖκα αὐτοῦ, καὶ γαμήσῃ ἄλλην μοιχᾶται.	Πᾶς ὁ ἀπολύων τὴν γυναῖκα αὐτοῦ καὶ γαμῶν ἑτέραν μοιχεύει.

It cannot, obviously, be rightly affirmed that Athenagoras must have derived this from Luke, and the sense of the passage in that Gospel, compared with the passage in Matthew xix. 9, on the contrary, rather makes it certain that the reading of Athenagoras was derived from a source combining the language of the one and the thought of the other. In Mark x. 11, the reading is nearer that of Athenagoras and confirms this conclusion; and the addition there of ἐπ' αὐτήν "against her" after

---

[1] Ὃς γὰρ ἂν ἀπολύσῃ, φησὶ, τὴν γυναῖκα αὐτοῦ, καὶ γαμήσῃ ἄλλην, μοιχᾶται. Leg. pro Chr., § 33.

[2] Ἐγὼ δὲ λέγω ὑμῖν ὅτι ὃς ἂν ἀπολύσῃ τὴν γυναῖκα αὐτοῦ παρεκτὸς λόγου πορνείας ποιεῖ αὐτὴν μοιχευθῆναι, καὶ ὃς ἂν ἀπολελυμένην γαμήσῃ, μοιχᾶται· Matt. v. 32. πᾶς ὁ ἀπολύων is the older and better reading, but we give ὃς ἂν ἀπολύσῃ as favouring the similarity.

[3] Lardner, indeed, points to the passage as a quotation from the third Gospel. Works, ii. p. 183.

μοιχᾶται, further tends to prove that his source was not that Gospel.

We may at once give the last passage which is supposed to be a quotation from our Synoptics, and it is that which is affirmed to be a reference to Mark. Athenagoras states in almost immediate context with the above: "for in the beginning God formed one man and one woman."[1] This is compared with Mark x. 6: "But from the beginning of the creation God made them male and female":

ATHENAGORAS.	MARK x. 6.
Ὅτι ἐν ἀρχῇ ὁ Θεὸς ἕνα ἄνδρα ἔπλασε καὶ μίαν γυναῖκα.	Ἀπὸ δὲ ἀρχῆς κτίσεως ἄρσεν καὶ θῆλυ ἐποίησεν αὐτοὺς ὁ Θεός.

Now this passage differs materially in every way from the second Synoptic. The reference to "one man" and "one woman" is used in a totally different sense, and enforces the previous assertion that a man may only marry one wife. Such an argument directly derived from the Old Testament is perfectly natural to one who, like Athenagoras, derived all his authority from it alone. It is not permissible to claim it as evidence of the use of Mark.

Now we must repeat that Athenagoras does not name any source from which he derives his knowledge of the sayings of Jesus. These sayings are all from the Sermon on the Mount, and are introduced by the indefinite phrase φησί, and it is remarkable that all differ distinctly from the parallels in our Gospels. The whole must be taken together as coming from one source, and while the decided variation excludes the inference that they must have been taken from our Gospels, there is reasonable ground for assigning them to a different

[1] Leg. pro Chr., § 33.

source. Dr. Donaldson states the case with great fairness: "Athenagoras makes no allusion to the inspiration of any of the New Testament writers. He does not mention one of them by name, and one cannot be sure that he quotes from any except Paul. All the passages taken from the Gospels are parts of our Lord's discourses, and may have come down to Athenagoras by tradition."[1] He might have added that they might also have been derived from the gospel according to the Hebrews or many another collection now unhappily lost.

One circumstance strongly confirming this conclusion is the fact already mentioned, that Athenagoras, in the same chapter in which one of these quotations occurs, introduces an apocryphal saying of the Logos, and connects it with previous sayings by the expression "The Logos *again* (πάλιν) saying to us." This can only refer to the sayings previously introduced by the indefinite φησί. The sentence, which is in reference to the Christian salutation of peace, is as follows: "The Logos again saying to us: 'If any one for this reason kiss a second time because it pleased him (he sins);' and adding: 'Thus the kiss or rather the salutation must be used with caution, as, if it be defiled even a little by thought, it excludes us from the life eternal.'"[2] This saying, which is directly attributed to the Logos, is not found in our Gospels. The only natural deduction is that it comes from the same source as the other sayings, and that source was not our synoptic Gospels.

---

[1] Hist. Chr. Lit. and Doctr., iii. p. 172.
De Wette says regarding Athenagoras: "The quotations of evangelical passages prove nothing." Einl. A. T., 1852, p. 25.

[2] Πάλιν ἡμῖν λέγοντος τοῦ Λόγου· 'Εάν τις διὰ τοῦτο ἐκ δευτέρου καταφιλήσῃ, ὅτι ἤρεσεν αὐτῷ· καὶ ἐπιφέροντος· Οὕτως οὖν ἀκριβώσασθαι τὸ φίλημα, μᾶλλον δὲ τὸ προσκύνημα δεῖ· ὡς εἴπου μικρὸν τῇ διανοίᾳ παραθολωθείη, ἔξω ἡμᾶς τῆς αἰωνίου τιθέντος ζωῆς. Leg. pro Christ., § 32.

The total absence of any allusion to New Testament Scriptures in Athenagoras, however, is rendered more striking and significant by the marked expression of his belief in the inspiration of the Old Testament.[1] He appeals to the prophets for testimony as to the truth of the opinions of Christians: men, he says, who spoke by the inspiration of God, whose Spirit moved their mouths to express God's will as musical instruments are played upon:[2] "But since the voices of the prophets support our arguments, I think that you, being most learned and wise, cannot be ignorant of the writings of Moses, or of those of Isaiah and Jeremiah and of the other prophets, who being raised in ecstasy above the reasoning that was in themselves, uttered the things which were wrought in them, when the Divine Spirit moved them, the Spirit using them as a flute player would blow into the flute."[3] He thus enunciates the theory of the mechanical inspiration of the writers of the Old Testament, in the clearese manner,[4] and it would indeed have been strange, on the supposition that he extended his views of inspiration to any of the Scriptures of the New Testament, that he never names a single one of them, nor indicates to the Emperors in the same way, as worthy of their attention, any of these Scriptures along with the Law and the Prophets. There can be no doubt that he nowhere gives reason for supposing that he regarded any other writings than the Old Testament as inspired or "Holy Scripture."[5]

[1] *Credner*, Beiträge, i. p. 54 f.
[2] Leg. pro Christ., § 7.
[3] Leg. pro Christ., § 9.
[4] *Credner*, Beiträge, i. p. 54 f.; *Donaldson*, Hist. Chr. Lit. and Doctr., iii. p. 171 f.
[5] In the treatise on the Resurrection there are no arguments derived from Scripture.

4.

In the 17th year of the reign of Marcus Aurelius, between the 7th March, 177-178, a fierce persecution was, it is said,[1] commenced against the Christians in Gaul, and more especially at Vienne and Lyons, during the course of which the aged Bishop Pothinus, the predecessor of Irenæus, suffered martyrdom for the faith. The two communities some time after addressed an Epistle to their brethren in Asia and Phrygia, and also to Eleutherus, Bishop of Rome,[2] relating the events which had occurred, and the noble testimony which had been borne to Christ by the numerous martyrs who had been cruelly put to death. The Epistle has in great part been preserved by Eusebius,[3] and critics generally agree in dating it about A.D. 177,[4] although it was most probably not written until the following year.[5]

No writing of the New Testament is mentioned in this Epistle,[6] but it is asserted that there are "unequivocal coincidences of language"[7] with the Gospel of Luke, and others of its books. The passage which is referred to as

---

[1] *Eusebius*, H. E., v. Proem.   [2] *Ib.*, H. E., v. 3.
[3] *Ib.*, II. E., v. 1 f.
[4] *Anger*, Synops. Ev. Proleg., p. xxxii.; *Donaldson*, Hist. Chr. Lit. and Doctr., iii. p. 255 ff.; *Hilgenfeld*, Der Kanon, p. 10, p. 32; *Lipsius*, Chronologie d. röm. Bischöfe, p. 185; *Lardner*, Works, ii. p. 149; *Mosheim*, Observ. Sacr. et Hist., i. 3, § 10; *Neander*, K. G., i. p. 190 f.; *Routh*, Reliq. Sacræ, i. p. 289 f., p. 326 f.; *Scholten*, Die ält. Zeugnisse, p. 110 f.; *Tillemont*, Mém. Hist. Eccl., iii. art. 2, et note 1; *Tischendorf*, Wann wurden, u. s. w., p. 80 f., an. 1; *Volkmar*, Der Ursprung, p. 164, p. 156; *Westcott*, On the Canon, p. 295.
[5] *Baronius* dates the death of Pothinus in A.D. 179; *Valesius*, ad Euseb. H. E., v. 5.
[6] *Donaldson*, Hist. Chr. Lit. and Doctr., iii. p. 285; *Lardner*, Works, ii. p. 153; *Westcott*, On the Canon, p. 295.
[7] *Westcott*, On the Canon, p. 295.

showing knowledge of our Synoptic, is as follows. The letter speaks of one of the sufferers, a certain Vettius Epagathus, whose life was so austere that, although a young man, "he was thought worthy of the testimony (μαρτυρία) borne by the elder (πρεσβυτέρου) Zacharias. He had walked, of a truth, in all the commandments and ordinances of the Lord blameless, and was untiring in every kind office towards his neighbour; having much zeal for God and being fervent in spirit."[1] This is compared with the description of Zacharias and Elizabeth in Luke i. 6: "And they were both righteous before God, walking in all the commandments and ordinances of the Lord blameless."[2] A little further on in the Epistle it is said of the same person: "Having in himself the advocate (παράκλητον), the spirit (τὸ πνεῦμα), more abundantly than Zacharias," &c.[3] which again is referred to Luke i. 67, "And his father Zacharias was filled with the Holy Spirit and prophesied, saying," &c.[4]

A few words must be said regarding the phrase τῇ τοῦ πρεσβυτέρου Ζαχαρίου μαρτυρίᾳ, "the testimony of the presbyter Zacharias." This, of course, may either be rendered: "the testimony borne to Zacharias," that is to say, borne by others to his holy life; or, "the testi-

---

[1] .... συνεξισοῦσθαι τῇ τοῦ πρεσβυτέρου Ζαχαρίου μαρτυρίᾳ. ἐπεπόρευτο γοῦν ἐν πάσαις ταῖς ἐντολαῖς καὶ δικαιώμασι τοῦ Κυρίου ἄμεμπτος, καὶ πάσῃ τῇ πρὸς τὸν πλησίον λειτουργίᾳ ἄοκνος, ζῆλον Θεοῦ πολὺν ἔχων, καὶ ζέων τῷ πνεύματι, κ.τ.λ. *Euseb.*, H. E., v. 1. By a vexatious mistake, "to" was accidentally substituted for "by" in the above translation, in a very few early copies of the sixth edition. The error was almost immediately observed and corrected.

[2] ἦσαν δὲ δίκαιοι ἀμφότεροι ἐνώπιον τοῦ θεοῦ, πορευόμενοι ἐν πάσαις ταῖς ἐντολαῖς καὶ δικαιώμασιν τοῦ κυρίου ἄμεμπτοι. Luke i. 6.

[3] ἔχων δὲ τὸν παράκλητον ἐν ἑαυτῷ, τὸ πνεῦμα πλεῖον τοῦ Ζαχαρίου. *Euseb.*, H. E., v. i.

[4] Καὶ Ζαχαρίας ὁ πατὴρ αὐτοῦ ἐπλήσθη πνεύματος ἁγίου καὶ ἐπροφήτευσεν λέγων, κ.τ.λ. Luke i. 67.

mony borne by Zacharias," his own testimony to the
Faith: his martyrdom. We adopt the latter rendering for
various reasons. The Epistle is an account of the persecution of the Christian community of Vienne and Lyons,
and Vettius Epagathus is the first of the martyrs who
is named in it: μαρτυρία was at that time the term
used to express the supreme testimony of Christians—
martyrdom, and the Epistle seems here simply to refer
to the martyrdom, the honour of which he shared with
Zacharias. It is, we think, very improbable that, under
such circumstances, the word μαρτυρία would have been
used to express a mere description of the character of
Zacharias given by some other writer. The interpretation which we prefer is that adopted by Tischendorf.[1]
We must add that the Zacharias here spoken of is
generally understood to be the father of John the Baptist,
and no critic, so far as we can remember, has suggested
that the reference in Luke xi. 51, applies to him.[2] Since
the Epistle, therefore, refers to the martyrdom of Zacharias,
the father of John the Baptist, when using the expressions
which are supposed to be taken from our third Synoptic,
is it not reasonable to suppose that those expressions
were derived from some work which likewise contained
an account of his death, which is not found in the
Synoptic? When we examine the matter more closely,
we find that, although none of the Canonical Gospels,
except the third, gives any narrative of the birth of John
the Baptist, that portion of the Gospel, in which are the
words we are discussing, cannot be considered an original

---

[1] Wann wurden, u. s. w., p. 80 n. 1. So also *Hilgenfeld*, Die Evv.
Justin's, p. 155, and others.

[2] The great majority of critics consider it a reference to 2 Chron. xxiv.,
21, though some apply it to a later Zacharias.

production by the third Synoptist, but like the rest of his work is merely a composition based upon earlier written narratives.[1] Ewald, for instance, assigns the whole of the first chapters of Luke (i. 5—ii. 40) to what he terms "the eighth recognizable book."[2]

However this may be, the fact that other works existed at an earlier period in which the history of Zacharias the father of the Baptist was given, and in which not only the words used in the Epistle were found but also the martyrdom, is in the highest degree probable, and, so far as the history is concerned, this is placed almost beyond doubt by the Protevangelium Jacobi which contains it. Tischendorf, who does not make use of this Epistle at all as evidence for the Scriptures of the New Testament, does refer to it, and to this very allusion in it to the martyrdom of Zacharias, as testimony to the existence and use of the Protevangelium Jacobi, a work whose origin he dates so far back as the first three decades of the second century,[3] and which he considers was also used by Justin, as Hilgenfeld had already observed.[4] Tischendorf and Hilgenfeld, therefore, agree in affirming that the reference to Zacharias which we have quoted, indicates acquaintance with a different Gospel from our third Synoptic. Hilgenfeld rightly maintains that the Protevangelium Jacobi in its present shape is merely an

---

[1] Without referring to many critics in confirmation of this generally recognized fact, we may point out the following : *Bleek*, Synopt. Erklärung d. drei erst. Evv., 1862, i. p. 130, ff. ; *Ewald*, Die drei erst. Evv., 1850, pp. 97 ff., 177 ff. ; cf. Die Bücher d. N. B., 1871, i. p. 216 ff. ; *Holtzmann*, Die synopt. Evv., 1863, p. 210 ff. ; *Meyer*, Ev. des Markus u. Lukas, 1867, p. 240.

[2] Die drei erst. Evv. pp. 97 ff.

[3] Wann wurden, u. s. w., p. 76 ff., 80, anm. 1 ; cf. Evang. Apocr. Proleg., p. xii. f.

[4] Wann wurden, u. s. w., p. 76 f., p. 80. anm. 1 ; *Hilgenfeld*, Die Evv. Justin's p. 154 f.

altered form of an older work,[1] which he conjectures to have been the Gospel according to Peter, or the Gnostic work Γέννα Μαρίας,[2] and both he and Tischendorf show that many of the Fathers[3] were either acquainted with the Protevangelium itself or the works on which it was based.

The state of the case, then, is as follows: We find a coincidence in a few words in connection with Zacharias between the Epistle and our third Gospel, but so far from the Gospel being in any way indicated as their source, the words in question are connected with a reference to events unknown to our Gospel, but which were indubitably chronicled elsewhere. As part of the passage in the epistle, therefore, could not have been derived from our third Synoptic, the natural inference is that the whole emanates from a Gospel, different from ours, which likewise contained that part. In any case, the agreement of these few words, without the slightest mention of the third Synoptic in the epistle, cannot be admitted as proof that they must necessarily have been derived from it and from no other source.

[1] Die Evv. Justin's, p. 154 f. [2] *Ib.*, p. 160 f.
[3] *Tischendorf*, Wann wurden, u. s. w., p. 76 ff.; cf. Evang. Apoc., Proleg., p. xii. f.; *Hilgenfeld*, Die Evv. J., p. 154 ff.

CHAPTER X.

PTOLEMÆUS AND HERACLEON—CELSUS—THE CANON OF MURATORI—RESULTS.

WE have now reached the extreme limit of time within which we think it in any degree worth while to seek for evidence as to the date and authorship of the synoptic Gospels, and we might now proceed to the fourth Gospel; but before doing so it may be well to examine one or two other witnesses whose support has been claimed by apologists, although our attention may be chiefly confined to an inquiry into the date of such testimony, upon which its value, even if real, mainly depends so far as we are concerned. The first of these whom we must notice are the two Gnostic leaders, Ptolemæus and Heracleon.

Epiphanius has preserved a certain "Epistle to Flora" ascribed to Ptolemæus, in which, it is contended, there are "several quotations from Matthew, and one from the first chapter of John."[1] What date must be assigned to this Epistle? In reply to those who date it about the end of the second century, Tischendorf produces the evidence for an earlier period to which he assigns it. He says: "He (Ptolemæus) appears in all the oldest sources

---

[1] *Tischendorf*, Wann wurden, u. s. w., p. 46. Canon Westcott with greater caution says: "He quoted words of our Lord recorded by St. Matthew, the prologue of St. John's Gospel, &c." On the Canon, p. 267.

as one of the most important, most influential of the disciples of Valentinus. As the period at which the latter himself flourished falls about 140, do we say too much when we represent Ptolemæus as working at the latest about 160 ? Irenæus (in the 2nd Book) and Hippolytus name him together with Heracleon; likewise pseudo-Tertullian (in the appendix to *De Præscriptionibus Hæreticorum*) and Philastrius make him appear immediately after Valentinus. Irenæus wrote the first and second books of his great work most probably (höchst warscheinlich) before 180, and in both he occupies himself much with Ptolemæus."[1] Canon Westcott, beyond calling Ptolemæus and Heracleon disciples of Valentinus, does not assign any date to either, and does not of course offer any further evidence on the point, although, in regard to Heracleon, he admits the ignorance in which we are as to all points of his history,[2] and states generally, in treating of him, that "the exact chronology of the early heretics is very uncertain."[3]

Let us, however, examine the evidence upon which Tischendorf relies for the date he assigns to Ptolemæus. He states in vague terms that Ptolemæus appears "in all the oldest sources" (in allen den ältesten Quellen) as one of the most important disciples of Valentinus. We shall presently see what these sources are, but must now follow the argument: "As the date of Valentinus falls about 140, do we say too much when we represent Ptolemæus as working at the latest about 160?" It is obvious that there is no evidence here, but merely assumption, and the manner in which the period "about 160" is begged, is a clear admission that there are no certain data. The year

---

[1] Wann wurden, u. s. w., p. 46 f.
[2] On the Canon, p. 263.
[3] *Ib.*, p. 264, note 2.

might with equal propriety upon those grounds have been put ten years earlier or ten years later. The deceptive and arbitrary character of the conclusion, however, will be more apparent when we examine the grounds upon which the relative dates 140 and 160 rest. Tischendorf here states that the time at which Valentinus flourished falls about A.D. 140, but the fact is that, as all critics are agreed,[1] and as even Tischendorf himself elsewhere states,[2] Valentinus came out of Egypt to Rome in that year, when his public career practically commenced, and he continued to flourish for at least twenty years after.[3] Tischendorf's pretended moderation, therefore, consists in dating the period when Valentinus flourished from the very year of his first appearance, and in assigning the active career of Ptolemæus to 160 when Valentinus was still alive and teaching. He might on the same principle be dated 180, and even in that case there could be no reason for ascribing the Epistle to Flora to so early a period of his career. Tischendorf never even pretends to state any ground upon which Ptolemæus must be connected with any precise part of the public life of Valentinus, and still less for discriminating the period of the career of Ptolemæus at which the Epistle may have been composed. It is obvious that a wide limit for date thus exists.

After these general statements Tischendorf details the only evidence which is available. (1) "Irenæus (in the 2nd Book) and Hippolytus name him together with Heracleon; likewise (2) pseudo-Tertullian (in the

---

[1] See authorities, Vol. ii. p. 55, note 2. Cf. *Mansel*, The Gnostic Heresies, 1875, p. 166.

[2] Wann wurden, u. s. w., p. 43. "Valentinus, der um 140 aus Ægypten nach Rom kam und darauf noch 20 Jahre gelebt haben mag."

[3] Cf. *Irenæus*, Adv. Hær., iii. 4, § 3; *Eusebius*, H. E., iv. 11.

appendix to *De Præscriptionibus Hæreticorum*) and Philastrius make him appear immediately after Valentinus," &c. We must first examine these two points a little more closely in order to ascertain the value of such statements. With regard to the first (1) of these points, we shall presently see that the mention of the name of Ptolemæus along with that of Heracleon throws no light upon the matter from any point of view, inasmuch as Tischendorf has as little authority for the date he assigns to the latter, and is in as complete ignorance concerning him, as in the case of Ptolemæus. It is amusing, moreover, that Tischendorf employs the very same argument, which sounds well although it means nothing, inversely to establish the date of Heracleon. Here, he argues: "Irenæus and Hippolytus name him (Ptolemæus) together with Heracleon;"[1] there, he reasons: "Irenæus names Heracleon together with Ptolemæus,"[2] &c. As neither the date assigned to the one nor to the other can stand alone, he tries to get them into something like an upright position by propping the one against the other, an expedient which, naturally, meets with little success. We shall in dealing with the case of Heracleon show how untenable is the argument from the mere order in which such names are mentioned by these writers; meantime we may simply say that Irenæus only once mentions the name of Heracleon in his works, and that the occasion on which he does so, and to which reference is here made, is merely an allusion to the Æons "of Ptolemæus himself, and of Heracleon, and all the rest who hold these views."[3] This phrase might have been used, exactly as it stands, with

[1] Wann wurden, u. s. w., p. 47. [2] *Ib.*, p. 48.
[3] Ipsius Ptolemæi et Heracleonis, et reliquorum omnium qui eadem opinantur. Adv. Hær., ii. 4, § 1.

perfect propriety even if Ptolemæus and Heracleon had been separated by a century. The only point which can be deduced from this mere coupling of names is that, in using the present tense, Irenæus is speaking of his own contemporaries. We may make the same remark regarding Hippolytus, for, if his mention of Ptolemæus and Heracleon has any weight at all, it is to prove that they were flourishing in his time: "Those who are of Italy, of whom *is* Heracleon and Ptolemæus, say . . ."[1] &c. We shall have to go further into this point presently. As to (2) pseudo-Tertullian and Philastrius we need only say that even if the fact of the names of the two Gnostics being coupled together could prove anything in regard to the date, the repetition by these writers could have no importance for us, their works being altogether based on those of Irenæus and Hippolytus,[2] and scarcely, if at all, conveying independent information.[3] We have merely indicated the weakness of these arguments in passing, but shall again take them up further on.

The next and final consideration advanced by Tischendorf is the only one which merits serious attention. "Irenæus wrote the first and second book of his great work most probably before 180, and in both he occupies himself much with Ptolemæus." Before proceeding to examine the accuracy of this statement regarding the time at which Irenæus wrote, we may ask what conclusion would be involved if Irenæus really did compose the two books in A.D. 180 in which he mentions

---

[1] Οἱ μὲν ἀπὸ τῆς 'Ιταλίας, ὧν ἐστιν 'Ηρακλέων καὶ Πτολεμαιος . . . . φασι. Ref. Omn. Hær., vi. 35.

[2] Cf. *Lipsius*, Zur Quellenkritik des Epiphanius, 1865.

[3] Indeed the direct and avowed dependence of Hippolytus himself upon the work of Irenæus deprives the Philosophumena, in many parts, of all separate authority.

our Gnostics in the present tense? Nothing more than the simple fact that Ptolemæus and Heracleon were promulgating their doctrines at that time. There is not a single word to show that they did not continue to flourish long after; and as to the "Epistle to Flora" Irenæus apparently knows nothing of it, nor has any attempt been made to assign it to an early part of the Gnostic's career. Tischendorf, in fact, does not produce a single passage nor the slightest argument to show that Irenæus treats our two Gnostics as men of the past, or otherwise than as heretics then actively disseminating their heterodox opinions, and, even taken literally, the argument of Tischendorf would simply go to prove that about A.D. 180 Irenæus wrote part of a work in which he attacks Ptolemæus and mentions Heracleon.

When did Irenæus, however, really write his work against Heresies? Although our sources of credible information regarding him are exceedingly limited, we are not without materials for forming a judgment on the point. Irenæus was probably born about A.D. 140-145, and is generally supposed to have died at the beginning of the third century (A.D. 202).[1] We know that he was deputed by the Church of Lyons to bear to Eleutherus, then Bishop of Rome, the Epistle of that Christian community describing their sufferings during the persecution commenced against them in the seventeenth year of the reign of Marcus Aurelius Antoninus (7th March, 177—178).[2] It is very improbable that this journey was undertaken, in any case, before the spring of A.D. 178 at the earliest, and, indeed, in accordance with the given data, the persecu-

---

[1] Cf. vol. i. p.274. *Scholten*, Die ält. Zeugnisse, p. 118 f.; *Tischendorf*, Wann wurden, u. s. w., p. 11, 12; *Volkmar*, Der Ursprung, p. 24; *Ziegler*, Irenæus, Bisch. v. Lyon, 1871, pp. 15 f. 30.

[2] *Eusebius*, H. E., v. 1; Præf. § 1, 3, 4.

tion itself may not have commenced earlier than the beginning of that year, so that his journey need not have been undertaken before the close of 178 or the spring of 179, to which epoch other circumstances might lead us.[1] There is reason to believe that he remained some time in Rome. Baronius states that Irenæus was not appointed Bishop of Lyons till A.D. 180, for he says that the see remained vacant for that period after the death of Pothinus in consequence of the persecution. Now certain expressions in his work show that Irenæus did not write it until he became Bishop.[2] It is not known how long Irenæus remained in Rome, but there is every probability that he must have made a somewhat protracted stay, for the purpose of making himself acquainted with the various tenets of Gnostic and other heretics then being actively taught, and the preface to the first Book refers to the pains he took. He wrote his work in Gaul, however, after his return from this visit to Rome. This is apparent from what he himself states in the Preface to the first Book : " I have thought it necessary," he says, " after having read the Memoirs (ὑπομνήμασι) of the disciples of Valentinus as they call themselves, and *having had personal intercourse with some of them* and acquired full knowledge of their opinions, to unfold to thee,"[3] &c. A little further on, he claims from the friend to whom he addresses his work indulgence for any defects of style on the score of his being resident amongst the Keltæ.[4] Irenæus no doubt during his stay in Rome came in

---

[1] Baronius (Ann. Eccles.) sets the death of Pothinus in A.D. 179.

[2] Cf. Adv. Hær., v. Præf. ; *Massuet*, Dissert. in Iren., ii. art. ii. § 49 ; *Lardner*, Works, ii. p. 157.

[3] Adv. Hær., i. Præf. § 2. See the passage quoted, vol. ii. p. 59.

[4] Οὐκ ἐπιζητήσεις δὲ παρ' ἡμῶν τῶν ἐν Κελτοῖς διατριβόντων, κ.τ.λ. Adv. Hær., i. Præf. § 3.

contact with the school of Ptolemæus and Heracleon, if not with the Gnostic leaders themselves, and shocked as he describes himself as being at the doctrines which they insidiously taught, he undertook, on his return to Lyons, to explain them that others might be exhorted to avoid such an "abyss of madness and blasphemy against Christ."[1] Irenæus gives us other materials for assigning a date to his work. In the third Book he enumerates the bishops who had filled the Episcopal Chair of Rome, and the last whom he names is Eleutherus (A.D. 177—190), who, he says, "now in the twelfth place from the apostles, holds the inheritance of the episcopate."[2] There is, however, another clue which, taken along with this, leads us to a close approximation to the actual date. In the same Book, Irenæus mentions Theodotion's version of the Old Testament: "But not as some of those say," he writes, "who now (νῦν) presume to alter the interpretation of the Scripture: 'Behold the young woman shall conceive, and bring forth a son,' as Theodotion, the Ephesian, translated it, and Aquila of Pontus, both Jewish proselytes."[3] Now we are informed by Epiphanius that Theodotion published his translation during the reign of the Emperor Commodus[4] (A.D. 180—192). The Chronicon Paschale adds that it was during the Consulship of Marcellus, or as Massuet[5] proposes to read Marullus, who, jointly with Ælianus, assumed office A.D. 184. These dates decidedly agree with the passage of Irenæus and with the other data, all of which lead

---

[1] Adv. Hær., i. Præf. § 2.
[2] Adv. Hær., iii. 3, § 3; Eusebius, II. E., v. 6.
[3] Ἀλλ' οὐχ ὡς ἔνιοί φασι τῶν νῦν τολμώντων μεθερμηνεύειν τὴν γραφὴν . . . ὡς Θεοδοτίων ἡρμήνευσεν ὁ Ἐφέσιος, καὶ Ἀκύλας ὁ Ποντικὸς, κ.τ.λ. Adv. Hær. iii. 21, § 1. Euseb., II. E., v. 8.
[4] De Ponderib. et Mens., 17.
[5] Dissert. in Iren., ii. art. ii. xcvii. § 47.

us to about the same period within the episcopate of Eleutherus († c. 190).[1] We have here, therefore, a clue to the date at which Irenæus wrote. It must be remembered that at that period the multiplication and dissemination of books was a very slow process. A work published about 184 or 185 could scarcely have come into the possession of Irenæus in Gaul till some years later, and we are, therefore, brought towards the end of the episcopate of Eleutherus as the earliest date at which the first three books of his work against Heresies can well have been written, and the rest must be assigned to a later period under the episcopate of Victor († 198—199).[2]

At this point we must pause and turn to the evidence which Tischendorf offers regarding the date to be assigned to Heracleon.[3] As in the case of Ptolemæus, we shall give it entire and then examine it in detail. To the all-important question: "How old is Heracleon?" Tischendorf replies: "Irenæus names Heracleon, together

[1] Cf. *Credner*, Beiträge, ii. p. 253 ff.; *De Wette*, Einl. A. T., 1852, p. 61 ff., p. 62, anm. d.; *Lardner*, "He also speaks of the translation of Theodotion, which is generally allowed to have been published in the reign of Commodus." Works, ii. p. 156 f.; *Massuet*, Dissert. in Iren., ii. art. ii. xcvii. § 47.

[2] *Massuet*, Dissert. in Iren., ii. art. ii. xcvii. (§ 47), xcix. (§ 50); *Volkmar*, Der Ursprung, p. 24; cf. *De Wette*, Einl. A. T., p. 62, anm. d. ("Er schrieb zw., 177—192"); cf. *Credner*, Beiträge, ii. p. 255. The late Dr. Mansel places the work "between A.D. 182 and 188." The Gnostic Heresies, p. 240. This date is partly based upon the mention of Eleutherus (cf. p. 240, note 2), which, it must be remembered, however, occurs in the third book. Jerome says: "Hoc ille scripsit ante annos circiter trecentos." Epist. ad Theod., § 53, al. 29. If instead of "trecentos," which is an evident slip of the pen, we read "ducentos," his testimony as to the date exactly agrees.

[3] Canon Westcott adds no separate testimony. He admits that: "The history of Heracleon, the great Valentinian Commentator, is full of uncertainty. Nothing is known of his country or parentage." On the Canon, p. 263, and in a note: "The exact chronology of the early heretics is very uncertain," p. 264, note 2.

with Ptolemæus II. 4, § 1, in a way which makes them appear as well-known representatives of the Valentinian school. This interpretation of his words is all the more authorized because he never again mentions Heracleon. Clement, in the 4th Book of his Stromata, written shortly after the death of Commodus (193), recalls an explanation by Heracleon of Luke xii. 8, when he calls him the most noted man of the Valentinian school (ὁ τῆς Οὐαλεντίνου σχολῆς δοκιμώτατος is Clement's expression). Origen, at the beginning of his quotation from Heracleon, says that he was held to be a friend of Valentinus (τὸν Οὐαλεντίνου λεγόμενον εἶναι γνώριμον Ἡρακλέωνα). Hippolytus mentions him, for instance, in the following way: (vi. 29); 'Valentinus, and Heracleon, and Ptolemæus, and the whole school of these, disciples of Pythagoras and Plato. . . .' Epiphanius says (Hær. 41): 'Cerdo (the same who, according to Irenæus III. 4, § 3, was in Rome under Bishop Hyginus with Valentinus) follows these (the Ophites, Kainites, Sethiani), and Heracleon.' After all this Heracleon certainly cannot be placed later than 150 to 160. The expression which Origen uses regarding his relation to Valentinus must, according to linguistic usage, be understood of a personal relation."[1]

We have already pointed out that the fact that the names of Ptolemæus and Heracleon are thus coupled together affords no clue in itself to the date of either, and their being mentioned as leading representatives of the school of Valentinus does not in any way involve the inference that they were not contemporaries of Irenæus, living and working at the time he wrote. The way in which Irenæus mentions them in this the only passage throughout his whole work in which he names

[1] Wann wurden, u. s. w., p. 48 f.

Heracleon, and to which Tischendorf pointedly refers, is as follows: "But if it was not produced, but was generated by itself, then that which is void is both like, and brother to, and of the same honour with, that Father who has before been mentioned by Valentinus; but it is really more ancient, having existed long before, and is more exalted than the rest of the Æons of Ptolemæus himself, and of Heracleon, and all the rest who hold these views."[1] We fail to recognize anything special, here, of the kind inferred by Tischendorf, in the way in which mention is made of the two later Gnostics. If anything be clear, on the contrary, it is that a distinction is drawn between Valentinus and Ptolemæus and Heracleon, and that Irenæus points out inconsistencies between the doctrines of the founder and those of his later followers. It is quite irrelevant to insist merely, as Tischendorf does, that Irenæus and subsequent writers represent Ptolemæus and Heracleon and other Gnostics of his time as of "the school" of Valentinus. The question simply is, whether in doing so they at all imply that these men were not contemporaries of Irenæus, or necessarily assign their period of independent activity to the lifetime of Valentinus, as Tischendorf appears to argue? Most certainly they do not, and Tischendorf does not attempt to offer any evidence that they do so. We may perceive how utterly worthless such a fact is for the purpose of affixing an early date by merely considering the quotation which Tischendorf himself makes from Hippolytus: "Valentinus, therefore, and Heracleon and Ptolemæus, and

---

[1] Si autem non prolatum est, sed a se generatum est; et simile est, et fraternum, et ejusdem honoris id quod est vacuum, ei Patri qui prædictus est a Valentino: antiquius autem et multo ante exsistens, et honorificentius reliquis Æonibus ipsius Ptolemæi et Heracleonis, et reliquorum omnium qui eadem opinantur. Adv. Hær., ii. 4, § 1.

the whole school of these, disciples of Pythagoras and Plato. . . . "[1] If the statement that men are of a certain school involves the supposition of coincidence of time, the three Gnostic leaders must be considered contemporaries of Pythagoras or Plato, whose disciples they are said to be. Again, if the order in which names are mentioned, as Tischendorf contends by inference throughout his whole argument, is to involve strict similar sequence of date, the principle applied to the whole of the early writers would lead to the most ridiculous confusion. Tischendorf quotes Epiphanius: "Cerdo follows these (the Ophites, Kainites, Sethiani), and Heracleon." Why he does so it is difficult to understand, unless it be to give the appearance of multiplying testimonies, for two sentences further on he is obliged to admit: "Epiphanius has certainly made a mistake, as in such things not unfrequently happens to him, when he makes Cerdo, who, however, is to be placed about 140, follow Heracleon."[2] This kind of mistake is, indeed, common to all the writers quoted, and when it is remembered that such an error is committed where a distinct and deliberate affirmation of the point is concerned, it will easily be conceived how little dependence is to be placed on the mere mention of names in the course of argument. We find Irenæus saying that "neither Valentinus, nor Marcion, nor Saturninus, nor Basilides" possesses certain knowledge,[3] and elsewhere: "of such an one as Valentinus, or Ptolemæus, or Basilides."[4] To base

---

[1] Οὐαλεντῖνος τοίνυν καὶ Ἡρακλέων καὶ Πτολεμαῖος καὶ πᾶσα ἡ τούτων σχολή οἱ Πυθαγόρου καὶ Πλάτωνος μαθηταί, κ.τ.λ. Ref. Omn. Hær., vi. 29.

[2] Wann wurden, u. s. w., p. 49.

We do not here enter into the discussion of the nature of this error. (See *Volkmar*, Der Ursprung, p. 129 f.; *Scholten*, Die ält. Zeugnisse, p. 91; *Riggenbach*, Die Zeugn. f. d. Ev. Johan., 1866, p. 79.)

[3] Adv. Hær.. ii. 28, § 6.   [4] *Ib.*, ii. 28, § 9.

an argument as to date on the order in which names appear in such writers is preposterous.

Tischendorf draws an inference from the statement that Heracleon was said to be a γνώριμος of Valentinus, that Origen declares him to have been his friend, holding personal intercourse with him. Origen, however, evidently knew nothing individually on the point, and speaks from mere hearsay, guardedly using the expression "said to be" (λεγόμενον εἶναι γνώριμον). But according to the later and patristic use of the word, γνώριμος meant nothing more than a "disciple," and it cannot here be necessarily interpreted into a "contemporary."[1] Under no circumstances could such a phrase, avowedly limited to hearsay, have any weight. The loose manner in which the Fathers repeat each other, even in serious matters, is too well known to every one acquainted with their writings to require any remark. Their inaccuracy keeps pace with their want of critical judgment. We have seen one of the mistakes of Epiphanius, admitted by Tischendorf to be only too common with him, which illustrates how little such data are to be relied on. We may point out another of the same kind committed by him in common with Hippolytus, pseudo-Tertullian and Philastrius. Mistaking a passage of Irenæus,[2] regarding the sacred Tetrad (Kol-Arbas) of the Valentinian Gnosis, Hippolytus supposes Irenæus to refer to another heretic leader. He at once treats the Tetrad as such a leader named "Kolarbasus," and after dealing (vi. 4) with the doctrines of Secundus, and Ptolemæus, and Heracleon, he proposes, § 5, to show "what are the opinions held by Marcus and

[1] *Volkmar*, Der Ursprung, p. 127; *Scholten*, Die ält. Zeugnisse, p. 89; cf. *Lipsius*, Zeitschr. wiss. Theol., 1867, p. 82; *Stephanus*, Thesaurus Ling. Gr.; *Suidas*, Lexicon, in voce. [2] Adv. Hær., i. 14.

Kolarbasus."[1] At the end of the same book he declares that Irenæus, to whom he states that he is indebted for a knowledge of their inventions, has completely refuted the opinions of these heretics, and he proceeds to treat of Basilides, considering that it has been sufficiently demonstrated " whose disciples are Marcus and Kolarbasus, the successors of the school of Valentinus."[2] At an earlier part of the work he had spoken in a more independent way in reference to certain who had promulgated great heresies: " Of these," he says, " one is Kolarbasus, who endeavours to explain religion by measures and numbers."[3] The same mistake is committed by pseudo-Tertullian,[4] and Philastrius,[5] each of whom devotes a chapter to this supposed heretic. Epiphanius, as might have been expected, fell into the same error, and he proceeds elaborately to refute the heresy of the Kolarbasians, " which is Heresy XV." He states that Kolarbasus follows Marcus and Ptolemæus,[6] and after discussing the opinions of this mythical heretic he devotes the next chapter, " which is Heresy XVI.," to the Heracleonites, commencing it with the information that : " A certain Heracleon follows after Kolarbasus."[7] This absurd mistake[8] shows how little these writers

---

[1] Τίνα τὰ Μάρκῳ καὶ Κολαρβάσῳ νομισθέντα. Ref. Omn. Hær., vi. § 5. There can be no doubt that a chapter on Kolarbasus is omitted from the MS. of Hippolytus which we possess. Cf. *Bunsen*, Hippolytus u. s. Zeit, 1852, p. 54 f.

[2] . . . . τίνων εἶεν μαθηταὶ Μάρκος τε καὶ Κολάρβασος, οἱ τῆς Οὐαλεντίνου σχολῆς διάδοχοι γενόμενοι, κ.τ.λ. Ref. Omn. Hær., vi. § 55.

[3] Ὧν εἷς μὲν Κολάρβασος, ὃς διὰ μέτρων καὶ ἀριθμῶν ἐκτίθεσθαι θεοσέβειαν ἐπιχειρεῖ. Ref. Omn. Hær., iv. § 13.

[4] Hær., 15.   [5] *Ib.*, 43.

[6] *Ib.*, xxxv. § 1, p. 258.

[7] Ἡρακλέων τις τοῦτον τὸν Κολόρβασον διαδέχεται, κ.τ.λ. Hær., xxxvi. § 1, p. 262.

[8] *Volkmar*, Die Colarbasus-gnosis in Niedner's Zeitschr. hist. Theol., 1855 ; Der Ursprung, p. 128 f. ; *Baur*, K. G. d. drei erst. Jahrh., p. 204 ;

knew of the Gnostics of whom they wrote, and how the one ignorantly follows the other.

The order, moreover, in which they set the heretic leaders varies considerably. It will be sufficient for us merely to remark here that while pseudo-Tertullian [1] and Philastrius [2] adopt the following order after the Valentinians: Ptolemæus, Secundus, Heracleon, Marcus, and Kolarbasus, Epiphanius [3] places them: Secundus, Ptolemæus, Marcosians, Kolarbasus, and Heracleon; and Hippolytus [4] again: Secundus, Ptolemæus, Heracleon, Marcus, and Kolarbasus. The vagueness of Irenæus had left some latitude here, and his followers were uncertain. The somewhat singular fact that Irenæus only once mentions Heracleon whilst he so constantly refers to Ptolemæus, taken in connection with this order, in which Heracleon is always placed after Ptolemæus,[5] and by Epiphanius after Marcus, may be reasonably explained by the fact that whilst Ptolemæus had already gained considerable notoriety when Irenæus wrote, Heracleon may only have begun to come into notice. Since Tischendorf lays so much stress upon pseudo-Tertullian and Philastrius making Ptolemæus appear immediately after Valentinus, this explanation is after his own principle.

We have already pointed out that there is not a single passage in Irenæus, or any other early writer, assigning Ptolemæus and Heracleon to a period anterior to the time when Irenæus undertook to refute their opinions. Indeed, Tischendorf has not attempted to show that

anm. 1; *Lipsius*, Der Gnosticismus, in Ersch. u. Grubers Real. Encykl.; Zur Quellenkritik des Epiph., p. 166 f., 168 f.; *Scholten*, Die ält. Zeugnisse, p. 91.
 [1] Hær., 13 ff. [2] *Ib.*, 39 ff. [3] *Ib.*, 32 ff.
 [4] Ref. Omn. Hær., vi. § 3, 4, 5.
 [5] Tertullian also makes Heracleon follow Ptolemæus. Adv. Val., 4.

they do, and he has merely, on the strength of the general expression that these Gnostics were of the school of Valentinus, boldly assigned to them an early date. Now, as we have stated, he himself admits that Valentinus only came from Egypt to Rome in A.D. 140, and continued teaching till 160,[1] and these dates are most clearly given by Irenæus himself.[2] Why then should Ptolemæus and Heracleon, to take an extreme case, not have known Valentinus in their youth, and yet have flourished chiefly during the last two decades of the second century? Irenæus himself may be cited as a parallel case, which Tischendorf at least cannot gainsay. He is never tired of telling us that Irenæus was the disciple of Polycarp,[3] whose martyrdom he sets about A.D. 165, and he considers that the intercourse of Irenæus with the aged Father must properly be put about A.D. 150,[4] yet he himself dates the death of Irenæus, A.D. 202,[5] and nothing is more certain than that the period of his greatest activity and influence falls precisely in the last twenty years of the second century. Upon his own data, therefore, that Valentinus may have taught for twenty years after his first appearance in Rome in A.D. 140—and there is no ground whatever for asserting that he did not teach for even a much longer period—Ptolemæus and Heracleon might well have personally sat at the feet of Valentinus in their youth, as Irenæus is said to have done about the very same period at those of Polycarp, and yet, like him, have flourished chiefly towards the end of the century.

[1] Wann wurden, u. s. w., p. 43.
[2] Adv. Hær., iii. 4, § 3; Euseb., H. E., iv. 11.
[3] Wann wurden, u. s. w., p. 25, p. 11.
[4] Ib., p. 12. Compare, however, vol. i. p. 274.   [5] Ib., p. 11 f.

Although there is not the slightest ground for asserting that Ptolemæus and Heracleon were not contemporaries with Irenæus, flourishing like him towards the end of the second century, there are, on the other hand, many circumstances which altogether establish the conclusion that they were. We have already shown, in treating of Valentinus,[1] that Irenæus principally directs his work against the followers of Valentinus living at the time he wrote, and notably of Ptolemæus and his school.[2] In the preface to the first book, having stated that he writes after personal intercourse with some of the disciples of Valentinus,[3] he more definitely declares his purpose: "We will, then, to the best of our ability, clearly and concisely set forth the opinions of those who are *now* (νῦν) teaching heresy, *I speak particularly of the disciples of Ptolemæus* (τῶν περὶ Πτολεμαῖον) whose system is an offshoot from the school of Valentinus."[4] Nothing could be more explicit. Irenæus in this passage distinctly represents Ptolemæus as teaching at the time he is writing, and this statement alone is decisive, more especially as there is not a single known fact which is either directly or indirectly opposed to it.

Tischendorf lays much stress on the evidence of Hippolytus in coupling together the names of Ptolemæus and Heracleon with that of Valentinus; similar testimony of the same writer, fully confirming the above statement of Irenæus, will, therefore, have the greater force. Hippolytus says that the Valentinians differed materially among themselves regarding certain points which led to divisions, one party being called the

---

[1] Vol. ii. p. 59 ff.
[2] Canon Westcott admits this. On the Canon, p. 266 f.
[3] See passage quoted, vol. ii. p. 59 f.
[4] Adv. Hær., i. Præf. § 2. See Greek quoted, vol. ii. p. 60, note 1.

Oriental and the other the Italian. "They of the Italian party, of whom *is* Heracleon and Ptolemæus, *say*, &c. . . . They, however, who are of the Oriental party, of whom is Axionicus and Bardesanes, maintain," &c.[1] Now, Ptolemæus and Heracleon are here quite clearly represented as being contemporary with Axionicus and Bardesanes, and without discussing whether Hippolytus does not, in continuation, describe them as all living at the time he wrote,[2] there can be no doubt that some of them were, and that this evidence confirms again the statement of Irenæus. Hippolytus, in a subsequent part of his work, states that a certain Prepon, a Marcionite, has introduced something new, and "now in our own time (ἐν τοῖς καθ᾿ ἡμᾶς χρόνοις νῦν) has written a work regarding the heresy in reply to Bardesanes."[3] The researches of Hilgenfeld have proved that Bardesanes lived at least over the reign of Heliogabalus (218—222), and the statement of Hippolytus is thus confirmed.[4] Axionicus again was still flourishing when Tertullian wrote his work against the Valentinians

---

[1] Οἱ μὲν ἀπὸ τῆς Ἰταλίας, ὧν ἐστὶν Ἡρακλέων καὶ Πτολεμαῖος . . . φασι . . .

Οἱ δ᾿ αὖ ἀπὸ τῆς ἀνατολῆς λέγουσιν, ὧν ἐστὶν Ἀξιόνικος καὶ Βαρδησάνης, κ.τ.λ. Ref. Omn. Hær., vi. 35.

[2] Tischendorf did not refer to these passages at all originally, and only does so in the second and subsequent editions of his book, in reply to Volkmar and others in the Vorwort (p. ix. f.), and in a note (p. 49, note 2). Volkmar argues from the opening of the next chapter (36), Ταῦτα οὖν ἐκεῖνοι ζητείτωσαν κατ᾿ αὐτούς. (Let those heretics, therefore, discuss these points amongst themselves), that they are represented as contemporaries of Hippolytus himself at the time he wrote (A.D. 225—235), *Der Ursprung*, p. 23, p. 130 f. It is not our purpose to pursue this discussion, but whatever may be the conclusion as regards the extreme deduction of Volkmar, there can be no doubt that the passage proves at least the date which was assigned to them against Tischendorf.

[3] Ref. Omn. Hær., vii. 31.

[4] *Hilgenfeld*, Bardesanes, 1864, p. 11 ff.; *Volkmar*, Der Ursprung, p. 131, p. 23; *Lipsius*, Zeitschr. wiss. Theol., 1867, p. 80 ff.; *Riggenbach*,

(201—226). Tertullian says: "Axionicus of Antioch alone to the present day (ad hodiernum) respects the memory of Valentinus, by keeping fully the rules of his system."[1] Although on the whole they may be considered to have flourished somewhat earlier, Ptolemæus and Heracleon are thus shown to have been for a time at least contemporaries of Axionicus and Bardesanes.[2]

Moreover, it is evident that the doctrines of Ptolemæus and Heracleon represent a much later form of Gnosticism than that of Valentinus. It is generally admitted that Ptolemæus reduced the system of Valentinus to consistency,[3] and the inconsistencies which existed between the views of the Master and these later followers, and which indicate a much more advanced stage of development, are constantly pointed out by Irenæus and the Fathers who wrote in refutation of heresy. Origen also represents Heracleon as amongst those who held opinions sanctioned by the Church,[4] and both he and Ptolemæus must indubitably be classed amongst the latest Gnostics.[5] It is clear, therefore, that Ptolemæus and Heracleon were contemporaries of Irenæus[6] at the time he composed his work against Heresies (185—195), both, and especially

---

Die Zeugnisse f. d. Ev. Johannis, 1866, p. 78 f.; *Scholten*, Die ält. Zeugnisse, p. 90.

[1] Adv. Val., 4; *Hilgenfeld*, Bardesanes, p. 15; *Volkmar*, Der Ursprung, p. 130 f.; *Lipsius*, Zeitschr. wiss. Theol., 1867, p. 81.

[2] *Volkmar*, Der Ursprung, p. 23 f., p. 130 f.; *Lipsius*, Zeitschr. wiss. Theol., 1867, p. 82; *Scholten*, Die ält. Zeugnisse, p. 90.

[3] *Westcott*, On the Canon, p. 276.

[4] In Joh., T. xvi. p. 236 f.; *Grabe*, Spicil. Patr., ii. p. 105.

[5] *Hilgenfeld*, Die Evangelien, p. 346; *Volkmar*, Der Ursprung, p. 127 ff.; *Scholten*, Die ält. Zeugnisse, p. 89 ff.; *Lipsius*, Zeitschr. wiss. Theol., 1867, p. 82; *Riggenbach*, Die Zeugn. f. d. Ev. Johann., p. 78.

[6] *Volkmar*, Der Ursprung, p. 22 ff., p. 126 ff.; *Scholten*, Die ält. Zeugnisse, p. 88 ff.; *Lipsius*, Zeitschr. wiss. Theol., 1867, p. 81, 83; *Davidson*, Introd. N. T., ii. p. 391; *Riggenbach*, Die Zeugn. f. d. Ev. Johann., p. 78; *Mangold*, Zu Bleek's Einl. N. T., 1875, p. 263, anm.

the latter, flourishing and writing towards the end of the second century.[1]

We mentioned, in first speaking of these Gnostics, that Epiphanius has preserved an Epistle, attributed to Ptolemæus, which is addressed to Flora, one of his disciples.[2] This Epistle is neither mentioned by Irenæus nor by any other writer before Epiphanius. There is nothing in the Epistle itself to show that it was really written by Ptolemæus himself. Assuming it to be by him, however, the Epistle was in all probability written towards the end of the second century, and it does not, therefore, come within the scope of our inquiry. We may, however, briefly notice the supposed references to our Gospels which it contains. The writer of the Epistle, without any indication whatever of a written source from which he derived them, quotes sayings of Jesus for which parallels are found in our first Gospel. These sayings are introduced by such expressions as "he said," "our Saviour declared," but never as quotations from any Scripture. Now, in affirming that they are taken from the Gospel according to Matthew, Apologists exhibit their usual arbitrary haste, for we must clearly and decidedly state that there is not a single one of the passages which does not present decided variations from the parallel passages in our first Synoptic. We subjoin for comparison in parallel columns the passages from the Epistle and Gospel:—

Epistle.	Matt. xii. 25.
Οἰκία γὰρ ἢ πόλις μερισθεῖσα ἐφ' ἑαυτὴν ὅτι μὴ δύναται στῆναι, ὁ σωτὴρ ἡμῶν ἀπεφήνατο.[3]	. . . . πᾶσα πόλις ἢ οἰκία μερισθεῖσα καθ' ἑαυτῆς οὐ σταθήσεται.

[1] *Volkmar*, Der Ursprung, p. 22 ff., 126 ff.; *Scholten*, Die ält. Zeugnisse, p. 88 ff.; *Ebrard*, Evang. Gesch., p. 874, § 142; *Lipsius*, Zeitschr. wiss. Theol., 1867, p. 81 ff.; *Mangold*, Zu Bleek's Einl. N. T. p. 263, anm.*
[2] *Epiphanius*, Hær., xxxiii. 3—7.   [3] *Ib.*, § 3.

EPISTLE.	MATT. XIX. 8, and 6.
ἔφη αὐτοῖς ὅτι Μωϋσῆς πρὸς τὴν σκληροκαρδίαν ὑμῶν ἐπέτρεψε τὸ ἀπολύειν τὴν γυναῖκα αὐτοῦ· ἀπ' ἀρχῆς γὰρ οὐ γέγονεν οὕτως. Θεὸς γάρ, φησὶ, συνέζευξε ταύτην τὴν συζυγίαν, καὶ ὃ συνέζευξεν ὁ κύριος, ἄνθρωπος μὴ χωριζέτω, ἔφη.[1]	λέγει αὐτοῖς Ὅτι Μωϋσῆς πρὸς τὴν σκληροκαρδίαν ὑμῶν ἐπέτρεψεν ὑμῖν ἀπολῦσαι τὰς γυναῖκας ὑμῶν· ἀπ' ἀρχῆς δὲ οὐ γέγονεν οὕτως. 6..... ὃ οὖν ὁ θεὸς συρέζευξεν, ἄνθρωπος μὴ χωριζέτω.
	MATT. XV. 4–8.
Ὁ γὰρ θεὸς, φησίν, εἶπε, τίμα τὸν πατέρα σου καὶ τὴν μητέρα σου, ἵνα εὖ σοι γένηται. ὑμεῖς δέ, φησὶν, εἰρήκατε, τοῖς πρεσβυτέροις λέγων, δῶρον τῷ θεῷ ὃ ἐὰν ὠφεληθῇς ἐξ ἐμοῦ,	Ὁ γὰρ θεὸς ἐνετείλατο, λέγων· Τίμα τὸν πατέρα καὶ τὴν μητέρα, καί Ὁ κακολογῶν, κ.τ.λ.[2] 5. ὑμεῖς δὲ λέγετε· Ὃς ἂν εἴπῃ τῷ πατρὶ ἢ τῇ μητρί, Δῶρον, ὃ ἐὰν ἐξ ἐμοῦ ὠφεληθῇς, καὶ οὐ μὴ τιμήσει τὸν πατέρα αὐτοῦ, ἢ τὴν μητέρα αὐτοῦ·
καὶ ἠκυρώσατε τὸν νόμον τοῦ θεοῦ, διὰ τὴν παράδοσιν τῶν πρεσβυτέρων ὑμῶν. Τοῦτο δὲ Ἡσαΐας ἐξεφώνησεν εἰπών,	6. καὶ ἠκυρώσατε τὸν νόμον τοῦ θεοῦ διὰ τὴν παράδοσιν ὑμῶν. 7. ὑποκριταί, καλῶς ἐπροφήτευσεν περὶ ὑμῶν Ἡσαΐας, λέγων,
Ὁ λαὸς οὗτος, κ.τ.γ.[3]	8. Ὁ λαὸς οὗτος, κ.τ.λ.
	MATT. V. 38—39.
τὸ γὰρ, Ὀφθαλμὸν ἀντὶ ὀφθαλμοῦ, καὶ ὀδόντα ἀντὶ ὀδόντος . . . ἐγὼ γὰρ λέγω ὑμῖν μὴ ἀντιστῆναι ὅλως τῷ πονηρῷ ἀλλὰ ἐάν τίς σε ῥαπίσῃ στρέψον αὐτῷ καὶ τὴν ἄλλην σιαγόνα.[4]	Ἠκούσατε ὅτι ἐρρέθη· Ὀφθαλμὸν ἀντὶ ὀφθαλμοῦ, καὶ ὀδόντα ἀντὶ ὀδόντος. 39. ἐγὼ δὲ λέγω ὑμῖν, μὴ ἀντιστῆναι τῷ πονηρῷ· ἀλλ' ὅστις σε ῥαπίσει ἐπὶ τὴν δεξιάν σου σιαγόνα, στρέψον αὐτῷ καὶ τὴν ἄλλην·

It must not be forgotten that Irenæus makes very explicit statements as to the recognition of other sources of evangelical truth than our Gospels by the Valentinians, regarding which we have fully written when discussing the founder of that sect.[5] We know that they professed to have direct traditions from the Apostles through Theodas, a disciple of the Apostle Paul;[6] and in the

---

[1] *Epiph.*, Hær., xxxiii. 4.
[2] This phrase, from Leviticus xx. 9, occurs further on in the next chapter.
[3] *Epiph.*, Hær., xxxiii. § 4.
[4] *Ib.*, § 6. In the next chapter, § 7, there is ἕνα γὰρ μόνον εἶναι ἀγαθὸν θεὸν τὸν ἑαυτοῦ πατέρα ὁ σωτὴρ ἡμῶν ἀπεφήνατο, κ.τ.λ. cf. Matt. xix. 17. . . . εἶς ἐστιν ὁ ἀγαθός.
[5] See Vol. ii. p. 75 ff.
[6] *Clemens Al.*, Strom., vii. 17.

Epistle to Flora allusion is made to the succession of doctrine received by direct tradition from the Apostles.[1] Irenæus says that the Valentinians profess to derive their views from unwritten sources,[2] and he accuses them of rejecting the Gospels of the Church,[3] but, on the other hand, he states that they had many Gospels different from what he calls the Gospels of the Apostles.[4]

With regard to Heracleon, it is said that he wrote Commentaries on the third and fourth Gospels. The authority for this statement is very insufficient. The assertion with reference to the third Gospel is based solely upon a passage in the Stromata of the Alexandrian Clement. Clement quotes a passage found in Luke xii. 8, 11, 12, and says: "Expounding this passage, Heracleon, the most distinguished of the School of Valentinus, says as follows," &c.[5] This is immediately interpreted into a quotation from a Commentary on Luke.[6] We merely point out that from Clement's remark it by no means follows that Heracleon wrote a Commentary at all, and further there is no evidence that the passage commented upon was actually from our third Gospel.[7] The Stromata of Clement were not written until after A.D. 193, and in them we find the first and only reference to this supposed Commentary. We need not here refer to the Commentary on the fourth Gospel, which is merely

---

[1] *Epiphanius*, Hær., xxxiii. 7.
[2] Adv. Hær., i. 8, § 1. [3] *Ib.*, iii. 2, § 1. [4] *Ib.*, iii. 11, § 9.
[5] Τοῦτον ἐξηγούμενος τὸν τόπον Ἡρακλέων, ὁ τῆς Οὐαλεντίνου σχολῆς δοκιμώτατος, κατὰ λέξιν φησίν, κ.τ.λ. Strom., iv. 9, § 73.
[6] In Lucæ igitur Evangelium Commentaria edidit Heracleon, &c. *Grabe*, Spicil. Patr., ii. p. 83.
[7] The second reference by Clement to Heracleon is in the fragment § 25; but it is doubted by apologists (cf. *Westcott*, On the Canon, p. 264). It would, however, tend to show that the supposed Commentary could not be upon our Luke, as it refers to an apostolic injunction regarding baptism not found in our Gospels.

inferred from references in Origen (c. A.D. 225), but of which we have neither earlier nor fuller information.[1] We must, however, before leaving this subject, mention that Origen informs us that Heracleon quotes from the Preaching of Peter (Κήρυγμα Πέτρου, Prædicatio Petri), a work which, as we have already several times mentioned, was cited by Clement of Alexandria as authentic and inspired Holy Scripture.[2]

The epoch at which Ptolemæus and Heracleon flourished would in any case render testimony regarding our Gospels of little value. The actual evidence which they furnish, however, is not of a character to prove even the existence of our Synoptics, and much less does it in any way bear upon their character or authenticity.

2.

A similar question of date arises regarding Celsus, who wrote a work, entitled Λόγος ἀληθής, True Doctrine, which is no longer extant, of which Origen composed an elaborate refutation. The Christian writer takes the arguments of Celsus in detail, presenting to us, therefore, its general features, and giving many extracts; and as Celsus professes to base much of his accusation upon the writings in use amongst Christians, although he does not name a single one of them, it becomes desirable to ascertain what those works were, and the date at which

---

[1] Neither of the works, whatever they were, could have been written before the end of the second century. *Volkmar*, Der Ursprung, p. 22 f., 130 f., 165; *Scholten*, Die ält. Zeugnisse, p. 91 f.; *Ebrard*, Evang. Gesch., p. 874, § 142; *Lipsius*, Zeitschr. wiss. Theol., 1867, p. 81 f.

[2] *Clem. Al.*, Strom., vi. 5, § 39, 6, § 48, 7, § 58, 15, § 128. Canon Westcott says regarding Ptolemæus: "Two statements however which he makes are at variance with the Gospels: that our Lord's ministry was completed in a year; and that He continued for eighteen months with his disciples after His Resurrection." On the Canon, p. 268.

Celsus wrote. As usual, we shall state the case by giving the reasons assigned for an early date.

Arguing against Volkmar and others, who maintain, from a passage at the close of his work, that Origen, writing about the second quarter of the third century, represents Celsus as his contemporary,[1] Tischendorf, referring to the passage, which we shall give in its place, proceeds to assign an earlier date upon the following grounds: "But indeed, even in the first book, at the commencement of the whole work, Origen says: 'Therefore, I cannot compliment a Christian whose faith is in danger of being shaken by Celsus, who yet does not even (οὐδὲ) still (ἔτι) live the common life among men, but already and long since (ἤδη καὶ πάλαι) is dead.' . . . . . In the same first book Origen says: 'We have heard that there were two men of the name of Celsus, Epicureans, the first under Nero; this one' (that is to say, ours) 'under Hadrian and later.' It is not impossible that Origen mistakes when he identified his Celsus with the Epicurean living 'under Hadrian and later;' but it is impossible to convert the same Celsus of whom Origen says this into a contemporary of Origen. Or would Origen himself in the first book really have set his Celsus 'under Hadrian (117—138) and later,' yet in the eighth have said: 'We will wait (about 225), to see whether he will still accomplish this design of making another work follow?' Now, until some better discovery regarding Celsus is attained, it will be well to hold to the old opinion that Celsus wrote his book about the middle of the second century, probably between 150—160," &c.[2]

---

[1] *Volkmar*, Der Ursprung, p. 80; *Scholten*, Die ält. Zeugnisse, p. 99 f.

[2] Aber auch schon im ersten Buche zu Anfang der ganzen Schrift sagt Origenes: "Daher kann ich mich nicht eines Christen freuen, dessen

It is scarcely necessary to point out that the only argument advanced by Tischendorf bears solely against the assertion that Celsus was a contemporary of Origen, "about 225," and leaves the actual date entirely unsettled. He not only admits that the statement of Origen regarding the identity of his opponent with the Epicurean of the reign of Hadrian "and later," may be erroneous, but he tacitly rejects it, and having abandoned the conjecture of Origen as groundless and untenable, he substitutes a conjecture of his own, equally unsupported by reasons, that Celsus probably wrote between 150—160. Indeed, he does not attempt to justify this date, but arbitrarily decides to hold by it until a better can be demonstrated. He is forced to admit the ignorance of Origen on the point, and he does not conceal his own.

Now it is clear that the statement of Origen in the preface to his work, quoted above, that Celsus, against whom he writes, is long since dead,[1] is made in the belief that this Celsus was the Epicurean who lived under Hadrian,[2]

Glaube Gefahr läuft durch Celsus wankend gemacht zu werden, der doch nicht einmal (οὐδέ) mehr (ἔτι) das gemeine Leben unter den Menschen lebt, sondern bereits und längst (ἤδη καὶ πάλαι) verstorben ist." . . . .
In demselben ersten Buche sagt Origenes : "Wir haben erfahren, dass zwei Männer Namens Celsus Epikuräer gewesen, der erste unter Nero, dieser" (d. h. der unsrige) "unter Hadrian und später." Es ist nicht unmöglich, dass sich Origenes irrte, wenn er in seinem Celsus den "unter Hadrian und später" lebenden Epikuräer wiederfand ; aber es ist unmöglich, denselben Celsus, von welchem Origenes dies aussagt, zu einem Zeitgenossen des Origenes zu machen. Oder hätte wirklich gar Origenes selbst im 1. Buche seinen Celsus "unter Hadrian (117—138) und später" gesetzt, im 8. aber gesagt : "Wir wollen abwarten (um 225) ob er dieses Vorhaben, eine andere Schrift folgen zu lassen, noch ausführen werde ? Nun so lange keine bessere Entdeckung über Celsus gelingt, wirds wol beim Alten bleiben mit der Annahme, dass Celsus um die Mitte des 2. Jahrhunderts, vielleicht zwischen 150 und 160 sein Buch verfasst, &c." Wann wurden, u. s. w., p. 74.

[1] Contra Cels., præf., § 4. [2] Ib., i. 8.

which Tischendorf, although he avoids explanation of the reason, rightly recognizes to be a mistake. Origen undoubtedly knew nothing of his adversary, and it obviously follows that, his impression that he is Celsus the Epicurean being erroneous, his statement that he was long since dead, which is based upon that impression, loses all its value. Origen certainly at one time conjectured his Celsus to be the Epicurean of the reign of Hadrian, for he not only says so directly in the passage quoted, but on the strength of his belief in the fact, he accuses him of inconsistency: "But Celsus," he says, "must be convicted of contradicting himself; for he is discovered from other of his works to have been an Epicurean, but here, because he considered that he could attack the Word more effectively by not avowing the views of Epicurus, he pretends, &c. . . . Remark, therefore, the falseness of his mind," &c.[1] And from time to time he continues to refer to him as an Epicurean,[2] although it is evident that in the writing before him he constantly finds evidence that he is of a wholly different school. Beyond this belief, founded avowedly on mere hearsay, Origen absolutely knows nothing whatever as to the personality of Celsus, or the time at which he wrote,[3] and he sometimes very naïvely expresses his uncertainty regarding him. Referring in one place to certain passages which seem to imply a belief in magic on the part of Celsus, Origen adds: "I do not know whether he is the same who has written several books

---

[1] Ἐλεγκτέον δὴ ὡς τὰ ἐναντία ἑαυτῷ λέγοντα τὸν Κέλσον. Εὑρίσκεται μὲν γὰρ ἐξ ἄλλων συγγραμμάτων Ἐπικούρειος ὤν· ἐνταῦθα δὲ, διὰ τὸ δοκεῖν εὐλογώτερον κατηγορεῖν τοῦ λόγου, μὴ ὁμολογῶν τὰ Ἐπικούρου, προσποιεῖται, κ.τ.λ. . . . Ὅρα οὖν τὸ νόθον αὐτοῦ τῆς ψυχῆς, κ.τ.λ. Contra Cels., i. 8.

[2] Cf. Contra Cels., i. 10, 21, iii. 75, 80, iv. 36.

[3] Neander, K. G., 1842, i. p. 274.

against magic."[1] Elsewhere he says: ". . . the Epicurean Celsus (if he be the same who composed two other books against Christians)," &c.[2]

Not only is it apparent that Origen knows nothing of the Celsus with whom he is dealing, however, but it is almost impossible to avoid the conviction that during the time he was composing his work his impressions concerning the date and identity of his opponent became considerably modified. In the earlier portion of the first book[3] he has heard that his Celsus is the Epicurean of the reign of Hadrian, but a little further on,[4] he confesses his ignorance as to whether he is the same Celsus who wrote against magic, which Celsus the Epicurean actually did. In the fourth book[5] he expresses uncertainty as to whether the Epicurean Celsus had composed the work against Christians which he is refuting, and at the close of his treatise he seems to treat him as a contemporary. He writes to his friend Ambrosius, at whose request the refutation of Celsus was undertaken: "Know, however, that Celsus has promised to write another treatise after this one. . . . If, therefore, he has not fulfilled his promise to write a second book, we may well be satisfied with the eight books in reply to his Discourse. If, how-

---

[1] Οὐκ οἶδα, εἰ ὁ αὐτὸς ὢν τῷ γράψαντι κατὰ μαγείας βιβλία πλείονα. Contra Cels., i. 68.

[2] . . . ὁ Ἐπικούρειος Κέλσος (εἴ γε οὗτός ἐστι καὶ ὁ κατὰ Χριστιανῶν ἄλλα δύο βιβλία συντάξας,) κ.τ.λ. Contra Cels., iv. 36. With regard to the word ἄλλα, the most competent critics have determined that the doubt expressed is whether the Epicurean Celsus wrote the work against Christians which Origen is here refuting. Such a remark applied to any books against Christians of which no information is given would be absurdly irrelevant. Neander, K. G., i. p. 273, anm. 2; Baur, K. G. d. drei erst. Jahrh., i. p. 383 f., anm. 1; Scholten, Die ält. Zeugnisse, p. 99. We may point out that the opening passage of the 4th book of Origen's work, as well as subsequent extracts, seems to indicate a distinct division of the treatise of Celsus into two parts which may fully explain the δύο βιβλία of this sentence.

[3] i. 8. [4] i. 68. [5] iv. 36.

ever, he has commenced and finished this work also, seek it and send it in order that we may answer it also, and confute the false teaching in it," &c.[1] From this passage, and supported by other considerations, Volkmar and others assert that Celsus was really a contemporary of Origen.[2] To this, as we have seen, Tischendorf merely replies by pointing out that Origen in the preface says that Celsus was already dead, and that he was identical with the Epicurean Celsus who flourished under Hadrian and later. The former of these statements, however, was made under the impression that the latter was correct, and as it is generally agreed that Origen was mistaken in supposing that Celsus the Epicurean was the author of the Λόγος ἀληθής,[3] and Tischendorf himself admits the fact, the two earlier statements, that Celsus flourished under Hadrian and consequently that he had long been dead, fall together, whilst the subsequent doubts regarding his identity not only stand, but

---

[1] Ἴσθι μέντοι ἐπαγγελλόμενον τὸν Κέλσον ἄλλο σύνταγμα μετὰ τοῦτο ποιήσειν, ... Εἰ μὲν οὖν οὐκ ἔγραψεν ὑποσχόμενος τὸν δεύτερον λόγον, εὖ ἂν ἔχοι ἀρκεῖσθαι ἡμᾶς τοῖς ὀκτὼ πρὸς τὸν λόγον αὐτοῦ ὑπαγορευθεῖσι βιβλίοις. Εἰ δὲ κἀκεῖνον ἀρξάμενος συνετέλεσε, ζήτησον, καὶ πέμψον τὸ σύγγραμμα, ἵνα καὶ πρὸς ἐκεῖνο .... ὑπαγορεύσαντες, καὶ τὴν ἐν ἐκείνῳ ψευδοδοξίαν ἀνατρέψωμεν' κ.τ.λ. Contra Cels., viii. 76. We quote, above, the rendering of the passage referred to, p. 228, upon which Tischendorf (Wann wurden, u. s. w. p. 73 f.) insists. We may mention that in strictness the original Greek reads: "promises" instead of "has promised;" .... "did not write" instead of "has not written;" and "commenced and finished," instead of "has commenced and finished." This, however, does not materially affect the argument of Volkmar.

[2] *Volkmar*, Der Ursprung, p. 80, cf. 165; *Scholten*, Die ält. Zeugnisse, p. 100; cf. *Riggenbach*, Die Zeugn. f. d. Ev. Johann., p. 83; *Ueberweg*, Grundriss der Gesch. der Philos. des Alterth., 1867, i. p. 237.

[3] *Baur*, K. G. d. drei erst. Jahrh., p. 383 f., anm. 1; *Davidson*, Introd. N. T., ii. p. 398; *Keim*, Celsus Wahres Wort, 1873, p. 275 ff. *Mosheim*, Instit. Hist. Eccles., P. i. lib. i. sæc. ii. cap. 2, § 8; De Rebus Christ. sæc. ii. § 19, note *; *Neander*, K. G., i. p. 273 f.; *Scholten*, Die ält. Zeugnisse, p. 99 f.; *Volkmar*, Der Ursprung, p. 80. Cf. *Riggenbach*, Die Zeugn. f. d. Ev. Johann., p. 83.

rise into assurance at the close of the work in the final request to Ambrosius.[1] There can be no doubt that the first statements and the closing paragraphs are contradictory, and whilst almost all critics pronounce against the accuracy of the former, the inferences from the latter retain full force, confirmed as they are by the intermediate doubts expressed by Origen himself.

Even those who, like Tischendorf, in an arbitrary manner assign an early date to Celsus, although they do not support their conjectures by any satisfactory reasons of their own, all tacitly set aside those of Origen.[2] It is generally admitted by these, with Lardner[3] and Michaelis,[4] that the Epicurean Celsus to whom Origen was at one time disposed to refer the work against Christianity, was the writer of that name to whom Lucian, his friend and contemporary, addressed his Alexander or Pseudomantis, and who really wrote against magic,[5] as Origen mentions.[6] But although on this account Lardner assigns to him the date of A.D. 176, the fact is that Lucian did not write his Pseudomantis, as Lardner is obliged to admit,[7] until the reign of the

---

[1] Contra Cels., viii. 76.

[2] *Kirchhofer* says that Origen himself does not assign a date to the work of Celsus: "but as he (Celsus) speaks of the Marcionites, he must, in any case, be set in the second half of the second century." Quellensamml., p. 330, anm. 1; *Lardner* decides that Celsus wrote under Marcus Aurelius, and chooses to date him A.D. 176. Works, viii. p. 6. *Bindemann* dates between 170—180; Zeitschr. f. d. Hist. Theol., 1842, II. 2, p. 60, 107 ff.; cf. *Anger*, Synops. Ev. Proleg., p. xl.; *Michaelis*, Einl. N. B., 1788, i. p. 41; *Riggenbach*, Die Zeugn. f. d. Ev. Johan., p. 83; *Zeller*, Theol. Jahrb., 1845, p. 629. Canon *Westcott* dates Celsus "towards the close of the second century." On the Canon, p. 356. *Keim* dates the work about A.D. 178. Celsus' Wahres Wort, 1873, p. 261 ff. So also *Pélagaud*, Et. sur Celse, 1878, p. 207 ff.

[3] Works, viii. p. 6. [4] Einl. N. B., i. p. 41. [5] Ψευδόμαντις, § 21.

[6] Contra Cels., i. 68; *Neander*, K. G., i. p. 275; *Baur*, K. G. drei erst. Jahrh., p. 383, anm. 1; cf. *Keim*, Celsus' Wahres Wort, 1873, p. 275 ff.

[7] Works, viii. p. 6; cf. *Bindemann*, Zeitschr. hist. Theol. 1842, II. 2, p. 107.

Emperor Commodus (180—193), and even upon the supposition that this Celsus wrote against Christianity, of which there is not the slightest evidence, there would be no ground whatever for dating the work before A.D. 180. On the contrary, as Lucian does not in any way refer to such a writing by his friend, there would be strong reason for assigning the work, if it be supposed to be written by him, to a date subsequent to the Pseudomantis. It need not be remarked that the references of Celsus to the Marcionites,[1] and to the followers of Marcellina,[2] only so far bear upon the matter as to exclude an early date.[3]

It requires very slight examination of the numerous extracts from, and references to, the work which Origen seeks to refute, however, to convince any impartial mind that the doubts of Origen were well founded as to whether Celsus the Epicurean were really the author of the Λόγος ἀληθής. As many critics of all shades of opinion have long since determined, so far from being an Epicurean, the Celsus attacked by Origen, as the philosophical opinions which he everywhere expresses clearly show, was a Neo-Platonist.[4] Indeed, although Origen seems to retain some impression that his antagonist must be an Epicurean, as he had heard, and frequently refers to him as such, he does not point out Epicurean senti-

---

[1] Contra Cels., v. 62, vi. 53, 74.   [2] Ib., v. 62.
[3] *Irenæus* says that Marcellina came to Rome under Anicetus (157—168) and made many followers. *Adv. Hær.*, i. 25, § 6; cf. *Epiphanius*, Hær., xxvii. 6.
[4] *Baur*, K. G. drei erst. Jahrh., p. 383 ff., anm. 1; *Davidson*, Introd. N. T., ii. p. 398; *Mosheim*, Instit. Hist. Eccles., lib. i. sæc. ii. p. i. cap. 2, § 8; De Rebus Christ., sæc. ii. § 19, note *; *Neander*, K. G., i. p. 273 ff., 278 f.; *Schollen*, Die ält. Zeugnisse, p. 99; *Volkmar*, Der Ursprung, p. 80. Cf. *Bindemann*, Zeitschr. hist. Theol. 1842, H. 2, p. 62 ff., 108 f.; *Keim*, Celsus' Wahres Wort, 1873, p. 286 f.; *Pélagaud*, Et. sur Celse, 1878, pp. 224 ff., 239 ff.

ments in his writings, but on the contrary, not only calls upon him no longer to conceal the school to which he belongs and avow himself an Epicurean,[1] which Celsus evidently does not, but accuses him of expressing views inconsistent with that philosophy,[2] or of so concealing his Epicurean opinions that it might be said that he is an Epicurean only in name.[3] On the other hand, Origen is clearly surprised to find that he quotes so largely from the writings, and shows such marked leaning towards the teaching, of Plato, in which Celsus indeed finds the original and purer form of many Christian doctrines,[4] and Origen is constantly forced to discuss Plato in meeting the arguments of Celsus.

The author of the work which Origen refuted, therefore, instead of being an Epicurean, as Origen supposed merely from there having been an Epicurean of the same name, was undoubtedly a Neo-Platonist, as Mosheim long ago demonstrated, of the School of Ammonius, who founded the sect at the close of the second century.[5] The promise of Celsus to write a second book with practical rules for living in accordance with the philosophy he promulgates, to which Origen refers at the close of his work, confirms this conclusion, and indicates a new and recent system of philosophy.[6] An Epicurean would not have thought of such a work—it would have been both appropriate and necessary in connection with Neo-Platonism.

We are, therefore, constrained to assign the work of

[1] Contra Cels., iii. 80, iv. 54.
[2] Contra Cels., i. 8.   [3] Ib., iv. 54.
[4] Ib., i. 32, iii. 63, iv. 54, 55, 83, vi. 1, 6, 8, 9, 10, 12, 13, 15, 16, 17, 18, 19, 20, 47, vii. 28, 31, 42, 58 f., &c., &c.
[5] Inst. Hist. Eccles., lib. i. sœc. ii. p. i. cap. 2, § 8; De Rebus Christ. sæc. ii. § 19, § 27.
[6] Cf. Neander, K. G., i. p. 278.

Celsus to at least the early part of the third century, and to the reign of Septimius Severus. Celsus repeatedly accuses Christians, in it, of teaching their doctrines secretly and against the law, which seeks them out and punishes them with death,[1] and this indicates a period of persecution. Lardner, assuming the writer to be the Epicurean friend of Lucian, from this clue supposes that the persecution referred to must have been that under Marcus Aurelius († 180), and practically rejecting the data of Origen himself, without advancing sufficient reasons of his own, dates Celsus A.D. 176.[2] As a Neo-Platonist, however, we are more accurately led to the period of persecution which, from embers never wholly extinct since the time of Marcus Aurelius, burst into fierce flame more especially in the tenth year of the reign of Severus[3] (A.D. 202), and continued for many years to afflict Christians.

It is evident that the dates assigned by apologists are wholly arbitrary, and even if our argument for the later epoch were very much less conclusive than it is, the total absence of evidence for an earlier date would completely nullify any testimony derived from Celsus. It is sufficient for us to add that, whilst he refers to incidents of Gospel history and quotes some sayings which have parallels, with more or less of variation, in our Gospels, Celsus nowhere mentions the name of any Christian book, unless we except the Book of Enoch;[4] and he accuses Christians, not without reason, of interpolating the books of the Sibyl, whose authority, he states, some of them acknowledged.[5]

---

[1] *Origen*, Contra Cels., i. 1, 3, 7, viii. 69.
[2] Works, viii. p. 6.
[3] *Eusebius*, II. E., vi. 1, 2.
[4] Contra Cels., v. 54, 55.
[5] *Ib.*, vii. 53, 56.

3.

The last document which we need examine in connection with the synoptic Gospels is the list of New Testament and other writings held in consideration by the Church, which is generally called, after its discoverer and first editor, the Canon of Muratori. This interesting fragment, which was published in 1740 by Muratori in his collection of Italian antiquities,[1] at one time belonged to the monastery of Bobbio, founded by the Irish monk Columban, and was found by Muratori in the Ambrosian Library at Milan in a MS. containing extracts of little interest from writings of Eucherius, Ambrose, Chrysostom, and others. Muratori estimated the age of the MS. at about a thousand years, but so far as we are aware no thoroughly competent judge has since expressed any opinion upon the point. The fragment, which is defective both at the commencement and at the end, is written in an apologetic tone, and professes to give a list of the writings which are recognised by the Christian Church. It is a document which has no official character,[2] but which merely conveys the private views and information of the anonymous writer, regarding whom nothing whatever is known. From any point of view, the composition is of a nature permitting the widest differences of opinion. It is by some affirmed to be a complete treatise on the books received by the Church, from which fragments have been lost;[3] whilst

---

[1] Antiquit. Ital. Med. Ævi, iii. p. 851 ff.

[2] *Reuss*, Gesch. N. T., p. 303 f.; Hist. du Canon, p. 109; *Scholz*, Einl. A. u. N. T., i. p. 272; *Tregelles*, Canon Muratorianus, 1867, p. 1 ff.; *Westcott*, On the Canon, p. 186.

[3] *Credner*, Gesch. N. T. Kanon, p. 143; *Volkmar*, Anhang, p. 341 ff., p. 355.

others consider it a mere fragment in itself.¹ It is written in Latin which by some is represented as most corrupt,² whilst others uphold it as most correct.³ The text is further rendered almost unintelligible by every possible inaccuracy of orthography and grammar, which is ascribed diversely to the transcriber, to the translator, and to both.⁴ Indeed such is the elastic condition of the text, resulting from errors and obscurity of every imaginable description, that by means of ingenious conjectures critics are able to find in it almost any sense they desire.⁵ Considerable difference of opinion exists as to the original language of the fragment, the greater number of critics maintaining that the composition is a translation from the Greek,⁶ whilst others assert it to

---

[1] *Hilgenfeld*, Der Kanon, p. 39; *Mayerhoff*, Einl. petr. Schr., p. 147; *Westcott*, On the Canon, p. 186, note 5; *Tregelles*, Can. Murat., p. 29 f.

[2] *Bleek*, Einl. N. T., p. 640; *Credner*, Zur. Gesch. d. Kanons, p. 72; *Donaldson*, Hist. Chr. Lit. and Doctr., iii. p. 205 ff.; *Guericke*, Beiträge Einl. N. T., p. 13; *Reuss*, Gesch. N. T., p. 303; *Scholz*, Einl. N. T., i. p. 271 f.; *Tregelles*, Can. Murat., p. 6 f., p. 27 f.; *Westcott*, On the Canon, p. 185.

[3] *Volkmar* considers it in reality the reverse of corrupt. After allowing for peculiarities of speech, and for the results of an Irish-English pronunciation by the monk who transcribed it, he finds the characteristic original Latin, the old *lingua vulgata* which, in the Roman Provinces, such as Africa, &c., was the written as well as the spoken language. Anhang zu *Credner's* Gesch. N. T. Kanon, p. 341 ff.

[4] *Credner*, Zur. Gesch. d. Kanons, p. 72; *Hilgenfeld*, Der Kanon, p. 39 f.; *Mayerhoff*, Einl. petr. Schr., p. 147 f.; *Scholz*, Einl. A. u. N. T., i. p. 271 f.; *Tregelles*, Can. Murat., p. 2; *Westcott*, On the Canon, p. 185.

[5] *Reuss*, Gesch. N. T., p. 303; Hist. du Canon, p. 101; *Eichhorn*, Einl. N. T., iv. p. 34.

[6] *Bunsen*, Analecta Ante-Nic., 1854, i. p. 137 f.; *Bötticher*, Zeitschr. f. d. gesammte luth. Theol. u. Kirche, 1854, p. 127 f.; *Ewald*, Gesch. d. V. Isr., vii. p. 497; cf. p. 340, anm. 2; *Guericke*, Gesammtgesch. N. T., p. 593, anm.; *Hilgenfeld*, Der Kanon, p. 39 f.; Zeitschr. w. Th. 1872, p. 560 ff.; Einl. N. T. 1875, p. 89 ff.; *Hug*, Einl. N. T., i. p. 106; *Simon de Magistris*, Daniel, sec. lxx. iv. p. 467; *Mangold*, Zu Bleek's Einl. N. T. 1875, p. 746, anm.; *Muratori*, Antiq. Ital., iii. p. 851 ff.; *Nolte*, Tüb. Quartalschr., 1860, p. 193 ff.; *Routh*, Rel. Sacr., i. p. 402; *Scholz*, Einl.

have been originally written in Latin.¹ Its composition is variously attributed to the Church of Africa² and to a member of the Church in Rome.³

The fragment commences with the concluding portion of a sentence. . . . "quibus tamen interfuit et ita posuit"—"at which nevertheless he was present, and thus he placed it." The MS. then proceeds: "Third book of the Gospel according to Luke. Luke, that physician, after the ascension of Christ when Paul took him with him . . ., wrote it in his name as he deemed best (ex opinione)—nevertheless he had not himself seen the Lord in the flesh,—and he too, as far as he could obtain information, also begins to speak from the nativity of John." The text, at the sense of which this is a closely approximate guess, though several other in-

---

A. u. N. T., i. p. 271 f.; *Thiersch*, Versuch. u. s. w., p. 385; *Tregelles*, Can. Murat. p. 4; *Volkmar*, Der Ursprung, p. 28; *Westcott*, On the Canon, p. 185. Cf. *Donaldson*, Hist. Chr. Lit. and Doctr., iii. p. 204, p. 210 f.

¹ *Bleek*, Einl. N. T., p. 640; *Credner*, Zur. Gesch. d. Kanons, p. 93; Gesch. N. T. Kanon, p. 144; *Freimüller*, Apud *Routh*, Rel. Sacr., i. p. 401 f.; *Hesse*, Das Murat. Fragment, 1873, p. 25 ff.; *Laurent*, Neutest. Stud., 1866, p. 198 f.; *Mayerhoff*, Einl. petr. Schr., p. 147; *Reuss*, Gesch. N. T., p. 305 f.; *Steckhoven*, Het Fragm. van Muratori, 1877; *Stosch*, Comm. Hist. Crit. de Libr. N. T. Can., 1755, §§ lxi. f. Cf. *Donaldson*, Hist. Chr. Lit. and Doctr., iii. p. 210 f. If the fragment, as there is some reason to believe, was originally written in Latin, it furnishes evidence that it was not written till the third century. Canon Westcott, who concludes from the order of the Gospels, &c., that it was not written in Africa, admits that: "There is no evidence of the existence of Christian Latin Literature out of Africa till about the close of the second century."

² *Credner*, Gesch. N. T. Kanon, p. 141 ff., p. 168 ff.; *Donaldson*, Hist. Chr. Lit. and Doctr. iii. p. 211; *Reuss*, Gesch. N. T., p. 303; Hist. du Canon, p. 109. Cf. *Volkmar*, Anhang zu *Credner's* Gesch. N. T. Kan., p. 341 f.

³ *Guericke*, Beiträge N. T., 1828, p. 7; *Hilgenfeld*, Der Kanon, p. 39; *Loman*, Joh. in het Fragm. v. Muratori, 1865, p. 11 f.; *Meyer*, H'buch Hebräerbr., 1867, p. 7; *Reithmayr*, Einl. Can. B. N. B., p. 65; *Scholz*, Einl. A. u. N. T., i. p. 271; *Tischendorf*, Wann wurden, u. s. w., p. 9; *Volkmar*, Der Ursprung, p. 27 f.; cf. Anh. z. *Credner's* Gesch. N. T. Kan., p. 341 f.; *Westcott*, On the Canon, p. 186.

terpretations might be maintained, is as follows: Tertio evangelii librum secundo Lucan Lucas iste medicus post ascensum Christi cum eo Paulus quasi ut juris studiosum secundum adsumsisset numeni suo ex opinione concribset dominum tamen nec ipse vidit in carne et idem prout asequi potuit ita et ad nativitate Johannis incipet dicere.

The MS. goes on to speak in more intelligible language "of the fourth of the Gospels of John, one of the disciples." (Quarti evangeliorum Johannis ex decipolis) regarding the composition of which the writer relates a legend, which we shall quote when we come to deal with that Gospel. The fragment then proceeds to mention the Acts of the Apostles,—which is ascribed to Luke—thirteen epistles of Paul in peculiar order, and it then refers to an Epistle to the Laodiceans and another to the Alexandrians, forged, in the name of Paul, after the heresy of Marcion, "and many others which cannot be received by the Catholic Church, as gall must not be mixed with vinegar." The Epistle to the Ephesians bore the name of Epistle to the Laodiceans in the list of Marcion, and this may be a reference to it.[1] The Epistle to the Alexandrians is generally identified with the Epistle to the Hebrews,[2] although some critics think this doubtful, or deny the fact, and consider both Epistles referred to pseudographs

---

[1] *Tertullian*, Adv. Marc., v. 17. *Hilgenfeld*, Der Kanon, p. 42; *Scholten*, Die ält. Zeugnisse, p. 129; *Westcott*, On the Canon, p. 190, note 1. Cf. *Schneckenburger*, Beitr. Einl. N. T. 1832, p. 153 ff. It will be remembered that reference is made in the Epist. to the Colossians to an Epistle to the Laodiceans which is lost. Col. iv. 16.

[2] *Hilgenfeld*, Der Kanon, p. 42; *Köstlin*, Theol. Jahrb., 1854, p. 416; *Scholten*, Die ält. Zeugnisse, p. 129; *Wieseler*, Th. Stud. u. Krit., 1847, p. 840, 1857, p. 97 f., and so also, *Credner*, *Eichhorn*, *Hug*, *Münster*, *Schleiermacher*, *Semler*, *Volkmar*, &c., &c.

attributed to the Apostle Paul.[1] The Epistle of Jude, and two (the second and third) Epistles of John are, with some tone of doubt, mentioned amongst the received books, and so is the Book of Wisdom. The Apocalypses of John and of Peter only are received, but some object to the latter being read in church.

The Epistle of James, both Epistles of Peter, the Epistle to the Hebrews (which is, however, probably indicated as the Epistle to the Alexandrians), and the first Epistle of John are omitted altogether, with the exception of a quotation which is supposed to be from the last-named Epistle, to which we shall hereafter refer. Special reference is made to the Pastor of Hermas, which we shall presently discuss, regarding which the writer expresses his opinion that it should be read privately but not publicly in church, as it can neither be classed amongst the books of the prophets nor of the apostles. The fragment concludes with the rejection of the writings of several heretics.[2]

It is inferred that, in the missing commencement of the fragment, the first two Synoptics must have been mentioned. This, however, though of course most probable, cannot actually be ascertained, and so far as these Gospels are concerned, therefore, the "Canon of Muratori" only furnishes conjectural evidence. The statement regarding the third Synoptic merely proves the existence of that Gospel at the time the fragment

---

[1] *Guericke*, Beiträge, N. T., p. 7 f.; *Thiersch*, Versuch, u. s. w., p. 385; *Westcott*, On the Canon, p. 190, note 1.

[2] The text of the fragment may be found in the following amongst many other books, of which we only mention some of the more accessible. *Bunsen*, Analecta Ante-Nic., i. p. 125 ff.; *Credner*, Zur Gesch. d. Kanons, p. 73 ff.; Gesh. N. T. Kanon, p. 153 ff.; *Hilgenfeld*, Der Kanon, p. 40 ff.; *Kirchhofer*, Quellensamml., p. 1 ff.; *Routh*, Reliq. Sacr., i. p. 394 ff.; *Tregelles*, Canon Murat., p. 17 ff.; *Westcott*, On the Canon, p. 467 ff.

was composed, and we shall presently endeavour to form some idea of that date, but beyond this fact the information given anything but tends to establish the unusual credibility claimed for the Gospels. It is declared by the fragment, as we have seen, that the third Synoptic was written by Luke, who had not himself seen the Lord, but narrated the history as best he was able. It is worthy of remark, moreover, that even the Apostle Paul, who took Luke with him after the Ascension, had not been a follower of Jesus either, nor had seen him in the flesh, and certainly he did not, by the showing of his own Epistles, associate much with the other Apostles, so that Luke could not have had much opportunity while with him of acquiring from them any intimate knowledge of the events of Gospel history. It is undeniable that the third Synoptic is not the narrative of an eye-witness, and the occurrences which it records did not take place in the presence, or within the personal knowledge, of the writer, but were derived from tradition, or from written sources. Such testimony, therefore, could not in any case be of much service to our third Synoptic; but when we consider the uncertainty of the date at which the fragment was composed, and the certainty that it could not have been written at an early period, it will become apparent that the value of its evidence is reduced to a minimum.

We have already incidentally mentioned that the writer of this fragment is totally unknown, nor does there exist any clue by which he can be identified. All the critics who have assigned an early date to the composition of the fragment have based their conclusion, almost solely, upon a statement made by the Author regarding the Pastor of Hermas. He says: " Hermas in truth composed the Pastor very recently in our times in the city of Rome, the Bishop Pius his brother, sitting in the chair of the church of the city of Rome. And, therefore, it should indeed be read, but it cannot be published in the church to the people, neither being among the prophets, whose number is complete, nor amongst the apostles in the latter days."

"Pastorem vero nuperrime temporibus nostris in urbe Roma Herma conscripsit sedente cathedra urbis Romæ ecclesiæ Pio episcopus fratre ejus et ideo legi cum quidem oportet se publicare vero in ecclesia populo neque inter prophetas completum numero neque inter apostolos in fine temporum potest." [1]

Muratori, the discoverer of the MS., conjectured for various reasons, which need not be here detailed, that the fragment was written by Caius the Roman Presbyter, who flourished at the end of the second (c. A.D. 196) and beginning of the third century, and in this he was followed by a few others.[2] The great mass of critics, however, have rejected this conjecture, as they have likewise negatived the fanciful ascription of the composition by Simon de Magistris to Papias of Hierapolis,[3] and by Bunsen to Hegesippus.[4] Such attempts to identify the unknown author are obviously mere speculation, and it is impossible to suppose that, had Papias, Hegesippus, or any other well-known writer of the same period composed such a list, Eusebius could have failed to refer to

---

[1] With the exception of a few trifling alterations we give these quotations as they stand in the MS.

[2] Antiq. Ital., iii. p. 854 ff.; *Gallandi*, Bibl. Vet. Patr., 1788, ii. p. xxxiii.; *Freindaller*, apud *Routh*, Rel. Sacr., i. p. 401; cf. *Hefele*, Patr. Ap. Proleg. p. lxiii.

[3] Daniel secundum LXX. 1772; Dissert., iv. p. 467 ff.

[4] Analecta Ante-Nic., 1854, i. p. 125; Hippolytus and his Age, i. p. 314.

it, as so immediately relevant to the purpose of his work. Thiersch even expressed a suspicion that the fragment was a literary mystification on the part of Muratori himself.[1]

The mass of critics, with very little independent consideration, have taken literally the statement of the author regarding the composition of the Pastor "very recently in our times" (nuperrime temporibus nostris), during the Episcopate of Pius (A.D. 142—157), and have concluded the fragment to have been written towards the end of the second century, though we need scarcely say that a few writers would date it even earlier.[2] On the other hand, and we consider with reason, many critics,

---

[1] Versuch, u. s. w., p. 387.

[2] *Bleek*, Einl. N. T., p. 640; Hebräerbr., 1828, i. 1, p. 121, anm.; *Credner*, Zur Gesch. d. Kan., p. 84, p. 92 f., Gesch. N. T. Kanon, p. 167; *Corrodi*, Versuch ein. Beleucht. d. Gesch. jüd. u. chr. Bibel-Kanons, 1792, ii. p. 219 f.; *Davidson*, Introd. N. T., i. p. 7; *Feilmoser*, Einl. N. T., p. 203, anm.; *Guericke*, Gesammtgesch. N. T., p. 587 f.; Beiträge N. T., p. 7; *Hilgenfeld*, Der Canon, p. 39; Zeitschr. w. Theol. 1872, p. 575; *Lumper*, Hist. de Vita, Script., &c., SS. Patr., vii. 1790; p. 26 ff.; *Lücke*, Einl. Offenb. Joh., 1852, ii. p. 595; *Mosheim*, De Rebus Christ., p. 164 ff.; *Meyer*, Krit., ex. H'buch. üb. d. Hebräerbr., 1867, p. 7; *Olshausen*, Echth. d. vier kan. Evv., p. 281 ff.; *Reuss*, Gesch. N. T., p. 303, p. 305; Hist. du Canon, p. 108; *Reithmayr*, Einl. N. B., p. 65, anm. 1; *Routh*, Reliq. Sacr., i. p. 397 ff.; *Chr. F. Schmid*, Unters. Offenb. Joh., u. s. w., 1771, p. 101 ff.; Hist. Antiq. et Vindic. Canonis, 1775, p. 308 f.; *Schröckh*, Chr. K. G., iii. 1777, p. 426 ff.; *Stosch*, Comment. Hist. Crit. de libris N. T. Can., 1755, §§ lxi. ff.; *Scholten*, Die ält. Zeugnisse, p. 127; *Scholz*, Einl. A. u. N. T., i. p. 272; *Thiersch* (if not spurious), Versuch, u. s. w., p. 384 f., cf. 315; *Volkmar*, (A.D. 190—200) Anh. zu *Credner's* Gesch. N. T. Kan., p. 359; *Wieseler*, Th. Stud. u. Krit., 1847, p. 815 ff.

Ewald (in late middle of 2nd century), Gesch. d. V. Isr., vii. p. 497; *Hesse* (before Irenæus, Clement Al., and Tertullian, perhaps in 3rd quarter, 2nd cent.), Das Muratori'sche Fargment, 1873, p. 48, cf. p. 56, *Laurent* (c. A.D. 160), Neutest. Studien, p. 198; *Luthardt* (c. A.D. 170), Das Joh. Ev. 1875, p. 228; *Sanday* (A.D. 170—180), Gospels in Sec. Cent., p. 266; *Steckhoven* (c. A.D. 170), Het Fragm. v. Muratori, 1877; *Tischendorf* (A.D. 160—170), Wann wurden, u. s. w., p. 9; *Tregelles* (c. A.D. 170), Canon Murat., p. 1 f., p. 4, note c.; *Westcott* (not much later than A.D. 170), On the Canon, p. 185.

including men who will not be accused of opposition to an early Canon, assign the composition to a later period, between the end of the second or beginning of the third century and the fourth century.[1]

When we examine the ground upon which alone an early date can be supported, it becomes apparent how slight the foundation is. The only argument of any weight is the statement with regard to the composition of the Pastor, but with the exception of the few apologists who do not hesitate to assign a date totally inconsistent with the state of the Canon described in the fragment, the great majority of critics feel that they are forced to place the composition at least towards the end of the second century, at a period when the statement in the composition may agree with the actual opinions in the Church, and yet in a sufficient degree accord with the expression "very recently in our times," as applied to the period of Pius of Rome, 142—157. It must be evident that, taken literally, a very arbitrary interpretation is given to this indication, and in supposing that the writer may have appropriately used the phrase thirty or forty years after the time of Pius, so much licence is taken that there is absolutely no reason why a still greater interval may not be allowed. With this sole exception, there is not a single word or statement in the fragment which would oppose our assigning the

[1] End of 2nd, or beginning of 3rd century: *Eichhorn*, Einl. N. T., iv. p. 34; *Keil* ad *Fabric.* Bibl. Græce, vii. 1801, p. 285; *Loman*, Joh. in het Fragm. Murat., 1865, p. 30; *Mayerhoff*, Einl. petr. Schr., p. 147; *Tayler*, The Fourth Gospel, 1867, p. 38; *Zimmermann*, Diss. Crit. Script., &c. &c., a Murat. rep. exhib., 1805, and to these may be added all those who assign the fragment to Caius. *Hug* (beginning 3rd century), Einl. N. T., i. p. 105 f.; *Donaldson* (end of first half of 3rd century), Hist. Chr. Lit. and Doctr., iii. p. 212.

composition to a late period of the third century. Volkmar has very justly pointed out, however, that in saying "very recently in our times" the writer merely intended to distinguish the Pastor of Hermas from the writings of the Prophets and Apostles: It cannot be classed amongst the Prophets whose number is complete, nor amongst the Apostles, inasmuch as it was only written in our post-apostolic time. This is an accurate interpretation of the expression,[1] which might with perfect propriety be used a century after the time of Pius. We have seen that there has not appeared a single trace of any Canon in the writings of any of the Fathers whom we have examined, and that the Old Testament has been the only Holy Scripture they have acknowledged; and it is therefore unsafe, upon the mere interpretation of a phrase which would be applicable even a century later, to date this anonymous fragment, regarding which we know nothing, earlier than the very end of the second or beginning of the third century, and it is still more probable that it was not written until an advanced period of the third century. The expression used with regard to Pius: "Sitting in the chair of the church," is quite unprecedented in the second century or until a very much later date.[2] It is argued that the fragment is imperfect, and that sentences have fallen out; and in regard to this, and to the assertion that it is a translation from the Greek, it has been well remarked by a writer whose judgment on the point will scarcely be called prejudiced: "If it is thus mutilated, why might it not also be interpolated? If moreover the translator

---

[1] Cf. *Donaldson*, Hist. Chr. Lit. and Doctr., iii. p. 212; *Scholten*, Die ält. Zeugnisse, p. 127; *Volkmar*, Der Ursprung, p. 28.

[2] *Donaldson*, Hist. Chr. Lit. and Doctr., iii. p. 212.

was so ignorant of Latin, can we trust his translation? and what guarantee have we that he has not paraphrased and expanded the original? The force of these remarks is peculiarly felt in dealing with the paragraph which gives the date. The Pastor of Hermas was not well known to the Western Church, and it was not highly esteemed. It was regarded as inspired by the Eastern, and read in the Eastern Churches. We have seen, moreover, that it was extremely unlikely that Hermas was a real personage. It would be, therefore, far more probable that we have here an interpolation, or addition by a member of the Roman or African Church, probably by the translator, made expressly for the purpose of serving as proof that the Pastor of Hermas was not inspired. The paragraph itself bears unquestionable mark of tampering,"[1] &c. It would take us too far were we to discuss the various statements of the fragment as indications of date, and the matter is not of sufficient importance. It contains nothing involving an earlier date than the third century.

The facts of the case may be briefly summed up as follows, so far as our object is concerned. The third Synoptic is mentioned by a totally unknown writer, at an unknown, but certainly not early, date, in all probability during the third century, in a fragment which we possess in a very corrupt version very far from free from suspicion of interpolation in the precise part from which the early date is inferred. The Gospel is attributed to Luke, who was not one of the followers of Jesus, and of whom it is expressly said that "he himself had not seen the Lord in the flesh," but wrote " as he deemed best (ex opinione)," and followed his history as he was able (et

[1] Donaldson, Hist. Chr. Lit. and Doctr., iii. p. 209.

idem prout assequi potuit).[1] If the fragment of Muratori, therefore, even came within our limits as to date, its evidence would be of no value, for, instead of establishing the trustworthiness and absolute accuracy of the narrative of the third Synoptic, it distinctly tends to discredit it, inasmuch as it declares it to be the composition of one who undeniably was not an eye-witness of the miracles reported, but collected his materials, long after, as best he could.[2]

4.

We may now briefly sum up the results of our examination of the evidence for the synoptic Gospels. After having exhausted the literature and the testimony bearing on the point, we have not found a single distinct trace of any of those Gospels, with the exception of the third, during the first century and a half after the death of Jesus. Only once during the whole of that period do we find even a tradition that any of our Evangelists composed a Gospel at all, and that tradition, so far from favouring our Synoptics, is fatal to the claims of the first and second. Papias, about the middle of

---

[1] The passage is freely rendered thus by Canon Westcott: "The Gospel of St. Luke, it is then said, stands third in order [in the Canon], having been written by 'Luke the physician,' the companion of St. Paul, who, not being himself an eye-witness, based his narrative on such information as he could obtain, beginning from the birth of John." On the Canon, p. 187.

[2] We do not propose to consider the Ophites and Peratici, obscure Gnostic sects towards the end of the second century. There is no direct evidence regarding them, and the testimony of writers in the third century, like Hippolytus, is of no value for the Gospels.

the second century, on the occasion to which we refer, records that Matthew composed the Discourses of the Lord in the Hebrew tongue, a statement which totally excludes the claim of our Greek Gospel to apostolic origin. Mark, he said, wrote down from the casual preaching of Peter the sayings and doings of Jesus, but without orderly arrangement, as he was not himself a follower of the Master, and merely recorded what fell from the Apostle. This description, likewise, shows that our actual second Gospel could not, in its present form, have been the work of Mark. There is no other reference during the period to any writing of Matthew or Mark, and no mention at all of any work ascribed to Luke. The identification of Marcion's Gospel with our third Synoptic proves the existence of that work before A.D. 140, but no evidence is thus obtained either as to the author or the character of his work, but on the contrary the testimony of the great heresiarch is so far unfavourable to that Gospel, as it involves a charge against it, of being interpolated and debased by Jewish elements. The freedom with which Marcion expurgated and altered it clearly shows that he did not regard it either as a sacred or canonical work. Any argument for the mere existence of our Synoptics based upon their supposed rejection by heretical leaders and sects has the inevitable disadvantage, that the very testimony which would show their existence would oppose their authenticity. There is no evidence of their use by heretical leaders, however, and no direct reference to them by any writer, heretical or orthodox, whom we have examined. It is unnecessary to add that no reason whatever has been shown for accepting the testimony of these Gospels as sufficient to establish the reality of miracles and of a direct Divine Revelation.[1] It is not pretended that more than one of the synoptic Gospels was written by an eye-witness of the miraculous occurrences reported, and whilst no evidence has been, or can be, produced even of the historical accuracy of the narratives, no testimony as to the correctness of the inferences from the external phenomena exists, or is now even conceivable. The discrepancy between the amount of evidence required and that which is forthcoming, however, is greater than under the circumstances could have been thought possible.

[1] A comparison of the contents of the three Synoptics would have confirmed this conclusion, but this is not at present necessary, and we must hasten on.

PART III.

THE FOURTH GOSPEL.

CHAPTER I.

THE EXTERNAL EVIDENCE.

WE shall now examine, in the same order, the witnesses already cited in connection with the Synoptics, and ascertain what evidence they furnish for the date and authenticity of the fourth Gospel.

Apologists do not even allege that there is any reference to the fourth Gospel in the so-called Epistle of Clement of Rome to the Corinthians.[1]

A few critics[2] pretend to find a trace of it in the Epistle of Barnabas, in the reference to the brazen Serpent as a type of Jesus. Tischendorf states the case as follows:—

---

[1] Canon Westcott, however, cannot resist the temptation to press Clement into service. He says: "In other passages it is possible to trace the influence of St. John, 'The blood of Christ hath gained for the whole world the offer of the grace of repentance.' 'Through Him we look steadfastly on the heights of heaven; through Him we view as in a glass ($\dot{\epsilon}\nu o \pi \tau \rho \iota \zeta \acute{o} \mu \epsilon \theta a$) His spotless and most excellent visage; through Him the eyes of our heart were opened; through Him our dull and darkened understanding is quickened with new vigour on turning to his marvellous light.'" He does not indicate more clearly the nature and marks of the "influence" to which he refers. As he also asserts that the Epistle "affirms the teaching of St. Paul and St. James," and that the Epistle to the Hebrews is "wholly transfused into Clement's mind," such an argument does not require a single remark. On the Canon, p. 23 f.

[2] Lardner, Canon Westcott, and others do not refer to it at all.

"And when in the same chapter xii. it is shown how Moses in the brazen serpent made a type of Jesus 'who should suffer (die) and yet himself make alive,' the natural inference is that Barnabas connected therewith John iii. 14, f. even if the use of this passage in particular cannot be proved. Although this connection cannot be affirmed, since the author of the Epistle, in this passage as in many others, may be independent, yet it is justifiable to ascribe the greatest probability to its dependence on the passage in John, as the tendency of the Epistle in no way required a particular leaning to the expression of John. The disproportionately more abundant use of express quotations from the Old Testament in Barnabas is, on the contrary, connected most intimately with the tendency of his whole composition."[1]

It will be observed that the suggestion of reference to the fourth Gospel is here advanced in a very hesitating way, and does not indeed go beyond an assertion of probability. We might, therefore, well leave the matter without further notice, as the reference in no case could be of any weight as evidence. On examination of the context, however, we find that there is every reason to conclude that the reference to the brazen serpent is made direct to the Old Testament. The author who delights in typology is bent upon showing that the cross is prefigured in the Old Testament. He gives a number of instances, involving the necessity for a display of ridiculous ingenuity of explanation, which should prepare us to find the comparatively simple type of the brazen serpent naturally selected. After pointing out that Moses, with his arms stretched out in prayer that the Israelites might prevail in the fight, was a type of the

[1] Wann wurden, u. s. w., 96 f.

cross, he goes on to say: "Again Moses makes a type of Jesus, that he must suffer and himself make alive (καὶ αὐτὸς ζωοποιήσει), whom they will appear to have destroyed, in a figure, while Israel was falling;"[1] and connecting the circumstance that the people were bit by serpents and died with the transgression of Eve by means of the serpent, he goes on to narrate minutely the story of Moses and the brazen serpent, and then winds up with the words: "Thou hast in this the glory of Jesus; that in him are all things and for him."[2] No one can read the whole passage carefully without seeing that the reference is direct to the Old Testament.[3] There is no ground for supposing that the author was acquainted with the fourth Gospel.

To the Pastor of Hermas Tischendorf devotes only two lines, in which he states that "it has neither quotations from the Old nor from the New Testament."[4] Canon

---

[1] Πάλιν Μωϋσῆς ποιεῖ τύπον τοῦ Ἰησοῦ, ὅτι δεῖ αὐτὸν παθεῖν, καὶ αὐτὸς ζωοποιήσει, ὃν δόξουσιν ἀπολωλεκέναι ἐν σημείῳ, πίπτοντος τοῦ Ἰσραήλ. Ch xii.

[2] Ἔχεις πάλιν καὶ ἐν τούτοις τὴν δόξαν τοῦ Ἰησοῦ, ὅτι ἐν αὐτῷ πάντα καὶ εἰς αὐτόν. Ch. xii.; cf. Heb. ii. 10; Rom. xi. 36.

[3] *Hilgenfeld*, Die ap. Väter, p. 50, anm. 8; Theol. Jahrb., 1850, p. 396; Zeitschr. wiss. Theol., 1868, p. 215 ff.; Einl. N. T., 1877, p. 733; *Holtzmann*, Zeitschr. w. Th., 1877, p. 400 f.; *Müller*, Das Barnabasbr., p. 281; *Scholten*, Die ält. Zeugnisse, p. 14: *Volkmar*, Der Ursprung, p. 66 ff. So also probably *Westcott* ("or at least not from John iii.") on the Canon 4th ed. p. 61. *Scholten* rightly points out that the distinguishing ὑψοῦσθαι of the fourth Gospel is totally lacking in the Epistle. Die ält. Zeugn., p. 14. The brazen serpent is also referred to in the Wisdom of Solomon, xvi. 5, 6, and by *Philo*, Leg. Alleg., ii. § 20; De Agricultura, § 22. Cf. *Volkmar*, Der Ursprung, p. 67 f.; *Tobler*, Zeitschr. wiss. Theol., 1860, p. 190 f. Justin Martyr also refers to the type of the brazen serpent without any connection with the fourth Gospel, Dial., 91, 94.

[4] Wann wurden, u. s. w., p. 20, anm. 1; *Lücke* makes no claim to its testimony, the analogies being "too slight and distant." Comment. Ev. Joh., 1840, i. p. 44, anm. 2. The use of the fourth Gospel (and Eps. of John) is denied by the following, amongst other writers: *Davidson*, Canon of the Bible, 1877, p. 93 f.; *Hilgenfeld*, Zeitschr. wiss. Th., 1868, p. 217 f.; *Holtzmann*, Zeitschr. wiss. Th., 1875, p. 40 ff. Cf. *Sanday*, Gospels in Sec. Cent., p. 272 f.

Westcott makes the same statement,[1] but, unlike the German apologist, he proceeds subsequently to affirm that Hermas makes " clear allusions to St. John ; " which few or no apologists support. This assertion he elaborates and illustrates as follows :—

" The view which Hermas gives of Christ's nature and work is no less harmonious with apostolic doctrine, and it offers striking analogies to the Gospel of St. John. Not only did the Son ' appoint angels to preserve each of those whom the Father gave to him ; ' but ' He himself toiled very much and suffered very much to cleanse our sins. . . . And so when he himself had cleansed the sins of the people, he showed them the paths of life by giving them the Law which he received from his Father.'[2] He is ' a Rock higher than the mountains, able to hold the whole world, ancient, and yet having a new gate.'[3] ' His name is great and infinite, and the whole world is supported by him.'[4] ' He is older than Creation, so that he took counsel with the Father about the

---

[1] On the Canon, p. 175.

[2] Καὶ αὐτὸς τὰς ἁμαρτίας αὐτῶν ἐκαθάρισε πολλὰ κοπιάσας καὶ πολλοὺς κόπους ἠντληκώς· . . . . αὐτὸς οὖν καθαρίσας τὰς ἁμαρτίας τοῦ λαοῦ ἔδειξεν αὐτοῖς τὰς τρίβους τῆς ζωῆς, δοὺς αὐτοῖς τὸν νόμον ὃν ἔλαβε παρὰ τοῦ πατρὸς αὐτοῦ. Sim., v. 6.

[3] εἰς μέσον δὲ τοῦ πεδίου ἔδειξέ μοι πέτραν μεγάλην λευκὴν ἐκ τοῦ πεδίου ἀναβεβηκυῖαν. ἡ δὲ πέτρα ὑψηλοτέρα ἦν τῶν ὀρέων, τετράγωνος ὥστε δύνασθαι ὅλον τὸν κόσμον χωρῆσαι· παλαιὰ δὲ ἦν ἡ πέτρα ἐκείνη, πύλην ἐκκεκομμένην ἔχουσα· ὡς πρόσφατος δὲ ἐδόκει μοι εἶναι ἡ ἐκκόλαψις τῆς πύλης. ἡ δὲ πύλη οὕτως ἔστιλβεν ὑπὲρ τὸν ἥλιον, ὥστε με θαυμάζειν ἐπὶ τῇ λαμπηδόνι τῆς πύλης· Simil., ix. 2.

ἡ πέτρα, φησίν, αὕτη καὶ ἡ πύλη ὁ υἱὸς τοῦ θεοῦ ἐστί. Πῶς, φημί, κύριε, ἡ πέτρα παλαιά ἐστιν, ἡ δὲ πύλη καινή; Ἄκουε, φησί, καὶ σύνιε, ἀσύνετε. Ὁ μὲν υἱὸς τοῦ θεοῦ πάσης τῆς κτίσεως αὐτοῦ προγενέστερός ἐστιν, ὥστε σύμβουλον αὐτὸν γενέσθαι τῷ πατρὶ τῆς κτίσεως αὐτοῦ· διὰ τοῦτο καὶ παλαιός ἐστιν. ἡ δὲ πύλη διὰ τί καινή, φημί, κύριε ; Ὅτι, φησίν, ἐπ᾽ ἐσχάτων τῶν ἡμερῶν τῆς συντελείας φανερὸς ἐγένετο, διὰ τοῦτο καινὴ ἐγένετο ἡ πύλη, ἵνα οἱ μέλλοντες σώζεσθαι δι᾽ αὐτῆς εἰς τὴν βασιλείαν εἰσέλθωσι τοῦ θεοῦ. Simil., ix. 12.

[4] τὸ ὄνομα τοῦ υἱοῦ τοῦ θεοῦ μέγα ἐστὶ καὶ ἀχώρητον καὶ τὸν κόσμον ὅλον βαστάζει. Simil., ix. 14.

creation which he made.'[1] 'He is the sole way of access to the Lord; and no one shall enter in unto him otherwise than by his Son.'"[2]

This is all Canon Westcott says on the subject.[3] He does not attempt to point out any precise portions of the fourth Gospel with which to compare these "striking analogies," nor does he produce any instances of similarity of language, or of the use of the same terminology as the Gospel in this apocalyptic allegory. It is evident that such evidence could in no case be of any value for the fourth Gospel.

When we examine more closely, however, it becomes certain that these passages possess no real analogy with the fourth Gospel, and were not derived from it. There is no part of them that has not close parallels in writings antecedent to our Gospel, and there is no use of terminology peculiar to it. The author does not even once use the term Logos. Canon Westcott makes no mention of the fact that the doctrine of the Logos and of the pre-existence of Jesus was enunciated long before the composition of the fourth Gospel, with almost equal clearness and fulness, and that its development can be traced through the Septuagint translation, the "Proverbs of Solomon," some of the Apocryphal works of the Old Testament, the writings of Philo, and in the Apocalypse, Epistle to the Hebrews, as well as the Pauline Epistles. To any one who examines the passages cited from the works of Hermas, and still more to any one acquainted with the history of the Logos doctrine, it will, we fear,

[1] Simil., ix. 12, quoted above.
[2] ἡ δὲ πύλη ὁ υἱὸς τοῦ θεοῦ ἐστίν. αὕτη μία εἴσοδός ἐστι πρὸς τὸν κύριον. ἄλλως οὖν οὐδεὶς εἰσελεύσεται πρὸς αὐτὸν εἰ μὴ διὰ τοῦ υἱοῦ αὐτοῦ. Sim., ix. 12.
[3] On the Canon, p. 177 f. We give the Greek quotations as they stand in Canon Westcott's notes: and also the translations in his text, without, however, adopting them.

seem wasted time to enter upon any minute refutation of such imaginary "analogies." We shall, however, as briefly as possible refer to each passage quoted.

The first is taken from an elaborate similitude with regard to true fasting, in which the world is likened to a vineyard and, in explaining his parable, the Shepherd says: "God planted the vineyard, that is, he created the people and gave them to his Son: and the Son appointed his angels over them to keep them: and he himself cleansed their sins, having suffered many things and endured many labours. . . . He himself, therefore, having cleansed the sins of the people, showed them the paths of life by giving them the Law which he received from his Father."[1]

It is difficult indeed to find anything in this passage which is in the slightest degree peculiar to the fourth Gospel, or apart from the whole course of what is taught in the Epistles, and more especially the Epistle to the Hebrews. We may point out a few passages for comparison: Heb. i. 2—4; ii. 10—11; v. 8—9; vii. 12, 17—19; viii. 6—10; x. 10—16; Romans viii. 24—17; Matt. xxi. 33; Mark xii. 1; Isaiah v. 7, liii.

The second passage is taken from an elaborate parable on the building of the Church: (a) "And in the middle of the plain he showed me a great white rock which had risen out of the plain, and the rock was higher than the mountains, rectangular so as to be able to hold the whole world, but that rock was old having a gate ($\pi \acute{\upsilon} \lambda \eta$) hewn out of it, and the hewing out of the gate ($\pi \acute{\upsilon} \lambda \eta$) seemed to me to be recent."[2] Upon this rock the tower of the Church is built. Further on an explanation is given of the similitude, in which occurs another of the

---

[1] Simil., v. 6.   [2] Ib., ix. 2.

passages referred to. (β) "This rock (πέτρα) and this gate (πύλη) are the Son of God. 'How, Lord,' I said, 'is the rock old and the gate new?' 'Listen,' he said, 'and understand, thou ignorant man. (γ) The Son of God is older than all of his creation (ὁ μὲν υἱὸς τοῦ θεοῦ πάσης τῆς κτίσεως αὐτοῦ προγενέστερός ἐστιν), so that he was a councillor with the Father in his work of creation; and for this is he old.' (δ) 'And why is the gate new, Lord?' I said; 'Because,' he replied, 'he was manifested at the last days (ἐπ᾽ ἐσχάτων τῶν ἡμερῶν) of the dispensation; for this cause the gate was made new, in order that they who shall be saved might enter by it into the kingdom of God.'"[1]

And a few lines lower down the Shepherd further explains, referring to entrance through the gate, and introducing another of the passages cited: (ε) "'In this way,' he said, 'no one shall enter into the kingdom of God unless he receive his holy name. If, therefore, you cannot enter into the City unless through its gate, so also,' he said, 'a man cannot enter in any other way into the kingdom of God than by the name of his Son beloved by him' . . . 'and the gate (πύλη) is the Son of God. This is the one entrance to the Lord.' In no other way, therefore, shall any one enter in to him, except through his Son."[2]

Now with regard to the similitude of a rock we need scarcely say that the Old Testament teems with it; and we need not point to the parable of the house built upon a rock in the first Gospel.[3] A more apt illustration is the famous saying with regard to Peter: "And upon this rock (πέτρα) I will build my Church," upon which

[1] Simil., ix. 12. *Philo* represents the Logos as a Rock (πέτρα). Quod det. potiori insid., § 31, *Mangey*, i. 213.
[2] Simil., ix. 12.   [3] Matt. vii. 24.

indeed the whole similitude of Hermas turns; and in 1 Cor. x. 4, we read: "For they drank of the Spiritual Rock accompanying them; but the Rock was Christ" (ἡ πέτρα δὲ ἦν ὁ Χριστός). There is no such similitude in the fourth Gospel at all.

We then have the "gate," on which we presume Canon Westcott chiefly relies. The parable in John x. 1—9 is quite different from that of Hermas,[1] and there is a persistent use of different terminology. The door into the sheepfold is always θύρα, the gate in the rock always πύλη. "I am the door,"[2] (ἐγώ εἰμι ἡ θύρα) is twice repeated in the fourth Gospel. "The gate is the Son of God" (ἡ πύλη ὁ υἱὸς τοῦ θεοῦ ἐστίν) is the declaration of Hermas. On the other hand, there are numerous passages, elsewhere, analogous to that in the Pastor of Hermas. Every one will remember the injunction in the Sermon on the Mount: Matth. vii. 13, 14. "Enter in through the strait gate (πύλη), for wide is the gate (πύλη), &c., 14. Because narrow is the gate (πύλη) and straitened is the way which leadeth unto life, and few there be that find it."[3] The limitation to the one way of entrance into the kingdom of God: "by the name of his Son," is also found everywhere throughout the Epistles, and likewise in the Acts of the Apostles; as for instance: Acts iv. 12, "And there is no salvation in any other: for neither is there any other name under heaven given among men whereby we must be saved."

The reasons given why the rock is old and the gate new (γ, δ) have anything but special analogy with

---

[1] Cf. Heb. ix. 24, 11—12, &c.   [2] John x. 7, 9.

[3] Compare the account of the new Jerusalem, Rev. xxi. 12 ff.; cf. xxii. 4, 14. In Simil. ix. 13, it is insisted that, to enter into the kingdom, not only "his name" must be borne, but that we must put on certain clothing.

the fourth Gospel. We are, on the contrary, taken directly to the Epistle to the Hebrews in which the preexistence of Jesus is prominently asserted, and between which and the Pastor, as in a former passage, we find singular linguistic analogies. For instance, take the whole opening portion of Heb. i. 1: "God having at many times and in many manners spoken in times past to the fathers by the prophets, 2. At the end of these days (ἐπ' ἐσχάτου τῶν ἡμερῶν τούτων) spake to us in the Son whom he appointed heir (κληρονόμος)[1] of all things, by whom he also made the worlds, 3. Who being the brightness of his glory and the express image of his substance, upholding all things by the word of his power, when he had made by himself a cleansing of our sins sat down at the right hand of Majesty on high, 4. Having become so much better than the angels,"[2] &c., &c.; and if we take the different clauses we may also find them elsewhere constantly repeated, as for instance: (γ) The son older than all his creation: compare 2 Tim. i. 9, Colossians i. 15 ("who is . . . the first born of all creation"—ὅς ἐστιν . . . . πρωτότοκος πάσης κτίσεως), 16, 17, 18, Rev. iii. 14, x. 6. The works of Philo are full of this representation of the Logos. For example: "For the Word of God is over all the universe, and the oldest and most universal of all things created" (καὶ ὁ Λόγος δὲ

[1] We may remark that in the parable Hermas speaks of the son as the heir (κληρονόμος), and of the slave—who is the true son—also as co-heir (συγκληρονόμος), and a few lines below the passage above quoted, of the hoirship (κληρονομίας). This is another indication of the use of this Epistle, the peculiar expression in regard to the son "whom he appointed heir (κληρονόμος) of all things" occurring here. Cf. Simil., v. 2, 6.

[2] Heb. i. 1. Πολυμερῶς καὶ πολυτρόπως πάλαι ὁ θεὸς λαλήσας τοῖς πατράσιν ἐν τοῖς προφήταις ἐπ' ἐσχάτου τῶν ἡμερῶν τούτων ἐλάλησεν ἡμῖν ἐν υἱῷ, (2) ὃν ἔθηκεν κληρονόμον πάντων, δι' οὗ καὶ ἐποίησεν τοὺς αἰῶνας, (3) ὃς ὢν ἀπαύγασμα τῆς δόξης καὶ χαρακτὴρ τῆς ὑποστάσεως αὐτοῦ φέρων τε τὰ πάντα τῷ ῥήματι τῆς δυνάμεως αὐτοῦ, δι' ἑαυτοῦ καθαρισμὸν ποιησάμενος τῶν ἁμαρτιῶν ἐκάθισεν ἐν δεξιᾷ τῆς μεγαλωσύνης ἐν ὑψηλοῖς, (4) τοσούτῳ κρείττων γενόμενος τῶν ἀγγέλων, κ.τ.λ.

τοῦ θεοῦ ὑπεράνω παντός ἐστι τοῦ κόσμου, καὶ πρεσ-βύτατος καὶ γενικώτατος τῶν ὅσα γέγονε).[1] Again, as to the second clause, that he assisted the Father in the work of creation, compare Heb. ii. 10, i. 2, xi. 3, Rom. xi. 36, 1 Cor. viii. 6, Coloss. i. 15, 16.[2]

The only remaining passage is the following: "The name of the Son of God is great and infinite and supports the whole world." For the first phrase, compare 2 Tim. iv. 18, Heb. i. 8; and for the second part of the sentence, Heb. i. 3, Coloss. i. 17, and many other passages quoted above.[3]

The whole assertion[4] is devoid of foundation, and might well have been left unnoticed. The attention called to it, however, may not be wasted in observing the kind of evidence with which apologists are compelled to be content.

Tischendorf points out two passages in the Epistles of pseudo-Ignatius which, he considers, show the use of the fourth Gospel.[5] They are as follows—Epistle to the Romans vii.: "I desire the bread of God, the bread of

---

[1] Leg. Alleg., iii. § 61, *Mangey*, i. p. 121; cf. De Confus. Ling., § 28, *Mang.*, i. p. 427, § 14, *ib.* i. p. 414; De Profugis, § 19, *Mang.*, i. 561; De Caritate, § 2, *Mang.*, ii. 385, &c., &c. The Logos is constantly called by *Philo* "the first-begotten of God" (πρωτόγονος Θεοῦ Λόγος); "the most ancient son of God" (πρεσβύτατος υἱὸς Θεοῦ).

[2] Cf. *Philo*, Leg. Alleg., iii. § 31, *Mangey*, i. 106; De Cherubim, § 35, *Mang.*, i. 162, &c., &c.

[3] Cf. *Philo*, De Profugis, § 20, *Mangey*, i. 562; *Frag. Mangey*, ii. 655; De Somniis, i. § 41, *Mang.*, i. 656.

[4] Canon Westcott also says: "In several places also St. John's teaching on 'the Truth' lies at the ground of Hermas' words," and in a note he refers to "Mand. iii.=1 John ii. 27; iv. 6," without specifying any passage of the book. (On the Canon, p. 176, and note 4.) Such unqualified assertions unsupported by any evidence cannot be too strongly condemned. Dr. Westcott's own words may be quoted against himself: "It is impossible to exaggerate the mischief done by these vague general statements, which produce a permanent impression wholly out of proportion with the minute element of truth which is hidden in them." On the Canon, 4th ed. p. 156, n. 1.

[5] Wann wurden, u. s. w., p. 22 f. *Lücke* does not attach much weight to

heaven, the bread of life, which is the flesh of Jesus Christ the son of God, who was born at a later time of the seed of David and Abraham; and I desire the drink of God (πόμα θεοῦ), that is his blood, which is love incorruptible, and eternal life" (ἀένναος ζωή).[1] This is compared with John vi. 41 : "I am the bread which came down from heaven" 48. . . . "I am the bread of life," 51. . . . "And the bread that I will give is my flesh;" 54. "He who eateth my flesh and drinketh my blood hath everlasting life" (ζωὴν αἰώνιον). Scholten has pointed out that the reference to Jesus as "born of the seed of David and Abraham" is not in the spirit of the fourth Gospel; and the use of πόμα θεοῦ for the πόσις of vi. 55, and ἀένναος ζωή instead of ζωὴ αἰώνιος are also opposed to the connection with that Gospel.[2] On the other hand, in the institution of the Supper, the bread is described as the body of Jesus, and the wine as his blood; and reference is made there, and elsewhere, to eating bread and drinking wine in the kingdom of God,[3] and the passage seems to be nothing but a development of this teaching.[4] Nothing could be proved by such an analogy.[5]

The second passage referred to by Tischendorf is in the Epistle to the Philadelphians vii. : "For if some

any of the supposed allusions in these Epistles. Comm. Ev. Joh., i. p. 43. Cf. *Sanday*, Gospels in Sec. Cent., p. 273 f.

[1] Ἄρτον Θεοῦ θέλω, ἄρτον οὐράνιον, ἄρτον ζωῆς, ὅς ἐστιν σὰρξ Ἰησοῦ Χριστοῦ τοῦ υἱοῦ τοῦ Θεοῦ, τοῦ γενομένου ἐν ὑστέρῳ ἐκ σπέρματος Λαβὶδ καὶ Ἀβραάμ· καὶ πόμα Θεοῦ θέλω, τὸ αἷμα αὐτοῦ, ὅ ἐστιν ἀγάπη ἄφθαρτος, καὶ ἀένναος ζωή. Ad Rom., vii.

[2] Die ält. Zeugnisse, p. 54.

[3] Matt. xxvi. 26—29; Mark xiv. 22—25; Luke xxii. 17—20; 1 Cor. xi. 23—25; cf. Luke xiv. 15.

[4] Cf. *Scholten*, Die ält. Zeugnisse, p. 54.

[5] Cf. *De Wette*, Einl. N. T., p. 225 f.; *Scholten*, Die ält. Zeugnisse, p. 54.

would have led me astray according to the flesh, yet the Spirit is not led astray, being from God, for it knoweth whence it cometh and whither it goeth, and detecteth the things that are hidden."[1] Tischendorf considers that these words are based upon John iii. 6—8, and the last phrase: "And detecteth the hidden things," upon verse 20. The sense of the Epistle, however, is precisely the reverse of that of the Gospel, which reads: "The wind bloweth where it listeth; and thou hearest the sound thereof but *knowest not* whence it cometh and whither it goeth; so is every one that is born of the Spirit;"[2] whilst the Epistle does not refer to the wind at all, but affirms that the Spirit of God does know whence it cometh, &c. The analogy in verse 20 is still more remote: "For every one that doeth evil hateth the light, neither cometh to the light, lest his deeds should be detected."[3] In 1 Cor. ii. 10, the sense is found more closely: "For the Spirit searcheth all things, yea, even the deep things of God."[4] It is evidently unreasonable to assert from such a passage the use of the fourth Gospel.[5] Even Tischendorf recognizes that in themselves the phrases which he points out in pseudo-Ignatius could not, unsupported by other corroboration, possess much weight as testimony for the use of our Gospels. He says: "Were these allusions of Ignatius to Matthew and John a wholly isolated phenomenon, and one which perhaps other undoubted results

---

[1] Εἰ γὰρ καὶ κατὰ σάρκα με τινες ἠθέλησαν πλανῆσαι, ἀλλὰ τὸ πνεῦμα οὐ πλανᾶται, ἀπὸ θεοῦ ὄν· οἶδεν γὰρ πόθεν ἔρχεται, καὶ ποῦ ὑπάγει, καὶ τὰ κρυπτὰ ἐλέγχει. Ad Philadelph., vii.

[2] τὸ πνεῦμα ὅπου θέλει πνεῖ, καὶ τὴν φωνὴν αὐτοῦ ἀκούεις, ἀλλ' οὐκ οἶδας πόθεν ἔρχεται καὶ ποῦ ὑπάγει· οὕτως ἐστὶν πᾶς ὁ γεγεννημένος ἐκ τοῦ πνεύματος. John iii. 8.

[3] πᾶς γὰρ ὁ φαῦλα πράσσων μισεῖ τὸ φῶς καὶ οὐκ ἔρχεται πρὸς τὸ φῶς, ἵνα μὴ ἐλεγχθῇ τὰ ἔργα αὐτοῦ. John iii. 20.

[4] τὸ γὰρ πνεῦμα πάντα ἐρευνᾷ, καὶ τὰ βάθη τοῦ θεοῦ. 1 Cor. ii. 10.

[5] Cf. *De Wette*, Einl. N. T., p. 225 f; *Lücke*, Comm. Ev. Joh. i. p. 43 f.

of inquiry wholly contradicted, they would hardly have any conclusive weight. But ———."[1] Canon Westcott says: "The Ignatian writings, as might be expected, are not without traces of the influence of St. John. The circumstances in which he was placed required a special enunciation of Pauline doctrine; but this is not so expressed as to exclude the parallel lines of Christian thought. Love is 'the stamp of the Christian.' (Ad Magn. v.) 'Faith is the beginning and love the end of life.' (Ad Ephes. xiv.) 'Faith is our guide upward' (ἀναγωγεύς), but love is the road that 'leads to God.' (Ad Eph. ix.) 'The Eternal (ἀίδιος) Word is the manifestation of God' (Ad Magn. viii.), 'the door by which we come to the Father' (Ad Philad. ix., cf. John x. 7), 'and without Him we have not the principle of true life' (Ad Trall. ix.: οὗ χωρὶς τὸ ἀληθινὸν ζῆν οὐκ ἔχομεν. cf. Ad Eph. iii. : 'I.X. τὸ ἀδιάκριτον ἡμῶν ζῆν). The true meat of the Christian is the 'bread of God, the bread of heaven, the bread of life, which is the flesh of Jesus Christ,' and his drink is 'Christ's blood, which is love incorruptible' (Ad Rom. vii., cf. John vi. 32, 51, 53). He has no love of this life; 'his love has been crucified, and he has in him no burning passion for the world, but living water (as the spring of a new life) speaking within him, and bidding him come to his Father' (Ad Rom. l. c.). Meanwhile his enemy is the enemy of his Master, even the 'ruler of this age.' (Ad Rom. l. c., ὁ ἄρχων τοῦ αἰῶνος τούτου. Cf. John xii. 31, xvi. 11 : ὁ ἄρχων τοῦ κόσμου τούτου· and see 1 Cor. ii. 6, 8.[2])"

Part of these references we have already considered;

---

[1] Wann wurden, u. s. w., p. 23.
[2] *Westcott*, On the Canon, p. 32 f., and notes. We have inserted in the text the references given in the notes.

others of them really do not require any notice whatever, and the only one to which we need to direct our attention for a moment may be the passage from the Epistle to the Philadelphians ix., which reads: He is the door of the Father, by which enter in Abraham, Isaac, and Jacob and the prophets, and the apostles, and the Church."[1] This is compared with John x. 7. "Therefore said Jesus again: Verily, verily, I say unto you, I am the door of the Sheep" (ἐγώ εἰμι ἡ θύρα τῶν προβάτων). We have already referred, a few pages back,[2] to the image of the door. Here again it is obvious that there is a marked difference in the sense of the Epistle from that of the Gospel. In the latter Jesus is said to be the door into the Sheepfold;[3] whilst in the Epistle, he is the door into the Father, through which not only the patriarchs, prophets, and apostles enter, but also the Church itself. Such distant analogy cannot warrant the conclusion that the passage shows any acquaintance with the fourth Gospel.[4] As for the other phrases, they are not only without special bearing upon the fourth Gospel, but they are everywhere found in the canonical Epistles, as well as elsewhere. Regarding love and faith, for instance, compare Gal. v. 6, 14, 22; Rom. xii. 9, 10, viii. 39, xiii. 9; 1 Cor. ii. 9, viii. 3; Ephes. iii. 17, v. 1, 2, vi. 23; Philip. i. 9, ii. 2; 2 Thess. iii. 5; 1 Tim. i. 14, vi. 11; 2 Tim. i. 13; Heb. x. 38 f., xi., &c., &c.

We might point out many equally close analogies in

---

[1] Αὐτὸς ὢν θύρα τοῦ πατρὸς, δι᾽ ἧς εἰσέρχονται Ἀβραὰμ καὶ Ἰσαὰκ καὶ Ἰακὼβ καὶ οἱ προφῆται, καὶ οἱ ἀπόστολοι, καὶ ἡ ἐκκλησία. Ad Philad., ix.

[2] Vol. ii. p. 256 ff.

[3] Compare the whole passage, John x. 1—16.

[4] Cf. *Davidson*, Introd. N. T., ii. p. 368 f.; *Lücke*, Com. Ev. Joh., i. p. 43 ff.; *Scholten*, Die ält. Zeugnisse, p. 54 f.; *De Wette*, Einl. N. T., p. 225 f.

EXTERNAL EVIDENCE FOR THE FOURTH GOSPEL.

the works of Philo,[1] but it is unnecessary to do so, although we may indicate one or two which first present themselves. Philo equally has "the Eternal Logos" (ὁ ἀίδιος Λόγος),[2] whom he represents as the manifestation of God in every way. "The Word is the likeness of God, by whom the universe was created" (Λόγος δέ ἐστιν εἰκὼν θεοῦ, δι᾽ οὗ σύμπας ὁ κόσμος ἐδημιουργεῖτο).[3] He is "the vicegerent" (ὕπαρχος) of God,[4] "the heavenly incorruptible food of the soul," "the bread (ἄρτος) from heaven." In one place he says: "and they who inquired what is the food of the soul . . . learnt at last that it is the Word of God, and the Divine Logos. . . . This is the heavenly nourishment, and it is mentioned in the holy Scriptures . . . saying, 'Lo! I rain upon you bread (ἄρτος) from heaven.' (Exod. xvi. 4.) 'This is the bread (ἄρτος) which the Lord has given them to eat'" (Exod. xvi. 15).[5] And again: "For the one indeed raises his eyes towards the sky, contemplating the manna, the divine Word, the heavenly incorruptible food of the longing soul."[6] Elsewhere: " . . . but it is

---

[1] Philo's birth is dated at least 20 to 30 years before our era, and his death about A.D. 40. His principal works were certainly written before his embassy to Caius. *Dähne*, Gesch. Darstell. jüd. alex. Religions-Philos., 1834, 1 abth. p. 98, anm. 2; *Delaunay*, Philon d'Alexandrie, 1867, p. 11 f.; *Ewald*, Gesch. d. V. Isr., vi. p. 239; *Gfrörer*, Gesch. des Urchristenthums I., i. p. 5, p. 37 ff., p. 45.

[2] De plant. Noe, § 5, *Mang.*, i. 332; De Mundo, § 2, *Mang.*, ii. 604.

[3] De Monarchia, ii. § 5; *Mang.*, ii. 225.

[4] De Agricult., § 12, *Mang.*, i. 308; De Somniis, i. § 41, *Mang.*, i. 656; cf. Coloss. i. 15; Heb. i. 3; 2 Cor. iv. 4.

[5] Ζητήσαντες καὶ τί τὸ τρέφον ἐστὶ τὴν ψυχήν . . . . εὗρον μαθόντες ῥῆμα θεοῦ καὶ λόγον θεῖον . . . . . ῾Η δ᾽ ἐστὶν ἡ οὐράνιος τροφή, μηνύεται δὲ ἐν ταῖς ἱεραῖς ἀναγραφαῖς . . . . λέγοντος. "'Ἰδοὺ ἐγὼ ὕω ὑμῖν ἄρτους ἐκ τοῦ οὐρανοῦ." De Profugis, § 25, *Mangey*, i. 566.

[6] Ὁ μὲν γὰρ τὰς ὄψεις ἀνατείνει πρὸς αἰθέρα, ἀφορῶν τὸ μάννα, τὸν θεῖον λόγον, τὴν οὐράνιον φιλοθεάμονος ψυχῆς ἄφθαρτον τροφήν. Quis rerum Div. Heres., § 15, *Mang.*, i. 484; Quod det. potiori insid., § 31, *Mang.*, i. 213 . . . . Μάννα, τὸν πρεσβύτατον τῶν ὄντων Λόγον θεῖον, κ.τ.λ.

taught by the Hierophant and Prophet Moses, who will say: 'This is the bread (ἄρτος), the nourishment which God gave to the soul'—that he offered his own Word and his own Logos; for this is bread (ἄρτος) which he has given us to eat, this is the Word (τὸ ῥῆμα)."[1] He also says: "Therefore he exhorts him that can run swiftly to strive with breathless eagerness towards the Divine Word who is above all things, the fountain of Wisdom, in order that by drinking of the stream, instead of death he may for his reward obtain eternal life."[2] It is the Logos who guides us to the Father, God "by the same Logos both creating all things and leading up (ἀνάγων) the perfect man from the things of earth to himself."[3] These are very imperfect examples, but it may be asserted that there is not a representation of the Logos in the fourth Gospel which has not close parallels in the works of Philo.

We have given these passages of the pseudo-Ignatian Epistles which are pointed out as indicating acquaintance with the fourth Gospel, in order that the whole case might be stated and appreciated. The analogies are too distant to prove anything, but were they fifty times more close, they could do little or nothing to establish an early origin for the fourth Gospel, and nothing at all to elucidate the question as to its character and authorship.[4]

---

[1] διδάσκεται δὲ ὑπὸ τοῦ ἱεροφάντου καὶ προφήτου Μωυσέως, ὃς ἐρεῖ· "Οὗτός ἐστιν ὁ ἄρτος, ἡ τροφή, ἣν ἔδωκεν ὁ θεὸς τῇ ψυχῇ," προσενέγκασθαι τὸ ἑαυτοῦ ῥῆμα καὶ τὸν ἑαυτοῦ Λόγον· οὗτος γὰρ ὁ ἄρτος, ὃν δέδωκεν ἡμῖν φαγεῖν, τοῦτο τὸ ῥῆμα. Leg. Alleg., iii. § 60, Mang., i. 121; cf. ib., §§ 61, 62.

[2] Προτρέπει δὲ οὖν τὸν μὲν ὠκυδρομεῖν ἱκανὸν συντείνειν ἀπνευστὶ πρὸς τὸν ἀνωτάτω Λόγον θεῖον, ὃς σοφίας ἐστὶ πηγή, ἵνα ἀρυσάμενος τοῦ νάματος ἀντὶ θανάτου ζωὴν ἀΐδιον ἆθλον εὕρηται. De Profugis, § 18, Mang., i. 560.

[3] . . . . τῷ αὐτῷ Λόγῳ καὶ τὸ πᾶν ἐργαζόμενος καὶ τὸν τέλειον ἀπὸ τῶν περιγείων ἀνάγων ὡς ἑαυτόν. De Sacrif. Abelis et Caini, § 3; Mang., i. 165.

[4] In general the Epistles follow the Synoptic narratives, and not the account of the fourth Gospel. See for instance the reference to the

The Epistles in which the passages occur are spurious and of no value as evidence for the fourth Gospel. Only one of them is found in the three Syriac Epistles. We have already stated the facts connected with the so-called Epistles of Ignatius,[1] and no one who has attentively examined them can fail to see that the testimony of such documents cannot be considered of any historic weight, except for a period when evidence of the use of the fourth Gospel ceases to be of any significance.

There are fifteen Epistles ascribed to Ignatius — of these eight are universally recognized to be spurious. Of the remaining seven, there are two Greek and Latin versions, the one much longer than the other. The longer version is almost unanimously rejected as interpolated. The discovery of a still shorter Syriac version of "the three Epistles of Ignatius," convinced the majority of critics that even the shorter Greek version of seven Epistles must be condemned, and that whatever matter could be ascribed to Ignatius himself, if any, must be looked for in these three Epistles alone. The three martyrologies of Ignatius are likewise universally repudiated as mere fictions. From such a mass of forgery, in which it is impossible to identify even a kernel of truth, no testimony could be produced which could in any degree establish the apostolic origin and authenticity of our Gospels.

It is not pretended that the so-called Epistle of Polycarp to the Philippians contains any references to the fourth Gospel. Tischendorf, however, affirms that it is weighty testimony for that Gospel, inasmuch as he discovers in it a certain trace of the first "Epistle of

anointing of Jesus, Ad Eph. xvii., cf. Matt. xxvi. 7 ff. ; Mark xiv. 3 ff. ; cf. John xii. 1 ff.

[1] Vol. i. p. 258 ff. Preface to 6th ed. p. xliv. ff.

John," and as he maintains that the Epistle and the Gospel are the works of the same author, any evidence for the one is at the same time evidence for the other.[1] We shall hereafter consider the point of the common authorship of the Epistles and fourth Gospel, and here confine ourselves chiefly to the alleged fact of the reference.

The passage to which Tischendorf alludes we subjoin, with the supposed parallel in the Epistle.

Epistle of Polycarp, vii.	1 Epistle of John, iv. 3.
For whosoever doth not confess that Jesus Christ hath come in the flesh is Antichrist, and whosoever doth not confess the martyrdom of the cross is of the devil, and whosoever doth pervert the oracles of the Lord to his own lusts, and saith that there is neither resurrection nor judgment, he is a firstborn of Satan.	And every spirit that confesseth not the Lord Jesus come in the flesh is not of God, and this is the (*spirit*) of Antichrist of which ye have heard that it cometh, and now already it is in the world.
Πᾶς γὰρ, ὃς ἂν μὴ ὁμολογῇ, Ἰησοῦν Χριστὸν ἐν σαρκὶ ἐληλυθέναι, ἀντίχριστός ἐστιν· καὶ ὃς ἂν μὴ ὁμολογῇ τὸ μαρτύριον τοῦ σταυροῦ, ἐκ τοῦ διαβόλου ἐστίν· καὶ ὃς ἂν μεθοδεύῃ τὰ λόγια τοῦ κυρίου πρὸς τὰς ἰδίας ἐπιθυμίας, καὶ λέγῃ μήτε ἀνάστασιν μήτε κρίσιν εἶναι, οὗτος πρωτότοκός ἐστι τοῦ Σατανᾶ.	Καὶ πᾶν πνεῦμα ὃ μὴ ὁμολογεῖ Ἰησοῦν κύριον ἐν σαρκὶ ἐληλυθότα, ἐκ τοῦ θεοῦ οὐκ ἔστιν, καὶ τοῦτό ἐστιν τὸ τοῦ ἀντιχρίστου, ὅ τι ἀκηκόαμεν ὅτι ἔρχεται, καὶ νῦν ἐν τῷ κόσμῳ ἐστὶν ἤδη.[2]

[1] Wann wurden, u. s. w., p. 24 f.
[2] We give the text of the Sinaitic Codex as the most favourable. A great majority of the other MSS., and all the more important, present very marked difference from this reading. [In reference to this, Dr. Westcott has the following note in the 4th edition of his work on the Canon (p. 50, n. 2): "The author of *Supern. Relig.* gives (ii. p. 268) a good example of the facility with which similar phrases are mixed up, when, with the Greek text of St. John before him, he quotes as '1 John iv. 3,' καὶ πᾶν πνεῦμα, κ. τ. λ. (quoting the passage in the text above). Is this also taken from an apocryphal writing?" No, as was clearly stated in the note, it is taken from the Codex Sinaiticus. Dr. Westcott ought to have observed this. At the end of his volume, in a page of "addenda,"

This passage does not occur as a quotation, and the utmost that can be said of the few words with which it opens is that a phrase somewhat resembling, but at the same time materially differing from, the Epistle of John is interwoven with the text of the Epistle to the Philippians. If this were really a quotation from the canonical Epistle, it would indeed be singular that, considering the supposed relations of Polycarp and John, the name of the apostle should not have been mentioned, and a quotation have been distinctly and correctly made.[1] On the other hand, there is no earlier trace of the canonical Epistle, and, as Volkmar argues, it may well be doubted whether it may not rather be dependent on the Epistle to the Philippians, than the latter upon the Epistle of John.[2]

We believe with Scholten that neither is dependent on the other, but that both adopted a formula in use in the early Church against various heresies,[3] the superficial coincidence of which is without any weight as evidence for the use of either Epistle by the writer of the other. Moreover, it is clear that the writers refer to different classes of heretics. Polycarp attacks the Docetæ who deny that Jesus Christ has come in the flesh, that is with a human body of flesh and blood; whilst the Epistle of John is directed against those who deny that Jesus who has come in the flesh is the

he says: "I should have added that the singular combination of phrases which is quoted is taken from *Cod. Sin.* The words as they stand are liable to be misunderstood." In this he does himself injustice. It would not be easy to misunderstand the sarcastic question, and still less the curious addition made when his mistake was pointed out to him.]

[1] *Scholten*, Die ält. Zeugnisse, p. 46. [2] *Volkmar*, Der Ursprung, p. 48 f.
[3] *Scholten*, Die ält. Zeugnisse, p. 45 f.; cf. *Volkmar*, Der Ursprung, p. 48 f.; cf. *Irenæus*, Adv. Hær., i. 24, § 4; pseudo-*Ignatius*, Ad Smyrn., v., vi.

Christ the Son of God.[1] Volkmar points out that in Polycarp the word "Antichrist" is made a proper name, whilst in the Epistle the expression used is the abstract "Spirit of Antichrist." Polycarp in fact says that whoever denies the flesh of Christ is no Christian but Antichrist, and Volkmar finds this direct assertion more original than the assertion of the Epistle ; "Every spirit that confesseth that Jesus Christ is come in the flesh is of God,"[2] &c. In any case it seems to us clear that in both writings we have only the independent enunciation, with decided difference of language and sense, of a formula current in the Church, and that neither writer can be held to have originated the condemnation, in these words, of heresies which the Church had begun vehemently to oppose, and which were merely an application of ideas already well known, as we see from the expression of the Epistle in reference to the " Spirit of Antichrist, of which ye have heard that it cometh." Whether this phrase be an allusion to the Apocalypse xiii., or to 2 Thessalonians ii., or to traditions current in the Church, we need not inquire ; it is sufficient that the Epistle of John avowedly applies a prophecy regarding Antichrist already known amongst Christians, which was equally open to the other writer and probably familiar in the Church. This cannot under any circumstances be admitted as evidence of weight for the use of the 1st Epistle of John. There is no testimony whatever of the existence of the Epistles ascribed to John previous to this date, and that fact would have to

---

[1] *Scholten*, Die ält. Zeugnisse, p. 46 ff. ; *Volkmar*, Der Ursprung, p. 48 ff. ; cf. 1 John ii. 22 ; iv. 2, 3 ; v. 1, 5 ff.

[2] *Volkmar*, Der Ursprung, p. 49 ff. ; *Scholten*, Die ält. Zeugnisse, p. 46 ff.

be established on sure grounds before the argument we are considering can have any value.

On the other hand, we have already seen[1] that there is strong reason to doubt the authenticity of the Epistle attributed to Polycarp, and a certainty that in any case it is, in its present form, considerably interpolated. Even if genuine in any part, the use of the 1st Epistle of John, if established, could not be of much value as evidence for the fourth Gospel, of which the writing does not show a trace. So far from there being any evidence that Polycarp knew the fourth Gospel, however, everything points to the opposite conclusion. About A.D. 154-155 we find him taking part in the Paschal controversy,[2] contradicting the statements of the fourth Gospel,[3] and supporting the Synoptic view, contending that the Christian festival should be celebrated on the 14th Nisan, the day on which he affirmed that the Apostle John himself had observed it.[4] Irenæus, who represents Polycarp as the disciple of John, says of him: "For neither was Anicetus able to persuade Polycarp not to observe it (on the 14th) because he had always observed it with John the disciple of our Lord, and with the rest of the apostles with whom he consorted."[5] Not only, therefore, does Polycarp not refer to the fourth Gospel, but he is on the

---

[1] Vol. i. p. 273 ff.

[2] The date has, hitherto, generally been fixed at A.D. 160, but the recent investigations referred to in vol. i. p. 274 f. have led to the adoption of this earlier date, and the visit to Rome must, therefore, probably have taken place just after the accession of Anicetus to the Roman bishopric. Cf. *Lipsius*, Zeitschr. w. Theol. 1874, p. 205 f.

[3] John xiii. 1, xvii. 28, xix. 14, 31; cf. Matt. xxvi. 17; Mark xiv. 12; Luke xxii. 8.

[4] Cf. *Irenæus*, Adv. Hær., iii. 3, § 4; *Eusebius*, H. E., iv. 14, v. 24.

[5] *Eusebius*, H. E., v. 24.

contrary an important witness against it as the work of John, for he represents that apostle as practically contradicting the Gospel of which he is said to be the author.

The fulness with which we have discussed the character of the evangelical quotations of Justin Martyr renders the task of ascertaining whether his works indicate any acquaintance with the fourth Gospel comparatively easy. The detailed statements already made enable us without preliminary explanation directly to attack the problem, and we are freed from the necessity of making extensive quotations to illustrate the facts of the case.

Whilst apologists assert with some boldness that Justin made use of our Synoptics, they are evidently, and with good reason, less confident in maintaining his acquaintance with the fourth Gospel. Canon Westcott states : " His references to St. John are uncertain ; but this, as has been already remarked, follows from the character of the fourth Gospel. It was unlikely that he should quote its peculiar teaching in apologetic writings addressed to Jews and heathens; and at the same time he exhibits types of language and doctrine which, if not immediately drawn from St. John, yet mark the presence of his influence and the recognition of his authority."[1] This apology for the neglect of the fourth Gospel illus-

---

[1] On the Canon, p. 145. In a note Canon Westcott refers to *Credner*, Beiträge, i. p. 253 ff. *Credner*, however, pronounces against the use of the fourth Gospel by Justin. Dr. Westcott adds the singular argument: "Justin's acquaintance with the Valentinians proves that the Gospel could not have been unknown to him." (Dial. 35.) We have already proved that there is no evidence that Valentinus and his earlier followers knew anything of our Synoptics, and we shall presently show that this is likewise the case with the fourth Gospel.

trates the obvious scantiness of the evidence furnished by Justin.

Tischendorf, however, with his usual temerity, claims Justin as a powerful witness for the fourth Gospel. He says: "According to our judgment there are convincing grounds of proof for the fact that John also was known and used by Justin, provided that an unprejudiced consideration be not made to give way to the antagonistic predilection against the Johannine Gospel." In order fully and fairly to state the case which he puts forward, we shall quote his own words, but to avoid repetition we shall permit ourselves to interrupt him by remarks and by parallel passages from other writings for comparison with Justin. Tischendorf says: "The representation of the person of Christ altogether peculiar to John as it is given particularly in his Prologue i. 1 ("In the beginning was the Word and the Word was with God, and the Word was God"), and verse 14 ("and the word became flesh"), in the designation of him as Logos, as the Word of God, unmistakably re-echoes in not a few passages in Justin; for instance:[1] 'And Jesus Christ is alone the special Son begotten by God, being his Word and first-begotten and power.'"[2]

With this we may compare another passage of Justin from the second Apology. "But his son, who alone is rightly called Son, the Word before the works of creation,

---

[1] Tischendorf uses great liberty in translating some of these passages, abbreviating and otherwise altering them as it suits him. We shall therefore give his German translation below, and we add the Greek which Tischendorf does not quote—indeed he does not, in most cases, even state where the passages are to be found.

[2] "Und Jesus Christus ist allein in einzig eigenthümlicher Weise als Sohn Gottes gezeugt worden, indem er das Wort (Logos) desselben ist." Wann wurden, u. s. w., p. 32.

Καὶ Ἰησοῦς Χριστὸς μόνος ἰδίως υἱὸς τῷ θεῷ γεγέννηται, Λόγος αὐτοῦ ὑπάρχων καὶ πρωτότοκος καὶ δύναμις. Apol., i. 23.

who was both with him and begotten when in the beginning he created and ordered all things by him,"[1] &c.

Now the same words and ideas are to be found throughout the Canonical Epistles and other writings, as well as in earlier works. In the Apocalypse,[2] the only book of the New Testament mentioned by Justin, and which is directly ascribed by him to John,[3] the term Logos is applied to Jesus "the Lamb," (xix. 13) : "and his name is called the Word of God" (καὶ κέκληται τὸ ὄνομα αὐτοῦ ὁ Λόγος τοῦ θεοῦ). Elsewhere (iii. 14) he is called "the Beginning of the Creation of God" (ἡ ἀρχὴ τῆς κτίσεως τοῦ θεοῦ) ; and again in the same book (i. 5) he is "the first-begotten of the dead" (ὁ πρωτότοκος τῶν νεκρῶν). In Heb. i. 6 he is the "first-born" (πρωτότοκος), as in Coloss. i. 15 he is "the first-born of every creature" (πρωτότοκος πάσης κτίσεως) ; and in 1 Cor. i. 24 we have : "Christ the Power of God and the Wisdom of God" (Χριστὸν θεοῦ δύναμιν καὶ θεοῦ σοφίαν), and it will be remembered that "Wisdom" was the earlier term which became an alternative with "Word" for the intermediate Being. In Heb. i. 2, God is represented as speaking to us "in the Son . . . . by whom he also made the worlds" (ἐν υἱῷ, ... δι' οὗ καὶ ἐποίησεν τοὺς αἰῶνας). In 2 Tim. i. 9, he is "before all worlds" (πρὸ χρόνων αἰωνίων), cf. Heb. i. 10, ii. 10, Rom. xi. 36, 1 Cor. viii. 6, Ephes. iii. 9.

The works of Philo are filled with similar representations of the Logos, but we must restrict ourselves to a very

---

[1] Ὁ δὲ υἱὸς ἐκείνου, ὁ μόνος λεγόμενος κυρίως υἱός, ὁ Λόγος πρὸ τῶν ποιημάτων, καὶ συνὼν καὶ γεννώμενος, ὅτε τὴν ἀρχὴν δι' αὐτοῦ πάντα ἔκτισε καὶ ἐκόσμησε. Apol. ii. 6.

[2] Written c. A.D. 68—69; *Credner*, Einl. N. T., i. p. 704 f.; *Beiträge*, ii. p. 294; *Lücke*, Comm. Offenb. Joh., 1852, ii. p. 840 ff.; *Ewald*, Jahrb. bibl. Wiss., 1852—53, p. 182; Gesch. d. V. Isr., vi. p. 643, &c. &c.

[3] Dial., 81.

few. God as a Shepherd and King governs the universe "having appointed his true Logos, his first begotten Son, to have the care of this sacred flock, as the Vicegerent of a great King."[1] In another place Philo exhorts men to strive to become like God's "first begotten Word" (τὸν πρωτόγονον αὐτοῦ Λόγον),[2] and he adds, a few lines further on: "for the most ancient Word is the image of God" (θεοῦ γὰρ εἰκὼν Λόγος ὁ πρεσβύτατος). The high priest of God in the world is "the divine Word, his firstbegotten son" (ὁ πρωτόγονος αὐτοῦ θεῖος Λόγος).[3] Speaking of the creation of the world Philo says: "The instrument by which it was formed is the Word of God" (ὄργανον δὲ Λόγον θεοῦ, δι' οὗ κατεσκευάσθη).[4] Elsewhere: "For the Word is the image of God by which the whole world was created" (Λόγος δέ ἐστιν εἰκὼν θεοῦ, δι' οὗ σύμπας ὁ κόσμος ἐδημιουργεῖτο).[5] These passages might be indefinitely multiplied.

Tischendorf's next passage is: "The first power (δύναμις) after the Father of all and God the Lord, and Son, is the Word (Logos); in what manner having been made flesh (σαρκοποιηθείς) he became man, we shall in what follows relate."[6]

---

[1] .... προστησάμενος τὸν ὀρθὸν αὐτοῦ Λόγον, πρωτόγονον υἱόν, ὃς τὴν ἐπιμέλειαν τῆς ἱερᾶς ταύτης ἀγέλης οἷά τις μεγάλου βασιλέως ὕπαρχος διαδέξεται. De Agricult., § 12, *Mangey*, i. 308.

[2] De Confus. ling., § 28, *Mang.*, i. 427, cf. § 14, *ib.*, i. 414; cf. De Migrat. Abrahami, § 1, *Mang.*, i. 437; cf. Heb. i. 3; 2 Cor. iv. 4.

[3] De Somniis, i. § 37, *Mang.*, i. 653.

[4] De Cherubim, § 35, *Mang.*, i. 162.

[5] De Monarchia, ii. § 5, *Mang.*, ii. 225.

[6] "Die erste Urkraft (δύναμις) nach dem Vater des Alles und Gott dem Herrn ist der Sohn, ist das Wort (Logos); wie derselbe durch die Fleischwerdung (σαρκοποιηθείς) Mensch geworden, das werden wir in folgenden darthun." Wann wurden, u. s. w., p. 32.

Ἡ δὲ πρώτη δύναμις μετὰ τὸν Πατέρα πάντων καὶ Δεσπότην Θεὸν, καὶ υἱὸς, ὁ Λόγος ἐστίν· ὃς τίνα τρόπον σαρκοποιηθεὶς ἄνθρωπος γέγονεν, ἐν τοῖς ἑξῆς ἐροῦμεν. Apol., i. 32.

We find everywhere parallels for this passage without seeking them in the fourth Gospel. In 1 Cor. i. 24, "Christ the Power (δύναμις) of God and the Wisdom of God;" cf. Heb. i. 2, 3, 4, 6, 8; ii. 8. In Heb. ii. 14—18, there is a distinct account of his becoming flesh; cf. verse 7. In Phil. ii. 6—8: "Who (Jesus Christ) being in the form of God, deemed it not grasping to be equal with God, (7) But gave himself up, taking the form of a servant, being made in the likeness of men," &c. In Rom. viii. 3 we have: "God sending his own Son in the likeness of the flesh of sin," &c. (ὁ θεὸς τὸν ἑαυτοῦ υἱὸν πέμψας ἐν ὁμοιώματι σαρκὸς ἁμαρτίας.) It must be borne in mind that the terminology of John i. 14, "and the word became flesh" (σὰρξ ἐγένετο) is different from that of Justin, who uses the word σαρκοποιηθείς. The sense and language here is, therefore, quite as close as that of the fourth Gospel. We have also another parallel in 1 Tim. iii. 16, "Who (God) was manifested in the flesh" (ὃς ἐφανερώθη ἐν σαρκί), cf. 1 Cor. xv. 4, 47.

In like manner we find many similar passages in the Works of Philo. He says in one place that man was not made in the likeness of the most high God the Father of the universe, but in that of the "Second God who is his Word" (ἀλλὰ πρὸς τὸν δεύτερον θεόν, ὅς ἐστιν ἐκείνου Λόγος).[1] In another place the Logos is said to be the interpreter of the highest God, and he continues: "that must be God of us imperfect beings" (Οὗτος γὰρ ἡμῶν τῶν ἀτελῶν ἂν εἴη θεός).[2] Elsewhere he says: "But the

---

[1] *Philo*, Fragm. i. ex. *Euseb.*, Praepar. Evang., vii. 13, *Mang.*, ii. 625; cf. De Somniis, i. § 41, *Mang.*, i. 656; Leg. Alleg., ii. § 21, *ib.*, i. 83.

[2] Leg. Alleg., iii. § 73, *Mang.*, i. 128.

divine Word which is above these (the Winged Cherubim) .... but being itself the image of God, at once the most ancient of all conceivable things, and the one placed nearest to the only true and absolute existence without any separation or distance between them ";[1] and a few lines further on he explains the cities of refuge to be : "The Word of the Governor (of all things) and his creative and kingly power, for of these are the heavens and the whole world."[2] "The Logos of God is above all things in the world, and is the most ancient and the most universal of all things which are."[3] The Word is also the "Ambassador sent by the Governor (of the universe) to his subject (man)" (πρεσβευτὴς δὲ τοῦ ἡγεμόνος πρὸς τὸ ὑπήκοον).[4] Such views of the Logos are everywhere met with in the pages of Philo.

Tischendorf continues: "The Word (Logos) of God is his Son."[5] We have already in the preceding paragraphs abundantly illustrated this sentence, and may proceed to the next: "But since they did not know all things concerning the Logos, which is Christ, they have frequently contradicted each other."[6] These words are

[1] Ὁ δὲ ὑπεράνω τούτων Λόγος θεῖος. .... ἀλλ' αὐτὸς εἰκὼν ὑπάρχων θεοῦ, τῶν νοητῶν ἅπαξ ἁπάντων ὁ πρεσβύτατος, ὁ ἐγγυτάτω, μηδενὸς ὄντος μεθορίου διαστήματος, τοῦ μόνου ὅ ἐστιν ἀψευδῶς ἀφιδρυμένος. De Profugis, § 19, Mang., i. 561.

[2] Ὁ τοῦ ἡγεμόνος Λόγος, καὶ ἡ ποιητικὴ καὶ βασιλικὴ δύναμις αὐτοῦ· τούτων γὰρ ὅ τε οὐρανὸς καὶ σύμπας ὁ κόσμος ἐστί. De Profugis, § 19.

[3] Καὶ ὁ Λόγος δὲ τοῦ θεοῦ ὑπεράνω παντός ἐστι τοῦ κόσμου, καὶ πρεσβύτατος καὶ γενικώτατος τῶν ὅσα γέγονε. Leg. Alleg., iii. § 61, Mang., i. 121; cf. De Somniis, i. § 41, Mang., i. 656.

[4] Quis rerum div. Heres., § 42, Mang., i. 501.

[5] "Das Wort (Logos) Gottes ist der Sohn desselben." Wann wurden, u. s. w., p. 32.
Ὁ Λόγος δὲ τοῦ θεοῦ ἐστιν ὁ υἱὸς αὐτοῦ. Apol., i. 63.

[6] "Da sie nicht alles was dem Logos, welcher Christus ist, angehört erkannten, so haben sie oft einander widersprechendes gesagt."
Ἐπειδὴ δὲ οὐ πάντα τὰ τοῦ Λόγου ἐγνώρισαν, ὅς ἐστι Χριστός, καὶ ἐναντία ἑαυτοῖς πολλάκις εἶπον. Apol., ii. 10.

used with reference to Lawgivers and philosophers. Justin, who frankly admits the delight he took in the writings of Plato[1] and other Greek philosophers, held the view that Socrates and Plato had in an elementary form enunciated the doctrine of the Logos,[2] although he contends that they borrowed it from the writings of Moses, and with a largeness of mind very uncommon in the early Church, and indeed, we might add, in any age, he believed Socrates and such philosophers to have been Christians, even although they had been considered Atheists.[3] As they did not of course know Christ to be the Logos, he makes the assertion just quoted. Now the only point in the passage which requires notice is the identification of the Logos with Jesus, which has already been dealt with, and as this was asserted in the Apocalypse xix. 13, before the fourth Gospel was written, no evidence in its favour is deducible from the statement. We shall have more to say regarding this presently.

Tischendorf continues: "But in what manner through the Word of God, Jesus Christ our Saviour having been made flesh,"[4] &c.

It must be apparent that the doctrine here is not that of the fourth Gospel which makes "the word become flesh" simply, whilst Justin, representing a less advanced form, and more uncertain stage, of its development, draws a distinction between the Logos and Jesus, and describes Jesus Christ as being made flesh by the power

---

[1] Apol., ii. 12 ; cf. Dial., 2 ff.
[2] Apol., i. 60, &c., &c. ; cf. 5.
[3] Apol., i. 46.
[4] "Vermittels des Worts (Logos) Gottes ist Jesus Christus unser Heiland Fleisch goworden (σαρκοποιηθείς)." Wann wurden, u. s. w., p. 32.
ἀλλ' ὃν τρόπον διὰ Λόγου θεοῦ σαρκοποιηθεὶς Ἰησοῦς Χριστὸς ὁ Σωτὴρ ἡμῶν, κ.τ.λ. Apol. i. 66.

of the Logos. This is no accidental use of words, for he repeatedly states the same fact, as for instance: "But why through the power of the Word, according to the will of God the Father and Lord of all, he was born a man of a Virgin,"[1] &c.

Tischendorf continues: "To these passages out of the short second Apology we extract from the first (cap. 33).[2] By the Spirit, therefore, and power of God (in reference to Luke i. 35: 'The Holy Spirit shall come upon thee, and the power of the Highest shall overshadow thee') we have nothing else to understand but the Logos, which is the first-born of God."[3]

Here again we have the same difference from the doctrine of the fourth Gospel which we have just pointed out, which is, however, so completely in agreement with the views of Philo,[4] and characteristic of a less developed form of the idea. We shall further refer to the terminology hereafter, and meantime we proceed to the last illustration given by Tischendorf.

"Out of the Dialogue (c. 105): 'For that he was the only-begotten of the Father of all, in peculiar wise begotten of him as Word and Power ($\delta \acute{\upsilon} \nu \alpha \mu \iota \varsigma$), and afterwards became man through the Virgin, as we have learnt from the Memoirs, I have already stated.'"[5]

---

[1] Δι' ἣν δ'αἰτίαν διὰ δυνάμεως τοῦ Λόγου κατὰ τὴν τοῦ Πατρὸς πάντων καὶ δεσπότου Θεοῦ βουλὴν, διὰ παρθένου ἄνθρωπος ἀπεκυήθη, κ.τ.λ. Apol., i. 46.

[2] This is an error. Several of the preceding passages are out of the first Apology. No references, however, are given to the source of any of them. We have added them.

[3] "Unter dem Geiste nun und der Kraft von Gott (zu Luk. i. 35, 'der heilige Geist wird über dich kommen und die Kraft des Höchsten wird dich überschatten,') haben wir nichts anders zu verstehen als den Logos, welcher der Erstgeborne Gottes ist." Wann wurden, u. s. w., p. 32.

Τὸ πνεῦμα οὖν καὶ τὴν δύναμιν τὴν παρὰ τοῦ Θεοῦ οὐδὲν ἄλλο νοῆσαι θέμις, ἢ τὸν Λόγον, ὃς καὶ πρωτότοκος τῷ θεῷ ἐστι, κ.τ.λ. Apol., i. 33.

[4] Cf. *Gfrörer*, Gesch. des Urchristenthums, 1835, I. i. pp. 229—243.

[5] Aus dem Dialog (Kap. 105): "Dass derselbe dem Vater des Alls

The allusion here is to the preceding chapters of the Dialogue, wherein, with special reference (c. 100) to the passage which has a parallel in Luke i. 35, quoted by Tischendorf in the preceding illustration, Justin narrates the birth of Jesus.

This reference very appropriately leads us to a more general discussion of the real source of the terminology and Logos doctrine of Justin. We do not propose, in this work, to enter fully into the history of the Logos doctrine, and we must confine ourselves strictly to showing, in the most simple manner possible, that not only is there no evidence whatever that Justin derived his ideas regarding it from the fourth Gospel, but that, on the contrary, his terminology and doctrine may be traced to another source. Now, in the very chapter (100) from which this last illustration is taken, Justin shows clearly whence he derives the expression: "only-begotten." In chap. 97 he refers to the Ps. xxii. (Sept. xxi.) as a prophecy applying to Jesus, quotes the whole Psalm, and comments upon it in the following chapters; refers to Ps. ii. 7 : "Thou art my Son, this day have I begotten thee," uttered by the voice at the baptism, in ch. 103, in illustration of it; and in ch. 105 he arrives, in his exposition of it, at Verse 20 : "Deliver my soul from the sword, and my[1] only-begotten (μονογενῆ) from the hand of the dog." Then follows the passage we are discussing, in which Justin affirms that

---

eingeboren in einziger Weise aus ihm heraus als Wort (Logos) und Kraft (δύναμις) gezeugt worden und hernach Mensch vermittels der Jungfrau Maria geworden, wie wir aus den Denkwürdigkeiten gelernt haben, das habe ich vorher dargelegt." Wann wurden, u. s. w., p. 32.

Μονογενὴς γὰρ ὅτι ἦν τῷ Πατρὶ τῶν ὅλων οὗτος, ἰδίως ἐξ αὐτοῦ Λόγος καὶ δύναμις γεγενημένος, καὶ ὕστερον ἄνθρωπος διὰ τῆς παρθένου γενόμενος, ὡς ἀπὸ τῶν ἀπομνημονευμάτων ἐμάθομεν, προεδήλωσα. Dial. c. Tryph., 105.

[1] This should probably be "thy."

he has proved that he was the only-begotten (μονογενής) of the Father, and at the close he again quotes the verse as indicative of his sufferings. The Memoirs are referred to in regard to the fulfilment of this prophecy, and his birth as man through the Virgin. The phrase in Justin is quite different from that in the fourth Gospel, i. 14: "And the Word became flesh (σὰρξ ἐγένετο) and tabernacled among us, and we beheld his glory, glory as of the only-begotten from the Father" (ὡς μονογενοῦς παρὰ πατρός), &c. In Justin he is "the only-begotten of the Father of all" (μονογενὴς τῷ Πατρὶ τῶν ὅλων), and he "became man (ἄνθρωπος γενόμενος) through the Virgin," and Justin never once employs the peculiar terminology of the fourth Gospel, σὰρξ ἐγένετο, in any part of his writings.

There can be no doubt that, however the Christian doctrine of the Logos may at one period of its development have been influenced by Greek philosophy, it was in its central idea mainly of Jewish origin, and the mere application to an individual of a theory which had long occupied the Hebrew mind. After the original simplicity which represented God as holding personal intercourse with the Patriarchs, and communing face to face with the great leaders of Israel, had been outgrown, an increasing tendency set in to shroud the Divinity in impenetrable mystery, and to regard him as unapproachable and undiscernible by man. This led to the recognition of a Divine representative and substitute of the Highest God and Father, who communicated with his creatures, and through whom alone he revealed himself. A new system of interpretation of the ancient traditions of the nation was rendered necessary, and in the Septuagint translation of the Bible we are fortunately able to trace the progress of the theory which culminated in the Christian doctrine of the Logos. Wherever in the sacred records God had been represented as holding intercourse with man, the translators either symbolized the appearance or interposed an angel, who was afterwards understood to be the Divine Word. The first name under which the Divine Mediator was known in the Old Testament was Wisdom (Σοφία), although in its Apocrypha the term Logos was not unknown. The personification of the idea was very rapidly effected, and in the Book of Proverbs, as well as in the later Apocrypha based upon it: the Wisdom of Solomon, and the Wisdom of Sirach, "Ecclesiasticus;" we find it in ever increasing clearness and concretion. In the School of Alexandria the active Jewish intellect eagerly occupied itself with the speculation, and in the writings of Philo especially we find the doctrine of the Logos—the term which by that time had almost entirely supplanted that of Wisdom—elaborated to almost its final point, and wanting little or nothing but its application in an incarnate form to an individual man to represent the doctrine of the earlier Canonical writings of the New Testament, and notably the Epistle to the Hebrews,— the work of a Christian Philo,[1]—the Pauline Epistles, and lastly the fourth Gospel.[2]

[1] *Ewald* freely recognises that the author of this Epistle, written about A.D. 66, transferred Philo's doctrine of the Logos to Christianity. Apollos, whom he considers its probable author, impregnated the Apostle Paul with the doctrine. Gesch. des V. Isr., vi., p. 474 f., p. 638 ff.; Das Sendschr. an d. Hebräer, p. 9 f.

[2] Compare generally *Gfrörer*, Gesch. des Urchristenthums, i. 1, 1 und 2 Abth., 1835; *Keferstein*, Philo's Lehre v. d. göttl. Mittelwesen, 1846; *Vacherot*, Hist. crit. de l'Ecole d'Alexandrie, 1846, i. p. 125 ff.; *Delaunay*, Philon d'Alexandrie, 1867, i. p. 40 ff.; *Franck*, La Kabbale, 1843, p. 269 ff., 293 ff.; *Hilgenfeld*, Die Evv. Justin's, p. 292 ff.; *Niedner*,

In Proverbs viii. 22 ff., we have a representation of Wisdom corresponding closely with the prelude to the fourth Gospel, and still more so with the doctrine enunciated by Justin : 22. "The Lord created me the Beginning of his ways for his works. 23. Before the ages he established me, in the beginning before he made the earth. 24. And before he made the abysses, before the springs of the waters issued forth. 25. Before the mountains were settled, and before all the hills he begets me. 26. The Lord made the lands, both those which are uninhabited and the inhabited heights of the earth beneath the sky. 27. When he prepared the heavens I was present with him, and when he set his throne upon the winds, 28, and made strong the high clouds, and the deeps under the heaven made secure, 29, and made strong the foundations of the earth, 30, I was with him adjusting, I was that in which he delighted; daily I rejoiced in his presence at all times."[1] In the "Wisdom of Solomon" we find the writer addressing God : ix. 1 . . . "Who madest all things by thy Word" (ὁ ποιήσας τὰ πάντα ἐν Λόγῳ σου); and further on in the same chapter, v. 9, "And Wisdom was with thee who knoweth thy works, and was present when thou madest the world, and knew what was acceptable

Zeitschr. f. hist. Theol., 1849, h. 3, p. 337—381; *Lücke*, Comm. Evang. Joh., i. p. 283 ff. ; cf. p. 210 ff.

[1] Proverbs viii. 22. Κύριος ἔκτισέ με ἀρχὴν ὁδῶν αὐτοῦ εἰς ἔργα αὐτοῦ, 23. πρὸ τοῦ αἰῶνος ἐθεμελίωσέ με, ἐν ἀρχῇ πρὸ τοῦ τὴν γῆν ποιῆσαι, 24. καὶ πρὸ τοῦ τὰς ἀβύσσους ποιῆσαι, πρὸ τοῦ προελθεῖν τὰς πηγὰς τῶν ὑδάτων· 25. πρὸ τοῦ ὄρη ἑδρασθῆναι, πρὸ δὲ πάντων βουνῶν, γεννᾷ με. 26. Κύριος ἐποίησε χώρας καὶ ἀοικήτους, καὶ ἄκρα οἰκούμενα τῆς ὑπ᾽ οὐρανῶν. 27. Ἡνίκα ἡτοίμαζε τὸν οὐρανὸν, συμπαρήμην αὐτῷ, καὶ ὅτε ἀφώριζε τὸν ἑαυτοῦ θρόνον ἐπ᾽ ἀνέμων, 28. καὶ ὡς ἰσχυρὰ ἐποίει τὰ ἄνω νέφη, καὶ ὡς ἀσφαλεῖς ἐτίθει πηγὰς τῆς ὑπ᾽ οὐρανὸν, 29. καὶ ὡς ἰσχυρὰ ἐποίει τὰ θεμέλια τῆς γῆς, 30. ἤμην παρ᾽ αὐτῷ ἁρμόζουσα· ἐγὼ ἤμην ᾗ προσέχαιρε· καθ᾽ ἡμέραν δὲ εὐφραινόμην ἐν προσώπῳ αὐτοῦ ἐν παντὶ καιρῷ, κ.τ.λ. Sept. vers.

in thy sight, and right in thy commandments."[1] In verse 4, the writer prays: "Give me Wisdom that sitteth by thy thrones" (Δός μοι τὴν τῶν σῶν θρόνων πάρεδρον σοφίαν).[2] In a similar way the son of Sirach makes Wisdom say (Ecclesiast. xxiv. 9): "He (the Most High) created me from the beginning before the world, and as long as the world I shall not fail."[3] We have already incidentally seen how these thoughts grew into an elaborate doctrine of the Logos in the works of Philo.

Now Justin, whilst he nowhere adopts the terminology of the fourth Gospel, and nowhere refers to its introductory condensed statement of the Logos doctrine, closely follows Philo and, like him, traces it back to the Old Testament in the most direct way, accounting for the interposition of the divine Mediator in precisely the same manner as Philo, and expressing the views which had led the Seventy to modify the statement of the Hebrew original in their Greek translation. He is, in fact, thoroughly acquainted with the history of the Logos doctrine and its earlier enunciation under the symbol of Wisdom, and his knowledge of it is clearly independent of, and antecedent to, the statements of the fourth Gospel.

Referring to various episodes of the Old Testament in which God is represented as appearing to Moses and the Patriarchs, and in which it is said that "God went up from Abraham,"[4] or "The Lord spake to Moses,"[5] or "The Lord came down to behold the town," &c.,[6] or "God

---

[1] Καὶ μετὰ σοῦ ἡ σοφία ἡ εἰδυῖα τὰ ἔργα σου, καὶ παροῦσα ὅτε ἐποίεις τὸν κόσμον, καὶ ἐπισταμένη τί ἀρεστὸν ἐν ὀφθαλμοῖς σου, καὶ τί εὐθὲς ἐν ἐντολαῖς σου· Wisdom of Solom., ix. 9.   [2] Cf. ch. viii.—xi.

[3] Πρὸ τοῦ αἰῶνος ἀπ' ἀρχῆς ἔκτισέ με, καὶ ἕως αἰῶνος οὐ μὴ ἐκλίπω. Ecclesiastic. xxiv. 9.

[4] Gen. xviii. 22.   [5] Exod. vi. 29.
[6] Gen. xi. 5.

shut Noah into the ark,"[1] and so on, Justin warns his antagonist that he is not to suppose that "the unbegotten God" (ἀγέννητος θεός) did any of these things, for he has neither to come to any place, nor walks, but from his own place, wherever it may be, knows everything although he has neither eyes nor ears. Therefore he could not talk with anyone, nor be seen by anyone, and none of the Patriarchs saw the Father at all, but they saw "him who was according to his will both his Son (being God) and the Angel, in that he ministered to his purpose, whom also he willed to be born man by the Virgin, who became fire when he spoke with Moses from the bush."[2] He refers throughout his writings to the various appearances of God to the Patriarchs, all of which he ascribes to the pre-existent Jesus, the Word,[3] and in the very next chapter, after alluding to some of these, he says : "he is called Angel because he came to men, since by him the decrees of the Father are announced to men . . . At other times he is also called Man and human being, because he appears clothed in these forms as the Father wills, and they call him Logos because

[1] Gen. vii. 16.

[2] ἀλλ' ἐκεῖνον τὸν κατὰ βουλὴν τὴν ἐκείνου καὶ θεὸν ὄντα υἱὸν αὐτοῦ, καὶ ἄγγελον ἐκ τοῦ ὑπηρετεῖν τῇ γνώμῃ αὐτοῦ· ὃν καὶ ἄνθρωπον γεννηθῆναι διὰ τῆς παρθένου βεβούληται· ὃς καὶ πῦρ ποτε γέγονε τῇ πρὸς Μωϋσέα ὁμιλίᾳ τῇ ἀπὸ τῆς βάτου. Dial. 127 ; cf. 128, 63 ; cf. *Philo*, De Somniis, i. §§ 11 f., *Mang.*, i. 630 f. ; § 31. *ib.*, i. 648; §§ 33 ff., *ib.*, i. 649 ff. ; §§ 39 ff., *ib.*, i. 655 ff. Nothing in fact could show more clearly the indebtedness of Justin to Philo than this argument (Dial. 100) regarding the inapplicability of such descriptions to the "unbegotten God." Philo in one treatise from which we are constantly obliged to take passages as parallels for those of Justin (de Confusione linguarum) argues from the very same text : "The Lord went down to see that city and tower," almost in the very same words as Justin, § 27. The passage is unfortunately too long for quotation.

[3] Dial. 56, 57, 58, 59, 60, 126, 127, 128, &c., &c. ; Apol., i. 62, 63 ; cf. *Philo*, Vita Mosis, §§ 12 ff., *Mangey*, i. 91 ff. ; Leg. Alleg., iii. §§ 25 ff., *ib.*, i. 103 f., &c., &c.

he bears the communications of the Father to mankind."[1]

Justin, moreover, repeatedly refers to the fact that he was called Wisdom by Solomon, and quotes the passage we have indicated in Proverbs. In one place he says, in proof of his assertion that the God who appeared to Moses and the Patriarchs was distinguished from the Father, and was in fact the Word (ch. 66—70): "Another testimony I will give you, my friends, I said, from the Scriptures that God begat before all of the creatures (πρὸ πάντων τῶν κτισμάτων) a Beginning (ἀρχὴν),[2] a certain rational Power (δύναμιν λογικὴν) out of himself, who is called by the Holy Spirit, now the Glory of the Lord, then the Son, again Wisdom, again Angel, again God, and again Lord and Logos;" &c., and a little further on: "The Word of Wisdom will testify to me, who is himself this God begotten of the Father of the universe, being Word, and Wisdom, and Power (δύναμις), and the Glory of the Begetter," &c.,[3] and he quotes, from the Septuagint version, Proverbs viii. 22—36, part of which we have given above, and indeed, elsewhere (ch. 129), he quotes the passage a second time as evidence, with a similar context. Justin refers to it

---

[1] . . . ."Ἄγγελον καλεῖσθαι ἐν τῇ πρὸς ἀνθρώπους προόδῳ, ἐπειδὴ δι' αὐτῆς τὰ παρὰ τοῦ Πατρὸς τοῖς ἀνθρώποις ἀγγέλλεται· . . . . ἄνδρα δέ ποτε καὶ ἄνθρωπον καλεῖσθαι, ἐπειδὴ ἐν μορφαῖς τοιαύταις σχηματιζόμενος φαίνεται, αἷσπερ βούλεται ὁ Πατήρ· καὶ Λόγον καλοῦσιν, ἐπειδὴ καὶ τὰς παρὰ τοῦ Πατρὸς ὁμιλίας φέρει τοῖς ἀνθρώποις. Dial. 128; cf. Apol. i. 63; Dial. 60.

[2] Cf. Apoc., iii. 14.

[3] Μαρτύριον δὲ καὶ ἄλλο ὑμῖν, ὦ φίλοι, ἔφην, ἀπὸ τῶν γραφῶν δώσω, ὅτι Ἀρχὴν πρὸ πάντων τῶν κτισμάτων ὁ Θεὸς γεγέννηκε δύναμίν τινα ἐξ ἑαυτοῦ λογικήν, ἥτις καὶ Δόξα Κυρίου ὑπὸ τοῦ Πνεύματος τοῦ ἁγίου καλεῖται, ποτὲ δὲ Υἱὸς, ποτὲ δὲ Σοφία, ποτὲ δὲ Ἄγγελος, ποτὲ δὲ Θεὸς, ποτὲ δὲ Κύριος καὶ Λόγος· . . . Μαρτυρήσει δέ μοι ὁ λόγος τῆς σοφίας, αὐτὸς ὢν οὗτος ὁ Θεὸς ἀπὸ τοῦ Πατρὸς τῶν ὅλων γεννηθείς, καὶ Λόγος, καὶ Σοφία, καὶ Δύναμις, καὶ Δόξα τοῦ γεννήσαντος ὑπάρχων, κ.τ.λ. Dial. 61.

again in the next chapter, and the peculiarity of his terminology in all these passages, so markedly different from, and indeed opposed to, that of the fourth Gospel, will naturally strike the reader: "But this offspring (γέννημα) being truly brought forth by the Father was with the Father before all created beings (πρὸ πάντων τῶν ποιημάτων), and the Father communes with him, as the Logos declared through Solomon, that this same, who is called Wisdom by Solomon, had been begotten of God before all created beings (πρὸ πάντων τῶν ποιημάτων), both Beginning (ἀρχή) and Offspring (γέννημα)," &c.[1] In another place after quoting the words: "No man knoweth the Father but the Son, nor the Son but the Father, and they to whom the Son will reveal him," Justin continues: "Therefore he revealed to us all that we have by his grace understood out of the Scriptures, recognizing him to be indeed the first-begotten (πρωτότοκος) of God, and before all creatures (πρὸ πάντων τῶν κτισμάτων) . . . . and calling him Son, we have understood that he proceeded from the Father by his power and will before all created beings (πρὸ πάντων ποιημάτων), for in one form or another he is spoken of in the writings of the prophets as Wisdom," &c.;[2] and again, in two other places he refers to the same fact.[3]

On further examination, we find on every side still

---

[1] Ἀλλὰ τοῦτο τὸ τῷ ὄντι ἀπὸ τοῦ Πατρὸς προβληθὲν γέννημα, πρὸ πάντων τῶν ποιημάτων συνῆν τῷ Πατρί, καὶ τούτῳ ὁ Πατὴρ προσομιλεῖ, ὡς ὁ Λόγος διὰ τοῦ Σολομῶνος ἐδήλωσεν, ὅτι καὶ Ἀρχὴ πρὸ πάντων τῶν ποιημάτων τοῦτ' αὐτὸ καὶ γέννημα ὑπὸ τοῦ Θεοῦ ἐγεγέννητο, ὃ Σοφία διὰ Σολομῶνος καλεῖται, κ.τ.λ. Dial. 62.

[2] Ἀπεκάλυψεν οὖν ἡμῖν πάντα ὅσα καὶ ἀπὸ τῶν γραφῶν διὰ τῆς χάριτος αὐτοῦ νενοήκαμεν, γνόντες αὐτὸν πρωτότοκον μὲν τοῦ Θεοῦ, καὶ πρὸ πάντων τῶν κτισμάτων· . . . . καὶ Υἱὸν αὐτὸν λέγοντες, νενοήκαμεν, καὶ πρὸ πάντων ποιημάτων, ἀπὸ τοῦ Πατρὸς δυνάμει αὐτοῦ καὶ βουλῇ προελθόντα, ὃς καὶ Σοφία, κ.τ.λ. Dial. 100.

[3] Dial., 126, 129.

stronger confirmation of the conclusion that Justin derived his Logos doctrine from the Old Testament and Philo, together with early New Testament writings. We have quoted several passages in which Justin details the various names of the Logos, and we may add one more. Referring to Ps. lxxii., which the Jews apply to Solomon, but which Justin maintains to be applicable to Christ, he says: "For Christ is King, and Priest, and God, and Lord, and Angel, and Man, and Captain, and Stone, and a Son born (παιδίον γεννώμενον), &c. &c., as I prove by all of the Scriptures."[1] Now these representations, which are constantly repeated throughout Justin's writings, are quite opposed to the Spirit of the fourth Gospel, but are on the other hand equally common in the works of Philo, and many of them also to be found in the Philonian Epistle to the Hebrews. Taking the chief amongst them we may briefly illustrate them. The Logos as King, Justin avowedly derives from Ps. lxxii., in which he finds that reference is made to the "Everlasting King, that is to say Christ."[2] We find this representation of the Logos throughout the writings of Philo. In one place already briefly referred to,[3] but which we shall now more fully quote, he says: "For God as Shepherd and King governs according to Law and justice like a flock of sheep, the earth, and water, and air, and fire, and all the plants and living things that are in them, whether they be mortal or divine, as well as the course of heaven, and the periods of sun and moon, and the variations and harmonious revolutions of the other stars; having appointed his true Word (τὸν ὀρθὸν αὐτοῦ

---

[1] Ὁ γὰρ Χριστὸς Βασιλεὺς, καὶ Ἱερεὺς, καὶ Θεὸς, καὶ Κύριος, καὶ Ἄγγελος, καὶ Ἄνθρωπος, καὶ Ἀρχιστράτηγος, καὶ Λίθος, καὶ Παιδίον γεννώμενον, κ.τ.λ. Dial. 34.
[2] Dial., 34.   [3] p. 274.

Λόγον) his first-begotten Son (πρωτόγονον υἱόν) to have the care of this sacred flock as the Vicegerent of a great King;"[1] and a little further on, he says: "very reasonably, therefore, he will assume the name of a King, being addressed as a Shepherd."[2] In another place, Philo speaks of the "Logos of the Governor, and his creative and kingly power, for of these is the heaven and the whole world."[3]

Then if we take the second epithet, the Logos as Priest (ἱερεύς), which is quite foreign to the fourth Gospel, we find it repeated by Justin, as for instance: "Christ the eternal Priest" (ἱερεύς),[4] and it is not only a favourite representation of Philo, but is almost the leading idea of the Epistle to the Hebrews, in connection with the episode of Melchisedec, in whom also both Philo,[5] and Justin,[6] recognize the Logos. In the Epistle to the Hebrews, vii. 3, speaking of Melchisedec: "but likened to the Son of God, abideth a Priest for ever:"[7] again in iv. 14: "Seeing then that we have a great High Priest that is passed through the heavens, Jesus the Son

---

[1] καθάπερ γάρ τινα ποίμνην γῆν καὶ ὕδωρ καὶ ἀέρα καὶ πῦρ καὶ ὅσα ἐν τούτοις φυτά τε αὖ καὶ ζῶα, τὰ μὲν θνητά, τὰ δὲ θεῖα, ἔτι δὲ οὐρανοῦ φύσιν καὶ ἡλίου καὶ σελήνης περιόδους καὶ τῶν ἄλλων ἀστέρων τροπάς τε αὖ καὶ χορείας ἐναρμονίους ὡς ποιμὴν καὶ Βασιλεὺς ὁ θεὸς ἄγει κατὰ δίκην καὶ νόμον, προστησάμενος τὸν ὀρθὸν αὑτοῦ Λόγον, πρωτόγονον υἱόν, ὃς τὴν ἐπιμέλειαν τῆς ἱερᾶς ταύτης ἀγέλης οἷά τις μεγάλου βασιλέως ὕπαρχος διαδέξεται. De Agricult., § 12, Mangey, i. 308.

[2] Εἰκότως τοίνυν ὁ μὲν βασιλέως ὄνομα ὑποδύσεται, ποιμὴν προσαγορευθείς, κ.τ.λ. § 14, cf. De Profugis, § 20, Mang., i. 562; De Somniis, ii. § 37, Mang., i. 691.

[3] Ὁ τοῦ ἡγεμόνος Λόγος, καὶ ἡ ποιητικὴ καὶ βασιλικὴ δύναμις αὐτοῦ· τούτων γὰρ ὅ τε οὐρανὸς καὶ σύμπας ὁ κόσμος ἐστί. De Profugis, § 19, Mang., i. 561; cf. de Migrat. Abrahami, § 1, Mang., i. 437.

[4] Dial., 42.   [5] Legis Alleg., § 26, Mang., i. 104, &c., &c.

[6] Dial., 34, 83, &c., &c.

[7] .... ἀφομοιωμένος δὲ τῷ υἱῷ τοῦ θεοῦ, μένει ἱερεὺς εἰς τὸ διηνεκές. Heb. vii. 3.

of God," &c.;[1] ix. 11: "Christ having appeared a High Priest of the good things to come;"[2] xii. 21: "Thou art a Priest for ever."[3] The passages are indeed far too numerous to quote.[4] They are equally numerous in the writings of Philo. In one place already quoted,[5] he says: "For there are as it seems two temples of God, one of which is this world, in which the High Priest is the divine Word, his first-begotten Son" (Δύο γὰρ, ὡς ἔοικεν, ἱερὰ θεοῦ, ἓν μὲν ὅδε ὁ κόσμος, ἐν ᾧ καὶ ἀρχιερεύς, ὁ πρωτόγονος αὐτοῦ θεῖος Λόγος).[6] Elsewhere, speaking of the period for the return of fugitives, the death of the high priest, which taken literally would embarrass him in his allegory, Philo says: "For we maintain the High Priest not to be a man, but the divine Word, who is without participation not only in voluntary but also in involuntary sins;"[7] and he goes on to speak of this priest as "the most sacred Word" (ὁ ἱερώτατος Λόγος).[8] Indeed, in many long passages he descants upon the "high priest Word" (ὁ ἀρχιερεὺς Λόγος).[9]

Proceeding to the next representations of the Logos

---

[1] Ἔχοντες οὖν ἀρχιερέα μέγαν διεληλυθότα τοὺς οὐρανούς, Ἰησοῦν τὸν υἱὸν τοῦ θεοῦ, κ.τ.λ. Heb. iv. 14.

[2] Χριστὸς δὲ παραγενόμενος ἀρχιερεὺς τῶν μελλόντων ἀγαθῶν, κ.τ.λ. Heb. ix. 11.

[3] Σὺ ἱερεὺς εἰς τὸν αἰῶνα. Heb. vii. 21.

[4] Heb. vii. 11, 15, 17, 21 f., 26 ff.; viii. 1 ff.; ii. 6, 17; v. 5, 6, 10.

[5] ii. p. 273.

[6] *Philo*, De Somniis, i. § 37, *Mangey*, i. 653.

[7] Λέγομεν γάρ, τὸν ἀρχιερέα οὐκ ἄνθρωπον, ἀλλὰ Λόγον θεῖον εἶναι, πάντων οὐχ ἑκουσίων μόνον, ἀλλὰ καὶ ἀκουσίων ἀδικημάτων ἀμέτοχον. De Profugis, § 20, *Mang.*, i. 562. Philo continues: that this priest, the Logos, must be pure, "God indeed being his Father, who is also the Father of all things, and Wisdom his mother, by whom the universe came into being." (πατρὸς μὲν θεοῦ, ὃς καὶ τῶν συμπάντων ἐστὶ πατήρ, μητρὸς δὲ Σοφίας, δι' ἧς τὰ ὅλα ἦλθεν εἰς γένεσιν.)

[8] *Ib.*, § 21.   [9] De Migrat. Abrahami, § 18, *Mang.*, i. 452.

as "God and Lord," we meet with the idea everywhere. In Hebrews i. 8 : " But regarding the Son he saith : Thy throne, O God, is for ever and ever" (πρὸς δὲ τὸν υἱὸν Ὁ θρόνος σου, ὁ Θεὸς, εἰς τὸν αἰῶνα τοῦ αἰῶνος), &c., and again in the Epistle to the Philippians, ii. 6, "Who (Jesus Christ) being in the form of God, deemed it not grasping to be equal with God" (ὃς ἐν μορφῇ θεοῦ ὑπάρχων οὐχ ἁρπαγμὸν ἡγήσατο τὸ εἶναι ἴσα θεῷ), &c. &c.[1] Philo, in the fragment preserved by Eusebius, to which we have already referred,[2] calls the Logos the "Second God" (δεύτερος θεός).[3] In another passage he has : " But he calls the most ancient God his present Logos," &c. (καλεῖ δὲ θεὸν τὸν πρεσβύτατον αὐτοῦ νυνὶ Λόγον) ;[4] and a little further on, speaking of the inability of men to look on the Father himself : "thus they regard the image of God, his Angel Word, as himself" (οὕτως καὶ τὴν τοῦ θεοῦ εἰκόνα, τὸν ἄγγελον αὐτοῦ Λόγον, ὡς αὐτὸν κατανοοῦσιν).[5] Elsewhere discussing the possibility of God's swearing by himself, which he applies to the Logos, he says : "For in regard to us imperfect beings he will be a God, but in regard to wise and perfect beings the first. And yet Moses, in awe of the superiority of the unbegotten (ἀγεννήτου) God, says : 'And thou shalt swear by his name,' not by himself ; for it is sufficient for the creature to receive assurance and testimony by the divine Word."[6]

It must be remarked, however, that both Justin and

---

[1] Cf. verse 11.   [2] ii. p. 277.
[3] Fragm. i., Mang., ii. 625 ; cf. Leg. Alleg., ii. § 21, Mang., i. 83.
[4] Philo, De Somniis, i. 39, Mang., i. 655.
[5] De Somniis, i. § 41, Mang., i. 656.
[6] Οὗτος γὰρ ἡμῶν τῶν ἀτελῶν ἂν εἴη θεός, τῶν δὲ σοφῶν καὶ τελείων ὁ πρῶτος. Καὶ Μωϋσῆς μέντοι τὴν ὑπερβολὴν θαυμάσας τοῦ ἀγεννήτου φησίν· "Καὶ τῷ ὀνόματι αὐτοῦ ὀμῇ," οὐχὶ αὐτῷ· ἱκανὸν γὰρ τῷ γεννητῷ πιστοῦσθαι καὶ μαρτυρεῖσθαι Λόγῳ θείῳ. Leg. Alleg., iii. § 73, Mang., i. 128.

Philo place the Logos in a position more clearly secondary to God the Father, than the prelude to the fourth Gospel i. 1. Both Justin and Philo apply the term θεός to the Logos without the article. Justin distinctly says that Christians worship Jesus Christ as the Son of the true God, holding him in the second place (ἐν δευτέρᾳ χώρᾳ ἔχοντες),[1] and this secondary position is systematically defined through Justin's writings in a very decided way, as it is in the works of Philo by the contrast of the begotten Logos with the unbegotten God. Justin speaks of the Word as "the first-born of the unbegotten God" (πρωτότοκος τῷ ἀγεννήτῳ θεῷ),[2] and the distinctive appellation of the "unbegotten God" applied to the Father is most common throughout his writings.[3] We may in continuation of this remark point out another phrase of Justin which is continually repeated, but is thoroughly opposed both to the spirit and to the terminology of the fourth Gospel, and which likewise indicates the secondary consideration in which he held the Logos. He calls the Word constantly "the first-born of all created beings" (πρωτότοκος τῶν πάντων ποιημάτων,[4] or πρωτότοκος πρὸ πάντων τῶν κτισμάτων,[5] or πρωτότοκος πάσης κτίσεως,[6]) "the first-born of all creation," echoing the expression of Col. i. 15. (The Son) "who is the image of the invisible God, the first-born of all creation" (πρωτότοκος πάσης κτίσεως). This is a totally different view from that of the fourth Gospel, which in so emphatic a manner

---

[1] Apol., i. 13, cf. 60, where he shows that Plato gives the second place to the Logos.
[2] Apol., i. 53, compare quotation from Philo, p. 291, note 2.
[3] Apol., i. 49, Apol., ii. 6, 13; Dial., 126, 127.
[4] Dial., 62, 84, 100, &c., &c.
[5] Dial., 61, 100, 125, 129, &c., &c. [6] Dial., 85, 138, &c.

enunciates the doctrine: "In the beginning was the Word and the Word was with God, and the Word was God," a statement which Justin, with Philo, only makes in a very modified sense.

To return, however, the next representation of the Logos by Justin is as "Angel." This perpetually recurs in his writings.[1] In one place, to which we have already referred, he says: "The Word of God is his Son, as we have already stated, and he is also called Messenger (Ἄγγελος) and Apostle, for he brings the message of all we need to know, and is sent an Apostle to declare all the message contains."[2] In the same chapter reference is again made to passages quoted for the sake of proving: "that Jesus Christ is the Son of God and Apostle, being aforetime the Word and having appeared now in the form of fire, and now in the likeness of incorporeal beings;"[3] and he gives many illustrations.[4] The passages, however, in which the Logos is called Angel, are too numerous to be more fully dealt with here. It is scarcely necessary to point out that this representation of the Logos as Angel, is not only foreign to, but opposed to the spirit of, the fourth Gospel, although it is thoroughly in harmony with the writings of Philo. Before illustrating this, however, we may incidentally remark that the ascription to the Logos of the name "Apostle" which occurs in the two passages just quoted above, as well as in other parts of the writings of Justin,[5]

---

[1] Apol., i. 63; Dial., 34, 56, 57, 58, 59, 60, 61, 127; cf. Apol., i. 6.

[2] Ὁ Λόγος δὲ τοῦ θεοῦ ἐστιν ὁ υἱὸς αὐτοῦ, ὡς προέφημεν· καὶ Ἄγγελος δὲ καλεῖται, καὶ Ἀπόστολος. Αὐτὸς γάρ ἀπαγγέλλει ὅσα δεῖ γνωσθῆναι, καὶ ἀποστέλλεται μηνύσων ὅσα ἀγγέλλεται, κ.τ.λ. Apol., i. 63.

[3] ὅτι υἱὸς θεοῦ καὶ Ἀπόστολος Ἰησοῦς ὁ Χριστός ἐστι, πρότερον Λόγος ὤν, καὶ ἐν ἰδέᾳ πυρὸς ποτὲ φανείς, ποτὲ δὲ καὶ ἐν εἰκόνι ἀσωμάτων, κ.τ.λ. Apol., i. 63.

[4] Cf. Dial., 56—60, 127, 128.

[5] Apol., i. 12, &c.

is likewise opposed to the fourth Gospel, although it is found in earlier writings, exhibiting a less developed form of the Logos doctrine; for the Epistle to the Hebrews iii. 1, has: "Consider the Apostle and High Priest of our confession, Jesus," &c. (κατανοήσατε τὸν ἀπόστολον καὶ ἀρχιερέα τῆς ὁμολογίας ἡμῶν Ἰησοῦν). We are, in fact, constantly directed by the remarks of Justin to other sources of the Logos doctrine, and never to the fourth Gospel, with which his tone and terminology do not agree. Everywhere in the writings of Philo we meet with the Logos as Angel. He speaks "of the Angel Word of God" in a sentence already quoted,[1] and elsewhere in a passage, one of many others, upon which the lines of Justin which we are now considering (as well as several similar passages)[2] are in all probability moulded. Philo calls upon men to "strive earnestly to be fashioned according to God's first-begotten Word, the eldest Angel, who is the Archangel bearing many names, for he is called

---

[1] *Philo*, De Somniis, i. § 41, *Mang.*, i. 656, see ii. p. 289.

[2] For instance, in the quotations at p. 286 f. from Dial. 61, and also that from Dial. 62, in which the Logos is also called the Beginning (ἀρχή). Both Philo and Justin, no doubt, had in mind Prov. viii. 22. In Dial. 100, for example, there is a passage, part of which we have quoted, which reads as follows: "for in one form or another he is spoken of in the writings of the prophets as Wisdom, and the Day, and the East, and a Sword, and a Stone, and a Rod, and Jacob, and Israel, &c." Now in the writings of Philo these passages in the Old Testament are discussed, and applied to the Logos, and one in particular we may refer to as an illustration. Philo says: "I have also heard of a certain associate of Moses having pronounced the following saying: 'Behold a man whose name is the East.' (Zech. vi. 12.) A most novel designation if you consider it to be spoken regarding one composed of body and soul, but if regarding that incorporeal Being who does not differ from the divine image, you will agree that the name of the East is perfectly appropriate to him. For indeed the Father of the Universe caused this eldest son (πρεσβύτατον υἱὸν) to rise (ἀνέτειλε), whom elsewhere he names his first-begotten (πρωτόγονον), &c." De Confus. Ling., § 14. Can it be doubted that Justin follows Philo in such exegesis?

the Beginning (ἀρχή), and Name of God, and Logos, and the Man according to his image, and the Seer of Israel."[1] Elsewhere, in a remarkable passage, he says: "To his Archangel and eldest Word, the Father, who created the universe, gave the supreme gift that having stood on the confine he may separate the creature from the Creator. The same is an intercessor on behalf of the ever wasting mortal to the immortal; he is also the ambassador of the Ruler to his subjects. And he rejoices in the gift, and the majesty of it he describes, saying: 'And I stood in the midst between the Lord and you' (Numbers xvi. 48); being neither unbegotten like God, nor begotten like you, but between the two extremes," &c.[2] We have been tempted to give more of this passage than is necessary for our immediate purpose, because it affords the reader another glimpse of Philo's doctrine of the Logos, and generally illustrates its position in connection with the Christian doctrine.

The last of Justin's names which we shall here notice is the Logos as "Man" as well as God. In another place Justin explains that he is sometimes called a Man and human being, because he appears in these forms as the Father wills.[3] But here confining ourselves merely

---

[1] .... σπουδαζέτω κοσμεῖσθαι κατὰ τὸν πρωτόγονον αὐτοῦ λόγον, τὸν ἄγγελον πρεσβύτατον, ὡς ἀρχάγγελον πολυώνυμον ὑπάρχοντα· καὶ γὰρ ἀρχή, καὶ ὄνομα θεοῦ, καὶ λόγος, καὶ ὁ κατ' εἰκόνα ἄνθρωπος, καὶ ὁρῶν Ἰσραὴλ προσαγορεύεται. De Confus. Ling., § 28, *Mang.*, i. 427; cf. De Migrat. Abrahami, § 31, *Mang.*, i. 463.

[2] Τῷ δὲ ἀρχαγγέλῳ καὶ πρεσβυτάτῳ Λόγῳ δωρεὰν ἐξαίρετον ἔδωκεν ὁ τὰ ὅλα γεννήσας πατήρ, ἵνα μεθόριος στὰς τὸ γενόμενον διακρίνῃ τοῦ πεποιηκότος. Ὁ δ' αὐτὸς ἱκέτης μέν ἐστι τοῦ θνητοῦ κηραίνοντος ἀεὶ πρὸς τὸ ἄφθαρτον, πρεσβευτὴς δὲ τοῦ ἡγεμόνος πρὸς τὸ ὑπήκοον. Ἀγάλλεται δὲ ἐπὶ τῇ δωρεᾷ, καὶ σεμνυνόμενος αὐτὴν ἐκδιηγεῖται φάσκων· "Καὶ ἐγὼ εἱστήκειν ἀνὰ μέσον κυρίου καὶ ὑμῶν" (Num. xvi. 48), οὔτε ἀγέννητος ὡς ὁ θεὸς ὤν, οὔτε γεννητὸς ὡς ὑμεῖς, ἀλλὰ μέσος τῶν ἄκρων, κ.τ.λ. Quis rerum div. Heres., § 42, *Mang.*, i. 501 f.

[3] Dial., 128, see the quotation, ii. p. 283 ff.

to the concrete idea, we find a striking representation of it in 1 Tim. ii. 5: "For there is one God and one mediator between God and man, the Man Christ Jesus" (εἷς γὰρ θεός, εἷς καὶ μεσίτης θεοῦ καὶ ἀνθρώπων, ἄνθρωπος Χριστὸς Ἰησοῦς); and again in Rom. v. 15: " . . . by the grace of the one man Jesus Christ" (τοῦ ἑνὸς ἀνθρώπου Ἰησοῦ Χριστοῦ), as well as other passages.[1] We have already seen in the passage quoted above from "De Confus. Ling." § 28, that Philo mentions, among the many names of the Logos, that of "the Man according to (God's) image" (ὁ κατ' εἰκόνα ἄνθρωπος,[2] or "the typical man"). If, however, we pass to the application of the Logos doctrine to Jesus, we have the strongest reason for inferring Justin's total independence of the fourth Gospel. We have already pointed out that the title of Logos is given to Jesus in New Testament writings earlier than the fourth Gospel. We have remarked that, although the passages are innumerable in which Justin speaks of the Word having become man through the Virgin, he never once throughout his writings makes use of the peculiar expression of the fourth Gospel: "the Word became flesh" (ὁ Λόγος σὰρξ ἐγένετο). On the few occasions on which he speaks of the Word having been *made* flesh, he uses the term σαρκοποιηθείς.[3] In one instance he has σάρκα ἔχειν,[4] and speaking of the Eucharist Justin once explains that it is in memory of Christ's having made himself *body*, σωματοποιήσασθαι.[5] Justin's most common phrase,

---

[1] Phil. ii. 8; 1 Cor. xv. 47.
[2] Elsewhere Philo says that the Word was the archetypal model after which man and the human mind were formed. De Exsecrat., § 8, *Mang.*, i. 436; De Mundi Opificio, § 6, *Mang.*, i. 6.
[3] Apol., i. 66 (twice); Dial., 45, 100.
[4] Dial., 48.   [5] Dial., 70.

however, and he repeats it in numberless instances, is that the Logos submitted to be born, and become man (γεννηθῆναι ἄνθρωπον γενόμενον ὑπέμεινεν), by a Virgin, or he uses variously the expressions : ἄνθρωπος γέγονε, ἄνθρωπος γενόμενος, γενέσθαι ἄνθρωπον.[1] In several places he speaks of him as the first production or offspring (γέννημα) of God before all created beings, as, for instance : " The Logos ... who is the first offspring of God" (ὅ ἐστι πρῶτον γέννημα τοῦ θεοῦ);[2] and again, "and that this offspring was begotten of the Father absolutely before all creatures the Word was declaring" (καὶ ὅτι γεγεννῆσθαι ὑπὸ τοῦ πατρὸς τοῦτο τὸ γέννημα πρὸ πάντων ἁπλῶς τῶν κτισμάτων ὁ λόγος ἐδήλου).[3] We need not say more of the expressions : "first-born" (πρωτότοκος), "first-begotten" (πρωτόγονος), so constantly applied to the Logos by Justin, in agreement with Philo; nor to "only begotten" (μονογενής), directly derived from Ps. xxii. 20 (Ps. xxi. 20, Sept.).

It must be apparent to everyone who seriously examines the subject, that Justin's terminology is markedly different from, and in spirit sometimes opposed to, that of the fourth Gospel, and in fact that the peculiarities of the Gospel are not found in Justin's writings at all.[4] On the

[1] Apol., i. 5, 23, 63; Apol., ii. 6, 13 ; Dial., 34, 45, 48, 57, 63, 75, 84, 85, 105, 113, 125, 127, &c., &c.   [2] Apol., i. 21.
[3] Dial., 129. cf. 62.
[4] A passage is sometimes quoted in which Justin reproaches the Jews for spreading injurious and unjust reports " concerning the only blameless and righteous Light sent by God to man," (Κατὰ οὖν τοῦ μόνου ἀμώμου καὶ δικαίου φωτὸς τοῖς ἀνθρώποις πεμφθέντος παρὰ τοῦ θεοῦ κ.τ.λ. Dial. 17), and this is claimed as an echo of the Gospel ; cf. John i. 9, viii. 12, xii. 46, &c. Now here again we have in Philo the elaborate representation of the Logos as the sun and Light of the world ; as for instance in a long passage in the treatise De Somniis, i. §§ 13 ff., *Mang.*, i. 631 ff., of which we can only give the slightest quotation. Philo argues that Moses only speaks of the sun by symbols, and that it is easy to prove

other hand, his doctrine of the Logos is precisely that of Philo,[1] and of writings long antecedent to the fourth Gospel, and there can be no doubt, we think, that it was derived from them.[2]

---

this; "since in the first place God is Light. 'For the Lord is my Light and my Saviour,' it is said in hymns, and not only Light, but archetype of every other light, nay rather more ancient and more perfect than archetype, having the Logos for an exemplar. For indeed the exemplar was his most perfect Logos, Light," &c. (. . . . ἐπειδὴ πρῶτον μὲν ὁ θεὸς φῶς ἐστι· "Κύριος γὰρ φῶς μου καὶ σωτήρ μου" ἐν ὕμνοις ᾄδεται· Καὶ οὐ μόνον φῶς, ἀλλὰ καὶ παντὸς ἑτέρου φωτὸς ἀρχέτυπον, μᾶλλον δὲ ἀρχετύπου πρεσβύτερον καὶ ἀνώτερον, λόγον ἔχον παραδείγματος· τὸ μὲν γὰρ παράδειγμα ὁ πληρέστατος ἦν αὐτοῦ Λόγος, φῶς, κ.τ.λ. De Somniis, i. § 13, *Mang.*, i. 632). And again: "But according to the third meaning, he calls the divine Word the sun" (κατὰ δὲ τρίτον σημαινόμενον ἥλιον καλεῖ τὸν θεῖον Λόγον), and proceeds to show how by this sun all wickedness is brought to light, and the sins done secretly and in darkness are made manifest. De Somniis, i. § 15, *Mang.*, i. 634; cf. *ib.*, § 19.

[1] If the Cohort. ad Græcos be assigned to Justin, it directly refers to Philo's works, c. ix.

[2] *Baur*, Unters. kan. Evv., p. 351; Theol. Jahrb., 1857, p. 223 ff.; *Bretschneider*, Probabilia de Ev. et Ep. Joan. Apost., p. 191 f.; *Credner*, Beiträge, i. p. 251 ff.; *Davidson*, Introd. N. T., ii. p. 380 ff.; *Hilgenfeld*, Die Evv. Justin's, p. 298 ff.; *Réville*, Hist. du Dogme de la Div. de J. C., 1869, p. 45 ff.; *Scholten*, Das Ev. u. Johann., p. 9 f.; Die ält. Zeugnisse, p. 24 ff.; *Vacherot*, Hist. de l'Ecole d'Alexandrie, i. p. 230 ff.; *Volkmar*, Zeitschr. wiss. Theol., 1860, p. 300; Der Ursprung, p. 92 ff.; *Tjeenk Willink*, Justinus Mart., p. 108 f.; cf. *Dorner*, Die Lehre v. d. Pers. Christi, 1845, i. p. 414 ff.; *Siegfried*, Philo. v. Alex. 1875, p. 332 ff. J. T. *Tobler* derives the Johannine Logos doctrine from Philo, Theol. Jahrb., 1860, p. 180 ff. *Ewald* holds that the Epistle to the Hebrews transfers the Logos doctrine of Philo to Christianity; and that the Apostle Paul's mind was filled with it from the same sources: Gesch. d. Volkes Isr., vi. p. 474 f., p. 638 ff.; Das Sendschr. a. d. Hebräer, p. 9 ff. Cf. *Bleek*, Hebräerbr. 1828, i. p. 398 ff.; *Hausrath*, N. T. Zeitgesch., 1874, iii. p. 561 f.; *Holsten*, Zeitschr. wiss. Theol., 1861, p. 233 f., anm. 2; Zum Ev. d. Paulus u. Petrus, 1868, p. 72 ff.; *Hilgenfeld*, Zeitschr. wiss. Theol., 1871, p. 189 ff.; *Köstlin*, Joh. Lehrbegriff, p. 357 ff., p. 392 ff.; *Lücke*, Comment. Ev. Joh., i. p. 283 ff.; *Pfleiderer*, Zeitschr. wiss. Theol., 1869, p. 400 ff.; *Schwegler*, Das nachap. Zeit., ii. p. 286 ff., pp. 298, 313, 365; Der Montanismus, 1841, p. 155; *Siegfried*, Philo. v. Alex. pp. 304 ff., 321 ff. That the doctrine of the Logos was enunciated in the Κήρυγμα Πέτρου we know from the quotations of Clement of Alexandria. Strom., vi. 5, § 39, 7, § 58.

We may now proceed to consider other passages adduced by Tischendorf to support his assertion that Justin made use of the fourth Gospel. He says: "Passages of the Johannine Gospel, however, are also not wanting to which passages in Justin refer back. In the Dialogue, ch. 88, he writes of John the Baptist: 'The people believed that he was the Christ, but he cried to them: I am not the Christ, but the voice of a preacher.' This is connected with John i. 20 and 23; for no other Evangelist has reported the first words in the Baptist's reply."[1] Now the passage in Justin, with its context, reads as follows: "For John sat by the Jordan (καθεζομένου ἐπὶ τοῦ Ἰορδάνου) and preached the Baptism of repentance, wearing only a leathern girdle and raiment of camel's hair, and eating nothing but locusts and wild honey; men supposed (ὑπελάμβανον) him to be the Christ, wherefore he himself cried to them: 'I am not the Christ, but the voice of one crying: For he shall come (ἥξει) who is stronger than I, whose shoes I am not meet (ἱκανός) to bear.'"[2] Now the only ground upon which this passage can be compared with the fourth Gospel is the reply: "I am not the Christ" (οὐκ εἰμὶ ὁ Χριστός), which in John i. 20 reads: ὅτι ἐγὼ οὐκ εἰμὶ ὁ

---

[1] Es fehlt aber auch nicht an einzelnen Stellen des Johanneischen Evangeliums, auf welche sich Stellen bei Justin zurückbeziehen. Im Dialog Kap. 88 schreibt er von Johannes dem Täufer: "Die Leute glaubten dass er der Christ sei; aber er rief ihnen zu: Ich bin nicht Christus, sondern Stimme eines Predigers." Dies lehnt sich an Joh. i. 20 und 23 an; denn die ersten Worte in der Antwort des Täufers hat kein anderer Evangelist berichtet. Wann wurden, u. s. w. p. 33.

[2] Ἰωάννου γὰρ καθεζομένου ἐπὶ τοῦ Ἰορδάνου, καὶ κηρύσσοντος βάπτισμα μετανοίας, καὶ ζώνην δερματίνην καὶ ἔνδυμα ἀπὸ τριχῶν καμήλου μόνον φοροῦντος, καὶ μηδὲν ἐσθίοντος πλὴν ἀκρίδας καὶ μέλι ἄγριον, οἱ ἄνθρωποι ὑπελάμβανον αὐτὸν εἶναι τὸν Χριστόν· πρὸς οὓς καὶ αὐτὸς ἐβόα· Οὐκ εἰμὶ ὁ Χριστὸς, ἀλλὰ φωνὴ βοῶντος· Ἥξει γὰρ ὁ ἰσχυρότερός μου· οὗ οὐκ εἰμὶ ἱκανὸς τὰ ὑποδήματα βαστάσαι. Dial. 88.

Χριστός: and it is perfectly clear that, if the direct negation occurred in any other Gospel, the difference of the whole passage in the Dialogue would prevent even an apologist from advancing any claim to its dependence on that Gospel. In order to appreciate the nature of the two passages, it may be well to collect the nearest parallels in the Gospel, and compare them with Justin's narrative.

JUSTIN, DIAL. 88.	JOHN I. 19—27.
Men (οἱ ἄνθρωποι) supposed him to be the Christ;	19. And this is the testimony of John, when the Jews sent priests and Levites from Jerusalem to ask him: Who art thou? 24. And they were sent by the Pharisees. 20. And he confessed, and denied not: and confessed[2] that: I am not the Christ (ὅτι ἐγὼ οὐκ εἰμὶ ὁ Χριστός). 21. And they asked again: Who then? Art thou, Elias? &c. &c. 22. . . . Who art thou? &c. &c.
wherefore he cried to them: I am not the Christ (οὐκ εἰμὶ ὁ Χριστός),	
but the voice, of one crying:	23. He said: I am the voice of one crying in the desert: Make straight the way of the Lord, as said the prophet Isaiah. 25. . . . Why baptisest thou? &c., &c. 26. John answered them, saying: I baptise with water, but in the midst of you standeth one whom ye know not.
For he shall come (ἥξει) who is stronger than I (ὁ ἰσχυρότερός μου), whose shoes I am not meet (ἱκανὸς) to bear.[1]	27. Who cometh after me (ὁ ὀπίσω μου ἐρχόμενος) who is become before me (ὃς ἔμπροσθέν μου γέγονεν),[3] the thong of whose shoes I am not worthy (ἄξιος) to unloose.

[1] Matt. iii. 11 reads: "but he that cometh after me is stronger than I whose shoes I am not worthy to bear." (ὁ δὲ ὀπίσω μου ἐρχόμενος ἰσχυρότερός μου ἐστίν, οὗ οὐκ εἰμὶ ἱκανὸς τὰ ὑποδήματα βαστάσαι.) The context is quite different. Luke iii. 16, more closely resembles the version of the fourth Gospel in this part with the context of the first Synoptic.

[2] The second καὶ ὡμολόγησεν is omitted by the Cod. Sin.

[3] The Cod. Sinaiticus, as well as most other important MSS., omits this phrase.

The introductory description of John's dress and habits is quite contrary to the fourth Gospel, but corresponds to some extent with Matt. iii. 4. It is difficult to conceive two accounts more fundamentally different, and the discrepancy becomes more apparent when we consider the scene and actors in the episode. In Justin, it is evident that the hearers of John had received the impression that he was the Christ, and the Baptist becoming aware of it voluntarily disabused their minds of this idea. In the fourth Gospel the words of John are extracted from him ("he confessed and denied not") by emissaries sent by the Pharisees of Jerusalem specially to question him on the subject. The account of Justin betrays no knowledge of any such interrogation. The utter difference is brought to a climax by the concluding statement of the fourth Gospel:—

JUSTIN.	JOHN I. 28.
For John sat by the Jordan and preached the Baptism of repentance, wearing, &c.	These things were done in Bethany beyond the river Jordan, where John was baptizing.

In fact the scene in the two narratives is as little the same as their details. One can scarcely avoid the conclusion, in reading the fourth Gospel, that it quotes some other account and does not pretend to report the scene direct. For instance, i. 15, "John beareth witness of him, and cried, saying: 'This was he *of whom I said:* He that cometh after me is become before me, because he was before me,'" &c. V. 19: "And this is the testimony of John, *when the Jews sent priests and Levites from Jerusalem to ask him: Who art thou?* and he confessed and denied not, and confessed that I am not the Christ," &c. Now, as usual, the Gospel which Justin uses more nearly approximates to our first Synoptic than the other Gospels, although it differs in very important points from that also—still, taken in connection with the third Synoptic, and Acts xiii. 25, this indicates the great probability of the existence of other writings combining the particulars as they occur in Justin. Luke iii. 15, reads: "And as the people were in expectation, and all mused in their hearts concerning John whether he were the Christ, 16. John answered, saying to them all: I indeed baptize you with water, but he that is stronger than I cometh, the latchet of whose shoes I am not worthy to unloose: he shall baptize you with the Holy Spirit and with fire," &c.

Whilst, however, with the sole exception of the simple statement of the Baptist that he was not the Christ, which in all the accounts is clearly involved in the rest of the reply, there is no analogy whatever between the parallel in the fourth Gospel and the passage in Justin, many important circumstances render it certain that Justin did not derive his narrative from that source. We have already[1] fully discussed the peculiarities of Justin's account of the Baptist, and in the context to the very passage before us there are details quite foreign to our Gospels which show that Justin made use of another and different work. When Jesus stepped into the water to be baptized a fire was kindled in the Jordan, and the voice from heaven makes use of words not found in our Gospels; but both the incident and the words are known to have been contained in the Gospel according to the Hebrews and other works. Justin likewise states, in immediate continuation of the passage before us, that Jesus was considered the son of

[1] Vol. i. p. 316 ff.

Joseph the carpenter, and himself was a carpenter and accustomed to make ploughs and yokes.[1] The Evangelical work of which Justin made use was obviously different from our Gospels, therefore, and the evident conclusion to which any impartial mind must arrive is, that there is not only not the slightest ground for affirming that Justin quoted the passage before us from the fourth Gospel, from which he so fundamentally differs, but every reason on the contrary to believe that he derived it from a Gospel different from ours.[2]

The next point advanced by Tischendorf is, that on two occasions he speaks of the restoration of sight to persons born blind,[3] the only instance of which in our Gospels is that recorded, John ix. 1. The references in Justin are very vague and general. In the first place he is speaking of the analogies in the life of Jesus with events believed in connection with mythological deities, and he says that he would appear to relate acts very similar to those attributed to Æsculapius when he says that Jesus "healed the lame and paralytic, and the maimed from birth (ἐκ γενετῆς πονηρούς), and raised the dead."[4] In the Dialogue, again referring to Æsculapius, he says that Christ "healed those who were from birth and according to the flesh blind (τοὺς ἐκ γενετῆς καὶ κατὰ τὴν σάρκα πηρούς), and deaf, and lame."[5] In the fourth Gospel

---

[1] Dial., 88.

[2] *Bretschneider*, Probabilia, p. 192 f.; *Credner*, Beiträge, i. p. 218; *Hilgenfeld*, Die Evv. Justin's, p. 162 ff.; *Scholten*, Die ält. Zeugnisse, p. 33; *Volkmar*, Der Ursprung, p. 97, p. 156; *Zeller*, Theol. Jahrb., 1845, p. 613 f., 1847, p. 150 ff. Cf. *Davidson*, Introd. N. T., ii. p. 377 f. *Ebrard* thinks it a combination of Matt. iii. 11, and John i. 19, but admits that it may be from oral tradition: Die evang. Gesch., p. 813.

[3] Apol., i. 22, Dial., 69. On the second occasion Justin seems to apply the "from their birth" not only to the blind, but to the lame and deaf.

[4] Apol., i. 22.   [5] Dial. 69.

the born-blind is described as (ix. 1) ἄνθρωπος τυφλὸς ἐκ γενετῆς. There is a variation it will be observed in the term employed by Justin, and that such a remark should be seized upon as an argument for the use of the fourth Gospel serves to show the poverty of the evidence for the existence of that work. Without seeking any further, we might at once reply that such general references as those of Justin might well be referred to the common tradition of the Church, which certainly ascribed all kinds of marvellous cures and miracles to Jesus. It is moreover unreasonable to suppose that the only Gospel in which the cure of one born blind was narrated was that which is the fourth in our Canon. Such a miracle may have formed part of a dozen similar collections extant at the time of Justin, and in no case could such an allusion be recognized as evidence of the use of the fourth Gospel. But in the Dialogue, along with this remark, Justin couples the statement that although the people saw such cures: "They asserted them to be magical illusion; for they also ventured to call him a magician and deceiver of the people."[1] This is not found in our Gospels, but traces of the same tradition are met with elsewhere, as we have already mentioned;[2] and it is probable that Justin either found all these particulars in the Gospel of which he made use, or that he refers to traditions familiar amongst the early Christians.

Tischendorf's next point is that Justin quotes the words of Zechariah xii. 10, with the same variation from the text of the Septuagint as John xix. 37—"They shall look on him whom they pierced" (ὄψονται εἰς ὃν

---

[1] .... φαντασίαν μαγικὴν γίνεσθαι ἔλεγον. Καὶ γὰρ μάγον εἶναι αὐτὸν ἐτόλμων λέγειν καὶ λαοπλάνον. Dial. 69.
[2] Vol. i. p. 324 f.

ἐξεκέντησαν[1] instead of ἐπιβλέψονται πρὸς μὲ, ἀνθ' ὧν κατωρχήσαντο), arising out of an emendation of the translation of the Hebrew original. Tischendorf says: "Nothing can be more opposed to probability, than the supposition that John and Justin have here, independently of each other, followed a translation of the Hebrew text which elsewhere has remained unknown to us."[2] The fact is, however, that the translation which has been followed is not elsewhere unknown. We meet with the same variation, much earlier, in the only book of the New Testament which Justin mentions, and with which, therefore, he was beyond any doubt well acquainted, Rev. i. 7: "Behold he cometh with clouds, and every eye shall see him (ὄψεται αὐτόν), and they which pierced (ἐξεκέντησαν) him, and all the tribes of the earth shall bewail him. Yea, Amen." This is a direct reference to the passage in Zech. xii. 10. It will be remembered that the quotation in the Gospel: "They shall look upon him whom they pierced," is made solely in reference to the thrust of the lance in the side of Jesus, while that of the Apocalypse is a connection of the prophecy with the second coming of Christ, which, except in a spiritual sense, is opposed to the fourth Gospel. Now, Justin upon each occasion quotes the whole passage also in reference to the second coming of Christ as the Apocalypse does, and this alone settles the point so far as these two sources are concerned. If Justin derived his variation from either of the Canonical works,

[1] Justin has, Apol. i. 52, ὄψονται εἰς ὃν ἐξεκέντησαν. Dial. 14, καὶ ὄψεται ὁ λαὸς ὑμῶν καὶ γνωριεῖ εἰς ὃν ἐξεκέντησαν, and, Dial. 32, speaking of the two comings of Christ; the first, in which he was pierced, (ἐξεκεντήθη), "and the second in which ye shall know whom ye have pierced;" δευτέραν δὲ ὅτε ἐπιγνώσεσθε εἰς ὃν ἐξεκεντήσατε.

[2] Wann wurden, u. s. w., p. 34.

therefore, we should be bound to conclude that it must have been from the Apocalypse. The correction of the Septuagint version, which has thus been traced back as far as A.D. 68 when the Apocalypse was composed, was noticed by Jerome in his Commentary on the text;[1] and Aquila, a contemporary of Irenæus, and later Symmachus and Theodotion, as well as others, similarly adopted ἐξεκέντησαν. Ten important MSS., of the Septuagint, at least, have the reading of Justin and of the Apocalypse, and these MSS. likewise frequently agree with the other peculiarities of Justin's text. In all probability, as Credner, who long ago pointed out all these circumstances, conjectured, an emendation of the rendering of the LXX. had early been made, partly in Christian interest and partly for the critical improvement of the text,[2] and this amended version was used by Justin and earlier Christian writers. Ewald[3] and some others suggest that probably ἐκκεντεῖν originally stood in the Septuagint text. Every consideration is opposed to the dependence of Justin upon the fourth Gospel for the variation.[4]

The next and last point advanced by Tischendorf is a passage in Apol. i. 61, which is compared with John iii.

---

[1] "Quod ibi (1 Regg. ii. 18) errore interpretationis accidit, etiam hic factum deprehendimus. Si enim legatur *Dacaru*, ἐξεκέντησαν, i.e., compunxerunt sive confixerunt accipitur: sin autem contrario ordine, literis commutatis *Racadu*, ὠρχήσαντο, i.e., saltaverunt intelligitur et ob similitudinem literarum error est natus."

[2] *Credner*, Beiträge, ii. p. 293 ff. Cf. *Sanday*, Gospels in Sec. Cent. p. 281.

[3] Comm. in Apoc. Joh. 1829, p. 93, anm. 1; cf. Die Joh. Schriften, 1862, p. 112 anm. 1; *Lücke*, Offenb. Joh. ii. p. 446 f.

[4] *Davidson*, Introd. N. T., ii. p. 378; *Hilgenfeld*, Die Evv. Justin's, p. 49 ff.; Theol. Jahrb. 1850, p. 415 f.; *Scholten*, Die ält. Zeugnisse, p. 37; Ilet Evang. n. Joh. 1864, p. 437 f.; *Volkmar*, Offenb. Joh., 1862, p. 58; Der Ursprung, p. 97.

3—5, and in order to show the exact character of the two passages, we shall at once place them in parallel columns :—

JUSTIN, APOL. I. 61.	JOHN III. 3—5.
For the Christ also said :	3. Jesus answered and said unto him : Verily, verily, I say unto thee : Except a man be born from above (γεννηθῇ ἄνωθεν) he cannot see the kingdom of God.
Unless ye be born again (ἀναγεννη-θῆτε) ye shall not enter into the kingdom of heaven.	
Now that it is impossible for those who have once been born to go (ἐμβῆναι) into the matrices of the parents[1] (εἰς τὰς μήτρας τῶν τεκουσῶν) is evident to all.	4. Nicodemus saith unto him : How can a man be born when he is old ? Can he enter (εἰσελθεῖν) a second time into his mother's womb (εἰς τὴν κοιλίαν τῆς μητρὸς αὐτοῦ) and be born ?
	5. Jesus answered : Verily, verily, I say unto thee : Except a man be born of water and of the Spirit, he cannot enter into[2] the kingdom of God.[3]
Καὶ γὰρ ὁ Χριστὸς εἶπεν· Ἂν μὴ ἀναγεννηθῆτε, οὐ μὴ εἰσέλθητε εἰς τὴν βασιλείαν τῶν οὐρανῶν. Ὅτι δὲ καὶ ἀδύνατον εἰς τὰς μήτρας τῶν τεκουσῶν τοὺς ἅπαξ γεννωμένους ἐμβῆναι, φανερὸν πᾶσίν ἐστι.	3. Ἀπεκρίθη Ἰησοῦς καὶ εἶπεν αὐτῷ· Ἀμὴν ἀμὴν λέγω σοι, ἐὰν μή τις γεννηθῇ ἄνωθεν, οὐ δύναται ἰδεῖν τὴν βασιλείαν τοῦ θεοῦ.
	4. Λέγει πρὸς αὐτὸν ὁ Νικόδημος· Πῶς δύναται ἄνθρωπος γεννηθῆναι γέρων ὤν ; μὴ δύναται εἰς τὴν κοιλίαν τῆς μητρὸς αὐτοῦ δεύτερον εἰσελθεῖν καὶ γεννηθῆναι ;
	5. Ἀπεκρίθη Ἰησοῦς· Ἀμὴν ἀμὴν λέγω σοι, ἐὰν μή τις γεννηθῇ ἐξ ὕδατος καὶ πνεύματος, οὐ δύναται εἰσελθεῖν εἰς[4] τὴν βασιλείαν τοῦ θεοῦ.[5]

This is the most important passage by which apologists endeavour to establish the use by Justin of the

[1] Τεκοῦσα, a mother, instead of μήτηρ.
[2] The Cod. Sinaiticus reads : " he cannot see."
[3] The Cod. Sinaiticus has been altered here to : " of heaven."
[4] The Cod. Sinaiticus reads ἰδεῖν for εἰσελθεῖν εἰς here.
[5] The Cod. Sin. has τῶν οὐρανῶν, but τοῦ θεοῦ is substituted by a later hand. The former reading is only supported by a very few obscure and unimportant codices. The Codices Alex. (A) and Vatic. (B), as well as all the most ancient MSS., read τοῦ θεοῦ.

fourth Gospel, and it is that upon which the whole claim may be said to rest. We shall be able to appreciate the nature of the case by the weakness of its strongest evidence. The first point which must have struck any attentive reader, must have been the singular difference of the language of Justin, and the absence of the characteristic peculiarities of the Johannine Gospel. The double "verily, verily," which occurs twice even in these three verses, and constantly throughout the Gospel¹, is absent in Justin; and apart from the total difference of the form in which the whole passage is given (the episode of Nicodemus being entirely ignored), and omitting minor differences, the following linguistic variations occur:

Justin has:

ἂν μὴ ἀναγεννηθῆτε	instead of	ἐὰν μή τις γεννηθῇ ἄνωθεν
οὐ μὴ εἰσέλθητε εἰς	,,	οὐ δύναται ἰδεῖν²
βασιλείᾳ τῶν οὐρανῶν	,,	βασιλείᾳ τοῦ θεοῦ
ἀδύνατον	,,	μὴ δύναται
τὰς μήτρας	,,	τὴν κοιλίαν
τῶν τεκουσῶν	,,	τῆς μητρὸς αὐτοῦ
ἐμβῆναι	,,	εἰσελθεῖν
τοὺς ἅπαξ γεννωμένους	,,	ἄνθρωπος γεννηθῆναι γέρων ὤν.

Indeed it is almost impossible to imagine a more complete difference, both in form and language, and it seems to us that there does not exist a single linguistic trace by which the passage in Justin can be connected with the fourth Gospel. The fact that Justin knows nothing of the expression γεννηθῇ ἄνωθεν ("born from above"), upon which the whole statement in the fourth Gospel turns, but uses a totally different word, ἀναγεννηθῆτε (born again),

¹ Cf. i. 51; iii. 11; v. 19, 24, 25; vi. 26, 32, 47, 53; viii. 34, 51, 58; x. 1, 7; xii. 24; xiii. 16, 20, 21, 38; xiv. 12; xvi. 20, 23; xxi. 18, &c., &c.

² It is very forced to jump to the end of the fifth verse to get εἰσελθεῖν εἰς and even in that case the Cod. Sin. reads again, precisely as in the third, ἰδεῖν.

is of great significance. Tischendorf wishes to translate ἄνωθεν "anew" (or again), as the version of Luther and the authorised English translation read, and thus render the ἀναγεννηθῆναι of Justin a fair equivalent for it; but even this would not alter the fact that so little does Justin quote the fourth Gospel, that he has not even the test word of the passage. The word ἄνωθεν, however, certainly cannot here be taken to signify anything but "from above"[1]—from God, from heaven,—and this is not only its natural meaning, but the term is several times used in other parts of the fourth Gospel, always with this same sense,[2] and there is nothing which warrants a different interpretation in this place. On the contrary, the same signification is manifestly indicated by the context, and forms the point of the whole lesson. "Except a man be born of water and *of Spirit*[3] he cannot enter into the kingdom of God. 6. That which hath been born of the flesh is flesh, and that which hath been born of the Spirit is Spirit. 7. Marvel not that I said unto thee: ye must be born from above" (γεννηθῆναι ἄνωθεν). The explanation of ἄνωθεν is given in verse 6. The birth "of the Spirit" is the birth "from above," which is essential to entrance into the kingdom of God.[4]

[1] *Credner*, Beiträge, i. p. 253; *Davidson*, Introd. N. T., ii. p. 375; *Hilgenfeld*, Die Evv. Justin's, p. 214; *Lange*, Ev. n. Joh., 1862, p. 84 f.; *Lightfoot*, Horæ Hebr. et Talm. on John iii. 3; Works, xii. p. 254 ff.; *J. B. Lightfoot*, on a Fresh Revision of the New Test., 1871, p. 142; *Lücke*, Comment. Ev. Joh., i. p. 516 ff.; *Meyer*, Ev. Joh., 1869, p. 154 f.; *Reuss*, Hist. Théol. Chrét. ii., pp. 521 ff., 523 n. 2; *Scholten*, Die ält. Zeugnisse, p. 36; Het. Ev. n. Joh., 1864, pp. 21, 105, 237, 272, 387; *Späth*, Protestanten Bibel, 1874, p. 276 f.; *Stemler*, Het. Ev. v. Joh., 1868, pp. 250, 338, 344, 400; *Suicer*, Thesaurus s. v. ἄνωθεν; *de Wette*, Ev. n. Br. Joh., 1863, p. 61; *Wordsworth*, Gk. Test., The Four Gospels, p. 280; *Zeller*, Theol. Jahrb., 1855, p. 140. Cf. *Bretschneider*, Probabilia, p. 193.

[2] Cf. i. 31; xix. 11, 23.

[3] Cf. Ezekiel xxxvi. 25—27.

[4] Cf. *Lightfoot*, Horæ Hebr. et Talm. Works, xii. p. 256.

The sense of the passage in Justin is different and much more simple. He is speaking of regeneration through baptism, and the manner in which converts are consecrated to God when they are made new (καινοποιηθέντες) through Christ. After they are taught to fast and pray for the remission of their sins, he says: "They are then taken by us where there is water, that they may be regenerated ("born again," ἀναγεννῶνται), by the same manner of regeneration (being born again, ἀναγεννήσεως) by which we also were regenerated (born again, ἀναγεννήθημεν). For in the name of the Father of the Universe the Lord God, and of our Saviour Jesus Christ, and of the Holy Spirit they then make the washing with the water. For the Christ also said, 'unless ye be born again (ἀναγεννηθῆτε), ye shall not enter into the kingdom of heaven.' Now that it is impossible for those who have once been born to go into the matrices of the parents is evident to all." And then he quotes Isaiah i. 16—20, "Wash you, make you clean, &c.," and then proceeds: "And regarding this (Baptism) we have been taught this reason. Since at our first birth we were born without our knowledge, and perforce, &c., and brought up in evil habits and wicked ways, therefore in order that we should not continue children of necessity and ignorance, but become children of election and knowledge, and obtain in the water remission of sins which we had previously committed, the name of the Father of the Universe and Lord God is pronounced over him who desires to be born again (ἀναγεννηθῆναι), and has repented of his sins, &c."[1] Now it is clear that whereas Justin speaks simply of regeneration by baptism, the fourth Gospel indicates a later development of the doctrine by spiritualizing the idea,

---

[1] Apol. i. 61.

and requiring not only regeneration through the water ("Except a man be born of water"), but that a man should be born from above ("and of the Spirit"), not merely ἀναγεννηθῆναι, but ἄνωθεν γεννηθῆναι. The word used by Justin is that which was commonly employed in the Church for regeneration, and other instances of it occur in the New Testament.[1]

The idea of regeneration or being born again, as essential to conversion, was quite familiar to the Jews themselves, and Lightfoot gives instances of this from Talmudic writings: "If any one become a proselyte he is like a child 'new born.' The Gentile that is made a proselyte and the servant that is made free he is like a child new born."[2] This is, of course, based upon the belief in special privileges granted to the Jews, and the Gentile convert admitted to a share in the benefits of the Messiah became a Jew by spiritual new birth. Justin in giving the words of Jesus clearly professed to make an exact quotation:[3] "For Christ also said: Unless ye be born again, &c." It must be remembered, however, that Justin is addressing the Roman emperors, who would not understand the expression that it was necessary to be "born again" in order to enter the kingdom of heaven. He, therefore, explains that he does not mean a physical new birth by men already born; and this explanation may be regarded as natural, under the circumstances, and independent of any written source. In any case, the striking difference of his language from that of the fourth Gospel at least forbids the inference that it must necessarily have been derived from that Gospel.

---

[1] Cf. 1 Peter i. 3, 23.   [2] *Lightfoot*, Works, xii. p. 255 ff.
[3] *Bretschneider*, Probabilia, p. 193.

To argue otherwise would be to assume the utterly untenable premiss that sayings of Jesus which are maintained to be historical were not recorded in more than four Gospels, and indeed in this instance were limited to one. This is not only in itself inadmissible, but historically untrue,[1] and a moment of consideration must convince every impartial mind that it cannot legitimately be asserted that an express quotation of a supposed historical saying must have been taken from a parallel in one of our Gospels, from which it differs so materially in language and circumstance, simply because that Gospel happens to be the only one now surviving which contains particulars somewhat similar. The express quotation fundamentally differs from the fourth Gospel, and the natural explanation of Justin which follows is not a quotation at all, and likewise fundamentally differs from the Johannine parallel. Justin not only ignores the peculiar episode in the fourth Gospel in which the passage occurs, but neither here nor anywhere throughout his writings makes any mention of Nicodemus. The accident of survival is almost the only justification of the affirmation that the fourth Gospel is the source of Justin's quotation. On the other hand, we have many strong indications of another source. In our first Synoptic (xviii. 3), we find traces of another version of the saying of Jesus, much more nearly corresponding with the quotation of Justin: "And he said, verily I say unto you: Except ye be turned and become as the little children ye shall not enter into the kingdom of heaven."[2] The last phrase of this saying is literally the same as the quotation of Justin,

---

[1] Cf. Luke i. 1.

[2] καὶ εἶπεν, Ἀμὴν λέγω ὑμῖν, ἐὰν μὴ στραφῆτε καὶ γένησθε ὡς τὰ παιδία, οὐ μὴ εἰσέλθητε εἰς τὴν βασιλείαν τῶν οὐρανῶν. Matt. xviii. 3.

EXTERNAL EVIDENCE FOR THE FOURTH GOSPEL. 311

and gives his expression, "kingdom of heaven," so characteristic of his Gospel, and so foreign to the Johannine. We meet with a similar quotation in connection with baptism, still more closely agreeing with Justin, in the Clementine Homilies, xi. 26 : " Verily I say unto you : Except ye be born again (ἀναγεννηθῆτε) by living water in the name of Father, Son, and Holy Spirit, ye shall not enter into the kingdom of heaven."[1] Here again we have both the ἀναγεννηθῆτε, and the βασιλεία τῶν οὐρανῶν, as well as the reference only to water in the baptism, and this is strong confirmation of the existence of a version of the passage, different from the Johannine, from which Justin quotes. As both the author of the Clementines and Justin probably made use of the Gospel according to the Hebrews, some most competent critics have, with reason, adopted the conclusion that the passage we are discussing was probably derived from that Gospel; at any rate it cannot be maintained as a quotation from our fourth Gospel,[2] and it is, therefore, of no value as evidence even

---

[1] Ἀμὴν ὑμῖν λέγω, ἐὰν μὴ ἀναγεννηθῆτε ὕδατι ζῶντι, εἰς ὄνομα Πατρὸς, Υἱοῦ, ἁγίου Πνεύματος, οὐ μὴ εἰσέλθητε εἰς τὴν βασιλείαν τῶν οὐρανῶν. Hom. xi. 26. Cf. Recogn. vi. 9: " Amen dico vobis, nisi quis denuo renatus fuerit ex aqua, non introibit in regna coelorum." Cf. Clem. Hom. Epitome, § 18. In this much later compilation the passage, altered and manipulated, is of no interest. *Uhlhorn*, Die Homilien u. Recogn., 1854, p. 43 ff.; *Schliemann*, Die Clementinen, 1844, p. 334 ff.

[2] *Baur*, Unters. kan. Evv., p. 352; Theol. Jahrb., 1849, p. 366 ff.; 1857, p. 230 ff.; *Bretschneider*, Probabilia, p. 179 ff., p. 192 f.; *Credner*, Beiträge, i. p. 252 ff.; *Davidson*, Introd. N. T., ii. p. 374 f.; *Ewald*, Die Bücher d. N. B., 1871, i. 1, p. 170; *Gieseler*, Enst. schr. Evv., p. 14, cf. p. 145 ff.; *Hilgenfeld*, Die Evv. Justin's, p. 214 ff., p. 358 ff.; Das Evang. Joh. u. s. w., 1849, p. 151, anm. 1; *Lützelberger*, Die kirchl. Tradition üb. Ap. Joh., u. s. w., 1840, p. 122 ff.; *Scholten*, Die ält. Zeugnisse, p. 34 ff.; Das Ev. Joh., p. 8 f.; *Schwegler*, Der Montanismus, p. 184, anm. 86; Das nachap. Zeit., i. p. 218 ff.; *Volkmar*, Justin d. Märt., 1853, p. 18 ff.; *Zeller*, Theol. Jahrb., 1845, p. 614; 1847, p. 152; 1855, p. 138 ff.

for its existence. Were it successfully traced to that work, however, the passage would throw no light on the authorship and character of the fourth Gospel.

If we turn for a moment from this last of the points of evidence adduced by Tischendorf for the use of the fourth Gospel by Justin, to consider how far the circumstances of the history of Jesus narrated by Justin bear upon this quotation, we have a striking confirmation of the results we have otherwise attained. Not only is there a total absence from his writings of the peculiar terminology and characteristic expressions of the fourth Gospel, but there is not an allusion made to any one of the occurrences exclusively narrated by that Gospel, although many of these, and many parts of the Johannine discourses of Jesus, would have been peculiarly suitable for his purpose. We have already pointed out the remarkable absence of any use of the expressions by which the Logos doctrine is stated in the prologue. We may now point out that Justin makes no reference whatever to any of the special miracles of the fourth Gospel. He is apparently quite ignorant even of the raising of Lazarus: on the other hand, he gives representations of the birth, life, and death of Jesus, which are ignored by the Johannine Gospel, and are indeed opposed to its whole conception of Jesus as the Logos; and when he refers to circumstances which are also narrated in that Gospel, his account is different from that which it gives. Justin perpetually refers to the birth of Jesus by the Virgin of the race of David and the Patriarchs; his Logos thus becomes man,[1] (not "*flesh*,"—ἄνθρωπος, not σάρξ); he is born in a cave in Bethlehem;[2] he grows in stature and intellect by the use of ordinary means like other men; he is accounted

[1] Dial., 100, &c., &c.   [2] Dial., 78.

the son of Joseph the carpenter and Mary: he himself works as a carpenter, and makes ploughs and yokes.[1] When Jesus is baptized by John, a fire is kindled in Jordan; and Justin evidently knows nothing of John's express declaration in the fourth Gospel, that Jesus is the Messiah, the Son of God.[2] Justin refers to the change of name of Simon in connection with his recognition of the Master as "Christ the Son of God,"[3] which is narrated quite differently in the fourth Gospel (i. 40—42), where, indeed, such a declaration is put into the mouth of Nathaniel (i. 49), which Justin ignores. Justin does not mention Nicodemus either in connection with the statement regarding the necessity of being "born from above," or with the entombment (xix. 39). He has the prayer and agony in the garden,[4] which the fourth Gospel excludes, as well as the cries on the cross, which that Gospel ignores. Then, according to Justin, the last supper takes place on the 14th Nisan,[5] whilst the fourth Gospel, ignoring the Passover and last supper, represents the last meal as eaten on the 13th Nisan (John xiii. 1 f., cf. xviii. 28). He likewise contradicts the fourth Gospel, in limiting the work of Jesus to one year. In fact, it is impossible for writings, so full of quotations of the words of Jesus and of allusions to the events of his life, more completely to ignore or vary from the fourth Gospel throughout; and if it could be shown that Justin was acquainted with such a work, it would follow certainly that he did not consider it an Apostolical or authoritative composition.

[1] Dial., 88.   [2] Dial., 88.   [3] Dial., 100.
[4] Dial., 99, 103.
[5] "And it is written that on the day of the Passover you seized him, and likewise during the Passover you crucified him." Dial., 111; cf. Dial. 70; Matt. xxvi. 2, 17 ff., 30, 57.

We may add that, as Justin so distinctly and directly refers to the Apostle John as the author of the Apocalypse,[1] there is confirmation of the conclusion, otherwise arrived at, that he did not, and could not, know the Gospel and also ascribe it to him. Finally, the description which Justin gives of the manner of teaching of Jesus excludes the idea that he knew the fourth Gospel. "Brief and concise were the sentences uttered by him: for he was no Sophist, but his word was the power of God."[2] No one could for a moment assert that this description applies to the long and artificial discourses of the fourth Gospel, whilst, on the other hand, it eminently describes the style of teaching in the Synoptics, with which the numerous Gospels in circulation amongst early Christians were, of course, more nearly allied.

The inevitable conclusion at which we must arrive is that, so far from indicating any acquaintance with the fourth Gospel, the writings of Justin not only do not furnish the slightest evidence of its existence, but offer presumptive testimony against its Apostolical origin.

Tischendorf only devotes a short note to Hegesippus,[3] and does not pretend to find in the fragments of his writings, preserved to us by Eusebius, or the details of his life which he has recorded, any evidence for our Gospels. Apologists generally admit that this source, at least, is barren of all testimony for the fourth Gospel, but Canon Westcott cannot renounce so important a witness without an effort, and he therefore boldly says: "When he, (Hegesippus) speaks of 'the door of Jesus' in his account of the death of St. James, there can be little

---

[1] Dial., 81.

[2] Βραχεῖς δὲ καὶ σύντομοι παρ' αὐτοῦ λόγοι γεγόνασιν. Οὐ γὰρ σοφιστὴς ὑπῆρχεν, ἀλλὰ δύναμις θεοῦ ὁ λόγος αὐτοῦ ἦν. Apol. i. 14.

[3] Wann wurden, u. s. w., p. 19, anm. 1.

doubt that he alludes to the language of our Lord recorded by St. John."[1] The passage to which Canon Westcott refers, but which he does not quote, is as follows :—" Certain, therefore, of the seven heretical parties amongst the people, already described by me in the Memoirs, inquired of him, what was the door of Jesus; and he declared this (τοῦτον—Jesus) to be the Saviour. From which some believed that Jesus is the Christ. But the aforementioned heretics did not believe either a resurrection, or that he shall come to render to every one according to his works. As many as believed, however, did so, through James." The rulers fearing that the people would cause a tumult, from considering Jesus to be the Messiah (Χριστός), entreat James to persuade them concerning Jesus, and prevent their being deceived by him; and in order that he may be heard by the multitude, they place James upon a wing of the temple, and cry to him: "O just man, whom we all are bound to believe, inasmuch as the people are led astray after Jesus, the crucified, declare plainly to us what is the door of Jesus."[2] To find in this a reference to the fourth Gospel, requires a good deal of apologetic ingenuity. It is perfectly clear that, as an allusion to John x. 7, 9: "I am the door," the question: "What is the door of Jesus?" is mere nonsense, and the reply of James totally irrelevant. Such a question in reference to the discourse

---

[1] On the Canon, p. 182 f.

[2] Τινές οὖν τῶν ἑπτὰ αἱρέσεων τῶν ἐν τῷ λαῷ, τῶν προγεγραμμένων μοι ἐν τοῖς ὑπομνήμασιν, ἐπυνθάνοντο αὐτοῦ, τίς ἡ θύρα τοῦ Ἰησοῦ. Καὶ ἔλεγε τοῦτον εἶναι τὸν Σωτῆρα. Ἐξ ὧν τινες ἐπίστευσαν, ὅτι Ἰησοῦς ἐστὶν ὁ Χριστός. Αἱ δὲ αἱρέσεις αἱ προειρημέναι οὐκ ἐπίστευον οὔτε ἀνάστασιν, οὔτε ἐρχόμενον ἀποδοῦναι ἑκάστῳ κατὰ τὰ ἔργα αὐτοῦ. Ὅσοι δὲ καὶ ἐπίστευσαν, διὰ Ἰάκωβον. . . . . Δίκαιε, ᾧ πάντες πείθεσθαι ὀφείλομεν, ἐπεὶ ὁ λαὸς πλανᾶται ὀπίσω Ἰησοῦ τοῦ σταυρωθέντος, ἀπάγγειλον ἡμῖν τίς ἡ θύρα τοῦ Ἰησοῦ. Eusebius, H. E., ii. 23.

in the fourth Gospel, moreover, in the mouths of the antagonistic Scribes and Pharisees, is quite inconceivable, and it is unreasonable to suppose that it has any connection with it. Various emendations of the text have been proposed to obviate the difficulty of the question, but none of these have been adopted, and it has now been generally accepted, that θύρα is used in an idiomatic sense. The word is very frequently employed in such a manner, or symbolically, in the New Testament,[1] and by the Fathers. The Jews were well acquainted with a similar use of the word in the Old Testament, in some of the Messianic Psalms, as for instance: Ps. cxviii. 19, 20 (cxvii. 19, 20 Sept.). 19, "Open to me the gates (πύλας) of righteousness; entering into them, I will give praise to the Lord;" 20, "This is the gate (ἡ πύλη) of the Lord, the righteous shall enter into it."[2] Quoting this passage, Clement of Alexandria remarks: "But explaining the saying of the prophet, Barnabas adds: Many gates (πυλῶν) being open, that which is in righteousness is in Christ, in which all those who enter are blessed."[3] Grabe explains the passage of Hegesippus, by a reference to the frequent allusions in Scripture to the two ways: one of light, the other of darkness; the one leading to life, the other to death; as well as the simile of two gates which is coupled with them, as in Matt. vii. 13 ff. He, therefore, explains the question of the rulers: "What is the door of Jesus?" as an inquiry into the judgment of James concerning him:

---

[1] Cf. Acts xiv. 27; 1 Cor. xvi. 9; 2 Cor. ii. 12; Col. iv. 3; James v. 9; Rev. iii. 8, 20; iv. 1.

[2] Cf. Ps. xxiv. 7—8 (xxiii. 7—8 Sept.).

[3] ἐξηγούμενος δὲ τὸ ῥητὸν τοῦ προφήτου Βαρνάβας ἐπιφέρει· "πολλῶν πυλῶν ἀνεῳγυιῶν, ἡ ἐν δικαιοσύνῃ αὕτη ἐστὶν ἡ ἐν Χριστῷ, ἐν ᾗ μακάριοι πάντες οἱ εἰσελθόντες." Strom. vi. 8, § 64. This passage is not to be found in the Epistle of Barnabas.

whether he was a teacher of truth or a deceiver of the people; whether belief in him was the way and gate of life and salvation, or of death and perdition.[1] He refers as an illustration to the Epistle of Barnabas, xviii.: "There are two ways of teaching and of power: one of light, the other of darkness. But there is a great difference between the two ways."[2] The Epistle, under the symbol of the two ways, classifies the whole of the moral law.[3] In the Clementine Homilies, xviii. 17, there is a version of the saying, Matt. vii. 13f., derived from another source, in which "way" is more decidedly even than in our first Synoptic made the equivalent of "gate:" "Enter ye through the narrow and straitened way (ὁδός) through which ye shall enter into life." Eusebius himself, who has preserved the fragment, evidently understood it distinctly in the same sense, and he gave its true meaning in another of his works, where he paraphrases the question into an enquiry, as to the opinion which James held concerning Jesus (τίνα περὶ τοῦ Ἰησοῦ ἔχοι δόξαν).[4] This view is supported by many learned men, and Routh has pointed out that Ernesti considered he would have been right in making διδαχή, doctrine, teaching, the equivalent of θύρα, although he admits that Eusebius does not once use it in his history, in connection with Christian doctrine.[5]

[1] Spicil. Patr., ii. p. 254.
[2] Ὁδοὶ δύο εἰσὶν διδαχῆς καὶ ἐξουσίας, ἥ τε τοῦ φωτὸς, καὶ ἡ τοῦ σκότους. Διαφορὰ δὲ πολλὴ τῶν δύο ὁδῶν. Barnabæ Ep. xviii.
[3] In like manner the Clementine Homilies give a peculiar version of Deut. xxx. 15: "Behold I have set before thy face the way of life, and the way of death." Ἰδοὺ τέθεικα πρὸ προσώπου σου τὴν ὁδὸν τῆς ζωῆς, καὶ τὴν ὁδὸν τοῦ θανάτου. Hom. xviii. 17, cf. vii. 7.
[4] Demonstrat. Evang. iii. 7. Routh, Rel. Sacr. i. p. 235.
[5] Si ego in Glossis ponerem: θύρα, διδαχή, rectum esset. Sed respicerem ad loca Græcorum theologorum v. c. Eusebii in Hist. Eccl. ubi non

He might, however, have instanced this passage, in which it is clearly used in this sense, and so explained by Eusebius. In any other sense the question is simple nonsense. There is evidently no intention on the part of the Scribes and Pharisees here to ridicule, in asking: "What is the door of Jesus?" but they desire James to declare plainly to the people, what is the teaching of Jesus, and his personal pretension. To suppose that the rulers of the Jews set James upon a wing of the temple, in order that they might ask him a question, for the benefit of the multitude, based upon a discourse in the fourth Gospel, unknown to the Synoptics, and even in relation to which such an inquiry as: "What is the door of Jesus?" becomes mere ironical nonsense, surpasses all that we could have imagined even of apologetic zeal.

We have already[1] said all that is necessary with regard to Hegesippus, in connection with the Synoptics, and need not add more here. It is certain that had he said anything interesting about our Gospels and, we may say, particularly about the fourth, the fact would have been recorded by Eusebius.

Nor need we add much to our remarks regarding Papias of Hierapolis.[2] It is perfectly clear that the works of Matthew and Mark,[3] regarding which he records

semel θύρα Χριστοῦ (sic) de doctrina Christiana dicitur." *Dissert. De Usu Glossariorum.* Routh, Reliq. Sacræ. i. p. 236. Donaldson gives as the most probable meaning: "To what is it that Jesus is to lead us? And James' answer is therefore: 'To salvation.'" Hist. Chr. Lit. and Doctr., iii. p. 190, note.

[1] Vol. i. p. 429 ff.; Preface to 6th ed. p. xviii. ff.
[2] See vol. i. p. 443 ff.; Preface to 6th ed., p. xxi. f.
[3] It is evident that Papias did not regard the works by "Matthew" and "Mark" which he mentions, as of any authority. Indeed, all that he reports regarding the latter is merely apologetic, and in deprecation of criticism.

such important particulars, are not the Gospels in our Canon, which pass under their names; he does not seem to have known anything of the third Synoptic; and there is no reason to suppose that he referred to the fourth Gospel or made use of it. He is, therefore, at least, a total blank so far as the Johannine Gospel and our third Synoptic are concerned, but he is more than this, and it may, we think, be concluded that Papias was not acquainted with any such Gospels which he regarded as Apostolic compositions, or authoritative documents. Had he said anything regarding the composition or authorship of the fourth Gospel, Eusebius would certainly have mentioned the fact, and this silence of Papias is strong presumptive evidence against the Johannine Gospel.[1] Tischendorf's argument in regard to the Phrygian Bishop is mainly directed to this point, and he maintains that the silence of Eusebius does not make Papias a witness against the fourth Gospel, and does not involve the conclusion that he did not know it, inasmuch as it was not, he affirms, the purpose of Eusebius to record the mention or use of the books of the New Testament which were not disputed.[2] It might be contended that this reasoning is opposed to the practice and express declaration of Eusebius himself, who says: "But in the course of the history I shall, with the successions (from the Apostles), carefully intimate what ecclesiastical writers of the various periods made use of

---

[1] *Credner*, Beiträge, i. p. 23 f.; *Davidson*, Introd. N. T., ii. p. 371; *Hilgenfeld*, Die Evangelien, p. 344; Zeitschr. wiss. Theol., 1865, p. 334; Einl. N. T., 1875, pp. 55, 59 ff.; *Lützelberger*, Die kirchl. Tradition üb. Ap. Joh., u. s. w., 1840 p. 89 ff.; *Renan*, Vie de Jésus, xiiime ed., 1867, p. lviii. f.; *Scholten*, Die ält. Zeugnisse, p. 16 ff.; *Strauss*, Das Leben Jesu, 1864, p. 62; *Volkmar*, Der Ursprung, p. 61; *Zeller*, Theol. Jahrb., 1845, p. 652 ff.; 1847, p. 148 f.   [2] Wann wurden, u. s. w., p. 112 ff.

the Antilegomena (or disputed writings), and which of them, and what has been stated by these as well regarding the collected (ἐνδιαθήκοι) and Homologumena (or accepted writings), as regarding those which are not of this kind."[1] It is not worth while, however, to dwell upon this, here. The argument in the case of Papias stands upon a broader basis. It is admitted that Eusebius engages carefully to record what ecclesiastical writers state regarding the Homologumena, and that he actually does so. Now Papias has himself expressed the high value he attached to tradition, and his eagerness in seeking information from the Presbyters. The statements regarding the Gospels composed by Matthew and Mark, quoted by Eusebius, are illustrative at once both of the information collected by Papias and of that cited by Eusebius. How comes it, then, that nothing whatever is said about the fourth Gospel, a work so peculiar and of such exceptional importance, said to be composed by the Apostle whom Jesus loved? Is it possible to suppose that when Papias collected from the Presbyter the facts which he has recorded concerning Matthew and Mark he would not also have inquired about a Gospel by John had he known of it? Is it possible that he could have had nothing interesting to tell about a work presenting so many striking and distinctive features? Had he collected any information on the subject he would certainly have recorded it, and as certainly Eusebius would have quoted what he said,[2] as he did the account of the other two Gospels, for he even mentions that Papias

---

[1] Προϊούσης δὲ τῆς ἱστορίας, προὔργου ποιήσομαι σὺν ταῖς διαδοχαῖς ὑποσημήνασθαι, τίνες τῶν κατὰ χρόνους ἐκκλησιαστικῶν συγγραφέων ὁποίαις κέχρηνται τῶν ἀντιλεγομένων, τίνα τε περὶ τῶν ἐνδιαθήκων καὶ ὁμολογουμένων γραφῶν, καὶ ὅσα περὶ τῶν μὴ τοιούτων αὐτοῖς εἴρηται. *Eusebius*, H. E., iii. 3; cf. iii. 24.

[2] Cf. Preface to 6th ed., pp. xi ff., xxi f.

made use of the 1st Epistle of John, and 1st Epistle of Peter, two equally accepted writings. The legitimate presumption, therefore, is that, as Eusebius did not mention the fact, he did not find anything regarding the fourth Gospel in the work of Papias, and that Papias was not acquainted with it. This presumption is confirmed by the circumstance that when Eusebius writes, elsewhere (H. E. iii. 24), of the order of the Gospels, and the composition of John's Gospel, he has no greater authority to give for his account than mere tradition: "they say" (φασί).

Proceeding from this merely negative argument, Tischendorf endeavours to show that not only is Papias not a witness against the fourth Gospel, but that he presents testimony in its favour. The first reason he advances is that Eusebius states: "The same (Papias) made use of testimonies out of the first Epistle of John, and likewise out of that of Peter."[1] On the supposed identity of the authorship of the Epistle and Gospel, Tischendorf, as in the case of Polycarp, claims this as evidence for the fourth Gospel. Eusebius, however, does not quote the passages upon which he bases this statement, and knowing his inaccuracy and the hasty and uncritical manner in which he and the Fathers generally jump at such conclusions, we must reject this as sufficient evidence that Papias really did use the Epistle, and that Eusebius did not adopt his opinion from a mere superficial analogy of passages.[2] But if it were certain that Papias actually quoted from the Epistle, it does not in the least follow that he

---

[1] Κέχρηται δ' ὁ αὐτὸς μαρτυρίαις ἀπὸ τῆς Ἰωάννου προτέρας ἐπιστολῆς, καὶ ἀπὸ τῆς Πέτρου ὁμοίως. *Eusebius*, H. E., iii. 39.

[2] *Zeller*, Theol. Jahrb., 1845, p. 652 ff., 1847, p. 148 f.; *Scholten*, Die alt. Zeugnisse, p. 17; Das Evang. Johan., p. 8; *Lützelberger*, Die kirchl. Tradition üb. Ap. Joh., p. 92 ff. Cf. *Davidson*, Introd. N. T., ii. p. 373.

ascribed it to the Apostle John, and the use of the Epistle would scarcely affect the question as to the character and authorship of the fourth Gospel.

The next testimony advanced by Tischendorf is indeed of an extraordinary character. There is a Latin MS. (Vat. Alex. 14) in the Vatican, which Tischendorf assigns to the ninth century, in which there is a preface by an unknown hand to the Gospel according to John, which commences as follows : " Evangelium iohannis manifestatum et datum est ecclesiis ab iohanne adhuc in corpore constituto, sicut papias nomine hierapolitanus discipulus iohannis carus in exotericis id est in extremis quinque libris retulit." "The Gospel of John was published and given to the churches by John whilst he was still in the flesh, as Papias, named of Hierapolis, an esteemed disciple of John, related in his 'Exoterics' that is his last five books." Tischendorf says : " There can, therefore, be no more decided declaration made of the testimony of Papias for the Johannine Gospel."[1] He wishes to end the quotation here, and only refers to the continuation, which he is obliged to admit to be untenable, in a note. The passage proceeds : " Disscripsit vero evangelium dictante iohanne recte." " He (Papias) indeed wrote out the Gospel, John duly dictating ;" then follows another passage regarding Marcion, representing him also as a contemporary of John, which Tischendorf likewise confesses to be untrue.[2] Now Tischendorf admits that the writer desires it to be understood that he derived the information that Papias wrote the fourth Gospel at the dictation of John likewise from the work of Papias, and as it is perfectly impossible, by his own admissions, that Papias, who was not a con-

[1] Wann wurden, u. s. w., p. 119.
[2] Wann wurden, u. s. w., p. 119, anm. 1.

temporary of the Apostle, could have stated this, the whole passage is clearly fabulous and written by a person who never saw the book at all. This extraordinary piece of evidence is so obviously absurd that it is passed over in silence by other critics, even of the strongest apologetic tendency, and it stands here a pitiable instance of the arguments to which destitute criticism can be reduced.

In order to do full justice to the last of the arguments of Tischendorf, we shall give it in his own words: "Before we separate from Papias, we have still to consider one testimony for the Gospel of John which Irenæus, v. 36, § 2, quotes out of the very mouth of the Presbyters, those high authorities of Papias: 'And therefore, say they, the Lord declared: In my Father's house are many mansions' (John xiv. 2). As the Presbyters set this declaration in connection with the blessedness of the righteous in the City of God, in Paradise, in Heaven, according as they bear thirty, sixty, or one hundred-fold fruit, nothing is more probable than that Irenæus takes this whole declaration of the Presbyters, which he gives, §§ 1-2, like the preceding description of the thousand years' reign, from the work of Papias. But whether this be its origin or not, the authority of the Presbyters is in any case higher than that of Papias," &c.[1] Now in the quotation from Irenæus given in this

[1] Ehe wir aber von Papias scheiden, haben wir noch eines Zeugnisses für das Johannesevangelium zu gedenken, das Irenäus, v. 36, 2 sogar aus dem Munde der Presbyter, jener hohen Autoritäten des Papias anführt. "Und deshalb sagen sie habe der Herr den Ausspruch gethan: In meines Vaters Hause sind viele Wohnungen" (Joh. 14, 2). Da die Presbyter diesen Ausspruch in Verbindung setzten mit den Seligkeitsstufen der Gerechten in der Gottesstadt, im Paradiese, im Himmel, je nachdem sie dreissig- oder sechzig- oder hundertfältig Frucht tragen, so ist nichts wahrscheinlicher als dass Irenäus diese ganze Aussage der Presbyter, die er a. a. O. 1—2 gibt, gleich der vorhergegangenen Schilderung des

passage, Tischendorf renders the oblique construction of the text by inserting "say they," referring to the Presbyters of Papias, and, as he does not give the original, he should at least have indicated that these words are supplementary. We shall endeavour as briefly as possible to state the facts of the case.

Irenæus, with many quotations from Scripture, is arguing that our bodies are preserved, and that the Saints who have suffered so much in the flesh shall in that flesh receive the fruits of their labours. In v. 33, § 2, he refers to the saying given in Matt. xix. 29 (Luke xviii. 29, 30) that whosoever has left lands, &c., because of Christ shall receive a hundred-fold in this world, and in the next, eternal life; and then, enlarging on the abundance of the blessings in the Millennial kingdom, he affirms that Creation will be renovated, and the Earth acquire wonderful fertility, and he adds: § 3, "As the Presbyters who saw John the disciple of the Lord, remember that they heard from him, how the Lord taught concerning those times and said:" &c. ("Quemadmodum presbyteri meminerunt, qui Joannem discipulum Domini viderunt, audisse se ab eo, quemadmodum de temporibus illis docebat Dominus, et dicebat," &c.), and then he quotes the passage: "The days will come in which vines will grow each having ten thousand Branches," &c.; and "In like manner that a grain of wheat would produce ten thousand ears," &c. With regard to these he says, at the beginning of the next paragraph, v. 33, § 4, "These things are testified in writing by Papias, a hearer of John and associate of Polycarp, an ancient

---

tausendjährigen Reichs, dem Werke des Papias entlehnte. Mag sie aber daher stammen oder nicht, jedenfalls steht die Autorität der Presbyter höher als die des Papias; u. s. w. Wann wurden, u. s. w., p. 119 f.

man, in the fourth of his books: for there were five books composed by him.[1] And he added saying : ' But these things are credible to believers. And Judas the traitor not believing, and asking how shall such growths be effected by the Lord, the Lord said : They who shall come to them shall see.' Prophesying of these times, therefore, Isaiah says : 'The Wolf also shall feed with the Lamb,' &c. &c. (quoting Isaiah xi. 6—9), and again he says, recapitulating : ' Wolves and lambs shall then feed together,' " &c. (quoting Isaiah lxv. 25), and so on, continuing his argument. It is clear that Irenæus introduces the quotation from Papias, and ending his reference at : " They who shall come to them shall see," he continues, with a quotation from Isaiah, his own train of reasoning. We give this passage to show the manner in which Irenæus proceeds. He then continues with the same subject, quoting (v. 34, 35) Isaiah, Ezekiel, Jeremiah, Daniel, the Apocalypse, and sayings found in the New Testament bearing upon the Millennium. In c. 35 he argues that the prophecies he quotes of Isaiah, Jeremiah, and the Apocalypse must not be allegorized away, but that they literally describe the blessings to be enjoyed, after the coming of Antichrist and the resurrection, in the New Jerusalem on earth, and he quotes Isaiah vi. 12, lx. 5, 21, and a long passage from Baruch iv. 36, v. 9 (which he ascribes to Jeremiah), Isaiah xlix. 16, Galatians iv. 26, Rev. xxi. 2, xx. 2—15, xxi. 1—6, all descriptive, as he maintains, of the Millennial kingdom prepared for the Saints; and then in v. 36, the last chapter of his work on Heresies, as if resuming his pre-

---

[1] *Eusebius* has preserved the Greek of this passage (H. E., iii. 39), and goes on to contradict the statement of Irenæus that Papias was a hearer and contemporary of the Apostles. Eusebius states that Papias in his preface by no means asserts that he was.

vious argument, he proceeds:[1] § 1. "And that these things shall ever remain without end Isaiah says: 'For like as the new heaven and the new earth which I make remain before me, saith the Lord, so shall your seed and your name continue,'[2] and as the Presbyters say, then those who have been deemed worthy of living in heaven shall go thither, and others shall enjoy the delights of Paradise, and others shall possess the glory of the City; for everywhere the Saviour shall be seen as those who see him shall be worthy. § 2. But that there is this distinction of dwelling (εἶναι δὲ τὴν διαστολὴν ταύτην τῆς οἰκήσεως) of those bearing fruit the hundred fold, and of the (bearers) of the sixty fold, and of the (bearers of) the thirty fold: of whom some indeed shall be taken up into the heavens, some shall live in Paradise, and some shall inhabit the City, and that for this reason (διὰ τοῦτο—propter hoc) the Lord declared: In the ... (plural) of my Father are many mansions (ἐν τοῖς τοῦ πατρός μου μονὰς εἶναι πολλάς).[3] For all things are of God, who prepares for all the fitting habitation, as his Word says, that distribution is made to all by the Father according

---

[1] We have the following passage only in the old Latin version, with fragments of the Greek preserved by Andrew of Cæsarea in his *Comment. in Apoc.*, xviii., lxiv., and elsewhere.

[2] Isaiah lxvi. 22, Sept.

[3] With this may be compared John xiv. 2, ἐν τῇ οἰκίᾳ τοῦ πατρός μου μοναὶ πολλαί εἰσιν. If the passage be maintained to be from the Presbyters, the variations from the text of the Gospel are important. Doubtless the expression τὰ τοῦ πατρός μου may mean "my father's house," and this sense is ancient, but a wider sense is far from excluded, and the plural is used. In Luke ii. 49, the very phrase occurs, ἐν τοῖς τοῦ πατρός μου, and in the authorized version is translated "about my father's business," cf. 1 Tim. iv. 15. The best commentators are divided in opinion regarding the passage in Luke. It is necessary, in a case like the present, to convey the distinct difference between the words as they stand in Irenæus, and the saying in the fourth Gospel. Dr. Sanday has: "In my Father's realm," Gospels in Sec. Cent., p. 297.

as each is or shall be worthy. And this is the couch upon which they recline who are invited to banquet at the Wedding. The Presbyters disciples of the Apostles state that this is the order and arrangement of those who are saved, and that by such steps they advance," [1] &c. &c.

Now it is impossible for any one who attentively considers the whole of this passage, and who makes himself acquainted with the manner in which Irenæus conducts his argument, and interweaves it with quotations, to assert that the phrase we are considering must have been taken from a book referred to three chapters earlier, and was not introduced by Irenæus from some other source. In the passage from the commencement of the second paragraph Irenæus enlarges upon, and illustrates, what "the Presbyters say" regarding the blessedness of the saints, by quoting the view held as to the distinction between those bearing fruit thirty fold, sixty fold, and one hundred fold,[2] and the interpretation given of the

---

[1] .... φησὶν γὰρ Ἡσαΐας "' Ὃν τρόπον γὰρ ὁ οὐρανὸς καινὸς καὶ ἡ γῆ καινή, ἃ ἐγὼ ποιῶ, μένει ἐνώπιον ἐμοῦ, λέγει Κύριος, οὕτω στήσεται τὸ σπέρμα ὑμῶν καὶ τὸ ὄνομα ὑμῶν ..." ὡς οἱ πρεσβύτεροι λέγουσι, τότε καὶ οἱ μὲν καταξιωθέντες τῆς ἐν οὐρανῷ διατριβῆς ἐκεῖσε χωρήσουσιν, οἱ δὲ τῆς τοῦ παραδείσου τρυφῆς ἀπολαύσουσιν, οἱ δὲ τὴν λαμπρότητα τῆς πόλεως καθέξουσιν· πανταχοῦ γὰρ ὁ Σωτὴρ ὁραθήσεται, καθὼς ἄξιοι ἔσονται οἱ ὁρῶντες αὐτόν.

2. Εἶναι δὲ τὴν διαστολὴν ταύτην τῆς οἰκήσεως τῶν τὰ ἑκατὸν καρποφορούντων, καὶ τῶν τὰ ἑξήκοντα, καὶ τῶν τὰ τριάκοντα· ὧν οἱ μὲν εἰς τοὺς οὐρανοὺς ἀναληφθήσονται, οἱ δὲ ἐν τῷ παραδείσῳ διατρίψωσιν, οἱ δὲ τὴν πόλιν κατοικήσουσιν· καὶ διὰ τοῦτο εἰρηκέναι τὸν Κύριον, ἐν τοῖς τοῦ πατρός μου μονὰς εἶναι πολλάς· τὰ πάντα γὰρ τοῦ θεοῦ, ὃς τοῖς πᾶσι τὴν ἁρμόζουσαν οἴκησιν παρέχει. Quemadmodum Verbum ejus ait, omnibus divisum esse a Patro secundum quod quis ost dignus, aut erit. Et hoc est triclinium, in quo recumbent ii qui epulantur vocati ad nuptias. Hanc esse adordinationem et dispositionem eorum qui salvantur, dicunt presbyteri apostolorum discipuli, et per hujusmodi gradus proficere, &c., &c. *Irenæus*, Adv. Hær., v. 36, §§ 1, 2.

[2] Matt. xiii. 8; Mark iv. 20; cf. Matt. xxv. 14—29; Luke xix. 12—26; xii. 47, 48.

saying regarding " many mansions," but the source of his quotation is quite indefinite, and may simply be the exegesis of his own day. That this is probably the case is shown by the continuation: " And this is the Couch upon which they recline who are invited to banquet at the Wedding "—an allusion to the marriage supper upon which Irenæus had previously enlarged;[1] immediately after which phrase, introduced by Irenæus himself, he says: " The Presbyters, the disciples of the apostles, state that this is the order and arrangement of those who are saved," &c. Now, if the preceding passages had been a mere quotation from the Presbyters of Papias, such a remark would have been out of place and useless, but being the exposition of the prevailing views, Irenæus confirms it and prepares to wind up the whole subject by the general statement that the Presbyters, the disciples of the Apostles, affirm that this is the order and arrangement of those who are saved, and that by such steps they advance and ascend through the Spirit to the Son, and through the Son to the Father, &c., and a few sentences after he closes his work.

In no case, however, can it be legitimately affirmed that the citation of " the Presbyters," and the " Presbyters, disciples of the Apostles," is a reference to the work of Papias. When quoting " the Presbyters who saw John the disciple of the Lord," three chapters before, Irenæus distinctly states that Papias testifies what he quotes in writing in the fourth of his books, but there is nothing whatever to indicate that " the Presbyters," and " the Presbyters, disciples of the Apostles," subsequently referred to, after a complete change of context, have anything to do with Papias. The references to Presbyters in this

[1] Adv. Hær., iv. 36, §§ 5, 6.

work of Irenæus are very numerous, and when we remember the importance which the Bishop of Lyons attached to "that tradition which comes from the Apostles, which is preserved in the churches by a succession of Presbyters,"[1] the reference before us assumes a very different complexion. In one place, Irenæus quotes "the divine Presbyter" (ὁ θεῖος πρεσβύτης), "the God-loving Presbyter" (ὁ θεοφιλὴς πρεσβύτης),[2] who wrote verses against the heretic Marcus. Elsewhere he supports his extraordinary statement that the public career of Jesus, instead of being limited to a single year, extended over a period of twenty years, and that he was nearly fifty when he suffered,[3] by the appeal: "As the gospel and all the Presbyters testify, who in Asia met with John the disciple of the Lord (stating) that these things were transmitted to them by John. For he continued among them till the times of Trajan."[4] That these Presbyters are not quoted from the work of Papias may be inferred from the fact that Eusebius, who had his work, quotes the passage from Irenæus without allusion to Papias, and as he adduces two witnesses only, Irenæus and Clement of Alexandria, to prove the assertion regarding John, he would certainly have referred to the earlier authority, had the work of Papias contained the statement, as he does for the stories regarding the

[1] Adv. Hær., iii. 2, § 2; cf. i. 10, § 1; 27, §§ 1, 2; ii. 22, § 5; iii. præf. 3, § 4; 21, § 3; iv. 27, § 1; 32, § 1; v. 20, § 2; 30, § 1.
[2] Ib., i. 15, § 6.   [3] Ib., ii. 22, §§ 4, 6.
[4] . . . sicut Evangelium, καὶ πάντες οἱ πρεσβύτεροι μαρτυροῦσιν, οἱ κατὰ τὴν Ἀσίαν Ἰωάννῃ τῷ τοῦ κυρίου μαθητῇ συμβεβληκότες, παραδεδωκέναι ταῦτα τὸν Ἰωάννην. Παρέμεινε γὰρ αὐτοῖς μέχρι τῶν Τραϊανοῦ χρόνων. Adv. Hær., ii. 22, § 5. Cf. Eusebius, H. E., iii. 23. "In Asia" evidently refers chiefly to Ephesus, as is shown by the passage immediately after quoted by Eusebius from Adv. Hær., iii. 3, § 4. "the Church in Ephesus also . . . where John continued until the times of Trajan, is a witness to the truth of the apostolic tradition."

daughters of the Apostle Philip; the miracle in favour of Justus, and other matters.[1] We need not refer to Clement, nor to Polycarp, who had been "taught by Apostles," and the latter of whom Irenæus knew in his youth.[2] Irenæus in one place also gives a long account of the teaching of some one upon the sins of David and other men of old, which he introduces: "As I have heard from a certain Presbyter, who had heard it from those who had seen the Apostles, and from those who learnt from them,"[3] &c. Further on, speaking evidently of a different person, he says: "In this manner also a Presbyter disciple of the Apostles, reasoned regarding the two Testaments:"[4] and quotes fully. In another place Irenæus, after quoting Gen. ii. 8, "And God planted a Paradise eastward in Eden," &c., states: "Wherefore the Presbyters who are disciples of the Apostles (οἱ πρεσ-βύτεροι, τῶν ἀποστόλων μαθηταί), say that those who were translated had been translated thither," there to remain till the consummation of all things awaiting immortality, and Irenæus explains that it was into this Paradise that Paul was caught up (2 Cor. xii. 4).[5] It seems highly probable that these "Presbyters the disciples of the Apostles" who are quoted on Paradise, are the same "Presbyters the disciples of the Apostles" referred to on the same subject (v. 36, §§ 1, 2) whom we

---

[1] *Eusebius*, H. E., iii. 39.

[2] Adv. Hær., iii. 3, §§ 3, 4. Fragment from his Epistle to Florinus preserved by Eusebius, H. E., v. 20.

[3] Quemadmodum audivi a quodam presbytero, qui audierat ab his qui apostolos viderant, et ab his qui didicerant, &c. Adv. Hær., iv. 27, § 1, cf. § 2; 30, § 1. This has been variously conjectured to be a reference to Polycarp, Papias, and Pothinus his predecessor at Lyons, but it is admitted by all to be impossible to decide upon the point.

[4] Hujusmodi quoque de duobus testamentis senior apostolorum discipulus disputabat, &c. Adv. Hær., iv. 32, § 1.

[5] Adv. Hær., v. 5, § 1

are discussing, but there is nothing whatever to connect them with Papias. He also speaks of the Septuagint translation of the Bible as the version of the "Presbyters,"[1] and on several occasions he calls Luke "the follower and disciple of the Apostles" (Sectator et discipulus apostolorum)[2], and characterizes Mark as "the interpreter and follower of Peter" (interpres et sectator Petri)[3], and refers to both as having learnt from the words of the Apostles.[4] Here is, therefore, a wide choice of Presbyters, including even Evangelists, to whom the reference of Irenæus may with equal right be ascribed,[5] so that it is unreasonable to claim it as an allusion to the work of Papias.[6] In fact, Dr. Tischendorf and Canon Westcott[7] stand almost alone in ad-

---

[1] Adv. Hær., iii. 21, §§ 3, 4.   [2] Ib., i. 23, § 1; iii. 10, § 1; 14, § 1.
[3] Ib., iii. 10, § 6.   [4] Ib., iii. 15, § 3.
[5] In the New Testament the term Presbyter is even used in reference to Patriarchs and Prophets. Heb. xi. 2; cf. Matt. xv. 2; Mark vii. 3, 5.
[6] With regard to the Presbyters quoted by Irenæus generally. Cf. Routh, Reliq. Sacræ, i. p. 47 ff.
[7] Canon Westcott affirms: "In addition to the Gospels of St. Matthew and St. Mark, Papias appears to have been acquainted with the Gospel of St. John."(³) He says no more, and offers no evidence whatever for this assertion in the text. There are two notes, however, on the same page, which we shall now quote, the second being that to which (³) above refers. "² No conclusion can be drawn from Eusebius' silence as to express testimonies of Papias to the Gospel of St. John, as we are ignorant of his special plan, and the title of his book shows that it was not intended to include 'all the oracles of the Lord,' see p. 61, note 2." The second note is: "³ There is also (!?) an allusion to it in the quotation from the 'Elders' found in Irenæus (lib. v. ad. f.) which probably was taken from Papias (fr. v. Routh et Nott.). The Latin passage containing a reference to the Gospel which is published as a fragment of 'Papias' by Grabe and Routh (fr. xi.), is taken from the 'Dictionary' of a mediæval Papias quoted by Grabe upon the passage, and not from the present Papias. The 'Dictionary' exists in MS. both at Oxford and Cambridge. I am indebted to the kindness of a friend for this explanation of what seemed to be a strange forgery." On the Canon, p. 65. The note 2, p. 61, referred to in note 2 quoted above, says on this subject: "The passage quoted by Irenæus from 'the Elders' may probably be taken as a specimen of his style of interpretation" (!) and then follows a quotation: "as the Pres-

vancing this passage as evidence that either Papias or his Presbyters[1] were acquainted with the fourth Gospel, and this renders the statement which is made by them without any discussion all the more indefensible. Scarcely a single writer, however apologetic, seriously cites it amongst the external testimonies for the early existence of the Gospel, and the few who do refer to the passage merely mention, in order to abandon, it.[2] So far as the question as to whether the fourth Gospel was mentioned in the work of Papias is concerned, the passage has practically never entered into the controversy at all, the great mass of critics having recognized that it is of no evidential value whatever, and, by common consent, tacitly excluded it.[3] It is

---

byters say:" down "to many mansions." Dr. Westcott then continues: "Indeed from the similar mode of introducing the story of the vine which is afterwards referred to Papias, it is reasonable to conjecture that this interpretation is one from Papias' '*Exposition*.'" We have given the whole of the passages to show how little evidence there is for the statement which is made. The isolated assertion in the text, which is all that most readers would see, is supported by no better testimony than that in the preceding note inserted at the foot of an earlier page.

[1] *Routh* (Reliq. Sacræ, i. p. 10 f., 31) also referred the passage to the work of Papias, and he was followed in this conjecture by *Dorner*, Lehre Pers. Christi, i. p. 217, anm. 56, p. 218, anm. 62.

[2] *Riggenbach* (Die Zeugnisse f. d. Ev. Johannes, 1866, p. 116) admits that there is no evidence that the passage was derived from Papias, but merely asserts that the "Presbyters" were men of the generation to which Papias and Polycarp belonged, and that the quotation therefore dates from the first half of the second century. Cf. *Anger*, Synops. Ev. Proleg. p. xxxi; *Hofstede de Groot*, Basilides, p. 110 f.; *Luthardt*, Der johann. Urspr. des viert. Evang. 1874, p. 72; *Meyer*, Komm. Ev. des Johannes, p. 6 f.; *Zahn*, Th. Stud. u. Krit., 1866, p. 674.

[3] The following writers directly refer to and reject it: *Zeller*, Theol. Jahrb., 1845, p. 593, anm. 2, cf. 1847, p. 160, anm. 1; *Hilgenfeld*, Zeitschr. wiss. Theol., 1867, p. 186, anm. 1, 1868, p. 219, anm. 4, cf. 1865, p. 334 ff., Die Evangelien, p. 339, anm. 4; *Davidson*, Introd. N. T., ii. pp. 372, 424 f. Distinguished apologetic writers like Bleek, Ebrard, Olshausen, Guericke, Kirchhofer, Thiersch, and Tholuck, and eminent critics like Credner, de Wette, Gfrörer, Lücke and others do not even

admitted that the Bishop of Hierapolis cannot be shown to have known the fourth Gospel, and the majority affirm that he actually was not acquainted with it. Being, therefore, so completely detached from Papias, it is obvious that the passage does not in any way assist the fourth Gospel, but becomes assignable to vague tradition, and subject to the cumulative force of objections, which prohibit an early date being ascribed to so indefinite a reference.

Before passing on there is one other point to mention: Andrew of Cæsarea, in the preface to his Commentary on the Apocalypse, mentions that Papias maintained "the credibility" (τὸ ἀξιόπιστον) of that book, or in other words, its apostolic origin.[1] His strong millenarian opinions would naturally make such a composition stand high in his esteem, if indeed it did not materially contribute to the formation of his views, which is still more probable. Apologists admit the genuineness of this statement, nay, claim it as undoubted evidence of the acquaintance of Papias with the Apocalypse.[2] Canon Westcott, for instance, says: "He maintained, moreover, 'the divine inspiration' of the Apocalypse, and commented, at least, upon part of it."[3] Now, he must, therefore, have recognized the book as the work of the Apostle John, and we shall, hereafter, show that it is impossible that the author of the Apocalypse is the author of the Gospel; therefore, in this way also, Papias

---

notice it, although they were all acquainted with the article of Zeller in which the passage is discussed.

[1] *Andreas*, Prolog. in Apocalypsin; *Routh*, Rel. Sacræ, i. p. 15.

[2] *Lücke*, Einl. Offenb. Joh., 1852, ii. p. 526; *Ewald*, Die Joh. Schriften, ii. p. 371 f.; *Guericke*, Gesammtgesch. N. T., p. 536; *Tischendorf*, Wann wurden, u. s. w., p. 116, &c., &c.

[3] On the Canon, p. 65.

is a witness against the Apostolic origin of the fourth Gospel.

We must now turn to the Clementine Homilies, although, as we have shown,[1] the uncertainty as to the date of this spurious work, and the late period which must undoubtedly be assigned to its composition, render its evidence of very little value for the canonical Gospels. The passages pointed out in the Homilies as indicating acquaintance with the fourth Gospel were long advanced with hesitation, and were generally felt to be inconclusive, but on the discovery of the concluding portion of the work and its publication by Dressel in 1853, it was found to contain a passage which apologists now claim as decisive evidence of the use of the Gospel, and which even succeeded in converting some independent critics.[2] Tischendorf[3] and Canon Westcott,[4] in the few lines devoted to the Clementines, do not refer to the earlier proof passages, but rely entirely upon that last discovered. With a view, however, to making the whole of the evidence clear, we shall give all of the supposed allusions to the fourth Gospel, confronting them with the text. The first is as follows :—

Hom. iii. 52.	John x. 9.
Wherefore he, being the true prophet, said :	
I am the gate of life : he coming in through me cometh in unto life, as there is no other teaching which is able to save.	I am the door (of the sheepfold), if anyone enter through me he shall be saved, and shall go in and shall go out and shall find pasture.

[1] Vol. ii., p. 1 ff.

[2] *Hilgenfeld*, who had maintained that the Clementines did not use the fourth Gospel, was induced by the passage to which we refer to admit its use. Cf. Die Evv. Justin's, p. 385 ff. ; Die Evangelien, p. 346 f. ; Der Kanon, p. 29 ; Theol. Jahrb., 1854, p. 534, anm. 1 ; Zeitschr. wiss. Theol., 1865, p. 338 ; *Volkmar* is inclined to the same opinion, although not with the same decision. Theol. Jahrb., 1854, p. 448 ff.

[3] Wann wurden, u. s. w., p. 90 f.   [4] On the Canon, p. 252.

Hom. III. 52.	John x. 9.
Διὰ τοῦτο αὐτὸς ἀληθὴς ὢν προφήτης ἔλεγεν· 'Εγώ εἰμι ἡ πύλη τῆς ζωῆς· ὁ δι' ἐμοῦ εἰσερχόμενος εἰσέρχεται εἰς τὴν ζωήν ὡς οὐκ οὔσης ἑτέρας τῆς σώζειν δυναμένης διδασκαλίας.	'Εγώ εἰμι ἡ θύρα· δι' ἐμοῦ ἐάν τις εἰσέλθῃ, σωθήσεται, καὶ εἰσελεύσεται καὶ ἐξελεύσεται καὶ νομὴν εὑρήσει.

The first point which is apparent here is that there is a total difference both in the language and real meaning of these two passages. The Homily uses the word πύλη instead of the θύρα of the Gospel, and speaks of the gate of life, instead of the door of the Sheepfold. We have already[1] discussed the passage in the Pastor of Hermas in which similar reference is made to the gate (πύλη) into the kingdom of God, and need not here repeat our argument. In Matt. vii. 13, 14, we have the direct description of the gate (πύλη) which leads to life (εἰς τὴν ζωήν), and we have elsewhere quoted the Messianic Psalm cxviii. 19, 20 : " This is the gate of the Lord (αὕτη ἡ πύλη τοῦ Κυρίου),[2] the righteous shall enter into it." In another place, the author of the Homilies, referring to a passage parallel to, but differing from, Matt. xxiii. 2, which we have elsewhere considered,[3] and which is derived from a Gospel different from ours, says : " Hear *them* (Scribes and Pharisees who sit upon Moses' seat), he said, as entrusted with the key of the kingdom which is knowledge, which alone is able to open the gate of life (πύλη τῆς ζωῆς), through which alone is the entrance to Eternal life."[4] Now in the very next chapter to that in which the saying which we are discussing occurs, a very few lines after it indeed, we have the following passage : " Indeed he said further : ' I am he concern-

---

[1] ii. p. 256 f. [2] Ps. cxvii. 20, Sept. [3] ii. p. 18 ff.
[4] Hom. iii. 18.

ing whom Moses prophesied, saying: 'a prophet shall the Lord our God raise up to you from among your brethren as also (he raised) me; hear ye him regarding all things, but whosoever will not hear that prophet he shall die.'"[1] There is no such saying in the canonical Gospels or other books of the New Testament attributed to Jesus, but a quotation from Deuteronomy xviii. 15 f., materially different from this, occurs twice in the Acts of the Apostles, once being put into the mouth of Peter applied to Jesus,[2] and the second time also applied to him, being quoted by Stephen.[3] It is quite clear that the writer is quoting from uncanonical sources, and here is another express declaration regarding himself: "I am he," &c., which is quite in the spirit of the preceding passage which we are discussing, and probably derived from the same source. In another place we find the following argument: "But the way is the manner of life, as also Moses says: 'Behold I have set before thy face the way of life, and the way of death'[4] and in agreement the teacher said: 'Enter ye through the narrow and straitened way through which ye shall enter into life,' and in another place a certain person inquiring: 'What shall I do to inherit eternal life?' he intimated the Commandments of the Law."[5] It has to be observed that the Homilies teach the doctrine

---

[1] "Ετι μὴν ἔλεγεν· Ἐγώ εἰμι περὶ οὗ Μωϋσῆς προεφήτευσεν εἰπών· Προφήτην ἐγερεῖ ὑμῖν Κύριος ὁ θεὸς ἡμῶν, ἐκ τῶν ἀδελφῶν ὑμῶν, ὥσπερ καὶ ἐμέ, αὐτοῦ ἀκούετε κατὰ πάντα· ὃς ἂν δὲ μὴ ἀκούσῃ τοῦ προφήτου ἐκείνου, ἀποθανεῖται. Hom. iii. 53. This differs from the text of the Sept.

[2] Acts iii. 22. [3] Acts vii. 37. [4] Deut. xxx. 15.

[5] 'Οδὸς δὲ ἡ πολιτεία ἐστίν, τῷ καὶ τὸν Μωϋσῆν λέγειν· Ἰδοὺ τέθεικα πρὸ προσώπου σου τὴν ὁδὸν τῆς ζωῆς, καὶ τὴν ὁδὸν τοῦ θανάτου. Καὶ ὁ διδάσκαλος συμφώνως εἶπεν· Εἰσέλθετε διὰ τῆς στενῆς καὶ τεθλιμμένης ὁδοῦ, δι' ἧς εἰσελεύσεσθε εἰς τὴν ζωήν. Καὶ ἀλλαχοῦ που, ἐρωτήσαντός τινος, Τί ποιήσας ζωὴν αἰώνιον κληρονομήσω; τὰς τοῦ νόμου ἐντολὰς ὑπέδειξεν. Hom. xviii. 17.

that the spirit in Jesus Christ had already appeared in Adam, and by a species of transmigration passed through Moses and the Patriarchs and prophets: "who from the beginning of the world, changing names and forms, passes through Time (τὸν αἰῶνα τρέχει) until, attaining his own seasons, being on account of his labours anointed by the mercy of God, he shall have rest for ever."[1] Just in the same way, therefore, as the Homilies represent Jesus as quoting a prophecy of Moses, and altering it to a personal declaration: "I am the prophet," &c., so here again they make him adopt this saying of Moses and, "being the true prophet," declare: "I am the gate or the way of life,"—inculcating the same commandments of the law which the Gospel of the Homilies represents Jesus as coming to confirm and not to abolish. The whole system of doctrine of the Clementines, as we shall presently see, indicated here even by the definition of "the true prophet," is so fundamentally opposed to that of the fourth Gospel that there is no reasonable ground for supposing that the author made use of it, and this brief saying, varying as it does in language and sense from the parallel in that work, cannot prove acquaintance with it. There is good reason to believe that the author of the fourth Gospel, who most undeniably derived materials from earlier Evangelical works, may have drawn from a source likewise used by the Gospel according to the Hebrews, and thence many analogies might well be presented with quotations from that or kindred Gospels.[2] We find, further, this community of source in the fact,

---

[1] . . . . ὃς ἀπ᾽ ἀρχῆς αἰῶνος ἅμα τοῖς ὀνόμασι μορφὰς ἀλλάσσων τὸν αἰῶνα τρέχει, μέχρις ὅτε ἰδίων χρόνων τυχὼν, διὰ τοὺς καμάτους θεοῦ ἐλέει χρισθεὶς, εἰς ἀεὶ ἕξει τὴν ἀνάπαυσιν. Hom. iii. 20.

[2] Credner, Beiträge, i. p. 326; Neander, K. G., 1843, ii. p. 624 f., anm. 1; Scholten, Die ält. Zeugnisse, p. 59 f.; Das Ev. Johan., p. 12.

that in the fourth Gospel, without actual quotation, there is a reference to Moses, and, no doubt, to the very passage (Deut. xviii. 15), which the Gospel of the Clementines puts into the mouth of Jesus, John v. 46: "For had ye believed Moses ye would believe me, for he wrote of me." Whilst the Ebionite Gospel gave prominence to this view of the case, the dogmatic system of the Logos Gospel did not permit of more than mere reference to it.

The next passage pointed out as derived from the Johannine Gospel occurs in the same chapter: "My sheep hear my voice."

Hom. iii. 52.	John x. 27.
Τὰ ἐμὰ πρόβατα ἀκούει τῆς ἐμῆς φωνῆς.	Τὰ πρόβατα τὰ ἐμὰ τῆς φωνῆς μου ἀκούει.

There was no more common representation amongst the Jews of the relation between God and his people than that of a Shepherd and his Sheep,[1] nor any more current expression than: hearing his voice. This brief anonymous saying was in all probability derived from the same source as the preceding,[2] which cannot be identified with the fourth Gospel. Tradition, and the acknowledged existence of other written records of the teaching of Jesus oppose any exclusive claim to this fragmentary saying.

We have already discussed the third passage regarding the new birth in connection with Justin,[3] and may therefore pass on to the last and most important passage, to which we have referred as contained in the concluding portion of the Homilies first published by Dressel in

---

[1] Cf. Isaiah xl. 11; liii. 6; Ezek. xxxiv.; Zech. xi.; Hebrews xiii. 20.
[2] *Credner*, Beiträge, i. p. 326; *Scholten*, Die ält. Zeugnisse, p. 60; Das Evang. Johan., p. 12.   [3] p. 311 f.

1853. We subjoin it in contrast with the parallel in the fourth Gospel.

Hom. xix. 22.	John ix. 1—3.
Wherefore also our Teacher when we inquired regarding the man blind from birth and whose sight was restored by him, if this man had sinned or his parents that he should be born blind, answered in explanation: Neither this man sinned at all nor his parents, but that through him the power of God might be made manifest healing the sins of ignorance.	And as he was passing by, he saw a man blind from birth. 2. And his disciples asked him saying: Rabbi, who sinned, this man or his parents that he should be born blind? 3. Jesus answered, Neither this man sinned, nor his parents, but that the works of God might be made manifest in him.
Ὅθεν καὶ διδάσκαλος ἡμῶν περὶ τοῦ ἐκ γενετῆς πηροῦ καὶ ἀναβλέψαντος παρ' αὐτοῦ ἐξετάζων ἐρωτήσασιν, εἰ οὗτος ἥμαρτεν ἢ οἱ γονεῖς αὐτοῦ, ἵνα τυφλὸς γεννηθῇ, ἀπεκρίνατο· οὔτε οὗτός τι ἥμαρτεν, οὔτε οἱ γονεῖς αὐτοῦ, ἀλλ' ἵνα δι' αὐτοῦ φανερωθῇ ἡ δύναμις τοῦ θεοῦ τῆς ἀγνοίας ἰωμένη τὰ ἁμαρτήματα.	1. Καὶ παράγων εἶδεν ἄνθρωπον τυφλὸν ἐκ γενετῆς. 2. Καὶ ἠρώτησαν αὐτὸν οἱ μαθηταὶ αὐτοῦ λέγοντες· Ῥαββεί, τίς ἥμαρτεν, οὗτος ἢ οἱ γονεῖς αὐτοῦ, ἵνα τυφλὸς γεννηθῇ; 3. Ἀπεκρίθη Ἰησοῦς· Οὔτε οὗτος ἥμαρτεν οὔτε οἱ γονεῖς αὐτοῦ, ἀλλ' ἵνα φανερωθῇ τὰ ἔργα τοῦ θεοῦ ἐν αὐτῷ.

It is necessary that we should consider the context of this passage in the Homily, the characteristics of which are markedly opposed to the theory that it was derived from the fourth Gospel. We must mention that, in the Clementines, the Apostle Peter is represented as maintaining that the Scriptures are not all true, but are mixed up with what is false, and that on this account, and in order to inculcate the necessity of distinguishing between the true and the false, Jesus taught his disciples, "Be ye approved money changers,"[1] an injunction not found in our Gospels. One of the points which Peter denies is the fall of Adam, a doctrine which, as Neander remarked, "he must combat as blasphemy."[2] At the part we are consider-

---

[1] Hom. iii. 50, cf. 9, 42 ff.; ii. 38. The author denies that Moses wrote the Pentateuch, Hom. iii. 47 ff.

[2] Hom. iii. 20 ff., 42 ff., viii. 10. "Die Lehre von einem Sündenfalle

ing he is discussing with Simon,—under whose detested personality, as we have elsewhere shown, the Apostle Paul is really attacked,—and refuting the charges he brings forward regarding the origin and continuance of evil. The Apostle Peter in the course of the discussion asserts that evil is the same as pain and death, but that evil does not exist eternally and, indeed, does not really exist at all, for pain and death are only accidents without permanent force—pain is merely the disturbance of harmony, and death nothing but the separation of soul from body.[1] The passions also must be classed amongst the things which are accidental, and are not always to exist; but these, although capable of abuse, are in reality beneficial to the soul when properly restrained, and carry out the will of God. The man who gives them unbridled course ensures his own punishment.[2] Simon inquires why men die prematurely and periodical diseases come, and also visitations of demons and of madness and other afflictions; in reply to which Peter explains that parents by following their own pleasure in all things and neglecting proper sanitary considerations, produce a multitude of evils for their children, and this either through care-

---

des ersten Menschen musste der Verfasser der Clementinen als Gotteslästerung bekämpfen." *Neander*, K. G., ii. p. 612 f. The Jews at that period held a similar belief. *Eisenmenger*, Entd. Judenthum, i. p. 336. Adam, according to the Homilies, not only did not sin but, as a true prophet possessed of the Spirit of God which afterwards was in Jesus, he was incapable of sin. *Schliemann*, Die Clementinen, p. 130, p. 176 f., p. 178 f.

[1] Hom. xix. 20.

[2] Hom. xix. 21. According to the author of the Clementines, evil is the consequence of sin, and is on one hand necessary for the punishment of sin, but on the other beneficial as leading men to improvement and upward progress. Suffering is represented as wholesome, and intended for the elevation of man. Cf. Hom., ii. 13; vii. 2; viii. 11. Death was originally designed for man, and was not introduced by Adam's "fall," but is really necessary to nature, the Homilist considers. Cf. *Schliemann*, Die Clementinen, p. 177, p. 168 f.

lessness or ignorance.[1] And then follows the passage we are discussing: "Wherefore also our Teacher," &c., and at the end of the quotation, he continues: "and truly such sufferings ensue in consequence of ignorance," and giving an instance,[2] he proceeds: "Now the sufferings which you before mentioned are the consequence of ignorance, and certainly not of an evil act, which has been committed,"[3] &c. Now it is quite apparent that the peculiar variation from the parallel in the fourth Gospel in the latter part of the quotation is not accidental, but is the point upon which the whole propriety of the quotation depends. In the Gospel of the Clementines the man is not blind from his birth, "that the works of God might be made manifest in him,"—a doctrine which would be revolting to the author of the Homilies,—but the calamity has befallen him in consequence of some error of ignorance on the part of his parents which brings its punishment; but "the power of God" is made manifest in healing the sins of ignorance. The reply of Jesus is a professed quotation, and it varies very substantially from the parallel in the Gospel, presenting evidently a distinctly different version of the episode. The substitution of πηρός for τυφλός in the opening is also significant, more especially as Justin likewise in his general remark, which we have discussed, uses the same word. Assuming the passage in the fourth Gospel to be the account of a historical episode, as apologists, of course, maintain, the case stands thus:—The author of the Homilies introduces a narrative of a historical inci-

[1] Hom. xix. 22.
[2] Καὶ ἀληθῶς ἀγνοίας αἰτίᾳ τὰ τοιαῦτα γίνεται, ἤτοι τῷ μὴ εἰδέναι πότε δεῖ κοινωνεῖν τῇ γαμετῇ, εἰ καθαρὰ ἐξ ἀφέδρου τυγχάνει. Hom. xix. 22.
[3] Πλὴν ἃ προείρηκας πάθη ἐξ ἀγνοίας ἐστίν, οὐ μέντοι ἐκ πονηροῦ εἰργασμένου. Hom. xix. 22.

dent in the life of Jesus, which may have been, and probably was, reported in many early gospels in language which, though analogous to, is at the same time decidedly different, in the part which is a professed quotation, from that of the fourth Gospel, and presents another and natural comment upon the central event. The reference to the historical incident is, of course, no evidence whatever of dependence on the fourth Gospel, which, although it may be the only accidentally surviving work which contains the narrative, had no prescriptive and exclusive property in it, and so far from the partial agreement in the narrative proving the use of the fourth Gospel, the only remarkable point is, that all narratives of the same event and reports of words actually spoken do not more perfectly agree, while, on the other hand, the very decided variation in the reply of Jesus, according to the Homily, from that given in the fourth Gospel leads to the distinct presumption that it is not the source of the quotation.

It is perfectly unreasonable to assert that such a reference, without the slightest indication of the source from which the author derived his information, must be dependent on one particular work, more especially when the part which is given as distinct quotation substantially differs from the record in that work. We have already illustrated this on several occasions, and may once more offer an instance. If the first Synoptic had unfortunately perished, like so many other gospels of the early Church, and in the Clementines we met with the quotation: " Blessed are the poor in spirit, for theirs is the kingdom of heaven" (Μακάριοι οἱ πτωχοὶ τῷ πνεύματι, ὅτι αὐτῶν ἐστὶν ἡ βασιλεία τῶν οὐρανῶν), apologists would certainly assert, according to the principle upon which they act in the present case, that this quotation was clear evidence of the use of Luke vi. 20 : " Blessed are ye poor, for yours is the kingdom of God." (Μακάριοι οἱ πτωχοί, ὅτι ὑμετέρα ἐστὶν ἡ βασιλεία τοῦ θεοῦ), more especially as a few codices actually insert τῷ πνεύματι, the slight variations being merely ascribed to free quotation from memory. In point of fact, however, the third Synoptic might not at the time have been in existence, and the quotation might have been derived, as it is, from Matt. v. 3. Nothing is more certain and undeniable than the fact that the author of the fourth Gospel made use of materials derived from oral tradition and earlier records for its composition.[1] It is equally undeniable that other gospels had access to the same materials, and made use of them; and a comparison of our three Synoptics renders very evident the community of materials, including the use of the one by the other, as well as the diversity of literary handling to which those materials were subjected. It is impossible with reason to deny that the Gospel according to the Hebrews, for instance, as well as other earlier evangelical works now lost, may have drawn from the same sources as the fourth Gospel, and that narratives derived from the one may, therefore, present analogies with the other whilst still perfectly independent of it.[2] Whatever private opinion, therefore, any one may form as to the source of the anonymous quotations which we have been considering, it is evident that they are totally insufficient to prove that the Author of

---

[1] *Bleek*, Beiträge, 1846, p. 268 f.; Einl. N. T., p. 308 f.; *Ewald*, Jahrb. bibl. Wiss., 1849, p. 196 ff., 1851, p. 164, p. 166, anm. 2; Die Joh. Schriften, 1861, i. p. 24 f.; *Hilgenfeld*, Die Evangelien, p. 325 ff.; *de Wette*, Einl. N. T., p. 209 f.

[2] *Neander*, K. G., ii. p. 624 f., anm. 1.

the Clementine Homilies must have made use of the fourth Gospel, and consequently they do not establish even the contemporary existence of that work. If such quotations, moreover, could be traced with fifty times greater probability to the fourth Gospel, it is obvious that they could do nothing towards establishing its historical character and apostolic origin.

Leaving, however, the few and feeble analogies by which apologists vainly seek to establish the existence of the fourth Gospel and its use by the author of the pseudo-Clementine Homilies, and considering the question for a moment from a wider point of view, the results already attained are more than confirmed. The doctrines held and strongly enunciated in the Clementines seem to us to exclude the supposition that the author can have made use of a work so fundamentally at variance with all his views as the fourth Gospel, and it is certain that, holding those opinions, he could hardly have regarded such a Gospel as an apostolic and authoritative document. Space will not permit our entering adequately into this argument, and we must refer our readers to works more immediately devoted to the examination of the Homilies for a close analysis of their dogmatic teaching,[1] but we may in the briefest manner point out some of their more prominent doctrines in contrast with those of the Johannine Gospel.

---

[1] *Baur*, Gesch. chr. Kirche, i. p. 85 ff., p. 218 ff.; Chr. Gnosis, p. 300 ff.; Tüb. Zeitschr., 1831, iv. p. 114 ff., p. 174 ff., 1836, iii. p. 123 ff., p. 182 ff.; *Credner*, Winer's Zeitschr. wiss. Theol., 1829, i. h. 2, p. 237 ff.; *Dorner*, Entw. Gesch. der Lehre v. d. Person Christi, i. p. 324 ff.; *Neander*, K. G., ii. p. 610 ff., Genet. Entw. d. Gnost. Systeme, Beilage, p. 361 ff.; *Schliemann*, Die Clementinen, 1844, p. 130—229; *Schwegler*, Das nachap. Zeit., i. p. 363 ff.; Der Montanismus, 1841, p. 145 ff.; *Uhlhorn*, Die Homilien und Recogn., 1854, p. 153—230. Compare also *Mansel*, The Gnostic Heresies, 1875, p. 222 ff., and especially p. 229 ff.

One of the leading and most characteristic ideas of the Clementine Homilies is the essential identity of Judaism and Christianity. Christ revealed nothing new with regard to God, but promulgated the very same truth concerning him as Adam, Moses, and the Patriarchs, and in fact the right belief is that Moses and Jesus were essentially one and the same.[1] Indeed, it may be said that the teaching of the Homilies is more Jewish than Christian.[2] In the preliminary Epistle of the Apostle Peter to the Apostle James, when sending the book, Peter entreats that James will not give it to any of the Gentiles,[3] and James says: "Necessarily and rightly our Peter reminded us to take precautions for the security of the truth, that we should not communicate the books of his preachings, sent to us, indiscriminately to all, but to him who is good and discreet and chosen to teach, and who is *circumcised*,[4] being faithful."[5] &c. Clement also is represented as describing his conversion to Christianity in the following terms: "For this cause I fled for refuge to the Holy God and Law of the Jews, with faith in the certain conclusion that, by the righteous judgment of God, both the Law is prescribed, and the soul beyond doubt everywhere receives

---

[1] Hom. xvii. 4; xviii. 14; viii. 6. *Baur*, K. G., i. p. 85 ff.; *Dorner*, Lehre Pers. Christi, i. p. 325, p. 343 ff.; *Mansel*, The Gnostic Heresies, p. 230; *Neander*, K. G., ii. p. 611 ff., p. 621 ff.; *Schliemann*, Die Clem., p. 215 ff.; *Schwegler*, Das nachap. Zeit., i. p. 365 ff., p. 379 ff.; *Uhlhorn*, Die Homilien, p. 212.

[2] *Dorner*, Lehre Pers. Christi, i. p. 325; *Schwegler*, Das nachap. Zeit., i. p. 365.

[3] Ep. Petri ad Jacob. § 1.   [4] Cf. Galatians, ii. 7.

[5] Ἀναγκαίως καὶ πρεπόντως περὶ τῆς ἀληθείας ἀσφαλίζεσθαι ὁ ἡμέτερος ὑπέμνησε Πέτρος, ὅπως τὰς τῶν αὐτοῦ κηρυγμάτων διαπεμφθείσας ἡμῖν βίβλους μηδενὶ μεταδώσωμεν ὡς ἔτυχεν, ἢ ἀγαθῷ τινι καὶ εὐλαβεῖ, τῷ καὶ διδάσκειν αἱρουμένῳ ἐμπεριτύμῳ τε ὄντι πιστῷ, κ.τ.λ. Contestatio, § 1.

the desert of its actions."[1] Peter recommends the inhabitants of Tyre to follow what are really Jewish rites, and to hear " as the God-fearing Jews have heard."[2] The Jew has the same truth as the Christian: "For as there is one teaching by both (Moses and Jesus), God accepts him who believes either of these."[3] The Law was in fact given by Adam as a true prophet knowing all things, and it is called "Eternal," and neither to be abrogated by enemies nor falsified by the impious.[4] The author, therefore, protests against the idea that Christianity is any new thing, and insists that Jesus came to confirm, not abrogate, the Mosaic Law.[5] On the other hand the author of the fourth Gospel represents Christianity in strong contrast and antagonism to Judaism.[6] In his antithetical system, the religion of Jesus is opposed to Judaism as well as all other belief, as Light to Darkness and Life to Death.[7] The Law which Moses gave is treated as merely national, and neither of

[1] Διὰ τοῦτο ἐγὼ τῷ ἁγίῳ τῶν Ἰουδαίων θεῷ καὶ νόμῳ προσέφυγον, ἀποδεδωκὼς τὴν πίστιν ἀσφαλεῖ τῇ κρίσει, ὅτι ἐκ τῆς τοῦ θεοῦ δικαίας κρίσεως καὶ νόμος ὥρισται, καὶ ἡ ψυχὴ πάντως τὰ κατ' ἀξίαν ὧν ἔπραξεν ὁπουδήποτε ἀπολαμβάνει. Hom. iv. 22.

[2] ὡς οἱ θεὸν σέβοντες ἤκουσαν Ἰουδαῖοι. Hom. vii. 4; cf. ii. 19, 20; xiii. 4; *Schliemann*, Die Clementinen, p. 221 f.; *Schwegler*, Das nachap. Zeit., i. p. 368 ff.

[3] Μιᾶς γὰρ δι' ἀμφοτέρων διδασκαλίας οὔσης τὸν τούτων τινὶ πεπιστευκότα ὁ θεὸς ἀποδέχεται. Hom. viii. 6, cf. 7; *Uhlhorn*, Die Homilien, p. 212; *Schwegler*, Das nachap. Zeit., i. p. 366 f.; *Schliemann*, Die Clementinen, p. 221 f. [4] Hom. viii. 10.

[5] Hom. iii. 51; *Dorner*, Lehre Pers. Christi, i. p. 325; *Schwegler*, Das nachap. Zeit., i. p. 366.

[6] *Baur*, Unters. kan. Evv., p. 311 ff., p. 327; *Hilgenfeld*, Die Evangelien, p. 330 ff.; Das Evang. u. d. Br. Joh., p. 188 ff.; *Köstlin*, Lehrbegriff des Ev. u. Br. Johannes, 1843, p. 40 ff., p. 48 ff.; *Schwegler*, Das nachap. Zeit., ii. p. 292 f., p. 359 ff.; *Westcott*, On the Canon, p. 276, note 1.

[7] John xii. 46; i. 4, 5, 7 ff.; iii. 19—21; v. 24; viii. 12; ix. 5; xii. 35 ff.; xiv. 6; *Köstlin*, Lehrb. Ev. Joh., p. 40 f.; *Hilgenfeld*, Die Evangelien, p. 330 f.

general application nor intended to be permanent, being only addressed to the Jews. It is perpetually referred to as the "Law of the Jews," "your Law,"—and the Jewish festivals as Feasts of the Jews, and Jesus neither held the one in any consideration nor did he scruple to shew his indifference to the other.[1] The very name of "the Jews" indeed is used as an equivalent for the enemies of Christ.[2] The religion of Jesus is not only absolute, but it communicates knowledge of the Father which the Jews did not previously possess.[3] The inferiority of Mosaism is everywhere represented: "and out of his fulness all we received, and grace for grace. *Because* the *Law* was given through Moses; *grace and truth* came through Jesus Christ."[4] "Verily verily I say unto you: Moses did not give you the bread from heaven, but my Father giveth you the true bread from heaven."[5] The fundamental difference of Christianity from Judaism will further appear as we proceed.

The most essential principle of the Clementines, again, is Monotheism,—the absolute oneness of God,—which the author vehemently maintains as well against the ascription of divinity to Christ as against heathen Polytheism and the Gnostic theory of the Demiurge as distinguished from the Supreme God.[6] Christ not only is not God,

---

[1] John ii. 13; iv. 20 ff.; v. 1, 16, 18; vi. 4; vii. 2, 19, 22; viii. 17; ix. 16, 28, 29; x. 34; xv. 25, &c. *Baur*, Theol. Jahrb., 1844, 4, p. 624; *Hilgenfeld*, Die Evangelien, p. 330 ff.; *Schwegler*, Das nachap. Zeit., ii. p. 364 f.

[2] John vi. 42, 52, &c., &c. *Baur*, Unters. kan. Evv., p. 163, p. 317 f.; *Fischer*, Tüb. Zeitschr., 1840, h. 2, p. 96 f.; *Hilgenfeld*, Die Evang. Joh., p. 193 f.; *Schwegler*, Das nachap. Zeit., ii. p. 360 f.

[3] John i. 18; viii. 19, 31 ff., 54, 55; xv. 21 f.; xvii. 25, 26.

[4] John i. 16, 17; cf. x. 1, 8.   [5] John vi. 32 ff.

[6] Hom. xvi. 15 ff.; ii. 12; iii. 57, 59; x. 19; xiii. 4; *Baur*, Gnosis, p. 380 ff.; *Dorner*, Lehre Pers. Christi, i. p. 296 ff., p. 325 f., p. 343 ff.; *Hilgenfeld*, Das Ev. Johan., p. 286 f.; *Mansel*, The Gnostic Heresies,

but he never asserted himself to be so.[1] He wholly ignores the doctrine of the Logos, and his speculation is confined to the Σοφία, the Wisdom of Proverbs viii., &c., and is, as we shall see, at the same time a less developed and very different doctrine from that of the fourth Gospel.[2] The idea of a hypostatic Trinity seems to be quite unknown to him, and would have been utterly abhorrent to his mind as sheer Polytheism. On the other hand, the fourth Gospel proclaims the doctrine of a hypostatic Trinity in a more advanced form than any other writing of the New Testament. It is, indeed, the fundamental principle of the work,[3] as the doctrine of the Logos is its most characteristic feature. In the beginning the Word not only was with God, but "the Word was God" (θεὸς ἦν ὁ Λόγος).[4] He is the "only begotten God" (μονογενὴς θεός),[5] equivalent to the "Second God" (δεύτερος θεός) of Philo, and, throughout, his absolutely divine nature is asserted both by the Evangelist, and in express terms in the discourses of Jesus.[6] Nothing could be more opposed to the principles of the Clementines.

p. 227, p. 230; *Schliemann*, Die Clementinen, p. 130, p. 134 ff., 144 f., 200; *Schwegler*, Das nachap. Zeit., i. p. 367, p. 376 f.; cf. ii. p. 270 ff.; Der Montanismus, p. 148 ff.; *Uhlhorn*, Die Hom. u. Recogn., p. 167 ff.

[1] Hom. xvi. 15 f.

[2] Cf. *Dorner*, Lehre Pers. Christi, i. p. 334; *Schwegler*, Das nachap. Zeit., ii. p. 294 f.

[3] *Hilgenfeld*, Das Ev. Joh., p. 113 ff.; *Köstlin*, Lehrbegriff, p. 56 f., 83 ff.; *Reuss*, Hist. de la Théol. Chrétienne au siècle apost., 1864, ii. p. 435 ff.; *Schwegler*, Das nachap. Zeit., ii. p. 369 ff.

[4] John i. 1.

[5] John i. 18. This is the reading of the Cod. Sinaiticus, of the Cod. Vaticanus, and Cod. C., as well as of other ancient MSS., and it must be accepted as the best authenticated.

[6] John i. 2; v. 17 ff.; x. 30 ff., 38; xiv. 7 f., 23; xvii. 5, 21 f., &c.; *Baur*, Unters. kan. Evv. p. 312 ff.; *Ewald*, Die Joh. Schriften, i. p. 116 ff.; *Hilgenfeld*, Das Ev. Joh., p. 84 ff.; *Köstlin*, Lehrbegriff, p. 45 f., 55, 89 ff.; *Reuss*, Hist. Théol. Chrét., ii. p. 435.

According to the Homilies, the same Spirit, the Σοφία, appeared in Adam, Enoch, Noah, Abraham, Isaac, Jacob, Moses, and finally in Jesus, who are the only "true prophets" and are called the seven Pillars (ἑπτὰ στῦλοι) of the world.[1] These seven[2] persons, therefore, are identical, the same true Prophet and Spirit "who from the beginning of the world, changing names and forms, passes through Time,"[3] and these men were thus essentially the same as Jesus.[4] As Neander rightly observes, the author of the Homilies "saw in Jesus a new appearance of that Adam whom he had ever venerated as the source of all the true and divine in man."[5] We need not point out how different these views are from the Logos doctrine of the fourth Gospel.[6] In other points there is an equally wide gulf between the Clementines and the fourth Gospel. According to the author of the Homilies, the chief dogma of

---

[1] Hom. iii. 20 f.; ii. 15; viii. 10; xvii. 4; xviii. 14.

[2] *Credner* considers that only Adam, Moses, and Christ are recognized as identical (W. Zeitschr. wiss. Theol., 1829, 1 h. 2, p. 247 ff.), and so also *Uhlhorn* (Die Homilien, p. 164 ff.); Gfrörer thinks the idea limited to Adam and Christ. (Jahrh. des Heils, i. p. 337). The other authorities referred to below in note 4 hold to the seven. [3] Hom. iii. 20.

[4] *Dorner*, Lehre Pers. Christi, i. pp. 332, 335 ff.; *Mansel*, The Gnostic Heresies, p. 229 ff.; *Neander*, K. G., ii. pp. 612 ff., 621; Genet. Entw. Gnost. Syst., p. 380; *Schliemann*, Die Clementinen, pp. 130, 141 ff., 176, 191 ff., 199 f.; as also, with the sole difference as to number, the authorities quoted in note 2.

[5] K. G., ii. p. 622; cf. Hom. iii. 18 ff.

[6] It is very uncertain by what means the author of the Homilies considered this periodical reappearance to be effected, whether by a kind of transmigration or otherwise. Critics consider it very doubtful whether he admitted the supernatural birth of Jesus (though some hold it to be probable), but at any rate he does not explain the matter: *Uhlhorn*, Die Homilien, p. 209 f.; *Neander*, K. G., ii. p. 618, anm. 1; *Credner* thought that he did not admit it, l. c. p. 253; *Schliemann*, whilst thinking that he did admit it, considers that in that case he equally attributed a supernatural birth to the other seven prophets: Die Clementinen, p. 207 ff.

true Religion is Monotheism. Belief in Christ, in the specific Johannine sense, is nowhere inculcated, and where belief is spoken of, it is merely belief in God. No dogmatic importance whatever is attached to faith in Christ or to his sufferings, death, and resurrection, and of the doctrines of Atonement and Redemption there is nothing in the Homilies,[1]—everyone must make his own reconciliation with God, and bear the punishment of his own sins.[2] On the other hand, the representation of Jesus as the Lamb of God taking away the sins of the world,[3] is the very basis of the fourth Gospel. The passages are innumerable in which belief in Jesus is insisted upon as essential. "He that believeth in the Son hath eternal life, but he that believeth not the Son shall not see life, but the wrath of God abideth on him"[4] . . . . "for if ye believe not that I am he, ye shall die in your sins."[5] In fact, the whole of Christianity according to the author of the fourth Gospel is concentrated in the possession of faith in Christ.[6] Belief in God alone is never held to be sufficient; belief in Christ is necessary for salvation; he died for the sins of the world, and is the object of faith, by which alone forgiveness and justification before God can be secured.[7] The same discrepancy is apparent in smaller details. In the Clementines the Apostle Peter

---

[1] *Schliemann*, ib., p. 217 ff.; *Uhlhorn*, ib., p. 211 f.; *Dorner*, Lehre Pers. Chr., i. p. 338 f.; *Schwegler*, Das nachap. Zeit., i. p. 367 f.

[2] Hom. iii. 6 f.; *Uhlhorn*, ib., p. 212.

[3] John i. 29; cf. iii. 14 ff., iv. 42, &c., &c.

[4] John iii. 36; cf. 16 f.   [5] Ib., viii. 24.

[6] Ib., iii. 14 ff.; v. 24 ff.; vi. 29, 35 ff., 40, 47, 65; vii. 38; viii. 24, 51; ix. 35 ff.; x. 9, 28; xi. 25 ff.; xii. 47; xiv. 6; xv. 5 f.; xvi. 9; xvii. 2 ff.; xx. 31.

[7] *Baur*, Unters. kan. Evv., p. 312; *Hilgenfeld*, Das Ev. Joh., pp. 256 ff., 285 ff.; *Köstlin*, Lehrbegriff, pp. 57, 178 ff.; *Reuss*, Hist. Théol. Chrét., ii. pp. 427 f., 491 ff., 508 ff.

is the principal actor, and is represented as the chief amongst the Apostles. In the Epistle of Clement to James, which precedes the Homilies, Peter is described in the following terms: "Simon, who, on account of his true faith and of the principles of his doctrine, which were most sure, was appointed to be the foundation of the Church, and for this reason his name was by the unerring voice of Jesus himself changed to Peter; the first-fruit of our Lord; the first of the Apostles to whom first the Father revealed the Son; whom the Christ deservedly pronounced blessed; the called and chosen and companion and fellow-traveller (of Jesus); the admirable and approved disciple, who as fittest of all was commanded to enlighten the West, the darker part of the world, and was enabled to guide it aright," &c.[1] He is here represented as the Apostle to the Heathen, the hated Apostle Paul being robbed of that honourable title, and he is, in the spirit of this introduction, made to play, throughout, the first part amongst the Apostles.[2] In the fourth Gospel, however, he is assigned a place quite secondary to John,[3] who is the disciple whom Jesus loved and who leans on his bosom.[4] We shall only mention one other point. The Homilist, when attacking the Apostle Paul, under the

---

[1] Σίμων, ὁ διὰ τὴν ἀληθῆ πίστιν καὶ τὴν ἀσφαλεστάτην αὐτοῦ τῆς διδασκαλίας ὑπόθεσιν τῆς Ἐκκλησίας θεμέλιος εἶναι ὁρισθεὶς καὶ δι' αὐτὸ τοῦτο ὑπ' αὐτοῦ τοῦ Ἰησοῦ ἀψευδεῖ στόματι μετονομασθεὶς Πέτρος· ἡ ἀπαρχὴ τοῦ Κυρίου ἡμῶν· ὁ τῶν ἀποστόλων πρῶτος, ᾧ πρώτῳ ὁ Πατὴρ τὸν Υἱὸν ἀπεκάλυψεν· ὃν ὁ Χριστὸς εὐλόγως ἐμακάρισεν· ὁ κλητὸς καὶ ἐκλεκτὸς καὶ συνέστιος καὶ συνοδοίπορος· ὁ καλὸς καὶ δόκιμος μαθητής· ὁ τῆς δύσεως τὸ σκοτεινότερον τοῦ κόσμου μέρος ὡς πάντων ἱκανώτερος φωτίσαι κελευσθεὶς καὶ κατορθῶσαι δυνηθείς, κ.τ.λ. Ep. Clem. ad Jacobum, § 1.

[2] Baur, K. G., i. p. 104 ff.

[3] Baur, Theol. Jahrb., 1844, 4, p. 627 ff.; Unters. Kan. Evv., p. 320 ff.; Hilgenfeld, Die Evangelien, p. 335; Schwegler, Das nachap. Zeit., ii. p. 355 ff.

[4] Cf. John xiii. 23—25; xix. 26 f.; xx. 2 f.; xxi. 3 ff., 7, 20 ff.

name of Simon the Magician, for his boast that he had not been taught by man, but by a revelation of Jesus Christ,[1] whom he had only seen in a vision, inquires: Why, then, did the Teacher remain and discourse a whole year to us who were awake, if you became his Apostle after a single hour of instruction?[2] As Neander aptly remarks: "But if the author had known from the Johannine Gospel that the teaching of Christ had continued for *several years,* he would certainly have had particularly good reason instead of one year to set *several.*"[3] It is obvious that an author with so vehement an animosity against Paul would assuredly have strengthened his argument, by adopting the more favourable statement of the fourth Gospel as to the duration of the ministry of Jesus, had he been acquainted with that work.

Our attention must now be turned to the anonymous composition, known as the "Epistle to Diognetus," general particulars regarding which we have elsewhere given.[4] This epistle, it is admitted, does not contain any quotation from any evangelical work, but on the strength of some supposed references it is claimed by apologists as evidence for the existence of the fourth Gospel. Tischendorf, who only devotes a dozen lines to this work, states his case as follows: "Although this short apologetic epistle contains no precise quotation from any gospel, yet it contains repeated references to evangelical, and particularly to Johannine, passages. For when the author writes, ch. 6: 'Christians dwell in the world, but they are not of the world;' and in

[1] Gal. i. 12 f.
[2] Hom., xvii. 19.
[3] K. G., ii. p. 624, anm. 1.
[4] Vol. ii. p. 38 ff.

ch. 10: 'For God has loved men, for whose sakes he made the world .... to whom he sent his only begotten Son,' the reference to John xvii. 11 ('But they are in the world'); 14 ('The world hateth them, for they are not of the world'); 16 ('They are not of the world as I am not of the world'); and to John iii. 16 ('God so loved the world that he gave his only begotten Son'), is hardly to be mistaken."[1]

Dr. Westcott still more emphatically claims the epistle as evidence for the fourth Gospel, and we shall, in order impartially to consider the question, likewise quote his remarks in full upon the point, but as he introduces his own paraphrase of the context in a manner which does not properly convey its true nature to a reader who has not the epistle before him, we shall take the liberty of putting the actual quotations in italics, and the rest must be taken as purely the language of Canon Westcott. We shall hereafter show also the exact separation which exists between phrases which are here, with the mere indication of some omission, brought together to form the supposed references to the fourth Gospel. Canon Westcott says: "In one respect the two parts of the book are united,[2] inasmuch as they both exhibit a combination of the teaching of St. Paul and St. John. The love of God, it is said in the letter to Diognetus, is the source of love in the Christian, who must needs '*love God who thus first loved him*' (προαγαπήσαντα), and find an expression for this love by loving his neighbour,

---

[1] Wann wurden, u. s. w., p. 40. We may mention that neither Tischendorf nor Dr. Westcott gives the Greek of any of the passages pointed out in the Epistle, nor do they give the original text of the parallels in the Gospel.

[2] This is a reference to the admitted fact that the first ten chapters are by a different author from the writer of the last two.

whereby he will be '*an imitator of God.*' '*For God loved men, for whose sakes He made the world, to whom He subjected all things that are in the earth . . . . unto whom* (πρός) *He sent His only begotten Son, to whom He promised the kingdom in heaven* (τὴν ἐν οὐρανῷ βασιλείαν), *and will give it to those who love Him.*' God's will is mercy; '*He sent His Son as wishing to save* (ὡς σώζων) . . . . *and not to condemn,*' and as witnesses of this, '*Christians dwell in the world, though they are not of the world.*'[1] At the close of the paragraph he proceeds: "The presence of the teaching of St. John is here placed beyond all doubt. There are, however, no direct references to the Gospels throughout the letter, nor indeed any allusions to our Lord's discourses."[2]

It is clear that as there is no direct reference to any Gospel in the Epistle to Diognetus, even if it were ascertained to be a composition dating from the middle of the second century, which it is not, and even if the indirect allusions were ten times more probable than they are, this anonymous work could do nothing towards establishing the apostolic origin and historical character

[1] On the Canon, p. 77. Dr. Westcott continues, referring to the later and more recent part of the Epistle: "So in the conclusion we read that 'the Word who was from the beginning . . . at His appearance speaking boldly manifested the mysteries of the Father to those who were judged faithful by Him.' And these again to whom the Word speaks 'from love of that which is revealed to them,' share their knowledge with others." It is not necessary to discuss this, both because of the late date of the two chapters, and because there is certainly no reference at all to the Gospel in the words. We must, however, add, that as the quotation is given it conveys quite a false impression of the text. We may just mention that the phrase which Dr. Westcott quotes as: "the Word who was from the beginning," is in the text: "This is he who was from the beginning" (οὗτος ὁ ἀπ' ἀρχῆς) although "the Word" is in the context, and no doubt intended.

[2] *Ib.*, p. 78.

of the fourth Gospel. Written, however, as we believe it to have been, at a much later period, it scarcely requires any consideration here.

We shall, however, for those who may be interested in more minutely discussing the point, at once proceed to examine whether the composition even indicates the existence of the Gospel, and for this purpose we shall take each of the passages in question and place them with their context before the reader; and we only regret that the examination of a document which, neither from its date nor evidence can be of any real weight, should detain us so long. The first passage is: "Christians dwell in the world but are not of the world" (χριστιανοὶ ἐν κόσμῳ οἰκοῦσιν, οὐκ εἰσὶ δὲ ἐκ τοῦ κόσμου). Dr. Westcott, who reverses the order of all the passages indicated, introduces this sentence (which occurs in chapter vi.) as the consequence of a passage following it in chapter vii. by the words "and as witnesses of this: Christians," &c. . . . The first parallel which is pointed out in the Gospel reads, John xvii. 11: "And I am no more in the world, and these are in the world (καὶ οὗτοι ἐν τῷ κόσμῳ εἰσίν), and I come to thee, Holy Father keep them," &c. Now it must be evident that in mere direct point of language and sense there is no parallel here at all. In the Gospel, the disciples are referred to as being left behind in the world by Jesus who goes to the Father, whilst, in the Epistle, the object is the antithesis that while Christians *dwell* in the world they are not of the world. In the second parallel, which is supposed to complete the analogy, the Gospel reads: v. 14, "I have given them thy word: and the world hated them because they are not of the world, (καὶ ὁ κόσμος ἐμίσησεν αὐτούς, ὅτι οὐκ εἰσὶν ἐκ τοῦ κόσμου) even as I am not of the world." Here, again, the parallel words are merely introduced as a reason why the world hated them, and not antithetically, and from this very connection we shall see that the resemblance between the Epistle and the Gospel is merely superficial.

In order to form a correct judgment regarding the nature of the passage in the Epistle, we must carefully examine the context. In chapter v. the author is speaking of the manners of Christians, and he says that they are not distinguished from others either by country or language or by their customs, for they have neither cities nor speech of their own, nor do they lead a singular life. They dwell in their native countries, but only as sojourners (πάροικοι), and the writer proceeds by a long sequence of antithetical sentences to depict their habits. "Every foreign land is as their native country, yet the land of their birth is a foreign land" (πᾶσα ξένη, πατρίς ἐστιν αὐτῶν· καὶ πᾶσα πατρὶς, ξένη), and so on. Now this epistle is in great part a mere plagiarism of the Pauline and other canonical epistles, whilst professing to describe the actual life of Christians, and the fifth and sixth chapters, particularly, are based upon the epistles of Paul and notably the 2nd Epistle to the Corinthians, from which even the antithetical style is derived. We may give a specimen of this in referring to the context of the passage before us, and it is important that we should do so. After a few sentences like the above the fifth chapter continues: "They are in the flesh, but do not live according to the flesh. They continue on earth, but are citizens of heaven" (ἐπὶ γῆς διατρίβουσιν ἀλλ' ἐν οὐρανῷ πολιτεύονται).[1]

[1] The whole passage in the Epistle recalls many passages in the works of Philo, with which the writer was evidently well acquainted. One occurs to us. Speaking of Laban and his family, that "they dwelt as in their native country, not as in a foreign land" (ὡς ἐν πατρίδι, οὐχ ὡς ἐπὶ ξένης παρῴκησαν), he continues after a few reflections: "For this reason all the wise men according to Moses are represented as sojourners, (παροικοῦντες), for their souls are indeed sent from heaven to earth as to a colony. . . . . they return thither again whence they first proceeded, regarding indeed as their native land the heavenly country in which they are citizens, but as a foreign land the earthly dwelling in which they sojourn" (πατρίδα μὲν τὸν οὐράνιον χῶρον ἐν ᾧ πολιτεύονται, ξένον δὲ τὸν περίγειον ἐν ᾧ παρῴκησαν νομίζουσαι). And a little further on: "But Moses saith: 'I am a stranger in a foreign land,' regarding with perfect distinction the abiding in the body not only as a foreign land, as sojourners do, but also as worthy of estrangement, not considering it one's own home." De Confus. Ling., § 17, Mangey, i. 416. One more instance: "First that God does not grant to the lover of virtue to dwell in the body as in his own native land, but only permits him to sojourn in it as in a strange country. . . . . But the country of the body is kindred to every bad man, in which he is careful to dwell, not to sojourn," &c. Quis Rerum Div. Heres, § 54, Mang., i. 512. Cf. § 55; De Confus. Ling., § 22, ib., i. 421; De Migrat. Abrahami, § 2, ib., i. 438, § 28, ib., i. 460.

EPISTLE TO DIOGNETUS, V.	2ND EP. TO CORINTHIANS.
They obey the prescribed laws and exceed the laws in their own lives. They love all and are persecuted by all.	A paraphrase of vi. 3—6 (cf. iv. 2, 8—9).
They are unknown and are condemned.	vi. 9. As unknown and well known; as dying and behold we live; as chastened and not put to death.
They are put to death and are made alive.	
They are poor and make many rich; they are in need of all things and in all abound.	10. . . . . As poor yet making many rich; as having nothing and possessing all.
They are dishonoured and in their dishonour honoured; they are profanely reported[1] and are justified.	8. Through honour and dishonour; through evil report and good report; as deceivers; and true.
They are reviled and bless,[2] &c., &c.	1 Cor. iv. 12. Being reviled we bless.[3]

It is very evident here, and throughout the Epistle, that the Epistles of Paul chiefly, together with the other canonical Epistles, are the sources of the writer's inspiration. The next chapter (vi.) begins and proceeds as follows: "To say all in a word: what the soul is in the body, that Christians are in the world. The soul is dispersed throughout all the members of the body, and Christians throughout all the cities of the world. The soul dwells in the body but is not of the body, and Christians dwell in the world, but are not of the world. (Οἰκεῖ μὲν ἐν τῷ σώματι ψυχή, οὐκ ἔστι δὲ ἐκ τοῦ σώματος· καὶ Χριστιανοὶ ἐν κόσμῳ οἰκοῦσιν, οὐκ εἰσὶ δὲ ἐκ τοῦ κόσμου.) The invisible soul is kept in the visible body, and Christians are known, indeed, to be in the world, but their worship of God remains invisible. The flesh hates the soul and wages war against it, although in no way wronged by it, because it is restrained from indulgence in sensual pleasures, and the world hates Christians,

---

[1] Cf. 1 Cor. iv. 13.

[2] Ἀγνοοῦνται, καὶ κατακρίνονται. Θανατοῦνται, καὶ ζωοποιοῦνται· πτωχεύουσι, καὶ πλουτίζουσι πολλούς. Πάντων ὑστεροῦνται, καὶ ἐν πᾶσι περισσεύουσιν. Ἀτιμοῦνται, καὶ ἐν ταῖς ἀτιμίαις δοξάζονται· βλασφημοῦνται, καὶ δικαιοῦνται· λοιδοροῦνται, καὶ εὐλογοῦσιν κ.τ.λ. Ep. ad Diogn. v.

[3] 2 Cor. vi. 9, ὡς ἀγνοούμενοι καὶ ἐπιγινωσκόμενοι, ὡς ἀποθνῄσκοντες καὶ ἰδοὺ ζῶμεν, ὡς παιδευόμενοι καὶ μὴ θανατούμενοι, 10 . . . . ὡς πτωχοὶ πολλοὺς δὲ πλουτίζοντες, ὡς μηδὲν ἔχοντες καὶ πάντα κατέχοντες. 8. διὰ δόξης καὶ ἀτιμίας, διὰ δυσφημίας καὶ εὐφημίας· ὡς πλάνοι καὶ ἀληθεῖς. 1 Cor. iv. 12 . . . . λοιδορούμενοι εὐλογοῦμεν, κ.τ.λ.

although in no way wronged by them, because they are opposed to sensual pleasures (μισεῖ καὶ Χριστιανοὺς ὁ κόσμος μηδὲν ἀδικούμενος, ὅτι ταῖς ἡδοναῖς ἀντιτάσσονται). The soul loves the flesh that hates it, and the members, and Christians love those who hate them" (καὶ Χριστιανοὶ τοὺς μισοῦντας ἀγαπῶσιν). And so on with three or four similar sentences, one of which, at least, is taken from the Epistle to the Corinthians,[1] to the end of the chapter.

Now the passages pointed out as references to the fourth Gospel, it will be remembered, distinctly differ from the parallels in the Gospel, and it seems to us clear that they arise naturally out of the antithetical manner which the writer adopts from the Epistles of Paul, and are based upon passages in those Epistles closely allied to them in sense and also in language. The simile in connection with which the words occur is commenced at the beginning of the preceding chapter, where Christians are represented as living as strangers even in their native land, and the very essence of the passage in dispute is given in the two sentences: "They are in the flesh, but do not live according to the flesh" (ἐν σαρκὶ τυγχάνουσιν, ἀλλ' οὐ κατὰ σάρκα ζῶσιν), which is based upon 2 Cor. x. 3, "For we walk in the flesh, but do not war[2] according to the flesh" (ἐν σαρκὶ γὰρ περιπατοῦντες οὐ κατὰ σάρκα στρατευόμεθα), and similar passages abound; as for instance, Rom. viii. 4 . . . "in us who walk not according to the flesh, but according to the Spirit; 9. But ye are not in the flesh but in the Spirit (ὑμεῖς δὲ οὐκ ἐστὲ ἐν σαρκὶ ἀλλὰ ἐν πνεύματι): 12 . . . So then, brethren, we are debtors not to the flesh, that we should live after the flesh" (οὐ τῇ σαρκὶ τοῦ κατὰ σάρκα ζῆν) &c., &c. (Cf. 4, 14.). And the second: "They continue on earth but are citizens of heaven" (ἐπὶ γῆς διατρίβουσιν, ἀλλ' ἐν οὐρανῷ πολιτεύονται), which recalls Philip. iii. 20: "For our country (our citizenship) is in heaven" (ἡμῶν γὰρ τὸ πολίτευμα ἐν οὐρανοῖς ὑπάρχει).[3] The sense of the passage is everywhere found, and nothing is more natural than

---

[1] "The immortal soul dwells in a mortal tabernacle, and Christians dwell as strangers in corruptible (bodies), awaiting the incorruption in the heavens (καὶ Χριστιανοὶ παροικοῦσιν ἐν φθαρτοῖς, τὴν ἐν οὐρανοῖς ἀφθαρσίαν προσδεχόμενοι). Ep. ad Diogn. vi. Cf. 1 Cor. xv. 53, 54; 2 Cor. v. 1 ff.

[2] The preceding verse has "walk," instead of "war."

[3] Cf. Ephes. ii. 19; Heb. xii. 22; xiii. 14.

the use of the words arising both out of the previous reference to the position of Christians as mere sojourners in the world, and as the antithesis to the preceding part of the sentence: "The soul dwells in the body, but is not of the body," and: "Christians dwell in the world but are not of the world." Cf. 1 Cor. ii. 12; vii. 31; 2 Cor. i. 12. Gal. iv. 29, v. 16 ff. 24, 25, vi. 14. Rom. viii. 3 ff. Ephes. ii. 2, 3, 11 ff. Coloss. iii. 2 ff: Titus ii. 12. James i. 27. There is one point, however, which we think shows that the words were not derived from the fourth Gospel. The parallel with the Epistle can only be made by taking a few words out of xvii. 11 and adding to them a few words in verse 14, where they stand in the following connection " And the world hated them, *because they are not of the world*" (καὶ ὁ κόσμος ἐμίσησεν αὐτούς, ὅτι οὐκ εἰσὶν ἐκ τοῦ κόσμου). In the Epistle, in a passage quoted above, we have: "The flesh hates the soul, and wages war against it, although unjustly, because it is restrained from indulgence in sensual pleasures, and the world hates Christians, *although in no way wronged by them, because they are opposed to sensual pleasures*." (Μισεῖ τὴν ψυχὴν ἡ σάρξ, καὶ πολεμεῖ, μηδὲν ἀδικουμένη, διότι ταῖς ἡδοναῖς κωλύεται χρῆσθαι· μισεῖ καὶ Χριστιανοὺς ὁ κόσμος μηδὲν ἀδικούμενος, ὅτι ταῖς ἡδοναῖς ἀντιτάσσονται.)

Now nothing could more clearly show that these analogies are mere accidental coincidence, and not derived from the fourth Gospel, than this passage. If the writer had really had the passage in the Gospel in his mind, it is impossible that he could in this manner have completely broken it up and changed its whole context and language. The phrase: "they are not of the world" would have been introduced here as the reason for the hatred, instead of being used with quite different context elsewhere in the passage. In fact, in the only place in which the words would have presented a true parallel with the Gospel, they are not used. Not the slightest reference is made throughout the Epistle to Diognetus to any of the discourses of Jesus. On the other hand, we have seen that the whole of the passage in the Epistle in which these sentences occur is based both in matter, and in its peculiar antithetical form, upon the Epistles of Paul, and in these and other canonical Epistles again, we find the source of the sentence just quoted: Gal. iv. 29. "But as then, he that was born after the flesh persecuted him (that was born) after the Spirit, even so it is now."[1] v. 16. " Walk by the Spirit, and ye shall not fulfil the lust of the flesh. 17. For the flesh lusteth against the Spirit and the Spirit against the flesh : for these are contrary the one to the other, that ye may not do the things that ye would."[2] There are innumerable passages in the Pauline Epistles to the same effect.

We pass on now to the next passage in the order of the Epistle. It is not mentioned at all by Tischendorf : Dr. Westcott introduces it with the words : " God's will is mercy," by which we presume that he means to paraphrase the context. " He sent his Son as wishing to save (ὡς σώζων) . . . . and not to condemn."[3] This sentence, however, which is given as quotation without any explanation, is purely a composition by Canon Westcott himself out of different materials which he finds in the Epistle, and is not a quotation at all. The actual passage in the Epistle, with its immediate context, is as follows : " This (Messenger—the Truth, the holy Word) he sent to them; now, was it, as one of men might reason, for tyranny and to cause fear and consternation ? Not so, but in clemency and gentleness, as a King sending his Son (πέμπων υἱόν) a king, he sent (ἔπεμψεν); as God he sent (him) ; as towards men he sent ; as saving he sent (ὡς σώζων ἔπεμψεν) (him) ; as persuading (ὡς πείθων), not forcing, for violence has no place with God. He sent as inviting, not vindictively pursuing ; he sent as loving, not condemning (ἔπεμψεν ὡς ἀγαπῶν, οὐ κρίνων). For he will send him to judge, and who shall abide his presence?"[4] The supposed parallel in the Gospel is as follows (John iii. 17) : " For God sent not his Son into the world that he might condemn the

---

[1] Ἀλλ' ὥσπερ τότε ὁ κατὰ σάρκα γεννηθεὶς ἐδίωκεν τὸν κατὰ πνεῦμα, οὕτως καὶ νῦν. Gal. iv. 29.

[2] Gal. v. 16, πνεύματι περιπατεῖτε καὶ ἐπιθυμίαν σαρκὸς οὐ μὴ τελέσητε· 17, ἡ γὰρ σὰρξ ἐπιθυμεῖ κατὰ τοῦ πνεύματος, τὸ δὲ πνεῦμα κατὰ τῆς σαρκός· ταῦτα δὲ ἀλλήλοις ἀντίκειται, ἵνα μὴ ἃ ἂν θέλητε ταῦτα ποιῆτε. Cf. 18—25 ; Titus ii. 12. [3] On the Canon, p. 77.

[4] Τοῦτον πρὸς αὐτοὺς ἀπέστειλεν, ἆρά γες ὡς ἀνθρώπων ἄν τις λογίσαιτο, ἐπὶ τυραννίδι καὶ φόβῳ καὶ καταπλήξει ; Οὐμενοῦν, ἀλλ' ἐν ἐπιεικείᾳ, πραΰτητι· ὡς βασιλεὺς πέμπων υἱὸν βασιλέα ἔπεμψεν· ὡς θεὸν ἔπεμψεν, ὡς πρὸς ἀνθρώπους ἔπεμψεν, ὡς σώζων ἔπεμψεν· ὡς πείθων, οὐ βιαζόμενος· βία γὰρ οὐ πρόσεστι τῷ θεῷ. Ἔπεμψεν ὡς καλῶν, οὐ διώκων· ἔπεμψεν ὡς ἀγαπῶν, οὐ κρίνων. Πέμψει γὰρ αὐτὸν κρίνοντα, καὶ τίς αὐτοῦ τὴν παρουσίαν ὑποστήσεται ; C. vii.

world, but that the world through him might be saved"[1] (οὐ γὰρ ἀπέστειλεν ὁ Θεὸς τὸν υἱὸν αὐτοῦ εἰς τὸν κόσμον ἵνα κρίνῃ τὸν κόσμον, ἀλλ' ἵνα σωθῇ ὁ κόσμος δι' αὐτοῦ). Now, it is obvious at a glance that the passage in the Epistle is completely different from that in the Gospel in every material point of construction and language, and the only similarity consists in the idea that God's intention in sending his Son was to save and not to condemn, and it is important to notice that the letter does not, either here or elsewhere, refer to the condition attached to salvation so clearly enunciated in the preceding verse: "That whosoever believeth in him might not perish." The doctrine enunciated in this passage is the fundamental principle of much of the New Testament, and it is expressed with more especial clearness and force, and close analogy with the language of the letter, in the Epistles of Paul, to which the letter more particularly leads us, as well as in other canonical Epistles, and in these we find analogies with the context quoted above, which confirm our belief that they, and not the Gospel, are the source of the passage—Rom. v. 8 : "But God proveth his own love towards us, in that while we were yet sinners Christ died for us. 9. Much more then . . . . shall we be saved (σωθησόμεθα) through him from the wrath (to come)." Cf. 16, 17. Rom. viii. 1 : "There is, therefore, now no condemnation (κατάκριμα) to them which are in Christ Jesus.[2] 3 . . . . God sending his own Son" (ὁ θεὸς τὸν ἑαυτοῦ υἱὸν πέμψας),[3] &c. And coming to the very 2nd Epistle to the Corinthians, from which we find the writer borrowing wholesale, we meet with the different members of the passage we have quoted : v. 19 . . . . "God was reconciling the world unto himself in Christ, not reckoning unto them their trespasses. . . . . 20. On Christ's behalf, then, we are ambassadors, as though God were entreating by us ; we pray on Christ's behalf: Be reconciled to God. v. 10. For we must all appear before the judgment seat of Christ, &c. 11. Knowing, then, the fear of

---

[1] The previous verse which we shall more particularly have to consider with the next passage, reads: 16. "For God so loved the world that he gave his only begotten son, that whosoever believeth in him might not perish, but have eternal life."

[2] The Cod. Alex., and some other ancient MSS. add : "who walk not after the flesh," μὴ κατὰ σάρκα περιπατοῦσιν.

[3] Cf. vv. 32—35, 39.

the Lord, we persuade (πείθομεν) men," &c. Galatians iv. 4: "But when the fulness of time came, God sent out his Son (ἐξαπέστειλεν ὁ θεὸς τὸν υἱὸν αὐτοῦ), 5. That he might redeem them that were under the law, that we might receive the adoption of sons,"[1] &c. Ephes. ii. 4. "But God being rich in mercy because of his great love wherewith he loved us, 5. Even when we were dead in our trespasses, quickened us together with Christ—by grace ye have been saved"—cf. verses 7, 8. 1 Thess. v. 9. "For God appointed us not to wrath, but to the obtaining salvation (σωτηρίας) through our Lord Jesus Christ." 1 Tim. i. 15. "This is a faithful saying . . . . that Christ Jesus came into the world to save sinners" (ἁμαρτωλοὺς σῶσαι). 1 Tim. ii. 3. "For this is good and acceptable in the sight of God our Saviour (τοῦ σωτῆρος ἡμῶν θεοῦ). 4. Who willeth all men to be saved" (ὃς πάντας ἀνθρώπους θέλει σωθῆναι). Cf. v. 5, 6. 2 Tim. i. 9. "Who saved us (σώσαντος ἡμᾶς), and called us with a holy calling, not according to our works, but according to his own purpose, and the grace which was given to us in Christ Jesus before time began; 10. But hath been made manifest by the appearing of our Saviour (σωτῆρος) Jesus Christ."[2] These passages might be indefinitely multiplied; and they contain the sense of the passage, and in many cases the language, more closely than the fourth Gospel, with which the construction and form of the sentence has no analogy.

Now, with regard to the Logos doctrine of the Epistle to

[1] The letter to Diognetus may further be connected with the Ep. to the Galatians in the remarks which the writer makes (iv.) on the observance of days, &c., by the Jews: "But regarding their attending to the stars and moon, observing the months and days," &c. (παρατήρησιν τῶν μηνῶν καὶ τῶν ἡμερῶν, κ.τ.λ.). Cf. Gal. iv. 10. "Are ye observing days and months, and times and years?" &c. (ἡμέρας παρατηρεῖσθε καὶ μῆνας καὶ καιροὺς καὶ ἐνιαυτούς;)

[2] In Ch. xi. which, it will be remembered, is acknowledged to be of later date, and not by the writer of the earlier part, the author, an admitted falsifier therefore, represents himself, as the writer of the letter, as: "having been a disciple of the Apostles, I am become a teacher of the Gentiles." (ἀποστόλων γενόμενος μαθητής, γίνομαι διδάσκαλος ἐθνῶν· c. xi.) Having observed the imitation in the earlier part of the letter of the Pauline Epistles, the writer of the last two chapters is induced to make this statement after an Epistle ascribed to Paul: 2 Tim. i. 11: "For which I was appointed a herald, and an Apostle, and a teacher of the Gentiles." (καὶ ἀπόστολος καὶ διδάσκαλος ἐθνῶν.)

Diognetus, to which we may appropriately here refer, although we must deal with it in the briefest manner possible, so far is it from connecting the Epistle with the fourth Gospel, that it much more proves the writer's ignorance of that Gospel. The peculiar terminology of the prologue to the Gospel is nowhere found in the Epistle, and we have already seen that the term Logos was applied to Jesus in works of the New Testament, acknowledged by all to have been written long before the fourth Gospel. Indeed, it is quite certain, not only historically, but also from the abrupt enunciation of the doctrine in the prologue, that the theory of the Logos was well known and already applied to Jesus before the Gospel was composed. The author knew that his statement would be understood without explanation. Although the writer of the Epistle makes use of the designation "Logos," he shows his Greek culture by giving the precedence to the term Truth or Reason. It has indeed been remarked[1] that the name Jesus or Christ does not occur anywhere in the Epistle. By way of showing the manner in which "the Word" is spoken of, we will give the entire passage, part of which is quoted above; the first and only one in the first ten chapters in which the term is used: "For, as I said, this was not an earthly invention which was delivered to them (Christians), neither is it a mortal system which they deem it right to maintain so carefully; nor is an administration of human mysteries entrusted to them, but the Almighty and invisible God himself, the Creator of all things (ἀλλ' αὐτὸς ὁ παντοκράτωρ καὶ παντοκτίστης καὶ ἀόρατος θεός) has implanted in men, and established in their hearts from heaven, the Truth and the Word, the holy and incomprehensible (τὴν Ἀλήθειαν καὶ τὸν Λόγον τὸν ἅγιον καὶ ἀπερινόητον), not as one might suppose, sending to men some servant or angel or ruler (ἄρχοντα), or one of those ordering earthly affairs, or one of those entrusted with the government of heavenly things, but the artificer and creator of the universe (τὸν τεχνίτην καὶ δημιουργὸν τῶν ὅλων) himself, by whom he created the heavens (ᾧ τοὺς οὐρανοὺς ἔκτισεν);[2] by

[1] *Donaldson*, Hist. Chr. Lit. and Doctr. ii. p. 127.

[2] John i. 3. "All things were made by him; and without him was not anything made that hath been made (πάντα δι' αὐτοῦ ἐγένετο, καὶ χωρὶς αὐτοῦ ἐγένετο οὐδὲ ἓν ὃ γέγονεν.) The difference of this language will be remarked.

whom he confined the sea within its own bounds; whose commands (μυστήρια—mysteries) all the stars (στοιχεῖα—elements) faithfully observe; from whom (the sun) has received the measure of the daily course to observe; whom the moon obeys, being bidden to shine at night; whom the stars obey, following in the course of the moon; by whom all things have been arranged and limited and subjected, the heavens and the things in the heavens, the earth and the things in the earth, the sea and the things in the sea (οὐρανοὶ καὶ τὰ ἐν οὐρανοῖς, γῇ καὶ τὰ ἐν τῇ γῇ, θάλασσα καὶ τὰ ἐν τῇ θαλάσσῃ), fire, air, abyss, the things in the heights, the things in the depths, the things in the space between. This (Messenger—the truth, the Word) he sent to them. Now, was it, as one of men might reason, for tyranny and to cause fear and consternation? Not so, but in clemency and gentleness, as a King sending his Son, a king, he sent; as God he sent (him); as towards men he sent, as saving he sent (him); as persuading," &c., &c.[1] The description here given, how God in fact by Reason or Wisdom created the Universe, has much closer analogy with earlier representations of the doctrine than with that in the fourth Gospel, and if the writer does also represent the Reason in a hypostatic form, it is by no means with the concreteness of the Gospel doctrine of the Logos, with which linguistically, moreover, as we have observed, it has no similarity. There can be no doubt that his Christology presents differences from that of the fourth Gospel.[2]

We have already seen how Jesus is called the Word in works of the New Testament earlier than the fourth Gospel,[3] and how the doctrine is constantly referred to in the Pauline Epistles and the Epistle to the Hebrews, and it is to these, and not to the fourth Gospel, that the account in the Epistle to Diognetus may be more properly traced. Heb. i. 2. "The Son of God by whom also he made the worlds. 10. The heavens are works of thy hands" (ἔργα τῶν χειρῶν σου εἰσὶν οἱ οὐρανοί). xi. 3. "By faith we understand that the worlds were framed (κατηρτίσθαι), by the word of God" (ῥήματι θεοῦ). 1 Cor. viii. 6. "Jesus Christ by whom are all things" (δι' οὗ τὰ πάντα). Coloss. i. 13. ". . . The

---

[1] Ep. ad Diogn., vii.

[2] Cf. *Dorner*, Lehre Pers. Christi, i. p. 413 ff.; *Donaldson*, Hist. Chr. Lit. and Doctr., ii. p. 127 ff.

[3] Rev. xix. 13; vi. 9; xx. 4; Heb. iv. 12, 13; xi. 3.

Son of his love: 15. Who is the image of the invisible God (τοῦ Θεοῦ τοῦ ἀοράτου) the first-born of all creation; 16. Because in him were all things created, the things in the heavens, and the things in the earth, the things visible and the things invisible (ὅτι ἐν αὐτῷ ἐκτίσθη τὰ πάντα τὰ ἐν τοῖς οὐρανοῖς καὶ τὰ ἐπὶ τῆς γῆς, τὰ ὁρατὰ, καὶ τὰ ἀόρατα) whether they be thrones or dominions, or principalities, or powers; All things have been created by him and for him (τὰ πάντα δι' αὐτοῦ καὶ εἰς αὐτὸν ἔκτισται). 17. And he is before all things, and in him all things subsist. 18. And he is the head of the body, the Church, who is the Beginning[1] (ὅς ἐστιν ἀρχή); the first-born from the dead; that in all things he might be the first. 19. Because he was well pleased that in him should all the fulness dwell. 20. And through him to reconcile all things unto himself," &c., &c. These passages might be greatly multiplied, but it is unnecessary, for the matter of the letter is substantially here. As to the titles of King and God they are everywhere to be found. In the Apocalypse, the Lamb whose name is "The Word of God" (ὁ Λόγος τοῦ Θεοῦ), (xix. 13) has also his name written (xix. 16), "King of kings and Lord of lords" (Βασιλεὺς βασιλέων καὶ Κύριος κυρίων).[2] We have already quoted the views of Philo regarding the Logos, which also merit comparison with the passage of the Epistle, but we cannot repeat them here.

The last passage to which we have to refer is the following: "For God loved men, for whose sakes He made the world, to whom He subjected all things that are in the earth ... Unto whom (πρός) He sent his only-begotten Son, to whom He promised the kingdom in heaven (τὴν ἐν οὐρανῷ βασιλείαν) and will give it to those who love Him."[3] The context is as follows: "For God loved men (ὁ γὰρ θεὸς τοὺς ἀνθρώπους ἠγάπησε) for whose sake he made the world, to whom he subjected all things that are in it, to whom he gave reason and intelligence, to whom alone he granted the right of looking towards him, whom he formed after his own image, to whom he sent his only begotten son (πρὸς οὓς ἀπέστειλε τὸν υἱὸν αὐτοῦ τὸν μονογενῆ), to whom he has promised the kingdom in heaven, and will give it to those who have loved him. And when you know this, with what

---

[1] Cf. Rev. iii. 14.
[2] Cf. Rev. xvii. 14; Coloss. i. 15; Phil. ii. 6; 2 Cor. iv. 4; Heb. i. 8, 2 f.
[3] On the Canon, p. 77.

gladness, think you, you will be filled? Or how will you love him, who beforehand so loved you? (προαγαπήσαντά σε). But if you love, you will be an *imitator of his kindness*," &c. (μιμητὴς ἔσῃ αὐτοῦ τῆς χρηστότητος).[1] This is claimed as a reference to John iii. 16 f. "For God so loved the world (οὕτως γὰρ ἠγάπησεν ὁ θεὸς τὸν κόσμον) that he gave his only begotten son (ὥστε τὸν υἱὸν αὐτοῦ τὸν μονογενῆ ἔδωκεν) that whosoever believeth in him might not perish," &c. 17. "For God sent not his son into the world that he might judge the world," &c. (οὐ γὰρ ἀπέστειλεν ὁ θεὸς τὸν υἱὸν αὐτοῦ εἰς τὸν κόσμον ἵνα κρίνῃ τὸν κόσμον). Here, again, a sentence is patched together by taking fragments from the beginning and middle of a passage, and finding in them a superficial resemblance to words in the Gospel. We find parallels for the passage, however, in the Epistles from which the unknown writer obviously derives so much of his matter. Rom. v. 8 : "But God giveth proof of his love towards us, in that while we were yet sinners Christ died for us. 10. . . . through the death of his son." Chap. viii. 3, "God sending his son, &c. 29. . . . Them he also foreordained to bear the likeness of the image of his son, &c. 32. He that spared not his own son, but delivered him up for us all," &c. 39. (Nothing can separate us) "from the love of God which is in Christ Jesus our Lord." Gal. ii. 20. . . . "by the faith of the Son of God who loved me and gave himself for me." Chap. iv. 4. "God sent out his son (ἐξαπέστειλεν ὁ θεὸς τὸν υἱὸν αὐτοῦ). 5. . . . that he might redeem," &c. Ephes. ii. 4. "But God being rich in mercy because of his great love wherewith he loved us. 5. Even when we were dead in our trespasses hath quickened us together with Christ. 7. That he might show forth the exceeding riches of his grace in *kindness* (χρηστότης) towards us in Christ Jesus." Chap. iv. 32. "Be ye *kind* (χρηστοί) one to another, tender-hearted, forgiving one another, even as God also in Christ forgave you."[2] Chap. v. 1. "Be ye therefore imitators (μιμηταὶ) of God as beloved children. 2. And walk

---

[1] Ep. ad Diogn. x., Ὁ γὰρ θεὸς τοὺς ἀνθρώπους ἠγάπησε, δι' οὓς ἐποίησε τὸν κόσμον, οἷς ὑπέταξε πάντα τὰ ἐν . . . . . οἷς λόγιον ἔδωκεν, οἷς νοῦν· οἷς μόνοις πρὸς αὐτὸν ὁρᾶν ἐπέτρεψε· οὓς ἐκ τῆς ἰδίας εἰκόνος ἔπλασε· πρὸς οὓς ἀπέστειλε τὸν υἱὸν αὐτοῦ τὸν μονογενῆ· οἷς τὴν ἐν οὐρανῷ βασιλείαν ἐπηγγείλατο, καὶ δώσει τοῖς ἀγαπήσασιν αὐτόν. Ἐπιγνοὺς δέ, τίνος οἴει πληρωθήσεσθαι χαρᾶς; ἢ πῶς ἀγαπήσεις τὸν οὕτως προαγαπήσαντά σε; ἀγαπήσας δέ, μιμητής ἔσῃ αὐτοῦ τῆς χρηστότητος· κ.τ.λ.   [2] Cf. Coloss. iii. 12—14.

in love (ἐν ἀγάπῃ) even as Christ also loved you (ὁ Χριστὸς ἠγάπησεν ὑμᾶς), and gave himself for us," &c., &c. Titus iii. 4. "But when the kindness (χρηστότης) and love towards men (φιλανθρωπία) of our Saviour God was manifested. 5. . . . according to his mercy he saved us. . . . 6. . . . through Jesus Christ our Saviour. 7. That being justified by his grace, we should become heirs according to the hope of Eternal life."[1]

The words: "Or how will you love him who so beforehand loved you?" (ἢ πῶς ἀγαπήσεις τὸν οὕτως προαγαπήσαντά σε;), Canon Westcott refers to 1 John iv. 19, "We love God[2] because he first loved us" (ἡμεῖς ἀγαπῶμεν τὸν θεόν, ὅτι αὐτὸς πρῶτος ἠγάπησεν ἡμᾶς.) The linguistic differences, however, and specially the substitution of προαγαπήσαντα for πρῶτος ἠγάπησεν, distinctly oppose the claim. The words are a perfectly natural comment upon the words in Ephesians, from which it is obvious the writer derived other parts of the sentence, as the striking word "kindness" (χρηστότης), which is commonly used in the Pauline Epistles, but nowhere else in the New Testament,[3] shows.

Dr. Westcott "cannot call to mind a parallel to the phrase 'the kingdom in heaven'"[4] which occurs above in the phrase "to whom he has promised the kingdom in heaven, and will give it to those who have loved him" (οἷς τὴν ἐν οὐρανῷ βασιλείαν ἐπηγγείλατο, καὶ δώσει τοῖς ἀγαπήσασιν αὐτόν). This also we find in the Epistles to which the writer exclusively refers in this letter: James ii. 5, "heirs of the kingdom which he promised to them that love him" (τῆς βασιλείας ἧς ἐπηγγείλατο τοῖς ἀγαπῶσιν αὐτόν) i. 12. ". . . he shall receive the crown of life which he promised to them that love him" (ὃν ἐπηγγείλατο τοῖς ἀγαπῶσιν αὐτόν). In 2 Tim. iv. 18, we have: "The Lord . . . shall preserve me safe unto his heavenly kingdom" (εἰς τὴν βασιλείαν αὐτοῦ τὴν ἐπουράνιον).[5] The very fact that there is no exact parallel to the phrase "kingdom in heaven" in our Gospels is unfavourable to the argument that they were used by the author. Whatever evangelical works he may have read,

---

[1] Cf. 2 Thess. ii. 16; 1 Thess. ii. 12, iv. 9.

[2] We quote the reading of the Cod. Sinaiticus as most favourable to Dr. Westcott; the Alexandrian and Vatican MSS. have simply: "we love," omitting both "God" and "him."

[3] Cf. Rom. ii. 4; iii. 12; xi. 22 (thrice); 2 Cor. vi. 6; Gal. v. 22; Ephes. ii. 7. Cf. iv. 32; Coloss. iii. 12; Titus, iii. 4; cf. 1 Peter, ii. 3.

[4] On the Canon, p. 77, note 4.   [5] Cf. 2 Tim. iv. 8; 2 Thess. i. 5.

it is indisputable that the writer of this Epistle does not quote any of them, and he uses no expressions and no terminology which warrants the inference that he must have been acquainted with the fourth Gospel.

As we have already stated, the writer of the Epistle to Diognetus is unknown; Diognetus, the friend to whom it is addressed, is equally unknown; the letter is neither mentioned nor quoted by any of the Fathers, nor by any ancient writer, and there is no external evidence as to the date of the composition. It existed only in one codex, destroyed at Strasburg during the Franco-German war, the handwriting of which was referred to the thirteenth or fourteenth century, but it is far from certain that it was so old. The last two chapters are a falsification by a later writer than the author of the first ten. There is no internal evidence whatever in this brief didactic composition requiring or even suggesting its assignment to the second or third centuries, but on the contrary, we venture to assert that there is evidence, both internal and external, justifying the belief that it was written at a comparatively recent date. Apart from the uncertainty of date, however, there is no allusion in it to any Gospel. Even if there were, the testimony of a letter by an unknown writer at an unknown period could not have any weight, but under the actual circumstances the Epistle to Diognetus furnishes absolutely no testimony at all for the apostolical origin and historical character of the fourth Gospel.[1]

The fulness with which we have discussed the supposed testimony of Basilides[2] renders it unnecessary for us to re-enter at any length into the argument as to his knowledge of the fourth Gospel. Tischendorf[3] and

[1] See note 3, p. 39. [2] Vol. ii. p. 41 ff. [3] Wann wurden, u. s. w., p. 52.

EXTERNAL EVIDENCE FOR THE FOURTH GOSPEL. 369

Canon Westcott[1] assert that two passages, namely: "The true light which lighteth every man came into the world," corresponding with John i. 9, and: "mine hour is not yet come," agreeing with John ii. 4, which are introduced by Hippolytus in his work against Heresies[2] with a subjectless φησί "he says," are quotations made in some lost work by Basilides. We have shown that Hippolytus and other writers of his time were in the habit of quoting passages from works by the founders of sects and by their later followers without any distinction, an utterly vague φησί doing service equally for all. This is the case in the present instance, and there is no legitimate reason for assigning these passages to Basilides himself,[3] but on the contrary many considerations which forbid our doing so, which we have elsewhere detailed.

These remarks most fully apply to Valentinus, whose supposed quotations we have exhaustively discussed,[4] as well as the one passage given by Hippolytus containing a sentence found in John x. 8,[5] the only one which can be pointed out. We have distinctly proved that the quotations in question are not assignable to Valentinus himself, a fact which even apologists admit. There is no just ground for asserting that his terminology was derived from the fourth Gospel, the whole having been in current use long before that Gospel was composed.

---

[1] On the Canon, p. 256, note 3.   [2] vii. 22, 27.
[3] *Davidson*, Introd. N. T., ii. p. 388 f.; *Hilgenfeld*, Die Evangelien, p. 345, anm. 5; cf. Zeitschr. wiss. Theol., 1862, p. 453 ff.; *Luthardt*, Der johann. Urspr. d. viert. Ev. p. 85 f.; Das Joh. Evang., 1875, i. p. 235; *Rumpf*, Rev. de Théol., 1867, p. 18 ff., p. 366; *Scholten*, Die ält. Zeugnisse, p. 65 f.; *Strauss*, Das Leben Jesu, 1864, p. 67 f.; *Volkmar*, Theol. Jahrb., 1854, p. 108, p. 125 f.; Der Ursprung, p. 71, anm.; *Zeller*, Theol. Jahrb., 1853, p. 148 ff. Cf. *Guericke*, H'buch. K. G., i. p. 184.
[4] Vol. ii. p. 55 ff.   [5] Adv. Hær., vi. 35.

There is no evidence whatever that Valentinus was acquainted with such a work.[1]

We must generally remark, however, with regard to Basilides, Valentinus and all such Heresiarchs and writers, that, even if it could be shown, as actually it cannot, that they were acquainted with the fourth Gospel, the fact would only prove the existence of the work at a late period in the second century, but would furnish no evidence of the slightest value regarding its apostolic origin, or towards establishing its historical value. On the other hand, if, as apologists assert, these heretics possessed the fourth Gospel, their deliberate and total rejection of the work furnishes evidence positively antagonistic to its claims. It is difficult to decide whether their rejection of the Gospel, or their ignorance of its existence is the more unfavourable alternative.

The dilemma is the very same in the case of Marcion. We have already fully discussed his knowledge of our Gospels,[2] and need not add anything here. It is not pretended that he made any use of the fourth Gospel, and the only ground upon which it is argued that he supplies evidence even of its existence is the vague general statement of Tertullian, that Marcion rejected the Gospels "which are put forth as genuine, and under the name of Apostles or at least of contemporaries of the Apostles," denying their truth and integrity, and maintaining the sole

---

[1] *Baur*, Unters. kan. Ev., p. 357 f.; *Bretschneider*, Probabilia, p. 212 ff.; *Davidson*, Introd. N. T., ii. p. 390; *Hilgenfeld*, Die Evangelien, p. 345; *Rumpf*, Rev. de Théol., 1867, p. 17; *Scholten*, Die ält. Zeugnisse, p. 67 ff.; *Strauss*, Das Leben Jesu, 1864, p. 67; *Volkmar*, Der Ursprung, p. 69 ff.; Theol. Jahrb., 1854, p. 108, p. 125 f.; *Weizsäcker*, Unters. Evang. Gesch., p. 234; *Zeller*, Die Apostelgesch., p. 65 ff.; Theol. Jahrb., 1853, p. 151 f.   [2] Vol. ii. p. 79 ff.

authority of his own Gospel.[1] We have shown[2] how unwarrantable it is to affirm from such data that Marcion knew, and deliberately repudiated, the four canonical Gospels. The Fathers, with uncritical haste and zeal, assumed that the Gospels adopted by the Church at the close of the second and beginning of the third centuries must equally have been invested with canonical authority from the first, and Tertullian took it for granted that Marcion, of whom he knew very little, must have actually rejected the four Gospels of his own Canon. Even Canon Westcott admits that : " it is uncertain whether Tertullian in the passage quoted speaks from a knowledge of what Marcion may have written on the subject, or simply from his own point of sight."[3] There is not the slightest evidence that Marcion knew the fourth Gospel,[4] and if he did, it is perfectly inexplicable that he did not adopt it as peculiarly favourable to his own views.[5] If he was acquainted with the work and, nevertheless, rejected it as false and adulterated, his testimony is obviously opposed to the Apostolic origin and historical accuracy of the fourth Gospel, and the critical acumen which he exhibited in his selection of the Pauline Epistles renders his judgment of greater weight than that of most of the Fathers.

We have now reached an epoch when no evidence regarding the fourth Gospel can have much weight,

---

[1] Adv. Marc., iv. 3, 4.   [2] Vol. ii. p. 141 ff.
[3] On the Canon, p. 276, note 1.
[4] *Eichhorn*, Einl. N. T., i. pp. 73 ff., 78 f., 84 ; *Gieseler*, Entst. schr. Evv., p. 25; *Hilgenfeld*, Die Evv. Justin's, p. 474; *Rumpf*, Rev. de Théol., 1867, p. 21; *Schleiermacher*, Einl. N. T., 1845, p. 214 f.; *Scholten*, Die ält. Zeugnisse, p. 76 ff.; *Schwegler*, Das nachap. Zeit., i. p. 282; *Volkmar*, Der Ursprung, p. 76.
[5] *Hilgenfeld*, Die Evv. Justin's, p. 474 ; *Scholten*, Die ält. Zeugnisse, p. 77 ; *Volkmar*, Der Ursprung, p. 76 ff.

and the remaining witnesses need not detain us long. We have discussed at length the Diatessaron of Tatian,[1] and shown that whilst there is no evidence that it was based upon our four Gospels, there is reason to believe that it may have been identical with the Gospel according to the Hebrews, by which name, as Epiphanius[2] states, it was actually called. We have only now briefly to refer to the address to the Greeks (Λόγος πρὸς Ἕλληνας), and to ascertain what testimony it bears regarding the fourth Gospel. It was composed after the death of Justin, and scarcely dates earlier than the beginning of the last quarter of the second century. No Gospel and no work of the New Testament is mentioned in this composition, but Tischendorf[3] and others point out one or two supposed references to passages in the fourth Gospel. The first of these in order, is one indicated by Canon Westcott,[4] but to which Tischendorf does not call attention: "God was in the beginning, but we have learned that the beginning is the power of Reason (Θεὸς ἦν ἐν ἀρχῇ, τὴν δὲ ἀρχὴν λόγου δύναμιν παρειλήφαμεν). For the Lord of the Universe (δεσπότης τῶν ὅλων) being himself the substance (ὑπόστασις) of all, in that creation had not been accomplished was alone, but inasmuch as he was all power, and himself the substance of things visible and invisible, all things were with him (σὺν αὐτῷ τὰ πάντα). With him by means of rational power the Reason (Λόγος) itself also which was in him subsisted. But by the will of his simplicity, Reason (Λόγος) springs forth; but the Reason (Λόγος) not

---

[1] Vol. ii. p. 148 ff.   [2] Hær., xlvi. § 1.
[3] Wann wurden, u. s. w., p. 17.
[4] On the Canon, p. 278, note 2. [In the 4th ed., however, Canon Westcott puts it within brackets, adding: "This reference is not certain." P. 317, n. 2.]

proceeding in vain, because the first-born work (ἔργον πρωτότοκον) of the Father. Him we know to be the Beginning of the world (Τοῦτον ἴσμεν τοῦ κόσμου τὴν ἀρχήν). But he came into existence by division, not by cutting off, for that which is cut off is separated from the first: but that which is divided, receiving the choice of administration, did not render him defective from whom it was taken, &c., &c. And as the Logos (Reason), in the beginning begotten, begat again our creation, himself for himself creating the matter (Καὶ καθάπερ ὁ Λόγος, ἐν ἀρχῇ γεννηθεὶς, ἀντεγέννησε τὴν καθ' ἡμᾶς ποίησιν, αὐτὸς ἑαυτῷ τὴν ὕλην δημιουργήσας), so I," &c., &c.[1]

It is quite evident that this doctrine of the Logos is not that of the fourth Gospel, from which it cannot have been derived. Tatian himself[2] seems to assert that he derived it from the Old Testament. We have quoted the passage at length that it might be clearly under-

---

[1] Orat. ad Græcos, § 5. As this passage is of some obscurity, we subjoin, for the sake of impartiality, an independent translation taken from Dr. Donaldson's able History of Christ. Lit. and Doctrine, iii. p. 42: "God was in the beginning, but we have understood that the beginning was a power of reason. For the Lord of all, Himself being the substance of all, was alone in so far as the creation had not yet taken place, but as far as He was all power and the substance of things seen and unseen, all things were with Him: along with Him also by means of rational power, the reason which was in Him supported them. But by the will of his simplicity, the reason leaps forth; but the reason, not having gone from one who became empty thereby, is the first-born work of the Father. Him we know to be the beginning of the world. But He came into existence by sharing (μερισμός) not by cutting off; for that which is cut off is separated from the first; but that which is shared, receiving a selection of the work, did not render Him defective from whom it was taken, &c., &c. And as the Word begotten in the beginning begot in his turn our creation, He Himself fashioning the material for Himself, so I, &c., &c." Cf. *Dorner*, Lehre Pers. Christi, i. p. 437 ff.

[2] § 12, cf. § 20. Cf. *Bretschneider*, Probabilia, p. 193 ff.; *Donaldson*, Hist. Chr. Lit. and Doctr., iii. p. 32.

stood; and with the opening words, we presume, for he does not quote at all but merely indicates the chapter, Canon Westcott compares John i. 1: "In the beginning was the Word, and the Word was with God, and the Word was God" (Ἐν ἀρχῇ ἦν ὁ Λόγος, κ.τ.λ.). The statement of Tatian is quite different; *God* was in the beginning" (Θεὸς ἦν ἐν ἀρχῇ), and he certainly did not identify the Word with God, so as to transform the statement of the Gospel into this simple affirmation. In all probability his formula was merely based upon Genesis i. 1: "In the beginning God created the heavens and the earth" (ἐν ἀρχῇ ἐποίησεν ὁ Θεὸς, κ.τ.λ.).[1] The expressions: "But we have learned that the Beginning (ἀρχή) was the power of Reason," &c., "but the Reason (Λόγος) not proceeding in vain became the first-born work (ἔργον πρωτότοκον) of the Father. Him we know to be the Beginning (ἀρχή) of the world," recall many early representations of the Logos, to which we have already referred: Prov. viii. 22: "The Lord created me the Beginning (ἀρχή) of his ways for his works (ἔργα), 23. Before the ages he established me, in the beginning (ἐν ἀρχῇ) before he made the earth," &c., &c. In the Apocalypse also the Word is called "the Beginning (ἀρχή) of the creation of God," and it will be remembered that Justin gives testimony from Prov. viii. 21 ff. "that God begat before all the creatures a Beginning (ἀρχήν) a certain rational Power (δύναμιν λογικήν), out of himself,"[2] &c., &c., and elsewhere: "As the Logos declared through Solomon, that this same . . . . . had been begotten of God, before all created beings, both Beginning (ἀρχή)," &c.[3] We need not, however, refer to

---

[1] *Donaldson*, Hist. Chr. Lit. and Doctr., iii. p. 43.
[2] Dial. 61, see vol. ii. p. 286.   [3] Dial. 62, see vol. ii. p. 284.

the numerous passages in Philo and in Justin, not derived from the fourth Gospel, which point to a different source for Tatian's doctrine. It is sufficient that both his opinions and his terminology differ distinctly from that Gospel.[1]

The next passage we at once subjoin in contrast with the parallel in the fourth Gospel:

Orat. ad Græcos, § xiii.	John i. 5.
And this, therefore, is (the meaning of) the saying: The darkness comprehends not the light.	And the light shineth in the darkness; and the darkness comprehended it not.
Καὶ τοῦτο ἔστιν ἄρα τὸ εἰρημένον· Ἡ σκοτία τὸ φῶς οὐ καταλαμβάνει.	Καὶ τὸ φῶς ἐν τῇ σκοτίᾳ φαίνει, καὶ ἡ σκοτία αὐτὸ οὐ κατέλαβεν.

The context to this passage in the Oration is as follows: Tatian is arguing about the immortality of the soul, and he states that the soul is not in itself immortal but mortal, but that nevertheless it is possible for it not to die. If it do not know the truth it dies, but rises again at the end of the world, receiving eternal death as a punishment. "Again, however, it does not die, though it be for a time dissolved, if it has acquired knowledge of God; for in itself it is darkness, and there is nothing luminous in it, and this, therefore, is (the meaning of) the saying: The darkness comprehends not the light. For the soul (ψυχή) did not itself save the spirit (πνεῦμα), but was saved by it, and the light comprehended the darkness. The Logos (Reason) truly is the light of God, but the ignorant soul is darkness (Ὁ Λόγος μέν ἐστι τὸ τοῦ Θεοῦ φῶς, σκότος δὲ ἡ ἀνεπιστήμων ψυχή). For this reason, if it remain

[1] We have already mentioned that the Gospel according to Peter contained the doctrine of the Logos.

alone, it tends downwards to matter, dying with the flesh," &c., &c.[1] The source of "the saying" is not mentioned, and it is evident that, even if it were taken to be a reference to the fourth Gospel, nothing would thereby be proved but the mere existence of the Gospel. "The saying," however, is distinctly different in language from the parallel in the Gospel, and it may be from a different Gospel. We have already remarked that Philo calls the Logos "the Light,"[2] and quoting in a peculiar form Ps. xxvi. 1 : "For the Lord is my light ($\phi\hat{\omega}s$) and my Saviour," he goes on to say that, as the sun divides day and night, so, Moses says, "God divides light and darkness" ($\tau\grave{o}\nu$ $\theta\epsilon\grave{o}\nu$ $\phi\hat{\omega}s$ $\kappa a\grave{\iota}$ $\sigma\kappa\acute{o}\tau os$ $\delta\iota a\tau\epsilon\iota\chi\acute{\iota}\sigma a\iota$).[3] When we turn away to things of sense we use "another light," which is in no way different from "darkness."[4] The constant use of the same similitude of Light and darkness in the Canonical Epistles[5] shows how current it was in the Church; and nothing is more certain than the fact that it was neither originated by, nor confined to, the fourth Gospel.

The third and last passage is as follows :

Orat. ad Græcos, xix.	John i. 3.
We being such as this, do not pursue us with hatred, but, rejecting the Demons, follow the one God.	
All things were by ($\dot{v}\pi\acute{o}$) him, and without him was not anything made.	All things were made by ($\delta\iota\acute{a}$) him, and without him was not anything made that was made.
Πάντα ὑπ' αὐτοῦ, καὶ χωρὶς αὐτοῦ γέγονεν οὐδὲ ἕν.	Πάντα δι' αὐτοῦ ἐγένετο, καὶ χωρὶς αὐτοῦ ἐγένετο οὐδὲ ἓν ὃ γέγονεν.

[1] Orat. ad Græcos, § 13.
[2] De Somniis, i. § 13, Mangey, i. 632; cf. §§ 14 ff., De Mundi op. § 9, ib., i. 7. See vol. ii. p. 295, note 4.
[3] De Somniis, i. § 13.   [4] Ib., i. § 14.
[5] 2 Cor. iv. 6; Ephes. v. 8—14; Coloss. i. 12, 13; 1 Thess. v. 5; 1 Tim. vi. 16; 1 Pet. ii. 9; cf. Rev. xxi. 23, 24; xxii. 5.

Tatian here speaks of God, and not of the Logos, and in this respect, as well as in language and context, the passage differs from the fourth Gospel. The phrase is not introduced as a quotation, and no reference is made to any Gospel. The purpose for which the words are used, again, rather points to the first chapters of Genesis than to the dogmatic prologue enunciating the doctrine of the Logos.[1] Under all these circumstances, the source from which the expression may have been derived cannot with certainty be ascertained and, as in the preceding instance, even if it be assumed that the words show acquaintance with the fourth Gospel, nothing could be proved but the mere existence of the work about a century and a half after the events which it records. It is obvious that in no case does Tatian afford the slightest evidence of the Apostolic origin or historical veracity of the fourth Gospel.

Dr. Lightfoot points out another passage, § 4, πνεῦμα ὁ Θεός, which he compares with John iv. 24, where the same words occur. It is right to add that he himself remarks: "If it had stood alone I should certainly not have regarded it as decisive. But the epigrammatic form is remarkable, and it is a characteristic passage of the fourth Gospel.[2] Neither Tischendorf nor Dr. Westcott refer to it. The fact is, however, that the epigrammatic form only exists when the phrase is quoted without its context. "God is a spirit, not pervading matter, but the creator of material spirits, and of the forms that are in it. He is invisible and impalpable," &c. &c. Further on, Tatian says (§ 15), "For the perfect God is without flesh, but man is flesh," &c. A large

---

[1] Cf. 1 Cor. viii. 6; Ephes. iii. 9; Heb. i. 2.
[2] Contemp. Rev., 1877, p. 1135.

part of the oration is devoted to discussing the nature of God, and the distinction between spirit (πνεῦμα) and soul (ψυχή), and it is unreasonable to assert that a man like Tatian could not make the declaration that God is a spirit without quoting the fourth Gospel.

We have generally discussed the testimony of Dionysius of Corinth,[1] Melito of Sardis,[2] and Claudius Apollinaris,[3] and need not say more here. The fragments attributed to them neither mention nor quote the fourth Gospel, but in no case could they furnish evidence to authenticate the work. The same remarks apply to Athenagoras.[4] Canon Westcott only ventures to say that he "appears to allude to passages in St. Mark and St. John, but they are all anonymous."[5] The passages in which he speaks of the Logos, which are those referred to here, are certainly not taken from the fourth Gospel, and his doctrine is expressed in terminology which is different from that of the Gospel, and is deeply tinged with Platonism.[6] He appeals to Proverbs viii. 22, already so frequently quoted by us, for confirmation by the Prophetic Spirit of his exposition of the Logos doctrine.[7] He nowhere identifies the Logos with Jesus;[8] indeed he does not once make use of the name of Christ in his works. He does not show the slightest knowledge of the doctrine of salvation so constantly enunciated in the fourth Gospel. There can be no doubt, as we have already shown,[9] that he considered the Old Testament to

---

[1] Vol. ii. p. 159 ff.   [2] Ib., p. 169 ff.   [3] Ib., p. 182 ff.
[4] Ib., p. 188 ff.   [5] On the Canon, p. 103.
[6] Cf. Dorner, Lehre Pers. Christi, i. p. 440 ff.; Donaldson, Hist. Chr. Lit. and Doctr., iii. p. 149 ff.   [7] Leg. pro Christ., § 10.
[8] Dorner, ib., i. p. 442; Donaldson, ib., iii. p. 154.
[9] Vol. ii. p. 197.

be the only inspired Holy Scriptures. Not only does he not mention nor quote any of our Gospels, but the only instance in which he makes any reference to sayings of Jesus, otherwise than by the indefinite φησί "he says," is one in which he introduces a saying which is not found in our Gospels by the words: "The Logos again saying to us:" (πάλιν ἡμῖν λέγοντος τοῦ Λόγου), &c. From the same source, which was obviously not our Canonical Gospels, we have, therefore, reason to conclude that Athenagoras derived all his knowledge of Gospel history and doctrine. We need not add that this writer affords no testimony whatever as to the origin or character of the fourth Gospel.

It is scarcely worth while to refer to the Epistle of Vienne and Lyons, a composition dating at the earliest A.D. 177-178, in which no direct reference is made to any writing of the New Testament.[1] Acquaintance with the fourth Gospel is argued from the following passage:

Epistle, § iv.	John xvi. 2.
And thus was fulfilled the saying of our Lord:	
The time shall come in which every one that killeth you shall think that he offereth a service unto God.	But the hour cometh that every one that killeth you may think that he offereth a service unto God.
Ἐλεύσεται καιρὸς ἐν ᾧ πᾶς ὁ ἀποκτείνας ὑμᾶς, δόξει λατρείαν προσφέρειν τῷ θεῷ.	ἀλλ' ἔρχεται ὥρα ἵνα πᾶς ὁ ἀποκτείνας ὑμᾶς δόξῃ λατρείαν προσφέρειν τῷ θεῷ.

Now such a passage cannot prove the use of the fourth Gospel. No source is indicated in the Epistle from which the saying of Jesus, which of course apologists assert to be historical, was derived. It presents decided variations from the parallel in the fourth Gospel; and in the

[1] Vol. ii. p. 198 ff.

Synoptics we find sufficient indications of similar discourses[1] to render it very probable that other Gospels may have contained the passage quoted in the Epistle. In no case could an anonymous reference like this be of any weight as evidence for the Apostolic origin of the fourth Gospel.

We need not further discuss Ptolemæus and Heracleon. We have shown[2] that the date at which these heretics flourished places them beyond the limits within which we propose to confine ourselves. In regard to Ptolemæus all that is affirmed is that, in the Epistle to Flora ascribed to him, expressions found in John i. 3 are used. The passage as it is given by Epiphanius is as follows: "Besides, that the world was created by the same, the Apostle states (saying all things have been made (γεγονέναι) by him and without him nothing was made)." (Ἔτι γε τὴν τοῦ κόσμου δημιουργίαν ἰδίαν λέγει εἶναι (ἅτε πάντα δι᾽ αὐτοῦ γεγονέναι, καὶ χωρὶς αὐτοῦ γέγονεν οὐδέν) ὁ ἀπόστολος).[3] Now the supposed quotation is introduced here in a parenthesis interrupting the sense, and there is every probability that it was added as an illustration by Epiphanius, and was not in the Epistle to Flora at all. Omitting the parenthesis, the sentence is a very palpable reference to the Apostle Paul, and Coloss. i. 16.[4] In regard to Heracleon, it is asserted from the unsupported references of Origen[5] that he wrote a commentary on the fourth Gospel. Even if this be a fact, there is not a single word of it preserved by Origen which in the least degree bears upon the Apostolic origin

---

[1] Matt. x. 16—22, xxiv. 9 f.; Mark xiii. 9—13; Luke xxi. 12—17.
[2] Vol. ii. p. 203 ff.
[3] *Epiphanius*, Hær., xxxiii. § 3.
[4] *Scholten*, Die ält. Zeugnisse, p. 68, anm. 4.
[5] The passages are quoted by *Grabe*, Spicil. Patr., ii. p. 85 ff.

and trustworthiness of the Gospel. Neither of these heresiarchs, therefore, is of any value as a witness for the authenticity of the fourth Gospel.

The heathen Celsus, as we have shown,[1] wrote at a period when no evidence which he could well give of his own could have been of much value in supporting our Gospels. He is pressed into service,[2] however, because after alluding to various circumstances of Gospel history he says: "These things, therefore, being taken out of your own writings, we have no need of other testimony, for you fall upon your own swords,"[3] and in another place he says that certain Christians "alter the Gospel from its first written form in three-fold, four-fold, and many-fold ways, and re-mould it in order to have the means of contradicting the arguments (of opponents)."[4] This is supposed to refer to the four Canonical Gospels. Apart from the fact that Origen replies to the first of these passages, that Celsus has brought forward much concerning Jesus which is not in accordance with the narratives of the Gospels, it is unreasonable to limit the accusation of "many-fold" corruption to four Gospels, when it is undeniable that the Gospels and writings long current in the Church were very numerous. In any case, what could such a statement as this do towards establishing the Apostolic origin and credibility of the fourth Gospel?

We might pass over the *Canon of Muratori* entirely,

---

[1] Vol. ii. p. 225 ff.

[2] Cf. *Tischendorf*, Wann wurden, u. s. w., p. 71 ff.; *Westcott*, On the Canon, p. 356.

[3] Ταῦτα μὲν οὖν ὑμῖν ἐκ τῶν ὑμετέρων συγγραμμάτων, ἐφ' οἷς οὐδενὸς ἄλλου μάρτυρος χρῄζομεν· αὐτοὶ γὰρ ἑαυτοῖς περιπίπτετε. *Origen*, Contra Cels., ii. 74.

[4] Ὡς ἐκ μέθης ἥκοντας εἰς τὸ ἐφεστάναι αὑτοῖς, μεταχαράττειν ἐκ τῆς πρώτης γραφῆς τὸ εὐαγγέλιον τριχῇ καὶ τετραχῇ καὶ πολλαχῇ, καὶ μεταπλάττειν, ἵν' ἔχοιεν πρὸς τοὺς ἐλέγχους ἀρνεῖσθαι. Contra Cels., ii. 27.

as being beyond the limit of time to which we confine ourselves,[1] but the unknown writer of the fragment gives a legend with regard to the composition of the fourth Gospel which we may quote here, although its obviously mythical character renders it of no value as evidence regarding the authorship of the Gospel. The writer says:

> Quarti euangeliorum Iohannis ex decipolis
> Cohortantibus condescipulis et episcopis suis
> dixit coniciunate mihi hodie triduo et quid
> cuique fuerit reuelatum alterutrum
> nobis ennarremus eadem nocte reue
> latum Andreae ex apostolis ut recognis
> centibus cunctis Iohannis suo nomine
> cuncta describeret et ideo ([2]) licit uaria sin
> culis euangeliorum libris principia
> doceantur nihil tamen differt creden
> tium fidei cum uno ac principali spiritu de
> clarata sint in omnibus omnia de natiui
> tate de passione de resurrectione
> de conuersatione cum decipulis suis
> ac de gemino eius aduentu
> primo in humilitate dispectus quod fo   . . .
> .u ([3]) secundum potestate regali . . .   pre
> clarum quod futurum est ([4]) quid ergo
> mirum si Iohannes tam constanter
> sincula etiam in epistulis suis proferat
> dicens in semeipsu quae uidimus oculis
> nostris et auribus audiuimus et manus
> nostrae palpauerunt haec scripsimus uobis
> sic enim non solum uisurem sed et auditorem
> sed et scriptorem omnium mirabilium domini per ordi
> nem profetetur

[1] Vol. ii. p. 235 ff.

[2] It is admitted that the whole passage from this point to "futurum est" is abrupt and without connection with the context, as well as most confused. Cf. *Tregelles*, Can. Murat., p. 36; *Donaldson*, Hist. Chr. Lit. and Doctr., iii. p. 205.

[3] Credner reads here "quod ratum est." Zur Gesch. d. Kan., p. 74. Dr. Westcott reads: "quod fuit." On the Canon, p. 478.

[4] Dr. Tregelles calls attention to the resemblance of this passage to one of Tertullian (Apol. § 21). "Duobus enim adventibus eius significatis, primo, qui iam expunctus est in humilitate conditionis humanae; secundo, qui concludendo seculo imminet in sublimitate divinitatis exsertae: primum non intelligendo, secundum, quem manifestius praedicatum sperant unum

EXTERNAL EVIDENCE FOR THE FOURTH GOSPEL. 383

"The fourth of the Gospels, of John, one of the disciples. To his fellow-disciples and bishops (Episcopis) urging him he said: 'Fast with me to-day for three days, and let us relate to each other that which shall be revealed to each.' On the same night it was revealed to Andrew, one of the Apostles, that, with the supervision of all, John should relate all things in his own name. And, therefore, though various principles (principia) are taught by each book of the Gospels, nevertheless it makes no difference to the faith of believers, since, in all, all things are declared by one ruling Spirit concerning the nativity, concerning the passion, concerning the resurrection, concerning the intercourse with the disciples, and concerning his double advent; the first in lowliness of estate, which has taken place, the second in regal power and splendour, which is still future. What wonder, therefore, if John should so constantly bring forward each thing (singula) also in his Epistles, saying in regard to himself: The things which we have seen with our eyes, and have heard with our ears, and our hands have handled, these things have we written unto you. For thus he professes himself not only an eye-witness and hearer, but also a writer of all the wonders of the Lord in order."

It is obvious that in this passage we have an apologetic defence of the fourth Gospel,[1] which unmistakably implies antecedent denial of its authority and apostolic origin. The writer not only ascribes it to John, but he clothes it with the united authority of the rest of the Apostles, in

---

existimaverunt." Can. Murat., p. 36. This is another reason for dating the fragment in the third century.

[1] *Credner*, Gesch. N. T. Kanon, p. 158 f. and *Volkmar*, Anhang, p. 360; Der Ursprung, p. 28; *Davidson*, Introd. N. T., ii. p. 402; *Hilgenfeld*, Der Kanon, pp. 41, 43; *Lomann*, Johannes in het Fragm. v. Muratori, 1865, p. 83 ff.; *Scholten*, Die ält. Zeugnisse, p. 150 f.

a manner which very possibly aims at explaining the supplementary chapter xxi., with its testimony to the truth of the preceding narrative. In his zeal, the writer goes so far as to falsify a passage of the Epistle, and convert it into a declaration by the author of the letter himself that he had written the Gospel. "'The things which we have seen, &c., these things have we written unto you' (hæc scripsimus vobis).[1] For thus he professes himself not only an eye-witness and hearer, but also a writer of all the wonders of the Lord in order." Credner argues that in speaking of John as "one of the disciples" (ex discipulis), and of Andrew as "one of the Apostles," the writer intends to distinguish between John the disciple, who wrote the Gospel and Epistle, and John the Apostle, who wrote the Apocalypse, and that it was for this reason that he sought to dignify him by a special revelation, through the Apostle Andrew, selecting him to write the Gospel. Credner, therefore, concludes that here we have an ancient ecclesiastical tradition ascribing the Gospel and first Epistle to one of the disciples of Jesus different from the Apostle John.[2] Into this, however, we need not enter, nor is it necessary for us to demonstrate the mythical nature of this narrative regarding the origin of the Gospel. We have merely given this extract from the fragment to make our statement regarding it complete. Not only is the evidence of the fragment of no value, from the lateness of its date and the uncritical character of its author, but a vague and fabulous tradition recorded by an unknown writer could not, in any case, furnish testimony calculated to establish the Apostolic origin and trustworthiness of the fourth Gospel.

[1] 1 John i. 1—3.
[2] *Credner*, Gesch. N. T. Kan., p. 158 ff.; Theol. Jahrb., 1857, p. 301.

CHAPTER II.

AUTHORSHIP AND CHARACTER OF THE FOURTH GOSPEL.

THE result of our inquiry into the evidence for the fourth Gospel is sufficiently decided to render further examination unnecessary. We have seen that, for some century and a half after the events recorded in the work, there is not only no testimony whatever connecting the fourth Gospel with the Apostle John, but no certain trace even of the existence of the Gospel. There has not been the slightest evidence in any of the writings of the Fathers which we have examined even of a tradition that the Apostle John had composed any evangelical work at all, and the claim advanced in favour of the Christian miracles to contemporaneous evidence of extraordinary force and veracity by undoubted eye-witnesses so completely falls to the ground, that we might here well bring this part of our inquiry to a close. There are, however, so many peculiar circumstances connected with the fourth Gospel, both in regard to its authorship and to its relationship with the three Synoptics, which invite further attention, that we propose briefly to review some of them. We must, however, carefully restrict ourselves to the limits of our inquiry, and resist any temptation to enter upon an exhaustive discussion of the problem presented by the fourth Gospel from a more general literary point of view.

The endeavour to obtain some positive, or at least negative, information regarding the author of the fourth Gospel is facilitated by the fact that several other works in the New Testament Canon are ascribed to him. These works present such marked and distinct characteristics that, apart from the fact that their number extends the range of evidence, they afford an unusual opportunity of testing the tradition which assigns them all to the Apostle John, by comparing the clear indications which they give of the idiosyncrasies of their author with the independent data which we possess regarding the history and character of the Apostle. It is asserted by the Church that John the son of Zebedee, one of the disciples of Jesus, is the composer of no less than five of our canonical writings, and it would be impossible to select any books of our New Testament presenting more distinct features, or more widely divergent views, than are to be found in the Apocalypse on the one hand, and the Gospel and three Epistles on the other. Whilst a strong family likeness exists between the Epistles and the Gospel, and they exhibit close analogies both in thought and language, the Apocalypse, on the contrary, is so different from them in language, in style, in religious views and terminology, that it is almost impossible to believe that the writer of the one could be the author of the other. The translators of our New Testament have laboured, and not in vain, to eliminate as far as possible all individuality of style and language, and to reduce the various books of which it is composed to one uniform smoothness of diction. It is, therefore, impossible for the mere English reader to appreciate the immense difference which exists between the harsh and Hebraistic Greek of the Apocalypse and the polished elegance of the fourth Gospel, and it is to be feared that the rarity of critical study has prevented any general recognition of the almost equally striking contrast of thought between the two works. The remarkable peculiarities which distinguish the Apocalypse and Gospel of John, however, were very early appreciated, and almost the first application of critical judgment to the Canonical books of the New Testament is the argument of Dionysius Bishop of Alexandria, about the middle of the third century, that the author of the fourth Gospel could not be the writer of the Book of Revelation.[1] The dogmatic predilections which at that time had begun to turn against the Apocalypse, the nonfulfilment of the prophecies of which disappointed and puzzled the early Church, led Dionysius to solve the difficulty by deciding in favour of the authenticity of the Gospel, but at least he recognized the dilemma which has since occupied so much of biblical criticism.

It is not necessary to enter upon any exhaustive analysis of the Apocalypse and Gospel to demonstrate anew that both works cannot have emanated from the same mind. This has already been conclusively done by others. Some apologetic writers,—greatly influenced, no doubt, by the express declaration of the Church, and satisfied by analogies which could scarcely fail to exist between two works dealing with a similar theme,— together with a very few independent critics, have asserted the authenticity of both works.[2] The great majority of

---

[1] *Eusebius*, H. E., vii. 25.

[2] *Alford*, Greek Testament, 1868, iv. pp. 198 ff., 229; *Bertholdt*, Einl. A. u. N. T., iv. p. 1800 ff. ; cf. iii. p. 1299 ff. ; *Ebrard*, Die evang. Gesch., p. 858 ff. ; Das evang. Johannis, 1845, p. 137 ff. ; *Eichhorn*, Einl. N. T., ii. p. 375 ff., cf. p. 223 ff. ; *Feilmoser*, Einl. N. T., p. 569 ff., cf. p. 199 ff. ; *Hase*, Die Tüb. Schule, 1855, p. 25 ff. ; *Hug*, Einl. N. T., ii. p. 496 ff., cf.

critics, however, have fully admitted the impossibility of recognizing a common source for the fourth Gospel and the Apocalypse of John.[1] The critical question regarding the two works has, in fact, reduced itself to the dilemma which may be expressed as follows, in the words of Lücke: "Either the Gospel and the first Epistle are genuine writings of the Apostle John, and in that case the Apocalypse is no genuine work of that Apostle, or the inverse."[2] After an elaborate comparison of the two writings, the same writer, who certainly will not be suspected of wilfully subversive criticism, resumes: "The difference between the language, way

p. 160 ff.; *Lechler*, Das ap. u. nachap. Zeit., p. 195 ff.; *Lightfoot*, Ep. to Galatians, 4th ed. p. 343 ff.; *Niemeyer*, Verhandl. over de echtheid der Johann. Schr., 1852; *de Pressensé*, Hist. des Trois prem. Siècles, 2e éd., p. 311 ff.; *Reithmayr*, Einl. N. T., p. 774 ff.; *Thiersch*, Die Kirche im ap. Zeit., pp. 245 f., 267—274; *Tholuck*, Glaubw. evang. Gesch., p. 280 ff., &c., &c.

[1] *Dionysius*, in *Euseb.*, H. E., vii. 24, 25; *Baur*, Unters. kan. Evv., p. 345 ff.; K. G. drei erst. Jahrh., 1863, p. 146 ff.; *Bleek*, Beiträge, p. 190—200; Einl. N. T., 1866, p. 625 ff.; 1875, p. 724 ff.; *Bretschneider*, Probabilia, p. 150 ff.; *Credner*, Einl. N. T., i. pp. 724 ff., 732 ff.; *Davidson*, Introd. N. T., i. p. 313 ff.; ii. p. 441; *Erasmus*, Annot. in Apoc. Johannis N. Test., p. 625; *Ewald*, Jahrb. bibl. Wiss., v. 1852—3, p. 179 ff.; x. 1859—60, p. 85 f.; Die Joh. Schr., ii. p. 59 ff.; Com. in Apoc. Joh., 1828, p. 67 ff.; *Hilgenfeld*, Die Evangelien, p. 338 ff.; *Hitzig*, Ueber Johannes Marcus u. s. Schriften, 1843; *Holtzmann*, in Schenkel's Bib. Lex. iii. p. 338 f.; *Kayser*, Rev. de Théol., 1856, xiii. p. 80 ff.; *Köstlin*, Lehrb., Ev. u. Br. Joh., p. 1 ff.; *Lücke*, Einl. Offenb. Joh., ii. pp. 659 ff., 680 ff., 744 ff.; *Michaelis*, Einl. N. T., p. 1598—1650; *Nicholas*, Et. Cr. sur la Bible, N. T., p. 183 ff.; *Renan*, L'Antechrist, 1873, p. xxv.; Les Évangiles, 1877, p. 431; *Reuss*, Gesch. N. T., p. 152 f.; *Réville*, Rev. de Théol., 1854, ix. pp. 332 ff., 354 ff., 1855, x. p. 1 ff.; Rev. des deux Mondes, Oct. 1863, p. 633 ff.; cf. La Vie de Jésus de M. Renan, 1864, p. 42, note 1; *Scholten*, Das Ev. Joh., p. 401 ff.; *Schnitzer*, Theol. Jahrb., 1842, p. 451 ff.; *Schleiermacher*, Einl. N. T., pp. 317, 449 ff., 466 ff.; *Schwegler*, Das nachap. Zeit., ii. p. 372 f.; *Späth*, Protestanten Bibel, N. T. 1874, p. 263; *Tayler*, The Fourth Gospel, 1867, p. 14; *de Wette*, Einl. N. T., p. 422; *Weizsäcker*, Unters. evang. Gesch., p. 237, p. 295; *Zeller*, Theol. Jahrb., 1845, p. 654 f.; Vorträge u. s. w., 1865, p. 255, &c., &c.

[2] Einl. Offenb. Johannes, ii. p. 504.

of expression, and mode of thought and doctrine of the Apocalypse and the rest of the Johannine writings, is so comprehensive and intense, so individual and so radical; the affinity and agreement, on the contrary, are so general, and in details so fragmentary and uncertain (zurückweichend), that the Apostle John, if he really be the author of the Gospel and of the Epistle—which we here assume—cannot have composed the Apocalypse either *before* or *after* the Gospel and the Epistle. If all critical experience and rules in such literary questions are not deceptive, it is certain that the Evangelist and Apocalyptist are two different persons of the name of John,"[1] &c.

De Wette, another conservative critic, speaks with equal decision. After an able comparison of the two works, he says: "From all this it follows (and in New Testament criticism no result is more certain), that the Apostle John, if he be the author of the fourth Gospel and of the Johannine Epistles, did not write the Apocalypse, or, if the Apocalypse be his work, that he is not the author of the other writings."[2] Ewald is equally positive: "Above all," he says, "we should err in tracing this work (the Gospel) to the Apostle, if the Apocalypse of the New Testament were by him. That this much earlier writing cannot have been composed by the author of the later is an axiom which I consider I have already, (in 1826-28) so convincingly demonstrated, that it would be superfluous now to return to it, especially as, since then, all men capable of forming a judgment are of the same opinion, and what has been brought forward by a few writers against it too clearly depends upon—in-

[1] Einl. Offenb. Joh., ii. p. 744 f. [2] Einl. N. T., § 189 c., p. 422.

fluences foreign to science."¹ We may, therefore, consider the point generally admitted, and proceed very briefly to discuss the question upon this basis.

The external evidence that the Apostle John wrote the Apocalypse is more ancient than that for the authorship of any book of the New Testament, excepting some of the Epistles of Paul, and this is admitted even by critics who ultimately deny the authenticity of the work.² Passing over the very probable statement of Andrew of Cæsarea,³ that Papias recognized the Apocalypse as an inspired work, and the inference drawn from this fact that he referred it to the Apostle, we at once proceed to Justin Martyr, who affirms in the clearest and most positive manner the Apostolic origin of the work. He speaks to Tryphon of "a certain man whose name was John, one of the Apostles of Christ, who prophesied by a revelation made to him," of the Millennium, and subsequent general resurrection and judgment.⁴ The statement of Justin is all the more important from the fact that he does not name any other writing of the New Testament, and that the Old Testament was still for him the only Holy Scripture. The genuineness of this testi-

---

¹ Jahrb. bibl. Wiss., v. p. 179.
² *Baur*, Theol. Jahrb., 1844, p. 660; *Credner*, Gesch. N. T. Kan., pp. 97, 180; *Davidson*, Int. N. T., i. p. 318; *Ebrard*, Die evang. Gesch., p. 854 ff.; *Feilmoser*, Einl. N. T., p. 578; *Hilgenfeld*, Die Evangelien, p. 339 f.; *Kayser*, Rev. de Théol., 1856, xiii. p. 80 f.; *Lechler*, Das ap. u. nachap. Zeit., p. 197 f.; *Lücke*, Einl. Offenb. Joh., ii. p. 657; *Réville*, Rev. des deux Mondes, Oct. 1863, p. 632; *Schwegler*, Das nachap. Zeit., ii. p. 249, &c., &c.
³ It is generally asserted both by apologists and others that this testimony is valid in favour of the recognition by Papias of the authenticity of the Apocalypse.
⁴ Dial. 81; cf. *Eusebius*, H. E., iv. 18 : Καὶ ἐπειδὴ καὶ παρ' ἡμῖν ἀνήρ τις, ᾧ ὄνομα Ἰωάννης, εἷς τῶν ἀποστόλων τοῦ Χριστοῦ, ἐν ἀποκαλύψει γενομένῃ αὐτῷ χίλια ἔτη ποιήσειν ἐν Ἱερουσαλήμ, κ.τ.λ.

mony is not called in question by any one. Eusebius states that Melito of Sardis wrote a work on the Apocalypse of John,[1] and Jerome mentions the treatise.[2] There can be no doubt that had Melito thrown the slightest doubt on the Apostolic origin of the Apocalypse, Eusebius, whose dogmatic views led him to depreciate that writing, would have referred to the fact. Eusebius also mentions that Apollonius, a Presbyter of Ephesus, quoted the Apocalypse against the Montanists, and there is reason to suppose that he did so as an Apostolic work.[3] Eusebius further states that Theophilus of Antioch made use of testimony from the Apocalypse of John;[4] but although, as Eusebius does not mention anything to the contrary, it is probable that Theophilus really recognized the book to be by John the Apostle, the uncritical haste of Eusebius renders his vague statement of little value. We do not think it worth while to quote the evidence of later writers. Although Irenæus, who repeatedly assigns the Apocalypse to John, the disciple of the Lord,[5] is cited by Apologists as a very important witness, more especially from his intercourse with Polycarp, we do not attribute any value to his testimony, both from the late date at which he wrote, and from the uncritical and credulous character of his mind. Although he appeals to the testimony of those "who saw John face to face" with regard to the number of the name of the Beast, his own utter ignorance of the interpretation shows how little information he can have derived from Polycarp.[6] The same remarks apply still more strongly to Tertullian, who, however, most un-

---

[1] *Eusebius*, H. E., iv. 26.
[2] De Vir. Ill., 24.
[3] *Eusebius*, H. E., v. 18.
[4] *Ib.*, H. E., iv. 24.
[5] Adv. Hær., iv. 20, § 11, 21, § 3, 30, § 4, &c., &c.
[6] *Ib.*, v. 30.

hesitatingly assigns the Apocalypse to the Apostle John.[1] It would be useless more particularly to refer to later evidence, however, or quote even the decided testimony in its favour of Clement of Alexandria,[2] or Origen.[3]

The first doubt cast upon the authenticity of the Apocalypse occurs in the argument of Dionysius of Alexandria, one of the disciples of Origen, in the middle of the third century. He mentions that some had objected to the whole work as without sense or reason, and as displaying such dense ignorance, that it was impossible that an Apostle or even one in the Church, could have written it, and they assigned it to Cerinthus, who held the doctrine of the reign of Christ on earth.[4] These objections, it is obvious, are merely dogmatic, and do not affect to be historical. They are in fact a good illustration of the method by which the Canon was formed. If the doctrine of any writing met with the approval of the early Church, it was accepted with unhesitating faith, and its pretension to Apostolic origin was admitted as a natural consequence; but if, on the other hand, the doctrine of the writing was not clearly that of the community, it was rejected without further examination. It is an undeniable fact, that not a single trace exists of the application of historical criticism to any book of the New Testament in the early ages of Christianity. The case of the Apocalypse is most intelligible :—so long as the expectation and hope of a second advent and of a personal reign of the risen and glorified Christ, of the prevalence of which we have abundant testimony in the Pauline Epistles and other early works, continued to animate the Church, the

---

[1] Adv. Marc., iii. 14, 24, &c., &c.   [2] Stromata, vi. 13, §§ 106, 141.
[3] *Eusebius*, H. E., vi. 25, in Joann. Opp. iv. p. 17.
[4] *Eusebius*, H. E., vii. 24.

Apocalypse which excited and fostered them was a popular volume: but as years passed away and the general longing of Christians, eagerly marking the signs of the times, was again and again disappointed, and the hope of a Millennium began either to be abandoned or indefinitely postponed, the Apocalypse proportionately lost favour, or was regarded as an incomprehensible book misleading the world by illusory promises. Its history is that of a highly dogmatic treatise esteemed or contemned in proportion to the ebb and flow of opinion regarding the doctrines which it expresses.

The objections of Dionysius, resting first upon dogmatic grounds and his inability to understand the Apocalyptic utterances of the book, took the shape we have mentioned of a critical dilemma:—The author of the Gospel could not at the same time be the author of the Apocalypse. Dogmatic predilection decided the question in favour of the apostolic origin of the fourth Gospel, and the reasoning by which that decision is arrived at has, therefore, no critical force or value. The fact still remains that Justin Martyr distinctly refers to the Apocalypse as the work of the Apostle John and, as we have seen, no similar testimony exists in support of the claims of the fourth Gospel.

As another most important point, we may mention that there is probably not another work of the New Testament the precise date of the composition of which, within a very few weeks, can so positively be affirmed. No result of criticism rests upon a more secure basis and is now more universally accepted by all competent critics than the fact that the Apocalypse was written in A.D. 68-69.[1] The writer distinctly and repeatedly mentions his name: i. 1, "The revelation of Jesus Christ . . . .

[1] *Credner*, Einl. N. T., i. p. 705 ff.; *Davidson*, Int. N. T., i. p. 347 ff.

unto his servant John;"[1] i. 4, "John to the seven churches which are in Asia;"[2] and he states that the work was written in the island of Patmos where he was "on account of the Word of God and the testimony of Jesus."[3] Ewald, who decides in the most arbitrary manner against the authenticity of the Apocalypse and in favour of the Johannine authorship of the Gospel, objects that the author, although he certainly calls himself John, does not assume to be an Apostle, but merely terms himself the servant (δοῦλος) of Christ like other true Christians, and distinctly classes himself amongst the Prophets[4] and not amongst the Apostles.[5] We find, however, that Paul, who was not apt to waive his claims to the Apostolate, was content to call himself: "Paul a servant (δοῦλος) of Jesus Christ, called to be an Apostle," in writing to the Romans; (i. 1) and the superscription of the Epistle to the Philippians is: "Paul and Timothy servants (δοῦλοι) of Christ Jesus."[6] There was, moreover, reason why

Ewald, Jahrb. bibl. Wiss., v. p. 181 ff.; Gesch. V. Isr., vii. p. 227; Comment. in Apoc. Joh., 1828; Die Joh. Schr., ii. p. 62; *Guericke*, Gesammtgesch., p. 171, p. 522 f.; *Hausrath*, in Schenkel's Bib. Lex., 1869, i. p. 156; *Hilgenfeld*, Die Evangelien, p. 338; Einl. N. T., 1875, p. 447; *Kayser*, Rev. de Théol., 1856, xiii. p. 80; *Lücke*, Einl. Offenb. Joh., 1852, p. 840 ff.; *Lützelberger*, Die kirchl. Trad. Joh., p. 234; *Renan*, Vie de Jésus, xiiime. ed. p. lxxi. f.; L'Antechrist, p. 354 ff.; *Reuss*, Hist. Théol. Chrét., i. p. 430 f.; Gesch. N. T., p. 151; L'Apocalypse, 1878, p. 24 ff.; *Réville*, Rev. des deux Mondes, Oct. 1863, p. 623; Rev. de Théol., 1855, x. p. 4; *Rothe*, Anfänge chr. Kirche, 1837, p. 323; *Scholten*, Das Ev. Joh., p. 401; *Volkmar*, Comment. zur Offenb. Joh., 1862, p. 7 ff.; Die Religion Jesu, p. 148; *Zeller*, Vorträge, u. s. w., 1865, p. 212.

[1] Ἀποκάλυψις Ἰησοῦ Χριστοῦ . . . . . τῷ δούλῳ αὐτοῦ Ἰωάννῃ.
[2] Ἰωάννης ταῖς ἑπτὰ ἐκκλησίαις ταῖς ἐν τῇ Ἀσίᾳ. Cf. i. 9; xxii. 8.
[3] i. 9, διὰ τὸν λόγον τοῦ θεοῦ καὶ τὴν μαρτυρίαν Ἰησοῦ . . .
[4] Cf. i. 1—3, 9 f.; xix. 9 f.; xxii. 6—9, 10, 16 f., 18 f.
[5] *Ewald*, Die Joh. Schr., ii. p. 55 ff.; Jahrb. bibl. Wiss., v. p. 179 ff.
[6] We do not refer to the opening of the Epistle to Titus, nor to that which commences, "James a servant (δοῦλος) of God," &c., nor to the so-called "Epistle of Jude," all being too much disputed or apocryphal.

the author of the Book of Revelation, a work the form of which was decidedly based upon that of Daniel and other Jewish Apocalyptic writings, should rather adopt the character of Prophet than the less suitable designation of Apostle upon such an occasion. It is clear that he counted fully upon being generally known under the simple designation of "John," and when we consider the unmistakeable terms of authority with which he addresses the Seven Churches, it is scarcely possible to deny that the writer either was the Apostle, or distinctly desired to assume his personality. It is not necessary for us here to enter into any discussion regarding the "Presbyter John," for it is generally admitted that even he could not have had at that time any position in Asia Minor which could have warranted such a tone. If the name of Apostle, therefore, be not directly assumed—and it was not necessary to assume it—the authority of one is undeniably inferred.

Ewald, however, argues that, on the contrary, the author could not more clearly express that he was not one of the Twelve, than when he imagines (Apoc. xxi. 14) the names of the 'twelve apostles of the Lamb' shining upon the twelve foundation stones of the wall of the future heavenly Jerusalem. He considers that no intelligent person could thus publicly glorify himself or anticipate the honour which God alone can bestow. "And can any one seriously believe," he indignantly inquires, "that one of the Twelve, yea, that even he whom we know as the most delicate and refined amongst them could have written this of himself?"[1] Now, in the first place, we must remark that in this discussion

[1] Jahrb. bibl. Wiss., v. p. 180 f.; cf. Die Joh. Schriften, 1862, ii. p. 56 f.

it is not permissible to speak of our knowing John the Apostle as distinguished above all the rest of the Twelve for such qualities. Nowhere do we find such a representation of him except in the fourth Gospel, if even there, but, as we shall presently see, rather the contrary, and the fourth Gospel cannot here be received as evidence. We might, by way of retort, point out to those who assert the inspiration of the Apocalypse, that the symbolical representation of the heavenly Jerusalem is held to be practically objective, a revelation of things that "must shortly come to pass," and not a mere subjective sketch coloured according to the phantasy of the writer. Passing on, however, it must be apparent that the whole account of the heavenly city is typical, and that in basing its walls upon the Twelve, he does not glorify himself personally, but simply gives its place to the idea which was symbolised when Jesus is represented as selecting twelve disciples, the number of the twelve tribes, upon whose preaching the spiritual city was to be built up. The Jewish belief in a special preference of the Jews before all nations doubtless suggested this, and it forms a leading feature in the strong Hebraistic form of the writer's Christianity. The heavenly city is simply a glorified Jerusalem; the twelve Apostles, representatives of the twelve tribes, set apart for the regeneration of Israel, are the foundation-stones of the New City with its twelve gates, on which are written the names of the twelve tribes of Israel[1] for whom the city is more particularly provided. For 144,000 of Israel are first sealed, 12,000 of each of the twelve tribes before the Seer beholds the great multitude of all nations and tribes and peoples.[2] The whole description is a

---

[1] Apoc. xxi. 12.   [2] *Ib.*, vii. 4—9.

mere allegory characterized by the strongest Jewish dogmatism, and it is of singular value for the purpose of identifying the author.

Moreover, the apparent glorification of the Twelve is more than justified by the promise which Jesus is represented by the Synoptics[1] as making to them in person. When Peter, in the name of the Twelve, asks what is reserved for those who have forsaken all and followed him, Jesus replies: "Verily I say unto you that ye which have followed me, in the regeneration when the Son of Man shall sit in the throne of his glory, ye also shall be set upon twelve thrones judging the twelve tribes of Israel."[2] Ewald himself, in his distribution of the materials of our existing first Synoptic to the supposed original sources, assigns this passage to the very oldest Gospel.[3] What impropriety is there, and what improbability, therefore, that an Apostle, in an apocalyptic allegory, should represent the names of the twelve Apostles as inscribed upon the twelve foundation stones of the spiritual Jerusalem, as the names of the twelve tribes of Israel were inscribed upon the twelve gates of the city? On the contrary, we submit that it is probable under the circumstances that an Apostle should make such a representation, and in view of the facts regarding the Apostle John himself which we have from the Synoptics, it is particularly in harmony with his character, and these characteristics directly tend to establish his identity with the author.

"How much less is it credible of the Apostle John," says Ewald, elsewhere, pursuing the same argument, " who, as a writer, is so incomparably modest and

---

[1] Matt. xix. 27, 28; Luke xii. 28—30.
[2] Matt. xix. 28.
[3] Die drei ersten Evv., p. 23.

delicate in feeling, and does not in a single one of the
writings really emanating from him name himself as
the author, or even proclaim his own praise."[1] This is
merely sentimental assumption of facts to which we shall
hereafter allude, but if the "incomparable modesty" of
which he speaks really existed, nothing could more conclusively separate the author of the fourth Gospel from the
son of Zebedee whom we know in the Synoptics, or more
support the claims of the Apocalypse. In the first
place, we must assert that, in writing a serious history
of the life and teaching of Jesus, full of marvellous
events and astounding doctrines, the omission of his
name by an Apostle can not only not be recognized as
genuine modesty, but must be condemned as culpable
neglect. It is perfectly incredible that an Apostle could
have written such a work without attaching his name as
the guarantee of his intimate acquaintance with the events
and statements he records. What would be thought of a
historian who published a history without a single reference to recognized authorities, and yet who did not
declare even his own name as some evidence of his truth?
The fact is, that the first two Synoptics bear no author's
name because they are not the work of any one man, but
the collected materials of many; the third Synoptic only
pretends to be a compilation for private use; and the
fourth Gospel bears no simple signature because it is
neither the work of an Apostle, nor of an eye-witness of
the events and hearer of the teaching it records.

If it be considered incredible, however, that an Apostle
could, even in an Allegory, represent the names of the
Twelve as written on the foundation stones of the New
Jerusalem, and the incomparable modesty and delicacy

[1] Die Joh. Schr., ii. p. 56 f.

of feeling of the assumed author of the fourth Gospel be contrasted with it so much to the disadvantage of the writer of the Apocalypse, we ask whether this reference to the collective Twelve can be considered at all on a par with the self-glorification of the disguised author of the Gospel, who, not content with the simple indication of himself as John a servant of Jesus Christ, and with sharing distinction equally with the rest of the Twelve, assumes to himself alone a pre-eminence in the favour and affection of his Master, as well as a distinction amongst his fellow disciples, of which we first hear from himself, and which is anything but corroborated by the three Synoptics? The supposed author of the fourth Gospel, it is true, does not plainly mention his name, but he distinguishes himself as "the disciple whom Jesus loved," and represents himself as "leaning on Jesus' breast at supper."[1] This distinction assumed to himself, and this preference over the other disciples in the love of him whom he represents as God, is much greater self-glorification than that of the author of the Apocalypse. We shall presently see how far Ewald is right in saying, moreover, that the author does not clearly indicate the person for whom at least he desires to be mistaken.

We must conclude that these objections have no weight, and that there is no internal evidence whatever against the supposition that the "John" who announces himself as the author of the Apocalypse was the Apostle. On the contrary, the tone of authority adopted throughout, and the evident certainty that his identity would everywhere be recognized, denote a position in the Church which no other person of the name of John could well have held at the time when the Apocalypse was written.

[1] John xiii. 23; xix. 26, 27; xx. 2 f.; cf. xxi. 20 ff.

The external evidence, therefore, which indicates the Apostle John as the author of the Apocalypse is quite in harmony with the internal testimony of the book itself. We have already pointed out the strong colouring of Judaism in the views of the writer. Its imagery is thoroughly Jewish, and its allegorical representations are entirely based upon Jewish traditions, and hopes. The heavenly City is a New Jerusalem; its twelve gates are dedicated to the twelve tribes of Israel; God and the Lamb are the Temple of it; and the sealed of the twelve tribes have the precedence over the nations, and stand with the Lamb on Mount Zion (xiv. 1) having his name and his Father's written on their foreheads. The language in which the book is written is the most Hebraistic Greek of the New Testament, as its contents are the most deeply tinged with Judaism. If, finally, we seek for some traces of the character of the writer, we see in every page the impress of an impetuous fiery spirit, whose symbol is the Eagle, breathing forth vengeance against the enemies of the Messiah and impatient till it be accomplished, and the whole of the visions of the Apocalypse proceed to the accompaniment of the rolling thunders of God's wrath.

We may now turn to examine such historical data as exist regarding John the son of Zebedee, and to inquire whether they accord better with the character and opinions of the author of the Apocalypse or of the Evangelist. John and his brother James are represented by the Synoptics as being the sons of Zebedee and Salome. They were fishermen on the sea of Galilee, and at the call of Jesus they left their ship and their father and followed him.[1] Their fiery and impetuous character led

[1] Matt. iv. 21 f.; Mark i. 19 f.; Luke v. 19 ff.

Jesus to give them the surname of Βοανηργές: "Sons of thunder,"[1] an epithet justified by several incidents which are related regarding them. Upon one occasion, John sees one casting out devils in his master's name, and in an intolerant spirit forbids him because he did not follow them, for which he is rebuked by Jesus.[2] Another time, when the inhabitants of a Samaritan village would not receive them, John and James angrily turn to Jesus and say: "Lord, wilt thou that we command fire to come down from heaven, and consume them, even as Elijah did?"[3] A remarkable episode will have presented itself already to the mind of every reader, which the second Synoptic Gospel narrates as follows: Mark x. 35, "And James and John the sons of Zebedee come unto him saying unto him: Teacher, we would that thou shouldest do for us whatsoever we shall ask thee. 36. And he said unto them: What would ye that I should do for you? 37. They said unto him: Grant that we may sit, one on thy right hand, and the other on thy left hand in thy glory. 38. But Jesus said to them: Ye know not what ye ask: can ye drink the cup that I drink? or be baptized with the baptism that I am baptized with? 39. And they said unto him: We can. And Jesus said unto them: The cup that I drink ye shall drink; and with the baptism that I am baptized withal shall ye be baptized: 40. But to sit on my right hand or on my left hand is not mine to give, but for whom it has been prepared. 41. And when the ten heard it they began to be much displeased with James and John." It is difficult to say whether the

---

[1] Mark iii. 17.
[2] Mark ix. 38 f.; Luke ix. 49 f.
[3] Luke ix. 54 ff.

effrontery and selfishness of the request, or the assurance with which the brethren assert their power to emulate the Master is more striking in this scene. Apparently, the grossness of the proceeding already began to be felt when our first Gospel was edited, for it represents the request as made by the mother of James and John; but that is a very slight decrease of the offence, inasmuch as the brethren are obviously consenting, if not inciting, parties to the prayer, and utter their "We can," with the same absence of "incomparable modesty."[1] After the death of Jesus, John remained in Jerusalem,[2] and chiefly confined his ministry to the city and its neighbourhood.[3] The account which Hegesippus gives of James the brother of Jesus who was appointed overseer of the Church in Jerusalem will not be forgotten,[4] and we refer to it merely in illustration of primitive Christianity. However mythical elements are worked up into the narrative, one point is undoubted fact, that the Christians of that community were but a sect of Judaism, merely superadding to Mosaic doctrines belief in the actual advent of the Messiah whom Moses and the prophets had foretold; and we find, in the Acts of the Apostles, Peter and John represented as "going up into the Temple at the hour of prayer,"[5] like other Jews. In the Epistle of Paul to the Galatians, we have most valuable evidence with regard to the Apostle John. Paul found him still in Jerusalem on the occasion of the visit referred to in that letter, about A.D. 50—53. We need not quote at length the important passage Gal. ii. 1 ff., but the fact

---

[1] Matt. xx. 20 ff.
[2] Acts i. 13; iii. 1.
[3] Acts viii. 25; xv. 1 ff.
[4] *Eusebius*, H. E., ii. 23; cf. vol. i. p. 430 f.
[5] Acts iii. 1. f.

is undeniable, and stands upon stronger evidence than almost any other particular regarding the early Church, being distinctly and directly stated by Paul himself: that the three "pillar" Apostles representing the Church there were James, Peter, and John. Peter is markedly termed the Apostle of the circumcision, and the differences between him and Paul are evidence of the opposition of their views. James and John are clearly represented as sharing the views of Peter, and whilst Paul finally agrees with them that he is to go to the Gentiles, the three στῦλοι elect to continue their ministry to the circumcision.[1] Here is John, therefore, clearly devoted to the Apostleship of the circumcision as opposed to Paul, whose views, as we gather from the whole of Paul's account, were little more than tolerated by the στῦλοι. Before leaving New Testament data, we may here point out the statement in the Acts of the Apostles that Peter and John were known to be "unlettered and ignorant men"[2] (ἄνθρωποι ἀγράμματοι καὶ ἰδιῶται). Later tradition mentions one or two circumstances regarding John to which we may briefly refer. Irenæus states: "There are those who heard him (Polycarp) say that John, the disciple of the Lord, going to bathe at Ephesus and perceiving Cerinthus within, rushed forth from the bath-house without bathing, but crying out: 'Let us fly lest the bath-house fall down: Cerinthus, the enemy of the truth, being within it.' . . . So great was the care which the Apostles and their disciples took not to hold even verbal intercourse with any of the corrupters of the truth,"[3] &c. Polycrates, who was Bishop of Ephesus

---

[1] Gal. ii. 8—9.
[2] Acts iv. 13.
[3] *Irenæus*, Adv. Hær., iii. 3, § 4; *Eusebius*, H. E., iv. 14.

about the beginning of the third century, states that the Apostle John wore the mitre and petalon of the high priest (ὃς ἐγενήθη ἱερεὺς τὸ πέταλον πεφορηκώς),[1] a tradition which agrees with the Jewish tendencies of the Apostle of the circumcision as Paul describes him.[2]

Now if we compare these data regarding John the son of Zebedee with the character of John the author of the Apocalypse, as we trace it in the work itself, it is impossible not to be struck by the singular agreement. The Hebraistic Greek and abrupt inelegant diction are natural to the unlettered fisherman of Galilee, and the fierce and intolerant spirit which pervades the book is precisely that which formerly forbade the working of miracles, even in the name of the Master, by any not of the immediate circle of Jesus, and which desired to consume an inhospitable village with fire from heaven.[3] The Judaistic form of Christianity which is represented throughout the Apocalypse, and the Jewish elements which enter so largely into its whole composition, are precisely those

---

[1] *Eusebius*, H. E., iii. 31.

[2] We need not refer to any of the other legends regarding John, but it may be well to mention the tradition common amongst the Fathers which assigned to him the cognomen of "the Virgin." One Codex gives as the superscription of the Apocalypse: "τοῦ ἁγίου ἐνδοξοτάτου ἀποστόλου καὶ εὐαγγελιστοῦ παρθένου ἠγαπημένου ἐπιστηθίου Ἰωάννου θεολόγου" and we know that it is reported in early writings that, of all the Apostles, only John and the Apostle Paul remained unmarried, whence probably, in part, this title. In connection with this we may point to the importance attached to virginity in the Apocalypse, xiv. 4; cf. *Schwegler*, Das nachap. Zeit., ii. p. 254; *Lücke*, Comm. üb. d. Br. Joh., 1836, p. 32 f.; *Credner*, Einl. N. T., i. p. 21.

[3] The very objection of Ewald regarding the glorification of the Twelve, if true, would be singularly in keeping with the audacious request of John and his brother, to sit on the right and left hand of the glorified Jesus, for we find none of the "incomparable modesty" which the imaginative critic attributes to the author of the fourth Gospel in the John of the Synoptics.

which we might expect from John the Apostle of the circumcision and the associate of James and of Peter in the very centre of Judaism. Parts of the Apocalypse, indeed, derive a new significance when we remember the opposition which the Apostle of the Gentiles met with from the Apostles of the circumcision, as plainly declared by Paul in his Epistle to the Galatians ii. 1. ff., and apparent in other parts of his writings.

We have already seen the scarcely disguised attack which is made on Paul in the Clementine Homilies under the name of Simon the Magician, the Apostle Peter following him from city to city for the purpose of denouncing and refuting his teaching. There can be no doubt that the animosity against Paul which was felt by the Ebionitic party, to which John as well as Peter belonged, was extreme, and when the novelty of the doctrine of justification by faith alone, taught by him, is considered, it is very comprehensible. In the Apocalypse, we find undeniable traces of it which accord with what Paul himself says, and with the undoubted tradition of the early Church. Not only is Paul silently excluded from the number of the Apostles, which might be intelligible when the typical nature of the number twelve is considered, but allusion is undoubtedly made to him, in the Epistles to the Churches. It is clear that Paul is referred to in the address to the Church of Ephesus: "And thou didst try them which say that they are Apostles and are not, and didst find them false;"[1] and also in the words to the Church of Smyrna: "But I have a few things against thee, because thou hast there them that hold the teaching of Balaam, who taught

---

[1] Apoc., ii. 2.

Balak to cast a stumbling block before the sons of Israel, to eat things sacrificed unto idols,"[1] &c., as well as elsewhere.[2] Without dwelling on this point, however, we think it must be apparent to every unprejudiced person that the Apocalypse singularly corresponds in every respect—language, construction, and thought—with what we are told of the character of the Apostle John by the Synoptic Gospels and by tradition, and that the internal evidence, therefore, accords with the external in attributing the composition of the Apocalypse to that Apostle.[3]

---

[1] Apoc., ii. 14, iii. 9.

[2] *Baur*, Gesch. christl. Kirche, i. p. 80 ff.; *Hilgenfeld*, Einl. N. T., 1875, p. 413 ff.; *Keim*, Jesu v. Nazara, i. p. 160, anm. 2; *Krenkel*, Protestanten Bibel, N. T. 1874, p. 1003; *Renan*, St. Paul, 1869, p. 303 ff., 367 f.; *Rovers*, Heeft Paulus zich ter verdedig. v. zijn Apostelschap op Wonderen beroepen?, 1870, p. 32 f.; *Schenkel*, Das Christusbild d. Apostel, 1879, p. 103 ff.; *Schwegler*, Das nachap. Zeit. i. p. 172 f., ii. p. 116; *Volkmar*, Comm. z. Offenb. Johannis, 1862, p. 26 ff., p. 80 ff.; *Tjeenk Willink*, Justinus Mart., 1868, p. 44; *Zeller*, Vorträge u. s. w., 1865, p. 215 f. Cf. *Hausrath*, in Schenkel's Bib. Lex., 1869, i. p. 163; *Köstlin*, Lehrb. d. Ev. u. Br. Johannis, 1843, p. 486 f.; *Ritschl*, Entst. altk. Kirche, p. 134 f.

[3] *Baur*, Unters. kan. Evv., pp. 345 ff., 376 ff.; Theol. Jahrb., 1844, p. 661 ff.; *Bertholdt*, Einl. A. u. N. T., iv. p. 1800—1875; *Christianus*, Das Ev. d. Reichs, 1859, p. 900; *A. C. Dannemann*, Wer ist der Verfasser der Offenb. Johannis? 1841; *Ebrard*, Das Ev. Johann., p. 137 ff.; Die ovang. Gesch., p. 847 ff.; *Eichhorn*, Einl. N. T., ii. p. 375 ff.; *Feilmoser*, Einl. N. B., p. 569 ff.; *Gebhardt*, Lehrbegriff d. Apokalypse, 1873; *Guericke*, Gesammtgesch., p. 498 ff.; Beiträge, p. 181 ff.; *Hase*, Die Tüb. Schule, p. 25 ff.; *Hänlein*, Einl. N. T., i. p. 220 ff.; *Hartwig*, Apol. d. Apoc., u. s. w., 1780; *Hävernick*, Lucubr. crit. ad Apoc. spectantur, 1842; *Hengstenberg*, Die Offenb. d. heil. Johann., 1849; *Hilgenfeld*, Die Evangelien, p. 338; Zeitschr. wiss. Theol., 1872, p. 372 ff., 1873, p. 102 ff., 1874, p. 305 ff.; Einl. N. T., 1875, p. 395 ff.; p. 407 ff.; *Hug*, Einl. N. T., ii. p. 496 ff.; *Kliefoth*, Die Offenb. Joh., 1874, p. 4 ff.; *Kolthof*, Apoc. Joanni apost. vindicata, 1834; *J. P. Lange*, in Tholuck's Lit. Anzeiger, 1838, No. 20 ff.; Vermischt. Schr., ii. p. 173 ff.; Das ap. Zeit., 1853, p. 83; *Lechler*, Das ap. u. nachap. Zeit., p. 197 ff.; *Lightfoot*, Ep. to Galatians, 4th ed. p. 343 f.; *Lüderwald*, Beurth. u. Erkl. Offenb. Johann., 1788; *Luthardt*, Lehre v. d. letzt. Dingen, 1861, p. 165 ff.; *Niermeyer*, Verhandel. over Echth. Joh. Schr., 1852; *Olshausen*, Echtheit. d. v. kan. Evv., 1832; *de Pressensé*, Hist. Trois prem. Siècles. 2e éd. p. 311 ff.; *Reithmayr*, Einl. N. T., p. 774 ff.; *Réville* (doubtful), Rev. des Deux Mondes, Oct. 1863,

We may without hesitation affirm, at least, that with the exception of one or two of the Epistles of Paul there is

p. 633; *Riggenbach*, Die Zeugn. Evang. Joh., p. 30 ff.; *Schwegler*, Das nachap. Zeit., ii. p. 249 ff.; *Schnitzer*, Theol. Jahrb., 1842, 'p. 451 ff.; *Storr*, N. Apol. d. Offenb. Joh. 1783; Zweck d. evang. Gesch. u. Br. Joh., 1786, pp. 70 ff., 83, 163; *Thiersch*, Die Kirche im. ap. Zeit., p. 245 f.; *Tholuck*, Glaubw. evang. Gesch., p. 280 ff.; *Volkmar*, Comment. Offenb. Joh., 1862, p. 38 ff.; *Zeller*, Theol. Jahrb., 1842, p. 654 ff., Vorträge u. s. w. p. 212 f., &c., &c. Cf. *Krenkel*, Protestanten Bibel, N. T. 1874, p. 998 f., Der Ap. Johannes, 1871, p. 113 ff.; *Renan*, Vie de Jésus, xiiime éd. p. lxxi. f.; L'Antechrist, 1873, p. xxii. ff., p. 340 ff.; *Spüth*, Protestanten Bibel, N. T. 1874, p. 263 f.; *Weisse*, Die evang. Gesch., i. p. 98, anm. 3.

Although many of those who assign the Apocalypse to the Apostle John are apologists who likewise assert that he wrote the Gospel, very many accept the authenticity of the Apocalypse as opposed to that of the Gospel in the dilemma which we have stated. On the other hand not a few of those who reject the Apocalypse equally reject the Gospel, and consider that neither the one nor the other is apostolic.

We do not of course pretend to give a complete list of those who assert or deny the apostolic authorship of the Apocalypse, but merely refer to those whom we have noted down. The following deny the apostolic authorship: *Bleek*, Beiträge, p. 189—200; Einl. N. T., 1866, pp. 147 ff., 624 ff.; 1875, pp. 170 ff., 724 ff.; *Ballenstedt*, Philo u. Johannes, u. s. w., 1812; *Bretschneider*, Probabilia, p. 150 ff.; *Credner*, Einl. N. T., i. p. 732 ff.; *Corrodi*, Versuch Beleucht. d. Gesch. Bibelkanons, 1792, ii. p. 303 ff.; *Cludius*, Uransichten d. Christenth. Alt., 1808, p. 312 ff.; *Düsterdieck*, H'buch. Offenb. Joh., 1865, p. 62 ff.; *Ewald*, Jahrb. bibl. Wiss., v. 1852—53, p. 179 ff.; Comment. in Apoc. Joh., 1829, proleg. § 8; Die Joh. Schr., ii. p. 55 ff.; Gesch. V. Isr., vi. p. 694, vii. p. 227; *Hitzig*, Ueber Johan. Marcus u. s. Scriften; *Kayser* (doubtful), Rev. de Théol., 1856, xiii. p. 85; *Keim*, Jesu v. Nazara, i. p. 159 f.; *Lücke*, Einl. Offenb. Joh., ii. pp. 491 ff., 802; Th. Studien u. Krit., 1836, p. 654 ff.; *Luther*, Præf. in Apoc., 1552; *Lützelberger*, Die kirchl. Trad. ap. Joh., 1840, pp. 198 f., 210 ff.; *Mangold*, zu Bleek's Einl. N. T., 1875, p. 168 anm., p. 700 anm.*, p. 729 anm.; *Messner*, Lehre d. Apostel, 1856, p. 360 ff.; *Neander*, Gesch. Pflanz. u. s. w. Chr. Kirche, 1862, p. 481 f.; *Neudecker*, Einl. N. T., p. 757 ff.; *Schenkel*, Das Christusbild d. Apostel, 1879, p. 108 ff.; *Schleiermacher*, Einl. N. T., p. 470 f.; *Scholten*, De Apost. Johannes in Klein-Azië, 1871, p. 3 ff.; *Schott*, Isagoge, §§ 114 ff., p. 473 ff.; *Semler*, Neue Unters. über Apoc., 1776; Abhandl. Unters. d. Kanons, i. Anhang; *Stroth*, Freimüthige Unters. Offenb. Joh. betreffend, 1771; *Weizsäcker*, Unters. evang. Gesch., pp. 295, 235 ff.; *Wittichen*, Gesch. Charakter Ev. Joh., 1868, p. 101 ff. Cf. *Beyschlag*, Die Offenb. Johann., 1876, p. 22; *Holtzmann*, in Schenkel's Bib. Lex., iii. pp. 337 ff., 352 ff.; *Michaelis*, Einl. N. T., ii. p. 1573 ff.; *Reuss*, Gesch. N. T., p. 151 f.; L'Apocalypse, 1878, p. 27 ff.; *de Wette*, Einl. N. T., p. 422 ff.

no work of the New Testament which is supported by such close evidence.

We need not discuss the tradition as to the residence of the Apostle John in Asia Minor, regarding which much might be said. Those who accept the authenticity of the Apocalypse of course admit its composition in the neighbourhood of Ephesus,[1] and see in this the confirmation of the wide-spread tradition that the Apostle spent a considerable period of the latter part of his life in that city. We may merely mention, in passing, that a historical basis for the tradition has occasionally been disputed, and has latterly again been denied by some able critics.[2] The evidence for this, as for everything else connected with the early ages of Christianity, is extremely unsatisfactory. Nor need we trouble ourselves with the dispute as to the Presbyter John, to whom many ascribe the composition, on the one hand, of the Apocalypse and, on the other, of the Gospel, according as they finally accept the one or the other alternative of the critical dilemma which we have explained. We have only to do with the Apostle John and his connection with either of the two writings.

If we proceed to compare the character of the Apostle John, as we have it depicted in the Synoptics and other writings to which we have referred, with that of the author of the fourth Gospel, and to contrast the peculiarities of both, we have a very different result. Instead of the Hebraistic Greek and harsh diction which might

[1] Apoc. i. 9.
[2] *Keim*, Jesu v. Nazara, i. p. 162 ff.; *Wittichen*, Der gesch. Charakter Ev. Joh., 1868, p. 101 ff.; *Scholten*, De Apostel Johannes in Klein Azië, 1871; *Holtzmann*, in Schenkel's Bib. Lex. iii. pp. 332 ff., 352 ff.; Krit. d. Ephes. u. Kolosserbr., 1872, p. 314 ff. Cf. *Ziegler*, Irenäus, Bisch. v. Lyon, 1871, p. 127 ff.

be expected from the unlettered and ignorant fisherman of Galilee, we find, in the fourth Gospel, the purest and least Hebraistic Greek of any of the Gospels (some parts of the third Synoptic, perhaps, alone excepted), and a refinement and beauty of composition whose charm has captivated the world, and in too many cases prevented the calm exercise of judgment. Instead of the fierce and intolerant temper of the Son of thunder, we find a spirit breathing forth nothing but gentleness and love. Instead of the Judaistic Christianity of the Apostle of Circumcision who merely tolerates Paul, we find a mind which has so completely detached itself from Judaism that the writer makes the very appellation of "Jew" equivalent to that of an enemy of the truth. Not only are the customs and feasts of the Jews disregarded and spoken of as observances of a people with whom the writer has no concern, but he anticipates the day when neither on Mount Gerizim nor yet at Jerusalem men shall worship the Father, but when it shall be recognized that the only true worship is that which is offered in spirit and in truth. Faith in Jesus Christ and the merits of his death is the only way by which man can attain to eternal life, and the Mosaic Law is practically abolished. We venture to assert that, taking the portrait of John the son of Zebedee, which is drawn in the Synoptics and the Epistle of Paul to the Galatians, supplemented by later tradition, to which we have referred, and comparing it with that of the writer of the fourth Gospel, no unprejudiced mind can fail to recognize that there are not two features alike.

It is the misfortune of this case, that the beauty of the Gospel under trial has too frequently influenced the decision of the judges, and men who have, in other matters, exhibited sound critical judgment, in this abandon themselves to sheer sentimentality, and indulge in rhapsodies when reasons would be more appropriate. Bearing in mind that we have given the whole of the data regarding John the son of Zebedee furnished by New Testament writings,—excluding merely the fourth Gospel itself, which, of course, cannot at present be received in evidence,—as well as the only traditional information possessing, from its date and character, any appreciable value, it will become apparent that every argument which proceeds on the assumption that John was the beloved disciple, and possessed of characteristics quite different from those we meet with in the writings to which we have referred, is worthless and a mere petitio principii. We can, therefore, appreciate the state of the case when, for instance, we find an able man like Credner commencing his inquiry as to who was the author of the fourth Gospel, with such words as the following: "Were we entirely without historical data regarding the author of the fourth Gospel, who is not named in the writing itself, we should still, from internal grounds in the Gospel itself—from the nature of the language, from the freshness and perspicacity of the narrative, from the exactness and precision of the statements, from the peculiar manner of the mention of the Baptist and of the sons of Zebedee, from the love and fervour rising to ecstacy which the writer manifests towards Jesus, from the irresistible charm which is poured out over the whole ideally-composed evangelical history, from the philosophical considerations with which the Gospel begins—be led to the result: that the author of such a Gospel can only be a native of Palestine, can only be a direct eye-witness, can only be an Apostle, can only be a favourite of Jesus, can only be that John whom Jesus held captivated to himself by the whole heavenly spell of his teaching, that John who rested on the bosom of Jesus, stood beneath his cross, and whose later residence in a city like Ephesus proves that philosophical speculation not merely attracted him, but that he also knew how to maintain his place amongst philosophically cultivated Greeks."[1] It is almost impossible to proceed further in building up theory upon baseless assumption; but we shall hereafter see that he is kept in countenance by Ewald, who outstrips him in the boldness and minuteness of his conjectures. We must now more carefully examine the details of the case.

The language in which the Gospel is written, as we have already mentioned, is much less Hebraic than that of the other Gospels, with the exception of parts of the Gospel according to Luke, and its Hebraisms are not on the whole greater than was almost invariably the case with Hellenistic Greek, but its composition is distinguished by peculiar smoothness, grace, and beauty, and in this respect it is assigned the first rank amongst the Gospels. It may be remarked that the connection which Credner finds between the language and the Apostle John arises out of the supposition, that long residence in Ephesus had enabled him to acquire that facility of composition in the Greek language which is one of its characteristics. Ewald, who exaggerates the Hebraism of the work, resorts nevertheless to the conjecture, which we shall hereafter more fully consider, that the Gospel was written from dictation by young friends of John in Ephesus, who put the aged Apostle's thoughts, in many places, into purer Greek as they

[1] *Credner*, Einl. N. T., i. p. 208.

wrote them down.[1] The arbitrary nature of such an explanation, adopted in one shape or another by many apologists, requires no remark, but we shall at every turn meet with similar assumptions advanced to overcome difficulties. Now, although there is no certain information as to the time when, if ever, the Apostle removed into Asia Minor, it is at least pretty certain that he did not leave Palestine before A.D. 60.[2] We find him still at Jerusalem about A.D. 50—53, when Paul went thither, and he had not at that time any intention of leaving, but, on the contrary, his dedication of himself to the ministry of the circumcision is distinctly mentioned by the Apostle.[3] The "unlettered and ignorant" fisherman of Galilee, therefore, had obviously attained an age when habits of thought and expression have become fixed, and when a new language cannot without great difficulty be acquired. If we consider the Apocalypse to be his work, we find positive evidence of such markedly different thought and language actually existing when the Apostle must have been between sixty and seventy years of age, that it is quite impossible to conceive that he could have subsequently acquired the language and mental characteristics of the fourth Gospel.[4] It would be perfectly absurd, so far as language goes, to find in the fourth Gospel the slightest indication of the Apostle John, of whose language we have no information whatever except from the Apocalypse, a composition

---

[1] Die Joh. Schr., i. p. 50 f.

[2] It is almost certain that John did not remove to Asia Minor during Paul's time. There is no trace of his being there in the Pauline Epistles. Cf. de Wette, Einl. N. T., p. 221.   [3] Gal. ii. 9.

[4] Ewald, Die Joh. Schr., ii. p. 62 f.; Hilgenfeld, Die Evangelien, p. 340 f.; Keim, Jesu v. Nazara, i. p. 159; de Wette, Einl. N. T., p. 419, anm. d.

which, if accepted as written by the Apostle, would at once exclude all consideration of the Gospel as his work.

There are many circumstances, however, which seem clearly to indicate that the author of the fourth Gospel was neither a native of Palestine nor a Jew, and to some of these we must briefly refer. The philosophical statements with which the Gospel commences, it will be admitted, are anything but characteristic of the Son of thunder, the ignorant and unlearned fisherman of Galilee who, to a comparatively advanced period of life, continued preaching in his native country to his brethren of the circumcision. Attempts have been made to trace the Logos doctrine of the fourth Gospel to the purely Hebraic source of the Old Testament, but every impartial mind must perceive that here there is no direct and simple transformation of the theory of Wisdom of the Proverbs and Old Testament Apocrypha, and no mere development of the later Memra of the Targums, but a very advanced application to Christianity of Alexandrian philosophy, with which we have become familiar through the writings of Philo, to which reference has so frequently been made. It is quite true that a decided step beyond the doctrine of Philo is made when the Logos is represented as $\sigma \grave{\alpha} \rho \xi\ \grave{\epsilon} \gamma \acute{\epsilon} \nu \epsilon \tau o$ in the person of Jesus, but this argument is equally applicable to the Jewish doctrine of Wisdom, and that step had already been taken before the composition of the Gospel. In the Alexandrian philosophy everything was prepared for the final application of the doctrine, and nothing is more clear than the fact that the writer of the fourth Gospel was well acquainted with the teaching of the Alexandrian school, from which he derived his philosophy, and its elaborate and systematic application to Jesus alone indicates a late development of Christian doctrine, which we maintain could not have been attained by the Judaistic son of Zebedee.[1]

We have already on several occasions referred to the attitude which the writer of the fourth Gospel assumes towards the Jews. Apart from the fact that he places Christianity generally in strong antagonism to Judaism, as light to darkness, truth to a lie, and presents the doctrine of a hypostatic Trinity in the most developed form to be found in the New Testament, in striking contrast to the three Synoptics, and in contradiction to Hebrew Monotheism, he writes at all times as one who not only is not a Jew himself, but has nothing to do with their laws and customs. He speaks everywhere of the feasts " of the Jews," " the passover of the Jews," " the manner of the purifying of the Jews," " the Jews' feast of tabernacles," " as the manner of the Jews is to bury," " the Jews' preparation day," and so on.[2] The Law of Moses is spoken of as " your law," " their law," as of a people with which the writer was not connected.[3] Moreover, the Jews are represented as continually in virulent opposition to Jesus, and seeking to kill him ; and the word " Jew " is the unfailing indication of the enemies of the truth, and the persecutors of the Christ.[4] The Jews are not once spoken of as the favoured people of God, but they are denounced as " children of the devil," who is " the father of lies and a murderer from the beginning."[5] The author makes Caiaphas and the chief

[1] Most critics agree that the characteristics of the fourth Gospel render the supposition that it was the work of an old man untenable.
[2] John ii. 6, 13 ; v. 1 ; vi. 4 ; vii. 2 ; xix. 40, 42, &c., &c.
[3] *Ib.*, viii. 17 ; x. 34 ; xv. 25, &c., &c.
[4] *Ib.*, v. 16, 18 ; vii. 13, 19 f. ; viii. 40, 59 ; ix. 22, 28 ; xviii. 31 ff. ; xix. 12 ff.
[5] John viii. 44.

priests and Pharisees speak of the Jewish people not as ὁ λαός, but as τὸ ἔθνος, the term employed by the Jews to designate the Gentiles.[1] We need scarcely point out that the Jesus of the fourth Gospel is no longer of the race of David, but the Son of God. The expectation of the Jews that the Messiah should be of the seed of David is entirely set aside, and the genealogies of the first and third Synoptics tracing his descent are not only ignored, but the whole idea absolutely excluded.

Then the writer calls Annas the high priest, although at the same time Caiaphas is represented as holding that office.[2] The expression which he uses is: "Caiaphas being the high priest that year" (ἀρχιερεὺς ὢν τοῦ ἐνιαυτοῦ ἐκείνου). This statement, made more than once, indicates the belief that the office was merely annual, which is erroneous. Josephus states with regard to Caiaphas, that he was high priest for ten years from A.D. 25—36.[3] Ewald and others argue that the expression "that year" refers to the year in which the

---

[1] τὸ ἔθνος is applied to the Jewish people 14 times in the New Testament. It is so used five times in the fourth Gospel (xi. 48, 50, 51, 52, xviii. 35), and elsewhere, with one exception, only by the author of the third Synoptic and Acts (Luke vii. 5, xxiii. 2; Acts x. 22, xxiv. 3, 10, 17, xxvi. 4, xxviii. 19), who is almost universally believed to have been a Gentile convert and not a Jew. The exception referred to is 1 Pet. ii. 9, where, however, the use is justified: ἔθνος ἅγιον, λαὸς εἰς περιποίησιν. The word λαός is only twice used in the fourth Gospel, once in xi. 50, where ἔθνος occurs in the same verse, and again in xviii. 14, where the same words of Caiaphas, xi. 50, are quoted. It is found in viii. 2, but that episode does not belong to the fourth Gospel, but is probably taken from the Gospel according to the Hebrews. Ewald himself points out that the saying of Caiaphas is the purest Greek, and this is another proof that it could not proceed from the son of Zebedee. It could still less be, as it stands, an original speech in Greek of the high priest to the Jewish Council, a point which does not require remark. Cf. *Ewald*, Die Joh. Schr., i. p. 325, anm. 1.

[2] John xi. 49, 51; xviii. 13, 16, 19, 22, 24.

[3] Antiq. xviii. 2, § 2; 4, § 3; cf. Matt. xxvi. 3, 57.

death of Jesus, so memorable to the writer, took place, and that it does not exclude the possibility of his having been high priest for successive years also.[1] This explanation, however, is quite arbitrary and insufficient, and this is shown by the additional error in representing Annas as also high priest at the same time. The Synoptists know nothing of the preliminary examination before Annas, and the reason given by the writer of the fourth Gospel why the soldiers first took Jesus to Annas: "for he was father-in-law to Caiaphas, who was high priest that same year,"[2] is inadmissible. The assertion is a clear mistake, and it probably originated in a stranger, writing of facts and institutions with which he was not well acquainted, being misled by an error equally committed by the author of the third Gospel and of the Acts of the Apostles. In Luke iii. 2, the word of God is said to come to John the Baptist: "in the high priesthood of Annas and Caiaphas" (ἐπὶ ἀρχιερέως Ἄννα καὶ Καϊάφα), and again, in Acts iv. 6, Annas is spoken of as the high priest when Peter and John healed the lame man at the gate of the Temple which was called "Beautiful," and Caiaphas is mentioned immediately after: "and Annas the high priest, and Caiaphas, and John, and Alexander, and as many as were of the kindred of the high priest." Such statements, erroneous in themselves and not understood by the author of the fourth Gospel, may have led to the confusion in the narrative. Annas had previously been high priest, as we know from Josephus,[3] but nothing is more certain than the fact that the title was not continued after the office was resigned; and Ishmael

---

[1] Die Joh. Schr., i. p. 326, anm. 1; *Lücke*, Comment. Ev. Joh., ii. p. 484.
[2] John xviii. 13. [3] Antiq., xviii. 2, § 1.

Eleazar, and Simon, who succeeded Annas and separated his term of office from that of Caiaphas, did not subsequently bear the title. The narrative is a mistake, and such an error could not have been committed by a native of Palestine,[1] and much less by an acquaintance of the high priest.[2]

There are also several geographical errors committed which denote a foreigner. In i. 28, the writer speaks of a "Bethany beyond Jordan, where John was baptizing." The substitution of "Bethabara," mentioned by Origen, which has erroneously crept into the vulgar text, is of course repudiated by critics, "Bethany" standing in all the older codices. The alteration was evidently proposed to obviate the difficulty that, even in Origen's time, there did not exist any trace of a Bethany beyond Jordan in Peræa. The place could not be the Bethany near Jeru-

---

[1] *Baur*, Unters. kan. Evv., p. 332 f.; *Bretschneider*, Probabilia, p. 93 f.; *Davidson*, Int. N. T., ii. p. 429 f.; *Hilgenfeld*, Die Evangelien, p. 297, anm. 1; *Keim*, Jesu v. Nazara, iii. p. 321 ff.; *Nicolas*, Et. sur la Bible, N. T., p. 198 f.; *Schenkel*, Das Charakt. Jesu, p. 355; *Scholten*, Das Ev. Johannes, p. 300 ff.; *Volkmar*, Die Evangelien, p. 586 f.

[2] John xviii. 15. The author says, in relating the case of restoration of sight to a blind man, that Jesus desired him: (ix. 7) "Go wash in the pool of Siloam," and adds: "which is by interpretation: Sent." The writer evidently wishes to ascribe a prophetical character to the name, and thus increase the significance of the miracle, but the explanation of the Hebrew name, it is contended, is forced and incorrect, (*Bretschneider*, Probabilia, p. 93; *Davidson*, Int. N. T., ii. p. 428. Cf. *Gesenius*, Lex. Hebr., 1847, p. 925), and betrays a superficial knowledge of the language. At the best, the interpretation is a mere conceit, and *Lücke* (Ev. Joh. ii. p. 381) refuses to be persuaded that the parenthesis is by John at all, and prefers the conjecture that it is a gloss of some ancient allegorical interpreter introduced into the text. Other critics (*Kuinoel*, Com. in N. T., 1817, iii. p. 445; *Tholuck*, Com. Ev. Joh. 5te Aufl., 1837, p. 194. Cf. *Neander*, Leben J. C. 7te Ausg. p. 398, anm. 1; *Farrar*, Life of Christ, ii. p. 81, n. 3) express similar views; but this explanation is resisted by the evidence of MSS. As the balance of opinion pronounces the interpretation within grammatical *possibility*, and the interpolation of the phrase may be equally possible, the objection must not be pressed.

salem, and it is supposed that the writer either mistook its position or, inventing a second Bethany, which he described as "beyond Jordan," displayed an ignorance of the locality improbable either in a Jew or a Palestinian.[1] Again, in iii. 23, the writer says that "John was baptizing in Ænon, near to Salim, because there was much water there." This Ænon near to Salim was in Judæa, as is clearly stated in the previous verse. The place, however, was quite unknown even in the third century, and the nearest locality which could be indicated as possible was in the north of Samaria and, therefore, differing from the statements in iii. 22, iv. 3.[2] Ænon, however, signifies "springs," and the question arises whether the writer of the fourth Gospel, not knowing the real meaning of the word, did not simply mistake it for the name of a place.[3] In any case, there seems to be here another error into which the author of the fourth Gospel, had he been the Apostle John, could not have fallen.[4]

---

[1] *Baur*, Unters. kan. Evv., p. 331; *Bretschneider*, Probabilia, p. 95 f.; *Davidson*, Int. N. T., ii. p. 427; *Schenkel*, Das Charakt. Jesu, p. 354; *Scholten*, Het Ev. Joh. p. 207. *Keim* (Jes. v. Naz. i. p. 495, iii. p. 66, anm. 2) does not consider the events connected with the place historical. The reference is suggestively discussed by *Bleek*, Einl. N. T., p. 210 f.; Beiträge, p. 256 f.; *Caspari*, Chron. geogr. Einl., 1869, p. 79 f.; *Ebrard*, Ev. Joh., p. 68 f.; *Ewald*, Gesch. V. Isr., v. p. 262, anm. 1; *Farrar*, Life of Christ, i. p. 140, n. 1; *Grove*, in Smith's Dict. of Bible, i. p. 194 f.; *Hengstenberg*, Ev. Joh., i. p. 83 f.; *Holtzmann*, in Schenkel's Bib. Lex., i. p. 420 f.; *Meyer*, Ev. Joh., p. 103 f.; *Winer*, Bibl. Realwörterb. i. p. 167. The itinerary indicated in the following passages should be borne in mind: John i. 18, 43, ii. 1, x. 40, xi. 1–18. The recent apologetic attempt to identify this Bethany with Tell Anihje, "närrischer weise" as Keim contemptuously terms Caspari's proceeding, has signally failed.

[2] According to Eusebius and Jerome, it was shown in their day, near Salem and the Jordan, eight miles south of Scythopolis, but few critics adopt this site, which is, in fact, excluded by the statements of the evangelist himself.

[3] *Scholten*, Het Ev. Joh., p. 435.

[4] *Bretschneider*, Probabilia, p. 96 f.; *Nicolas*, Et. sur la Bible, N. T.,

The account of the miracle of the pool of Bethesda is a remarkable one for many reasons. The words which most pointedly relate the miraculous phenomena characterizing the pool, are rejected by many critics as an interpolation. In the following extract we put them in italics: v. 3.— "In these (five porches) lay a multitude of the sick, halt, withered, *waiting for the moving of the water.* 4. *For an angel went down at certain seasons into the pool and was troubling the water: he, therefore, who first went in after the troubling of the water was made whole of whatsoever disease he had.*" We maintain, however, that the obnoxious passage is no spurious interpolation, but that there is ample evidence, external and internal, to substantiate its claim to a place in the text. It is true that the whole passage is omitted by the Sinaitic and Vatican Codices, and by C: that A¹, L, 18, and others omit the last phrase of verse 3, and that D, 33, which contain that phrase, omit the whole of verse 4, together with 157, 314 and some other MSS.: that in many codices in which the passage is found it is marked by an asterisk or obelus, and that it presents considerable variation in readings. It is also true that it is omitted by Cureton's Syriac, by the Thebaic, and by most of the Memphitic versions. But, on the other hand, it exists in the Alexandrian Codex, C³, E, F, G, H, I, K, L, M, U, V, Γ, Δ and other MSS[1], and it forms part of the Peschito, Jerusalem Syriac, Vulgate, Watkin's Memphitic, Æthiopic and Armenian versions.[2]

p. 199 f.; *Scholten*, Het Ev. Joh., p. 207. Cf. *Ewald*, Gesch. V. Isr., v. p. 262, anm. 2; *Farrar*, Life of Christ, i. p. 202; *Grove*, in Smith's Dict. of Bible, i. p. 26; *Hengstenberg*, Ev. Joh. p. 223 f.; *Lücke*, Ev. Joh., i. p. 553 f.; *Meyer*, Ev. Joh. p. 174 f.; *Renan*, Vie de Jésus, xiiime éd. p. 105, n. 2; *Winer*, Bibl. Realw. i. p. 33 f.

[1] The italicised words in verse 3, as we have already pointed out, are only by the second hand in A, but they are originally given in D and 33.

[2] The English reader may refer to the following works for a statement

More important still is the fact that it existed in the ancient Latin version of Tertullian, who refers to the passage;[1] and it is quoted by Didymus, Chrysostom, Cyril, Ambrose, Theophylact, Euthymius, and other Fathers. Its presence in the Alexandrian Codex alone might not compensate for the omission of the passage by the Sinaitic and Vatican Codices and C, D, but when the Alexandrian MS. is supported by the version used by Tertullian, which is a couple of centuries older than any of the other authorities, as well as by the Peschito, not to mention other codices, the balance of external evidence is distinctly in its favour.

The internal evidence is altogether on the side of the authenticity of the passage. It is true that there are a considerable number of ἅπαξ λεγόμενα in the few lines: ἐκδέχεσθαι, κίνησις, ταραχή, νόσημα, κατέχεσθαι and perhaps δήποτε; but it must be remembered that the phenomena described are exceptional, and may well explain exceptional phraseology. On the other hand, ὑγιής is specially a Johannine word, used v. 4 and six times more in the fourth Gospel, but only five times in the rest of the New Testament; and ὑγιής with γίνεσθαι occurs in v. 4, 6, 9, 14, and with ποιεῖν in v. 11, 15, vii. 23 and nowhere else. ταράσσειν also may be indicated as employed in v. 4, 7 and five times more in other parts of the Gospel, and only eleven times in the rest of the New Testament, and the use of ταραχή in v. 4 is thus perhaps naturally

---

of the evidence of MSS.:—*Scrivener*, Int. to the Criticism of the N. T., 2nd ed., 1874, p. 527 ff.; *McClellan*, The New Test., 1875, i. p. 711; *Tregelles*, On the Printed Text of Gk. Test. 1854, p. 243 ff.

[1] Angelum aquis intervenire, si novum videtur, exemplum futuri praecucurrit. Piscinam Bethsaidam angelus interveniens commovebat. Observabant, qui valetudinem querebantur; nam si quis praevenerat descendere illuc, queri post lavacrum desinebat. *De Baptismo*, § 5.

accounted for. The context, however, forbids the removal of this passage. It is in the highest degree improbable that verse 3 could have ended with "withered" ξηρῶν, and although many critics wish to retain the last phrase in verse 3, in order to explain verse 7, this only shows the necessity, without justifying the arbitrary maintenance, of these words, whilst verse 4, which is still better attested, is excluded to get rid of the inconvenient angel. It is evident, however, that the expression: "when the water was troubled" (ὅταν ταραχθῇ τὸ ὕδωρ) of the undoubted verse 7 is unintelligible without the explanation that the angel "was troubling the water," (ἐτάρασσε τὸ ὕδωρ) of verse 4, and also that the statement of the verse 7, "but while I am coming, another goeth down before me" (ἐν ᾧ δὲ ἔρχομαι ἐγώ, ἄλλος πρὸ ἐμοῦ καταβαίνει) absolutely requires the account: "he, therefore, who first went in &c." (ὁ οὖν πρῶτος ἐμβάς κ. τ. λ.) of verse 4. The argument that the interpolation was made to explain the statement in verse 7 is untenable, for that statement necessarily presupposes the account in the verses under discussion, and cannot be severed from it. Even if the information that the water was "troubled" at certain seasons only could have been dispensed with, it is obvious that the explanation of the condition of healing, given in verse 4, is indispensable to the appreciation of the lame man's complaint in verse 7, for without knowing that priority was essential, the reason for the protracted waiting is inconceivable. It is also argued, that the passage about the angel may have been interpolated to bring out the presence of supernatural agency, but it is much more reasonable to believe that attempts have been made to omit these verses, of which there is such ancient attestation, in order to eliminate an embarrassing excess of supernatural agency, and get rid of the difficulty presented by the fact, for which even Tertullian[1] endeavoured to account, that the supposed pool had ceased to exhibit any miraculous phenomena. This natural explanation is illustrated by the alacrity with which apologists at the present day abandon the obnoxious passage.[2] The combined force of the external and internal evidence, however, cannot, we think, be fairly resisted.[3]

Now, not only is the pool of Bethesda totally unknown at the present day, but although possessed of such miraculous properties, it was not known even to Josephus, or any other writer of that time. It is inconceivable that, were the narrative genuine, the phenomena could have been unknown and unmentioned by the Jewish historian.[4] There is here evidently neither the narrative of an Apostle nor of an eye-witness.

Another very significant mistake occurs in the account of the conversation with the Samaritan woman, which is said to have taken place (iv. 5) near "a city of Samaria

---

[1] Adv. Judaeos, § 13.

[2] "The Biblical critic is glad that he can remove these words from the record, and cannot be called upon to explain them."—Rev. H. W. Watkins, M.A., in "A New Test. Commentary for English Readers," edited by Charles John Ellicott, D.D., Lord Bishop of Gloucester and Bristol, i. p. 416.

[3] Without pretending to give an exhaustive list, we may mention the views of the following critics:—*In favour of the authenticity:* Von Ammon, Bengel, Burton, Baumgarten-Crusius, Grotius, Hahn, Hengstenberg, Hilgenfeld, Hofmann, Lachmann, Lampe, Lange, McClellan, Reuss, Scholz, Scrivener (doubtful), Sepp, Stier, Strauss, Tittmann, Webster and Wilkinson, Weisse, Wetstein, Wordsworth. Ebrard and Ewald are disposed to accept verse 3, and to reject verse 4 only. *Against the authenticity:* Alford, Baeumlein, Brückner, Davidson, Farrar, Godet, Griesbach, Kuinoel, Lightfoot, Lücke, Luthardt, Meyer, Milligan, Neander, Olshausen, Sanday, Scholten, Semler, Späth, Stemler, Storr, Tischendorf, Tholuck, Tregelles, Trench, Weizsäcker, Westcott, and Hort. The following are *doubtful*,—Holtzmann, Schulz, Theile, de Wette.

[4] Cf. *Lücke*, Com. Ev. Joh., ii. p. 16 ff.; *Ewald*, Die Joh. Schr., i. p. 200 ff.

which is called Sychar." It is evident that there was
no such place—and apologetic ingenuity is severely
taxed to explain the difficulty. The common conjecture
has been that the town of Sichem is intended, but this
is rightly rejected by Delitzsch,[1] and Ewald.[2] Credner,[3]
not unsupported by others, and borne out in particular
by the theory of Ewald, conjectures that Sychar is a
corruption of Sichem, introduced into the Gospel by a
Greek secretary to whom this part of the Gospel was
dictated, and who mistook the Apostle's pronunciation
of the final syllable. We constantly meet with this
elastic explanation of difficulties in the Gospel, but its
mere enunciation displays at once the reality of the
difficulties and the imaginary nature of the explanation.
Hengstenberg adopts the view, and presses it with pious
earnestness, that the term is a mere nickname for the
city of Sichem, and that, by so slight a change in the
pronunciation, the Apostle called the place a city of Lies
(שֶׁקֶר a lie), a play upon words which he does not consider
unworthy.[4] The only support which this latter theory
can secure from internal evidence is to be derived from
the fact that the whole discourse with the woman is
ideal. Hengstenberg[5] conjectures that the five husbands
of the woman are typical of the Gods of the five nations
with which the King of Assyria peopled Samaria, II. Kings,
xvii. 24—41, and which they worshipped instead of the
God of Israel, and as the actual God of the Samaritans was
not recognized as the true God by the Jews, nor their

[1] Talmudische Stud. Zeitschr. gesammt. luth. Theol. u. Kirche, 1856, p. 240 ff.
[2] Die Joh. Schr., i. p. 181, anm. 1; Gesch. V. Isr., v. p. 348, anm. 1; Jahrb. bibl. Wiss., viii. p. 255 f.
[3] Einl. N. T., i. p. 264.
[4] Das Ev. des heil. Joh., 1867, i. p. 244. [5] Ib., i. p. 262 f.

worship of him on Mount Gerizim held to be valid, he considers that under the name of the City of Sychar, their whole religion, past and present, was denounced as a lie. There can be little doubt that the episode is allegorical, but such a defence of the geographical error, the reality of which is everywhere felt, whilst it is quite insufficient on the one hand, effectually destroys the historical character of the Gospel on the other.[1] The inferences from all of the foregoing examples are strengthened by the fact that, in the quotations from the Old Testament, the fourth Gospel in the main follows the Septuagint version, or shows its influence, and nowhere can be shown directly to translate from the Hebrew.

These instances might be multiplied, but we must proceed to examine more closely the indications given in the Gospel as to the identity of its author. We need not point out that the writer nowhere clearly states who he is, nor mentions his name, but expressions are frequently used which evidently show the desire that a particular person should be understood. He generally calls himself "the other disciple," or "the disciple whom Jesus loved."[2] It is universally understood that he repre-

---

[1] For orthodox theories regarding Sychar, in addition to the works already indicated, readers may be referred to the following:—*Bleek*, Einl. N. T., p. 211; *Bunsen*, Bibelwerk, iv. p. 219; *Farrar*, Life of Christ, i. p. 206, note 1; *Godet*, Com. sur l'Ev. de St. Jean, p. 475 f.; *Grove*, in Smith's Dictionary of the Bible, iii. p. 1395 f.; *Hug*, Einl. N. T., ii. p. 194 f.; *Lange*, Das Ev. Joh., p. 107; *Lightfoot*, Horae Hebr. et Talm., p. 938, Works, ed. Pitman, x. p. 339 f.; *Lücke*, Comm. Ev. des Joh., i. p. 577 f.; *Meyer*, Comm. Ev. n. Johan. p. 188 f.; *Neubauer*, La Géographie du Talmud, p. 170; *Olshausen*, Bibl. Comm., Das Ev. n. Johann., umgearb. Ebrard, ii. 1, p. 122 f.; *Riggenbach*, Die Zeugnisse, u. s. w., p. 21; *Sanday*, Authorship, &c. of Fourth Gospel, 1872, p. 92, p. 93, note 1; *de Wette*, Kurzgef. ex. H'buch N. T., i. 3, p. 84; *Wieseler*, Chron. Synops. d. vier Evv., p. 256, anm. 1.

[2] John i. 35 ff.; xiii. 23; xix. 26, 35; xx. 2.

sents himself as having previously been a disciple of John the Baptist (i. 35 ff.),[1] and also that he is "the other disciple" who was acquainted with the high priest (xviii. 15, 16),[2] if not an actual relative as Ewald and others assert.[3] The assumption that the disciple thus indicated is John, rests principally on the fact that whilst the author mentions the other Apostles, he seems studiously to avoid directly naming John, and also that he never distinguishes John the Baptist by the appellation ὁ βαπτιστής, whilst he carefully distinguishes the two disciples of the name of Judas, and always speaks of the Apostle Peter as "Simon Peter," or "Peter," but rarely as "Simon" only.[4] Without pausing to consider the slightness of this evidence, it is obvious that, supposing the disciple indicated to be John the son of Zebedee, the fourth Gospel gives a representation of him quite different from the Synoptics and other writings. In the fourth Gospel (i. 35 ff.) the calling of the Apostle is described in a peculiar manner. John (the Baptist) is standing with two of his disciples, and points out Jesus to them as "the Lamb of God," whereupon the two disciples follow Jesus and, finding out where he lives,

---

[1] *Credner*, Einl. N. T., i. p. 209; *Ewald*, Gesch. V. Isr., v. p. 323; Die Joh. Schr., i. p. 141 f.; *Hengstenberg*, Das Ev. d. heil. Joh., i. p. 106 f.; *Lücke*, Comm. Ev. Joh., i. p. 443 f.; *Michaelis*, Einl. N. T., ii. p. 1127; *Scholten*, Das Ev. Joh., p. 378; *Thiersch*, Die Kirche im ap. Zeit., p. 265 f.; *de Wette*, Einl. N. T., p. 229.

[2] *Bleek*, Einl. N. T., p. 151 f.; *Ewald*, Die Joh. Schr., i. p. 400; *Hengstenberg*, Das Ev. heil. Joh., iii. p. 196 f.; *Lücke*, Comm. Ev. Joh., ii. p. 703 f.

[3] *Ewald*, Die Joh. Schr., i. p. 400; *Bleek*, Einl. N. T., p. 151; *Ewald* considers the relationship to have been on the mother's side. *Hengstenberg* contradicts that strange assumption, Das Ev. heil. Joh. iii. p. 196.

[4] *Bleek*, Beiträge, p. 178; Einl. N. T., p. 150 f.; *Credner*, Einl. N. T., i. p. 209 f.; *Ebrard*, Die evang. Gesch., p. 835; *de Wette*, Einl. N. T., p. 230.

abide with him that day and subsequently attach themselves to his person. In verse 40 it is stated: "One of the two which heard John speak, and followed him, was Andrew, Simon Peter's brother." We are left to imagine who was the other, and the answer of critics is: John. Now, the "calling" of John is related in a totally different manner in the Synoptics—Jesus, walking by the Sea of Galilee, sees "two brethren, Simon called Peter and Andrew his brother, casting a net into the sea, for they were fishers, and he saith unto them: Follow me, and I will make you fishers of men. And they straightway left their nets and followed him. And when he had gone from thence, he saw other two brethren, James the son of Zebedee and John his brother, in the ship with Zebedee their father mending their nets; and he called them. And they immediately left the ship and their father and followed him."[1] These accounts are in complete contradiction to each other, and both cannot be true. We see, from the first introduction of "the other disciple" on the scene, in the fourth Gospel, the evident design to give him the precedence before Peter and the rest of the Apostles. We have above given the account of the first two Synoptists of the calling of Peter, according to which he is the first of the disciples who is selected, and he is directly invited by Jesus to follow him and become, with his brother Andrew, "fishers of men." James and John are not called till later in the day, and without the record of any special address. In the third Gospel, the calling of Peter is introduced with still more important details. Jesus enters the boat of Simon and bids him push out into the Lake and let down his net, and the miraculous draught of fishes is taken: "When Simon Peter

[1] Matt. iv. 18—22; Mark i. 16—20.

saw it, he fell down at Jesus' knees, saying: Depart from me, for I am a sinful man, O Lord. For he was astonished, and all that were with him, at the draught of fishes which they had taken." The calling of the sons of Zebedee becomes even less important here, for the account simply continues: "And so was also James and John, the sons of Zebedee, who were partners with Simon." Jesus then addresses his invitation to Simon, and the account concludes: "And when they had brought their boats to land, they forsook all, and followed him."[1] In the fourth Gospel, the calling of the two disciples of John is first narrated, as we have seen and the first call of Peter is from his brother Andrew, and not from Jesus himself. "He (Andrew) first findeth his own brother Simon, and saith unto him: We have found the Messias (which is, being interpreted, Christ), and he brought him to Jesus. Jesus looked on him and said: Thou art Simon, the son of Jonas;[2] thou shalt be called Cephas (which is by interpretation, Peter)."[3] This explanation of the manner in which the cognomen Peter is given, we need not point out, is likewise contradictory to the Synoptics, and betrays the same purpose of suppressing the prominence of Peter.

The fourth Gospel states that "the other disciple," who is declared to be John, the author of the Gospel, was known to the high priest, another trait amongst many others elevating him above the son of Zebedee as he is depicted elsewhere in the New Testament. The

[1] Luke v. 1—11.
[2] The author apparently considered that Jonas and John were the same name, another indication of a foreigner. Although some of the oldest Codices read John here and in xxi. 15—17, there is great authority for the reading Jona, which is considered by a majority of critics the original.
[3] John i. 41—42.

account which the fourth Gospel gives of the trial of Jesus is in very many important particulars at variance with that of the Synoptics. We need only mention here the point that the latter know nothing of the preliminary examination by Annas. We shall not discuss the question as to where the denial of Peter is represented as taking place in the fourth Gospel, but may merely say that no other disciple but Peter is mentioned in the Synoptics as having followed Jesus; and Peter enters without difficulty into the high priest's palace.[1] In the fourth Gospel, Peter is made to wait without at the door until John, who is a friend of the high priest and freely enters, obtains permission for Peter to go in, another instance of the precedence which is systematically given to John. The Synoptics do not in this particular case give any support to the statement in the fourth Gospel, and certainly in nothing that is said of John elsewhere do they render his acquaintance with the high priest in the least degree probable. It is, on the contrary, improbable in the extreme that the young fisherman of Galilee, who shows very little enlightenment in the anecdotes told of him in the Synoptics, and who is described as an "unlettered and ignorant" man in the Acts of the Apostles, could have any acquaintance with the high priest. Ewald, who, on the strength of the word γνωστός,[2] at once elevates him into a relation of the high priest, sees in the statement of Polycrates that late in life he wore the priestly πέταλον, a confirmation of the supposition that he was of the high priest's race and family.[3] The

---

[1] Matt. xxvi. 58, 69; Mark xiv. 54, 56; Luke xxii. 54 ff.
[2] John xviii. 15.
[3] Die Joh. Schr., i. p. 100, anm. 1; Bleek, Einl. N. T., p. 15,

evident Judaistic tendency, however, which made John wear the priestly mitre may distinguish him as author of the Apocalypse, but it is fatal to the theory which makes him author of the fourth Gospel, in which there is so complete a severance from Judaism.

A much more important point, however, is the designation of the author of the fourth Gospel, who is identified with the Apostle John, as "the disciple whom Jesus loved." It is scarcely too much to say, that this suggestive appellation alone has done more than any arguments to ensure the recognition of the work, and to overcome doubts as to its authenticity. Religious sentimentality, evoked by the influence of this tender epithet, has been blind to historical incongruities, and has been willing to accept with little question from the "beloved disciple" a portrait of Jesus totally unlike that of the Synoptics, and to elevate the dogmatic mysticism and artificial discourses of the one over the sublime morality and simple eloquence of the other. It is impossible to reflect seriously upon this representation of the relations between one of the disciples and Jesus without the conviction that every record of the life of the great Teacher must have borne distinct traces of the preference, and that the disciple so honoured must have attracted the notice of every early writer acquainted with the facts. If we seek for any evidence, however, that John was distinguished with such special affection,—that he lay on the breast of Jesus at supper—that even the Apostle Peter recognised his superior intimacy and influence[1]— and that he received at the foot of the cross the care of his mother from the dying Jesus,[2]—we seek in vain. The Synoptic Gospels, which minutely record the details

[1] John xiii. 23—26.   [2] Ib. xix. 25—27.

of the last supper and of the crucifixion, so far from reporting any such circumstances or such distinction of John, do not even mention his name, and Peter everywhere has precedence before the sons of Zebedee. Almost the only occasions upon which any prominence is given to them are episodes in which they incur the Master's displeasure, and the cognomen of "Sons of thunder" has certainly no suggestion in it of special affection, nor of personal qualities likely to attract the great Teacher. The selfish ambition of the brothers who desire to sit on thrones on his right and on his left, and the intolerant temper which would have called down fire from heaven to consume a Samaritan village, much rather contradict than support the representation of the fourth Gospel. Upon one occasion, indeed, Jesus in rebuking them, adds: "Ye know not what manner of spirit ye are of."[1] It is perfectly undeniable that John nowhere has any such position accorded to him in the Synoptics as this designation in the fourth Gospel implies. In the lists of the disciples he is always put in the fourth place,[2] and in the first two Gospels his only distinguishing designation is that of "the brother of James," or one of the sons of Zebedee. The Apostle Peter in all of the Synoptics is the leader of the disciples. He it is who alone is represented as the mouth-piece of the twelve or as holding conversation with Jesus; and the only occasions on which the sons of Zebedee address Jesus are those to which we have referred, upon which

[1] Luke ix. 55. These words are omitted from some of the oldest MSS., but they are in Cod. D (Bezæ) and many other very important texts, as well as in some of the oldest versions, besides being quoted by the Fathers. They were probably omitted after the claim of John to be the "beloved disciple" became admitted.

[2] Matt. x. 2—4; Mark, iii. 16—19; Luke vi. 14—16.

his displeasure was incurred. The angel who appears to the women after the resurrection desires them to tell his disciples "and Peter" that Jesus will meet them in Galilee,[1] but there is no message for any "disciple whom he loved." If Peter, James, and John accompany the Master to the mount of transfiguration, and are witnesses of his agony in the garden, regarding which, however, the fourth Gospel is totally silent, the two brethren remain in the back ground, and Peter alone acts a prominent part. If we turn to the Epistles of Paul, we do not find a single trace of acquaintance with the fact that Jesus honoured John with any special affection, and the opportunity of referring to such a distinction was not wanting when he writes to the Galatians of his visit to the "Pillar" Apostles in Jerusalem. Here again, however, we find no prominence given to John, but the contrary, his name still being mentioned last and without any special comment. In none of the Pauline or other Epistles is there any allusion, however distant, to any disciple whom Jesus specially loved. The Apocalypse, which, if any book of the New Testament can be traced to him, must be ascribed to the Apostle John, makes no claim whatever to such a distinction. In none of the Apocryphal Gospels is there the slightest indication of knowledge of the fact, and if we come to the Fathers even, it is a striking circumstance that there is not a trace of it in any early work, and not the most remote indication of any independent tradition that Jesus distinguished John or any other individual disciple with peculiar friendship. The Roman Clement, in referring to the example of the Apostles, only mentions Peter and Paul.[2] Polycarp, who is described as a disciple of the

[1] Mark xvi. 7.   [2] Ad Corinth., v.

Apostle John, apparently knows nothing of his having been especially loved by Jesus. Pseudo-Ignatius does not refer to him at all in the Syriac Epistles, or in either version of the seven Epistles.[1] Papias, in describing his interest in hearing what the Apostles said, gives John no prominence: "I inquired minutely after the words of the Presbyters: What Andrew, or what Peter said, or what Philip or what Thomas or James, or what John or Matthew, or what any other of the disciples of the Lord, and what Aristion and the Presbyter John, the disciples of the Lord, say,"[2] &c.

As a fact, it is undenied and undeniable that the representation of John, or of any other disciple, as specially beloved by Jesus, is limited solely and entirely to the fourth Gospel, and that there is not even a trace of independent tradition to support the claim, whilst on the other hand the total silence of the earlier Gospels and of the other New Testament writings on the point, and indeed their data of a positive and unmistakeable character, oppose rather than support the correctness of the later and mere personal assertion. Those who abandon sober criticism, and indulge in mere sentimental rhapsodies on the impossibility of the author of the fourth Gospel being any other than "the disciple whom Jesus loved," strangely ignore the fact that we have no reason whatever, except the assurance of the author himself, to believe that Jesus specially loved any disciple, and much less John the Son of Zebedee. Indeed, the statements of the fourth Gospel itself on the subject are

---

[1] Indeed in the universally repudiated Epistles, beyond the fact that two are addressed to John, in which he is not called "the disciple whom Jesus loved," the only mention of him is the statement, "John was banished to Patmos." Ad Tars., iii.

[2] *Eusebius*, H. E., iii. 39.

so indirect and intentionally vague that it is not absolutely clear what disciple is indicated as "the beloved," and it has even been maintained that not John the son of Zebedee, but Andrew the brother of Simon Peter was "the disciple whom Jesus loved," and consequently the supposed author of the fourth Gospel.[1]

We have hitherto refrained from referring to one of the most singular features of the fourth Gospel, the chapter xxi., which is by many cited as the most ancient testimony for the authenticity of the work, and which requires particular consideration. It is obvious that the Gospel is brought to a conclusion by verses 30, 31 of chapter xx., and critics are universally agreed at least that, whoever may be its author, chapter xxi. is a supplement only added after an interval. By whom was it written? As may be supposed, critics have given very different replies to this important question. Many affirm, and with much probability, that chapter xxi. was subsequently added to the Gospel by the author himself.[2] A few, however, exclude the last two verses, which they consider to have been added by another hand.[3] A much larger number assert that the whole

---

[1] *Lützelberger*, Die kirchl. Tradition über d. Apost. Joh., p. 199 ff.

[2] *Eichhorn*, Einl. N. T., ii. p. 213 ff.; *Godet*, Com. sur l'Év. de St. Jean, ii. p. 670 ff.; *Guericke*, Beiträge, p. 67 ff.; *Hengstenberg*, Das Ev. d. heil. Joh., p. 322 ff.; *Hilgenfeld*, Die Evangelien, p. 317 ff.; Zeitschr. wiss. Theol., 1868, p. 435 ff.; *Hug*, Einl. N. T., ii. p. 250 ff.; *J. P. Lange*, Gesch. chr. Kirche, 1854, ii. p. 421; *Luthardt*, Das Joh. Evang., i. p. 17 f., ii. p. 458 f.; *Meyer*, H'buch, Ev. des Johann. p. 664; *Michaelis*, Einl. N. T., ii. p. 1170 f.; *Olshausen*, Die Leidensgesch. des Herrn, rev. Ebrard, 4te Aufl. ii. 2, p. 235 ff; *Renan*, Vie de Jésus, xiiime éd., p. lxxiii.; *Schleiermacher*, Einl. N. T., p. 331; *Tholuck*, Com. z. Ev. Johann. 1857; Glaubw. ev. Gesch., p. 273 f.; *Weyscheider*, Einl. Ev. Joh., p. 173; *Weitzel*, Stud. u. Krit. 1849, p. 596 ff.; *Westcott*, Int. to the Study of the Gospels, 1872, p. 254. Cf. *Ewald*, references in note 1 on next page.

[3] *Godet, Guericke, Hug, J. P. Lange, Olshausen, Tholuck*. *Meyer* only excludes the last verse.

chapter is an ancient appendix to the Gospel by a writer who was not the author of the Gospel.[1] A few likewise reject the last two verses of the preceding chapter. In this supplement (v. 20), " the disciple whom Jesus loved, who also leaned on his breast at the supper and said: Lord, which is he that betrayeth thee?" is (v. 24) identified with the author of the Gospel.

We may here state the theory of Ewald with regard to the composition of the fourth Gospel, which is largely deduced from considerations connected with the last chapter, and which, although more audaciously minute in its positive and arbitrary statement of details than any other with which we are acquainted, introduces more or less the explanations generally given regarding the composition of chapter xxi. Out of all the indications in the work, Ewald decides:

" 1. That the Gospel, completed at the end of chapter xx., was composed by the Apostle about the year 80, with the free help of friends, not to be immediately circulated

---

[1] *Baur*, Unters. Kan. Evv., p. 235 ff.; *Bleek*, Einl. N. T., p. 219 f.; *Bertholdt*, Einl. A. u. N. T., iii. p. 1326; *Clericus*, Ad Hammondi in Ev. Joh. annott.; *Credner*, Einl. N. T., i. p. 222 f., p. 232 f.; *Davidson*, Int. N. T., ii. pp. 339, 426 f.; *Ewald*, Jahrb. bibl. Wiss., iii., 1850—51, p. 171 f.; x. 1859—60, p. 87; Die Joh. Schr., i. p. 54 ff.; *Ebrard*, Die Ev. Gesch. 2 Aufl. 1850, p. 838 ff.; *Gfrörer*, Das Heiligthum u. d. Wahrheit, 1838, p. 255 ff.; *Grotius*, Annot. ad Joh., xx. 30, xxi. 24; *Keim*, Jesu v. Nazara, i. p. 157 f.; *Lücke*, Comm. Ev. Joh., ii. p. 826 ff.; *Meijboom*, Het Geloof aan Jezus' Opstanding, 1865, p. 56; *Neudecker*, Einl. N. T., p. 334 f. anm. 4; *Paulus*, Repert. ii. p. 327; *Réville*, Rev. de Théol., 1854, ix. p. 345; *Reuss*, Gesch. N. T., p. 237; *Schott*, Comment. de origine et indole cap. ult. Ev. Joh., 1825; Isagoge, § 43, p. 155; *Schenkel*, Das Charakt. Jesu, p. 32; *Scholten*, Das Ev. Johan., pp. 4 ff., 57 ff.; *Schwegler*, Der Montanismus, p. 283 f.; *Späth*, Zeitschr. wiss. Theol., 1868, p. 192 ff.; *Semler*, Hist. Einl. Baumgarten's Unters. Theol. Streitigk., p. 62; *Volkmar*, Die Evangelien, p. 641 f.; *Weisse*, Die evang. Gesch., i. p. 99; *Weizsäcker*, Unters. evang. Gesch., p. 301 f.; *de Wette*, Einl. N. T. p. 238 f.; *Wieseler*, Chron. Synopse v. Evv., p. 418; Indagatur, num loci Marc. xvi. 9-20, et Joh. xxi. genuini sint nec ne &c., 1839.

throughout the world, but to remain limited to the narrower circle of friends until his death, and only then to be published as his legacy to the whole of Christendom. In this position it remained ten years, or even longer.

2. As the preconceived opinion regarding the life or death of the Apostle (xxi. 23) had perniciously spread itself throughout the whole of Christendom, the Apostle himself decided, even before his death, to counteract it in the right way by giving a correct statement of the circumstances. The same friends, therefore, assisted him to design the very important supplement, chapter xxi., and this could still be very easily added, as the book was not yet published. His friends proceeded, nevertheless, somewhat more freely in its composition than previously in writing the book itself, and allowed their own hand more clearly to gleam through, although here, as in the rest of the work, they conformed to the will of the Apostle, and did not, even in the supplement, openly declare his name as the author. As the supplement, however, was to form a closely connected part of the whole work, they gave at its end (verses 24 f.), as it now seemed to them suitable, a new conclusion to the augmented work.

3. As the Apostle himself desired that the preconceived opinion regarding him, which had been spread abroad to the prejudice of Christendom, should be contradicted as soon as possible, and even before his death, he now so far departed from his earlier wish, that he permitted the circulation of his Gospel before his death. We can accept this with all certainty, and have therein trustworthy testimony regarding the whole original history of our book.

4. When the Gospel was thus published it was for

the first time gradually named after our Apostle, even in its external superscription : a nomination which had then become all the more necessary and permanent for the purpose of distinction, as it was united in one whole with the other Gospels. The world, however, has at all times known it only under this wholly right title, and could in no way otherwise know it and otherwise name it." [1]

In addressing ourselves to each of these points in detail, we shall be able to discuss the principal questions connected with the fourth Gospel.

The theory of Ewald, that the fourth Gospel was written down with the assistance of friends in Ephesus, has been imagined solely to conciliate certain phenomena presented throughout the Gospel, and notably in the last chapter, with the foregone conclusion that it was written by the Apostle John. It is apparent that there is not a single word in the work itself explaining such a mode of composition, and that the hypothesis proceeds purely from the ingenious imagination of the critic. The character of the language, the manner in which the writer is indirectly indicated in the third person, and the reference, even in the body of the work (xix. 35), to the testimony of a third person, combined with the similarity of the style of the supplementary chapter, which is an obvious addition intended, however, to be understood as written by a different hand, have rendered these conjectures necessary to reconcile such obvious incongruities with the ascription of the work to the Apostle. The substantial identity of the style and vocabulary of chapter xxi. with the rest of the Gospel is asserted by a multitude of the most competent critics. Ewald, whilst he recognizes the great

[1] Dio Joh. Schr. i. p. 56 f. ; cf. Jahrb. bibl. Wiss., iii. p. 171 ff.

similarity, maintains at the same time a real dissimilarity, for which he accounts in the manner just quoted. The language, Ewald admits, agrees fully in many rare *nuances* with that of the rest of the Gospel, but he does not take the trouble to prove the decided dissimilarities which, he asserts, likewise exist. A less difference than that which he finds might, he thinks, be explained by the interval which had elapsed between the writing of the work and of the supplement, but "the wonderful similarity, in the midst of even greater dissimilarity, of the whole tone and particularly of the style of the composition is not thereby accounted for. This, therefore, leads us," he continues, "to the opinion: The Apostle made use, for writing down his words, of the hand and even of the skill of a trusted friend who later, on his own authority (für sich allein), wrote the supplement. The great similarity, as well as dissimilarity, of the style of both parts in this way becomes intelligible: the trusted friend (probably a Presbyter in Ephesus) adopted much of the language and mode of expression of the youthful old Apostle, without, however, where he wrote more in his own person, being carefully solicitous of imitating them. But even through this contrast, and the definite declaration in v. 24, the Apostolical origin of the book itself becomes all the more clearly apparent; and thus the supplement proves from the most diverse sides how certainly this Gospel was written by the trusted disciple."[1] Elsewhere, Ewald more clearly explains the share in the work which he assigns to the Apostle's disciple: "The proposition that the Apostle composed in a unique way our likewise unique Gospel is to be understood only with the im-

[1] Jahrb. bibl. Wiss., iii. 1850—51, p. 173.

portant limitation upon which I have always laid so much stress: for John himself did not compose this work quite so directly as Paul did most of his Epistles, but the young friend who wrote it down from his lips, and who, in the later appendix, chapter xxi., comes forward in the most open way, without desiring in the slightest to conceal his separate identity, does his work at other times somewhat freely, in that he never introduces the narrator speaking of himself and his participation in the events with 'I' or 'we,' but only indirectly indicates his presence at such events and, towards the end, in preference refers to him, from his altogether peculiar relation to Christ, as 'the disciple whom the Lord loved,' so that, in one passage, in regard to an important historical testimony (xix. 35), he even speaks of him as of a third person." Ewald then maintains that the agreement between the Gospel and the Epistles, and more especially the first, which he affirms, without vouchsafing a word of evidence, to have been written down by a different hand, proves that we have substantially only the Apostle's very peculiar composition, and that his friend as much as possible gave his own words.[1]

It is obvious from this elaborate explanation, which we need scarcely say is composed of mere assumptions, that, in order to connect the Apostle John with the Gospel, Ewald is obliged to assign him a very peculiar position in regard to it: he recognizes that some of the characteristics of the work exclude the supposition that the Apostle could himself have written the Gospel, so he represents him as dictating it, and his Secretary as taking considerable liberties with the composition as he writes it

[1] Jahrb. bibl. Wiss., x. 1859—60, p. 87 f.

down, and even as introducing references of his own; as, for instance, in the passage to which he refers, where, in regard to the statement that at the Crucifixion a soldier pierced the side of the already dead Jesus and that forthwith there came out blood and water (xix. 35), it is said: "And he that saw it hath borne witness, and his witness is true; and he knoweth that he saith true, that ye may believe."[1] It is perfectly clear that the writer refers to the testimony of another person[2]—the friend who is writing down the narrative, says Herr Ewald, refers to the Apostle who is actually dictating it. Again, in the last chapter, as elsewhere throughout the work, "the disciple whom Jesus loved," who is the author, is spoken of in the third person, and also in verse 24: "This is the disciple which testifieth of these things, and wrote these things" (καὶ γράψας ταῦτα). This, according to Ewald, is the same secretary, now writing in his own person. The similarity between this declaration and the appeal to the testimony of another person in xix. 35, is certainly complete, and there can be no doubt that both proceed from the same pen; but beyond the assertion of Herr Ewald there is not the slightest evidence that a secretary wrote the Gospel from the dictation of another, and ventured to interrupt the narrative by such a reference to testimony, which, upon the supposition that the

---

[1] We do not go into any discussion on the use of the word ἐκεῖνος. We believe that the reference is distinctly to another, but even if taken to be to himself in the third person, the passage is not less extraordinary, and the argument holds.

[2] *Davidson*, Int. N. T., ii. p. 436 f.; *Hilgenfeld*, Die Evangelien, p. 341; Zeitschr. wiss. Theol., 1859, p. 414 f., 1861, p. 313 ff.; *Köstlin*, Theol. Jahrb., 1851, p. 207; *Lützelberger*, Die kirchl. Trad. Ap. Joh., p. 205 ff.; *Schenkel*, Das Charakt. Jesu, 1864, p. 32; *Scholten*, Das Ev. Joh., p. 385; *Tobler*, Evangelienfrage, p. 33 ff.; Zeitschr. wiss. Theol., 1860, p. 177 f. Cf. *Weisse*, Die ev. Gesch., i. p. 101 ff., ii. p. 327 ff.; *Weizsäcker*, Unters. ev. Gesch., p. 300.

Apostle John was known as the actual author, is singularly out of place. If John wrote the Gospel, why should he appeal in utterly vague terms to his own testimony, and upon such a point, when the mere fact that he himself wrote the statement was the most direct testimony in itself? An author who composed a work which he desired to ascribe to a "disciple whom Jesus loved" might have made such a reference as xix. 35, in his anxiety to support such an affirmation, without supposing that he had really compromised his design, and might have naturally added such a statement as that in the last two verses, but nothing but the foregone conclusion that the Apostle John was the real author could have suggested such an explanation of these passages. It is throughout assumed by Ewald and others, that John wrote in the first instance, at least, specially for a narrow circle of friends, and the proof of this is considered to be the statement of the object with which it was written: "that ye may believe,"[1] &c., a phrase, we may remark, which is identical with that of the very verse (xix. 35) with which the secretary is supposed to have had so much to do. It is very remarkable, upon this hypothesis, that in xix. 35, it is considered necessary even for this narrow circle, who knew the Apostle so well, to make such an appeal, as well as to attach at its close (xxi. 24), for the benefit of the world in general as Ewald will have it, a certificate of the trustworthiness of the Gospel.

Upon no hypothesis which supposes the Apostle John the author of the fourth Gospel is such an explanation credible. That the Apostle himself could have written of himself the words in xix. 35 is impossible. After

[1] John xx. 31; *Ewald*, Die Joh. Schr., i. p. 56 f.; Jahrb. bibl. Wiss., iii. p. 171; *Bleek*, Einl. N. T., p. 303.

having stated so much that is much more surprising and contradictory to all experience without reference to any witness, it would indeed have been strange had he here appealed to himself as to a separate individual, and on the other hand it is quite inadmissible to assume that a friend to whom he is dictating should interrupt the narrative to introduce a passage so inappropriate to the work, and so unnecessary for any circle acquainted with the Apostolic author. If, as Ewald argues, the peculiarities of his style of composition were so well known that it was unnecessary for the writer more clearly to designate himself either for the first readers or for the Christian world, the passages we are discussing are all the more inappropriate. That any guarantee of the truth of the Gospel should have been thought desirable for readers who knew the work is to be composed by the Apostle John, and who believed him to be " the disciple whom Jesus loved," is inconceivable, and that any anonymous and quite indirect testimony to its genuineness should either have been considered necessary or of any value is still more incredible. It is impossible that nameless Presbyters of Ephesus could venture to accredit a Gospel written by the Apostle John; and any intended attestation must have taken the simple and direct course of stating that the work had been composed by the Apostle. The peculiarities we are discussing seem to us explicable only upon the supposition that the unknown writer of the Gospel desired that it should be understood to be written by a certain disciple whom Jesus loved, but did not choose distinctly to name him or directly to make such an affirmation.

It is, we assert, impossible that an Apostle who composed a history of the life and teaching of Jesus could have failed to attach his name, naturally and simply, as testimony of the trustworthiness of his statements, and of his fitness as an eye-witness to compose such a record. As the writer of the fourth Gospel does not state his name, Herr Ewald ascribes the omission to the "incomparable modesty and delicacy of feeling" of the Apostle John. We must further briefly examine the validity of this explanation. It is universally admitted, and by Ewald himself, that although the writer does not directly name himself, he very clearly indicates that he is "the other disciple" and "the disciple whom Jesus loved." We must affirm that such a mode of indicating himself is incomparably less modest than the simple statement of his name, and it is indeed a glorification of himself beyond anything in the Apocalypse. But not only is the explanation thus discredited but, in comparing the details of the Gospel with those of the Synoptics, we find still more certainly how little modesty had to do with the suppression of his name. In the Synoptics a very marked precedence of the rest of the disciples is ascribed to the Apostle Peter; and the sons of Zebedee are represented in all of them as holding a subordinate place. This representation is confirmed by the Pauline Epistles and by tradition. In the fourth Gospel, a very different account is given, and the author studiously elevates the Apostle John,—that is to say, according to the theory that he is the writer of the Gospel, himself,— in every way above the Apostle Peter. Apart from the general pre-eminence claimed for himself in the very name of "the disciple whom Jesus loved," we have seen that he deprives Peter in his own favour of the honour of being the first of the disciples who was called; he suppresses the account of the circumstances under which that Apostle was named Peter, and gives another and trifling version of the incident, reporting elsewhere indeed in a very subdued and modified form, and without the commendation of the Master, the recognition of the divinity of Jesus, which in the first Gospel is the cause of his change of name.[1] He is the intimate friend of the Master, and even Peter has to beg him to ask at the Supper who was the betrayer. He describes himself as the friend of the High Priest, and while Peter is excluded, he not only is able to enter into his palace, but he is the means of introducing Peter. The denial of Peter is given without mitigation, but his bitter repentance is not mentioned. He it is who is singled out by the dying Jesus and entrusted with the charge of his mother. He outruns Peter in their race to the Sepulchre, and in the final appearance of Jesus (xxi. 15) the more important position is assigned to the disciple whom Jesus loved. It is, therefore, absurd to speak of the incomparable modesty of the writer, who, if he does not give his name, not only clearly indicates himself, but throughout assumes a pre-eminence which is not supported by the authority of the Synoptics and other writings, but is heard of alone from his own narrative.

Ewald argues that chapter xxi. must have been written, and the Gospel as we have it, therefore, have been completed, before the death of the Apostle John. He considers the supplement to have been added specially to contradict the report regarding John (xxi. 23). "The supplement must have been written whilst John still lived," he asserts, "for only before his death was it worth while to contradict such a false hope; and if his death had actually taken place, the result itself would

---

[1] Matt. xvi. 13—19; cf. Mark viii. 29; Luke ix. 20.

have already refuted so erroneous an interpretation of the words of Christ, and it would then have been much more appropriate to explain afresh the sense of the words 'till I come.' Moreover, there is no reference here to the death as having already occurred, although a small addition to that effect in ver. 24 would have been so easy. But if we were to suppose that John had long been dead when this was written, the whole rectification as it is given would be utterly without sense."[1] On the contrary, we affirm that the whole history of the first two centuries renders it certain that the Apostle was already dead, and that the explanation was not a rectification of false hopes during his lifetime, but an explanation of the failure of expectations which had already taken place, and probably excited some scandal. We know how the early Church looked for the immediate coming of the glorified Christ, and how such hopes sustained persecuted Christians in their sorrow and suffering. This is very clearly expressed in 1 Thess. iv. 15—18, where the expectation of the second coming within the lifetime of the writer and readers of the Epistle is confidently stated, and elsewhere, and even in 1 John ii. 18, the belief that the "last times" had arrived is expressed. The history of the Apocalypse in relation to the Canon illustrates the case. So long as the belief in the early consummation of all things continued strong, the Apocalypse was the favourite writing of the early Church, but when time went on, and the second coming of Christ did not take place, the opinion of Christendom regarding the work changed, and disappointment, as well as the desire to explain the non-fulfilment of prophecies upon which so much hope had been based, led many to reject the Apocalypse

[1] Jahrb. bibl. Wiss., iii. 1850—51, p. 173.

as an unintelligible and fallacious book. We venture to conjecture that the tradition that John should not die until the second coming of Jesus may have originated with the Apocalypse, where that event is announced to John as immediately to take place, xxii. 7, 10, 12, and the words with which the book ends are of this nature, and express the expectation of the writer, 20 : "He which testifieth these things saith : Surely I come quickly. Amen. Come, Lord Jesus." It was not in the spirit of the age to hesitate about such anticipations, and so long as the Apostle lived, such a tradition would scarcely have required or received contradiction from any one, the belief being universal that the coming of Jesus might take place any day, and assuredly would not be long delayed. When the Apostle was dead, however, and the tradition that it had been foretold that he should live until the coming of the Lord exercised men's minds, and doubt and disappointment at the non-fulfilment of what may have been regarded as prophecy produced a prejudicial effect upon Christendom, it seemed to the writer of this Gospel a desirable thing to point out that too much stress had been laid upon the tradition, and that the words which had been relied upon in the first instance did not justify the expectations which had been formed from them. This also contradicts the hypothesis that the Apostle John was the author of the Gospel.

Such a passage as xix. 35, received in any natural sense, or interpreted in any way which can be supported by evidence, shows that the writer of the Gospel was not an eye-witness of the events recorded, but appeals to the testimony of others. It is generally admitted that the expressions in ch. i. 14 are of universal application, and capable of being adopted by all Christians, and, consequently, that they do not imply any direct claim on the part of the writer to personal knowledge of Jesus. We must now examine whether the Gospel itself bears special marks of having been written by an eye-witness, and how far in this respect it bears out the assertion that it was written by the Apostle John. It is constantly asserted that the minuteness of the details in the fourth Gospel indicates that it must have been written by one who was present at the scenes he records. With regard to this point we need only generally remark, that in the works of imagination of which the world is full, and the singular realism of many of which is recognized by all, we have the most minute and natural details of scenes which never occurred, and of conversations which never took place, the actors in which never actually existed. Ewald admits that it is undeniable that the fourth Gospel was written with a fixed purpose, and with artistic design and, indeed, he goes further and recognizes that the Apostle could not possibly so long have recollected the discourses of Jesus and verbally reproduced them, so that, in fact, we have only, at best, a substantial report of the matter of those discourses coloured by the mind of the author himself.[1] Details of scenes at which we were not present may be admirably supplied by imagination, and as we cannot compare what is here described as taking place with what actually took place, the argument that the author must have been an eye-witness because he gives such details is without validity. Moreover, the details of the fourth Gospel in many cases do not agree with those of the three Synoptics, and it is an undoubted fact that the author of the fourth Gospel gives the details of scenes at which the Apostle John was not

[1] Jahrb. bibl. Wiss., x. p. 91 ff.

present, and reports the discourses and conversations on such occasions, with the very same minuteness as those at which he is said to have been present; as, for instance, the interview between Jesus and the woman of Samaria. It is perfectly undeniable that the writer had other Gospels before him when he composed his work, and that he made use of other materials than his own.[1]

It is by no means difficult, however, to point out very clear indications that the author was not an eye-witness, but constructed his scenes and discourses artistically and for effect. We shall not, at present, dwell upon the almost uniform artifice adopted in most of the dialogues, in which the listeners either misunderstand altogether the words of Jesus, or interpret them in a foolish and material way, and thus afford him an opportunity of enlarging upon the theme. For instance, Nicodemus, a ruler of the Jews, misunderstands the expression of Jesus, that in order to see the kingdom of God a man must be born from above, and asks: "How can a man be born when he is old? can he enter a second time into his mother's womb and be born?"[2] Now, as it is well known, and as we have already shown, the common expression used in regard to a proselyte to Judaism was that of being born again, with which every Jew, and more especially every "ruler of the Jews," must have been well acquainted. The stupidity which he displays

---

[1] *Ewald*, Jahrb. bibl. Wiss., iii. p. 161; Die Joh. Schr., i. p. 7 ff. Cf. *Bertholdt*, Einl. A. u. N. T., iii. p. 1302; *Eichhorn*, Einl. N. T., ii. p. 127 ff.; *Hilgenfeld*, Die Evangelien, p. 329; *Holtzmann*, Zeitschr. wiss. Theol., 1869, pp. 62 ff., 155 ff.; *Hug*, Einl. N. T., ii. p. 191 ff.; *Keim*, Jesu v. Nazara, i. p. 118 ff.; *Lessing*, Neue Hypothese, § 51; *Lücke*, Comm. Ev. Joh., i. p. 197 ff.; *Schwegler*, Der Montanismus, p. 205, anm. 137; *Weisse*, Die ev. Gesch., i. p. 118 ff.; *Weizsäcker*, Unters. evang. Gesch., p. 270; *de Wette*, Einl. N. T., p. 209 f.

[2] John iii. 4.

in his conversation with Jesus, and with which the author endowed all who came in contact with him, in order, by the contrast, to mark more strongly the superiority of the Master, even draws from Jesus the remark: "Art thou the teacher of Israel and understandest not these things?"[1] There can be no doubt that the scene was ideal, and it is scarcely possible that a Jew could have written it. In the Synoptics, Jesus is reported as quoting against the people of his own city, Nazareth, who rejected him, the proverb: "A prophet has no honour in his own country."[2] The appropriateness of the remark here is obvious. The author of the fourth Gospel, however, shows clearly that he was neither an eye-witness nor acquainted with the subject or country when he introduces this proverb in a different place. Jesus is represented as staying two days at Sychar after his conversation with the Samaritan woman. "Now after the two days he departed thence into Galilee. For ($\gamma\acute{\alpha}\rho$) Jesus himself testified that a prophet hath no honour in his own country. When, therefore ($o\tilde{v}v$), he came into Galilee, the Galilæans received him, having seen all the things that he did in Jerusalem, at the feast—for they also went unto the feast."[3] Now it is manifest that the quotation here is quite out of place, and none of the ingenious but untenable explanations of apologists can make it appropriate. He is made to go into Galilee, which was his country, because a prophet has no honour in his country, and the Galilæans are represented as receiving him, which is a contradiction of the proverb. The writer evidently misunderstood the facts of the case or

---

[1] John iii. 10.
[2] Matt. xiii. 57; Mark vi. 4; Luke iv. 24.
[3] John iv. 43—45.

deliberately desired to deny the connection of Jesus with Nazareth and Galilee, in accordance with his evident intention of associating the Logos only with the Holy City. We must not pause to show that the author is generally unjust to the Galilæans, and displays an ignorance regarding them very unlike what we should expect from the fisherman of Galilee.[1] We have already alluded to the artificial character of the conversation with the woman of Samaria, which, although given with so much detail, occurred at a place totally unknown (perhaps allegorically called the "City of Lies"), at which the Apostle John was not present, and the substance of which was typical of Samaria and its five nations and false gods. The continuation in the Gospel is as unreal as the conversation.

Another instance displaying personal ignorance is the insertion into a discourse at the Last Supper, and without any appropriate connection with the context, the passage "Verily, verily, I say unto you : he that receiveth whomsoever I send, receiveth me, and he that receiveth me receiveth him that sent me."[2] In the Synoptics, this sentence is naturally represented as part of the address to the disciples who are to be sent forth to preach the Gospel;[3] but it is clear that its insertion here is a mistake.[4] Again, a very obvious slip, which betrays that what was intended for realistic detail is nothing but a reminiscence of some earlier Gospel misapplied, occurs in a later part

---

[1] We may merely refer to the remark of the Pharisees: search the Scriptures and see, "for out of Galilee ariseth no prophet" (vii. 52). The Pharisees could not have been ignorant of the fact that the prophets Jonah and Nahum were Galilæans, and the son of Zebedee could not have committed such an error. Cf. *Bretschneider*, Probabilia, p. 99 f.

[2] John xiii. 20.   [3] Matt. x. 40; cf. xviii. 5; Luke x. 16, cf. ix. 48.

[4] This is recognised by *de Wette*, Einl. N. T., p. 211 c.

of the discourses very inappropriately introduced as being delivered on the same occasion. At the end of xiv. 31, Jesus is represented, after saying that he would no more talk much with the disciples, as suddenly breaking off with the words: "Arise, let us go hence" (Ἐγείρεσθε, ἄγωμεν ἐντεῦθεν). They do not, however, arise and go thence, but, on the contrary, Jesus at once commences another long discourse: "I am the true vine," &c. The expression is merely introduced artistically to close one discourse, and enable the writer to begin another, and the idea is taken from some earlier work. For instance, in our first Synoptic, at the close of the Agony in the Garden which the fourth Gospel ignores altogether, Jesus says to the awakened disciples: "Rise, let us go" (Ἐγείρεσθε ἄγωμεν).[1] We need not go on with these illustrations, but the fact that the author is not an eye-witness recording scenes which he beheld and discourses which he heard, but a writer composing an ideal Gospel on a fixed plan, will become more palpable as we proceed.

It is not necessary to enter upon any argument to prove the fundamental difference which exists in every respect between the Synoptics and the fourth Gospel. This is admitted even by apologists, whose efforts to reconcile the discordant elements are totally unsuccessful. "It is impossible to pass from the Synoptic Gospels to that of St. John," says Canon Westcott, "without feeling that the transition involves the passage from one world of thought to another. No familiarity with the general teaching of the Gospels, no wide conception of the character of the Saviour is sufficient to destroy the

[1] Matt. xxvi. 46; Mark xiv. 42. *De Wette* likewise admits this mistaken reminiscence. Einl. N. T., p. 211 c.

contrast which exists in form and spirit between the earlier and later narratives."[1] The difference between the fourth Gospel and the Synoptics, not only as regards the teaching of Jesus but also the facts of the narrative, is so great that it is impossible to harmonize them, and no one who seriously considers the matter can fail to see that both cannot be accepted as correct. If we believe that the Synoptics give a truthful representation of the life and teaching of Jesus, it follows of necessity that, in whatever category we may decide to place the fourth Gospel, it must be rejected as a historical work. The theories which are most in favour as regards it may place the Gospel in a high position as an ideal composition, but sober criticism must infallibly pronounce that they exclude it altogether from the province of history. There is no option but to accept it as the only genuine report of the sayings and doings of Jesus, rejecting the Synoptics, or to remove it at once to another department of literature. The Synoptics certainly contradict each other in many minor details, but they are not in fundamental disagreement with each other and evidently present the same portrait of Jesus, and the same view of his teaching derived from the same sources.

The vast difference which exists between the representation of Jesus in the fourth Gospel and in the Synoptics is too well recognized to require minute demonstration. We must, however, point out some of the distinctive features. We need not do more here than refer to the fact that, whilst the Synoptics relate the circumstances of the birth of Jesus, two of them at least, and give some history of his family and origin, the fourth Gospel, ignoring all this, introduces the great

[1] Introd. to Study of the Gospels, p. 249.

Teacher at once as the Logos who from the beginning was with God and was himself God. The key-note is struck from the first, and in the philosophical prelude to the Gospel we have the announcement to those who have ears to hear, that here we need expect no simple history, but an artistic demonstration of the philosophical postulate. According to the Synoptics, Jesus is baptized by John, and as he goes out of the water the Holy Ghost descends upon him like a dove. The fourth Gospel says nothing of the baptism, and makes John the Baptist narrate vaguely that he saw the Holy Ghost descend like a dove and rest upon Jesus, as a sign previously indicated to him by God by which to recognize the Lamb of God.[1] From the very first, John the Baptist, in the fourth Gospel, recognizes and declares Jesus to be "the Christ,"[2] "the Lamb of God which taketh away the sins of the world."[3] According to the Synoptics, John comes preaching the baptism of repentance, and so far is he from making such declarations, or forming such distinct opinions concerning Jesus, that even after he has been cast into prison and just before his death,—when in fact his preaching was at an end,—he is represented as sending disciples to Jesus, on hearing in prison of his works, to ask him: "Art thou he that should come, or look we for another?"[4] Jesus carries on his ministry and baptizes simultaneously with John, according to the fourth Gospel, but his public career, according to the Synoptics, does not begin until after the Baptist's has concluded, and John is cast into prison.[5] The Synoptics clearly

---

[1] John i. 32—33. [2] *Ib.*, i. 15—27. [3] *Ib.*, i. 29.
[4] Matt. xi. 2 ff.; cf. Luke vii. 18 ff.
[5] John iii. 22; Matt. iv. 12, 17; Mark i. 14; Luke iii. 20, 23; iv. 1 ff.

represent the ministry of Jesus as having been limited to a single year,[1] and his preaching is confined to Galilee and Jerusalem, where his career culminates at the fatal Passover. The fourth Gospel distributes the teaching of Jesus between Galilee, Samaria, and Jerusalem, makes it extend at least over three years, and refers to three Passovers spent by Jesus at Jerusalem.[2] The Fathers felt this difficulty and expended a good deal of apologetic ingenuity upon it; but no one is now content with the explanation of Eusebius, that the Synoptics merely intended to write the history of Jesus during the one year after the imprisonment of the Baptist, whilst the fourth Evangelist recounted the events of the time not recorded by the others, a theory which is totally contradicted by the four Gospels themselves.[3]

The fourth Gospel represents the expulsion of the money-changers by Jesus as taking place at the very outset of his career,[4] when he could not have been known, and when such a proceeding is incredible; whilst the Synoptics place it at the very close of his ministry, after his triumphal entry into Jerusalem, when, if ever, such an act, which might have contributed to the final catastrophe, becomes conceivable.[5] The variation from the parallels in the Synoptics, moreover, is exceedingly instructive, and further indicates the amplification of a later writer imperfectly acquainted with the circumstances. The

---

[1] Apologists discover indications of a three years' ministry in Matt. xiii. 37, Luke xiii. 34: "How often," &c.; and also in Luke xiii. 32 f. "to-day, to-morrow and the third day."

[2] John ii. 13; vi. 40 f.; vii. 2; xiii. 1.

[3] *Eusebius*, H. E., iii. 24. We have already referred to the theory of Irenæus, which is at variance with all the Gospels, and extends the career of Jesus to many years of public life.

[4] John ii. 14 ff.

[5] Matt. xxi. 12 ff.; Mark xi. 15 ff.; Luke xix. 45 ff.

first and second Synoptists, in addition to the general expression "those buying and selling in the Temple," mention only that Jesus overthrew the tables of the money-changers and the seats of those selling doves. The third Synoptist does not even give these particulars. The author of the fourth Gospel, however, not only makes Jesus expel the sellers of doves and the money-changers, but adds: "those selling oxen and sheep." Now, not only is there not the slightest evidence that sheep and oxen were bought and sold in the Temple, but it is obvious that there was no room there to do so. On the contrary, it is known that the market for cattle was not only distant from the Temple, but even from the city.[1] The author himself betrays the foreign element in his account by making Jesus address his words, when driving them all out, only "to them selling doves." Why single these out and seem to exclude the sellers of sheep and oxen? He has apparently forgotten his own interpolation. In the first Gospel, the connection of the words of Jesus with the narrative suggests an explanation: xxi. 12 ". . . and overthrew the tables of the money-changers, and the seats *of those selling doves, and saith to them*, &c." Upon the occasion of this episode, the fourth Gospel represents Jesus as replying to the demand of the Jews for a sign why he did such things: "Destroy this temple, and within three days I will raise it up," which the Jews understand very naturally only in a material sense, and which even the disciples only comprehended and believed "after the resurrection." The Synoptists not only know nothing of this, but represent the saying as the false testimony which the false witnesses bare

---

[1] Cf. *Frankel*, Monatschr. f. Gesch. u. Wiss. d. Judenthums, 1877, p. 536 ff.

against Jesus.¹ No such charge is brought against Jesus at all in the fourth Gospel. So little do the Synoptists know of the conversation of Jesus with the Samaritan woman, and his sojourn for two days at Sychar, that in his instructions to his disciples, in the first Gospel, Jesus positively forbids them either to go to the Gentiles or to enter into any city of the Samaritans.²

The fourth Gospel has very few miracles in common with the Synoptics, and those few present notable variations. After the feeding of the five thousand, Jesus, according to the Synoptics, constrains his disciples to enter a ship and to go to the other side of the Lake of Gennesaret, whilst he himself goes up a mountain apart to pray. A storm arises, and Jesus appears walking to them over the sea, whereat the disciples are troubled, but Peter says to him: "Lord, if it be thou, bid me come unto thee over the water," and on his going out of the ship over the water, and beginning to sink, he cries: "Lord save me;" Jesus stretched out his hand and caught him, and when they had come into the ship, the wind ceased, and they that were in the ship came and worshipped him, saying: "Of a truth thou art the Son of God."³ The fourth Gospel, instead of representing Jesus as retiring to the mountain to pray, which would have been opposed to the author's idea of the Logos, makes the motive for going thither the knowledge of Jesus that the people "would come and take him by force that they might make him a king."⁴ The writer altogether ignores the episode of Peter walking on the sea, and adds a new miracle by stating that, as soon as Jesus was received on

---

[1] John ii. 18 ff.; Matt. xxvi. 60 ff.; cf. xxvii. 39 f.; Mark xiv. 57 f.; xv. 29.   [2] Matt. x. 5.
[3] Matt. xiv. 22, 23; cf. Mark vi. 46 ff.   [4] John vi. 15.

board, "the ship was at the land whither they were going."[1] The Synoptics go on to describe the devout excitement and faith of all the country round, but the fourth Gospel, limiting the effect on the multitude in the first instance to curiosity as to how Jesus had crossed the lake, represents Jesus as upbraiding them for following him, not because they saw miracles, but because they had eaten of the loaves and been filled,[2] and makes him deliver one of those long dogmatic discourses, interrupted by, and based upon, the remarks of the crowd, which so peculiarly distinguish the fourth Gospel.

Without dwelling upon such details of miracles, however, we proceed with our slight comparison. Whilst the fourth Gospel from the very commencement asserts the foreknowledge of Jesus as to who should betray him, and makes him inform the Twelve that one of them is a devil, alluding to Judas Iscariot,[3] the Synoptists represent Jesus as having so little foreknowledge that Judas should betray him that, shortly before the end and, indeed, according to the third Gospel, only at the last supper, Jesus promises that the disciples shall sit upon twelve thrones judging the twelve tribes of Israel,[4] and it is only at the last supper, after Judas has actually arranged with the chief priests, and apparently from knowledge of the fact, that Jesus for the first time speaks of his betrayal by him.[5] On his way to Jerusalem, two days before the Passover,[6] Jesus comes to Bethany where,

---

[1] John vi. 17—21.   [2] *Ib.*, vi. 26.
[3] *Ib.*, vi. 64, 70, 71; cf. ii. 25.
[4] Matt. xix. 28; cf. xvii. 22 f.; cf. Mark ix. 30 f., x. 32 f.; Luke xxii. 30; cf. ix. 22 f., 44 f.; xviii. 31 f.
[5] Matt. xxvi. 21 f., cf. 14 ff.; Mark xiv. 18 f., cf. 10 f.; Luke xxii. 21 f., cf. 3 ff.   [6] Mark xiv. 1.

according to the Synoptics, being in the house of Simon the leper, a woman with an alabaster box of very precious ointment came and poured the ointment upon his head, much to the indignation of the disciples, who say: "To what purpose is this waste? For this might have been sold for much, and given to the poor."[1] In the fourth Gospel the episode takes place six days before the Passover,[2] in the house of Lazarus, and it is his sister Mary who takes a pound of very costly ointment, but she anoints the feet of Jesus and wipes his feet with her hair. It is Judas Iscariot, and not the disciples, who says: "Why was not this ointment sold for three hundred pence and given to the poor?" And Jesus makes a similar reply to that in the Synoptics, showing the identity of the occurrence described so differently.[3]

The Synoptics represent most clearly that Jesus on the evening of the 14th Nisan, after the custom of the Jews, ate the Passover with his disciples,[4] and that he was arrested in the first hours of the 15th Nisan, the day on which he was put to death. Nothing can be more distinct than the statement that the last supper was the Paschal feast. "They made ready the Passover ($\dot{\eta}\tau o\acute{\iota}\mu\alpha\sigma\alpha\nu$ $\tau\grave{o}$ $\pi\acute{\alpha}\sigma\chi\alpha$), and when the hour was come, he sat down and the apostles with him, and he said to them: With desire I desired to eat this Passover with you before I suffer" ($'E\pi\iota\theta\upsilon\mu\acute{\iota}\alpha$ $\dot{\epsilon}\pi\epsilon\theta\acute{\upsilon}\mu\eta\sigma\alpha$ $\tau o\hat{\upsilon}\tau o$ $\tau\grave{o}$ $\pi\acute{\alpha}\sigma\chi\alpha$ $\phi\alpha\gamma\epsilon\hat{\iota}\nu$ $\mu\epsilon\theta'$ $\dot{\upsilon}\mu\hat{\omega}\nu$ $\pi\rho\grave{o}$ $\tau o\hat{\upsilon}$ $\mu\epsilon$ $\pi\alpha\theta\epsilon\hat{\iota}\nu$).[5] The fourth Gospel, however, in accordance with the principle which is dominant throughout, represents the last repast

[1] Matt. xxvi. 6—13; Mark xiv. 3—9.
[2] John xii. 1.   [3] Ib., xii. 1 ff.; cf. xi. 2.
[4] Matt. xxvi. 17 f., 19, 36 ff., 47 ff.; Mark xiv. 12 ff., 16 ff.; Luke xxii. 7 ff., 13 ff.
[5] Luke xxii. 13, 15; cf. Matt. xxvi. 19 ff.; Mark xiv. 16 ff.

which Jesus eats with his disciples as a common supper (δεῖπνον), which takes place, not on the 14th, but on the 13th Nisan, the day "before the feast of the Passover" (πρὸ τῆς ἑορτῆς τοῦ πάσχα),[1] and his death takes place on the 14th, the day on which the Paschal lamb was slain. Jesus is delivered by Pilate to the Jews to be crucified about the sixth hour of "the preparation of the Passover" (ἦν παρασκευὴ τοῦ πάσχα),[2] and because it was "the preparation," the legs of the two men crucified with Jesus were broken, that the bodies might not remain on the cross on the great day of the feast.[3] The fourth Gospel totally ignores the institution of the Christian festival at the last supper, but, instead, represents Jesus as washing the feet of the disciples, enjoining them also to wash each other's feet: "For I gave you an example that ye should do according as I did to you."[4] The Synoptics have no knowledge of this incident. Immediately after the warning to Peter of his future denial, Jesus goes out with the disciples to the Garden of Gethsemane and, taking Peter and the two sons of Zebedee apart, began to be sorrowful and very depressed and, as he prayed in his agony that if possible the cup might pass from him, an angel comforts him. Instead of this, the fourth Gospel represents Jesus as delivering, after the warning to Peter, the longest discourses in the Gospel: "Let not your heart be troubled," &c.; "I am the true vine,"[5] &c.; and, although said to be written by one of the sons of Zebedee who were with Jesus on the occasion, the fourth Gospel does not mention the agony in the garden but, on the contrary, makes Jesus utter the long

---

[1] John xiii. 1. [2] *Ib.*, xix. 14.
[3] *Ib.*, xix. 31 ff. [4] *Ib.*, xiii. 12, 15.
[5] *Ib.*, xiv. 1—31; xv. 1—27; xvi. 1—33; xvii. 1—26.

prayer xvii. 1—26, in a calm and even exulting spirit very far removed from the sorrow and depression of the more natural scene in Gethsemane. The prayer, like the rest of the prayers in the Gospel, is a mere didactic and dogmatic address for the benefit of the hearers.

The arrest of Jesus presents a similar contrast. In the Synoptics, Judas comes with a multitude from the chief priests and elders of the people armed with swords and staves, and, indicating his Master by a kiss, Jesus is simply arrested and, after the slight resistance of one of the disciples, is led away.[1] In the fourth Gospel, the case is very different. Judas comes with a band of men from the chief priests and Pharisees, with lanterns and torches and weapons, and Jesus—"knowing all things which were coming to pass"—himself goes towards them and asks: "Whom seek ye?" Judas plays no active part, and no kiss is given. The fourth Evangelist is, as ever, bent on showing that all which happens to the Logos is predetermined by himself and voluntarily encountered. As soon as Jesus replies: "I am he," the whole band of soldiers go backwards and fall to the ground, an incident thoroughly in the spirit of the early apocryphal Gospels still extant, and of an evidently legendary character. He is then led away first to Annas, who sends him to Caiaphas, whilst the Synoptics naturally know nothing of Annas, who was not the high priest and had no authority. We need not follow the trial, which is fundamentally different in the Synoptics and fourth Gospel; and we have already pointed out that, in the Synoptics, Jesus is crucified on the 15th Nisan, whereas in the fourth Gospel he is put to death—the spiritual Paschal lamb—on the 14th Nisan. According

[1] Matt. xxvi. 47 ff.; Mark xiv. 43 ff.; Luke xxii. 47 ff.

to the fourth Gospel, Jesus bears his own cross to Calvary,[1] but the Synoptics represent it as being borne by Simon of Cyrene.[2] As a very singular illustration of the inaccuracy of all the Gospels, we may point to the circumstance that no two of them agree even about so simple a matter of fact as the inscription on the cross, assuming that there was one at all. They give it respectively as follows: "This is Jesus the King of the Jews;" "The King of the Jews;" "This (is) the King of the Jews;" and the fourth Gospel: "Jesus the Nazarene the King of the Jews."[3] The occurrences during the Crucifixion are profoundly different in the fourth Gospel from those narrated in the Synoptics. In the latter, only the women are represented as beholding afar off,[4] but "the beloved disciple" is added in the fourth Gospel, and instead of being far off, they are close to the cross; and for the last cries of Jesus reported in the Synoptics we have the episode in which Jesus confides his mother to the disciple's care. We need not at present compare the other details of the Crucifixion and Resurrection, which are differently reported by each of the Gospels.

We have only indicated a few of the more salient differences between the fourth Gospel and the Synoptics, which are rendered much more striking, in the Gospels themselves, by the profound dissimilarity of the sentiments uttered by Jesus. We merely point out, in passing, the omission of important episodes from the fourth

[1] John xix. 17.
[2] Matt. xxvii. 32; Mark xv. 21; Luke xxii. 26.
[3] Οὗτός ἐστιν Ἰησοῦς ὁ βασιλεὺς τῶν Ἰουδαίων. Matt. xxvii. 37; Ὁ βασιλεὺς τῶν Ἰουδαίων. Mark xv. 26; Ὁ βασιλεὺς τῶν Ἰουδαίων οὗτος. Luke xxiii. 38; Ἰησοῦς ὁ Ναζωραῖος ὁ βασιλεὺς τῶν Ἰουδαίων. John xix. 19.
[4] Matt. xxvii. 55 f.; Mark xv. 40 f.; Luke xxiii. 49. In this last place all his acquaintance are added.

Gospel, such as the Temptation in the wilderness; the Transfiguration, at which, according to the Synoptics, the sons of Zebedee were present; the last Supper; the agony in the garden; the mournful cries on the cross; and, we may add, the Ascension; and if we turn to the miracles of Jesus, we find that almost all of those narrated by the Synoptics are ignored, whilst an almost entirely new series is introduced. There is not a single instance of the cure of demoniacal possession in any form recorded in the fourth Gospel. Indeed the number of miracles is reduced in that Gospel to a few typical cases; and although at the close it is generally said that Jesus did many other signs in the presence of his disciples, these alone are written with the declared purpose: "that ye might believe that Jesus is the Christ, the Son of God."[1]

We may briefly refer in detail to one miracle of the fourth Gospel—the raising of Lazarus. The extraordinary fact that the Synoptists are utterly ignorant of this the greatest of the miracles attributed to Jesus has been too frequently discussed to require much comment here. It will be remembered that, as the case of the daughter of Jairus is, by the express declaration of Jesus, one of mere suspension of consciousness,[2] the only instance in which a dead person is distinctly said, in any of the Synoptics, to have been restored to life by Jesus is that of the son of the widow of Nain.[3] It is, therefore, quite impossible to suppose that the Synoptists could have known of the raising of Lazarus and wilfully omitted it. It is equally impossible to believe that the authors of the Synoptic Gospels, from whatever sources they may have drawn their materials,

---

[1] John xx. 30 f.   [2] Matt. ix. 24; Mark v. 39; Luke viii. 52.
[3] Luke vii. 11 ff.

could have been ignorant of such a miracle had it really taken place. This astounding miracle, according to the fourth Gospel, created such general excitement that it was one of the leading events which led to the arrest and crucifixion of Jesus.[1] If, therefore, the Synoptics had any connection with the writers to whom they are referred, the raising of Lazarus must have been personally known to their reputed authors either directly or through the Apostles who are supposed to have inspired them, or even if they have any claim to contemporary origin the tradition of the greatest miracle of Jesus must have been fresh throughout the Church, if such a wonder had ever been performed.[2] The total ignorance of such a miracle displayed by the whole of the works of the New Testament, therefore, forms the strongest presumptive evidence that the narrative in the fourth Gospel is a mere imaginary scene, illustrative of the dogma : " I am the resurrection and the life," upon which it is based. This conclusion is confirmed by the peculiarities of the narrative itself. When Jesus first hears, from the message of the sisters, that Lazarus whom he loved was sick, he declares, xi. 4 : "This sickness is not unto death, but for the glory of God, that the Son of God may be glorified thereby ; " and v. 6 : " When, therefore (οὖν), he heard that he was sick, at that time he continued two days in the place where he was." After that time he proposes to go into Judæa, and explains to the disciples, v. 11 : " Our friend Lazarus is fallen asleep ; but I go that I may awake him out of sleep." The disciples reply, with the stupidity with which the fourth Evangelist endows all those who hold colloquy with Jesus,

[1] John xi. 45 ff., 53; xii. 9 ff., 17 ff.
[2] Cf. *Schleiermacher*, Einl. N. T., 1845, p. 282 f.

v. 12 : "Lord, if he is fallen asleep, he will recover. Howbeit, Jesus spake of his death; but they thought that he was speaking of the taking of rest in sleep. Then said Jesus unto them plainly : Lazarus is dead, and I am glad for your sakes that I was not there, to the intent that ye may believe." The artificial nature of all this introductory matter will not have escaped the reader, and it is further illustrated by that which follows. Arrived at Bethany, they find that Lazarus has lain in the grave already four days. Martha says to Jesus (v. 21 f.) : "Lord, if thou hadst been here, my brother had not died. And I know that even now whatsoever thou shalt ask of God, God will give thee. Jesus saith unto her : They brother shall rise again." Martha, of course, as usual, misunderstands this saying as applying to "the resurrection at the last day," in order to introduce the reply : "I am the resurrection and the life," &c. When they come to the house, and Jesus sees Mary and the Jews weeping, "he groaned in spirit and troubled himself," and on reaching the grave itself (v. 35. f.), "Jesus wept : Then said the Jews : Behold how he loved him !" Now this representation, which has ever since been the admiration of Christendom, presents the very strongest marks of unreality. Jesus, who loves Lazarus so much, disregards the urgent message of the sisters and, whilst openly declaring that his sickness is not unto death, intentionally lingers until his friend dies. When he does go to Bethany, and is on the very point of restoring Lazarus to life and dissipating the grief of his family and friends he actually weeps and groans in his spirit. There is so total an absence of reason for such grief at such a moment that these tears, to any sober reader, are unmistakably mere theatrical adjuncts of a scene elaborated out of the imagination of the writer. The suggestion of the bystanders (v. 37), that he might have prevented the death, is not more probable than the continuation (v. 38): "Jesus, therefore, again groaning in himself cometh to the grave." There, having ordered the stone to be removed, he delivers a prayer avowedly intended merely for the bystanders (v. 41 ff.): "And Jesus lifted up his eyes and said, Father, I thank thee that thou hast heard me, and I knew that thou hearest me always: but for the sake of the multitude which stand around I said this, that they may believe that thou hast sent me." This prayer is as evidently artificial as the rest of the details of the miracle but, as in other elaborately arranged scenic representations, the charm is altogether dispelled when closer examination shows the character of the dramatic elements. A careful consideration of the narrative and of all the facts of the case must, we think, lead to the conclusion that this miracle is not even a historical tradition of the life of Jesus, but is wholly an ideal composition by the author of the fourth Gospel. This being the case, the other miracles of the Gospel need not detain us.

If the historical part of the fourth Gospel be in irreconcilable contradiction to the Synoptics, the didactic is infinitely more so. The teaching of the one is totally different from that of the others, in spirit, form, and terminology; and although there are undoubtedly fine sayings throughout the work, in the prolix discourses of the fourth Gospel there is not a single characteristic of the simple eloquence of the Sermon on the Mount. In the diffuse mysticism of the Logos, we can scarcely recognise a trace of the terse practical wisdom of Jesus of Nazareth. It must, of course, be apparent even to the most superficial observer that, in the fourth Gospel, we are introduced to a perfectly new system of instruction, and to an order of ideas of which there is not a vestige in the Synoptics. Instead of short and concise lessons full of striking truth and point, we find nothing but long and involved dogmatic discourses of little practical utility. The limpid spontaneity of that earlier teaching, with its fresh illustrations and profound sentences uttered without effort and untinged by art, is exchanged for diffuse addresses and artificial dialogues, in which labour and design are everywhere apparent. From pure and living morality couched in brief incisive sayings, which enter the heart and dwell upon the ear, we turn to elaborate philosophical orations without clearness or order, and to doctrinal announcements unknown to the Synoptics. To the inquiry: "What shall I do to inherit eternal life?" Jesus replies, in the Synoptics: "Thou shalt love the Lord thy God with all thy heart, and with all thy soul, and with all thy mind; and thy neighbour as thyself, ... this do, and thou shalt live."[1] In the fourth Gospel, to the question: "What must we do, that we may work the works of God?" Jesus answers, "This is the work of God, that ye should believe in him whom he sent."[2] The teaching of Jesus, in the Synoptics, is almost wholly moral and, in the fourth Gospel, it is almost wholly dogmatic. If Christianity consist of the doctrines preached in the fourth Gospel, it is not too much to say that the Synoptics do not teach Christianity at all. The extraordinary phenomenon is presented of three Gospels, each professing to be complete in itself and to convey the good tidings of salvation to man,

---

[1] Luke x. 25—28; cf. Mark xix. 16 ff.; xxii. 36—40.
[2] John vi. 28, 29.

which have actually omitted the doctrines which are the condition of that salvation. The fourth Gospel practically expounds a new religion. It is undeniable that morality and precepts of love and charity for the conduct of life are the staple of the teaching of Jesus in the Synoptics, and that dogma occupies so small a place that it is regarded as a subordinate and secondary consideration. In the fourth Gospel, however, dogma is the one thing needful, and forms the whole substance of the preaching of the Logos. The burden of his teaching is: "He that believeth on the Son, hath eternal life, but he that believeth not the Son, shall not see life, but the wrath of God abideth on him."[1] It is scarcely possible to put the contrast between the Synoptics and the fourth Gospel in too strong a light. If we possessed the Synoptics without the fourth Gospel, we should have the exposition of pure morality based on perfect love to God and man. If we had the fourth Gospel without the Synoptics, we should have little more than a system of dogmatic theology without morality. Not only is the doctrine and the terminology of the Jesus of the fourth Gospel quite different from that of the Jesus of the Synoptics, but so is the teaching of John the Baptist. In the Synoptics, he comes preaching the Baptism of repentance[2] and, like the Master, inculcating principles of morality;[3] but in the fourth Gospel he has adopted the peculiar views of the author, proclaims "the Lamb of God which taketh away the sins of the world,"[4] and bears witness that he is "the Son of God."[5] We hear of the Paraclete for the first time in the fourth Gospel.

It is so impossible to ignore the distinct individuality

---

[1] John iii. 36. [2] Matt. iii. 1 ff.; Mark i. 4 ff.; Luke iii. 2 ff.
[3] Luke iii. 8, 10 ff. [4] John i. 29, 36. [5] *Ib.*, i. 34.

of the Jesus of the fourth Gospel, and of his teaching, that even apologists are obliged to admit that the peculiarities of the author have coloured the portrait, and introduced an element of subjectivity into the discourses. It was impossible, they confess, that the Apostle could remember verbally such long orations for half a century, and at best that they can only be accepted as substantially correct reports of the teaching of Jesus.[1] " Above all," says Ewald, " the discourses of Christ and of others in this Gospel are clothed as by an entirely new colour: on this account also scepticism has desired to conclude that the Apostle cannot have composed the Gospel; and yet no conclusion is more unfounded. When the Apostle at so late a period determined to compose the work, it was certainly impossible for him to reproduce all the words exactly as they were spoken, if he did not perhaps desire not merely to recall a few memorable sentences but, in longer discussions of more weighty subjects, to charm back all the animation with which they were once given. So he availed himself of that freedom in their revivification which is both quite intelligible in itself, and sufficiently warranted by the precedent of so many great examples of antiquity: and where the discourses extend to greater length, there entered involuntarily into the structure much of that fundamental conception and language regarding the

[1] *Bleek*, Einl. N. T., p. 200 f.; Beiträge, p. 242 f.; *Colani*, Rev. d. Théol. 1851, ii. p. 38 ff.; *Ewald*, Jahrb. bibl. Wiss., x. p. 91 f.; *Gfrörer*, Allg. K. G., i. p. 172 f.; Das Heiligthum u. d. Wahrheit, 1838, p. 331; *Kayser*, Rev. de Théol., 1856, xiii. p. 74 f.; *Lücke*, Comment. Ev. Joh., i. p. 242; *Mangold*, Zu Bleek's Einl. N. T., 1875, p. 232 anm.; *Reuss*, Gesch. N. T., p. 215 f.; *Watkins*, N. T. Comment. ed. Ellicott, p. 558, § 6.; *Weisse*, Die evang. Gesch., i. p. 105 ff.; *de Wette*, Einl. N. T., p. 212 ff., p. 232 ff., &c., &c. Cf. *Weizsäcker*, Unters. evang. Gesch., pp. 238 ff., 253 ff.

manifestation of Christ, which had long become deeply rooted in the Apostle's soul. But as certainly as these discourses bear upon them the colouring of the Apostle's mind, so certainly do they agree in their substantial contents with his best recollections—because the Spruchsammlung proves that the discourses of Christ in certain moments really could rise to the full elevation, which in John only surprises us throughout more than in Matthew. To deny the apostolical authorship of the Gospel for such reasons, therefore, were pure folly, and in the highest degree unjust. Moreover, the circumstance that, in the drawing up of such discourses, we sometimes see him reproduce or further develop sayings which had already been recorded in the older Gospels, can prove nothing against the apostolical origin of the Gospel, as he was indeed at perfect liberty, if he pleased, to make use of the contents of such older writings when he considered it desirable, and when they came to the help of his own memory of those long passed days: for he certainly retained many or all of such expressions also in his own memory."[1] Elsewhere, he describes the work as "glorified Gospel history," composed out of "glorified recollection."[2]

Another strenuous defender of the authenticity of the fourth Gospel wrote of it as follows: "Nevertheless, everything is reconcilable," says Gfrörer, "if one accepts that testimony of the elders as true. For as John must have written the Gospel as an old man, that is to say not before the year 90—95 of our era, there is an interval of more than half a century between the time

---

[1] Jahrb. bibl. Wiss., x. p. 90 f.
[2] "Verklärte evangelische Geschichte," — "verklärte eriunerung." Jahrb. bibl. Wiss., iii. p. 163, p. 166.

when the events which he relates really happened, and the time of the composition of his book,—space enough certainly to make a few mistakes conceivable, even presupposing a good memory and unshaken love of truth. Let us imagine, for instance, that to-day (in 1841) an old man of eighty to ninety years of age should write down from mere memory the occurrences of the American War (of Independence), in which he himself in his early youth played a part. Certainly in his narrative, even though it might otherwise be true, many traits would be found which would not agree with the original event. Moreover, another particular circumstance must be added in connection with the fourth Gospel. Two-thirds of it consist of discourses, which John places in the mouth of Jesus Christ. Now every day's experience proves that oral impressions are much more fleeting than those of sight. The happiest memory scarcely retains long orations after three or four years : how, then, could John with verbal accuracy report the discourses of Jesus after fifty or sixty years! We must be content if he truly render the chief contents and spirit of them, and that he does this, as a rule, can be proved. It has been shown above that already, before Christ, a very peculiar philosophy of religion had been formed among the Egyptian Jews, which found its way into Palestine through the Essenes, and also numbered numerous adherents amongst the Jews of the adjacent countries of Syria and Asia Minor. The Apostle Paul professed this : not less the Evangelist John. Undoubtedly, the latter allowed this Theosophy to exercise a strong influence upon his representation of the life-history of Jesus," [1] &c.

[1] *Gfrörer*, Allg. K. G., 1841, i. p. 172 f.

Now all such admissions, whilst they are absolutely requisite to explain the undeniable phenomena of the fourth Gospel, have one obvious consequence: The fourth Gospel, by whomsoever written,—even if it could be traced to the Apostle John himself,—has no real historical value, being at best the "glorified recollections" of an old man, written down half a century after the events recorded. The absolute difference between the teaching of this Gospel and of the Synoptics becomes perfectly intelligible, when the long discourses are recognized to be the result of Alexandrian Philosophy artistically interwoven with developed Pauline Christianity, and put into the mouth of Jesus. It will have been remarked that along with the admission of great subjectivity in the report of the discourses, and the plea that nothing beyond the mere substance of the original teaching can reasonably be looked for, there is, in the extracts we have given, an assertion that there actually is a faithful reproduction in this Gospel of the original substance. There is not a shadow of proof of this, but on the contrary the strongest reason for denying the fact; for, unless it be admitted that the Synoptics have so completely omitted the whole doctrinal part of the teaching of Jesus, have so carefully avoided the very peculiar terminology of the Logos Gospel, and have conveyed so unhistorical and erroneous an impression of the life and religious system of Jesus that, without the fourth Gospel, we should not actually have had an idea of his fundamental doctrines, we must inevitably recognize that the fourth Gospel cannot possibly be a true reproduction of his teaching. It is impossible that Jesus can have had two such diametrically opposed systems of teaching,—one purely moral, the other wholly dogmatic; one expressed in wonderfully terse, clear, brief sayings and parables, the other in long, involved, and diffuse discourses; one clothed in the great language of humanity, the other concealed in obscure philosophic terminology;—and that these should have been kept so distinct as they are in the Synoptics, on the one hand, and the fourth Gospel, on the other. The tradition of Justin Martin applies solely to the system of the Synoptics: "Brief and concise were the sentences uttered by him: for he was no Sophist, but his word was the power of God."[1]

We have already pointed out the evident traces of artificial construction in the discourses and dialogues of the fourth Gospel, and the more closely these are examined, the more clear does it become that they are not genuine reports of the teaching of Jesus, but mere ideal compositions by the author of the fourth Gospel. The speeches of John the Baptist, the discourses of Jesus, and the reflections of the Evangelist himself,[2] are marked by the same peculiarity of style and proceed from the same mind. It is scarcely possible to determine where the one begins and the other ends.[3] It is quite clear, for instance, that the author himself, without a break, continues the words which he puts into the mouth of Jesus, in the colloquy with Nicodemus, but it is not easy to determine where. The whole dialogue is artificial in the extreme, and is certainly not genuine, and this is apparent not only from the replies attributed to the "teacher of Israel," but to the irrelevant manner in which the reflections loosely ramble from the new birth to the dogmatic statements in the thirteenth and following verses, which are the never-failing resource of the

[1] Apol., i. 14, see vol. ii. p. 314.
[2] John i. 1—18, &c., &c.   [3] Cf. *ib.*, i. 15 ff., iii. 27 ff., 10—21.

Evangelist when other subjects are exhausted. The sentiments and almost the words either attributed to Jesus, or added by the writer, to which we are now referring, iii. 12 ff., we find again in the very same chapter, either put into the mouth of John the Baptist, or as reflections of the author, verses 31—36, for again we add that it is difficult anywhere to discriminate the speaker. Indeed, while the Synoptics are rich in the abundance of practical counsel and profound moral insight, as well as in variety of illustrative parables, it is remarkable how much sameness there is in all the discourses of the fourth Gospel, a very few ideas being constantly reproduced. Whilst the teaching of Jesus in the Synoptics is singularly universal and impersonal, in the fourth Gospel it is purely personal, and rarely passes beyond the declaration of his own dignity, and the inculcation of belief in him as the only means of salvation. There are certainly some sayings of rare beauty which tradition or earlier records may have preserved, but these may easily be distinguished from the mass of the work. A very distinct trace of ideal composition is found in xvii. 3 : " And this is eternal life, to know thee the only true God, and him whom thou didst send, even Jesus Christ." Even apologists admit that it is impossible that Jesus could speak of himself as " Jesus Christ." We need not, however, proceed further with such analysis. We believe that no one can calmly and impartially examine the fourth Gospel without being convinced of its artificial character. If some portions possess real charm, it is of a purely ideal kind, and their attraction consists chiefly in the presence of a certain vague but suggestive mysticism. The natural longing of humanity for any revelation regarding a future state has not been appealed to in vain. That the diffuse and often monotonous discourses of this Gospel, however, should ever have been preferred to the grand simplicity of the teaching of the Synoptics, illustrated by such parables as the wise and foolish virgins, the sower, and the Prodigal Son, and culminating in the Sermon on the Mount, each sentence of which is so full of profound truth and beauty, is little to the credit of critical sense and judgment.

The elaborate explanations by which the phenomena of the fourth Gospel are reconciled with the assumption that it was composed by the Apostle John are in vain, and there is not a single item of evidence within the first century and a half which does not agree with internal testimony in opposing the supposition. To one point, however, we must briefly refer in connection with this statement. It is asserted that the Gospel and Epistles—or at least the first Epistle—of the Canon ascribed to the Apostle John are by one author, although this is not without contradiction,[1] and very many of those who agree as to the identity of authorship by no means admit the author to have been the Apostle John. It is argued, therefore, that the use of the Epistle by Polycarp and Papias is evidence of the apostolic origin of the Gospel. We have, however, seen, that not only is it very uncertain that Polycarp made use of the Epistle at all, but that he does not in any case mention its author's name. There is not a particle of evidence that he ascribed the Epistle, even supposing he knew it, to the

[1] *Baur*, Theol. Jahrb., 1844, p. 666 f., 1848, pp. 293—337; Unters. kan. Evv., p. 350; *Davidson*, Int. N. T., ii. p. 293 ff.; *Zeller*, Theol. Jahrb. 1845, p. 588 f., 1847, p. 137. *Credner* assigns the second and third Epistle not to the Apostle but to the Presbyter John. Einl. N. T., i. p. 687 ff.

Apostle John. With regard to Papias, the only authority for the assertion that he knew the Epistle is the statement of Eusebius already quoted and discussed, that: "He used testimonies out of John's first Epistle,"[1] There is no evidence, however, even supposing the statement of Eusebius to be correct, that he ascribed it to the Apostle. The earliest undoubted references to the Epistle, in fact, are by Irenæus and Clement of Alexandria, so that this evidence is of little avail for the Gospel. There is no name attached to the first Epistle, and the second and third have the superscription of "the Presbyter," which, applying the argument of Ewald regarding the author of the Apocalypse, ought to be conclusive against their being written by an Apostle. As all three are evidently by the same writer, and intended to be understood as by the author of the Gospel, and that writer does not pretend to be an Apostle, but calls himself a simple Presbyter, the Epistles likewise give presumptive evidence against the apostolic authorship of the Gospel.

There is another important testimony against the Johannine origin of the fourth Gospel to which we must briefly refer. We have pointed out that, according to the fourth Gospel, Jesus did not eat the Paschal Supper with his disciples, but that being arrested on the 13th Nisan, he was put to death on the 14th, the actual day upon which the Paschal lamb was sacrificed. The Synoptics, on the contrary, represent that Jesus ate the Passover with his disciples on the evening of the 14th, and was crucified on the 15th Nisan. The difference of opinion indicated by these contradictory accounts actually prevailed in various Churches, and in the

[1] H. E., v. 8.

second half of the second century a violent discussion arose as to the day upon which "the true Passover of the Lord" should be celebrated, the Church in Asia Minor maintaining that it should be observed on the 14th Nisan,—the day on which, according to the Synoptics, Jesus himself celebrated the Passover and instituted the Christian festival,—whilst the Roman Church as well as most other Christians,—following the fourth Gospel, which represents Jesus as not celebrating the last Passover, but being himself slain upon the 14th Nisan, the true Paschal lamb,—had abandoned the day of the Jewish feast altogether, and celebrated the Christian festival on Easter Sunday, upon which the Resurrection was supposed to have taken place. Polycarp, who went to Rome to represent the Churches of Asia Minor in the discussions upon the subject, could not be induced to give up the celebration on the 14th Nisan, the day which, according to tradition, had always been observed, and he appealed to the practice of the Apostle John himself in support of that date. Eusebius quotes from Irenæus the statement of the case: "For neither could Anicetus persuade Polycarp not to observe it (the 14th Nisan), because he had ever observed it with John the disciple of our Lord, and with the rest of the Apostles with whom he consorted."[1] Towards the end of the century, Polycrates, the Bishop of Ephesus, likewise appeals to the practice of "John who reclined upon the bosom of the Lord," as well as of the Apostle Philip and his daughters, and of Polycarp and others in support of the same day: "All these observed

---

[1] Οὔτε γάρ ὁ Ἀνίκητος τὸν Πολύκαρπον πεῖσαι ἐδύνατο μὴ τηρεῖν, ἅτε μετὰ Ἰωάννου τοῦ μαθητοῦ τοῦ Κυρίου ἡμῶν, καὶ τῶν λοιπῶν ἀποστόλων οἷς συνδιέτριψεν, ἀεὶ τετηρηκότα, κ.τ.λ. *Irenæus*, Adv. Hær., iii. 3, § 4; *Eusebius*, H. E., v. 24.

the 14th day of the Passover, according to the Gospel, deviating from it in no respect, but following according to the rule of the faith."[1] Now it is evident that, according to this undoubted testimony, the Apostle John by his own practice, ratified the account of the Synoptics, and contradicted the data of the fourth Gospel, and upon the supposition that he so long lived in Asia Minor it is probable that his authority largely contributed to establish the observance of the 14th Nisan there. We must, therefore, either admit that the Apostle John by his practice reversed the statement of his own Gospel, or that he was not its author, which of course is the natural conclusion. Without going further into the discussion, which would detain us too long, it is clear that the Paschal controversy is opposed to the supposition that the Apostle John was the author of the fourth Gospel.[2]

We have seen that, whilst there is not one particle of evidence during a century and a half after the events recorded in the fourth Gospel that it was composed by the son of Zebedee, there is, on the contrary, the strongest reason for believing that he did not write it. The first writer who quotes a passage of the Gospel with the mention of his name is Theophilus of Antioch, who gives the few words : "In the beginning was the Word and the Word was with God," as spoken by "John," whom he considers amongst the divinely inspired (οἱ

---

[1] Οὗτοι πάντες ἐτήρησαν τὴν ἡμέραν τῆς τεσσαρεσκαιδεκάτης τοῦ πάσχα κατὰ τὸ εὐαγγέλιον, μηδὲν παρεκβαίνοντες, ἀλλὰ κατὰ τὸν κανόνα τῆς πίστεως ἀκολουθοῦντες. *Eusebius*, H. E., v. 24.

[2] *Baur*, Unters. kan. Evv., p. 334 ff.; Theol. Jahrb., 1857, p. 242 ff.; K. G. drei erst. Jahrh., p. 156 ff.; *Davidson*, Int. N. T., ii. p. 403 ff.; *Hilgenfeld*, Die Evangelien, p. 341 ff.; Der Paschastreit, u. s. w., Theol. Jahrb., 1849, p. 209 f.; Der Paschastreit, 1860; *Scholten*, Das Ev. Johan., p. 387 ff. De sterfdag van Jezus volgens het vierde Evangelie, 1856; *Schwegler*, Der Montanismus, p. 191 ff.

πνευματοφόροι),[1] though even he does not distinguish him as the Apostle. We have seen the legendary nature of the late traditions regarding the composition of the Gospel, of which a specimen was given in the defence of it in the Canon of Muratori, and we must not further quote them. The first writer who distinctly classes the four Gospels together is Irenæus; and the reasons which he gives for the existence of precisely that number in the Canon of the Church illustrate the thoroughly uncritical character of the Fathers, and the slight dependence which can be placed upon their judgments. "But neither can the Gospels be more in number than they are," says Irenæus, "nor, on the other hand, can they be fewer. For as there are four quarters of the world in which we are, and four general winds (καθολικὰ πνεύματα), and the Church is disseminated throughout all the world, and the Gospel is the pillar and prop of the Church and the spirit of life, it is right that she should have four pillars, on all sides breathing out immortality and revivifying men. From which it is manifest that the Word, the maker of all, he who sitteth upon the Cherubim and containeth all things, who was manifested to man, has given to us the Gospel, four-formed but possessed by one spirit; as David also says, supplicating his advent: 'Thou that sittest between the Cherubim, shine forth.' For the Cherubim also are four-faced, and their faces are symbols of the working of the Son of God . . . . and the Gospels, therefore, are in harmony with these amongst which Christ is seated. For the Gospel according to John relates his first effectual and glorious generation from the Father, saying: 'In the

---

[1] Ad Autolyc., ii. 22. *Tischendorf* dates this work about A.D. 180. Wann wurden, u. s. w., p. 16, anm. 1.

beginning was the Word, and the Word was with God, and the Word was God,' and 'all things were made by him, and without him nothing was made.' On this account also this Gospel is full of all trustworthiness, for such is his person.[1] But the Gospel according to Luke, being as it were of priestly character, opened with Zacharias the priest sacrificing to God . . . . . But Matthew narrates his generation as a man, saying : 'The book of the generation of Jesus Christ, the son of David, the son of Abraham,' and 'the birth of Jesus Christ was on this wise.' This Gospel, therefore, is anthropomorphic, and on this account a man, humble and mild in character, is presented throughout the Gospel. But Mark makes his commencement after a prophetic Spirit coming down from on high unto men, saying : 'The beginning of the Gospel of Jesus Christ, as it is written in Isaiah the prophet ;' indicating the winged form of the Gospel ; and for this reason he makes a compendious and precursory declaration, for this is the prophetic character. . . . . . Such, therefore, as was the course of the Son of God, such also is the form of the living creatures ; and such as is the form of the living creatures, such also is the character of the Gospel. For quadriform are the living creatures, quadriform is the Gospel, and quadriform the course of the Lord. And on this account four covenants were given to the human race . . . . . These things being thus : vain and ignorant and, moreover, audacious are those who set aside the form of the Gospel, and declare the aspects of the Gospels as either more or less than has been said."[2] As such principles of criticism presided

---

[1] The Greek of this rather unintelligible sentence is not preserved. The Latin version reads as follows: Propter hoc et omni fiducia plenum est Evangelium istud; talis est enim persona ejus.

[2] *Irenæus*, Adv. Hær., iii. 11, §§ 8, 9.

over the formation of the Canon, it is not singular that so many of the decisions of the Fathers have been reversed. Irenæus himself mentioned the existence of heretics who rejected the fourth Gospel,[1] and Epiphanius[2] refers to the Alogi, who equally denied its authenticity, but it is not needful for us further to discuss this point. Enough has been said to show that the testimony of the fourth Gospel is of no value towards establishing the truth of miracles and the reality of Divine Revelation.

[1] Adv. Hær., iii. 2, § 9.   [2] Hær., li. 3, 4, 28.

END OF VOL. II.

www.ingramcontent.com/pod-product-compliance
Lightning Source LLC
Chambersburg PA
CBHW020835020526
44114CB00040B/784